in canadian classrooms

sixth edition

margret winzer
university of lethbridge

Toronto

Canadian Cataloguing in Publication Data

Winzer, Margret, 1940-

Children with exceptionalities in Canadian classrooms.

6th ed.

Includes bibliographical references and index.

ISBN 0-13-091575-0

1. Special education —Canada. I. Title.

LC3984.W56 2001 371.9'0971 C00-933123-9

ISBN 0-13-091575-0

Vice President, Editorial Director: Michael Young
Editor-in-Chief: David Stover
Acquisitions Editor: Andrew Wellner
Marketing Manager: Christine Cozens
Developmental Editor: Marta Tomins
Production Editor: Susan Adlam
Copy Editor: Kelli Howey
Production Coordinator: Kathrine Pummell
Permissions/Photo Research: Susan Wallace-Cox
Page Layout: Gail Ferreira Ng-A-Kien
Art Direction: Julia Hall
Interior Design: Amy Harnden
Cover Design: Amy Harnden
Cover Image: Photonica, Geoff du Feu photographe

1 2 3 4 5 TR 05 04 03 02 01

Printed and bound in Canada

Visit the Pearson Education Canada web site! Send us your comments, browse our catalogues, and more at www.pearsoned.ca.

Contents

Preface

Children with Exceptionalities in Canadian Classrooms is designed to serve as a comprehensive introduction to children with exceptionalities in Canada and to Canadian special education. It is intended to be a practical and readily understandable guide for those who for the first time are studying children with exceptionalities, their special needs, and their education, as well as a resource for more advanced students. The text is directed toward a broad audience. It will interest students involved in special education, regular education, early childhood education, and early childhood special education. Students in psychology, rehabilitation, nursing, social work, and allied child care disciplines such as audiology, speech therapy, and language pathology will also find *Children with Exceptionalities* relevant.

The overarching theme of this text is an examination of students with exceptionalities within Canadian special education. We stress the psychological, cognitive, social, and physical differences that more and less able learners bring to the teaching/learning situation, the unique difficulties faced by children who are exceptional, the developmental consequences of various disabilities, and the multiple types of interventions necessary to accommodate these students effectively in local schools.

Founding an introductory text on children and their needs follows the general tenor of different strands of research in the field of special education as well as recent standards presented by the Council for Exceptional Children (CEC) for educators' basic knowledge and skills. One research strand shows that most general educators do not have a thorough understanding of students with exceptionalities and their skills and needs. If, however, professionals are to successfully identify, diagnose, prescribe treatment for, teach, remediate, motivate, or generally improve the life of a child with an exceptional condition, they first require an accurate and clear idea of the nature of the disability—its causes, developmental consequences, and prognosis.

Another research strand demonstrates that knowledge changes attitudes both toward people with disabilities and toward their education and place in society. The beliefs of school personnel can be a conservative force that impedes or obstructs change; teacher beliefs about the value of disability and professional responsibilities correlate with teaching practices in serving children who are exceptional. Teachers and others who hold a clear understanding of exceptional conditions tend to be more tolerant and accepting of the students themselves and of special education placements and interventions than are those who know little about the conditions and the way they affect development.

All of those involved in any way with children and education require knowledge of the philosophies, practices, and policies that determine the care and education of children and youth with special needs. The CEC guidelines, for example, point out that educators dealing with students with exceptionalities require a background in the professional, ethical, legal, historical, and philosophical aspects of the field; knowledge of the characteristics of children with exceptionalities and the ways that these characteristics may interact with culture and environment; assessment procedures for program implementation; and knowledge of effective instructional procedures and effective programs (see O'Shea, Hammitte, Mainzer, and Crutchfield, 2000). Each of these aspects is treated thoroughly in this text.

Canadian special education shares much with that of other countries in both its historical development and contemporary practice; however, there is also much that is unique and special to the Canadian situation. This book also aims to open a window on the Canadian experience and to capture the flavour of Canadian services. We provide recognition of the considerable Canadian achievements in the field and detail the exciting new advances that are occurring so that readers may discover the depth of the concern and care for children with exceptionalities being manifested in Canada.

Of particular importance and relevance is an understanding of the ideology and subsequent implementation of major movements in contemporary special education. In this age of greater teacher accountability and increased teacher decision-making, it is vital that those within the profession and those aspiring to join it fully understand the debates circulating in the field so that they can justify their own practice and explain it to others.

For example, the issue of inclusive schooling is one of the most controversial and even contentious debates in contemporary special education and one with fluid and rapidly changing parameters. Every author brings to a text opinions formed by experience and practice as well as conclusions based on research. However, when discussing inclusion—and other new movements and trends—we would be uncomfortable with presenting a single philosophical stance, adopting a single model as an unvarying theme, or promoting a particular service model. In the context of controversial issues, the author adopts a non-evaluative neutral position as far as possible and attempts to present all the arguments, based on the newest research and findings drawn from the special education literature and supported by relevant work from child development, educational psychology, and so on, and elaborated via styles of organization and models of best practice. Hence, in discussions about inclusion as an example, we outline the theory of inclusive schooling, detail the workable necessary technology, pinpoint barriers to successful implementation, and discuss current placement issues, service delivery models, and best practice in the field. Given the research base, the text discussions, and their own readings and observations, we hope that teachers and students will arrive at their own reasoned and flexible positions on these issues.

Throughout this text a categorical approach is adopted. Not only is this the most practical and logical manner in which to organize such a huge body of information, but it allows a focus on the specific needs of diverse groups of children and the medical, therapeutic, psychological, sociological, and educational aspects of the various categories of exceptionality. Within each chapter, the reader will find material dealing with etiology; developmental consequences; definitions and classification; prevalence; identification and measurement; and educational, medical, and technical interventions for each type of condition.

Such a categorical approach does not overlook the fact that there is much overlap between categories and that many instructional and other strategies are suitable for a range of learners. The In the Classroom features at the close of each categorical section link these aspects together. Readers who use this feature will be able to identify, for example, instructional approaches for students with learning disabilities as they appear in various parts of the text.

New to This Edition

In this sixth edition, many of the features of earlier editions have been retained and expanded. The presentation includes highly current topics, events, and relationships from various fields as these affect what does—or does not—happen in the lives of children who are exceptional. For example, chapters feature research notes that present new findings or directions. Glossary terms are set in bold type for ease of reference and enhanced by margin notations.

Other new improvements and revisions that distinguish the sixth edition:

- Debates designed to present both sides of certain critical issues have been expanded in this edition. Each debate springs from a dilemma found in contemporary special education. The notion of dilemmas and subsequent debates is a powerful lens through which to view the contemporary scene since, in general, a single argument is not sufficient in itself as it explains only one aspect of a complex phenomenon and comes from only one perspective. Hence, the ideals and reasoning presented in the Debates form a valid perspective by which to argue questions and approach dilemmas.
- Case studies. The profiles found in earlier editions have been expanded into case studies used to elaborate various aspects required to instruct a particular student. The case studies carry through the chapter and include Individual Education Plans. Pertinent discussions and questions related to the case studies are found in the Student Workbook.
- Instructional considerations. Although the stress in this text is on portraits of children with exceptionalities as learners with special needs rather than generic or specific teaching and instructional practices, more has been added about schooling, curriculum, and individualization. This aligns with emerging philosophies regarding inclusion and the need for every classroom teacher to be aware of methods, approaches, and techniques that enhance the learning of all students. Concrete examples and ideas are found in the In the Classroom sections that close each categorical section.
- Ordering of chapters. To further reflect the current inclusive movement, the chapters on mild disabilities have been grouped together in one section. In general, these students are served in general classrooms and many instructional approaches and techniques are similar. Although behavioural disorders are often considered with mild disabilities, we reserve a separate section for this increasing and worrying population of students.
- Expanded chapters in areas that reflect the realities of Canadian classrooms. For example, increasing numbers of children with specific health care needs are reaching our classrooms. In this edition, the chapter on health needs has been expanded in terms of medical and therapeutic interventions of which teachers must be aware. As well, students with behavioural disorders are a growing population and this chapter has been expanded to more comprehensively examine areas such as conduct disorders and school violence.
- Cultural differences. With a greater number of students from diverse cultural and linguistic backgrounds in our schools, educators must address their particular needs, learning styles, and so on. The issues surrounding cultural and linguistic differences when joined to an exceptionality are embedded in the relevant chapters.
- Found at the end of each chapter is a list of current Web sites where students can search for further information.

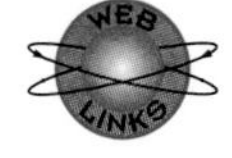

- Greater coherence with the Student Workbook.

Supplemental Teaching and Learning Aids

A Student Workbook accompanies the text. This workbook is designed as a study guide for students and contains key terms, concepts and names, and summaries of each chapter.

Review questions assist students in studying the material. Application questions and activities allow students to pursue areas of interest and research arising from the material presented.

For the instructor there is an Instructor's Manual, a Test Item File, and a Computerized Test Item File.

Acknowledgments

Of the many people who contributed to this edition, I want to especially thank Barbara Krushel who, with her usual patience and humour, assisted so competently. Thanks are also due to Jo-Ann Stocki, my graduate student who contributed much time and effort.

Finally, I wish to thank photographer Stephen Jones (Medicine Hat School District No. 76) and student Jessie Lee for the photos that appear on pages 456 and 504.

Dedication

For Marg Csapo, outstanding special educator, colleague, and friend.

Margret Winzer

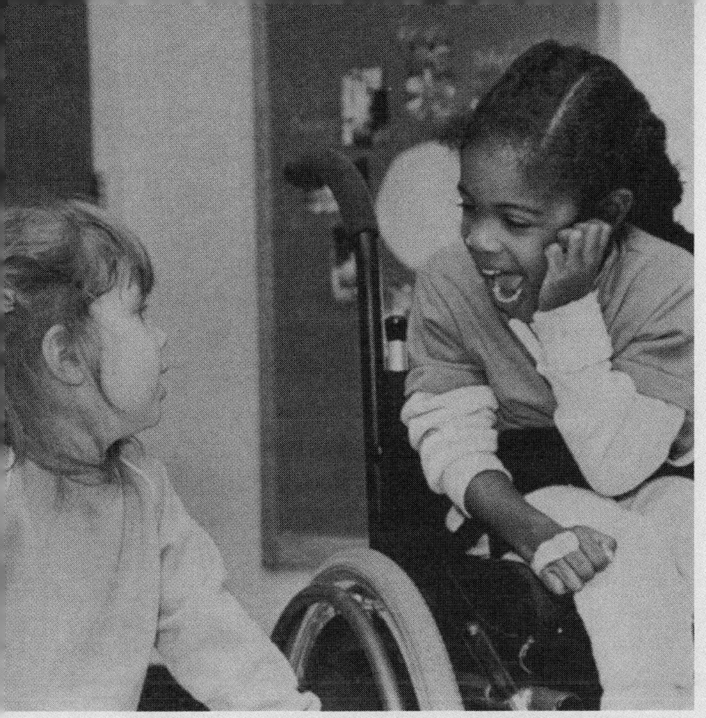

SECTION 1

Foundations of Special Education

In a philosophical and humanitarian sense, all children are special. All children have certain strengths and weaknesses, their own particular pattern of inter- and intra-individual differences. In most children, the strengths outweigh the weaknesses. In this text, however, we are concerned with children for whom the balance of strengths and weaknesses may tip a different way.

This book is about children with exceptionalities, those who have difficulty in realizing their full human potential. Their intellectual, emotional, physical, or social performance falls below that of other children. The differences may be related to physical, psychological, cognitive, emotional, or social factors, or a combination of these. Children who are gifted and talented are also included, although their patterns do not fall below but rise above those of average children.

In the past few decades, we have made such major gains in our ability to provide sophisticated services for individuals who are exceptional that the prospects for children and adults have altered dramatically. Medicine has made great strides in the prevention of disabling conditions, in intervention to ameliorate them, and in the care of children who must live with them. Genetic engineering and diagnosis are racing ahead. Closely linked to medicine, technological advances today provide a huge variety of adaptive devices and aids to help individuals with disabilities in education and in daily living.

In education, significant philosophical and program changes are ongoing. For students with special needs, the most fundamental social change of recent decades has been the clear and unequivocal statement of the responsibility of educational authorities to provide all children equal access to an education in the manner most appropriate to their needs. With equal educational opportunities for all children—including those who are exceptional—a dominant ideology, provincial governments and local school boards are increasingly obliged to make changes in the areas of school responsibility, program delivery, and program implementation.

In the wider social arena, an emphasis on the dignity and worth of each person has brought greater acceptance of individuals who are exceptional. Throughout Canada, the rights of persons with disabilities have emerged as key priorities, and public policies are changing as the authorities increasingly seek to develop the potential of individuals who are disabled and to make better use of their aptitudes. Together with a significant increase in public awareness and understanding, current social philosophy aims to provide such individuals with a lifestyle as close to normal as possible. The number of people with exceptional conditions who are living and working in home communities is testimony to positive social outcomes.

This opening section of the text is designed to introduce children and youth with exceptionalities, special education, and some general principles and practices that are germane to the care and education of individuals who are exceptional. The first chapter introduces the topic of exceptionality and children and adolescents who are seen to be exceptional within the school system. We consider the recognized exceptionalities; issues in classification, labelling, and prevalence; and the ways in which students with special needs are educated.

Educational services and the ideas that stimulate and direct their growth are never static. Changing needs lead to the formulation of new policies, legislation, and other administrative arrangements and practices. Nowhere is this more true than in the field of special education. In areas such as legislation, school placements, assessment, and teaching methodologies and approaches, today's special education is in a state of flux. Nearly all advocates for students with disabilities want "appropriate education in the least restrictive environment; public education that accommodates students with special problems; labels that carry the least possible social stigma; parental participation in decisions to provide special services; and collaboration among all service providers" (Kauffman, 1993, p. 10). How these ends are to be achieved remains the subject of intense debate. Special education is grappling with new and intriguing philosophies, innovative practices and approaches, and new forms of collaboration.

Chapter 2 explores some of the major issues, trends, and movements that surround contemporary special education and exceptionality. We place particular emphasis on the trend toward inclusive schooling and what it means to classroom teachers, to parents, and to students, both those with disabilities and their normally developing peers.

Considerations of etiology (causes) are generally the domain of medical personnel. Nevertheless, teachers need a working knowledge of causes and their consequences for learning and behaviour if they are to instruct children adequately. In Chapter 3, we outline some of the major etiologies and look, albeit briefly, at a huge group of children subsumed within the generic category of "at risk."

Chapter 1

Introduction to Children Who Are Exceptional

Learning Outcomes

After reading this chapter, you should be able to:

- Understand and describe the difficulties found in definitions, classification systems, and prevalence figures in contemporary special education;
- Detail the pros and cons about the use of labels in special education;
- Explain the various modes of intervention with children who are exceptional;
- Recognize and explain the continuum of educational services and the service delivery models found in current special education;
- Explain the process and practice of Individual Education Plans (IEPs).

Introduction

All children differ from one another to varying degrees. The colour of their eyes, hair, and skin differs; the way they dress and speak differs; and their physical, cognitive, social and emotional development, and skills differ. Every child possesses a unique combination of abilities and problems, interests and fears, successes and failures. These individual differences fall along a continuum and are characteristic of all humans.

We all have certain strengths, we all have some limitations on our mental and physical ability, and we all have some disabilities, however minor, when it comes to learning. Most of these problems fall into common areas—a tendency to be easily bored, distractibility, poor study habits, poor memory, inadequate motor control, family interference, and so on. Some of us have problems learning a foreign language; others forget directions or people's names. For most of us, a perfect backhand is an unreachable goal.

Classroom teachers see the same minor problems all the time. As they take these differences into account, teachers do not expect every student to learn the same things at the same pace, with the same materials, in the same time, and with the same amount of instruction. Good teachers always adapt to learning differences and minor learning difficulties.

In some students, the learning difficulties are more serious, and the children deviate more significantly in one way or another. These are students who are exceptional, those whose learning and behaviour deviates significantly from the norm.

THE STUDY OF EXCEPTIONALITY

The study of exceptionality is a complex undertaking. Of the many factors that contribute to the complexity, the differences, similarities, and diversity of the population of persons who are exceptional are at the forefront.

Because the child with an exceptionality is different from the average in some or many areas of functioning, the study of children with exceptionalities is the study of differences. People who are exceptional demonstrate differences in the physical, intellectual, communicative, social, or emotional domain, or in some combination of these areas.

However, we often are unable to make definitive statements about groups of children with the same exceptionality or even about a single child. Psychologists have not yet unravelled the mysteries of normal child development, so it is not surprising that understanding and explaining the course of development for children with disabilities poses a unique challenge to developmental researchers. Many of the aspects of atypical child development still remain unclear.

And, even as we examine differences, it is equally important that the similarities among children be given significant emphasis. Children with exceptionalities do not differ in every way from their normally developing peers. They are children first and exceptional second. Individuals with exceptionalities share many attitudes, needs, and perceptions with everyone else. They desire acceptance, approval, and affection as much as all children. These similarities are important, and we must always be aware of the danger of seeing only the disability and losing sight of how much children with exceptional conditions resemble other children.

SPECIAL EDUCATION

A dominant commonality found in children and youth with exceptionalities is the need for skilled intervention and special care from trained professionals. Intervention may take many forms—medical, technical, therapeutic, and educational. In an educational context, children are considered exceptional only when their educational program must be altered to meet their unique needs. They must demonstrate a clear need for special education support to reach their full potential.

special education

Special education means instruction that is specially designed to meet the unique needs of children and youth who are exceptional. Special education is provided for many students who display disparate characteristics. It encompasses students who are having problems adjusting to the regular school curriculum and those who encounter difficulties in conforming to the social needs of the classroom. Some pupils who are exceptional may require specific physical accommodations in the classroom and the school environment, such as a hearing aid or a wheelchair ramp. Children who are gifted and talented are recognized as exceptional because they too need specialized help from professionals to fully develop their unique abilities.

Until quite recently, special education was chiefly identified with the school system and with school-age children and their teachers. This is no longer true. In the past three decades, special education has expanded dramatically. It now includes infants and preschoolers and reaches up to encompass adolescents and young adults. Today, special education could be a mother using sign language with her deaf infant in the home, a caregiver in a nursery school modifying an activity for a preschooler, a classroom teacher using remedial techniques in the schoolroom, or a counsellor setting up a work experience program for a young adult with a disability.

Special education is founded on the proposition that all children can reach their full potential given the opportunity, effective teaching, and proper resources. As the Historical Notes feature at the end of this chapter shows, special education has both traditionally and currently been undertaken by different personnel in different settings. While the current trend in North America is toward inclusive settings (see Chapter 2), a few children may be placed in special schools or special classrooms with specially trained teachers. Others may be in the general classroom supported by paraprofessionals or provided adapted or modified instruction; still others may receive part-time special assistance in a resource room. Today, however, the majority of students with exceptionalities are in general classrooms, with instruction presented by classroom teachers who are increasingly required to tailor classroom instruction to the individual, not the group.

Although the onus for classroom instruction is increasingly being placed on general education teachers, they are not alone in their efforts. Psychologists, speech therapists,

Table 1-1 Sampling of disciplines involved with children who are exceptional

Medical	Paramedical	Educational	Psychological, social, behavioural
physician	audiologist	home-visiting teacher	intervenor
pediatrician	optometrist	infant stimulation therapist	social worker
neurologist	physical therapist	preschool teacher	school social worker
otolaryngologist	occupational therapist	regular classroom teacher	child care worker
ophthalmologist	public health nurse	special class teacher	guidance counsellor
dental surgeon	school nurse	remedial specialist	psychologist
psychiatrist		itinerant teacher	
nurse		learning assistant	
		school principal	
		speech therapist	
		language pathologist	
		paraprofessional	
		volunteer	

physical and occupational therapists, counsellors, and other professionals consult and collaborate with teachers to help them plan the best possible education for each student who is exceptional. These people form part of what is referred to as *related services, ancillary services, auxiliary services, the inter-disciplinary team,* or the *inclusion team.* We use the broad term **support services** to refer to those services that permit a child who is exceptional to benefit from special education. A sampling of the disciplines that may be involved is shown in Table 1-1.

support services

DEFINITIONS OF PERSONS WHO ARE EXCEPTIONAL

Children and youth who have differences that substantially change the way they learn, respond, or behave have been described in many ways. In fact, you will find these children referred to as children with exceptionalities, children with exceptional conditions, children with special needs, children with disabilities or disabling conditions, children who are challenged, and, occasionally, children who are handicapped. While the phrase **children with exceptionalities** tends to be the most encompassing, keep in mind that *exceptionality* can be defined and described in many ways, and that these ways constantly change in attempts to make descriptors more socially useful and relevant.

children with exceptionalities

Precise definitions of individual disabling conditions are vital. Definitions provide the basis for theories and hypotheses, for classifying disorders, for communicating with others, and for obtaining accurate prevalence figures. Nevertheless, while the search for universal or specific features of various conditions is ongoing, the results remain futile and frustrating. Even today, the entire area of disability is characterized by conceptual chaos. Children who are exceptional are constantly being reconceptualized, reconsidered, and renamed. Yet, perhaps such chaos is inevitable. It arises from the broad range of disciplines providing information and input, the various classification systems, the ongoing changes in terminology, and the continuing discovery of new etiologies (causes).

Many disciplines contribute to research and intervention for children who are exceptional. Alongside the expected areas of education, social work, medicine, and psychology, information is generated from such varied fields as genetics, sociology, economics, law, ethics, and politics. Many of these professionals have different ways of looking at exceptionalities and use slightly different frameworks for classification. This means that people working in biology, medicine, psychology, social work, or other disciplines may have different connotations of the term *exceptional* than do those in education.

Some people, for example, assess differences according to how far development deviates from the norm: a psychologist may report that a child's score on an IQ test is three standard deviations below the mean. Others classify differences in terms of some underlying organic or functional cause; for example, medical personnel would determine whether a child has *spastic* or *athetoid* cerebral palsy. Educators, of course, describe exceptional conditions in terms of educational functioning and achievement. If a child with athetoid cerebral palsy or mild mental retardation is in a classroom, the teacher is more likely to be concerned with the activities and techniques that will help the child learn than with the etiology of the condition or an exact IQ score.

SOME IMPORTANT TERMINOLOGY

Today's terminology, both specific and general, is relatively non-stigmatizing. For example, we no longer use emotionally laden and essentially incorrect terms such as *deaf and dumb* or *feeble-minded.* We know that deaf people are not "dumb" in any way and that people who are intellectually challenged in our society can learn and contribute.

Contemporary society holds a humanistic perception of the whole individual and sees the disorder or disability as only one part of the total person. Always, we use terms that place the child first, the disability second. Hence, we speak of *children with Down syndrome* or *children with intellectual disabilities* rather than of "Down-syndrome children" and "mentally disabled children." Or by simply saying "a person who uses a wheelchair" (rather than wheelchair-bound) one communicates information without using emotionally charged terms (McCrindle, 1995).

Further, *exceptional* is not the only generic term used to describe these children. Other terms are used synonymously, although the meanings are more restricted and slightly different. Some of the major descriptors are outlined below.

- **Impairments** are concerned with abnormalities of body structure and system function resulting from any cause. **impairments**
- **Disabilities** reflect the consequences of impairments in terms of functional performance and activity by the individual; an individual who is disabled suffers from a disability or impairment of function in one or more areas, such as vision, hearing, or mobility (World Health, 1980). In other words, a disability refers to the behaviour relevant to the completion of a task and obviously implies a limited aptitude in that task. **disabilities**
- **Handicaps** are concerned with the disadvantages experienced by individuals as a result of impairments or disability and reflect an interaction of the individual with the environment (World Health, 1980). A handicap, then, refers to environmental or functional demands *in a particular situation* that are placed on a person who is disabled. A disability is always with a person, a handicap is not. A disability becomes a handicap when the person who is disabled is unable to meet environmental demands and achieve personal goals. For example, a bright child with spina bifida could function well in math class but would be handicapped on the ball field. **handicaps**
- **Atypical** refers to youngsters who do not reach the norm in some functional area or areas, or who rise above the norm. **atypical**
- **Special needs** is an educational term used to designate pupils who require special education. **special needs**
- The terms *high risk* or **at risk** are widely used in contemporary special education. **Risk status** is a mechanism for describing the likelihood that a particular individual will experience a specific outcome given certain conditions (Planta, 1990). When the term *at risk* is used, children are seen to be vulnerable to some future condition. Some children are at risk for exceptional conditions that affect their functioning and achievement. Or a child may be at risk for learning and behavioural problems as a result of factors such as poverty or abuse, psychological disorders, or generally having an unproductive and **at risk** **risk status**

unrewarding childhood. Older students may be at risk for dropping out of school or for delinquency. At-risk status is discussed in Chapter 3.

developmental disability

- The original construct of **developmental disability**, introduced in the United States in 1970 with the passage of Public Law 91-517, included only individuals with mental retardation, epilepsy, and cerebral palsy. Current definitions are far broader and more encompassing. Today, a developmental disability/delay refers to "a condition which represents a significant delay in the process of development. It does not refer to a condition in which a child is slightly or momentarily lagging in development or is at risk of a delay. The presence of a developmental delay is an indication that the process of development is significantly affected and that without special intervention, it is likely that educational performance at school age will be affected" ("Developmental ...," 1991, p. 1).

special health management needs

- Children with **special health management needs** are those children who demonstrate a wide range of chronic and progressive illnesses and severe disabilities such as bronchiopulmonary dysplasia, cystic fibrosis, congenital malformations, neuromuscular diseases, and many others. Many of these children require technology, special services, or some form of ongoing medical support for survival (Prendergast, 1995).

medically fragile children

- **Medically fragile children** or those with extremely fragile physiological conditions are more extreme forms of the above. Students will certainly require ongoing medical support and care.
- Students with *severe handicaps* are part of the developmentally disabled population. This group is generically defined as "those who may possess severe language and/or perceptual/cognitive deprivations, and evidence abnormal behaviour such as failure to respond to pronounced social stimuli; self-mutilation; self-stimulation; manifestation of intense and prolonged temper tantrums; and the absence of rudimentary forms of verbal contact. Students also have extremely fragile physiological conditions" (U.S. Federal definition 20 USC 1401(7)).

MAJOR CATEGORIES OF EXCEPTIONALITY

The current classification systems used in special education evolved gradually, haphazardly, and inconsistently over the decades. As with definitions, classification systems remain imprecise. There is relatively little standardization in the study of children who are exceptional and a single consistent and universally accepted method of describing different groups of children with certain exceptional conditions does not exist.

Considerable overlap occurs in the classification of disabling conditions. Many children who are exceptional have more than one difficulty and, because they do not fall easily into one specific category, they are difficult to classify. Further, children who have been traditionally classified and grouped as mildly disabled—those described as *learning disabled, mildly mentally retarded,* and *mildly behaviourally disordered*—tend to share a variety of academic and behavioural characteristics that transcend traditional approaches to classification. These children often exhibit such similar behaviour that it is difficult to accurately differentiate the disability. This overlap of categories is discussed in the accompanying Research Notes box.

Research Notes

Overlap of Categories

Traditional special education was founded on the proposition that children with certain developmental characteristics required education matched to their individual needs. Students with mild disabilities—those labelled as *learning disabled, mildly mentally retarded,* and *mildly behaviourally disordered*—were not thought to share common etiological factors and behavioural characteristics. Among the three groups, differences were said to exist in the level of cognitive ability, in academic achievement, in patterns of cognitive performance, in degree of underachievement, and in adaptiveness of social and emotional development.

However, ongoing research finds that, in many respects, these students cannot be reliably distinguished from one another. Specific domains of development and the overlap of behaviours and learning are shown in table form below.

Ysseldyke (1987) observed that "There are no characteristics of behaviour specific to learning disabilities, there are no characteristics that students labelled as learning disabled evidence that are not demonstrated with equal frequency by low-achieving students who are not learning disabled." Not only is there almost no differentiation between learning disabilities and low achievers, but also researchers continue to find a considerable degree of overlap between the diagnostic areas of learning disabilities and behavioural disorders. Similarly, those with intellectual disabilities often exhibit behavioural disorders.

Multiple studies confirm the overlap. Research finds little evidence to support the contention that students with one disability should be taught differently from students with another mild disability. Special education students are generally most in need of remediation in reading, math, and written expression. On reading and phonological processing measures, for example, there are more similarities than differences (Gresham, 1997).

Similar instructional practices are effective in pro-

	LEARNING DISABLED	**MILDLY MENTALLY RETARDED**	**BEHAVIOURALLY DISORDERED**
Cognitive	Average or above average IQ	IQ below 75	Average IQ, mean around 90
Learning	Deficits in attention, memory, achievement	Deficits in memory, attention, and achievement	Deficits in memory, attention, and achievement
	Significantly more off-task behaviour	Significantly more off-task behaviour	Significantly more off-task behaviour
Social	Ignored or rejected by peers	Ignored or rejected by peers	Often actively disliked by peers
Physical	No physical anomalies	No physical anomalies	No physical anomalies
Communication	Speech and language difficulties	Speech and language difficulties	No language difficulties
Self-concept	Poor self-concept, outward locus of control	Poor self-concept, outward locus of control	Often outward locus of control, poor self-concept
Gender	4:1 boys to girls	5:1 boys to girls	6-12:1 boys to girls

moting student learning regardless of diagnostic category. One study (Algozzine, Morsink, and Algozzine, 1988) found that instruction in forty classrooms serving groups of students designated as behaviourally disordered, educable mentally retarded, or learning disabled did not differ to any degree. Not only do treatments and instructional methods often overlap, but also there are few differences on psycho-educational measures between students who are learning disabled and low-achieving students. In differential diagnosis, children with mild problems are difficult to categorize through formal methods such as diagnostic tests, WISC-III profile analyses, or behavioural checklists.

Keeping these caveats in mind, the following categories are used in this text to group the special traits of children who are exceptional.

- *Children and youth with mild disorders to learning.* Included in this category are students with intellectual differences—those who are intellectually disabled; those with learning disabilities; and those with communication disorders—children who have speech difficulties and language problems. Such a grouping reflects the contemporary movement toward inclusive schools, the overlap among categories, and the changing foci in dealing with students with mild disabilities in particular. Educators in inclusive classrooms are moving away from particular categories and stressing instead how to develop, implement, maintain, manage, and evaluate supportive classrooms that meet the needs of all students.
- *Children and youth with behavioural disorders.* Behavioural disorders include a wide variety of problems—conduct disorders, anxiety and withdrawal, attention deficit/hyperactivity disorder, social maladjustment, and juvenile delinquency.
- *Children and youth who are intellectually superior.* This category includes children who are gifted, creative, and talented learners.
- *Children and youth who have sensory disabilities.* This category includes children with auditory impairments and those with visual problems.
- *Children and youth who have physical disabilities and impaired health.* Included in this category are children with neurological defects, orthopedic conditions, birth defects, and conditions that are a result of infection and disease.
- *Children and youth who have developmental disabilities. Developmental disabilities* is an inclusive term. The category includes children with pervasive disorders such as severe mental retardation and infantile autism, and those with multiple disabilities such as cerebral palsy and mental retardation, or deafness and blindness.

Additional qualifiers may be used to provide more specificity to these general classifications. Degrees of severity are the most commonly used qualifiers. Conditions are described as *mild, moderate, severe,* or *profound.* When we speak of a child with mild mental retardation, we mean that the child has an IQ somewhere in the range of 55 to 70 and demonstrates deficits in **adaptive behaviour**—the ability to respond to and function in the environment according to age and social standards. On the other hand, a child with profound mental retardation would have an IQ below 25 and extreme difficulties in any form of adaptive behaviour.

adaptive behaviour

LOOKING AT LABELS

A central theme of this book is that children who are exceptional should be viewed first as individuals, and then as people who differ from the norm in some way. A child's functional level and behaviour should be the critical components analyzed for intervention, and we should be wary of supplying labels that are arbitrary and that permanently assign a child to a specific category of exceptionality.

labelling

Labelling refers to the categorizing of children on the basis of their primary disability. The practice evolved gradually; no one really planned it. Labels are products of the human mind—in special education they grew from a psychomedical model that encompassed diagnosis, classification, and placement. (The Historical Notes at the end of Chapter 3 explain the medical model and its genesis and development.)

There is much distrust of the labels and categorization that permeate today's special education. The term *special education* was probably first coined by Alexander Graham Bell in 1884 (Winzer, 1993). But even this broad designation of special services has now been called into question as an acceptable way of referring to the education of students with disabilities (Booth and Ainscow, 1998).

The major argument hinges on whether labels are "necessary conceptual shorthand in a busy world" or whether they are "subversive disempowerment" (McCrindle, 1995, p. 16). The research evidence is not very helpful here. While concerns exist about *labelling bias*—the expectations that others may develop for a person with a certain label—the results of research on labelling are ambiguous and inconclusive. In fact, some contend that concern for the negative effects of labelling appears to have little foundation in research evidence. Investigations suggest that stigma typically precedes a formal label and that labels do not add appreciably to stigma (see Kauffman, 1999; King-Sears, 1997).

Probably the best we can say is that while every situation has the potential for children to suffer adverse effects from labelling, in some cases labels may prove advantageous. Some of the many pros and cons of the labelling dilemma are shown in the accompanying Debate feature.

Despite the arguments, discrete categories of exceptionality and specific labels for particular conditions still abound. In Canada a number of provinces (Ontario, Saskatchewan, Alberta, and British Columbia) still include definitions of categories of exceptionality in special education policies.

What do persons with disabilities themselves say about labelling? The *Disability Rag*, a U.S. disability activist publication, periodically editorializes against euphemisms created by non-disabled people. They point out that disabilities are real, and present policies are needed to enable real choice, not euphemistic terms that gloss over the need for action (Sleeter and Grant, 1994). As Kate McCrindle points out, many people with disabilities object to "sugarcoated euphemisms" such as *handi-capable* and *physically challenged* because "they are condescending and reinforce the idea that a disability can't be dealt with in a straightforward manner" (1995, p. 22). Expressions that emphasize abilities and mirror advances are more constructive. These include words such as *choice, empowerment, inclusion, self-determination,* and *independence.*

A Matter of Debate

Labels in Special Education

The debate about labels in special education concerns whether or not to label, the validity of labels, the type of labels, and whether labelling creates stigma.

Arguments for labels	Cautions about labels
Problems cannot be identified or discussed lacking a descriptor or label.	Categorical definitions maintain the purity of each population by focusing on discrepant attributes, the unique and elusive characteristics that distinguish one defined population from another.
Categories provide a common language for professionals; a carefully considered classification can serve to simplify information for administrators, counsellors, educators, and parents.	Too often, a label describes only the problems and deficiencies of a person. It picks out a single quality, calls attention to it, stresses how this quality differs from the norm, and assumes that there is something wrong either in the family, the child, or the culture.
Labels promote effective communication among agencies, services, and professionals that deal with individuals who are exceptional.	An oversimplified label suggests that the child is an unhealthy, poorly functioning organism, deprived in some way. Strengths are obscured.
Labels are necessary for classification and funding.	Sometimes the labels are incorrect, as in making dyslexia synonymous with learning disabilities. Or labels may exaggerate the severity of a disability, as in the labelling of a child who is hard-of-hearing as deaf or a youngster who is visually impaired as blind.
Categories are necessary to ensure quality services. The rehabilitation and educational systems cannot disregard the fact that the unique needs of certain groups, such as those who are visually impaired, require the services of specialized professionals.	Labels do not automatically result in better services for a child.
When disability categories were completely abolished in England and Wales, there were negative consequences (Feniak, 1988).	Classification systems are too often unreliable and inconsistent, and labels seldom adequately reflect a child's educational and therapeutic needs.
The labels—and the influence they have—vary greatly, and often depend upon the labeller's perspective,	Parent and professional views may differ. For example, the term *mental retardation* is rejected by Puerto Rican

Arguments for labels	Cautions about labels
which may be shaped by cultural and/or professional background.	and African American parents in the United States; it is culturally offensive to them, as it is to parents in Pakistan (Harry, 1992; Mazurek and Winzer, 1994).
Labels may be helpful to parents, especially when a condition is initially diagnosed. Being able to use the name of a disability seems to give some control over it (Akerley, 1975).	Categorizing encourages educators to treat students as labels rather than as people.
Students with the same label may be assumed to share a common set of learning characteristics that may lead to efficient educational programming.	Decades of experience show that this approach does not work (Reschly and Ysseldyke, 1995).
Labels permit us to identify children whose learning and behavioural characteristics cause them to require differentiated instruction.	Although children may share a common exceptionality, they do not form homogeneous groups. Children exhibit different behaviours and are affected by the disability in various ways. And, as each disability ranges from mild to severe, a child who is mildly disabled functions quite differently than a child with a severe disability.
Teachers react to children differently according to the child's classroom behaviour, not the label or classification (Curci and Gottleib, 1990).	Labels may affect a teacher's interactions with students and may tend to absolve teachers of their responsibilities. If teachers are predisposed to expect behaviour consonant with a child's classification, it may negatively affect interactions with the child. For example, a teacher may not even try to help little Jimmy with arithmetic because Jimmy has been labelled as mildly disabled and the teacher does not believe that disabled children can learn to add and subtract.
Stigma precedes a label, not the other way around. That is, the disability and not the label is sufficient to generate stigma (Singer, 1988).	Other students are sensitive to labels and to the differences between peers who attend different educational placements. In one study (Bak, Cooper, Dobroth, and Siperstein, 1987), children responded to the resource room and special classroom pupils differently, with students going to resource room seen as significantly more capable than those in special classes.
Whinnery and colleagues (1995) found no differences in self-esteem.	Labelling negatively affects a child's self-esteem.
Labelling bias may not surface among educators. In a study using descriptions of mental retardation and	Labels result in lowered or negative expectations for those who are labelled.

Arguments for labels	Cautions about labels
learning disabilities, Pfieffer (1980) did not find bias among educators who worked as a team.	
Labels may be a necessary administrative lever within a school system to obtain funding for special services.	Labelling engenders unfortunate and often unanticipated consequences. Students may be misclassified and placed in unsuitable educational environments.
Labels result in increased visibility for groups of people with special needs.	People tend to view a labelled person differently from a non-labelled one.
Labels make others more tolerant of a disability. They may provide explanations for behaviour or appearance for which people may otherwise be blamed or stigmatized (Fiedler and Simpson, 1987).	People are more likely to expect deviant behaviour from labelled individuals.
The label *gifted* enhances a child's status in the family and affects the parents' perceptions of the child (Cornell 1983).	High expectations communicated through the labelling process for a gifted child may contribute to feelings of failure; the child never quite measures up to expectations (e.g. Buescher, 1991).

PREVALENCE OF EXCEPTIONAL CONDITIONS

Recent United Nations surveys estimate that there are 290 million people with moderate to severe physical and mental disabilities in the world today; their numbers are expected to double in the next 35 years. In developing countries, the catastrophic rates may be even greater than present figures suggest. The numbers of people affected by largely preventable diseases, such as water-borne blindness, tuberculosis, and leprosy, and from chronic debilitating conditions that stem from malnutrition, impure water, and inadequate sanitation, are simply staggering (Mazurek and Winzer, 1994).

In the United States, approximately 35 million people are considered exceptional. In Canada, there is not a federal office or national clearing house on special education or persons with disabilities, so data must be gathered from many diverse sources. Some studies point out that the number of Canadians who have some form of disability jumped more than 27 percent between 1986 and 1991, from 3.3 million to 4.2 million, or from 13.2 to 15.5 percent of the population ("Prevalence ...," 1995).

How many children among this number have disabilities? In 1986, there were an estimated 277 000 Canadian children with disabilities, representing 5 percent of all young people (Nessner, 1990). By 1991, numbers had risen. Of the 390 000 children reported as disabled, 89 percent had a mild disability, and 8 percent a moderate disability. About 3 percent, or 11 500 children, had a severe disability ("Prevalence ...," 1995).

Approximately 15.5 percent of the Canadian school-age population is considered to be exceptional.

Estimates of the numbers of individuals who are exceptional are generally reported as either *incidence* or *prevalence.* **Incidence** refers to the number of new cases of a particular condition identified over a given period of time, usually a year. Incidence is important for seeing trends, but for special education purposes prevalence has far more meaning, as disabilities often last through a lifetime.

incidence

Prevalence applies to the total number of existing cases, old and new. Prevalence is also used to refer to the percentage or proportion of the population that falls into a given category. The prevalence statistic tells teachers and others the total number of children.

prevalence

During the school years, approximately 15.5 percent of the Canadian school-age population is considered to be exceptional. Among these children and adolescents, boys are more likely to be classified as exceptional than girls. Table 1-2 shows the approximate proportions of various types of exceptional conditions drawn from the data on percentages and numbers that are presented throughout this text.

Table 1-2 Estimated prevalence of selected exceptional conditions

Exceptionality	General child population (%)
All exceptional conditions	15.5
Speech/language problems	2–4
Learning disabilities	2–4
Mental retardation	1–3
Behavioural disorders	1–3
Gifted and talented	2–5
Hearing impaired	0.5–0.7
Visually impaired	0.08–0.12
Health disabled	0.4–0.6
Neurological disorders	0.2–1.5
Pervasive developmental disorders	0.5–0.7

View this list with great caution. A precise determination of the incidence and prevalence rates for exceptional children and adolescents with specific conditions in Canada is very difficult. In general, estimates of the number of children with some identifiable special condition vary widely, particularly for those with high-incidence disabilities such as learning disabilities and behavioural disorders. It is easier to obtain accurate figures for low-incidence disabilities such as severe visual impairment. This fact is illustrated in Figure 1-1, which shows severity levels.

Prevalence estimates are influenced by a complex set of interacting factors. Contributing

Figure 1-1
Prevalence of disability by severity levels

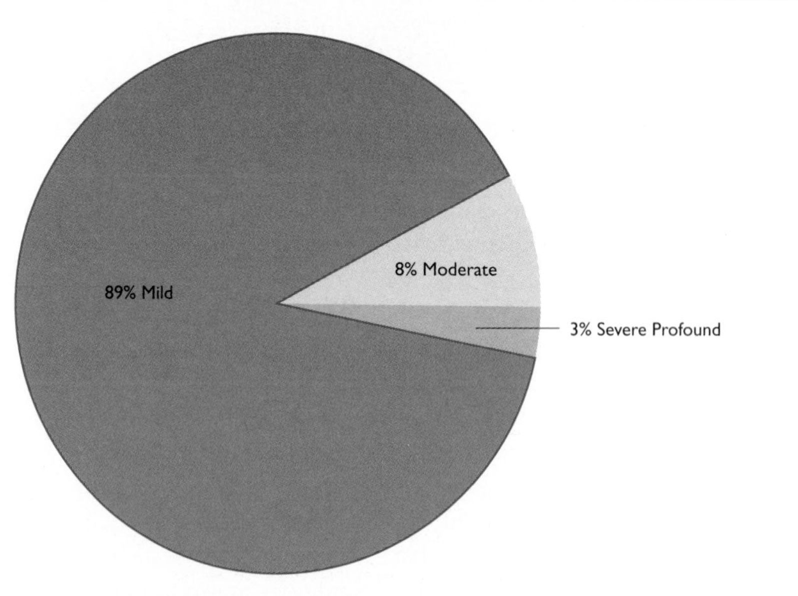

Sources: Oderkirk, 1993; "Prevalence of disability by severity levels," 1995

to the difficulties in obtaining accurate figures are the varying definitions and descriptions of disabilities, the methods of data collection, the interpretation of data, and social factors related to stigmatization and public perceptions.

Definitional Problems

We noted earlier that children with exceptional conditions require services from a range of professional disciplines, chiefly medical, therapeutic, and educational. These necessary services sometimes confound prevalence rates simply because each discipline brings its own definitions and characterizations of what is exceptional.

In the educational system, students are considered exceptional only when their educational program must be altered to meet their unique needs. They must demonstrate a clear need for support services to reach their full human potential. Although heart disease is a serious condition and physicians see it as an exceptionality, it may not have any impact on a student's learning, so a child with a heart disorder may not be counted among the special education population. On the other hand, a medical condition such as pediatric AIDS has major effects on learning, and a child with this condition would very likely require special education services.

Moreover, special education itself uses many vague and inconsistent definitions and, lacking clear definitions, it is almost impossible to estimate prevalence. Because school systems tend to interpret a child's condition according to services provided, a child may be called learning disabled in one school district and counted as a low achiever in another.

Changing Diagnoses

The diagnosis of a disabling condition is not, nor should it be, immutable. A diagnosis that is correct today could easily be inappropriate tomorrow. Sometimes, children diagnosed with behavioural disorders or learning disabilities—and, especially, speech defects—improve to such an extent that they are no longer considered disabled.

Another factor that confounds efforts to estimate prevalence is ongoing research that changes diagnoses by bringing new ways of looking at disabling conditions. For example, recent discoveries in neurology and genetics have altered traditional conceptions of the causes and nature of infantile autism; the condition is no longer classified as a severe emotional disturbance but as a neurological disability within the framework of pervasive developmental disorders.

Co-occurring and Multiple Disabilities

Confusion arises about the classification of children with dual or multiple disabilities. When children have more than one pertinent set of characteristics, such as mental retardation, cerebral palsy, and hearing impairment, or a speech disorder and visual impairment, children are often classified according to their major condition (called the **primary disability**). For example, a child who is deaf with an emotional problem may be classified as hearing impaired and receive services designed for deaf children; the emotional problem is presumed to be a secondary condition. Or, the child may be numbered in both categories, or simply described as multiply disabled. Obviously, such varied counting and categorization makes rates unstable.

primary disability

Early Identification

Low-incidence disabilities, such as severe retardation, serious physical impairment, or blindness, are usually identified early and involve more professional intervention than high-incidence conditions, such as mild intellectual disability. A mild intellectual disability, for example, may not be identified until the child has to confront the complexities of reading and writing in the classroom. As a result, low-incidence disabilities are more likely to be reported.

Changing Rates

Difficulties also spring from different prevalence figures at different points in the life cycle. As we just pointed out, children with mild intellectual disabilities are often not identified early. For these children, the most pronounced difficulties clearly relate to the structured environment of formal schooling. During the school years, therefore, the prevalence of mild intellectual disability tends to show a sharp increase. But since most of the adults who function in this range achieve personal and vocational independence, the estimated prevalence of mild disability decreases substantially as these adults enter the working world and assume their places as productive citizens.

The Stigma of Identification

The Canadian Office for Disability Issues (1997) pointed out that "Attitudes can be the most difficult barrier persons with disabilities must face in gaining full integration, acceptance and participation in society" (p. 1). In the face of such stereotypes and negative attitudes, it is not surprising that some parents are reluctant to have their child identified as exceptional. They may not report a condition, or they may opt for a different category.

Parents seem to see labels that specify a particular problem as less stigmatizing than those that imply a global, developmental impairment. For example, many parents find the term *learning disabilities* far preferable to *mild mental retardation.*

Survey Problems and Sampling Errors

epidemiology

Epidemiology refers to the study of the distribution and determinants of diseases and disabling conditions in a population. Survey problems result when epidemiologists and other researchers use varied definitions of an exceptionality. Surveys can also be misleading when figures from a small area are extrapolated to the rest of the country. Newfoundland, for example, has a high rate of spina bifida, and to extrapolate Newfoundland figures to the rest of Canada would clearly be unwise.

INTERVENTION WITH CHILDREN AND YOUTH WHO ARE EXCEPTIONAL

intervention
early intervention

Intervention is a general term that refers to the application of professional skills to maintain or improve a child's potential and functioning. **Early intervention**, a major trend in current special education practice, refers to the establishment of educational and support ser-

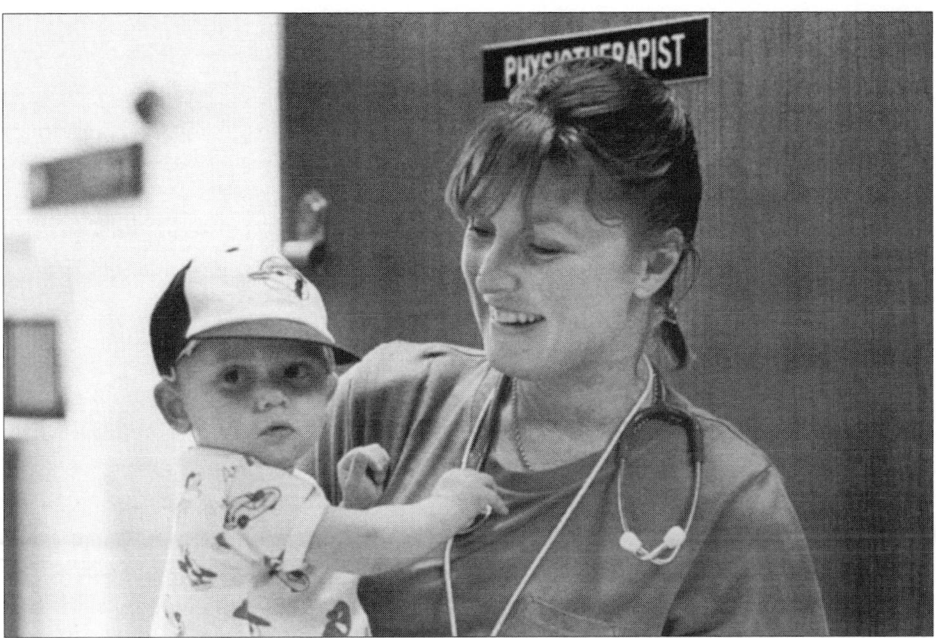

Intervention with children who are exceptional can involve a variety of specialists.

vices for young children who have disabilities or who are at risk for disabilities, and for their families. Although intervention is strongly associated with active educational programming, the term also includes medical intervention, mental health services, and welfare provisions for the family and the child.

habilitation

rehabilitation

remediation

A number of processes and terms are subsumed under the general rubric of intervention. First of all, there is **habilitation**, which comes from the Latin *habilitare,* "to make skilled." In habilitation, people in medical, social, psychological, and educational fields support and assist individuals with disabilities in their development and daily lives. Closely aligned to habilitation is **rehabilitation**, a therapeutic term that refers to procedures that endeavour to restore an individual to normal or optimal functioning. **Remediation** is an educational term that refers to helping a child to overcome, or compensate for, specific deficits in learning and development.

For the child who is exceptional, the basic approaches to care and education include four major forms of intervention—*medical, therapeutic, educational,* and *social.* We discuss some basic intervention techniques here; these are expanded upon in later chapters.

Medical Intervention

Medical intervention and treatment for children who are exceptional is a complex and highly sophisticated process that involves a variety of specialists with unique skills. Medical treatment is extremely varied. The most common forms involve surgery; treatment that is life saving, such as insulin; the controlled use of medication; and supportive therapy.

Surgery

In recent decades, many forms of surgical treatment for children who are exceptional have emerged, leading to the development of subspecialties within the field of pediatric surgery.

The most widely used surgical treatments currently include reconstructive surgery for repair of physical anomalies such as a cleft lip or palate; neurosurgery for disabling conditions of the brain and spinal cord; and orthopedic surgery for problems of the skeletal system that occur in youngsters with cerebral palsy or multiple physical anomalies. Other sophisticated techniques have also been developed to help children with Down syndrome, to insert cochlea implants in deaf individuals, and to transplant organs in children with cystic fibrosis.

Psychopharmacology

Of all the medical treatments for children with exceptional conditions, teachers are most likely to come into contact with psychopharmacology, or drug therapy. In 1937 Charles Bradley was the first to treat specific educational disabilities and hyperactive behaviour with a stimulant drug, Benzedrine. Bradley noticed an overall improvement in the children's mood, activity level, and educational achievement (Bradley, 1937). Since this seminal work, psychopharmacological approaches to treatment have increased dramatically and today drug therapy is used extensively with children who demonstrate physical and neurological complications. Reports indicate that perhaps as many as 2 to 3 percent of children in general education, 15 to 20 percent in special education, and 40 to 60 percent in residential facilities are on drug therapies (Forness, Kavale, Sweeney, and Gresham, 1999). We discuss drug therapy fully in Chapter 7.

Therapy

therapy

Therapy, the treatment of an illness or disabling condition, consists of a broad range of interventions to help children adapt to their particular disabilities. Physical, occupational, and speech/language therapists provide many essential treatments.

Physical and occupational therapy can help children to develop hand skills, body coordination, and other physical skills, and can aid in gross motor development, muscle relaxation, and fine motor control. Speech and language therapists/pathologists are trained in the evaluation and remedial treatment of speech and language problems in children and adults. They may develop appropriate augmentative communication for children who cannot talk and intervene with those children who have difficulty in controlling the fine motor muscles needed for eating.

There are different types of therapeutic intervention. Direct therapy occurs when therapeutic techniques are used in a treatment that only the therapist can safely carry out. *Monitoring* (sometimes called *consultative therapy*), in which teachers are involved, occurs when therapists monitor treatment carried out by parents, teachers, or classroom aides (Dunn, 1989).

Educational Intervention

service delivery models

Education for children who are exceptional is provided through a variety of educational arrangements, settings, and instructional alternatives. These **service delivery models**—plans for bringing together students, teachers, instruction, and learning—vary across the country, across provinces, and even across school districts. We look at some broad ideas here; each categorical chapter further explores educational intervention for specific populations.

Service Delivery Models

When it comes to service delivery models and **educational settings**—the place where students who are exceptional receive instruction—the alternatives are determined by the unique needs of each child. Many different kinds and combinations of programs are required to accommodate the wide range of conditions that occur in varying degrees of severity and the need for different types and degrees of assistance at various age levels. Even with today's strong movement toward inclusion (see Chapter 2), many experts in the field (e.g. Marston, 1996) recommend that to provide appropriate education for students who are exceptional a cascade, or continuum, of services is necessary, as represented in Figure 1-2.

educational settings

The continuum of educational services has been the blueprint for special education since 1975. It reflects a number of facets important in serving students who are exceptional within special education. First, a continuum manifests the concept of the **least restrictive environment** (LRE)—the most appropriate placement in which a student can receive instruction and services.

least restrictive environment

Settings on the continuum involve a series of options that move from contrived to more natural arrangements. The wider the pyramid, the more children are encompassed; throughout are increasingly restrictive environments, with the point of the triangle generally considered to be the most restrictive because it denotes children on homebound instruction, who have little opportunity for social interaction with their peers. We discuss the various settings below.

The continuum also reflects the intensity of a child's needs. With a full continuum of services, educators base their decision whether to place a student in an inclusive classroom or alternative setting on student outcomes—in which setting will the child succeed and be prepared to become a productive and active citizen ("Inclusion: Where ...," 1996). Whether this means receiving educational services in the general classroom; moving out of the classroom for remedial help for short periods of time; or working in a resource room, self-contained class, or even a separate setting must be determined individually.

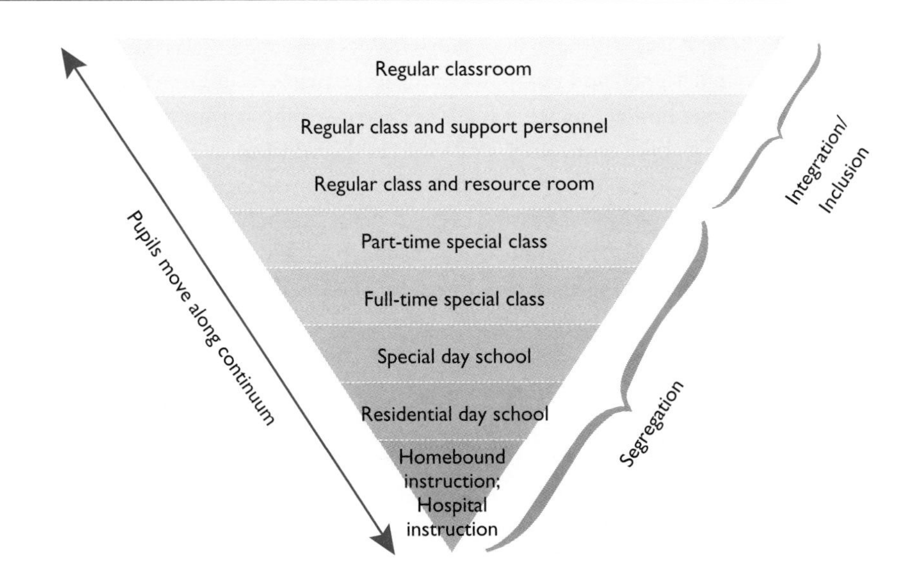

Figure 1-2 *Continuum of educational services*

The type and severity of disability affects placement. Students with mild disabilities are more likely to be in general classrooms, and those with more significant disabilities in special classes, schools, or facilities (Hobbs and Westling, 1998). Students who are deaf-blind, who have multiple disabilities, or who have serious emotional disorders comprise the largest proportions in separate schools (McLeskey, Henry, and Hodges, 1999).

Finally, the resources needed or available are an integral, if tacit, component of the LRE and the continuum. Lacking appropriate supports, a general classroom may not be the best placement for a student. Take, for example, a child with a profound hearing loss who uses American Sign Language as the primary mode of communication. Without amplification and access to an interpreter, the child would likely flounder in a general setting.

Home/Hospital Instruction

Homebound and hospital instruction are provided by local school boards for children who are confined because of illness, physical injury, or other problems (excluding suspension or expulsion). Intervention is initiated if the student's school absences begin to seriously affect progress.

Residential Schools

Special education in Canada began with residential institutions designed to serve the special needs of students who were blind, deaf, and mentally retarded. Provincially funded residential schools for children who are hearing impaired, visually impaired, and emotionally disturbed still function across Canada. In these settings, children live and are instructed with other youngsters who have the same exceptional conditions.

One of the problems with residential schools is that they separate the child from the home. However, the concept of full-time residential placement has changed substantially in recent years and many of these schools could more correctly be termed residential/day as more students are encouraged to commute.

Special Schools

During the late 1940s, it was felt that a logical extension of the special class was the special school. Schools were designed and equipped to meet the needs of discrete populations of students who were exceptional. Day schools allowed a core of specially trained teachers and professionals to guide a child's education while the child continued to live at home.

A few special day schools still provide special education services, usually to specific groups of children with exceptionalities and often at the preschool level for young children who are deaf. Other examples for school-aged students are Alberta's Horizon School in Olds, which specializes in assisting children with severe physical disabilities, and the Christine Meikle School for children with mental disabilities.

Special Classes

Traditionally, the full-time special class was the most popular vehicle for serving students with exceptional conditions. During the late 1960s, the notion of special classes was critically examined, and the resulting debates and evidence added impetus to the movement toward inclusion. Nevertheless, special classes remain a setting for a small number of students who are exceptional.

In special classrooms, which are staffed by specially trained teachers and are located within a regular school, children with similar disabilities are brought together for instruction and social interplay. Partial integration, when feasible, is a major aim.

Inclusion in the General Classroom

It is the general classroom that provides the student who is exceptional with the least restrictive environment and the opportunity for maximum social integration with normally developing peers. When a child is included in the general classroom, the classroom teacher holds primary responsibility for that child and must ensure that appropriate programs and curriculum modifications are made. The classroom teacher also works with a number of professionals to tailor education to the needs of the individual child.

Students in general classrooms and their teachers are supported in a number of ways that vary according to the needs of the child, the type of program espoused by the school, and the resources available. In very general terms, supports by both personnel and institutional arrangements are:

- *Itinerant teachers.* These are specially trained educators who give individual assistance to a child for specific periods during the normal school schedule. The type and intensity of itinerant intervention depend on the needs of the child. Some children may simply need tutoring to keep up in regular school subjects; others may require a specific program in one area, such as speech and auditory training. Itinerant teachers may work with classroom teachers on program preparation and offer in-service training. They may also help prepare the child's classmates by explaining the child's disabling condition. In some instances, the itinerant teacher serves as an advocate to ensure that the special child receives the best education possible in the most appropriate environment.
- *Educational consultants.* Consultants, sometimes referred to as *support facilitators* or *inclusion specialists,* usually do not have instructional responsibilities but serve to assist classroom teachers throughout a school district to maintain children who are exceptional in their regular school programs. As an indirect service provider, the consultant may function as a diagnostician, as a materials specialist, as an administrator of various services, and as an advocate.
- *Paraprofessionals.* Variously referred to as *teacher's aides, teaching assistants, classroom assistants, child care workers* and so on, paraprofessionals are an integral part of the instructional team that shares responsibility in the area of learning facilitation. The paraprofessional must be able, for example, to develop and/or select daily elements of the curriculum as defined in an individualized educational plan, deliver instruction, provide for remedial experiences, monitor a child's progress, make individual educational assessments, and record behaviour. The accompanying Research Notes provide more information about paraprofessionals in special education.
- *Therapists.* The speech/language, physical, and occupational therapists that we mentioned earlier are important in special education services. Often, the therapeutic services will be brought to the child in the classroom rather than the child being removed to access services.
- *Resource rooms.* Before the advent of resource rooms in the mid-1970s, children with mild learning difficulties floundered in the regular classroom, were placed in special classes, or were sent to special schools. Today, resource rooms stand at the point between

Research Notes

Paraprofessionals in Special Education

Assistance in the classroom is often offered by support personnel. These people have many titles but more and more often are being called *paraprofessionals*, "just as their counterparts in law and medicine are designated as paralegals and paramedics" (Pickett, 1989, p. 1).

Paraprofessionals first came into the schools in the 1950s. Since then, their roles have changed. What began as clerical and administrative supports for teachers has evolved from classroom helper to a greater emphasis on instructional support. Paraprofessionals now often fill roles that have traditionally been assigned to teachers. They may perform a variety of instructional and non-instructional tasks such as providing direct instruction to individuals or groups of students following the teacher's guidelines concerning choice of material and the instructional plan; tutoring and reinforcing previously taught material; providing behavioural management support; administering and scoring assessments; observing and recording data; being involved in preparation of Individual Education Plans; modifying educational materials; maintaining inventory; and ordering supplies.

As schools move toward inclusive programming, the roles of paraprofessionals will assume even greater importance. Nevertheless, while paraprofessionals are critical in the success of inclusionary practices, the mounting involvement of paraprofessionals has brought its own set of problems. Essentially, these problems revolve around the lack of a solid research base; ambivalence about the proper role of paraprofessionals by teachers, administrators, and the paraprofessionals themselves; teacher supervision of paraprofessionals; and the training, certification, and qualifications of the aides.

To date, the roles of paraprofessionals in the inclusive process have not been clearly delineated or even discussed in the literature on inclusion. Jones and Bender (1993) found only 13 experimental or quasi-experimental studies on the effects of paraprofessionals on student outcomes in special education from 1957 to 1993.

In a British Columbia study (Lamont and Hill, 1991), teachers, administrators, and paraprofessionals were asked which activities were appropriate for paraprofessionals to perform. There was general consensus that the tasks should be non-instructional and supportive in nature. A further small body of research agrees that non-teaching support personnel, whatever their title, are not meant to take away the authority of the teacher; they are to support the teacher. Teacher assistants are not to replace the educational decision making or to make plans; they are to assist the teacher in enacting plans.

For many schools, inclusion of students with special needs is a new phenomenon and learning to work with paraprofessionals is a new experience. Few teachers enter the profession with the expectation of having to direct adults, and certified teachers have little training in supervising paraprofessionals. When teachers have little or no preparation in supervision yet hold responsibility for assignments and outcomes, this can cause dissonance in some teachers; others are reluctant to supervise (French and Pickett, 1997; Salzburg and Morgan, 1995). When this situation occurs, teachers can make inappropriate decisions about the work of paraprofessionals that are driven by the teachers' fear of difference or change, their adherence to customary routines, and their reluctance to add another substantial task to what many already perceive are almost overwhelming responsibilities (Peters Goessling, 2000).

But teacher involvement and supervision is imperative as some current approaches to providing instructional assistant support might be counter-productive, and over-reliance on paraprofessionals might be a disservice to students. When aides have unfettered autonomy and are given ownership of children with special needs, two things can happen.

First, the proximity and availability of paraprofessionals can create a readily accessible opportunity for teachers to avoid assuming responsibility and ownership for the education of children with disabilities placed in their classes (see Giangreco, Edelman, MacFarland, and Luiselli, 1997). When this occurs, aides are making and implementing virtually all of the day-to-day curricula and instructional decisions. For example, in a British Columbia study (Lamont and Hill, 1991), one respondent wrote that "Behaviour management is left entirely to the judgment of the paraprofessional." Another said that "My paraprofessional is totally responsible for the personal care and well being of the child" (p. 21).

Second, aides regularly separate children with disabilities from the class group. This is not in the spirit of inclusion and, in this way, it may be that one-to-one aides are excessive and actually a barrier to inclusion by hindering a child's interaction with classmates.

As successful teaching and learning may be compromised when para-educators who have not received specialized training are providing services to students with disabilities, many jurisdictions are working to overcome problems. For example, the majority of boards in Alberta require a two-year diploma program from a recognized post-secondary institution. In British Columbia, qualifications vary by school district, but in general a one-year course or experience in a related field is required. Manitoba considers experience with children and youth an important asset. In Saskatchewan, the qualifications of paraprofessionals are set by individual school divisions. Some may require a course such as Early Childhood Education or Rehabilitation Worker ("At a glance ...," 1999). New Brunswick has the Teacher Assistance Guidelines for Standards and Evaluation (1994). In the province of Ontario, there is no provincial legislation that addresses the qualifications of paraprofessionals. However, in a position paper on professional standards and competencies for educational assistants released by the Ontario Council for Exceptional Children (CEC), a major recommendation was that all school boards should develop clear, written role descriptions for educational assistants that recognize their function as professional members of the school team (Ontario Council for Exceptional Children, 1997).

self-contained and regular classrooms. Pupils receive part of their education in the regular classroom and part of it in the resource room. This allows some learning to take place in an environment that is less distracting, less intense, and less competitive than the regular classroom. The regular classroom teacher still carries primary responsibility for program design, but works in close coordination with resource room personnel. Resource rooms have been described as "an island of learning opportunities" (Vergason and Anderegg, 1993, p. 475). Resource room teachers design, alter, and present instruction across a number of curriculum areas, and address elements that facilitate students' success in the regular environment. They may provide support in academic learning of both the core and remedial curricula, and training in social and communication skills that will help a student to interact better in the general classroom.

- *Collaboration and consultation.* Ideally, when children with disabilities are in general classrooms, teachers receive support in the form of training, help, and consultation from special education teachers and other personnel, instructional aides, and so on. Especially important is **collaboration**, a process that involves an interdependent relationship among two or more people to achieve a common goal (Salisbury, Evans, and Palombaro, 1997).

collaboration

Collaborative problem solving forges a different relationship between special education and general class teachers. By working with special education teachers, general educators learn about special education skills such as assessing learning styles and abilities, modifying curriculum, using various teaching strategies to meet student needs, and providing emotional support for students (Hanson, 1996).

Educational teams are a concrete manifestation of the collaborative process. The teacher may work on a school-based team with the principal, a psychologist, itinerant teachers, a speech therapist, a language therapist, and such allied child care personnel as audiologists and school nurses. Team collaboration provides a forum for regular and special educators to share ideas and concerns. The organization of a team is largely determined by the needs of a child and school policy (see Chapter 14).

One of the major duties of the team is to decide on both placement and program for a child who may be assigned to special education. First, the team considers a student's special difficulties in school and determines whether the student is eligible for special education. This often follows attempts at pre-referral interventions, discussed below. The team carefully considers placement. Finally (and often following further assessment) the team discusses and documents the accommodations, adaptations, and modifications that a student requires in order to succeed. The process is formalized in the preparation of an Individual Education Plan (IEP).

Pre-referral Interventions

In about 75 percent of cases, it is the general classroom teacher who refers a student for special education services (Lloyd, Kauffman, Lundrum, and Roe, 1991). Reading problems and behavioural disorders are the two main reasons that prompt teachers to refer.

pre-referral interventions

Before making such a referral, many authors suggest that teachers attempt **pre-referral interventions**. Essentially, this means making changes in the environment and instruction to see whether a child is not learning because of differences or because of disability.

Pre-referral is based on the assumption that learning problems are contextual and exist within the context of the classroom, where the curriculum design and the instructional strategies employed by the teacher influence the degree to which student needs are effectively met. If needs are not being met, then the environment should be changed.

Pre-referral interventions serve to gather data on a student's learning and behaviour. They may, though they do not necessarily, form part of the documentation that a team studies.

To implement pre-referral procedures, a teacher should

1. Gather data on behaviour, language, and achievement. Here the teacher should teach and assess basic skills to attempt to clarify the problem and determine discrepancies between a student's abilities and the demands of the classroom.
2. Look for influencing factors by examining the student's language, instructional achievements, and cultural influences.
3. Collaborate with other professionals. A common way to begin the process is to bring the problem to the attention of a team that can actively brainstorm intervention options.
4. Select the best option and determine changes that can be made in the classroom. For example, pre-referral for Native students may include peer tutoring, co-operative learn-

ing, and additional wait time with questions. For another child, a teacher may use observations, work samples, and error analysis.

5. Plan ways to implement the best option (see Winzer and Mazurek, 1998).

Individual Education Plans

The essence of special education is individualization. When educators specifically adjust the nature of student programs in response to individualization, their students learn reliably and learn dramatically more (see Fuchs, Fuchs, Hamlett, Phillips, and Karns, 1995).

Some people think that individualizing programs for pupils who are exceptional means that the teacher must work with that child on a one-to-one basis at all times. This is patently untrue. By individualizing the program for students who are exceptional, we attempt to fit the curriculum and the program to the child, rather than vice versa. The individualization is in the planning, not necessarily in the instruction. Hence, **individualization** is not a teaching method but a plan for instructional organization that may incorporate many methods. The defining characteristic of individual instruction is that each student works within learning plans designed to match his or her needs, interests, abilities, and pace of learning.

individualization

The process of adapting or modifying the regular curriculum and classroom environment often begins with an Individual Education Plan (IEP). In the United States, Individual Education Plans are mandated under federal special education legislation. Canadian jurisdictions are less prescriptive. A survey by the Canadian Council for Exceptional Children found that IEPs were mandated in eight provinces or territories (see Kasko, 2000).

In broad terms, the individual program is the manifestation of the philosophy of individualization as well as of pragmatic intentions concerning what to teach, who will teach it, and how it will be evaluated. Each student's IEP is a broad statement that assists teachers by pre-specifying the goals and objectives of instruction and ensuring that the educational program is appropriate to the child's specific needs. The plan of action outlines the short-term objectives and long-term goals, describes the methods and techniques that will be used to achieve them, and details the responsibilities of various people, such as the classroom teacher, the resource room teacher, or the speech therapist, who will help the child along the way.

The IEP is a personalized program that is prepared annually, usually at an early point in the year. It is filled in before programming begins, and therefore writing the first Individual Education Plan for a child with a disability is largely guesswork. The goals and objectives are hypotheses about what a child can and cannot do and about a child's critical needs. Moreover, the process of programming for needs is a dynamic one. An IEP is not a static document or a performance contract. Nor is it written in stone. The IEP is a communication document that is constantly modified and changed to match a child's progress and needs. A child who is visually impaired, for example, may in fact be visually impaired for life, but that child's needs will change, not merely each year but perhaps each week or even each day.

The major problem confronting teachers is determining and prioritizing the skills that are important to teach. Skill determination is easier for children with mild disabilities, who generally follow the curriculum designed for their normally developing peers, and the IEP shows the degree of involvement in the regular program as well as adaptations. These students may need only minor changes that can be documented on one page. On the other hand, the most complex IEPs are for children with communication disorders, because language comprises so many interdependent functions.

Format of Individual Education Plans

The actual formats of IEPs differ markedly. Most, however, contain certain components. These are:

1. IEP data. Many plans contain information about the preparation of the IEP. It may state the names and positions of those attending the team meeting when the IEP was drawn up and whether the IEP is an initial document, a second IEP, or an evaluation document.
2. Placement. This is a statement of the educational setting considered most appropriate for the student with special needs.
3. A summary of the student's present level of performance across a range of domains. Each individual plan is founded on an assessment designed to discover the child's strengths and weaknesses in the areas of cognitive development, physical and motor development, socio-emotional development, and adaptive behaviour. With a record of a child's performance based on information derived from an assessment or assessments, those preparing the IEP can pinpoint a child's present levels of performance and then determine the skills the child needs to acquire. That is, assessment data should tell us where a child is functioning and how that compares to normal developmental levels.

goal

4. Long-term or annual goals. A **goal** may be defined as a stated outcome desired as the result of some action. On an IEP, goals are broad general statements that help to focus on the general areas for which individualized programming is to be provided. They indicate the priorities for intervention—the major learning experiences the child will have and the broad range of skills that he or she can be expected to attain. Long-range goals are usually written for one year, except in the case of children with significant disabilities, who may have long-range goals over a greater period, up to five years.

   Taking assessment results, translating them into present levels of performance, and then using them in planning and individualized programming is not as straightforward as it may seem at first. In fact, the process is quite complicated and takes much careful thought. In using assessment information for IEPs, there are three basic steps. The present levels of functioning should provide a list of a child's strengths and weaknesses. These are divided into skills that need remediation, skills that are delayed, and skills within the normal ranges. Once this is done, skills are targeted for intervention (long-term goals). These are then written as short-term objectives. Typically, five to ten goals are identified in the domains of functioning where the child is showing the greatest lags. When they are written down, the goals should represent a specific expectation or skill (as opposed to a vague generic statement). For example, "Learn to read" is not specific enough, whereas "Will read books at grade one level" is.
5. Short-term objectives for each annual goal. An *objective* is a clear statement of exactly what a teacher wants a child to be able to do as a result of instruction. Objectives refer to increments in the progress of learning from the present level of functioning to the child's annual goals. Objectives are the steps toward achieving the goals, and they help to direct instruction and learning on a day-to-day basis. Short-term objectives are provided for each

annual goal. There is no rule, but generally three or four objectives are provided for each long-range goal.

The way to turn long-range goals into short-term objectives is through *task analysis,* breaking skills down into their component parts. All of the small tasks that make up the larger skill are listed. The number of sub-skills depends on the task and the individual needs of the child. Good behavioural objectives are written as brief action statements that use verbs that lend themselves to observation and measurement. Appropriate verbs include *apply, describe, recognize, repeat, copy, reproduce, choose, draw, classify, match, identify,* and *select.*

6. Specific educational and support services needed to attain each educational objective. Once goals and objectives are identified, the next step is to select and sequence the most appropriate learning experiences to achieve those aims and objectives. However, in a sense an IEP represents a philosophy of what should be taught rather than illustrations of how it should happen. Examples of how to accomplish an objective may appear, but every approach, activity, or group interaction will not.
7. Personnel who will hold primary responsibility for specific long-range goals and short-term objectives. The program outlines the responsibilities of various people, such as teachers or therapists, who will assist the child. It shows the kinds of services required (such as speech therapy), the type of instruction (individual or group), and the time to be spent in each activity (half an hour a day).
8. Individuals responsible for specific elements, such as a speech therapist.
9. Anticipated duration of the services.
10. Specific evaluation procedures for each objective. These are the criteria for determining whether the objectives have been attained.
11. Procedures for re-evaluating the total IEP document.

Instructional Practices

No universal conviction exists about how to teach children who are exceptional. There is no such thing as a panacea. Behaviour modification, individualized programming, direct instruction, and task analysis, along with children's own motivations and needs, cannot be administered through a generalized curriculum and set of techniques that are appropriate to all students and to all teachers at all times. Among educators, common ground is reached only concerning the necessity for a more detailed assessment of strengths and needs, greater individualization of instruction and curriculum (the IEP), and more careful and systematic monitoring of performance.

The techniques that often work with normally developing students do not always work with those who are exceptional. However, the reverse is true; the same instructional strategies that work with students with special needs are the ones that work with all students.

Teachers are therefore challenged to find innovative ways to enhance the learning environment to accommodate the learning differences and behavioural difficulties of pupils who are exceptional. They must adapt materials, teaching techniques, and activities to the particular needs of their students. When instructing, they should use concrete techniques, generalize skills, apply learning at the appropriate level, begin instruction at children's tolerance level, provide individual and small group instruction, chart progress regularly, and keep careful records.

Social Intervention

Social intervention covers a spectrum of services that can be grouped under the general category of *child welfare.* A primary concern is the care and treatment of the child within the family environment. A wide range of personnel are involved in service delivery—giving assistance to people who need it. They include social workers, family counsellors, foster parents, child advocates, child care workers, probation officers, and so on, who try to ensure that the child develops under the care of the family or surrogate family.

Child Advocacy

child advocacy
child advocate

Child advocacy can be defined as any social, political, or legal action that is intended to achieve a better life for children from infancy to late adolescence (Lourie, 1975). A **child advocate** is anyone who pleads a child's cause or defends a particular child-related cause.

Child advocacy is a wide-ranging movement that functions at several levels. It involves a spectrum of activities that identify the needs of children and try to rectify unsatisfactory practices. A major goal of advocacy is to stimulate public and professional response to the child's needs and problems. Increasingly, advocates are playing an integral part in the education of children who are exceptional.

Advocacy is one function of parent organizations that have initiated services in education, residential living (most specifically group homes), and vocational alternatives. Some parent groups have started and operated services, while others have been catalysts and now work with community organizations (see Chapter 15).

The efforts of parents have been supported and supplemented by professional and educational groups who also view advocacy as one of their primary functions. For example, parents are primary players in the Canadian Association for Community Living (formerly the Canadian Association for the Mentally Retarded) and the Canadian Learning Disabilities Association (formerly the Association for Children with Learning Disabilities).

SUMMARY

1. Children who are exceptional are those who deviate in some way from what society calls normal. However, the norm itself encompasses a wide range of behaviours from which everyone deviates to some degree.
2. Over the years, the way that professionals and society in general have described persons with exceptionalities has changed in a positive way. In the past, the terms used to describe people who were exceptional were value-laden and tended to emphasize the person's handicap, disorder, or disability. Today's terms are non-stigmatizing and as clear and unambiguous as possible.
3. In spite of the proliferation of labels in the health and education fields, and despite the fact that child-based categorical systems retain their popularity, many professionals see the traditional system of labelling children by their primary disability as not always useful. However, labels probably both stigmatize and help students.

Historical Notes

Society's attitude toward persons with disabilities has always been complex, fashioned at any given time by the prevailing culture, religion, government, and economic conditions. Because the care, training, and education of individuals with exceptionalities has tended to mirror societal attitudes, the history of disability and the history of special education can be seen as following historical trends, rather than creating them.

The history of disability extends far back in time. Persons with disabilities were mentioned by the ancient Egyptians, Greeks, and Romans, and in the Bible. The greatest attention was directed toward those considered mad or insane, a population that traditionally included persons with mental retardation and those with epilepsy. Hippocrates and the Roman physicians Galen and Celsus also intervened in cases of people with deafness, blindness, and overt physical disabilities.

Although the historical record is murky, it seems that from humanity's earliest beginnings and through many ages persons with disabilities were grossly mistreated. Their conditions were considered hopeless, and in most cultures they were scorned as degraded and inferior beings. A more humane climate emerged in the mid-1700s; it saw the development of treatment and the beginnings of special education.

Although the first documented reports of intervention with special students come from late-16th-century Spain, it was not until the middle decades of the 18th century that Britain and Europe turned their attention to the education of their disabled populations. In France, a new social philosophy, ushered in by Enlightenment thought, brought about major educational advances. The pioneer French educators such as Michel de l'Épée, Jacob Periere, Valentin Häuy, and Edouard Seguin adopted novel philosophical concepts about sensationalism, the psychology of language, and the use of alternate sensory stimuli, and joined them to the new concepts of social equality and individual rights. With their advances in establishing permanent schools and delineating specific methodologies, particularly for students who were deaf, blind, or mentally disabled, these French educators emerged as the founders of special education as we know it today.

North American special education began in 1817 with the founding of an institution for deaf students at Hartford, Connecticut. The first Canadian special school, again for persons who were deaf, opened near Montreal in 1831 but lack of funds forced it to close within five years, and it was not until 1848 that permanent residential schools were established in British North America.

For reasons of economy and convenience, students who were exceptional were chiefly educated in institutional settings. However, very few children were actually served. Differentiation among exceptional conditions was murky, and energies were directed to those with obvious and overt disabilities. Schooling was open to children with sensory impairments (those deaf and blind); to those with intellectual problems (known then as idiotic and feeble-minded); and to those considered to be socially at risk (vagrant, neglected, and delinquent children). A concern for children with mild disabilities and the emergence of categories such as *emotionally disturbed, childhood psychoses, physical and health disabilities,* and *learning disabilities* was largely a phenomenon of the first half of the 20th century.

For decades, students with disabilities were excluded from general classrooms and educated in residential institutions or the special segregated classes that began seriously in the public schools in about 1910 and expanded rapidly in the following decades. Placement in institutions, special classes, and special schools remained the common mode in the education of students with disabilities right into the 1960s.

But for many years there had been a simmering

controversy in the field revolving around the tension between training students with disabilities to fit into so-called normal society and training them in regard to their unique needs. The most salient manifestation of this tension was (and continues to be) the often acrimonious debate about students' school address; that is, their educational placement.

The 1960s was the benchmark era. It brought the philosophy of normalization (see Chapter 2), mounting and vexatious questioning of the value of special education, a series of efficacy studies that provided pessimistic evidence of just what special education was achieving, and shocking exposés of the conditions in institutions for persons with mental retardation and juvenile delinquents.

In the 1970s, intensive scrutiny of the knowledge and practices of special education continued, and simultaneous discontent with special classes peaked. Many questioned the necessity for a dual system of education, particularly the high proportion of educational funding directed toward special education; the fragmentary nature of so much of special education's service delivery; and the potential stigmatization of children identified for special education. Adding to this were concerns about the civil rights of children with disabilities; it was argued that segregated classes are inherently discriminatory and unequal. Agitation by parent and professional groups led to new legislation and many of the changes that are apparent in special education today. With enabling legislation passed in the United States in 1975 (Public Law 94-142), the way opened for large numbers of students with exceptional conditions to move into local schools and general classrooms.

The ripples of the 1970s turned into a strong tide in the 1980s as there were dramatic increases in the number of students mainstreamed into general classrooms. By 1991, only 26 percent of students with disabilities in Canada attended a special school or a special class in a regular school (Oderkirk, 1993).

Today we see continuing efforts by boards of education and other agencies to increase the universality of special education services. The trend is toward *inclusive schooling.* The term emerged in the professional literature in 1984 and has become the dominant discourse in special education since then. Inclusion in its various facets is addressed in every chapter of this text.

4. Children requiring special education may be taught in settings that range from the general classroom to a residential school or hospital program.
5. To fully accomplish the aim of individualizing instruction for children with exceptionalities, special education teachers and those involved in educationally integrating these students combine their resources with a wide range of personnel.
6. Many children with special needs require various types of therapy. A child with poor articulation may require help from a speech therapist; a child who has lost a limb will need physical therapy; an adolescent with cerebral palsy may benefit from occupational therapy.
7. Educational teams tend to be multidisciplinary in nature, with the major duties of planning, implementation, and evaluation of educational programs for special students.
8. The team prepares an Individual Education Plan (IEP), a written planning document that outlines educational services and learning objectives to meet the specific needs of a child. It aims to coordinate plans and services, personalize and individualize a child's program, and integrate the individual plan with the overall plans for the classroom group.

WEBLINKS

The Canadian Child Care Federation **www.cfc-efc.ca/cccf/**

The Council for Exceptional Children (CEC) **www.cec.sped.org**

Disability Information for Students **www.abilityinfo.com/**

Disabled Peoples' International **www.escape.ca/~dpi/**

ERIC Clearing House on Disabilities and Gifted Education **ericec.org**

General information on special education **www.pacer.org**; **www.fape.org**

IEP Guide (U.S.) **www.ed.gov.offices/OSERS/OSEP/IEP.Guide/**

The Integrated Network of Disability Information and Education **laurence.canlearn.ca/english/learn/newaccessguide/indie/**

Special Needs Education Network **www.schoolnet.ca/sne**

Special needs education project: Resources prepared under the auspices of SchoolNet, a co-operative initiative of Canada's provincial, territorial, and federal governments (also available in French) **www.schoolnet.ca/sne/**

Chapter 2

Issues and Trends in Canadian Special Education

Learning Outcomes

After reading this chapter, you should be able to:

Understand the debates in contemporary special education in relation to reforms in general education;

Recognize the changing paradigms in special education specifically as they relate to inclusive schooling;

Understand the importance of legislation and litigation in both Canada and the United States;

Detail and explain some major trends in contemporary special education;

Relate the procedures of early intervention to the types of intervention discussed in Chapter 1;

Understand the different stages of the assessment process and some of the procedures used, with particular reference to functional assessment.

Introduction

Social attitudes toward the education, care, and training of individuals who are exceptional usually reflect more general cultural attitudes toward the obligations of a society to its individual citizens. It is only recently that the creation of societies where persons who are exceptional can live productive and fulfilling lives has become an imperative, not just a dream.

In today's climate of heightened social identity, justice and equity are perceived in fundamentally different ways than in the past. As a newly evolving social philosophy has emphasized the value of the individual and the rights of every citizen, the prospects for people who are exceptional have altered positively in the social, occupational, and educational arenas.

In the past thirty years, education has seen a dramatic swing in ideas regarding educational placement as educators, officials, legislators, and parents attempt to reform, revamp, and generally improve services for students with special needs. Such reform efforts are not new—

they have characterized special education from its beginnings. As the Historical Notes at the end of this chapter show, the history of special education reveals a plethora of changes and reforms, all reflective of a gradual humanizing of attitudes toward persons with exceptionalities.

A field as historically complex and as diverse as special education is bound to reveal controversial issues and unsolved dilemmas and to reflect major social trends and movements. Over the years, both generic and category-specific controversies and dilemmas have emerged. In the contemporary arena, the most hotly debated general issue concerns inclusion, or inclusive schooling.

Inclusion in special education is not a minor reform; rather, it is a fundamental conceptual shift that involves the way in which people with disabilities and their place in society are seen and how educational rights are provided. Operationalized, inclusive schooling equates with school restructuring. In this way, it cannot be treated as a new program or innovation, as a discretionary responsibility rather than a core value. Inclusion must be seen as part of the fabric of a school's restructuring efforts. The focus is on all students, all teachers, all curricular reforms, all support personnel, all policies, all strategies for student assessment, and so on (see Ferguson, 1998). It follows, then, that a broad spectrum of other trends and movements, all related in some way to inclusion, are germane to contemporary special education.

The aim of this chapter is to familiarize readers with broad general issues that are currently under debate within special education and to present some of the relevant arguments. Dilemmas related to specific groups of students such as bilingual education for those who are deaf or acceleration practices in gifted education are reserved for the categorical chapters.

Here we direct the greatest attention to issues that directly impact on the teacher in the classroom. Of these, inclusion tops the list. It is important to understand the varied parameters of the movement, which include the development, the terminology, the debates, and the ways in which inclusion can be best implemented. Other current topics include legislation and litigation; early identification and intervention; transition services for adolescents; assessment practices and procedures; and students with cultural and linguistic differences.

To do justice to these issues would take an entire book for each. We can discuss only some of the major issues quite briefly in this chapter in an attempt to alert readers to the movements and trends and to lay the groundwork for later chapters in this text. Throughout the discussion, it should be kept in mind that reforms in education are continuous and that this text is a document written in a particular place at a particular time. It represents only a snapshot of special education and cannot faithfully reproduce the dynamic shifts that are occurring in the field. In addition, changes in special education are not always neat and may require many detours. Policy implementation is not so much an event but a process that is slow, multifaceted, and incremental, one that is ongoing and influenced by many external forces that include legislation, politics, medicine, ethics, and economics, to mention only a few.

CHANGING VIEWS OF EXCEPTIONALITY

Traditionally, North American society has not shown a high tolerance for persons who are exceptional. In the past, individuals were stigmatized and stereotyped by prevailing attitudes toward their disabilities. Special education was a service delivery system that adhered to contemporary social attitudes toward deviance. When the old adage "out of sight, out of mind" held sway, persons with exceptionalities were placed in institutions and other segregated settings for their care and training.

Recent decades have witnessed significant increases in public awareness and understanding of individuals who are exceptional. In general, our society has shifted from qualitative to quantitative conceptions of exceptionality. The qualitative model held that persons with disabilities were different and deviant—they learned, perceived, and thought in ways that were unlike the norm. Conversely, the quantitative model views differences as a matter of degree, not kind—people who are exceptional develop and function much as others do, but their progress may be slower and their achievements more restricted. Exceptionalities are no longer viewed as solely within the individual; a complex interplay of innate characteristics and environmental variables is instead considered.

The decade of the 1960s was a major crucible for changes in public perceptions and portrayals of persons with disabilities. Today's efforts to provide surroundings, opportunities, and programs much like those provided for non-disabled persons stem from programs originally undertaken in the Scandinavian countries in the mid-1960s. Most critical are ideas of **normalization**, the philosophical belief that all individuals who are exceptional, no matter what their level and type of disability, should be provided with an education and living environment as close to normal as possible. Normalization and its corollary, deinstitutionalization, are discussed in the accompanying Research Notes feature.

normalization

The new social philosophy emphasized the value of the individual and the rights of every citizen. Since then, overcoming barriers to allow persons with disabilities to fully participate in social and economic life has become a major policy concern in Canada. Promoted is an inclusive lifestyle that is defined as "Pervasive participation in family, friendships, school, work, and community life consistent with one's preferences and characterized by reponsive and reciprocal supports" (Turnbull and Reuf, 1997, p. 223).

Supporters of normalization argue that all people who are exceptional deserve an educational and living environment that is as close to normal as possible.

Research Notes

Normalization and Changes in Perceptions

During the 1960s, the civil rights movement brought about new conceptions of disability. Arguments held that persons with disabilities had a civil right to live, attend school, and work in the same environment as others. In Scandinavia, Bank-Mikkleson introduced the concept and incorporated the principle of normalization into Danish law in 1959. Benge Nirje, then Secretary General of the Swedish Association for Retarded Children, began to apply the ideas in about 1967.

Normalization, as defined by Nirje, was "making available to all mentally retarded people patterns of life and conditions of everyday living which are as close as possible to the regular circumstances of society" (Nirje, 1979, p. 173). The principles of normalization were rapidly translated to North America and Canada and expanded to include all persons with disabilities, along with those with mental retardation.

Normalization principles provide guidelines for the treatment of people with disabilities, as well as concrete suggestions for action. The major aim is for society to regard persons with disabilities as individuals and to treat them fairly and humanely. There will be a normal family and community life for all as the traditional boundaries raised by disabling conditions are broached and people who are exceptional fill a variety of roles in general society and are offered the chance of a normal life routine, normal developmental experiences, independent choices, and the right to live, work, and play in normal surroundings. Ultimately, normalization will have occurred when individuals who are exceptional live with members of the cultural group in a normal domicile within the community and have access to all the privileges and services that are available to others. This includes education in neighbourhood schools and general education classes.

An obvious outgrowth of the philosophy of normalization is the process of deinstitutionalization. In the physical sense, deinstitutionalization is the movement of individuals from large institutions into community-based living arrangements such as group homes and halfway houses. In the broader social context, deinstitutionalization addresses a return to the community, maintenance in the community, the respect of other citizens, and acceptance by peers and others in the culture.

An *institution* is defined as a publicly supported, professionally managed facility housing fifteen or more people with similar disabilities. In Canada, most provinces and territories have policies supporting deinstitutionalization. Any building of new institutions is being strongly resisted by citizens' groups, who are demanding community supports and services instead. Today the residential institution is rarely considered an option for children who are disabled.

REFORMS IN EDUCATION

Changes and reforms in contemporary special education cannot be fully appreciated without a digression into reforms within the entire educational arena. It was during the 1980s that the outcomes of general education became a key concern of reform and a top political priority. Parents, legislators, the general public, and educators themselves pointed to the gaps and deficiencies in the current educational system. Some critics went so far as to assert that education was tottering on the brink of chaos and failure and that educational reform had to be a major objective in North American education.

As Canada elevated school reform to a major movement for all levels and for all populations, the literature was replete with a myriad of initiatives to change the structure and culture of schools. Educational reforms generally focussed on six policy areas—standards, assessment, accountability, governance, teachers, and finance (Goertz and Friedman, 1996). Reformers called for greater accountability from schools and teachers; advanced academic achievement from students, especially in mathematics and science; improvement in literacy skills; a halting or lessening of dropout rates; the incorporation of multi-ethnic and multicultural perspectives into classrooms and schools; ways to promote bilingualism and to teach students with limited English proficiency; and the promotion of educational equality and opportunity for all students. A rash of terms and ideas emerged surrounding educational reform; ideas ranged from administrative practices such as lengthening the school day to full-scale restructuring of education systems (for example, providing open enrolment options).

One of the overarching objectives of the movement toward reforming and restructuring education was the creation of socially just and democratic communities by changing school communities to coordinate and bridge programs and services so as to transform schools to places where all students belong and learn together. The term that emerged to describe educational systems where equity was in place for all students was *inclusion,* or *inclusive schooling.* (For more on inclusive education in the general system in Canada see Dei, James, James-Wilson, Karumanchery, and Zine, 2000.)

REFORMS IN SPECIAL EDUCATION

The reform movement did not pass special education by. On the contrary: In the late 1980s, special education became deeply embroiled in reform efforts and was subjected to enormous pressures for change. Rhetoric called for special education to "break the mould," for "revolution," a "paradigm shift," a "fundamental reconceptualization," and "radical restructuring" (Kauffman, 1993, p. 10).

In many ways, the reform movement in special education articulated in the 1980s paralleled the reforms taking place in general education. But special education reform can trace its roots farther back—at least to the 1960s. As we point out in the Historical Notes and in the Research Notes on normalization, at the close of the 1960s the influence of the civil rights movement melded with pressure for normalization as espoused in the Scandinavian countries and a disenchantment with special education as it was then practised. All of this led eventually to the formulation of new policies and the adoption of new legislation and other administrative arrangements.

Our interest here is in changes in the ways that schools conceptualized the needs of students with exceptionalities and how they attended to those needs. From the late 1960s on, students with exceptionalities were increasingly drawn within the orbit of the public schools. The responsibility to provide equal access to an education in a manner most appropriate to their needs gradually became embedded in legislation and supported by ethical and philosophical precepts. Placement and instructional procedures that used terms such as *integration,* the *least restrictive environment* (LRE), and *mainstreaming* emerged and were practised.

Today, efforts to bring about basic structural changes in the fundamental operating mode of special education, to improve educational practice, and to operationalize a closer merger between general and special education are encompassed under a concept and practice variously termed *inclusion, inclusive schooling, inclusive education,* and, occasionally, *progressive inclusion.*

Development of the Inclusionary Movement

Over the past four decades, the gradual process of more and more children with exceptionalities receiving their special education while enrolled in general education classes and schools has been described in a number of ways. In the 1950s and 1960s, *integration* was the common term used to refer to the education of students with exceptionalities in general classrooms. The term is still popular.

Mainstreaming, often used as a synonym for integration, emerged in special education in the 1970s. The basic goal of mainstreaming was the provision of free, appropriate education in the most suitable setting for all youngsters with exceptionalities. Philosophically, mainstreaming focused on the integration of children with exceptionalities with their nondisabled peers within the context of the neighbourhood school. As a process, mainstreaming provided services along a continuum—a range of educational options and support services such as the resource rooms described in Chapter 1. This range of available services allowed pupils to be integrated in the least restrictive environment (LRE) in the manner best suited to their individual needs, supported by individual programming in the form of an Individual Education Plan (IEP).

During the 1980s, complaints about the mainstreaming movement were legion. Critics cried that special education "does not work. That is, it fails to serve well the students" (Lipsky and Gartner, 1991, p. 43). Only a small number of children were being mainstreamed, resource rooms were not functioning as effectively as they should, and the promises of the Individual Education Plan were not being met. As well, regular education and special education still functioned in the traditional way—as parallel rather than integrated enterprises.

The solution, the 1986 Regular Education Initiative (REI), reinterpreted mainstreaming. Essentially, the REI had two major processes. First, it required a closer merging of general and special education resources so that students with quite diverse, heterogeneous needs could be educated in the same classroom. Second, the REI advocated the integration of students with low-incidence and severe disabilities into the general educational system and the retention of students with mild and moderate disabilities in general classrooms where general educators would assume unequivocal, primary responsibility for all students.

The next step was *inclusion,* or *inclusive schooling,* which connotes subtle but real differences from integration or mainstreaming. Advocates of inclusive schooling argue that the social-cultural realities of mainstreaming and integration are that one group is viewed as the "mainstream" and one group is not; hence, one group must "push in" to the activities and settings occupied by the other (Salisbury, 1991).

Integration and mainstreaming sought to change individuals to fit the existing system; inclusion seeks to change the system so that exclusion and marginalization are avoided. Under the principles of inclusion children do not push into the mainstream, because the underlying supposition in inclusive programs is that all children will be based in the classrooms they would attend if they did not have a disability. Promoters insist that the most enlightened system alters classroom and school structures to allow all children to gain an education there.

Defining Inclusive Schooling

In the current climate, it is probably more apt to talk about inclusions rather than a single inclusion. The area is fluid and changing rapidly; swings and surges in philosophy remain the fundamental bottom line. The ideal of full inclusion, never universally shared or endorsed by all of those concerned with the education of children with exceptionalities, has ceded to discussions of selective or responsible inclusion, and implementation sees a variety of models and programs.

Inclusion hosts a range of theoretical positions related to the underlying philosophy, the relationship of those targeted for inclusion, the nature of the general educational provision, and the manner in which supports are provided. Inclusion means different things to different people, who see inclusion in different ways and want different things from it. Advocates for persons with severe and profound disabilities prompt full inclusion—the child in a general education setting full time. These proponents view inclusive schooling as an issue of access to education and stress its anticipated effects in the social domain. In contrast, those advocating for students with learning disabilities and other milder problems want services that address academic needs. They focus on whether inclusion represents another way to enhance academic and social achievement and wish to retain a continuum of education services.

Nor is there yet a solid research base to show the effectiveness (or ineffectiveness) of any type of inclusive model. The evidence for students with mild disabilities remains inconclusive (Manset and Semmel, 1997); that for students with significant disabilities is contentious (see Chapter 13). So far, there are no comprehensive data available on special education students' academic gains, graduation rates, preparation for post-secondary schooling or work, or involvement in community living.

With the varied perceptions and needs and the lack of robust data, it is easy to see why inclusive schooling defies easy interpretation and to understand why proponents of the various kinds of inclusion do not agree on definitions. Inclusive education is variously interpreted in the literature, and definitions of inclusive schooling abound.

For example, the (Canada) Council of Administrators of Special Education (CASE) (2000) states that: "Inclusion means that students with disabilities are educated in supported, heterogeneous, age appropriate, and natural and student-centred classrooms, school and community environments for the purpose of preparing them for full participation in a diverse and integrated society." The Council for Exceptional Children (CEC), the largest organization for special education professionals in the world, holds that "individuals with disabilities should be served whenever possible in general education classrooms in inclusive neighborhood schools and community settings" (1993).

Both the CEC and CASE recommend general classroom placements with appropriate supports for child and teacher. However, both also hold that "a continuum of service delivery options must always be available" (see CASE, 1997, p.3; CEC, 1993).

To reconcile different interpretations, we define inclusion in this text broadly. We see inclusive education as *a system of equity for students with exceptionalities that expresses a commitment to educate each child to the maximum extent through placement, instruction, and support in the most heterogeneous and appropriate educational environment.*

Each phrase in this and other conceptions of inclusive schooling is important. To wit:

- *Equity.* Equal opportunity implies equal educational rights for all children and youth. As Smith (1994) notes, "Young people with disabilities have an equal right to be in school and to have something meaningful happen once they are inside" (p. 7).
- *Heterogeneous.* Students of varied abilities and strengths will be in all classrooms. In such heterogeneous settings the learning/teaching bond is forged in normalized ways instead of in segregated settings where a disability classification is the common denominator.
- *Placement.* The general classroom is the least restrictive environment. But each child should be treated individually and a continuum of services is necessary to accommodate the diverse needs of students with exceptionalities. Location is not the key; the provision of supports and effective services and instruction is.

  The ultimate goal is integration in the general classroom with normally developing peers, but how much time in general classrooms is enough to be called inclusion? Usually, a minimum of 50 percent of the day is necessary, but each classroom is different (see Peters Goessling, 2000).
- *Supported.* The settings in which students are placed are strengthened and supported by an infusion of specially trained personnel and other appropriate supportive practices according to the individual needs of the child. Resources and supports include access to specialists, collaborative planning and decision making, appropriate environments and equipment, individual planning, and the availability of paraprofessionals.

Examining Inclusive Schooling

There is not an area in special education more difficult than inclusion. At the root of the difficulties is the fact that inclusion is both a philosophy and a practice. While the philosophy is fairly well accepted, the major difficulties come with attempting to translate the principles into efficient school-based service delivery models. As Lupart observes, "Although many Canadians agree with this goal in principle, few agree about how to achieve it" (Lupart, 1998, p. 256).

Figure 2-1 lays out the major philosophical strands of the inclusive movement and shows the processes needed for successful implementation. It also shows how both merge and collide with barriers in existing school systems. The major points are described below and further elucidated in the Debate box on p. 45.

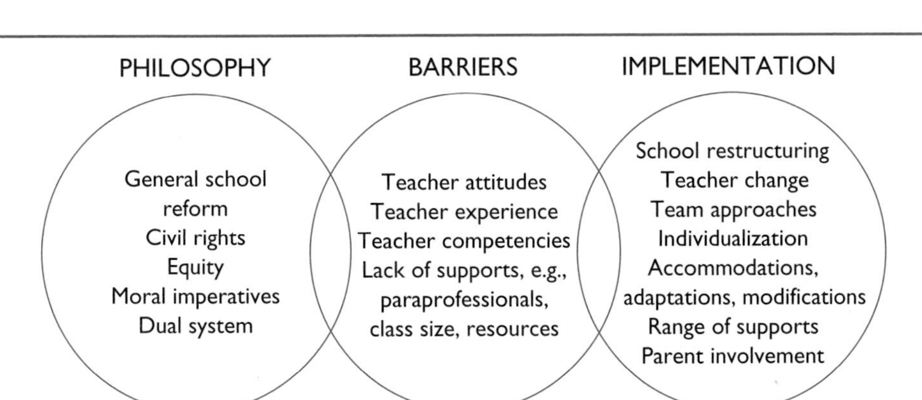

Figure 2-1 *Principles of inclusion*

Philosophy of Inclusion

The concept that school systems should provide for students with a wide range of needs can be supported from a relatively coherent set of basic assumptions. Essentially, these intertwined assumptions are:

- *General school reform.* As mentioned earlier, reforms in special education echo the thrust toward inclusion in general education.
- *Civil rights.* Special education is intimately connected to common views of social justice. The provision of less restrictive, more natural integrated environments for students with disabilities is an outgrowth of a social philosophy about individual civil rights that is so critical in the United States. Proponents argue that special classes are discriminatory and unequal and in violation of the democratic ethos that allows equal access to education for all students. That is, removal from the mainstream of education is inherently restrictive and limiting and the right to be educated with one's peers is a civil right (see Walmsley and Allington, 1995).
- *Equity.* Equity was discussed in our definition of inclusive schooling. It means that if all students are to gain the skills they need to meet the challenges of life then all must be assured the same opportunity to succeed in school regardless of differences in learning, behaviour, or other attributes.
- *Dual system.* Inclusion as a merger of regular and special education was mentioned in the mid-1980s (e.g., Will, 1986). In 1987, writers (Reynolds, Wang, and Walberg, 1987) called for "the joining of demonstrably effective practices from special, compensatory, and general education to establish a general educational system that is *more inclusive*, and better serves all students, particularly those who require greater-than-usual educational support" (p. 394, italics added).

Implementation

Inclusion is a radically different way of conceptualizing children and represents a fundamental change in who does what, to whom it is done, where it is done, and how resources support what is done. But many barriers continue to exist and concerns over practical implications on a wide scale have resulted in much divisiveness among parents and educators over the merits of the inclusionary ideal (Palmer, Borthwick-Duffy, and Widaman, 1998).

Inclusive schooling is complex, involving not only the children with special needs but also teachers, evaluation, and attitudes; indeed, it means restructuring of an entire school. The factors necessary for successful inclusionary practices are shown in the In the Classroom feature for Section 2 (see p. 202).

Barriers

Many contemporary educators hold that individuals with disabilities should be served whenever possible in general education classrooms in inclusive neighbourhood schools and community settings. But when implementation is broached, a consensus has not been reached, and there are often contradictions between espoused policy and actual practice. Some major barriers are outlined below.

- *Teacher attitudes.* Much recent work on school change emphasizes the key role of the individual teacher. It stresses that teachers' beliefs are powerful and enduring and act

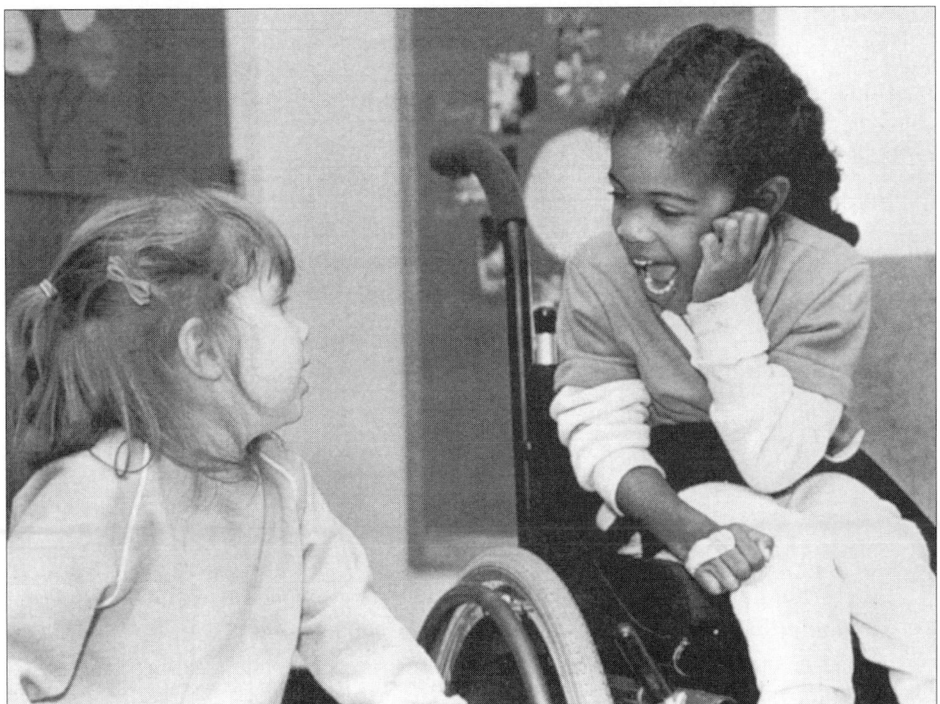

The social integration of children who are exceptional is essential to the success of inclusion.

as filters on teachers' construction of philosophy. As supportive attitudes by teachers are a condition without which inclusive programs cannot be effective, so policies for implementation must account for the pervasiveness of attitudes in shaping perceptions and actions.

Many teachers support the philosophy of inclusion. A recent national study of 1492 Canadian teachers found that more than two-thirds of teachers believe that inclusion is academically beneficial to children with special needs and their peers in regular classrooms, and 90 percent of teachers cite social benefits (Galt, 1997; "Resistance ...," 1997). Nevertheless, while many teachers express support for the principles of inclusion, they tend to articulate the weaknesses in the shifting propositions, to identify critical problems in implementation, and to show a persistent uneasiness about the practice. One recent survey of teachers (D'Alonzo, Giordano, and Vanleuven, 1997) found skepticism and mixed opinion about the potential benefits and an overwhelming expectation that problems would be inherent in a unified system of education.

Teachers' resistance should not be attributed to a dislike of children with disabilities, a rejection of inclusionary philosophies, or by characterizing teachers as the Achilles heel of educational reform. Many factors contribute. One may be that educators have had little input into the inclusionary process (Bradley and West, 1994). Writers observe that "Although a range of perceptions on the issue of inclusion have been aired, the views of classroom teachers are noticeably missing from the public discussion of inclusion" (Vaughn, Schumm, Jallad, Slushar, and Saunell, 1996, p. 96).

Lacking the required skills, teachers are often unwilling to make the pilgrimage toward meeting the needs of special learners. That is, teacher competencies form a substantial barrier. In fact, perhaps the most commonly cited source of resistance is a lack of skills necessary to teach students with disabilities (Minke, Bear, Deiner, and Griffin, 1996).

Concerns about inclusion are most acute in relation to novice teachers. Tomlinson and colleagues (1997) noted that novice teachers typically have a narrow understanding of student differences, use an apparently random selection of solutions for commonly occurring classroom problems, and apply a relatively limited range of instructional strategies with children. Goodlad and Field (1993) found in a national U.S. study that preservice teachers rated their own abilities to teach children with disabilities as the lowest of twelve domains of perceived instructional competence. They also found that many preservice general educators are aware of their own limited instructional competence with children with exceptionalities but are not inclined to do anything about it.

At the same time, many veteran teachers broadly resist mandates to differentiate curriculum and instruction for a wide range of learners (Behar and George, 1994) and make few modifications in general classrooms for learners who are gifted (Archambault, Westberg, Brown, Hallmark, Zhang, and Emmons, 1993) and those who qualify for special education (Bateman, 1993).

Special educators may also lack skills. In a recent survey by the Governmental Relations Committee of the Canadian Council for Exceptional Children, only three of the reporting ten provinces and territories noted that special education teachers need a certificate indicating their qualifications in the field (Kasko, 2000).

- *Conflicting principles.* Macro-reform is mediated by micro principles in school practices. Prevailing values define what is important and how such issues should be dealt with. Inclusion is not the only principle driving contemporary education. The values of inclusion may come into conflict with other values teachers hold dear, such as achievement and merit, and also with the dual restraints of heightened responsibilities and accountability. Hence, whether inclusion is right or wrong, effective or ineffective may not be as moot as how it merges with other principles.
- *Lack of supports.* Dissonance remains between policy aspirations and teachers' abilities. For a substantial number of educators, the controlling factors are concerns about workload and supports.

Implicitly, inclusion demands that supports be brought to the classroom to the child, not that the child be removed to the supports. Supports are varied, ranging from adaptive equipment to speech therapy to a paraprofessional. Supports for teachers include additional personnel assistance such as an aide or daily contact with special education teachers for collaborative teaming and teaching and shared planning, planning time, and small class sizes.

The target of equal education cannot be met by placing students with disabilities in the general system without the supports needed to accommodate their particular needs. However, the resource question is a major bone of contention between inclusion supporters and skeptics. Most general classroom teachers do not feel that inclusion is possible without a strong support system in place (Lamond, 1995). But at the moment there is too often an inadequate technology of inclusion. The best intentions are dragged down by large class sizes, inadequate teacher training, and lack of outside support for classroom teachers.

- *Outside forces.* The resolution of special education and inclusive education for learners with special needs will not emerge in a social vacuum. It will emerge, or sink, in an interplay of interests, politics, economics, and so on.

While there are many optimistic strands in the commentary, it is obvious that inclusion has not yet translated from a principled ideal into an attainable reality. So far reform efforts have been piecemeal and fragmented and clearly less effective than anticipated (Lupart, 1998). Debate, counter debate, discussion, and controversy still surround the many facets of the inclusionary movement. In the accompanying Debate box we show some of the major arguments. These should not be considered as black and white, but rather as advocacy and cautions.

A Matter of Debate

Inclusive Schooling

The inclusion of students who are exceptional into general education settings has been the dominant discourse among special educators for the past decade. No issue has both riven and riveted the profession of special education as has inclusion. Yet it is not a universally accepted movement; rather, as inclusive schooling is a fluid concept and practice, it is something that is still both evolving and changing, and open to many facets of debate.

Arguments for inclusion	Cautions about inclusion
Inclusion is the best way to educate all students with disabilities.	There is little evidence that one approach is better than another. There is no unified body of research findings that allow a rational choice.
All students with identified exceptionalities should be educated in the classrooms they would attend if not disabled.	It is a fundamental error to equate placement with schools and service.
All children can be taught successfully in regular classrooms.	There is no more sameness among children with disabilities than there is among anyone else. To place all students in general education is to deny students' unique characteristics as well as the right to an individual program.
The general classroom is appropriate for every child, regardless of degree and type of disability. We no longer need an array or continuum of placement options, as inclusion is a contrast to a continuum.	We do not need a retreat from the principles that support a continuum, but a thoughtful deployment of the ideas (Marston, 1996). Rather than following the traditional tendency in special education to focus on restructuring the instructional setting, we need to emphasize interventions applicable to varied settings.

Arguments for inclusion	Cautions about inclusion
Educational equity demands equal educational treatment and equal opportunity to learn with one's peers.	Equity does not mean the same treatment for all; it means equitable treatment despite individual differences and treatment that takes into consideration such differences.
Much of the zeal for the practice of inclusion stems from its anticipated effects in the socio-emotional domain. Students with disabilities are offered increased opportunities for interactions with non-disabled peers.	Evidence shows that children who are disabled are often perceived in negative and prejudiced ways by their non-disabled peers; integration may even increase prejudice, stereotyping, and rejection.
Students with and without disabilities have opportunities for interactions, which have many positive benefits for the social abilities of students with disabilities (Staub and Hunt, 1993).	Mere physical presence in a class does not seem to enhance social competence (Leffert and Siperstein, 1996). For example, the social outcomes of placing students with mental retardation in regular classrooms have been disappointing. Often these children occupy a marginal position in the social network of the class (see Siperstein and Leffert, 1997).
High-school students report positive outcomes of inclusion from either elementary or secondary experiences. Although Fisher (1999) found concerns about teasing, behaviour, and rules, the consensus was for inclusion. Respondents provided opinions, reflections, and insights that indicated the value of inclusive experiences.	Inclusion assumes that students with disabilities will be better accepted, have more friends, and feel better about themselves. There is little empirical data for this assumption (see Vaughn, Erlbaum, Schumm, and Hughes, 1998).
Many teachers express support for the principles of inclusion.	Many teachers prefer the current system and are satisfied with the pull-out model. The majority of teachers in one study (Semmel, Abernathy, Butera, and Lesar, 1991) perceived special education classrooms as more effective and more preferred than regular classrooms for students with mild disabilities.
Inclusion brings greater collaboration between special and general teachers.	Often, general and special education personnel are not motivated or prepared to participate in collaborative planning and instruction (Gersten, 1990). Many teachers feel that the hardest part of inclusion is planning with another person (Roach, 1995).
Successful inclusion functions via collaboration by general and special educators to bring support and services to the student.	Inclusion requires extensive retraining of both regular and special education teachers in teaching, teacher problem solving, and curricula frameworks.

Arguments for inclusion	Cautions about inclusion
General classroom teachers can teach all children. The same sort of generic teaching skills, attitudes, and beliefs will be effective regardless of students' characteristics.	Research does not support the contention that all students can be merged and taught successfully in general classes, and many disagree that regular educators can assume responsibility for special programming for all students with disabilities (e.g., Fuchs and Fuchs, 1995a,b).
Special education is really nothing more than a thoroughly good ordinary education. Good teachers can teach all students because only minor adjustments need to be made to accommodate special learners.	Enthusiasts have advocated for radical changes in teacher responsibility without showing that regular educators can actually support these changes (Minke, Bear, Deiner, and Griffin, 1996).
Schools can no longer operate on the conventional uniform curriculum at a conventional rate; on grade-level-driven requirements; on standard evaluation policies; and on traditional marking, reporting, and promotion practices.	Teaching that does not produce learning is not education; mere attendance at school is not education; and a primary measure of effectiveness is students' academic achievement.
The mere fact of school entry increases the probability of successful learning.	If it is the function of schools to help individuals meet their needs and prepare them to lead productive and rewarding lives, then specialized instruction is necessary.
The same sort of generic teaching skills, attitudes, and beliefs will be effective regardless of students' characteristics.	"One size fits all if your feet are of average size" (Detterman and Thompson, 1997, p. 1082).
General classrooms can provide for all students. The means that have always produced effective instruction and management work well in integrated settings (Weber, 1994).	General classrooms are not organized in ways that sustain direct attention to a few students. The planning frame of most teachers is the whole class; they teach to single large groups and incorporate little or no differentiation based on student need (Fuchs and Fuchs, 1995b).
All students need to learn in natural environments in which they are provided age-appropriate models for behaviour and communication. Inclusive schools provide a more real-life environment for learning.	Skills should be taught in the environment where they are most likely to occur—the community, home, or work setting. Students who are severely or profoundly disabled are best served in settings in which their cognitive development and social limitations can be addressed more intensively.
Students with exceptionalities are provided meaningful curriculum.	Many students with disabilities do not respond to traditional teaching techniques used in general educa-

Arguments for inclusion	Cautions about inclusion
	tion such as recitation, lecturing, rote learning, and so on (Boyle and Yeager, 1997).
Students will not suffer the social stigma of special classes or resource rooms, which can affect their behaviour, self-concept, and learning.	The research evidence on stigma is inconclusive. It is suggested that receiving pull-out services has a positive effect, if any, on self esteem (see Hallahan, Kauffman, and Lloyd, 1999).
Students who more fully participate in general education programs will develop more positive perceptions of themselves.	Pulling students aside for special instruction in the general class can be more stigmatizing than pull-out models. But studies of elementary children show that 44 percent did not like services in the general classroom (Whinnery, King, Evans, and Gable, 1995). When researchers (Nelson, Ferrante, and Mantella, 1999) asked 60 students in grades one, three, and five about their preferences, there was a general consensus that pull-out programs would benefit students with mild and severe learning problems more than in-class work. Consistent with Jenkins and Heinen (1989), younger students were less sure. Older students preferred pull-out models as less embarrassing and stigmatizing than in-class assistance.
Inclusion will unify special education and general education.	By eliminating special education, general education will have to deal with children it has avoided in the past and transform itself into a more responsive, resourceful, humane system (Fuchs and Fuchs, 1994).
Doubts about inclusion will be removed in direct proportion to demonstrations of effectiveness.	With the philosophical attraction is a responsibility to measure that it works. The current empirical research is modest in terms of the experiences of children in general classrooms, the strategies for assuring successful integration, and the effectiveness of inclusive practices.

TYPICAL SERVICES IN CANADA

It is difficult to make any broad statements about inclusive schooling across the whole of Canada. Not only is education a provincial responsibility, but on the Canadian vista, the "literature and research sources offering a national perspective [on inclusion] have been almost non-existent" (Lupart, 1998, p. 258). Moreover, schools are not fixed entities with determinate characteristics. We can rarely characterize a school as unequivocally inclusive or not inclusive and there is not an indisputable "best" form of provision.

Across Canada, the amount of integration into the regular classroom depends on provincial policy and the individual school district. Therefore, the implementation of inclusionary practices varies widely from province to province and even among neighbouring school boards.

Some programs label any planned participation as inclusion; others have a very specific meaning. Some systems support inclusive schooling and have made fundamental changes. New Brunswick and Nova Scotia, for example, have adopted integration. British Columbia has an inclusive schooling approach that identifies every student as unique. Some districts say that they support inclusive education, but have not made policy changes to ensure that integrated settings actually occur. Others treat inclusion programs as simply one more choice on the special education menu. Some schools and districts follow traditional eligibility criteria and a categorically based delivery system with autonomous special education and regular education.

A number of school districts in Canada have chosen to maintain a continuum of services and typically approach inclusion on a one-to-one basis. They maintain that inclusion is more than simply the place where students with disabilities receive services. Rather, it is a way to deliver services effectively where the opportunities made available by the setting, not the setting itself, become important.

It is held that case-by-case decisions are consistent with the essence of special education. Rather than a blanket policy, the special needs of each pupil must be carefully assessed and the most appropriate educational placement for that child judged. The challenge is to determine how all potential learning opportunities can be best used based on a student's needs. Opting for participation in any program is justified only if such programming meets the needs, wishes, and interests of the student.

LEGISLATION

law
school law

Law may be defined as a system of rules and regulations relating to the behaviour of individuals and society as a whole (Warren, 1988). **School law** is the legislation, regulations, bylaws, and judicial decisions that apply primarily to all or part of the public school system (Nicholls and Martin, 1983). School-based laws are important, designed to support teachers, school administrators, and parents in providing appropriate interventions for students in need of assistance in regular and special education (Cole and Brown, 1996).

The relationship between legislation and the quality of services is not a direct correlation. Attitudes cannot be legislated, nor can responsibility. In the final analysis, the measure of responsible education will not be the number and length of laws, court cases, and interpretative regulations. The quality of education will be determined by the nature of the direction provided by educational leaders and the commitment to quality by teachers and others as they attempt to implement the intent of the directions provided. Legislation therefore may not reshape special education, but it reflects the efforts that special educators have been working for years to achieve.

In Canada, special education has tended to follow the American model. Canadian educational issues—legislative, administrative, and curricular—are directly influenced by events, philosophies, and pedagogy from the United States. As a result, Canadians have a touchstone against which to critically assess their progress and greater freedom to meld practices and philosophies into Canada's unique educational system.

There are major differences between special education in Canada and in the United States, most particularly relating to legislation. In fact, since the late 1960s, educators and researchers have drawn attention to the shortcomings of Canadian legislation and the provision of special education services. Repeatedly, authors contrast the progress made in American special education, particularly with reference to PL 94-142, with the lack of progress in Canada (Carter and Rogers, 1989).

Canada does not have a federal office of education and therefore has no equivalent to the federal mandates in the United States. As a result, the differences between each province's special education programs and procedures tend to be greater than the differences between each U.S. state's special education programs and procedures.

Legislation in the United States

The United States has a long history of relying on legislative and judicial remedies for social issues, including special education. Recent years have seen an increasingly prominent role of the federal government in special education.

A number of important pieces of legislation related to individuals with disabilities—adults, school-age, and preschool-age children—have been passed and then amended in various ways. Four particular laws work together to ensure that persons with exceptionalities are not discriminated against, receive a free and appropriate public education, and have access to facilities.

A particularly important piece of legislation is the Americans with Disabilities Act (ADA) of 1990, which relates to people in general society. The ADA guarantees equal opportunity and access to all persons with disabilities, in and out of the school system.

An early and crucial educational law is Title V of the Rehabilitation Act, more commonly called Section 504, passed originally in 1974. Section 504 is a civil rights law that protects children and adults against discrimination. In the schools, it ensures that students can participate in educational programs. However, it compels schools only to make reasonable accommodations, not to provide substantial or expensive services. Students not included under other laws, such as those with Attention Deficit Hyperactivity Disorder, are served under Section 504. (Note that the IDEA amendments in 1997 allowed that Attention Deficit Hyperactivity Disorder and Attention Deficit Disorder may result in eligibility for special education under the category of "other health impairment.")

Public Law 94-142, the seminal law, came about in 1975 prompted by the civil rights movement, efficacy studies in special education, parent activism, professional pressure, and reports that four million of a total seven million youngsters with disabilities were being inappropriately or inadequately served (Meadow, 1980). When President Ford signed PL 94-142 (the Education for All Handicapped Children Act, or EHA) into law in November 1975, these children were ensured a free and appropriate education in the least restrictive environment. (Note that the numbers refer to the 142nd bill in the 94th Congress of the United States.)

As a legislative remedy to some of the past failures of schools in providing appropriate education, Public Law 94-142 had a tremendous impact on the provision of services to children who were in some way exceptional. It represented official recognition by the Congress of the United States of the growing dissatisfaction with placing students with disabilities in special classes. The Act and its amendments legitimized the notion of placing such students in the public schools and in general classroom settings. The legislation also promoted individualized instruction, increased the role of parents in the instruction of their children, and made education possible for previously unserved, seriously disabled children.

The least restrictive environment (LRE) was the cornerstone of Public Law 94-142. The law mandates that children with special needs must be educated in the LRE with an Individual Education Plan (IEP) developed, maintained, and evaluated for each child. States must assume non-discriminatory testing, confidentiality, and ensure due process procedures for all children with disabilities and their parents or guardians. As well, the states must actively attempt to identify children in need of special services and must provide a complete system of personnel development.

PL 94-142 is a grant-in-aid law, and responsibility for its implementation is shared by local, state, and federal governments. To be eligible for federal funds, state and local agencies must comply with the requirements of the law. All states have chosen to participate, so all are provided federal funds to support the education of students with disabilities.

PL 94-142 and its amendments adopt a categorical approach. While thirteen specific groups of students are now included, the law did not automatically apply to gifted and talented students. Their needs for financial assistance and programs were originally addressed in PL 95-561, the Gifted and Talented Children's Education Act of 1978.

Amendments

Although deeply significant, PL 94-142 was not model legislation. Like other comprehensive federal laws in the United States, PL 94-142 periodically undergoes re-authorization and amendments in response to changing circumstances. Under the original legislation, all states were mandated to serve children between the ages of six and eighteen. Ongoing amendments have extended the rights to preschool exceptional children and initiated transition programs for adolescents.

PL 99-457 (1986) amended PL 94-142 to give full services for three-year-olds by 1992 and dramatically increased funding for preschool programs. PL 99-457 divided the preschool population into two groups—infants and toddlers (birth to three years) and preschoolers (three to six years). Part H of PL 99-457 refers to infants; Part B to preschoolers. Early intervention is fully addressed in Chapter 15 of this book.

In 1990, the Individuals with Disabilities Education Act (IDEA) (PL 101-476) amended PL 94-142. IDEA retained all the basic provisions of the original legislation but was expanded to include thirteen types of disability when it added autism and traumatic brain injury as categories. The title of the law was also changed to stress people-first terminology; that is, to say "a child with a disability," rather than "a handicapped child."

IDEA was most recently amended on June 4, 1997, as PL 105-17. While most of the general requirements have been in the law since 1975, the IDEA of 1997 refined the basics, put new discipline provisions in place to ensure that schools are safe and conducive to learning, strengthened the role of parents, and added a new variable to the formula by changing the notion of a separate curriculum for individual children. The 1997 reauthorization makes special education teachers accountable for student progress, especially in relation to the general education curriculum. The Act requires that the general education curriculum be a starting place for all students and that outcome measures (goals and objectives) be tied directly to the general education curriculum goals and objectives. The classroom teacher is placed in a more central position and the concept of the LRE changed to include the extent to which a student is involved in the regular school curriculum. It is now expected that most children with IEPs will take the standard proficiency tests beginning as early as fourth grade (see Yell and Shriner, 1997).

Inclusion is a state-of-the art term; it is not mentioned in U.S. federal law. The IDEA of 1990 stipulates that children with disabilities must be provided with a free, appropriate public education in the least restrictive environment. IDEA requires a full continuum of services, which includes such environments as residential schools. Students can be placed in special settings only when the use of supplementary aids and services in the general classroom cannot achieve a satisfactory education (Culross, 1997).

Legislation in Canada

In the Canadian federal arena, it cannot be said that the law clearly and unequivocally obliges the publicly supported school system to provide appropriate forms of education for all students, exceptionality notwithstanding. Except for the Declaration of Human Rights, there is no federal law to outline or guarantee the rights of children who are exceptional; the right of every child to education is not entrenched by any constitutional provision. The 1867 British North America Act (Sec. 93) was chiefly concerned with protecting the educational rights of linguistic and religious minorities.

In the absence of constitutional provisions, the responsibility for education rests entirely with provincial legislation. Each of the ten provinces and three territories has its own school system based upon provincial (or territorial) education legislation that springs from diverse sources—federal and provincial constitutional provisions, federal and provincial statutory law, administrative rules and regulations, and case law.

Since 1969, all of the provinces and territories have enacted legislation guaranteeing education to all children, including those who are exceptional (Goguen, 1993). Within these guaranteed services, each government has developed its own legislation, regulations, policies, and procedures to ensure that all children receive a free and appropriate education. Educational goals and priorities occur in policy documents, the most relevant of which are issued by the ministries of education.

Only a few schools are controlled by the provincial governments directly, such as provincial resource centres for the deaf. The rest are administered through local school boards, each of which is responsible for a geographical school district. Funding stems from a combination of property taxes and provincial government grants, according to formulae that vary from province to province.

Legislation for special education occurs because school boards fail to develop thorough and systematic policies on their own initiative. Varying practices mean that some boards go well beyond official mandates in assessment and placement but others do not establish policies and procedures and do not systematically identify, assess, and place children who are exceptional. Legislation makes school boards implement fair and equitable provisions for special education assessment, placement, and programming.

Canadian provinces and territories have recognized the right to an education for all children in different ways, which can be broadly categorized as mandatory and permissive. The current legislation in each province and territory is summarized in Table 2-1.

Table 2-1 Canadian special education legislation and policies

Province/territory	Type	Policy
Newfoundland	Mandates boards to provide special education	"All students are entitled to programs designed to respond to their individual strengths and needs which are provided in the most enhancing environments. The policy promotes the idea of a continuum of supports."
Nova Scotia	Mandatory legislation; zero-reject policy (Education Act consolidated 1990; under amendment 1996)	"The issue is no longer whether students with exceptional needs should or should not be integrated, but what support is needed for integration to be successful."
Prince Edward Island	Mandatory, non-categorical, zero-reject	—
New Brunswick	Mandatory legislation introduced 1986	"Educational programs for exceptional students and inclusion emphasized placement of students with exceptionalities into regular classrooms."
Quebec	Mandatory; human rights approach with zero-reject and regulations	Amendments in 1979
Ontario	Mandatory legislation	Education Amendment Act (1980)
Manitoba	Mandatory legislation; all-inclusive policy	Amendment to the Public School Act of 1975; under revision
Saskatchewan	Mandatory	"Education in Saskatchewan is based on the belief of the innate value and dignity of all people and the understanding that the inclusion of people with exceptional needs into every aspect of community life benefits all ... in society."
Alberta	Permissive. Mandatory legislation proposed under C26 (1996), the Amended School Act (1988). School Act amended September 1990. Zero-reject. Policy formalized September 1993	"There is a need for a variety of partners to work together as a team, to meet each student's needs." Regular classroom is the first in a range of options. The School Act makes boards responsible for providing special education programs for students identified as having special needs, including

Table 2-1 continued

Province/territory	Type	Policy
		those who are gifted and talented. When this is not possible, alternative (and presumably more expensive) arrangements are made by the boards.
British Columbia	Permissive; inclusive; non-categorical. Amendment 1995; under provincial review 1999	"A board shall ensure that an administrative officer offers to consult with a parent of a student [with disabilities] regarding ... placement."
Yukon	Mandatory legislation; non-categorical School Act has sections based on least restrictive and most enabling environment	"The Education Act 1990 requires that all students with exceptionalities be provided with an IEP implemented in the least-restrictive and most-enabling environment."
Northwest Territories	Mandatory legislation; zero-reject inclusion	"Inclusive schooling shall be (a) characterized by equal access, (b) built on student strengths and needs, (c) community based, and (d) shall promote the involvement of parents ... in their child's education."

Individual provinces and territories have policies that are in a constant state of change and it is virtually impossible to pinpoint exact areas such as legislative progress toward inclusive schooling. Policy revisions are ongoing. For example, in the Northwest Territories, the Education Act and Developmental Directive on Inclusive Schooling of 1995 focused on all children receiving an education in the general classroom. In Newfoundland, the delivery models in special education are undergoing significant revisions along with a restructuring of the general school system.

Legislative activity has tended to focus on students with disabilities. Although gifted youngsters are considered to be exceptional in their need for special education, they have not fared as well in the legislative arena, perhaps because legal arguments for students who are gifted are different from those for children with disabilities; they are not fought on denial of access but denial of appropriate programs. In Canada, both territories and eight of the ten provinces include gifted students in some definition of *exceptional pupil,* either at the legislative, regulatory, or administrative policy level. The two provinces without a mention are Nova Scotia and Prince Edward Island (Ritchey, 1993). Three provinces—Alberta, Saskatchewan, and Ontario—have enacted legislation, developed regulations, and issued policy statements on the education of students who are gifted and talented. However, related funding is different in each of these provinces and only Alberta provides a funding formula that specifically includes programs to meet the needs of these students (McFadden and Ellis, 2000).

LITIGATION

Legislation refers to laws or bills enacted by lawmakers. *Litigation*, a process that occurs through the court system, is one of the principal means by which society exerts pressure over, and provides direction to, public schools. Litigious influence has altered public policy and the functioning of the school system in areas as diverse as architectural barriers, residential facilities, custody of children, life management and sterilization, inclusion, assessment and classification, and appropriate educational practices.

legislation

Litigation involves an individual or a small group of people filing a suit against another group. The suit represents a complaint against the status quo. For example, a parent of a child who is intellectually disabled may sue a school board on behalf of the child or as a class action for all children who are intellectually disabled.

litigation

In Canada, the emphasis on using the power of the courts to settle disputes of an educational nature is less pronounced than in the United States, but nevertheless does occur with some regularity. At the moment, judicial activity in Canada seems to be stimulated by three connected factors. These are the principles of the inclusion movement, the willingness of advocacy groups to support parents, and interpretations of the Canadian Charter of Rights and Freedoms.

Much litigation is initiated by parents. Sometimes, parents ask that a school district provide special educational services to a child or extend the amount of special education. In other cases, parents view the general school as the most appropriate educational setting for the special child and disagree with the decisions regarding their child's placement in a particular program or exclusion from a program.

Other Canadian litigation has involved the rights of people with disabilities, sometimes brought by individuals or sometimes brought on their behalf. In 1982 the Adult Mental Incompetency Act came under close scrutiny in the case of Clark vs. Clark heard in County Court, Lanark, Ontario (Baker, 1983). In this case, Justin Clark, a young person with cerebral palsy, won his rights. In British Columbia, the Stephen Dawson case involving sustaining life support was brought forward on Stephen's account (Savage, 1983).

The Charter is the federal and supreme law of Canada. Section 15 of the Charter, which came into effect in April 1985, states that every individual is "equal before and under the law and has the right to equal protection of the law without discrimination and in particular, without discrimination based on mental or physical disability" (s. 15 (1)).

Interpretations of the Charter mean that the courts are making complex and difficult decisions that ultimately influence educational policy and practice. A number of challenges to the existing educational structure heard under the Charter have already occurred.

One of the earliest cases was Elwood vs. Halifax County, Bedford School District, which arose because the school board insisted on a special placement for Luke Elwood, a boy with intellectual disabilities, and rejected his parents' requests for integration into the local school. The Elwoods went to court in 1987 in quest of the right of students with mental disabilities to be integrated into regular classrooms. When challenged on the grounds of discrimination on the basis of mental disability, the Board reversed its decision and negotiated under clauses of the Charter. A pretrial agreement signed between the Board and the family resulted in the child being integrated into the regular local public school classroom (MacKay, 1987).

Of particular relevance was Ontario's Eaton case against the Brant County Board of Education. Emily Eaton, at the time an eleven-year-old grade four student in Burford County, about 100 km southwest of Toronto, uses a wheelchair and a walker, cannot speak, and needs full assistance for personal care. Her teachers felt that, after three years in a regular class, Emily was increasingly isolated both intellectually and socially. The child's parents appealed the decision to place Emily in a special class and, after being frustrated at the board and district level, the case of Brant County Board of Education vs. Carol Eaton and Clayton Eaton was heard by the Ontario Court of Appeals. Here Madam Justice Louise Arbour ruled that under Section 15 of the Charter a placement cannot be made without parental consent, as placement without consent is discriminatory. The judge found that Emily Eaton had a constitutional right to attend school with fully able children despite the insistence of the Brant County Board of Education that she be placed in a segregated setting (Makin, 1997; Smith, 1995).

The Supreme Court of Canada reached a different conclusion when it decided that an individual child's needs are to be considered to determine the most appropriate placement from a range of options. As well, when an exceptional pupil has been placed in a general education class with appropriate supports and modifications and where objective evidence demonstrates that the child's needs are not being met, there is no violation of the Ontario Human Rights Code or the federal Charter of Rights and Freedoms in placing the child in a special class (Makin, 1997). Therefore, excluding some children from mainstream classes is an acceptable form of discrimination, provided that it is done in the best interests of the child. Unanimously, the Court rejected the idea of there being an automatic assumption that children with disabilities should gain entry into general classrooms if that is the wish of the parents. Instead, decisions should be made on a one-to-one basis, using the yardstick of the best interests of an individual child (Bogie, 1997; Makin, 1997).

This ruling parallels many in the United States. There, court actions have confirmed the rights of children who are exceptional to an appropriate education and have mandated public schools to provide that education. However, federal rulings about inclusion have also determined that the focus of an intervention should be on where a child can receive an appropriate education that meets his or her needs and that this may be a segregated or a regular setting. (On U.S. litigation, see McLaughlin and Henderson, 2000.)

TRENDS AND MOVEMENTS

As we point out in the introduction to this chapter, there are a number of issues germane to current special education. Most of them either directly or peripherally revolve around the notion of school restructuring and inclusion for students who are exceptional. In the following section we can only outline some of the most important and influential general trends.

Expansion of Services

As educational programming is provided for all children and youth, whatever the type and degree of their disability, there have been increasing pressures on special education to assume responsibility for the education of a greater proportion of the school population and a concomitant expansion of services. Programs are reaching down to encompass infants and preschoolers and up to provide transition programs and post-secondary education for students who are exceptional.

Early Intervention

Early identification and early intervention are two of the most promising areas of contemporary special education. **Early identification** is used to identify children with established disabilities, those who are at risk for problems, and those experiencing lags and delays. **Early intervention** refers to the establishment of educational and support services for preschool children and infants who are at risk for disabilities, and their families.

early identification
early intervention

Early identification and intervention are part of the broader construct of early childhood special education. This new direction in special education truly emerged in 1986 with the passage of PL 99-457, an amendment to PL 94-142. The many principles that underlie current early childhood special education are discussed in Chapter 15.

Transition

Many adults with disabilities do not fare well once they leave school. Increasingly, educators are becoming concerned with job placements, acquisition of a job, and maintenance of the job for young adults with disabilities. To ease the passage from school to work, transition programs are becoming more apparent in secondary special education.

Transition programs rest on the premise that the quality of life and the extent to which youth with disabilities achieve the desired goals of employment, community living, and social and leisure opportunities depend on the effectiveness and appropriateness of secondary school experiences as well as on co-operative service planning and the availability of needed adult services. The area of secondary programming and transitions is discussed in Chapter 16.

Parent Involvement

Reform efforts in general education stress the greater involvement of parents, as does the most recent amendment to IDEA in the United States. Research indicates that teachers should emphasize parental involvement if they wish to enhance the educational experience for all of their students. When educators involve parents as partners in their children's education, parents appear to develop a sense of efficacy that communicates itself to children with positive academic consequences.

Particularly for students with disabilities, communication and collaboration are critical if a child is to make educational gains in a planned and coordinated manner (Perl, 1995). For example, as a result of being tutored in how to assist their children, parents of students with disabilities have been able to ensure appropriate programming in the least restrictive environment; facilitate successful vocational/special education programs through collaborative consultation with the schools (Elksnin and Elksnin, 1989); and improve mathematical ability (Minner, 1989).

Technological Advances

Technology is changing the world in which we live and work. Today students use word processors to prepare written assignments, teachers maintain databases of their students' achievements, and administrators effectively track, maintain, and produce paperwork. And with the current proliferation of computer programs, CD-ROMS, and Web-based activities that provide swift access to multimedia (such as graphics, video, text, sound) both teachers and students are offered unlimited possibilities to experience novel and creative learning environments.

A broad range of technology is incorporated into the education and training of persons with disabilities. These are best seen on a continuum from high to low tech. High-tech solutions involve the use of sophisticated devices, such as computers, interactive multimedia systems, and high-technology communication aids that have speech output, printed output, or sometimes both output modes. Medium-tech solutions use less complicated electronic or mechanical devices, such as videocassette players and wheelchairs. Low-tech solutions are less sophisticated, such as adapted spoon handles, Velcro fasteners, or raised desks that can accommodate a wheelchair (see Maddux, 2000).

Computers are perhaps the technology that most obviously affects the lives of people who are disabled. Printed text is fixed and not flexible, and this creates barriers for students who have conditions such as learning disabilities, low vision, or blindness. Digital text on a computer, on the other hand, is not fixed but is flexible and can be easily transformed in size, shape, colour, and can be automatically transformed into spoken speech. Similarly, pencil and paper exercises are barriers to students who meet difficulties in handwriting, speed, note taking, or spelling. Provided in digital form, the same exercises can provide supports and alternatives for students. Examples include on-screen scanning keyboards, enlarged keyboards, word prediction, and spell checkers.

Computer technology can provide reading for blind students, language for those who are deaf, and speech for students deprived by serious disabilities. As technology to improve lifestyles, computers provide sensory input, enhance mobility, develop cognitive and language skills, strengthen motor and perceptual functioning, and facilitate communication.

In the classroom, computers are an effective supplement to classroom instruction—a tool that helps students learn more and have fun doing so. In special education, computer assisted instruction (CAI) has proven effective in influencing the educational outcomes of students of all ages. After a review of 133 research reports on the effectiveness of computer technology, one team (Sivin-Kachala and Bialo, 1995) reported that educational technologies have a significant and positive effect on achievement, self-concept, and attitudes in both general and special education.

Some children with disabilities may need peripherals to increase accessibility. Peripherals include a mouse, alternative keyboard, touch screen, single switches, trackball, key guard, head or mouth typing stick, or a hand splint for physical disabilities. Or, there may be special modifications to the software. For example, a word processor for individuals with limited fine-motor ability may present a grid of all the letters and other characters in the upper corner of the screen. Each character may be highlighted briefly and the user strikes the spacebar or uses another input aid when the desired character is highlighted (Maddux, 2000).

Of course, battles still rage over whether technology is actually improving teaching and learning. Some contend that "There is no good evidence that most uses of computers significantly improve teaching and learning" (Oppenheimer, 1997). Others (e.g., Stoll, 1995) warn that, although the Internet may spawn efficient information access, it does not teach students how to evaluate that information critically. In contrast, Maddux (2000) echoes many who do believe that efficient information technology is a boon to classroom instruction.

Adaptive equipment and other technology is fully addressed in the relevant chapters of this text.

Assessment Practices

Diagnosis is a term derived from the Greek root *dia* (apart) and *gignoskien* (to know). By definition, diagnosis is the art of identifying disease from its symptoms. **Differential diagnosis** implies the precise specification that a given set of symptoms is indicative of one disorder rather than another.

differential diagnosis

The word **assessment** is used rather than diagnosis in education because it is more relevant to instruction by stressing the current level of developmental functioning. The term refers to the process of gathering valid evidence to guide decisions about curriculum and instruction, and to evaluate the outcomes of instruction (Calfee, 1987).

assessment

All teachers are responsible for some assessment. Indeed, "The teacher who cannot or will not pinpoint and measure the relevant behavior of the students he or she is teaching is probably not going to be very effective" (Kauffman, 1997b, p. 514). In contemporary schools, assessment is undertaken with normally developing children and with those who appear to be making an inadequate adjustment in some aspect of their development, whether it be behavioural, social, emotional, or communicative, or some combination of these.

Effective classroom assessment is guided by three fundamental principles. Assessment should promote learning, use multiple sources of information, and provide fair, valid, and reliable information. The process is not intended to label a child or to propel him or her toward special education. Rather, the basic purpose is to collect information, to clarify the "whys" of a child's performance and behaviour. It targets behaviours—cognitive, social, communicative, motor, or self-care skills—to determine how a child learns best, the behavioural characteristics that will affect learning, and whether there are any sensory or motor impairments relevant to achievement and performance. Moreover, there is no clear line between assessment and intervention. The assessment process is vital in making decisions about the best educational placement for a child and is a first step toward preparing an IEP.

Over the years, the responsibility for assessing students with disabilities has come to be viewed as substantially different from assessment in general education. This is not correct. Assessment in special education is best viewed as an extension of the measurement and evaluation techniques used by all teachers to assess student learning, although the process tends to be more varied and complex. Assessment in special education is not a one-time or single procedure. A single test, person, or occasion is not a sufficient source of information; instead, a valid description of a child's status is generated from data collected from several sources, instruments, and settings, and on multiple occasions.

In recent years, practices in assessment for learning problems have progressed considerably, and a paradigm shift has occurred. There are changes in the preferred types of tools and measures, the environment used for assessment, the flexibility of the procedures, and the greater involvement of regular and special education personnel in the procedures.

No longer is assessment the sole responsibility of a psychologist in a clinic setting. There is increasing recognition of the importance of assessing student performance and learning outcomes in the context of the classroom and home environment. As this occurs, interest is being generated around methods that are relevant to the primary purposes of learning and that can be used to enhance teachers' instructional planning, such as curriculum-based assessment.

There is no such thing as a flawless diagnostic system, and quite a bit of controversy surrounds assessment in special education. One of the major arguments concerns the utility of traditional diagnostic models—that is, assessment based on the underlying assumption that a diagnosis can be formed on the basis of observations and tests of the individual and that there is a corresponding treatment for a rehabilitating effect. We can find out what is wrong with a person and then "fix" it. Diagnostic models feed into labelling (Chapter 1), categorical approaches (Chapter 1), and medical models (Chapter 3).

As special education moves away from traditional diagnostic models, many new approaches are emerging. In this short section, we could not possibly detail all of these, or even touch on the variety of information sources that are used as the basis for programming for students who are exceptional. We can only point out some single tools in a very large toolbox. We glance at promising methods that include the use of portfolios, functional analysis, and curriculum-based measurement. This summary lays the groundwork for discussions of assessment for special populations that are embedded in each chapter of the text.

Stages in Assessment

A good way to conceptualize the actual assessment process is as three interrelated stages: survey, or screening; specific, or diagnostic; and intensive, or medical and paraprofessional. Each of these stages involves different strategies and is undertaken by different professionals. All, however, focus on developing efficient treatment and educational programs for an individual child. The primary goal is to gather and analyze enough pertinent information to teach a child effectively.

Screening

The term *screening* originated in the medical literature. As its use becomes more prevalent in the behavioural sciences, screening is now used in medicine and education to refer to developmental and health activities that are intended to identify those children who have a high probability of exhibiting delayed or abnormal development.

screening

Screening in education refers to a classroom activity that generally occurs prior to direct testing. The procedures look at large groups of children and begin to identify those who may have difficulties in behaviour and learning. In this way, screening is a first step in determining whether a child may need intervention or special services for a condition that could prove disabling, or whether the child might profit from an adapted or individualized educational program due to disabilities or giftedness.

Screening procedures are broad. Included are interviews with parents, first-hand observations, child interviews, past records, developmental checklists, behaviour rating scales, inventories, teacher-made tests, criterion-referenced tests, group achievement tests, and error analysis.

On average, most educational screening identifies about 85 percent of children with exceptionalities (Lerner, Mardell-Czudnowski, and Goldenberg, 1981). An exception is students who are gifted, where screening procedures are less successful (see Chapter 8). Note, too, that many students with severe or multiple disabilities do not pass through the screening process as they are obviously disabled; the assessment process for them begins with psychoeducational testing.

Criterion-Referenced Measures

Criterion-referenced tests do not assess a child against some group norm but against the child's own individual progress toward pre-set criteria. Criterion-referenced tests may be commercially produced; many are designed by classroom teachers to assess the progress of an individual child.

Criterion-referenced testing is particularly easy to integrate with a child's individual educational program. The testing is performed simply to determine what needs to be taught. The teacher sets instructional objectives, or criteria, for the child to work toward. For example, if a short-term objective is for a child to learn the addition facts to nine, then the test would assess how that child achieved regarding that particular objective.

Curriculum-Referenced Measures

A special form of criterion-referenced test is referred to as *curriculum-referenced testing* or **curriculum-based assessment** (CBA). CBA is a procedure that directly assesses student performance within the course content for the purpose of determining a student's instructional needs.

curriculum-based assessment

Curriculum-referenced tools are similar to criterion-referenced tools, but they differ in that a predetermined criterion is not necessarily set and the test is always explicitly related to what was taught in the classroom. In brief, CBA indexes student proficiency directly to the curriculum and measures performance in a particular curriculum area.

Although the fundamental question of CBA is "How is the student progressing in the curriculum of his or her school?" there are a variety of models of CBA in use. All are guided by the premise that curricula should serve as the basis for assessment, and all emphasize measurement that is brief, frequent, based on the student's classroom curriculum, and that can be used to monitor instructional programs and effectiveness.

The core methods of CBA are frequent performance sampling, systematic recording and plotting of results, and results used to guide further teaching. To prepare CBA, teachers determine the annual curriculum goals for a student. They then devise and present short tests or **probes**—brief samples of academic behaviour. Two types of probes are commonly used—probes of basic skills in academic core areas and probes of content areas and the strategies needed, such as textbook reading and note taking. Teachers use the generated data to monitor student progress and to adjust programs.

probes

The measurement of progress by using actual curriculum-based items and by direct daily measurement has been found to have a noticeable effect on academic achievement when the results are used to modify instructional planning (Overton, 1992). Apart from progress monitoring, CBA can be used for screening, individual education planning, and program evaluation. It has been found an accurate screening measure for referral to special education, less influenced than other measures by teacher variables (Overton, 1992).

Portfolios

Used as authentic assessment measures in both general and special education, *portfolios* are highly popular—and becoming more so (see Harris and Curran, 1998). Portfolios serve to examine the learning process as well as the outcomes of learning. They stress products rather than tests and test scores; their use is appealing because of their instructional relevance. As well, portfolios may be a better predictor of future student achievement than most instruments (Johnsen, Ryser, and Dougherty, 1993).

Portfolios are joint projects between the teacher and a student. They include information selected by the student under the guidance of the teacher as well as a series of statements that reflect a student's thoughts about the contents. The portfolio will include work samples and projects, and may include the results of tests. As the portfolio is a continual collection of a student's work, developmental growth is evidenced through the work presented such as reports, artwork, poetry, and video.

rubric

To assist in evaluation, the teacher may prepare a **rubric**—a generic scoring tool used to evaluate the quality of products and performance in a given area. Rubrics consist of a fixed measuring scale (such as a four-point scale) and a list of criteria that describe the characteristics for each score point.

Functional Assessment

Functional analysis or functional assessment is a broad approach useful for all children with disabilities but particularly relevant to those with behavioural disorders and students with severe or multiple disabilities. As the name implies, *functional assessment* focuses on the functions that a behaviour serves for a student. It represents an assessment approach that is used to identify the possible relationship between events and people in the environment and student behaviour; that is, how a particular behaviour functions to obtain reinforcement for a child or avoid punishment.

At the moment, functional behaviour assessment is the subject of widespread debate (Conroy, Clark, Gable, and Fox, 1999). Many researchers (e.g., Slate and Jones, 2000) speak to the overwhelming advantage of functional analysis over other approaches. They note that functional assessment has demonstrated treatment utility because it directly addresses the causes of problematic behaviour by stressing the assessment of specific observable behaviours that form the mode of the current and future existence of a child.

Functional assessment is not a single thing or a single procedure; rather, it is a process, not a product. It contains overlapping and complementary components, some already mentioned in the section on screening. The major aims of functional assessment are to generate hypotheses about the possible causes of a student's behaviour and then develop intervention strategies that correlate with the hypotheses.

A complete functional analysis would describe the behaviour of interest, the situations in which the behaviour is likely or unlikely to occur, and the consequences that maintain or inhibit the behaviour. These data are gathered through procedures that range from structured interviews with the parents and target student, general observations, direct observations of naturally occurring behaviour, review of anecdotal records, and rating scales and checklists. Interviewing the parents and others who know the child is the functional assessment method most commonly used by practitioners (Horner and Carr, 1997).

We return to functional analysis in Chapters 7 and 14. For detailed information of functional analysis, see *Preventing School Failure,* 1998, volume 43, whole issue.

Parent Interviews

Parent conferences can be a source of apprehension for teachers, particularly when parents have requested the meeting or when the student is not adapting well at school (Perl, 1995). But information from parents or guardians is the backbone of functional assessment. Indeed, an assessment is incomplete without the careful collection of data from parent interviews. Parents offer the singular advantage of providing information about specific types of behaviour in a variety of settings over a long time. Parental insights about the child can complement information from other sources and paint a broader picture of the child's capabilities and educational needs. However, while valuable and oftentimes critical data are obtained through interviews, interviewers should be aware that the subjective and interpretative nature of interviews places limitations on their usefulness.

Specific Assessment

Direct testing (psycho-educational assessment) refers to testing children across a variety of domains relevant to social and educational performance. The aim is to gather further information on children who were identified as at-risk intellectually or behaviourally using primary screening measures. The process confirms or discounts the existence of a problem and helps determine what types of treatment and intervention are needed.

direct testing

Psycho-educational assessment relies heavily on testing. In general, the term *testing* means that explicit criteria for performance are established in advance. **Tests** are defined as controlled and structured procedures that attempt to elicit particular responses that the child might not demonstrate spontaneously (Bailey and Brochin, 1989). Many tests are standardized—they use standard materials, administrative procedures, scoring procedures, and score interpretation. The purpose of standardization is to ensure that all children taking the test receive essentially the same experience, are expected to perform the same tasks with the same set of materials, receive the same amount of assistance from the evaluator, and are evaluated according to a standard set of criteria. The overwhelming majority of standardized tests are norm-referenced—they indicate a child's developmental level in relation to that of other children of the same age, the normative group.

tests

IQ tests (measures of mental ability) are probably the best known and the most controversial of the norm-referenced measures. They provide an **intelligence quotient** (IQ), which is the relationship between a child's mental age (MA) and chronological age (CA). IQ reflects the difference between the child's performance on the tests and the normative performance for the child's age level.

intelligence quotient

Certain assumptions underlie the definition of IQ. The most crucial is the notion that intelligence, as measured on standardized tests of mental ability, is normally distributed. A normal distribution is a continuum of scores that vary from the average score by predictable amounts. Figure 2-2 shows the normal curve of intelligence, based on the scores of the *Wechsler Intelligence Scale for Children* (3rd edition) (WISC-III) (Wechsler, 1991). This widely used test of intelligence has an average score of 100 and a standard deviation of 15.

Teachers are not usually involved in assessing intelligence and cognitive functioning. Because IQ tests are delicate instruments and need careful interpretation, their use is restricted to psychologists and others who have received special training.

Many educators query the need for psychological services; they consider IQ scores to be of limited value in determining the needs and styles of inclusive classrooms. Nevertheless, psychometric assessment is still widely used. Advocates stress that an assessment of a child's cognitive skills is essential to a complete understanding of his or her development because cognitive skills are closely intertwined with skills in other domains, especially language, social functioning, and behaviour. Further, when properly used and interpreted, tests perform important functions. The greatest advantage of standardized tests is their potential for comparing a child's performance to that of other children (the norm group), and they are still

Figure 2-2
The normal curve of intelligence based on the WISC–III

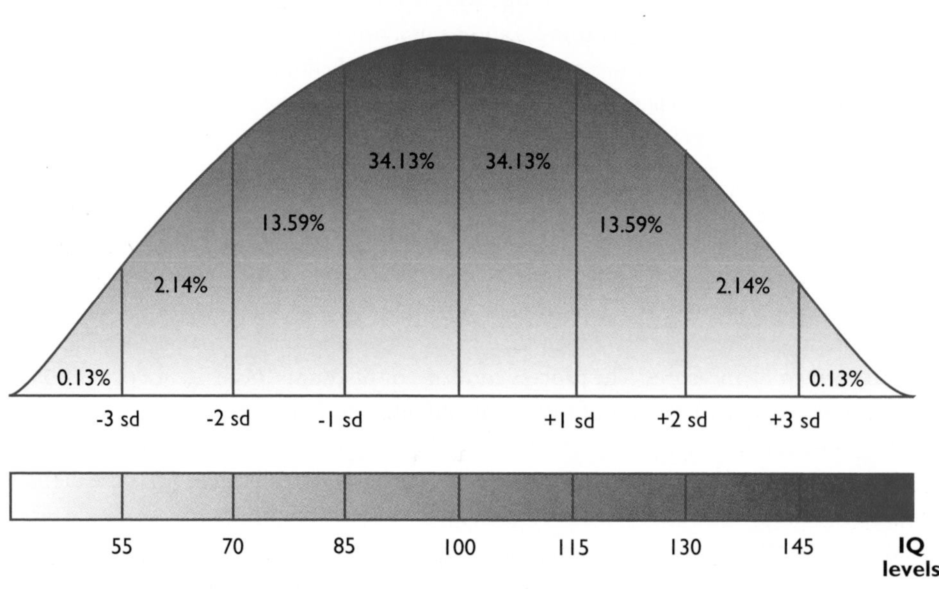

used with considerable success to predict academic achievement. As well, some school districts demand intellectual assessment as a major source of data in the designation and placement of students in special education (Wilson and Humphries, 1986).

The downside is that these measures are more important for defining delays than for program planning. Standardized measures tap isolated intellectual and language abilities but do not yield intervention-relevant information on functional skills that can be included in an individual child's program and easily integrated with daily activities.

Developmental Assessment

Developmental assessment is concerned with the location of a young child's skills within a specified hierarchy of skills (developmental milestones). The approach is founded on the assumption that children progress through specific patterns and that these patterns can be used in the detection of qualitative and quantitative differences among children.

The basis of the developmental approach is the use of developmental scales to establish lags or problems in one or more areas of growth. Sometimes teachers devise their own simple scales of developmental milestones that are compilations of developmental information taken from various developmental scales and charts. Just as often, they use norm-referenced tests to determine the extent of deviation from the norm.

The scales give a baseline to tell whether a child is progressing through the normal sequences of development or whether there are delays in development. If a child fails an item in the normal developmental sequence, it is rewritten as an instructional objective and the skill targeted for intervention. We readdress developmental assessment in Chapter 14.

Standards Testing

Although there is no finely tuned definition, *accountability* can be thought of as a system of informing those both inside and outside educational circles of the direction in which schools are moving (Westat, 1994). Accountability includes attainment of student goals and outcomes and is manifested as Canadian jurisdictions adopt province-wide testing for various grade levels.

As the stress on accountability and results of provincial examinations assume increasing importance, we must ask what is the status of students with disabilities. The Canadian Council for Exceptional Children (1998) reported on the different rules in some provinces and territories regarding standards testing and students who are exceptional. In British Columbia, for example, students who receive special services, including those who have little or no language skills in English, and those who would, at the administrator's discretion, be under undue stress, are exempt from participation. In Alberta, the superintendent may exempt individual students if the student can't respond to the instrument in its original or modified form or if participation would harm the student. In Saskatchewan, special provisions may be made for students with sensory disabilities, acute or chronic illness, and learning disabilities in the grade twelve departmental examinations. Manitoba allows exemptions for students with significant cognitive delays or if there would be harm to the student, and allows accommodations such as extra time to other students with special needs. In Ontario, a student can be fully exempt, partially exempt, or have accommodations. Newfoundland exempts students on individualized programs; other students with special needs may have accommodations.

Medical Assessment

Professionals involved at the medical level of assessment include school nurses, family doctors, pediatricians, neurologists, audiologists, and ophthalmologists, to mention only a few.

A huge variety of medical procedures are used with children with disabilities, often starting at birth or even before. The medical community uses a combination of testing devices to arrive at a diagnosis, including clinical history, physical examinations, and laboratory tests.

Screening may begin as early as the prenatal period with the use of amniocentesis to determine the presence of certain genetic disorders. Immediately following birth, screening occurs as physicians check for obvious disabilities or genetic and metabolic disorders. Later, a public health nurse using a sweep test to check hearing or a Snellen chart for visual acuity is screening for physical problems.

For a school-age child, a complete look at the child's health history and current medical status must form part of the total assessment. Suppose, for example, that a grade one child, who appears bright and outgoing, cannot seem to comprehend such sound–symbol associations as "S is for snake." Before any specific psycho-educational diagnosis is undertaken, the child should be referred to an audiologist for a complete assessment of hearing acuity.

Cultural and Linguistic Differences

Recent demographic data suggest that public schools are faced with increasing linguistic and cultural diversity. Winzer and Mazurek (2000) report that in 1986 some 6.3 percent of Canadians were members of a visible minority; the percentage increased to 9.4 percent in 1991, and to 11.2 percent in 1996. By 2005, the percentage will have risen to 16, and by 2016 it is expected that 20 percent of the Canadian population will be members of visible minorities. Of the more than one in 10 Canadians who are from visible minorities, 26.9 percent are

Chinese, 21 percent are South Asian, 17.9 percent are Black, 8 percent are Arab or West Asian, 7.7 percent are Filipino, 5.5 percent are Latin American, and 5.4 percent are Southeast Asian.

One result of these demographic changes is that the special education system is increasingly serving students who are in the process of acquiring a second language or who come from home backgrounds that differ culturally or linguistically from the Canadian majority. A second result is that schools and personnel must become more culturally aware and sensitive in order to include all students. A third result is that teachers must be especially sensitive when a child from a minority linguistic or cultural group also has an exceptional condition.

The influence of ethnicity on children is pervasive. Children do not shed their cultural differences at the school door; rather, they bring their socialization patterns, linguistic backgrounds, modes of communication, social mores, learning styles, and the manifestations of their culture and language to the classroom with them (Winzer and Mazurek, 1998).

One solution to the needs of students with cultural differences that simultaneously builds tolerance and understanding in other students is the process of multicultural education. Children with special needs also need to understand their own culture and those of others, they need to develop positive understandings of their own cultural heritage, and they need to explore similarities and differences.

Students with exceptionalities need multicultural special education that celebrates the first language and culture while building a second language and accommodating to the new culture. Multicultural special education can be defined as

> A set of perspectives and skills that change the climate, curriculum, and interactions in schools and classrooms so that all students, whatever their cultural and linguistic background or type and degree of disability, have equal respect, the opportunity to learn, and are given the skills to develop cross-cultural sensitivity and the competencies necessary to function in a pluralistic society. Multi-cultural perspectives and skills meld with special education practices, are infused throughout the curriculum, and are tailored to the unique strengths and needs of each child who is exceptional. (Winzer and Mazurek, 1998, pp. 104–105)

We discuss cultural and linguistic differences in Chapter 3 and throughout the text. Cooperative learning, a particularly potent instructional method, is discussed in the In the Classroom section at the close of Chapter 6.

SUMMARY

1. Contemporary special education is a vibrant and exciting area of education, alive with the pulse of new ideas. Issues, trends, and movements apparent in the field are all designed to ultimately improve conditions of living and learning for persons who are exceptional.
2. Many of the changes in attitudes and perceptions can be dated to the 1960s and the birth of the normalization movement. The ideological shift during the 1960s and the 1970s held that community settings were superior in their effects on social, vocational, and academic learning. By the mid-1970s, the treatment of persons with disabilities in non-restrictive, normalized settings gained priority.
3. Special education is deeply involved in reforming the system at various structural and theoretical levels. Probably no reform question has occupied special education professionals more in past decades than the effects, real and potential, of including children with disabilities into general classrooms.

Historical Notes

When special education began in North America, individuals with disabilities were believed to differ from the rest of the population in almost every domain. Because of this, and for reasons of economy and convenience, children with exceptionalities were educated chiefly in institutional settings designed as much to protect the rest of society from the so-called deviant child as to protect the children from an intolerant and prejudiced world.

Residential schools—variously referred to as *asylums, institutions, colonies,* or *training schools*—were first established in Canada in the 1860s to serve children described in the parlance of the day as deaf and dumb, blind, and idiotic or feeble-minded. In the United States and Canada these special schools were divorced from the general educational system and administered along with prisons, asylums, and public charities. Not until the early 1900s were special schools in most parts of Canada placed under provincial departments of education.

Schooling had become the social norm for most children in Canada by the early 1900s. As the public schools assumed responsibility for socializing and educating huge numbers of children, they were faced with an unforeseen problem. How could schools best provide for children who could not be handled in the regular classes? These difficult students, labelled as truant, delinquent, incorrigible, and feeble-minded, were those with mild disabilities in behaviour and learning. To keep order in the schools and to protect the education of other students and the time of teachers, special segregated classes seemed the ideal solution. Special classes, first known as ungraded classes, were first introduced in the United States in 1879. By 1910, segregated classrooms were a feature of most urban education systems.

In Canada the first special day classes were started in 1906 for children with physical problems—those described as crippled, sickly, and malnourished. These were followed by provisions for pupils who were mentally retarded, sight-saving classes, home instruction, speech correction, and lip-reading classes. There were also orthopedic classes, vocational and advancement classes, and remedial reading programs.

The late 1940s saw a huge expansion of special education due to simple demographics. The postwar baby boom increased the number of children with disabilities; advances in medical technology kept more children alive and limited degrees of impairment. Parents' associations formed and spearheaded a social movement to extend educational and treatment services to the most severely disabled children. In many cases, parents opened schools for children with moderate and severe disabilities.

The polio epidemic of the 1950s and the rubella epidemic of the 1960s generated still more demand for special education. However, the great majority of special education services were still provided in segregated settings—special classes or schools, clinics, hospitals, and so on.

The modern retelling of special education really began in the 1960s. Efforts to restructure special education, long-simmering and glacially paced, accelerated. As we mention in Chapter 1, parents, advocates, legislators, and educational systems began to reject the notion that students who were exceptional should be educated separately from their peers or that people with mental disabilities should be herded into large institutional settings.

Vehement critics of special education claimed that special classes were too often used as dumping grounds, they were often exclusionary rather than remedial, they did not appear to be returning a significant number of children to the regular classroom, and there was inherent discrimination in providing separate schooling for children based on presumed mental, physical, or behavioural incapacities. Still others castigated special education for the disproportionate number of ethnic- and minority-group children found in special segregated classrooms. Ethically, critics deplored labelling children and separating them from their normally developing peers. Not only did special education classes cast a stigma on exceptional children, but they provided low-quality education, and were often allotted inferior facilities and untrained teachers. Children from special classes were barely tolerated by regular classroom teachers and administrators. Grave dissatisfaction with special classes was bolstered by numerous efficacy studies. When the progress of children who were exceptional in segregated and regular classes was compared, these studies found that children performed no better in special classes than in general classrooms.

The late 1970s and early 1980s was the period in which the practice of special education came of age and the true movement toward integration got underway. In the 1970s, enormous changes came about as a result of enabling legislation in both the United States and Canada. The dual philosophies of normalization and mainstreaming impelled many children with mild to severe disabilities into the orbit of the public schools. Today we are witnessing the inclusion movement, which seeks regular education advantages for all children with disabilities.

4. Many educators support inclusionary philosophies but dispute inclusion as a universal template that assumes that only one solution exists to the various challenges faced by children with special needs. The philosophical ideal of inclusion is more accepted than the implementation. While Canadian studies show that a majority of teachers support the philosophical underpinnings of inclusion, many express a deep concern that in too many cases the inclusive process is not working.
5. Law and public policy have had a profound effect on the type and quality of education offered to children and youth who are exceptional. In some cases, they decide whether exceptional students are educated at all; in others, they determine how such children are educated. Litigation and legislation underlie much of the process of educational integration witnessed today. Parent groups, court decisions, escalating educational costs, and the example set by PL 94-142 have all exerted pressure on governments.
6. The U.S. Department of Education has taken a middle road on inclusive schooling—it supports inclusion, but cautions that there should be degrees of inclusion for individual learners. Canada follows suit. In Canada, there is no legal mandate on, or consistent definition of, inclusion; most Canadian legislation speaks to the idea of inclusion but not to the practice.
7. There is no single model of inclusive education. While some educators propose education for every child within the general classroom, others are more cautious within current educational realities. In schools, complex processes interact, and teachers face contradictory imperatives.
8. Successfully implementing inclusionary practices is a major challenge to school systems. Diverse and complex threads must draw together if the most appropriate education is to be provided for every child who is exceptional.
9. Before we can help children who are exceptional, we must accurately pinpoint their problems. For each child, we need a detailed picture of strengths and weaknesses in a variety of domains. Assessment serves little purpose if the process is undertaken merely to collect data. Data from screening and psycho-educational diagnosis are useful only when used to initiate more effective services and programming for children.

WEBLINKS

The Canadian Charter of Rights and Freedoms **canada.justice.gc.ca/en/laws/charter**

The Council for Exceptional Children **www.cec.sped.org/**

Education Quality and Accountability Office **www.eqao.com/**

IDEA Technical Assistance Project **www.ideapractices.org**

Internet Special Education Resources **www.iser.com/index.shtml**

Office of Learning Technologies **http://olt-bta.hrdc-drhc.gc.ca**

School Net, a co-operative venture of Canada's provincial, federal and territorial governments **www.schoolnet.ca/sne/**

Chapter 3

Risk Factors and Children at Risk

Learning Outcomes

After reading this chapter, you should be able to:

Understand the variety of risk factors and how they affect development;

Distinguish between established, biological, and environmental risk;

Understand the many familial and extra-familial factors that can place students at risk for learning and behavioural problems;

Understand the potential difficulties associated with cultural and linguistic differences.

Introduction

Dozens and dozens of factors surround children as they grow up. Some of them are related to the classroom; many more are familial or extra-familial factors. If teachers are to truly understand the pupils in their charge, they must be aware of a child's social world and a child's development; social skills and self-esteem; interactions with parents; and, in many cases, cultural and linguistic background. This is even more key when a child has a disability. Not only must teachers be aware of the psychological, social, and educational factors related to a disability, but they must also have a working knowledge of biomedical causes.

At risk is a term used in rather different ways to describe a number of different categories of children. Simply, children may be "at risk for" or "at risk because of." In the classroom, teachers will meet many students who are not designated as special education recipients, yet who are at risk for a number of unfortunate outcomes. In this usage of "at risk for," at-risk status includes, for example, young girls who become pregnant, adolescents involved in drugs and crime, those who have attempted suicide, school dropouts, and large groups of children for whom English is not the first language.

Large numbers of students are involved in the "at risk for" group. Studies find that between 25 and 35 percent of all students are seriously at risk (Frymier and Gansneder, 1989; Johnson, 1998). Causes are diverse. As it relates to school performance and success, at-risk status is associated with poverty in households, low-income families in which the parents' educational levels and occupational status are also low, single-parent families, and dysfunctional family backgrounds.

The second group, children who are "at risk because of," is smaller. In this sense, at risk refers to infants and young children who are physically, medically, or psychologically in danger of failing to thrive. When children are considered high risk or at risk, they are seen to be more prone to developing some form of disabling condition or for adverse effects on school learning and behaviour.

risk factors

This chapter is concerned chiefly with **risk factors**, the biological or environmental causes of potential disabilities and adverse outcomes. A huge variety of biological factors account for disabling or potentially disabling conditions in children. There are, for example, more than 200 known causes of mental retardation and perhaps nearly 2000 inborn errors of metabolism (Berlin, 1983); in total, more than 3500 genetic diseases have been identified. However, the etiology of a particular child's problem all too frequently remains obscure. Despite all that is known, nearly half of all childhood exceptionalities are attributable to unknown causes. We also discuss emerging causes of disabilities, referred to as the *new morbidity*.

It is almost impossible to determine the relative influences of heredity and environment on human behaviour, for every human life is a complex interplay of heredity and environment. The genes alone cannot produce a human being; an environment must also exist to provide nourishment, warmth, stimulation, and protection. Environmental causes that place students at risk are legion, although the most pervasive and important seem to be poverty, dysfunctional families, and cultural and linguistic differences. In this chapter we also examine, albeit briefly, some of the many environmental causes that increase the risk of a child developing a problem that affects learning and/or behaviour.

ETIOLOGICAL CONSIDERATIONS

etiology

As increasing numbers of children with exceptional conditions move into regular educational milieus, teachers will encounter far more students with problems such as epilepsy, Traumatic Brain Injury, visual and auditory impairment, and orthopedic and urologic difficulty. Fundamental to providing for the needs of these students is a basic understanding of **etiology**, the process of finding causes to explain how a particular problem came into existence.

teratology

Etiological considerations concern *symptoms*, the overt reactions or manifestations of the body to a certain condition, and *symptomology*, the study of symptoms and characteristics. Etiology likewise involves **teratology**, generally thought of as the study of the agents involved in major congenital malformations. The concept has recently been broadened to include more minor malformations and behavioural difficulties, and now involves the causes of malformations and looking at outcomes of long-term importance in the medical and psychological functioning of a child.

Keep in mind that a single cause can have various outcomes; causal agents are frequently not particular about what part of the human organism they attack. As well, a given agent may have different effects depending on timing, severity, genotype, and unknown factors. Deafness, for example, can have a pre-, peri-, or postnatal time of onset, and can be caused by agents such as rubella, syphilis, meningitis, or, in the past, drugs such as streptomycin.

Why is a knowledge of the pathophysiology, symptomology, and treatment of exceptional conditions important for education professionals? There are many reasons, which are summarized below.

- The causes of disabilities cannot easily be separated from the developmental consequences—the psychological, social, and educational implications that impact on learning and behaviour.
- Recent genetic research provides dramatic evidence that students affected by different genetic conditions present quite different profiles. This is most prominent in genetic causes of mental retardation. (Some examples are shown in Table 3-1.)
- Etiological knowledge leads to a better appreciation of a disability. Teachers' understanding of medical conditions aids them in becoming sensitized to the social, emotional, and educational problems resulting from a child's disabilities. It enhances an understanding relationship with the child, and creates an atmosphere of acceptance among classmates and others involved with the child. A child with spina bifida, for example, often requires an artificial bladder for urine drainage. The clinical manifestations of the child's urologic difficulties (incontinence) and the need for medical management (the bag worn on the stomach or flank) may create practical and psychological problems for the child. If the teacher is unable to assist and reassure the child, then the child's medical problems may create learning difficulties (Freund, Casey, and Bradley, 1982).
- Knowledge breeds tolerance. Research attests that teachers and others who hold a clear understanding of exceptional conditions tend to be more tolerant and accepting than those who know little about etiologies and developmental consequences.
- Effective treatment requires an appropriate theoretical understanding of a problem. Teachers' knowledge imparts confidence in their ability to program effectively for individual children. One teacher wrote, "The scariest thing about integration is the medical aspect of it. We're looking at giving out medication, injections, changing diapers and always having to be on guard for handicapped children's frailties in case they get a reaction to something or stop breathing for some reason" (Alberta Teachers' Association, 1993, p. 12). Understanding a condition leads to greater confidence in handling the medical aspects.
- Medical management for health problems can be a significant part of a child's daily life. In order to adequately assist children with exceptionalities in the classroom, teachers must be aware of physical deformities that may require special equipment or prosthetic devices; alterations that may be needed in work, play, and rest schedules; special positioning or handling techniques or special feeding techniques; and special arrangements that may be needed to accommodate seizure activity, medications, allergies, susceptibility to illness, poor muscle strength, and special feeding problems. They must also be willing to provide necessary assistance beyond that of an educational nature.
- Some children with disabilities require medication on a regular basis, such as anticonvulsants for seizures, muscle relaxants for spasticity, Ritalin for attention disorders, and a variety of medications for respiratory and cardiac problems. Depending on school-board policy, the teacher may be involved in the monitoring of drug dosages.
- Some children with disabilities have difficulty participating in certain physical activities. The teacher must be aware when certain activities must be limited, when to restrict the duration of an activity, and when to recommend an alternative learning experience.

Table 3-1 Examples of genetic and chromosomal anomalies

Condition	Anomalies	Social/cognitive effects
Angelman syndrome	Neurological and cranio-facial abnormalities; problems with gait and ambulation	Severe delays in motor and intellectual development, episodic laughter
Apert's syndrome	Incomplete fusion of the skull bones and malformation of the bones of skull and head	Associated mental retardation; often conductive hearing loss
Cri du chat syndrome	One in 50 000 live births; chromosomal	Unusual sounds; mental retardation
Fragile X syndrome	Genetic	Physical and mental aberrations, more obvious in males than females
Hunter's syndrome	Rare genetic lysosomal storage disorder; sex-linked	Progressive cognitive, physical disabilities
Lesch-Nyham syndrome	Chromosomal; x-linked	Often engage in self-biting
Prader-Willi syndrome	One in 15 000 live births	Almost obsessive desire for food. Much related maladaptive behaviour such as stereotyped skin picking
Turner's syndrome	Sex linked; chromosomal; affects females	Mental and physical anomalies
Smith-Magenis syndrome	One in 50 000 live births	Varied physical characteristics
Williams syndrome	Congenital heart and blood vessel defects, dental and kidney abnormalities, mild to serious mental retardation, hernias, low muscle tone; one in 25 000 live births	Unusual auditory hypersensitivity, good verbal but moderately low intellectual ability; visual/motor problems. Tend to be unusually friendly; strong interest in people

As well as etiological considerations, a general knowledge of the types of treatment that children with disabilities may be given is helpful. In general terms, treatment can be classified into five categories:

1. Treatment that is necessary and lifesaving, such as insulin for diabetes. (See also Chapter 11.)
2. Treatment that is ameliorative and avoids secondary complications, such as surgery for contractures in children with cerebral palsy. (See also Chapter 12.)
3. Treatment that is adaptive and facilitates development, such as total communication for individuals who are deaf. (See also Chapter 9.)

4. Treatment that is unproven but potentially useful, such as drug therapy. (See also Chapter 7.)
5. Treatment that is controversial, such as special diets in the control of hyperactivity (Kessler, 1977). (See also Chapter 5.)

The New Morbidity

In the past, conditions such as Rh factor and diseases such as whooping cough, measles, smallpox, enteric fever, meningitis, and scarlet fever seriously impaired or even destroyed the vision and hearing of many children, and left a range of other disabling conditions. Scarlet fever and other such conditions are virtually eliminated, but a new group of disorders related to new etiologies has emerged.

These new disorders have been characterized as "the new morbidity," referring to the fact that they result from newly discovered or new etiologies. Included are disorders such as Attention Deficit Hyperactivity Disorder (ADHD), Traumatic Brain Injury (TBI), Fetal Alcohol Syndrome (FAS), and fragile X syndrome. Of grave concern is **pediatric AIDS**—AIDS contracted by children under thirteen years—and the impairments caused because of the physical and chemical damage done to fetal brains by drug-abusing mothers.

pediatric AIDS

Another group of children included in this category is those whom medical technology helps survive. Even twenty years ago, many of these children would not have lived. Extremely premature babies, rescued by aggressive medical treatments, are at high risk for a number of neurological and physical impairments. In addition, many children with severe and profound disabilities and those with severe chronic illnesses can today expect a normal life span. The lowered mortality rate means that more severely impaired children are surviving and attending school.

We should mention that a relatively new educational term for co-occurring and multiple disabilities is surfacing in the literature. **Comorbidity** is the simultaneous occurrence of two or more unrelated conditions. The term, borrowed from medicine, should be regarded with some caution in special education.

comorbidity

RISK FACTORS AND DISABILITY

risk factors

Risk factors connote the range of biological and environmental conditions associated with increased probability of cognitive, social, affective, and physical problems. Risk factors may be intrinsic or extrinsic, although to some extent this is an arbitrary distinction as variables under these two classifications often interact. Extrinsic refers to the environment that elevates risk—physical, cultural, and social. Intrinsic refers to aspects of an individual's make-up.

Risk is basically a statistical concept. Risk status allows specialists to classify children in terms of the type and degree of potential disorders. Researchers who study risk identify the agent or situation, specify the effect, and then estimate the probability that they are associated.

There exist thousands upon thousands of risk factors. These can be slotted into three major categories—established risk, biological risk, and environmental risk. Much overlap exists between the categories. (See Table 3-2.)

Table 3-2 Sample of disabling conditions and sequelae

Condition	Classification	Timing	Major sequelae
CMV	Infection	Birth	Mental retardation; can be fatal
Cystic fibrosis	Hereditary anomaly	Conception	Involvement of digestive and respiratory systems
Down syndrome	Chromosomal aberration	Dysjunction at conception or soon after	Mental and physical anomalies
Fetal Alcohol Syndrome	Intoxication	Throughout pregnancy	Mental and physical anomalies
Fragile X syndrome	Chromosomal aberration	Conception	Mental and physical anomalies
Galactosemia	Hereditary anomaly	Conception	Untreated will result in mental retardation
Herpes	Infection	Birth	Mental retardation; often fatal
Muscular dystrophy	X-linked genetic anomaly	Conception	Muscle degeneration
Phenylketonuria (PKU)	Autosomal metabolic disorder	Conception	Untreated will lead to mental retardation
Rh factor	Genetic problem	Conception	Jaundice, mental retardation, deafness
Rubella	Infection	First trimester	Deafness, blindness, mental retardation, multiple handicaps
Spina bifida	Perhaps multifactorial inheritance		Neurological impairments of varying degrees
Syphilis	Infection	Second and third trimester	Physical handicaps, mental retardation, sensory disabilities

Table 3-2 continued

Condition	Classification	Timing	Major sequelae
Tay-Sachs disease	Autosomal hereditary anomaly	Conception	Fatal
Turner's syndrome	Chromosomal aberration	Conception	Mental and physical differences

Risk connotes a given probability but does not imply certainty, and not all children who fall within these categories of increased vulnerability become disabled. In fact, the majority of children deemed to be within the traditionally accepted categories of biological and environmental risk, such as those who were born prematurely and those who are raised by young unmarried mothers with low incomes, will develop normally. Nevertheless, when compared to the general population, a greater proportion of children who are exposed to risk factors will develop difficulties. Present estimates indicate that between 30 and 70 percent of infants classified at birth as at risk eventually develop problems that require some form of intervention.

Why are some at-risk children affected and not others? The answer is complex. One explanation is that even with heightened risk some children are simply more resilient. Resilience seems to be associated with high cognitive skills, curiosity, enthusiasm, ability to set goals for oneself, and high self-esteem (Hanson and Carta, 1995).

Established Risk

established risk

continuum of reproductive casualty

The established-risk category refers to medical conditions and anomalies that invariably result in a disability or developmental delay. **Established risk** can be described as a diagnosed medical disorder with a known etiology that bears "relatively well known" expectancies for developmental outcomes. This means that certain causes are known to relate to certain conditions and that there is a **continuum of reproductive casualty**; that is, the problems may range from relatively minor through to major difficulties. Established risk, most often related to genetic and chromosomal problems, includes conditions such as Down syndrome, fragile X syndrome, and infantile autism.

Genetic and Chromosomal Differences

All individuals are born with a unique combination of genes that is theirs alone from the moment of conception. Nothing will ever change. Individuals will die with the same number and set of genes and share these same genes with their offspring. Almost every human cell contains a complete package of hereditary instructions for the characteristics that comprise the individual. These instructions are located in 46 chromosomes, arranged in 23 pairs. Each pair carries one chromosome from each parent. The first 22 chromosomal pairs are autosomal (identical) and determine the thousands of traits that make up a human being, whether male or female. The twenty-third pair determines the sex of the individual. Each chromosome consists of thousands of genes, and each gene is made up of deoxyribonucleic acid (DNA), which in turn consists of thousands of combinations of four chemical sub-units. The order in which these sub-units are joined together spells out the gene's message in the genetic code. Whether a particular cell will become facial skin or ankle bone depends on which genes are "switched on." Many human traits such as skin and hair colour, height, and general body build, are controlled by the action of many genes operating together. Such interaction of numerous genes is known as *polygenic inheritance.*

Genes are responsible for more than just physical traits: genetics is involved in intellectual factors, including IQ; specific cognitive abilities; academic achievement; temperament in childhood; attitudes and beliefs; and personality factors, including extroversion and neuroticism. Genes are also involved in reading disability; some forms of mental retardation; and psychopathology, including schizophrenia, affective disorders, delinquent and criminal behaviour, and alcoholism (Plomin, 1989).

Just one misspelling in the DNA code throws off the entire process. This happens in the 3 to 5 percent of all babies born with a chromosomal abnormality, a clearly defined genetic disease, or a genetically influenced defect, such as malformation of the spine. Among these newborns, about 3 percent have some genetic birth defects. About one newborn in 200 has a chromosomal abnormality (Plomin, De Fries, and McClearn, 1990).

In recent decades, massive research has been undertaken in the field of **cytogenetics**, the study of the location and organization of genetic material from chromosomes. Research into genetic and chromosomal abnormalities has focused on the location, organization, and regulation of the genetic materials of the chromosomes, and on detecting a marker or unusual DNA sequence that is associated with a disease-causing gene (Nelkin and Tancredi, 1989).

cytogenetics

Genetic Disorders

As the embryo develops, DNA directs the chemical process within its cells. Scientists and researchers have looked for ways to locate and map defective genes to identify potential disabilities before birth. Much of the chromosomal territory is still unknown, but here and there are little pockets of well-covered ground. The X chromosome is the most explored, with about 115, or 10 percent, of its genes now mapped.

One tiny flaw in the genetic structure can have tragic results. A change in DNA may repair itself or lead to spontaneous abortion (miscarriage). The flaw may also create abnormalities present at birth, called **congenital abnormalities** or **hereditary anomalies**. Because hereditary anomalies are in the genes, they may be passed on to subsequent generations, the rate depending on the type of inheritance. With dominant inheritance, a child usually has parents with the same disorder. Dominant conditions tend to show marked variability, with different individuals having different degrees of symptoms, from none to severe.

congenital abnormalities
hereditary anomalies

The March of Dimes Birth Defects Foundation (1987) catalogued about 2000 confirmed or suspected dominant genetic disorders that can result in mental retardation and other disabilities. These include achondroplasia, a form of dwarfism; Huntington's disease, a progressive nervous system degeneration; and polydactyly, extra fingers or toes. There are about 1000 confirmed or suspected recessive disorders, which include cystic fibrosis, galactosemia, and Tay–Sachs disease. With recessive inheritance, the child must inherit a gene from both parents. Under simple Mendelian inheritance, each child runs a four-to-one risk of manifesting the disorder.

Some disorders are linked to the genes on the twenty-third pair of chromosomes. In X-linked inheritance, sons have a 50–50 chance of inheriting the condition though their mother. Of the more than 250 types of X-linked inheritance disorders identified, colour blindness, hemophilia, and muscular dystrophy are probably the best known.

Multifactorial inheritance results from the interaction of many genes with other genes and/or environmental factors. Patterns of transmission are poorly defined; some conditions thought to be multifactorial are spina bifida, clubfoot, and cleft lip or palate.

retinitis pigmentosa

In some cases, various types of transmission can account for a condition. For example, **retinitis pigmentosa** is a condition that affects the retina, the film-like layer in the back of the eye, and causes progressive visual loss. Retinitis pigmentosa is an inherited disease, transmitted through generations by a gene that may be recessive, dominant, or sex-linked. An estimated one person in eighty carries the gene for recessive retinitis pigmentosa. At present, however, it is rarely possible to detect the carriers ("Children should see ...," 1980).

Inborn Errors of Metabolism

While metabolic problems due to hereditary defects account for only a small percentage of disabilities, the study of these disorders has provided valuable knowledge for the prevention and treatment of disabilities due to other organic causes. Most inborn errors of metabolism are the result of the action of a single pair of genes. Many result in missing or defective *enzymes*, which are the proteins that help the body convert one substance into another as, for example, in the transformation of nutrients to chemicals usable by the cells. The absence of, or a defect in, one of the enzymes means that the normal chemistry of the cell is altered by the inability to provide or dispose of a critical chemical or protein, leading to unusual levels of particular chemicals in the body.

Tay-Sachs disease

Many of these conditions, such as phenylketonuria (PKU) and diabetes, can be treated or controlled; others, such as **Tay-Sachs disease**—a fatal deterioration of brain function—are untreatable. To provide examples, we describe a number of inborn errors of metabolism below. Diabetes is covered in Chapter 11.

Tay–Sachs disease is named after its discovers, Warren Tay, an English physician, and Bernard Sachs, an American physician, who identified the condition in 1877. Tay–Sachs results from an enzyme deficiency caused by a single autosomal recessive gene. Infants appear normal at birth, but the nervous system is gradually destroyed because of the missing enzyme, hexosamidose A. Lacking this enzyme, various fatty substances build up in the body cells, including those of the brain. The excessive glycolipid in the cells of the nervous system causes the cells to swell, rupture, and finally die. As the nerve cells die, the child becomes retarded, loses motor ability, and becomes deaf and blind. Effects of the condition can be seen at three to six months after birth. Death is inevitable, usually between four and six years of age.

The parents, who are heterozygous carriers, each have only about half of the regular amount of the enzyme, but this is sufficient for normal development. About one in thirty Jews carry the defective gene. Tay–Sachs is also found in non-Jewish persons, but is a hundred times less frequent.

phenylketonuria

Phenylketonuria (PKU), a relatively rare genetically transmitted metabolic disorder, was discovered in 1934 by physician and biochemist Dr. Ashborn Folling of Norway (Henderson, 1989). PKU is carried on a double recessive gene by about one in every 600 people, so the chance of two carriers marrying is statistically one in every 3600. The condition affects about one child in every 14 000 and accounts for approximately one percent of all institutionalized individuals who are mentally retarded. Phenylketonuria is primarily a condition that affects whites, with the highest incidence in the United States and Europe. It is rare in African, Jewish, or Japanese populations.

Some genes act on other genes. These *modifier genes* then determine how the other genes express themselves. This happens in PKU. The condition is marked by an inability to normally oxidize the amino acid phenylalanine, which is found in fish, dairy products, and most protein sources. Sustained hyperphenylalanin anemia in the early years is neurotoxic and almost invariably results in severe intellectual impairment (see Griffiths, Smith, and Harvie, 1997). Once in place, the effects are irreversible.

Early screening and a special diet eliminates or diminishes the effects of PKU. Screening procedures include urinalysis and blood tests shortly after birth. The most reliable test is the Guthrie blood test, developed by Dr. Robert Guthrie in 1961. It is performed between the third and sixth day after birth, with retesting after two weeks.

Early detection of PKU is vital, because the infant must immediately be restricted to a diet low in phenylalanine. Although phenylalanine cannot be completely eliminated from a child's diet, it can be severely restricted with a phenylalanine-deficient formula, Lofenalac, a prepared milk substitute. Low-phenylalanine foods include vegetables, fruits, juices, some cereals, breads, and starches. Milk and dairy foods are restricted and meat is eliminated from the child's daily intake.

Although the effects of phenylketonuria can be almost eliminated, some recent research has demonstrated mild problems, even in children on strict diets. One group of researchers found that some treated children showed neurophysiological dysfunctions that interfered with academic functioning. Others discovered that in treated PKU children, the IQs are within normal limits but they tend to be lower than those of parents, siblings, and non-sibling control subjects (see Ozanne, Kaimmer, and Murdoch, 1990). Many females fail to maintain the diet; when they bear children, the elevated levels of PKU increase the probability of having an impaired infant (Henderson, 1989).

Galactosemia is another metabolic disorder that can result in mental retardation. In this case, a child lacks the ability to metabolize galactose. As with PKU, successful treatment depends upon early detection and a special diet. *Tuberous sclerosis* is a complex disorder in which benign tumours grow in the brain, kidneys, eyes, and other organs causing seizures, mental retardation, and autism in about half of the affected group. The condition affects about one in every 6000 people, usually starting in childhood. Researchers believe that a third of the cases are passed from parents to their children; in the other two-thirds, a gene mutation arises spontaneously in a child with no affected parent (Painter, 1997).

Deletion Syndromes

In these rare diseases, it is not a case of aberrant genes. Rather, there is too little genetic material or there is at least one gene missing. Examples include Williams syndrome, Prader-Willi syndrome, and cri du chat. (See Table 3-1.)

Prader-Willi, for example, was reported in 1956 by Prader, Labhart, and Willi in Switzerland. It is associated with obesity, small stature, oligophrenia (less than normal mental development) and small hands and feet. It affects one in every 10 000 to 25 000 children. There are more boys than girls affected. The etiology is unknown (Otto and Barber, 1992).

Chromosomal Factors

Chromosomal problems result from chromosomal dysjunction, a malfunction in cell division. Problems occur when there is an extra chromosome, or when pieces or parts of chromosomes attach themselves to other chromosomes.

There are many different chromosomal disorders that affect children. The effects of the damage vary greatly. Wide variations occur in the onset of symptoms, the parts of the body involved, the nature of the symptoms, the degree of severity, and the possible multiplicity of impairments.

Down Syndrome

The most commonly occurring chromosomal aberration—and the most deeply researched—is Down syndrome. Almost half (46 percent) of all studies on any genetic disorder have focused on Down (Hodapp and Fidler, 1999).

Down syndrome occurs in approximately one in every 1000 live births (Plomin, De Fries, and McClearn, 1990). It is an equal-opportunity disability: it can occur in any family, regardless of race, socio-economic class, or the education of the parents. It usually happens only once in a family, and strikes most often when the mother is approaching the end of her child-bearing days.

The condition was first identified in 1866 by John Langton Down, a physician at the Earlswood Asylum in Surrey, England. The facial features of children with the condition prompted Down to refer to it as "Mongolian idiocy." He assumed that the condition represented a re-emergence of a more primitive evolutionary status, which he erroneously believed to also be that of the Mongolian race. The Mongolian resemblance, however, is due simply to the development of a fold in the upper eyelid, which is caused not by inheritance but by the failure of the root of the nose to develop normally (Montagu, 1977). Today we have discarded the term "mongoloid" as demeaning and developmentally inappropriate.

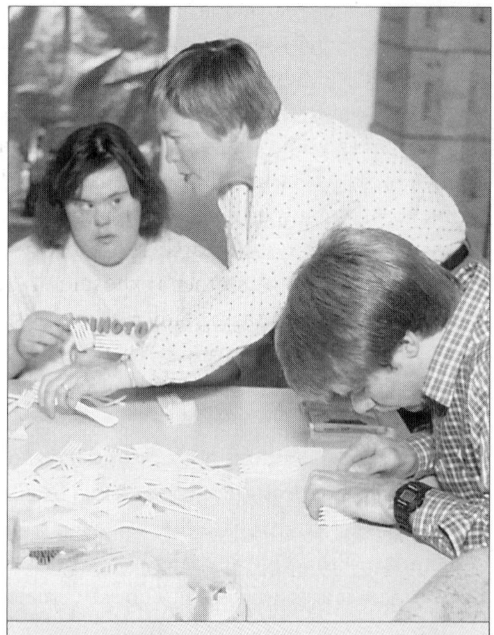

Down syndrome is the most common chromosomal aberration.

Down syndrome was one of the first conditions to be linked to a genetic abnormality. The major breakthrough came in 1959 when Swedish geneticists determined that the correct number of chromosomes in humans was 46. When they discovered the extra chromosome in Down, the link between Down syndrome and dysjunction was confirmed.

There are three major types of Down syndrome—Trisomy 21, translocation, and mosaicism. In each type, the mental and physical problems of the child are caused by extra chromosomal material, which somehow disturbs the orderly development of both body and brain.

Chromosome 21 is the smallest human chromosome; it contains only about 1.5 percent of the total genetic material (Patterson, 1987). Yet cases of Down syndrome are somehow linked to this tiny chromosome. There are no individuals with the clinical symptoms of Down syndrome who do not have at least partial Trisomy 21.

Trisomy 21 accounts for the great majority of children with Down syndrome (about 93 percent). There are actually fourteen different types of Trisomy 21. All are basically problems of dysjunction, which refers to the twenty-first pair of chromosomes containing three chromosomes instead of two. This may result from a mistake in chromosomal distribution in the egg or sperm, or happens when the chromosomes are distributed unequally when the fertilized egg began to divide.

Of the rest of the population with Down syndrome, 5 percent have *translocation*, in which only part of chromosome 21 is present in triplicate. In this condition, the extra chromosomal material most often attaches to chromosome 14, 15, 21, or 22 (Patterson, 1987). Although the actual chromosome count is 46, the affected child suffers from the same overdose of chromosome 21 as the child with standard trisomy. There may be hereditary components in translocation.

Mosaicism accounts for about 2 percent of Down syndrome cases. This condition results when there is a faulty distribution of chromosomes in later cell divisions. The child possesses some normal cells and some with a trisomy condition. Any resulting physical and mental anomalies depend on the number of affected cells.

More than 50 physical signs are listed as characteristic of Down syndrome. Some are apparent at birth, some appear much later, and some disappear with age. The number of physical features that a child displays bears no relationship to the degree of retardation. Few children have all the characteristics typical of the syndrome. Table 3-3 outlines the most common.

The chances of having a child with Down syndrome increase dramatically with the age of the parents, particularly the mother. (Very young mothers are an exception to this rule: they are more likely to have a Down syndrome baby than women in their twenties or thirties.) For the woman over 40, the chances of bearing a Down infant are approximately one in 80. For women over 45, the chances increase to one in 60 (Hansen, 1978).

Many authorities believe that Down syndrome may result from a combination of two factors—chemical changes in the egg cells due to the mother's aging ovaries, and a reduction in the secretion of various hormones in older women (Montagu, 1977). The mother's age may not be the only factor. Researchers are discovering possible links between Down syndrome and the amount of the mother's exposure to radiation and certain viruses. They are also exploring the role of the aging father, who contributes the extra chromosome in 20 to 25 percent of the cases (Abroms and Bennett, 1983). For men aged 41 and up, there is an increased risk of fathering children with Trisomy 21, regardless of the age of the mother.

Fragile X Syndrome

Fragile X syndrome is a relatively recent addition to the catalogue of causes of retardation. The fragile X chromosome was first reported in 1969, but the syndrome was not consistently diagnosed until the 1980s (Hagerman, 1988). Identification uses a karyotype with a special culture medium that is low in folic acid.

Today fragile X syndrome is second only to Down syndrome among cytogenetic abnormalities associated with mental retardation (Simen and Rogers, 1989). The prevalence of individuals affected by the fragile X syndrome is approximately one in 1000. The incidence

Table 3-3 Some observable physical characteristics associated with Down syndrome

Head	Hair	Face
distinctive shape; skull rounded and small	sparse, fine, and soft	flat profile
Nose	**Eyes**	**Ears**
small and "pug"; flat bridge; undeveloped or absent nasal cartilage; mucous discharge common	epicanthic fold; speckling of iris (Brushfield's spots); strabismus or nystagmus common	small and low-set; overlapping upper letices
Mouth	**Teeth**	**Tongue**
high-arched; thick, fissured lips; narrow palate	small, irregularly aligned; late erupting	coarse, protruding
Hands	**Muscles**	**Feet**
broad, stumpy, with short fingers; palmar crease (simian line) on one or both hands; incurved little finger (clindactly)	general hypotonia; flexible joints	broad and short; excessive space between first and second toes
Skin	**Abdomen**	**Stature**
thick, dry, rough; mottled or flushed	prominent umbilical hernia common	short; average height: male – 152.4 cm female – 139.7 cm

among live male births is about one in 1350; among female births, about one in 2033 (Webb, Bundey, Thake, and Todd, 1986). The prevalence of carriers is higher. Reports of the prevalence of fragile X syndrome (those affected and carriers) in the general population range from 1.9 to 5.9 percent (Blomquist, Gustavson, Holmgren, Nordenson, and Paslsson-Strade, 1983; Jacobs, Mayer, and Abruzzo, 1986).

Fragile X is a marker on the X chromosome at position 927. The syndrome is caused by an abnormal gene or genes at the lower end of the long arm of the X chromosome. The defective gene creates too long a stretch of DNA, which disrupts the structure of the X chromosome and creates a fragile area which then makes too many copies or repeats of a particular gene.

The genetics involved in fragile X seem to be unlike those of most typical X-linked recessive conditions. Santos (1992) notes that fragile X runs through a family tree in a multi-step process, resulting two or three generations later in full activation of the mutation. During this time many people can be affected to various degrees (physically, cognitively, and behaviourally) before a complete diagnosis is made.

Clinicians familiar with fragile X syndrome utilize physical findings to aid in diagnosis of affected males (see Table 3-4). Fragile X patients undergo changes in appearance from childhood through the adult years. During the growth period in males, testicular volume increases, the face grows in an elongated pattern, the forehead becomes more prominent, and the ears enlarge. The adult male patient typically has a long face, large ears, a prominent forehead, midface hypoplasia, and a prominent jaw. The most common feature seen in the postpubescent male is macro-orchidism (large testicles). However, among prepubertal males macro-orchidism is reported in only approximately 50 percent of the population (Simen and Rogers, 1989).

Some of the physical features typical of fragile X males can also be seen in female carriers, such as mildly prominent ears, a long face, and hyperextensible finger joints. Female carriers who are affected cognitively are more likely to show these physical features (Hagerman, 1988). Among fragile X–positive females, however, facial features are exceedingly variable and do not serve as an aid in diagnosis.

Turner's Syndrome

Turner's syndrome (TUS) is a condition affecting approximately one in every 2000 live female births. Diagnosis is made by karyotype. Women with TUS either lack an X chromosome or have a structural abnormality in one of the X chromosomes. The syndrome is characterized by short stature, growth failure, or gonadal dysgenesis (unformed reproductive sys-

Table 3-4 Features of fragile X syndrome

Physical	Non-physical
large head size	developmental delay
large flat ears	mental retardation
long narrow face	learning disabilities
prominent forehead	hyperactivity
broad nose	short attention span
high palate	autistic behaviours
large testicles	fearfulness, shyness
large hands; non-tapering fingers	rapid, repetitive speech
mitral valve prolapse (heart murmur)	talkativeness
increased birth-weight	difficulty adjusting to change
repeated ear infections	

tems) that inhibits spontaneous pubertal onset and fertility. Some women with TUS have abnormal appearances and/or medical problems such as problems of the aorta, hypertension, and renal abnormalities. Individuals with TUS also have a characteristic pattern of cognitive abilities consisting of normal verbal IQ and relatively lower performance IQ due to difficulty with space forms and number concepts (Downey, Elkin, Ehrhardt, Meyer-Bahlberg, Bell, and Morishima, 1991).

Biological Risk

biological risk

Biological risk relates to infants and toddlers with a history of prenatal, perinatal, neonatal, or early developmental events that can result in biological insults to developing systems. Documented biological risk includes children whose pediatric history or current circumstances reveal significant biological conditions that do not lead inevitably to developmental delay or disorder but carry a greater probability of delay or disability than that found in the general population (Shonkoff and Meisels, 1990).

For purposes of discussion, it is useful to group biological causes of exceptionality into some major categories and then discuss them in specific developmental periods: the *prenatal* or gestation period; the *perinatal* period, which extends from the seventh month of pregnancy and includes the delivery and birth period as well as the neonatal period, or first two weeks after birth; and the *postnatal* period.

Prenatal Period

Life begins not at birth, but at conception. At the beginning of life, a human being is smaller than the period at the end of this sentence. The individual is a single cell, barely visible to the naked eye, a tiny drop of fluid made up mainly of non-living material surrounding a minuscule nucleus of living matter. By the time of birth, some 38 weeks later, the individual weighs about 3.5 kilograms and contains 200 billion specialized cells (Montagu, 1977).

The prenatal period encompasses three stages. The first two weeks are known as the period of the *ovum*, or *zygote*. Next, the period of the *embryo* lasts until the beginning of the third month. The remaining gestation time is known as the period of the *fetus*. The change of labels charts the organism's growth from a simple cell to a recognizable human creature. Specific changes occur to the developing human at specific times. Every cell, every tissue, and every organ has its own timetable for coming into existence, for developing, and for beginning to carry out its functions. So consistent are these functions that embryologists can determine them with great accuracy.

From the moment of conception until delivery nine months later, the human being is more susceptible to environment than at any other time. The opening third of pregnancy, the

first trimester

first trimester, is the most important to development. Here the die is cast, so to speak, in that the organism is immutably affected. During this time, major organs and basic tissues take shape and develop into their finished forms; after this stage, it is difficult to affect their growth in any fundamental way (Montagu, 1977).

Infections and Intoxicants

During pregnancy, the mother's health and adequate nutrition are vital to the development of the fetus. Any maternal condition that impairs the transport of oxygen and nutrients to the fetus or the exchange of metabolic waste products has the potential to act deleteriously on fetal development. Etiologically, environmental agents that may harm the developing infant are known as **teratogens**, from the Greek *teros*, meaning monster. Teratogens that can cause damage include prescription drugs, hard drugs, nicotine, and alcohol.

teratogens

Rubella

Rubella (German measles) provides an example of a critical period when exposure to a certain teratogen is most harmful to the fetus. A *critical period* is a part of the life cycle during which the developing organism is particularly sensitive or responsive to specific environmental forces. Outside this period, the same event or influences are thought to have few if any lasting effects.

The rubella virus crosses the placenta and affects the developing fetus. The fetal organs likely to be affected are those whose development is underway when the mother contracts the virus. If this is during the first trimester of pregnancy, the eye, ear, nervous system, and heart are especially vulnerable. It is estimated that 50 percent of fetuses are damaged if the disease is contracted in the first month; 20 percent of embryos affected in the second month are born with defects (Rosenblith and Sims-Knight, 1985).

Severe sensorineural hearing loss is the major effect of maternal rubella; other major permanent features include cataracts, glaucoma, mental retardation, congenital heart disease, and cerebral palsy. There is also a significant occurrence of late-onset defects of rubella (conditions that are not apparent at birth but occur later), including vascular disease, growth hormone deficiency, thyroid dysfunction, and diabetes mellitus.

Rubella is often seen in epidemics that are estimated to occur in twenty-five-year cycles. In 1964, the last major rubella epidemic created a phenomenal spike in the charts measuring the numbers of special children who were left deaf and blind or with other multiple disabilities as a result of the disease. Vaccines developed in 1969 make a rubella baby rare today.

Syphilis

Syphilis, one of the venereal diseases, is produced by the bacterium *Treponema pallidum* (also called *Spirocheta pallida*). It does not affect the developing organs as does rubella but produces destructive lesions (abnormal changes in structure) in already developed organs.

While rubella is most critical during the first trimester of pregnancy, syphilis affects the fetus after the sixteenth or eighteenth week of gestation. If the disease is controlled by penicillin before that time, only about 2 percent of fetuses will contract it. After the fifth month, uncontrolled syphilis will affect about 40 percent of fetuses. Twenty-five percent of affected babies die before birth; 33 percent of those who survive die in early childhood.

Infants who survive may exhibit many disabilities, including mental retardation, blindness, and deafness. Other affected infants show liver problems, peritonitis, central nervous system disorders, and pegged teeth (Montagu, 1977; Rosenblith and Sims-Knight, 1985).

Drugs

When we talk about drugs, we are referring to a wide assortment of potentially harmful agents that range from hard drugs such as heroin, through prescription and over-the-counter drugs, to drugs widely used in Canadian society—nicotine and alcohol. The problem is significant, although there is not the bleak and panicked picture of numbers and effects that there was some years ago.

Researchers are unable to conclusively identify a set of characteristics that represent prenatal drug exposure so that "there is no typical profile of children prenatally exposed to drugs, though there seems to be a developmental continuum of vulnerabilities that persist into the preschool years" (Cole, Jones, and Sadofsky, 1990, p. 1). Generalizations about children exposed prenatally to drugs are troublesome for two main reasons.

First, it is extremely difficult to attribute specific characteristics to certain drugs, since abuse of multiple drugs is common. It is known that mothers who are multi-drug users (cocaine plus other drugs) have children with the most adverse outcomes (Van Dyke and Fox, 1990). Infants of multi-drug users fare worse than infants exposed to single drugs in regard to birth-weight, gestational age, withdrawal responses, and length of hospital stay (Kaye, Elkind, Goldberg, and Tytum, 1989).

Second, caregiving of the infant is vital in mitigating or exacerbating the prenatal exposure effects. Studies show, for example, that the behaviour seen in preschool children who are exposed to drugs prenatally appears to be the result of a constellation of risk factors resulting from possible organic damage and ongoing environmental instability (see Sinclair, 1998). Hence, prenatal exposure and later development is often compounded by the presence of social factors such as poverty, neglect, or drug use by others in the home. Mothers may be passive, lacking in emotional involvement and responsiveness, and more prone to abuse, which compromises a child's development.

PRESCRIPTION DRUGS

Prescription drugs have been shown to have an adverse effect on fetal development. Research has linked some antibiotic, anticonvulsant, and anticancer medications to fetal malformations (Batshaw and Perret, 1986). There is also evidence that pain-relieving drugs administered during labour and delivery can result in behavioural differences in infants (Rosenblith and Sims-Knight, 1985).

COCAINE

The 1980s saw an increase in the use of cocaine for all socio-economic classes, races, ages, and sexes. With increased use, there is growing concern about the long-term effects of cocaine on the fetus and the neonate.

Some neurochemical studies on cocaine in utero suggest that if the drug is present during gestation it may affect developing fetal neuromotor systems, which could have a significant impact on the developing nervous system. As well, cocaine affects the vascular system, causing the blood vessels to constrict in a state known as *vasoconstriction.* This condition in turn puts increasing pressure on the heart and the blood vessels, increases blood pressure, and restricts the flow of oxygen. Babies are therefore more prone to intercranial hemorrhages. (Chasnoff, 1987; Van Dyke and Fox, 1990).

Cocaine use during the last trimester may cause fetal hyperactivity, increased fetal blood pressure, or premature placental detachment from the uterus, which endangers both mother and child. Other research (Bingol, Schuster, Fuchs, and Iosub, 1987) has concluded that cocaine use in humans significantly reduces the weight of the fetus, increases the stillbirth rate related to *abruptio placentae*, and is associated with a higher malformation rate. Infants are likely to die before birth, to be born prematurely, and to be abnormally small for their ages (Rest, 1990).

Case histories of congenital abnormalities among cocaine-exposed children show missing fingers and forearm bones, cardiac anomalies, and microcephaly. Newborns may be born with deformed heads, lungs, digestive systems, or limbs. Researchers also describe children experiencing convulsions and stoppage of breathing (Chasnoff, Burns, Burns, and Schnoll, 1988; Chasnoff, Chisum, and Kaplan, 1988). Other reports point to poor baby state, which includes tremors, chronic irritability, and poor visual orientation. Later, in learning situations, these children may demonstrate poor abstract reasoning and memory, poor judgment, inability to concentrate, inability to deal with stress, frequent tantrums, a wide variety of behaviour disorders, and violent acting out.

In the late 1980s, crack, a relatively pure and inexpensive form of cocaine, emerged on the drug scene. As with cocaine, there is no single profile of an infant born to a crack-using mother. Some appear healthy. Others are adversely affected, more prone to having strokes and seizures, or are born with small heads, missing bowels, and malformed genitals. Crack babies are irritable, tremulous, and difficult to soothe for at least three months. They have a significantly higher rate of Sudden Infant Death Syndrome (SIDS) than do babies who are not prenatally exposed. Many suffer neurological damage from prenatal drug exposure (Rest, 1990).

As mentioned earlier, too often the infant's environment simply compounds the problems. Children born exposed to crack leave the hospital and enter homes often headed by poor, drug-addicted young mothers who are not able to cope with the demands of their own care, let alone the needs of a high-strung, difficult to soothe, unhealthy infant.

HEROIN

Heroin passes the placenta so that the infants of addicted women are born addicted. Withdrawal symptoms can prove fatal to the tiny infant. Survivors suffer a number of difficulties, but it is not known whether these extend beyond infancy. Methadone, the substitute used to withdraw heroin addicts, may cause even more physiological damage to the fetus. Children are small and subject to high mortality. They suffer more seizures and central nervous system damage, and seem to have altered breathing responses that persist twenty to forty days after methadone is no longer detected in their systems (Rosenblith and Sims-Knight, 1985).

FETAL ALCOHOL SYNDROME

Together with nicotine, alcohol is the drug most likely to be used and abused by Canadians. Alcohol in moderate amounts used to be thought safe during pregnancy. We now realize that even small amounts can damage the developing fetus. Alcohol ingestion by pregnant women can be more catastrophic to the growing fetus than illicit drugs such as crack cocaine or heroin (Phelp, 2000).

A small proportion of children of drinking mothers are born with a **syndrome**—a constellation of findings similar from patient to patient—known as *Fetal Alcohol Syndrome* (FAS), first reported in France in the late 1960s and then described in 1973 by Kenneth Jones and his colleagues.

syndrome

FAS exists on a continuum ranging from major to minor developmental defects. Children may have the full-blown syndrome (FAS) or Fetal Alcohol Effect (FAE). General estimates of the incidence of full-blown FAS are 1 to 2 per 1000 live births. Children who exhibit only FAE effects are thought to number 3 to 5 per 1000 (Sandor, 1981).

Full-blown FAS affects the whole body system. Mental retardation is a major characteristic in children affected by FAS. In fact, FAS is now considered to be the second major cause of mental retardation (Williams, Howard, and McLaughlin, 1994). As the condition varies in intensity, there are also differences in the degree of mental retardation involved.

FAS is associated with spontaneous abortions and miscarriages. In live births, as well as mental retardation there may be malformations and anomalies in the nervous system, the musculoskeletal structure, and the internal organs, especially the heart and urinogenital tracts. Children show a high rate of epilepsy, which may persist through the early school years (Williams, Howard, and McLaughlin, 1994).

Children with FAS often show specific physical stigmata, such as small eyes, a flat bridge of the nose, retarded growth, and a small head circumference, known as microcephaly. The more physical disabilities that are evident, the more severe the retardation is likely to be (Montagu, 1977). Examples of anomalies are shown in Table 3-5.

In the third trimester of pregnancy, the unborn child is gaining most of its eventual birth weight and the brain cells are rapidly multiplying and increasing in size. Some evidence indicates that the toxic effects of alcohol inhibit the development of nerve and other major tissues. Mental anomalies occur because alcohol hinders fetal growth and produces small babies with small brains. Fetal damage is caused when the ethanol in the alcohol takes fluid from the developing brain, causing the death of brain cells.

Physical anomalies may have earlier onset. Iber (1980) postulated that craniofacial abnormalities occur because particular parts of the face are dependent upon a brain of normal

Table 3-5 Specific sequelae associated with FAS

Neurological	Craniofacial
mental retardation	low-set ears
microcephalus	short low-bridged nose
seizures	epicanthic folds
tremors	short lower jaw
irritability	long upper lip
poor fine coordination	droopy eyelids
hyperactivity	high-arched palate
Skeletal	**Other**
clubfoot	cardiac defects
spinal fusion	kidney defects
growth deficiency	genital problems
abnormal palmar creases	poor weight gain

size to fill out the face. The critical period for the development of the facial features associated with FAS seems to be the third or fourth week of prenatal development, when the head is starting to take shape.

Much is still unknown about FAS; the connection between alcohol consumption and reproductive risk is not clear. The medical profession has not yet determined a safe level of alcohol for the pregnant woman, and the influence of moderate drinking is unknown. Certainly, infants of mothers who drink heavily are at greater risk. Recent reports note that of babies born to alcoholics and binge drinkers, 10 in every 100 have FAS; 10 in 30 have FAE; and the rest are normal (Phelp, 2000). Even in moderate drinkers there is evidence that the amount of alcohol consumed is related to the infant's arousal levels and central-nervous-system functioning.

It has been suggested that 90 millilitres of alcohol a day during pregnancy is heavy drinking (Landesman-Dwyer, Martin, Smith, and Streissguth, 1980). One study found that two ounces of alcohol in the first trimester (one six-pack of beer) led to 12 percent of the sample having infants with malformations, similar to children of chronic alcoholics (March of Dimes [1986]). However, given the metabolic variations between individuals, there is no correlation between the quantity and frequency of the ingestion of alcohol and the number of defects in a child.

MATERNAL SMOKING

When the mother smokes a cigarette, the fetus smokes it too. After the first few puffs its heart begins to beat faster, and it feels a drop in oxygen (hypoxia) and an increase in carbon dioxide. It stops moving and increases its fetal breathing to try to make up for the hypoxia. All these responses have a severe enough cumulative effect in heavy smokers to contribute to spontaneous abortions, bleeding during pregnancy, premature rupture of the amniotic sac, fetal deaths, and deaths of newborns (Salkind, 1990). Smokers are twice as likely as non-smokers to have low-birth-weight babies. The infants of smokers weigh an average of 200 grams less than infants of non-smokers (Vorhees and Mollnow, 1987). Infants are shorter, have smaller head, chest, arm, and thigh circumference, and have lower neurological scores than do infants of non-smokers (Metcoff, Cristiloe, Crosby, Sandstread, and Milne, 1989).

Maternal Nutrition

A mother's diet and nutrition play a significant role in the growth and development of her fetus. The importance of nutrition is suggested by the relationship between the mother's diet, the newborn's weight, and the child's eventual learning ability (see Salt, Galler, and Ramsey, 1988).

The period of intra-uterine development and the first eighteen months after birth are crucial to the physiological development of every organ system. This is especially true for the brain. Inadequate prenatal nutrition can affect the relationship between the body's biochemistry and the functioning of the brain. Severe malnutrition can stunt brain growth and produce a significant lowering of intellectual ability. Nutrition in the mother seems to be particularly important in the third trimester, when the fetus should be making rapid gains in weight and the nervous system is developing rapidly.

Postnatal nutrition, especially during the first six months of an infant's life, is similarly critical for brain development. Various important neural structures and interconnections between the brain cells develop during this period. In the postnatal period, research indicates that severe chronic deprivation of either general nutrition or certain special diet substances can cause behavioural disorders as well as physical disorders and mental retardation (Lahey and Ciminero, 1980). When prenatal and postnatal malnutrition both exist, problems are likely to be much more severe.

Maternal nutritional deficiency covers a wide range of problems and developmental consequences. In general, malnourished women are much more likely to produce low-birth-weight babies, although it may be that low birth-weight per se is not so much a problem as that maternal malnutrition increases the fetus's vulnerability to other risk factors. Severe malnutrition increases the risk of congenital defects, prolonged labour, stillbirth, and infant mortality during the first year.

Unknown Prenatal Influence

microcephaly
macrocephaly
hydrocephalus

There are a number of conditions present at or before birth for which there is no known cause. One such condition is **microcephaly**, a rare phenomenon in which brain development is impaired by an abnormally small cranium. Another is **macrocephaly**, which refers to an enlargement of the head, most frequently caused by **hydrocephalus**, a build-up of cerebrospinal fluid in the brain. Retardation may follow, but its severity can be reduced or eliminated by early diagnosis and treatment. To treat hydrocephalus, a shunt is surgically implanted to drain excess fluid away from the brain and into a vein behind the ear or in the neck. (See also Chapter 12.)

Birth and Neonatal Development

Birth is neither a beginning nor an ending, but a bridge between two stages of life. Birth takes place in three stages: labour, delivery, and afterbirth. It is a long process. An average first labour takes fourteen hours; the average for later labours is eight hours. In many areas of life, too much or too little is not a good thing. This is true of labour—labours that are too long or too short produce a greater likelihood of problems.

Birth can be dangerous for the child and/or the mother. The fetus may be in an unusual position, such as breech or transverse presentations. The membranes may rupture too early, leading to infection. An incorrectly placed placenta may mean excessive bleeding. Drugs and forceps used during delivery may cause harm to the fetus.

Before the child is born, there is no contact with the atmosphere. The oxygen that is necessary for fetal survival and to the orderly development of the body reaches the fetus by way of the mother's bloodstream. When the time of birth draws near, the oxygen level in the placenta and in the child's circulatory system drops sharply. During the birth process, the human fetus is squeezed through the birth canal for several hours, during which time the head sustains considerable pressure and the infant is intermittently deprived of oxygen. Most infants tolerate this without difficulty; in spite of surface appearances, the stresses of normal delivery are usually not harmful (Lagercrantz and Slotkin, 1986).

anoxia

Sometimes, however, inadequate uterine environments pose additional risks, and the infant cannot tolerate the normal changes of labour. If the child is overly deprived of oxygen, the condition is called **anoxia**. Most birth injuries result from deprivation of oxygen to the immature brain, which leads to abridgment of nervous system function.

If supplies of oxygen to the nerve cells of the brain are too greatly reduced, brain damage or death can result. When a portion of the brain is damaged, the part of the individual that is controlled by that portion of the brain is also damaged. Anoxia may be a villain in cerebral palsy, some types of epilepsy, and some mental retardation. Mild anoxia can also produce other subtle forms of childhood disability such as irritability, muscular tension, rigidity, learning disabilities, and motor defects.

Neurological Impairments

Neurological impairments can occur before, during, or after birth. Any factor that leads to hormonal, chemical, or blood-flow imbalances can cause central nervous system problems. While pre- and perinatal causes are crucial, the incidence of infant and preschool brain injury is increasing. Causes include household and auto accidents; meningitis and encephalitis; anoxia caused through such events as near-drowning, inhalation of toxic fumes, and choking; and periventricular hemorrhage (Ewing-Cobbs, Fletcher, and Levin, 1985). Chapter 12 details neurological disabilities.

Damage to the brain may be so mild as to be undetectable or so profound as to reduce the child to a very low level of functioning. There may be focal brain damage that involves a very specific and delimited area of the brain, or diffuse brain damage involving a large or poorly defined area. Depending on the degree and location of the damage, the child's behaviour will be affected. For example, one of the traditional etiologies of learning disabilities is minimal brain dysfunction. On the other hand, generalized and diffuse brain damage results in mental retardation; damage to the motor areas causes cerebral palsy. Children with cerebral palsy caused by brain damage often have impaired vision as a result of loss of control of ocular muscles.

Preterm and Low-Birth-Weight Infants

premature babies

Premature babies generally weigh 2500 grams or less, as compared to the usual birth weight of 3000 to 3500 grams. In terms of length of pregnancy, the earliest stage possible for survival outside the womb is now considered to be about twenty-seven weeks. Fetuses born before this have little chance of survival, primarily because of lung immaturity. Children born after twenty-two weeks of gestation have a survival rate of 60 percent, and those born at twenty-eight weeks have an 85 to 90 percent chance of survival (Musgrove, 1984). In Canada, about 75 percent of infants at twenty-five weeks gestation now survive, about half at twenty-four weeks, and about one-quarter at twenty-three weeks. Surviving infants now have a greater than 70 percent chance of being free of disability (Barrington, Papageorgiou, and Usher, 2001).

The most critical problem for preterm babies is obtaining enough oxygen. A preterm baby has very little surfactin, a substance that normally coats the lungs during the last three or four weeks of gestation to prevent them from collapsing. Respiratory distress syndrome is responsible for about half of all newborn deaths in North America. Research has also clearly established that preterm infants have a higher incidence of developmental problems in childhood than full-term infants.

Because of possible difficulties with placental nutrition, babies may be of low birth weight but not premature. Full-term but low-birth-weight infants are prone to a range of potentially dangerous conditions. In Ontario, Sagal, Rosenbaum, Stotskopf, and Milner (1982) studied the developmental progress of 294 low-birth-weight infants. Of the 179 children who survived, 30 showed neurological impairments, including microcephaly, blindness, deafness, mental retardation, and retrolental fibroplasia. As they grow, small-for-term babies as a group tend to remain shorter and lighter than their agemates, while preterm babies who survive are more likely to achieve normal heights and weights.

An overly long pregnancy can also be problematic. Infants born two weeks or more beyond the expected due date are said to be *postmature.* These children are in somewhat greater danger from anoxia and cerebral hemorrhage than children born at the normal 266 to 270 days. They also have a higher death rate and suffer more frequently from severe congenital abnormalities (Montagu, 1977).

CMV and Herpes

Some conditions are transmitted to the baby right at the time of delivery. Two potentially harmful or fatal conditions of this nature are cytomegalovirus (CMV) and herpes.

CMV, a form of herpes, is the most frequently occurring congenital virus among newborns. It affects about 3 percent of pregnant women (Kurant and Sever, 1977). When babies are born to mothers who have infections in the active stages, the mortality rate is about 50 percent. Of children that survive, about half suffer from conditions such as microcephaly, spasticity, paralysis, seizures, deafness, or blindness (McIntosh, 1984).

Herpes (HVH), actually less prevalent than CMV, is potentially as damaging and can be fatal. Although it is a rare occurrence, babies are infected as they pass through the cervix or vagina. Affected infants are treated with an antiviral drug, but survivors are still at considerable risk for permanent damage (Hetherington and Parke, 1986).

Pediatric AIDS

Acquired Immunodeficiency Syndrome (AIDS) was first reported in 1981 as a mysterious ailment that seemed to afflict only particular groups in society. However, within a few years AIDS was recognized as a condition resulting from a viral infection that can afflict anyone of any class, any age, or either sex.

The T-cell lymphotropic virus, Type III, is commonly called the human immunodeficiency virus (HIV), the cause of the deadly AIDS. The virus attacks and seriously disrupts the body's immune system, its defence against disease. Without the protection of the immune system, AIDS sufferers are prone to potentially fatal infections and cancers. HIV takes many forms.

AIDS in children may be the result of tainted blood transfusions or, rarely, it may be contracted through the mother's milk. Placental passage in utero and newborn contact with the mother's blood or vaginal fluids during the process of labour and delivery are the two major routes of perinatal HIV infection. Children infected with HIV will likely develop symptoms of AIDS; between 30 and 60 percent of children born to HIV-positive mothers will contract AIDS (Dokecki, Baumeister, and Kupstas, 1989).

Around the world, about 1000 children become infected with AIDS every day; three million children in all have the disease. In Canada from 1991 to 1998, there were 43 347 positive HIV tests and 16 236 AIDS cases from all provinces and territories. There were 243 children diagnosed with AIDS and another 1193 with HIV (Roberts, 2000).

At present, the numbers are either stable or in decline. Better treatments are keeping down infections and more children are living longer, so that it is now more a chronic than a terminal illness. Pediatric AIDS is readdressed in Chapter 12.

Postnatal Development

Postnatally, accidents are the most common cause of disabilities in children, followed by cancer in its various forms. As well, a variety of childhood diseases and infections can hinder children's progress.

Infections

Both meningitis and encephalitis can result in mental retardation, visual impairment, deafness, cerebral palsy, and other disabling conditions. Meningitis attacks the *meninges*, or coverings of the brain and spinal cord; it is accompanied by a high fever. Spinal meningitis has a mortality rate of about 10 percent in young children and is often an offshoot of influenza B. Recently, a new vaccine became available to protect children from spinal meningitis.

Encephalitis can be caused by viral, bacterial, or parasitic infections. More encephalitic children suffer retardation than do meningitic children.

Environmental Risk

environmental risk

Environmental risk refers to conditions that occur when a child is biologically normal but is at risk for not developing age-appropriate behaviour at the regular rate. In this sense, environmental risk applies to infants and toddlers who are biologically sound yet whose early life experiences (including maternal and family care, health care, nutrition, opportunities for expression of language, adaptive behaviour, and patterns of physical and social stimulation) are so limited that there is a probability of delayed development. But current efforts to predict which individual infants will develop subsequent disabilities using perinatal medical factors are not very successful. Thus, in populations of four-month-olds, it is often impossible to distinguish those who will be functioning normally at age two from those who will display serious developmental delays (Bricker and Squires, 1989).

Once in school, many students who are affected by adverse environmental factors perform poorly. As we pointed out at the opening of this chapter, in every classroom there are a large number of students who, to a greater or lesser degree, are not "getting" the curriculum. This group is not limited to students who have been identified as having disabilities and who are provided IEPs; it also includes those who are linguistically or culturally diverse, those who may be low achievers, and an amorphous group of unidentified students who may understand some of the subject matter but not enough to develop competency in it.

The environmental factors that place children at risk are legion. We cannot possibly describe here all the risk factors that exist; rather, we briefly examine three major environmental risk factors that are particularly relevant to classroom learning and behaviour. We touch on family structures and poverty, and then return to cultural and linguistic differences.

Family Structures

Students receive about 900 hours of instruction in school each year. However, they spend a great deal more time out of school; about 87 percent out of the classroom and only 13 percent in it (Monroe, 1991). What happens in the home, within the family, and in the neighbourhood that 87 percent of the time affects every aspect of a student's functioning and learning.

Teachers must be aware that the child population of today is different from earlier generations. Today's children are caught in the midst of rapid social changes. Many of the changes are positive; on the negative side are changing social and family structures that include everything from shortages in technical labour markets, to children living in poverty and homelessness, to destabilization of the institution of the family shown in mounting divorce rates and increases in the number of single-parent families.

High numbers of children (approximately 16 percent in 1985) are born to unmarried mothers. The Canadian divorce rate has increased 600 percent in the past 35 years. The number of single-parent families has likewise increased at a rate 2.5 times faster than two-parent families to 14 percent in 1995. Many children now have blended families that include stepbrothers and stepsisters moving in and out of children's lives.

The family is universally recognized as a fundamental influence on child behaviour. The family structure establishes the norms of behaviour and teaches, explicitly and implicitly, social, moral, and psychological lessons to the developing child. As families change, new problems emerge. This is not in any way to suggest that non-traditional, non-nuclear families are dysfunctional. However, research does support the contention that increasing family instability leads to dysfunctional relationships.

In children, dysfunctional relationships during childhood and adolescence have been found to be related to verbal and physical aggression against others; school truancy and dropping out; behavioural disorders; learning disabilities; mental retardation; juvenile crime and delinquency; social isolation and withdrawal; and bad-conduct discharges from the military (Bracken and Newman, 1994). The area of familial and non-familial influences on children's behaviour is discussed again in Chapter 7.

Poverty

Poverty is the most critical factor undermining families and one of the greatest risk factors in the development of children. Schorr (1988) observed that "Persistent and concentrated poverty virtually guarantees the presence of a vast collection of risk factors and their continuing destructive impact over time" (p. 30).

The collection of risk factors accompanying poverty serve to compromise a child's development to an extraordinary extent. In fact, living in poverty is associated with adverse mental health outcomes in both children and adults.

In the family setting, lower socio-economic status (SES) negatively correlates with eight adverse socializing factors—harsh discipline, lack of maternal warmth, exposure to aggressive adult models, maternal aggressive values, family life stressors, mother's lack of social support, peer group instability, and lack of cognitive stimulation (Dodge, Pettit, and Bates, 1994). Children of lower SES families are much more at risk for abuse than children from higher SES homes (Dodge, Bates, and Pettit, 1990).

Poor children can be adversely affected from the moment of conception. Poor families may not utilize adequate prenatal and postnatal health care. Children are more likely to suffer the consequences of poor maternal nutrition, complications of pregnancy and delivery, prematurity, and low birth weight.

Within the school system, children of poverty are at high risk for reading and writing difficulties. They make up a disproportionately large percentage of those who repeat a grade, are placed in special education, or drop out before completing school (see Winzer and Mazurek, 1998).

Cultural and Linguistic Differences

As pointed out in Chapter 2, it is estimated that in the year 2001 some 15 percent of the Canadian population will be members of a visible minority group; 20 percent by 2016. In cities such as Vancouver, Montreal, and Toronto, large numbers of students come from homes where English is not the first language.

Cultural and linguistic differences in the schools reflect the rapid demographic changes seen in society. They also have a huge impact on children's learning and achievement. This is not to suggest any firm equation between school problems and cultural and linguistic differences or that minority group status is necessarily a risk factor. But we must be aware of the cumulative effects when such variables as poverty, disability, limited English proficiency, and lack of appreciation of a child's cultural values and learning styles meld with cultural and linguistic diversity.

Students may be at risk because culturally diverse students are more likely than those from majority backgrounds to be poor. In general, children from minority families who have limited English proficiency and are impoverished have historically done poorly in school (Dao, 1991). In both the United States and Canada, these students show an unacceptable pattern of social separation and isolation, a growing gap between their achievement and that of majority group children, disproportionate referrals to special education, tracking to lower streams, lower scores on tests, lower grades, high rates of school failure, high dropout rates, and lower rates of college attendance (Winzer and Mazurek, 1998).

Limited English proficiency places a child at risk for learning lags. Research in Canadian schools suggests that students learning English as a second language take between four to six years to match the achievement levels of first-language students on achievement tests (Klesner,1994). Misunderstandings of the values of a child's culture, ignoring unique learning styles, or lack of knowledge and appreciation of a culture can further place students at risk. Language and colour barriers often separate students from the educational institutions that they attend and place them at risk for educational and behavioural difficulties as well as for cultural bias and discrimination.

Further risk occurs when educational programs have little or no relevance to a child's family and community culture, language, and values. Or students may be threatened by unrealistic expectations for academic and behavioural performance.

Other subtle biases may intrude. For example, misdiagnosis occurs when school psychologists are not trained or are at a loss considering cultural and linguistic differences in their testing. As well, teachers are often ill equipped to teach diverse populations. Typically, educators have not been prepared to be culturally sensitive and responsive and explicit efforts to prepare teachers in training to work with culturally diverse students is a relatively recent phenomena.

Culturally Different Students with Special Needs

To live and develop in two culturally different systems is sufficiently challenging for students without exceptional conditions. The difficulties multiply for students who are culturally and linguistically diverse and also disabled. When special problems in cognitive functioning, sensory use, communication, mobility, or social and behavioural interactions combine with cultural and linguistic diversity, individual differences increase dramatically, as do the chances of school failure, even when special services are provided.

Culturally diverse students are represented in all categories of exceptionality and can experience any disability that is found in other children: disabilities of the same type affect children from diverse cultural backgrounds just as they do those of the dominant culture. However, demographic information on the numbers of children with exceptionalities who have diverse cultural and linguistic backgrounds is difficult to extrapolate from sources because of a lack of consistency in identifying, defining, and reporting these populations. Hardman and colleagues (1993) estimate that among students with disabilities, 41 percent are from culturally diverse backgrounds.

To accommodate culturally diverse students with disabilities, educators must place high priority on positively recognizing individual differences relating to cultural backgrounds and attitudes. They must appreciate the values and beliefs, learning styles, communication and language patterns, behavioural and response mechanisms, and family and community roles and involvement that accompany these children to school. Multicultural special education, defined in Chapter 1, is critical.

PREVENTION

primary prevention

The prevention of disabilities and potentially disabling conditions and the elimination of risk factors is usually classified as *primary, secondary,* and *tertiary.* **Primary prevention** is concerned with establishing medical and social programs to reduce the occurrence of diseases and conditions that cause disabilities. The aim is to reduce the incidence of certain problems in the population, to remove the causative factors that account for the initial occurrence of a disorder, and to strengthen the well-being of individuals in the population as a form of inoculation against subsequent problems. For example, providing medical care and fluoridated water to all children prevents childhood diseases and tooth decay (Planta, 1990). Other examples of primary prevention include measures to counteract poor nutrition, poverty, and premature birth.

Genetic counselling and educational programs on conditions such as Down syndrome are also part of primary prevention. Genetic counselling deals with the human and medical problems associated with the occurrence of risk or recurrence of a genetic disorder in the family. The major goal is to convey an understanding of birth defects and genetic mechanisms to affected families to enable prospective parents to make informed decisions about childbearing.

secondary prevention

Once a disorder has emerged, primary prevention is not possible. **Secondary prevention** refers to ascertaining, as early as possible, the evidence of disorders that may cause disabilities, as well as allied attempts to keep the disorder from increasing in intensity. Successful secondary prevention programs provide services to high-risk groups to keep problems from becoming debilitating and to diminish the effects of dysfunctions that are identified early. There are two ways in which individuals are identified for secondary prevention. They manifest signs of potential dysfunction, or they are members of a high-risk group that has an elevated likelihood of having the problem but show no signs of problems as of yet (Planta, 1990).

In many cases, secondary prevention has proven very successful. For example, Tay–Sachs carriers are detected through a simple blood test. As a result of extensive testing and counselling, far fewer Tay–Sachs babies are conceived and born. In North America, the rate of Tay–Sachs among Jewish infants decreased by 95 percent in the 20 years from 1970 to 1990. As a result of prenatal testing, the incidence of Down syndrome dropped from one in 600 in 1970 to one in 1000 in 1990 (Plomin, De Fries, and McClearn, 1990).

The major method used in the prenatal diagnosis of Down syndrome and other genetic disorders is amniocentesis, usually performed between the tenth and nineteenth week of gestation. Amniocentesis can be used to detect about forty conditions, including abnormalities of the spinal cord such as spina bifida ("Pre-natal" [1987]; Rosenblith and Sims-

Knight, 1985). In this procedure, a needle is inserted through the mother's abdominal wall to extract 10 to 20 millilitres of amniotic fluid. A chromosomal analysis then checks whether free-floating fetal cells have karyotypes (genetic patterns) typical of specific disabling conditions. The procedure is relatively safe, with a total 2.5 to 3 percent risk of miscarriage, of which 0.5 percent is due to the amniocentesis itself ("Pre-natal" [1987]).

Another procedure, *chorionic villi sampling* (CVS) has a risk factor of about 4 to 5 percent ("Pre-natal" [1987]). CVS is performed between the ninth and twelfth week of pregnancy by removing a small amount of the tissue around the fetal sac that eventually becomes the placenta. The sample is removed using a catheter inserted through the vagina into the uterus under ultrasound guidance.

Other screening procedures include percutaneous umbilical blood sampling, ultrasonography, and fetoscopy. Ultrasound, which generates a picture (a sonogram), is used successfully in the prenatal diagnosis of hydrocephaly, anencephaly, and other multiple congenital deformities. Fetoscopy is used to evaluate fetuses that are at risk for certain genetic conditions. A fetoscope, equipped with a fibre-optic lens for viewing the fetus, is inserted into the amniotic sac. This process can be useful in determining whether a fetus has a congenital malformation that may be associated with mental retardation (Vitello and Soskin, 1985).

Secondary prevention also encompasses the management of conditions in order to ameliorate their impact. For example, certain organic conditions that cause mental retardation can be successfully managed when identified early. The effect of PKU can be prevented or diminished if a low-phenylalanine diet is introduced in infancy. Hydrocephalus can be surgically treated, even in the fetus, by the insertion of a shunt to remove excess cerebrospinal fluid (Henig, 1982). Examples of secondary prevention in the schools include dropout prevention programs.

tertiary prevention

Tertiary prevention consists of intervention strategies after a negative outcome has occurred. It is designed for disorders that have reached advanced stages and threaten to produce significant side effects or complications that may overwhelm the individual. The object of tertiary prevention is to minimize residual disabilities and maximize potential. Amelioration efforts seek to reduce the residual effects or adverse consequences of a disorder. Methods of intervention may be medical, psychological, social, or educational.

SUMMARY

1. Medical research is bringing a more complete understanding of the ways in which a child's psychological, social, and educational environments are related to learning. Teachers' understanding of the etiology, developmental consequences, treatments, and prognoses of exceptional conditions will serve to increase their interactions with and understanding of children with disabilities.
2. A huge range of disabilities affect children, the result of multiple etiologies. Disorders and diseases may arise from chromosomal or genetic aberrations, infections and intoxicants, malnutrition, deprivation of oxygen, and environmental hazards.
3. At-risk children are those not currently identified as disabled but more likely to develop some type of problem. Studies show that infants classified as at risk more often develop problems than those classified neonatally as well babies. Difficulties may be overcome in

Historical Notes

People with disabilities have probably been in society since its beginnings. Responses to individuals who were different or deviant were influenced by many factors—culture, religion, government, and economics. Educational and social intervention was little heeded until the middle of the 18th century.

Throughout history, exceptional conditions were bounded by medical paradigms. Those requiring medical treatment were the first to be addressed; the recognition and care of intellectually and sensorially deprived persons had to wait for more enlightened attitudes regarding social care, which historically tended to lag behind purely medical concerns. The medical stress largely determined societal attitudes and legal mandates for persons with disabilities.

In the mid-19th century there was enormous interest in human genetics and heredity stimulated by Darwin's work (1859). Major advances occurred in the etiology of disabilities, particularly mental retardation. One of the most important came when John Langdon Down in 1866 identified specific subcategories of retardation.

Constructs of disability shifted and evolved in concert with this new knowledge and spawned new beliefs about the nature of various conditions (especially mental retardation), the educability of affected children, and the type of training that should be offered. Many pioneer educators came from the medical profession and added a further medical slant. For example, all of the early superintendents of institutions for persons with mental retardation were physicians. Today's American Association on Mental Retardation (AAMR) began as the Association of Medical Superintendents of American Institutions for the Feeble Minded (Winzer, 1993).

Medical models became very prominent and many categories of disability emerged. Special education developed along the lines of a clinical individual service model attached to concepts of individual differences, intervention, and prevention. Because disorders were seen to have distinct patterns of symptoms and signs that resulted from different disease entities and causes, they responded to different treatments. In the schools, medical models translated to diagnostic-prescriptive approaches, where traits are diagnosed and then a prescription is written to address weaknesses. A condition within a child could be diagnosed, and the child could be labelled and then placed in a class consonant with that label. Each condition was slotted into a separate pigeonhole, then a particular treatment was designed for each condition. Teachers were trained for specific conditions and then seen to hold a unique body of expertise and to serve a specific clientele.

Medical models still remain important in special education, reflected in the current categorical systems. Today, though, many educators prefer to focus on the learning styles and behaviours of a child rather than the presumed underlying etiology. Contemporary systems tend to describe or profile children's behaviour patterns and move the field closer to models in which descriptions of children's needs, not etiological labels, drive intervention efforts.

a stable family environment; in unstable low-income families lacking decent housing and enough money, the difficulties present at birth may result in developmental delays and learning problems.

4. Changing demographics are accompanied by other major social changes such as pervasive violence, mounting divorce rates, increased foster care, and rising teenage preg-

nancies. Because of this, the schools will meet more students at risk for educational failure and dropping out, and special education is likely to serve a wider range of students.

5. The causes of childhood disabling conditions are changing; with the rapid advances in medical science, certain conditions have disappeared but others have filled their places. For example, premature babies are surviving, but a wide range of insults to the nervous and organic systems that can lead to mental retardation and other disabilities are possible with prematurity.
6. Biology is hardly destiny, and social influences combine with biological predispositions to shape behaviour and learning potential. A child's growth will be seriously hampered by restricted sensory stimulation, deprivation, and impoverishment.
7. While linguistic, cultural, socio-economic, and lifestyle differences are not of themselves disabling conditions, the consequences may place children at higher risk. Teachers must be aware of the myriad of economic, environmental, and geographic factors that influence the lives of children with exceptionalities.

WEBLINKS

Campaign 2000: Child Poverty in Canada **www.campaign2000.ca**

Canadian Institute of Child Health (CICH) **www.cich.ca/**

March of Dimes Birth Defects Foundation **www.modimes.org/**

Motherisk **www.motherisk.org/**

National Academy for Child Development **www.nacd.org**

SECTION 2

Children and Youth with Mild Disabilities

In this section, we discuss children and youth with mild disabilities. Two main ideas underlie these chapters. First, the contemporary movement toward inclusive classrooms is particularly relevant to students with mild disabilities to learning. Most, if not all, will be presented with the general curriculum in a general classroom. Instruction is the responsibility of the general classroom teacher with some type of support, either via collaboration with special education and other resource personnel, a paraprofessional for in-class assistance, or part-time resource room assistance for the students.

Next, although these conditions are referred to as mild, any condition or disability that can seriously disrupt a student's educational career should not be considered in anything less than a serious light. Finally, as we explained in Chapter 1, there is much overlap among these categories. The way these students learn, their manifested behaviours, and teachers' strategies and adaptations are similar.

Traditionally, the area of mild disabilities has included communication disorders, learning disabilities, mild mental retardation, and mild behavioural disorders. In this section, we examine children and youth with communication disorders, learning disabilities, and mental retardation. We glance at the full spectrum of retardation to keep the continuity of the material; readers will find more explicit information about students with severe and profound disabilities in Chapter 14. We also reserve a separate section for students with behavioural disorders. This varied and heterogeneous group often requires behavioural interventions that extend beyond those for other children and youth with mild disabilities.

The chapter on speech and language problems is the first of the categorical chapters because these types of problems affect almost all of the children we will meet in this text. While speech and language problems are a separate category of exceptionality, they also cut across other categories. Many, if not most, children with other disabling conditions also manifest speech and language problems that further hinder their optimal development. Children with hearing impairments, learning disabilities, intellectual disabilities, and severe emotional disturbance often display speech and language problems.

After learning disabilities, speech and language disorders are the most common problems seen in the schools. (In preschool children, speech and language disorders are the most common form of disability.) About 8 to 10 percent of school-aged children have some type of speech or language disorder. For some children, this is a short-term delay in acquiring articulation proficiency. Other children have chronic, recurrent speech and language difficulties, such as stuttering. For others, speech and language difficulties are part of a more complex constellation of disorders that may limit their lifetime options.

Learning disabilities adversely affect a child's functioning across domains. The common thread is the inability of these students to learn adequately in regular classrooms under traditional teaching approaches and methods. Youngsters who are learning disabled cannot conform to normal educational demands—there is a marked gap between capability and performance on academic tasks. Children are sound in mind and body but still cannot seem to get the hang of reading, writing, and arithmetic, and therefore lag noticeably in school. Students who have difficulty learning often have problems adjusting to the school, classroom routines, the pressures of daily life, peer groups, and a range of different teachers.

Many students diagnosed as learning disabled also meet problems in the areas of speech and language. The term *language learning disabilities* refers to the language disorder syndrome associated with learning disabilities. Studies suggest that language is the primary deficit for 60 percent of students with learning disabilities (LD), while for all LD students language is one component of their disorder (Wesanko, 1990).

Individuals who are described as intellectually disabled vary widely in almost every aspect of human behaviour, human personality, and human temperament. Students who are intellectually disabled will have difficulties with complex academic material; they are markedly slower than their agemates in using memory effectively, associating and classifying information, reasoning, and making judgments.

In this section, we first introduce the subject of speech and language disorders and illustrate how they affect children who have these as their sole disabilities. We then discuss the very special problems of children identified as learning disabled, with particular emphasis on aspects of speech and language. The final chapter in this section deals with mental retardation. The In the Classroom feature that closes the section presents ideas for specific approaches and techniques that are applicable to a variety of learners with special needs.

Chapter 4

Children with Speech and Language Differences

Learning Outcomes

After reading this chapter, you should be able to:

Understand the major elements of language and the stages and process of language acquisition in normally developing students;

Differentiate between language delays and language disorders;

Understand the major types of speech and language disorders, their developmental consequences, and the influence the various disorders have on children's behaviour and learning;

Apply incidental techniques for speech and language improvement in the classroom.

Introduction

In all the enormous repertoire of human skills and abilities, communication is one of the most critical tools. Communication is the essence of human socialization, the link that provides reciprocal interaction between the individual and the environment. It is through communication that human beings make their impact upon the world and establish and maintain relationships. Humans use communication to meet needs and desires, control environmental events, establish social relationships, and learn new skills and concepts. Of all the achievements of early childhood, the acquisition and development of speech and language is one of the most remarkable. Tiny infants, initially able to produce only vegetative sounds and reflexive cries, listen and respond to the language in their environments. Through exposure and experience, they typically make enormous progress in speech and language development and quite unconsciously learn to produce an infinite variety of intelligible utterances.

The first three years are critical in the development of speech and language: about twice as much language growth occurs between the first and third years as between the third and fifth years (Cratty, 1986). Without formal instruction, most children in those first three years develop a lexicon of spoken words and learn to form simple multilevel utterances.

The language explosion that occurs in the early years is most apparent in the growth of vocabulary—from about 110 words at 18 months to 300 words at age 2, to about 540 at 30 months (Fenson, Dale, Reznick, Bates, Thal, and Pethick, 1994). As children develop speech and language, they are also developing **communicative competence**—they know how to interact, how to communicate appropriately in various situations, and how to make sense of what others say and do in communicative interactions.

communicative competence

What happens in the early stages of acquisition of speech and language is critical: it reflects many aspects of development, is closely tied to cognitive development and self-concept, and affects a child's performance in the classroom later on. Problems can impair a child's functioning in play and with peers and can result in the development of secondary behavioural problems. As well, unresolved difficulties will hinder a child's academic progress. For many school-aged children, inferior communication skills inhibit learning and contribute to feelings of failure (Wesanko, 1990). Too, competence with language has a direct influence on a child's ability to learn to read and write. Children who meet problems in understanding and using language when they are in kindergarten and grade one typically have problems learning to read and are likely to be clearly identified as poor readers by grade three (see Seidenberg, 1997).

A basic understanding of the normal development of language and speech underlies an appreciation of the nature of communication disorders. We therefore begin this chapter with a brief overview of normal speech and language development.

OVERVIEW OF SPEECH AND LANGUAGE

Communication may be seen as the process of exchanging information and ideas between participants. All living things communicate in some way and, in this sense, communication includes the entire spectrum of acts performed by living creatures in order to pass on and respond to messages.

language
speech

Language and *speech* are the typically human activities in communication. **Language** is a system of symbols organized into conventional patterns to communicate meaning. **Speech** is essentially a mechanical production of language. Other methods than speech may be appropriately employed to express language—sign language and writing, for example. However, while it is possible to possess language and lack the ability to speak, it is not possible to have speech without language.

A number of important points characterize speech and language development. First, there are distinct stages. These should not be viewed as a set of discrete milestones through which children pass on the way to mastering adult communication. Rather, as language learning begins in infancy and continues throughout life, formal language use is one point on a continuum of communication behaviour that begins in non-verbal social exchanges during infancy and extends through the use of written language.

Another important aspect of language is the creativity involved. Children are not passive organisms into which language is poured; rather, they are catalytic agents. In other words, it is not so much that language *develops*, but that language is *acquired*. It is clear quite early that children do not put words together only if they have heard those words together in combination before; instead, they produce utterances they have never heard. As children develop vocabulary and internalize a knowledge of the rules of their native language they can potentially create an infinite number of unique utterances.

Finally, children acquiring language do so in essentially the same order. In English, children learn *in* and *on* before other prepositions such as *under*, and they learn the progressive form using *-ing* before other verb endings such as *-ed*. After they learn regular plurals and past tenses, as in *horses* and *skated*, they create some forms of their own, like *mouses* and *eated* (Gleason, 1985).

Elements of Language

Language consists of interrelated and intertwined components, all of which must be present or developing for appropriate usage. Children must simultaneously learn the sound structure of the language (the *phonology*), the rules that govern the ordering of words within sentences (the *syntax* or *grammar*), and the meaning of words and phrases (*semantics*). If their usage is to attain appropriate meaning, children must employ *pragmatics*—the use of language in its social context.

Syntax is the network of organizational principles underlying linguistic expression. Syntactic rules govern what we call the grammar of language. **syntax**

Children do not learn syntax all at one time, but progress through distinct stages. For example, in learning to express questions, children show a definite sequence of acquisition. In the first stage, the question is expressed by a slight rising of the voice. The second stage involves the use of an interrogative word, such as *who, what, where, which,* and *why*. These words are placed in front of a word, phrase, or complete sentence, resulting in such questions as "Who that?" "What this?" and "Why you cry?" The third stage involves the principle of *inversion*. The child places the verb before the subject of the sentence to ask "Is Daddy home?" and "Does it belong here?" Some children rely on the ubiquitous "Eh?" Tag questions, such as "You have one, don't you?" appear a little later (de Villiers and de Villiers, 1978).

Semantics is concerned specifically with meaning. The acquisition of words, their meanings, and the links between them does not usually happen at once. Words are clearly comprehended before they are spoken, and the number of words comprehended continues to be greater all through language development and in later life. Comprehension of the first word is about three months ahead of production of the first word, and the gap grows; comprehension of fifty words appears to occur five months before production of fifty words (Benedict, 1979). Moreover, children learn to produce fifty words before they string them together into sentences. Vocabulary growth begins slowly, but there is a great spurt in word learning between twenty-four and thirty months (Reich, 1986). **semantics**

Morphology is the system of word building in the language. *Morphemes* may be words or significant elements, such as prefixes and suffixes. Sound units that are not words by themselves are called *bound morphemes*, because they are units of meaning only when combined with words. For example, the suffix *-ness* can be added to many words in English. **morphology**

Phonology is the sound system of language; the smallest sound units are called *phonemes*. Phonology encompasses the rules for using the sounds of language, for combining phonemes in particular ways to form identifiable language units such as the /s/ that we add to make words plural. People who speak American or Canadian English recognize about forty-four phonemes. Other languages recognize different sounds. **phonology**

Phonetics is the description of the speech sounds of a language. There are only twenty-six letters—vowels and consonants—in the English alphabet, but they are pronounced in different ways. As noted above, combinations of just forty-four phonemes produce every English word. **phonetics**

pragmatics

Pragmatics is concerned with the ways in which we use language, the role of context in communicative interactions. Pragmatics develops from the early stages as children use their language to query, request, deny, and declare. How they use language—the content of their interactions—changes with the interaction and the situation. They can talk baby talk to infants, tell jokes and riddles, be rude to their friends and, usually, polite to their teachers and parents.

The Speech Mechanism

The act of speech is enormously complicated. English speakers talk at an average rate of 150 words a minute. A speaker produces 14 phonemes per second, using about 100 muscles that require 100 motor units apiece (Shames and Wiig, 1990).

The anatomical structures involved in the comprehension and production of language and speech include the nervous system, the respiratory system, the oral part of the digestive tract, and the auditory sense receptors. These physical structures function in a highly organized and integrated fashion. Each part is synchronized with other parts to produce a meaningful sequence of accurate speech sounds while maintaining proper levels of loudness and pitch and a pleasing voice quality.

In general terms, speech is produced in an airstream that is shaped and resonated by the lips, tongue, teeth, jaw, nasal cavity, larynx, and pharynx. Figure 4-1 shows the organs and musculature of speech.

More specifically, the physiological process of speech involves three stages—*vocaliza-*

Figure 4-1
The sound-producing mechanism in humans

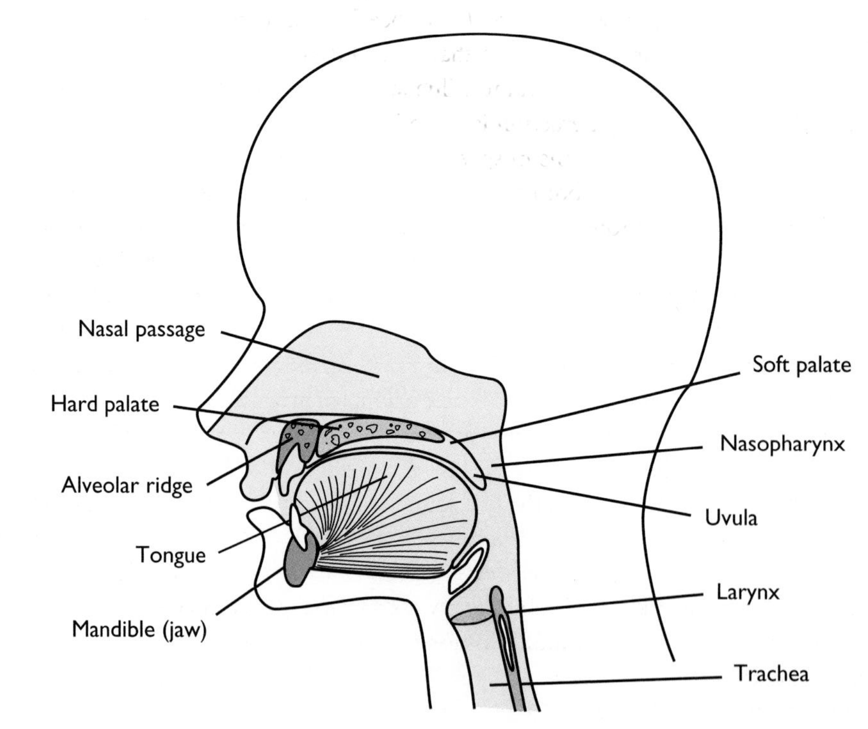

tion, articulation, and *modulation.* Vocalization is the ability to produce sound. Articulation involves the generation of speech sounds by modifications of the vocal tract, which consists basically of the mouth and nasal and pharyngeal cavities. Changes in placement and manner of articulators (lips, teeth, tongue, palate, pharynx) cause changes in speech sounds. For example, /t/ and /d/ are formed by closing the lips and then opening them to allow air to escape. The only difference between /t/ and /d/ or /p/ and /b/ is that /d/ and /b/ are voiced, while /t/ and /p/ are voiceless. Modulation is the ability to control the loudness of the sounds produced.

Within these major processes, *respiration, phonation,* and *resonance* are the necessary components. Respiration provides the airstream from which speech is developed; it depends on the lungs and various muscular and skeletal elements. Phonation, or vocal tone production, depends on the larynx, which produces a vibrating airstream. The larynx produces sound, and the pharynx modifies it, providing resonance. In addition to voice production, the larynx functions in crying, in keeping foreign objects out of the lungs, in coughing, and as a regulator of the exchange of oxygen and carbon dioxide in breathing. The pharynx changes its shape, size, and tension, and combines with the nose or mouth to form the resonating chambers for speech. As the larynx and resonating cavities develop, the voice becomes louder, the pitch becomes lower, and the vocal tone increases in variety and range of inflectional patterns.

Speech and Language Development

Language acquisition overlaps and relies upon social and cognitive growth. These aspects of development are closely intertwined, and really cannot be considered separately. Further, it is extremely difficult to separate speech and language development in the early years because language usage is expressed so cogently in speech forms in most children.

Language is first and foremost a social behaviour. At the outset, the quality of adult–child interactions is the single most important influence on the child's language development. Child–adult communicative interaction is sometimes called **motherese**, which is characterized by rather unique alterations in speech, meaning, form, and even language usage. When interacting with infants, both adults and children tend to use register changes—a higher pitch, exaggerated intonation, clear enunciation, a slower rate with more pauses between utterances, simplified speech sounds, repeated syllables, and simplified syntax.

motherese

How important is interaction in the early months? One report (Begley, 1996) notes that infants whose mothers spoke to them a lot knew 131 more words at 20 months than did babies of more taciturn, or less involved mothers. At 24 months, the gap widened to 295 words. When there is minimal or no social interaction, language acquisition will be severely hindered. Two children in quite different eras who were deprived of early stimulation are described in the profiles that follow.

Speech development begins with the first sound following the birth cry and ends with full articulatory control. Infants begin to experiment with sound in the early months of life and increase their sound-making capacity in conjunction with other aspects of development, specifically neural, motor, and social. In the very early stages, speech and motor development are seen as occurring in a synchronous fashion so that acquisition follows an orderly progression, with advances in speech and motor skills intertwined to a considerable extent.

Newborns have a limited range of vocalizations. They cry, burp, cough, and make a few other sounds. For the later development of language, **cooing**—the production of clear vow-

cooing

Case Study

Victor

Jean Marc Gaspard Itard (1755–1838), a French physician, is remembered for his intervention with the so-called wild boy of Aveyron. The boy was caught in the woods, and was reported to have been raised by wolves. When the lad finally reached Paris on Bastille Day, 1800, he was placed in the school for the deaf because of his muteness. Itard named him Victor.

Victor was stunted in growth, with a light complexion and scarred, pockmarked skin—probably the result of the smallpox he had caught in captivity. A huge scar ran across his larynx, suggesting that his throat had been cut before he was abandoned in the forest. Instead of resembling Rousseau's "noble savage," the boy was dirty, incapable of focusing attention, and insensitive to the basic sensations of heat and cold. He lapped his food, uttered inarticulate sounds, fixated on empty space, bit people who came too close, and spent most of his time sleeping or rocking back and forth. Observers concluded that Victor's constitution was defective; the boy was not an idiot because he had been left in the wilds, but had been left in the wilds because he was an idiot.

Itard could not accept that Victor was irreversibly idiotic. Instead, he believed that the child was mentally arrested due to social and educational neglect; Victor had acquired idiocy through isolation, suffering a sort of mental atrophy from disuse of his senses. Despite Victor's appearance and lack of responsiveness, Itard believed that appropriate environmental conditions could humanize the boy and decided to try to educate him rather than sending him to a lunatic hospital.

Itard began his work with little concept of the complexities involved in working with a severely disabled child. Using crude diagnostic methods, he determined that Victor's sense organs were intact, though "dull" or insensitive. Victor would not, for example, respond to loud noises, not even to the sound of a pistol shot. On the other hand, he would react to such subtle signals as the cracking of a walnut.

Itard used a variety of means to make Victor aware of sensation—hot baths, massages, tickling, emotional excitement, even electric shock. Along with sensory stimulation and discipline, Itard presented Victor with a systematic series of specific sense training activities designed to improve his visual, auditory, and motor skills. He taught the activities in order and at a variable rate tailored to fit Victor's progress. Especially, Itard tried to teach the boy to communicate through speech and sign language.

In time, Victor became moderately socialized but not, as Itard had naïvely hoped, normal. Victor's ability to communicate continued to increase, and he learned the basic skills of eating and dressing. Nevertheless, after five years, Itard concluded that his work had been a failure and left Victor in the care of a friendly housekeeper.

Genie

The story of Genie illustrates the severe effects of emotional and social deprivation on language and speech development. Genie's father believed her to be hopelessly retarded, and from the time she was twenty months old he confined her to a small room. The room was barren, completely unfurnished save for a small crib entirely covered with wire mesh and an infant potty. During the day, the child was strapped in the crib or tied to the potty chair. At night she was stuffed into a sleeping bag specially made to restrain her.

Genie's father never spoke to her and beat her if she made any noise. Sometimes, he pretended he was a dog, barking and growling and sometimes scratching the child with his fingernails. Genie's mother could only visit her for a few minutes each day to feed her. There was no radio or television in the house.

When Genie was thirteen and a half, the parents had an especially violent fight and the mother left. At about this time, in November 1970, Genie was discovered by the California authorities. Her father committed suicide on the day he was to be brought to trial.

When she was found, Genie weighed a mere 27 kg and was 137 cm tall. She could not chew solid food, was not toilet trained, was unable to stand erect, and could only shuffle, not walk. Genie was mute and could understand only a few simple commands. She appeared to have no comprehension of grammar. However, when tested at the hospital, Genie was found to have normal hearing, vision, and eye–hand coordination.

Genie was placed with a foster family who treated her much as they would a normal child. She began to develop speech, following a normal course of language development but with marked differences. After seven years of language acquisition, Genie continued to have articulation problems. She used 200 words before she began making two-word combinations. She did not ask questions spontaneously and she demonstrated inconsistencies in word order.

After many years of working with Genie, language therapists concluded that failure to acquire language during the normal period makes development laborious and incomplete, but that the similarities between delayed and normal acquisition outweigh the differences (de Villiers and de Villiers, 1978).

Early stimulation from parents and siblings aids in young children's language acquisition.

els, often in isolation—is the most important. By their eighth week, infants can usually produce various of these vowel sounds.

Because they require finer motor control of the tongue and lips, consonant sounds are more difficult to produce than vowel sounds. But as infants approach the six-month mark, the nature of cooing changes and consonant–vowel patterns begin to appear. This incorporation of vowel and consonant sounds is known as **babbling**—random sound play of almost infinite variety.

babbling

Babbling is an almost universal response during infancy and does not seem to require exposure to language or other environmental auditory input. Even infants who are deaf babble, although they do not babble in the same way; their babbling is substantially delayed and these sounds usually stop around one year of age (Pettito and Marenette, 1991). The exceptions to the universal nature of babbling behaviour are children who are autistic or neurologically damaged, who may not babble at all.

There is considerable controversy over the relationship between babbling and later speech. Most researchers now believe that babbling and early speech are one continuous phenomenon (e.g., Gleason, 1985), and that the babbling stage is a period of "tuning up" and establishing the necessary integrations between hearing/listening and sound production. Even if the sounds of babbling don't approximate speech, the intonation of babbling does. Babbling also helps to develop the musculature of the lips and the mouth necessary for the later articulation of speech sounds. Further, children begin to babble the sounds unique to their own language. By six months of age, infants in English-speaking homes have different auditory maps than do those in Swedish-speaking homes (Begley, 1996).

At the same time that infants begin to babble, they also show the first indications of comprehension. Babies at about six months of age begin to associate certain sounds with people, events, and objects in the environment. Their signals also take on a relatively consistent form, produced in the expectation that they will promote a consistent response from people in the environment.

Once infants are using consonants in their babbling, they attempt to imitate adult sounds. At about eight months of age, infants begin to use **echolalic speech**—speech that is an immediate imitation of that of some other speaker. Soon infants move into the jargon stage; they begin to imitate adults consistently and are able to reproduce the intonation patterns or melodies of the language they hear.

echolalic speech

At around one year of age, two new developments occur—expressive intonation in babbling and first words. By ten or eleven months children are babbling in sentences, combining several incomprehensible "words" and uttering them with correct inflections (Reich, 1986).

At the same time, children are having a great many experiences with listening to language, and they rapidly become adept at discerning meaning from contextual as well as voice clues. Children show comprehension of words; they learn to follow simple directions and associate many environmental clues with speech that they have heard and with gestures. Then, after months of coaxing and prompting the meaningless babble of their babies, parents are rewarded by the first word.

First words emerge when the infant's motor system for speech production has become coordinated with breath control and the movements of lips and tongue. The age for first words ranges from nine to nineteen months for normal children. As children move into using single words, there is a corresponding decrease in babbling.

Toddlers' first single-word utterances are remarkably efficient and maximally communicative. The speech is termed **holophrasic,** because a single word is used to express a more complex idea. Although the first words may differ markedly from adult pronunciation, they are likely to be simplifications of adult usage involving the omission of final consonants, the reduction of consonant clusters, the omission of unstressed syllables, or the reduplication of syllables (Lindfors, 1987).

holophrasic

Single words are used for naming favourite toys or foods, family members, or pets, and to make requests, comments, and enquiries. Children also incorporate single-word approximations of frequently used adult phrases such as "all gone" or "bad boy."

Several weeks after the first word, vocabulary begins to grow quite rapidly as new words are learned daily. Children learn to produce about fifty words before they string them together. Between eighteen and twenty-four months of age, they begin to combine words. These early phrases (presentences) are the precursors of true sentences. For example, the child may express phrases such as: "Me Mike," "Bump table," "Daddy no," "Car now," or "No more milk." Children show a wide range of variation in the number of presentences they use. Some children use only a few; others as many as a thousand.

The sentence is the key landmark in language acquisition. The first true sentences used by small children are described as **telegraphic speech**, because they resemble a telegram in that only the essential aspects of the message, those possessing meaning, are included. In these utterances, children begin to use syntax and morphology; inflections to signify plurality; possession; verb tense and subject-verb agreement; and comparative and superlative forms of adjectives. Children at this stage also use function words such as *in* and *on*, and the articles *a*, *an*, and *the*.

telegraphic speech

In first using language, young children tend to regularize the language because they have not yet learned the exceptions. A small child is likely to say, "He runned," or "He hurt his self." As well, small children often reach beyond the borders of word meaning and overextend their word usage, as in the little boy who calls every animal a doggie.

By the time they are using simple sentences, at about two years of age, children are about 70 to 80 percent intelligible in their speech. Yet the full development of all of the sounds of English is a slow process. It is not until they are about eight years old that children are able to produce all the speech sounds: vowels, consonants, diphthongs, and blends. The last English sound that most children acquire is the /zh/, as in leisure and measure.

By three years of age, most children demonstrate the construction of simple affirmative–declarative sentences. They put together a noun phrase for a subject and a verb phrase for a predicate. As syntax develops, the child learns how to change word order and add and replace words to express more complex grammatical relationships. These changes are called *transformations*; as syntax becomes more complex, many transformations are used within the same utterances.

By the age of four, most children have achieved a great deal of language maturity. They have usually mastered the basic structures of their language and have developed an array of conversational skills that enable them to engage in extensive social and play interactions with their peers and others in the environment. As children gain greater control over the speech mechanisms, pronunciation improves. Speech is now more than 90 percent intelligible. Children still have difficulty with /r/, /s/, /j/, and /z/, and blends such as /ch/ and /sh/.

By the time they arrive at school at about five or six years of age, children are sophisticated language users with a mastery over language, developing metalinguistic skills and a firm linguistic base on which teachers can formally build reading and writing.

When children enter first grade, they bring with them an impressive store of background knowledge and a vocabulary of between 5000 and 14 000 words with which to talk about their experiences (Carey, 1978; Chall, Jacobs, and Baldwin, 1990). Children now use a variety of language functions, a greater variety of discourse styles and organization, more abstract vocabulary, and more complex syntax. The developmental emphasis moves from semantics and syntax to pragmatics and **metalinguistics** (the ability to reflect on all the aspects of language). Children learn to recognize instructional discourse—the language that gives them information about the curriculum and feedback on their efforts in mastering it.

metalinguistics

During middle childhood, every subsystem of language improves. Children begin to use a number of complex grammatical forms that did not appear in their earlier speech, and correct many of their syntactical errors. They use past participles, such as *eaten,* and perfect tense, such as *has been*, personal pronouns, and passive voice. They develop wider metalinguistic skills: nine-year-olds are more likely than five-year-olds to recognize grammatical

Case Study

Ashley

Ashley is seven-and-a-half years old and in a grade two class in the local school. He is small for his age and lags behind in academic work. Although the teacher describes him as a "dear child," she is increasingly frustrated with Ashley's lack of progress and his diminishing motivation.

Before referring Ashley for an assessment, the classroom teacher undertook some pre-referral interventions that included observations of his behaviour, interactions with peers and on-task behaviour in the classroom. She also used some broad measures of reading. She tried a more structured approach to beginning reading, stressing phonological awareness activities. However, little improvement was seen, and in her referral for a full assessment the teacher noted that Ashley's reading was poor, showing a marked academic delay of about a year. Writing and spelling also lagged badly. Math performance was at grade level or slightly below.

Of all the areas that worried the teacher, oral language performance topped the list. Very often, Ashley's speech was difficult to understand, particularly when he was nervous, in a hurry, or attempting to read aloud. But Ashley did not talk a lot. The teacher observed that he often refused to speak, balked at reading orally, and would not join in during the morning opening exercises in songs, chants, or conversations. He answered questions with a shrug or a frown, and increasingly used gestures to express his wants.

The teacher tried to identify the mispronunciations in Ashley's speech. He appeared to be missing or substituting a number of consonant sounds. For example, a sentence such as "The little child sat under a tree," sounded to the teacher as "Ta wittle kild at una ta ree." Other children in the class were amused by Ashley's speech and called him Baby or other names.

After a meeting with the mother, the teacher became aware of Ashley's growing dislike of school. He complained at home that the work is too hard, that the teacher asked him too many questions, and that the other children did not like him. "They say I talk like a baby," he confided to his mother. "They laugh at me and call me names."

errors in sentences and to be able to correct them. They also use the prepositions *as, if, so,* and *because* more accurately than earlier, although full development does not occur until later. Conjunctions such as *although* don't come until the late elementary years or early adolescence.

Of course, language development does not stop in middle childhood; rather, it is a lifelong process. It will continue to develop in conjunction with expanding cognitive skills and learning. But the critical syntactic, morphological, and phonological bases are in place by school age and later development is in metalinguistics, semantics, and pragmatics.

SPEECH AND LANGUAGE DIFFERENCES

Learning to communicate and understand the communication of others is one of the biggest challenges young children face. It is little surprise, then, that delays and disorders in speech and language are the most common and varied disabilities that teachers, especially those involved with young children, will encounter.

Ashley, the child discussed in the case study, provides an example of the complexity of speech and language problems, the difficulties in accurate identification, and the secondary disabilities that can emerge. Rather than talking in school, Ashley is resorting to shrugs and gestures. His academic work is suffering and his social interactions are becoming more negative.

Communication disorders include a range of difficulties associated with speech, language, and hearing, or a combination of these. Within the generic classification of *communication disorders*, we find *speech disorders* (as in Ashley's case), *language delays and disorders*, and *problems subsequent to hearing loss.* Speech problems include delayed onset of speech, speech usage below age-level expectations, oddities in articulation, peculiar usage of grammar, stuttering, unusual intonations or voice quality, paucity of speech, inability to recall familiar words, poor self-expression, or total absence of speech. Language disorders include delayed language, different language, deviant language, or even no language. Typically, language disorders are more complex in identification, diagnosis, and remediation than are speech problems. Hearing impairments, as we discuss in Chapter 9, are the most complex. Table 4-1 lists some signs and effects of communication disorders.

The overlap between speech and language is considerable. For clarity, however, we describe speech and language disorders separately.

DEFINITIONS OF LANGUAGE PROBLEMS

language problems

Language problems refer to a range of difficulties with the linguistic code, or with the rules for linking the symbols and the symbol sequences. Children who demonstrate significant lags but whose language is still progressing according to the stages of normal language development are said to have **language delays**. Children with language delays characteristically use language infrequently; by the time they reach preschool age, they talk approximately half as much as their peers and are much less responsive to inquiries from teachers and peers (see Roth, McCaul, and Barnes, 1993).

language delays

language disorders

Language disorders are more complex than language delays. As defined by the American Speech and Hearing Association (1982), language disorders refer to impairment or deviant

Table 4-1 Signs and effects of communication disorders

Disorder	Signs	Effects
Language delay	More than six months behind norm in reaching language milestones	Slower in all the elements of language acquisition and usage
Language disorders	May show impaired comprehension and poor verbal expression	Failure to understand instructions; withdrawal from group situations
Aphasia	Impaired reception or production of oral language	Failure to understand speech or to produce meaningful sentences
Apraxia	Inability to sequence the muscle movements needed for speech	Failure to produce meaningful speech
Articulation disorders	Abnormal production of speech sounds; speech not typical of chronological age	May be ridiculed by peers; may have decoding and comprehension problems with respect to specific words
Dysfluency	Impaired fluency and rhythm	Peer ridicule, oral difficulties
Voice disorders	Abnormal vocal quality, pitch, loudness, or duration	Self-confidence may suffer; withdrawal
Orofacial defects	Variety of clefts, such as cleft lip or cleft palate	May have problems in feeding, speech, or respiration
Dysarthria	Paralysis of the muscles associated with speech	Distorted speech

development of comprehension or of the use of a spoken, written, or other symbol system. These disorders may involve form (phonological, morphological, and syntactical elements), content (semantics), function (pragmatics) or any combination of these.

Prevalence of Language Problems

Researchers and practitioners are no more adept at estimating the number of students with language delays and disorders than they are at pinpointing numbers for other forms of disability. The prevalence issue is particularly confused for language problems because:

- Researchers disagree on definitional and classification systems. Many types of language disorders remain ambiguous and controversial; a consensus has not been reached about the patterns of subtypes of language impairments or the criteria for classification.
- Varied terms are used to describe language disorders. These include *aphasia, dysphasia, communicatively impaired,* and *language learning disabled.* Some clinicians prefer the

terms aphasia or dysphasia because they suggest fairly specific conditions; others prefer the use of the general term *language disabled.*

- Some researchers (e.g., Shames and Wiig, 1990) define a language disorder as a form of speech disorder. Of children with speech disorders, they claim that 3 to 5 percent have language disabilities. Others (e.g., de Villiers and de Villiers, 1978) define language problems as separate from speech disorders. They estimate that 12 percent of children with communication problems have language delays or disorders.
- Surveys of language problems are often based on interviews of questionable validity, and there is likely a tendency to under-report the presence of communication disorders.
- Children in other categories of exceptionality often have language problems. For example, students who are learning disabled more often than not demonstrate deviations or delays in language; children who are intellectually disabled do not develop language commensurate with their intellectual ability; language problems are the chief difficulty of children who are hearing impaired.

As far as prevalence is concerned, therefore, the best we can say is that the overall number for communication disorders of all types in children and adults may be as high as 12 to 15 percent, and speech and language disorders are estimated at between 5 and 8 percent of school-aged children ("Children with communication ... ," 1995; Spitz, Tallal, Flax, Benasich, 1997).

Of all children with language disabilities, about two-thirds are boys (Silva, 1980). As well, there is an increase in communication disorders in people over the age of forty as a result of stroke and other conditions.

Classification of Language Problems

Communication disorders in general are usually classified according to their symptoms, their causes, or their subtypes. This classification is shown in Table 4-2.

Table 4-2 Classification of communication disorders

Symptoms	Causes	Types
Phonological disorders	Organic—show a demonstrable pathology	Language delay
Articulation disorders		Language disorder
Voice disorders	Functional—no identifiable pathology	Aphasia
Fluency disorders		Expressive disorder
Orofacial		Receptive disorder
Dysarthria		
Dyspraxia		
Language disorders		

Specifically, language problems relate to disorders in the recognition and understanding of spoken language or in the ability to formulate well-organized grammatical sentences. As we noted, children may be characterized as having delayed or disordered language, a distinction that depends on the type, intensity, and duration of the difficulties.

receptive disorders
expressive disorders

Language disorders may also be classified as receptive or expressive. **Receptive disorders** are those that interfere with the comprehension of spoken language; **expressive disorders** are those that affect the formulation of grammatical utterances. Language disorders in children frequently combine both receptive and expressive problems. They range in severity from mild language learning difficulties to profoundly debilitating disorders.

Delayed Language Development

A child with delayed language development learns language in an orderly progression but more slowly and less proficiently than normal-age peers. Minor delays in language development may be caused by generalized immaturity rather than a pervasive language problem. Clinicians sometimes use the "rule of six" in defining language delays; that is, if a child's language development lags six months behind what is considered to be normal, the child is said to have a delay.

Many young children who show minor delays catch up with their peers by the time they are five or six. Others may not close the gap in functioning.

Children with minor speech and language disorders can often receive adequate assistance within the school from a special education teacher or speech-and-language clinician.

Language Disorders

Children who are language impaired or disordered show a developmental language disorder that affects most or all aspects of expressive and receptive language. Some of these children show such difficulties in developing language in a normal progression that they may never attain adult levels. Others with language disorders may demonstrate bizarre language behaviour. The great majority meet difficulties with acquisition such that they require structured and systematic intervention. Another group shows deviant language secondary to other disabling conditions.

Aphasia

Of the many factors accounting for language problems, the most prominent are brain dysfunction and psychological problems. Neurological (brain) dysfunction underlies the most severe types of speech and language disorders. One of the most serious neurological language disorders is **aphasia**, a condition in which a child's primary impairment is the inability to communicate effectively with verbal language because of comprehension and/or production difficulties. Aphasia may be developmental (often referred to as *dysphasia*) or acquired. **aphasia**

Children with developmental aphasia show severe delays in the development of receptive and expressive language but do not suffer from any apparent additional disabling conditions.

Acquired aphasia refers to conditions (trauma) that occur after language has been developed. It is a loss in linguistic ability that usually results from brain damage arising from serious illness, trauma to the head, or stroke. Verbal output and understanding are diminished but not always altogether absent. Generally, children under eight years of age make excellent recoveries from acquired aphasia (Zemlin, 1990; see also Chapter 12 on Traumatic Brain Injury).

Aphasia is also classified as receptive or expressive. *Receptive aphasia* is the inability to understand speech symbols. Children with receptive aphasia appear to talk in a free-flowing manner, but their words are incomprehensible. *Expressive aphasia* manifests itself as trouble remembering words (**dysnomia**), blocking on a word, and hesitating often when speaking. *Severe global aphasia* means that both expressive and receptive aphasia are present to a severe degree, often associated with additional perceptual problems, such as sight or hearing. **dysnomia**

Mutism

The condition where there is no voice is known as **aphonia**. This is different from **mutism**, the total absence of speech. Mutism is a rare condition, related to severe emotional, neurological, or sensory deficit. **aphonia** **mutism**

The term *elective mutism* describes emotionally disturbed children who do not speak or who speak only in certain circumstances. Elective mutism may be associated with a traumatic event and is always symptomatic of a deep disturbance of psychological functioning.

Selective mutism seems to be a little different in intensity. This refers to the behaviour of children who generally have normal language development yet talk to only a small group of relatives or peers (Powell and Dalley, 1995). Selective mutism is found in less than one percent of all mental health referrals and found more often in females. It may be a variant of school phobia.

Etiology of Language Problems

As we have just discussed, damage to the speech/language centres of the brain can lead to aphasia or generalized communication disorders with varying characteristics depending on the site of the lesion. Head injuries, especially from motor vehicle accidents and diseases such as encephalitis, are the most common causes of aphasia in children, with stroke the most common cause in adults (Holland, Swindell, and Ruinmuth, 1990).

Disruptions in early social interactions may contribute to the particular difficulties experienced by some children. Language disorders may be exacerbated by the child's interactions with the family. Children who are neglected, for example, show delays in language development (Allen and Wasserman, 1985).

Parents of children with language disorders also engage in fewer play and language activities, unwittingly contributing to the language delay or disorder. For example, studies have found that mothers of three-month-old infants with minor facial anomalies (cleft lip and palate) were less active during interactions with their infants than were mothers of normal infants (Barden, Ford, Jensen, Rogers-Salyer, and Salyer, 1989). Other research indicates that in social interactions with their mothers, infants with Down syndrome show atypical interactive behaviours when compared with normal infants matched for mental age (Coggins and Morrison, 1981).

Children with other disabilities are doubly disadvantaged because the original disability may lead to secondary language problems. Children with disabilities may have fewer opportunities to learn the social, play, and communication skills that are unique to and emerge from child–child social interchange (Guralnick, 1986) and from adult–child interaction. They may hear less language than other children; adults tend to speak less *to* non-verbal or low-verbal children but to talk more *for* them.

DEFINITIONS OF SPEECH DISORDERS

speech disorders

Speech disorders are problems encountered in the oral production of language. "Speech is abnormal when it deviates so far from the speech of other people that it calls attention to itself, interferes with communication, or causes the speaker or his listeners to be distressed" (Van Riper and Emerick, 1990, p. 34).

Speech disorders should not be confused with the speech errors that all young children make when learning to talk. In small children, mispronunciations and dysfluencies are common; children are about eight years of age before they are relatively stable in the sounds of the English language. Even then, about 10 percent of eight-year-old children still have some trouble with /s/, /z/, /v/, /th/, and /zh/ (Rathus, 1988).

Mispronunciations and dysfluencies only become disorders when they persist as characteristics in the speech of children who should have acquired certain sounds. We would worry more, for example, about the seven-year-old who talks about his "Wittle wellow wabbit" than the child of the same age who could not get her tongue around the /zh/ sound in *leisure* and *measure.*

Prevalence of Speech Disorders

As with language problems, reliable figures on the prevalence of speech disorders among children are difficult to obtain. This happens for several reasons:

- Criteria and definitions of communication disorders vary.
- Many speech problems, such as articulation problems, simply disappear as children mature. When minor delays are due to general immaturity, most children catch up with their peers without special intervention.
- Prevalence varies according to age. It is estimated that 12 to 15 percent of children in kindergarten to grade four have speech problems. In grades five to eight, the proportion drops to four to five percent, and this remains constant after grade eight unless treatment intervenes.
- Speech problems are more common among boys than girls, especially in the early grades; this is particularly true in the case of stuttering.
- Of speech disorders, articulation problems are the most usual type, accounting for approximately 75 percent of all speech disorders. However, as we explain later, the terms *articulation disorder* and *phonological disorder* are often used synonymously although they refer to slightly different problems, and this can confuse prevalence.

Classification of Speech Disorders

There are many ways to classify speech disorders. For the sake of clarity and simplicity, we focus on specific major areas—phonological and articulation problems, voice disorders, problems with speech flow (dysfluency), orofacial defects, and problems associated with muscle control.

Articulation Disorders

Therapists talk about phonological difficulties and articulation disorders. Phonological difficulties are present if a person does not understand how to use speech sounds according to linguistic rules and to communicate meaning accurately. When a child has a sound and pronounces it correctly in some contexts but not in others, the child has a **phonological problem**. Children with phonological impairments are aware of the effect of their errors on a listener's comprehension and will make adjustments to enhance verbal comprehension (Owens, 1991).

phonological problem

Articulation problems are not related to use but to ability. With a phonological disorder, a child may have but not use a sound; with an **articulation disorder**, a child cannot actually make or produce a sound. Speech sounds are incorrect because of changes in the placement and manner of articulators. With a lisp, for example, the child's tongue is misplaced and says /th/ instead of /s/.

articulation disorder

Some articulation errors result from problems such as cleft palate, but in the large majority of cases the disorders appear to result simply from deficiencies in learning. When the child was first learning speech, for example, there may have been inadequate coordination of oral and facial muscles that eventually became habitual.

Articulation disorders are characterized by omissions, substitutions, distortions, and additions of speech sounds that may occur in the initial, medial, or final position in a word. The most commonly misarticulated sounds are /s/, /z/, voiceless /th/ as in *bath*, /r/, /l/, /sh/, and /j/ as in *judge* (Gearheart, Mullen, and Gearheart, 1993).

Omission errors are those in which one or more sounds are left out of words. Omissions occur most frequently with blended sounds, such as /bl/,/pl/, /pr/, /st/, /dr/, and /tr/. When words begin with a blend, children may drop one sound so that *smell* becomes *mell*, *break* is *reak*, *play* is *pay*, and *school* is *kool.*

Substitutions of speech sounds occur when one consonant is replaced by another: /b/ for /v/, /w/ for /r/, or /w/ for /l/, or *thunshine* for *sunshine.* A *lisp* is a substitution where /th/ is used for /s/ or /z/. Some children may substitute sounds in some words but not in others. A child may be able to say the word *yes* correctly, but substitute /l/ for /y/ in the word *yellow.*

Distortions involve deviations from normal speech sounds, often caused by placing the tongue or lips in the wrong position for the production of a particular sound, as *shoup* for *soup* or *ideer* for *idea.* Addition of sounds refers to the adding of a sound to a word. The extra sounds are usually added between blended sounds, such as *terain* for *train.*

Voice Disorders

Voice disorders are probably the least understood of all the various communication disorders. A voice that lacks power, is unpleasant, or abuses the vocal mechanism is likely to be considered defective.

Voice disorders include hoarseness (too nasal or rough), breathiness, loudness (too loud or too soft), pitch (too high or too low), and sudden breaks in pitch. They are frequently combined with other speech problems to form a complex communication disorder. Deviations may impair both speaking and singing.

The most common deviations in pitch seen by speech and language clinicians are levels that are too high or low and levels that are monotonous with little variation of pitch (Moore, 1986). Children who do not speak loudly enough for their needs may suffer from hearing loss, an organic disorder, or reticence about speaking. Some children do not know how to use a "big" voice without abusing the vocal mechanism (Moore, 1986).

For some people, pitch problems are caused by too small a larynx (too high) or too large a larynx (too low). Some may result from overall slow maturation. In children, however, most voice disorders are functional, related to poor learning of voice control. Children who scream or talk loudly are in danger of abusing their vocal cords. Vocal abuse can lead to vocal nodules or polyps that may have to be removed surgically.

The child who "talks through the nose" has hypernasal speech. This may result from a cleft palate, or from partial paralysis of the soft palate rendering the necessary closure of the nasal passages impossible.

Dysfluency

dysfluency

Fluency is the smoothness with which sounds, syllables, words, and phrases flow together; the opposite, **dysfluency**, describes conditions in which the flow of speech is interrupted with blocking, repetitions, or prolongations of sounds, words, phrases, or syllables.

stuttering

Stuttering, the major subcategory of dysfluency (speech flow) disorder, affects about five percent of children during language development (Guitar, 1998), usually beginning between the ages of two and five. Dysfluency affects approximately one percent of the entire population. Two to ten times more males than females stutter.

The condition is not related to social class or cognitive functioning; stuttering is found among all ethnic and socio-economic groups. Many famous people were stutterers, including Aesop, Aristotle, Demosthenes, Charles I, Winston Churchill, Charles Darwin, and George VI.

While persons who stutter are reported to make up about one percent of the entire population, this estimate may be low. It is estimated that teachers routinely identify only about one-half of the children who stutter in their classrooms because children hide the problem (see Williams, 1999).

As a serious communication problem, stuttering is both complicated and multidimensional. In terms of severity, it should be seen on a continuum. At one end is normal dysfluency, which is not stuttering but a part of speech development in young children at about three years of age. The progression is then to primary stuttering, which is characterized by breaks in speech caused by repetitions of syllables and sounds, and sometimes prolongations, but which is not usually accompanied by physical signs. The final stage is secondary stuttering, which is terse, non-fluent speech in which the rate and rhythm are severely affected. Secondary stutterers show symptoms such as eye blinking, head jerking, facial grimaces and tension, other types of body distortions, muscular tension, and forcing when they try to speak. Secondary stuttering is much harder to overcome than primary stuttering.

In terms of age of onset, the earliest onset of stuttering is generally around eighteen months, just when children begin to speak in short phrases. However, a child may begin to stutter at any time; the mean age of onset is 3.6 years and the incidence of onset declines each year from eighteen months on (Bloodstein, 1975). In some cases, stuttering progresses from a sporadic to a chronic problem. In others, it spontaneously disappears by adolescence; a greater number of females than males recover spontaneously. In another group, stuttering disappears only to resurface later.

The likelihood of spontaneous recovery is inversely related to the age of the child. Children who stop stuttering are generally younger than three years when they begin (Curlee and Yairi, 1997), and usually recover within twelve to fourteen months of onset (Yairi and Ambrose, 1992). Hence, by the time a child is four years of age, the stuttering may have progressed beyond the point where it will disappear without intervention.

Cluttering

Cluttered speech should not be confused with stuttering. Cluttering involves rapid, jerky, stumbling speech with marked omissions. Speakers may clip off speech sounds, omit sounds, and have rapid-fire bursts of speech. Cluttered speech shows excessive speed combined with disorganized sentence structure and articulation problems. It lacks appropriate phrasing or grouping of words within an utterance and is difficult to understand. In severe cases, the speech is confused, disorganized, and even chaotic (Van Riper and Emerick, 1990).

Muscle Control

dysarthria

Dysarthria refers to a group of speech disorders resulting from disturbed muscular control over the speech mechanisms. The articulation of speech sounds is disturbed when there is a partial or complete paralysis of the muscles associated with speech. When a child with dysarthria tries to talk, consonant sounds are distorted and efforts at speech may not be successful. Indeed, the harder the child tries to speak, the more difficult speech becomes.

apraxia

Apraxia is the inability to program, position, and sequence the muscle movements involved in speech. The child with apraxia can produce the movements involved in articulation, but often fails to combine these movements into meaningful speech.

Orofacial Defects

Clefts are known as *midline defects.* They are only one of the wide variety of craniofacial anomalies, but they are also one of the most common and generally least severe.

There are several patterns of clefting—for example, cleft mandible, double mouth, cleft tongue, cleft uvula, undeveloped tongue, cleft lip, cleft palate, and cleft lip and palate. Clefts also vary in severity. A cleft lip can range from a slight notch in the vermilion (coloured portion of the lip) to a complete separation of the lip extending up and into the nose. When there is a cleft lip, the alveolar ridge (upper gum ridge) may also be separated. Lip clefts can occur on one or both sides. Clefts may also be part of a disorder such as Crouzon's disease or Treacher Collins syndrome, both which are accompanied by facial anomalies.

Clefts occur in approximately one in every 750 live births (Moran and Pentz, 1995; Speltz, Endriga, Fisher, and Mason, 1997). Incidence varies by gender and ethnic group, but not by socio-economic status or maternal age. Incidence rates are higher among Native Americans and Asians, lower among Blacks (McWilliams, Morris, and Shelton, 1990). Among Black babies, the ratio is one in every 1000 to 1500. Usually more males than females are affected, except in the rare condition of a cleft palate only, in which case more females are affected.

The palate separates the respiratory and the digestive systems. Many children with clefts are born with a gap in the roof of the mouth (palate), which opens into the nasal cavity. Children with unrepaired cleft lip/palate have difficulties in the feeding process because of interruptions in the rhythm of feeding, or in mastication, swallowing, choking, and regurgitation.

There may be malocclusion (abnormality in the coming together of the teeth). As well, between 25 and 60 percent of children with cleft palates have a degree of hearing loss due to intermittent occurrence of middle-ear disease (Harrison and Philips, 1971).

Children with clefts may exhibit delayed language development and are more likely to have language-based learning disabilities (Moran and Pentz, 1995). Delayed articulation is not uncommon; children may have difficulty building and sustaining enough air pressure in the mouth to make pressure consonants such as /p/, /b/, /s/, /z/, and /ch/.

Etiology of Speech Disorders

Structural inadequacies are a major cause of speech disorders in children. These may be structural inadequacies in the vocal folds (larynx), tongue, teeth, lips, palate, and resonating cavities. Most defects of this type are of a developmental nature, although they can result from physical injury or disease.

Damage to or maldevelopment of the central and/or peripheral nervous system is another major cause. Dysarthria, for example, results from a fundamental disturbance in the movement or motoric function brought about by damage to the nervous system. Children with cerebral palsy often suffer from dysarthria. The motor impairment that affects the lips, tongue, jaw, and soft palate hinders the intelligibility of their speech. Inadequacy of the hearing mechanism, causing hearing impairment, is a third major cause of speech disorders.

The causes of clefts are confusing. While some result from arrests of midline facial development during the first trimester of pregnancy, clefts of the lip and palate seem to have distinct genetic etiologies. Others seem to result from an interaction of genetic and environmental influences. Numerous villains have been suggested, including alcohol, acetylsalicylic acid, certain foods, and an excess or lack of vitamin A.

Stuttering is known to have both biochemical and physiological indicators. There is also clear evidence of genetic transmissions of susceptibility that have been reported since the 1960s. Analysis of pedigrees—family trees—have found that much stuttering is familial (Ambrose, Cox, and Yairi, 1997). See the accompanying Research Notes feature for more on stuttering.

Research Notes

Stuttering

One of the most difficult things about stuttering is the inability to confidently point to a precise cause. The search for causes is long-standing and the assumptions underlying the research, theories, and therapies related to stuttering range from obvious to obscure. Reich (1986) points out that 20th-century explanations included lack of cerebral dominance, neurotic symptoms arising out of psychodynamic conflicts developed in early childhood, biochemical causes, perseveration, lateral auditory dominance, laryngeal dysfunction, and auditory feedback dysfunction. Genetic predisposition is a popular, but disputed, explanation. Some studies lean to learning rather than genetics. For example, Farber (1981) studied ninety-five sets of identical twins raised apart. A genetic predisposition would find pairs of stutterers, but only five individuals in the group stuttered, and in each case only one member of the pair stuttered. On the other hand, clear evidence of genetic transmissions of susceptibility have been reported since the 1960s. Stuttering is found in families as shown by analysis of pedigrees (family trees). For men who stutter, the chances of their children having the condition is 9 percent for daughters and 22 percent for sons. For stuttering women, the figures are 17 percent for daughters and 36 percent for sons (Andrews, Craig, Feyer, Hoddinott, Howie, and Neilson, 1983).

No one can be confident about the precise causes of stuttering (or about current treatment of the disorder). Probably the most useful approach is to view stuttering as the result of multiple causative factors including potential constitutional vulnerability, biochemical and physiological factors, the cumulative results of faulty learning, and resultant apprehension and anxiety related to speech. In correction, current practices tend to focus on three broad groupings of etiology. Some speech pathologists regard stuttering as a symptom of physical impairment or instability; others look at it as a symptom of personal maladjustment or emotional instability; still others are of the opinion that it is symptomatic of neither but simply a form of learned behaviour found in normal individuals.

When stuttering is regarded as a symptom of an underlying emotional problem, psychotherapeutic intervention is in order. The objective of treatment is to eliminate stuttering or to decrease its effect. Treatments that focus on organic causes include air flow techniques—breathing manoeuvres that release the laryngeal spasm (a locking of the vocal cords as speaking begins)—together with stress reduction and procedures that build confidence and develop self-motivation (Schwartz, 1988). Biofeedback, counselling, and speech therapy are also widely used.

Free-token response–cost programs have been used successfully to modify stuttering during speech therapy (Salend and Andress, 1984).

Whatever the intervention, the trend is to attempt to remediate the condition early. Clinicians stress the elimination of stuttered speech at the time it first appears. Researchers hold that optimal intervention involves early detection and prevention, and that there is less risk involved in over-diagnosis than under-diagnosis of stuttering (Moore and Perkins, 1990).

DEVELOPMENTAL CONSEQUENCES OF SPEECH AND LANGUAGE PROBLEMS

All types of speech and language disorders affect the ease with which children can communicate with people in their environment. As language is inextricably intertwined with perceiving, remembering, attending, comprehending, and thinking—in short, all of our attempts to make sense of our experiences with the world—children who communicate poorly, whether because of speech problems or language disorders, may be hindered in their academic performance and in almost every aspect of functioning.

Cognitive Development

No correlation exists between speech and language disorders and poor cognitive functioning. However, many cognitive abilities are clearly language-dependent, and children with language problems tend to be more rigid and literal in their thinking. They lack the flexibility required for pretending, for playing word games, for laughing at riddles and jokes, and for effective social interaction. For example, symbolic play in young children with language impairments is different from that of their peers, although the differences seem quite small (Casby, 1997).

Academic Achievement

As one would expect, children with language problems perform poorly in those aspects of learning that rely on language. Literacy skills suffer because children with problems in language acquisition and use invariably have difficulties learning to read. Further, the abstract and symbolic material that becomes important by about grade four makes it increasingly difficult for children with language disorders to cope with academic subjects.

Speech disorders bring their own set of difficulties. For example, students with articulation disorders, particularly those with multiple sound errors, also have difficulties with comprehension, syntax, and vocabulary (Bernthal and Bankston, 1981).

Clefts are not associated with lower cognitive ability. But there are problems with language deficits, and children tend to show poorer self-perception and lower school achievement than peers (Speltz, Endriga, Fisher, and Mason, 1997).

Social and Emotional Development

Any degree of disturbance in our communication with others in the environment has an impact on social adjustment. Although the link between language deficits and the development of behavioural problems is not well understood, it is known that there is a fairly strong relationship between communication disorders, emotional disorders, and behavioural disorders in children and adolescents.

Children with articulation problems and those with language problems tend to show a high prevalence of behavioural problems (Baker and Cantwell, 1982). As well, Speltz and colleagues (1997) reported on studies that indicate that children with craniofacial anomalies were two to three times more likely than peers to have parent and teacher reports of behavioural problems at school entry.

In children with speech and language disorders, teachers may observe behaviours such as short attention span, excitability, tantrums, and solitary behaviour. Some children find it so difficult to communicate that they become frustrated, withdrawn, and depressed. They may withdraw from social contact and talk only when absolutely necessary because of the negative feedback they have received in the past. They use physical means to gain others' attention, by relying on gesture and body language—a shake of the head or a shrug.

Children who stutter are very aware of listeners' reactions and often feel embarrassed, guilty, frustrated, and angry. Students may respond to their difficulties by becoming more anxious, less self-confident, and more socially withdrawn than non-stutterers. Some become aggressive; others deny they have a problem. Be aware that the longer people stutter, the more likely they are to have associated emotional problems.

The reactions of others in the environment add to the frustration. A British study (Hugh-Jones and Smith, 1999) found suggestions that bullying and peer relationships are related to children's dysfluency. In this study, 83 percent of the sample reported being bullied in school.

In some students, more serious psychiatric problems emerge. As disorders of the development of language are likely to be central to the development of human personality, researchers observe that "There appears to be a strong association between developmental language deficits and severe psychiatric disorders" (Gualtieri, Koriath, Van Bourgondien, and Saleeby, 1983, p. 168). (See Chapter 7.)

Cultural and Linguistic Differences

Special education is designed to accommodate students who are different from the average in some or many areas of functioning. The students served have traits and characteristics that demand unique and individual programming. But with the increasing linguistic and cultural diversity in our schools, the special education system is serving more students who are in the process of acquiring a second language or who come from home backgrounds where a language other than English is spoken.

Certainly, some of these students have disabilities that require special intervention. But be aware that far too many minority-group children who have linguistic difficulties within the regular system are misconstrued as having problems that require special education intervention. Within special education, language minority children are treated as a further differentiation of those with language problems. Limited English proficient (LEP) students make up an increasingly high proportion of special classes (Willig and Greenberg, 1986). For example, in the United States, Asian American children are over-represented in special education speech programs (Grossman, 1995).

Note that when students do have speech or language problems as well as being LEP, similar difficulties will emerge in both languages. For example, a Spanish-speaking child with substitutions in speech will make similar mistakes in English.

ASSESSMENT OF SPEECH AND LANGUAGE PROBLEMS

We must identify delays and disorders in speech and language as early as possible because such disorders affect other areas of development, impact negatively on social integration, and hinder educational and personal achievement. Because language and speech are so intimately connected, assessment usually includes both areas. However, language is far more complex both in assessment and remediation. Robert Owens, Jr. (1991) describes the evaluation of language as "part science and part art" (p. 290). This statement reflects the multiple contexts in which communication assessment should be implemented, the variability in children's functioning, the vast range of areas to be assessed, and a relative shortage of appropriate tools. Moreover, the types of measures used, the domains sampled, and the targeted skills are quite different for children with mild delays and for those with severe disabilities of which language is only one component. Students with severe or multiple disabilities may be functioning at prelinguistic or minimally linguistic levels (see Chapter 14).

Assessing Language Problems

Language problems are generally assessed by a team comprising a psychologist, a speech clinician, a physician, an educator, and possibly a neurologist. All physical and psychological disturbances to normal language development, such as hearing loss or low IQ, must first be ruled out. After that, assessment involves both linguistic and cognitive skills, since both are necessary for language competence. A comprehensive assessment consists of a range of tools and procedures. A sampling is shown in the assessment tables in this book's appendix, Tools for Assessment.

Assessing Speech Disorders

Assessment of articulatory, voice, and fluency disorders is undertaken by a speech/language therapist/pathologist in the school or in a clinic setting. Articulation assessment is a rapid and effective way of obtaining a sample of a child's speech.

In its crudest form, the articulation test is a test of a child's ability to pronounce correctly, in the view of the investigator, a certain number of words. Children under age four are usually tested on their ability to echo or imitate the clinician's model. Children over four are usually asked to name either objects or pictures. Older children may be asked to read words or sentences or to describe objects. We can see some of the procedures in the case study about Ashley.

INTERVENTION WITH CHILDREN WHO HAVE SPEECH AND LANGUAGE DISORDERS

Language specialists and educators have developed many new forms of treatment for children with speech and language disorders, both for the classroom and for the clinic. Nevertheless, a guaranteed method to correct speech and language difficulties simply does not exist, and diversity in remediation programs characterizes the status quo.

A range of methods are used depending on the needs of the child, the severity of the dis-

Case Study

Ashley (continued)

Once the teacher referred Ashley, a number of professionals using different tools and procedures assessed him. These included medical personnel, a psychologist, and a speech/language therapist.

Most often, children with articulation and voice disorders do not differ from others in anatomical variables, auditory variables, intelligence, or personality. To rule out any hearing or physical problems, medical and audiological assessment was first undertaken. Results showed Ashley to have normal hearing and no deviations in his speech mechanisms.

When a psychologist assessed Ashley, his performance on standardized tests showed a child of average-level abilities whose competence exceeded his performance. The poor academic progress in the classroom did not correlate with his cognitive levels, so other factors were intervening.

It was the speech/language therapist who found the root of Ashley's problems. During a speech/language assessment the therapist used a number of measures, beginning with language functioning and use and moving to speech production. She began with the Peabody Picture Vocabulary Test (PPVT) to assess receptive language. On this test, Ashley scored at the 84th percentile. However, he performed poorly on informal tests of phonological processing and auditory tasks involving discrimination, sequence, and memory. This may account for at least some anomalies in articulation, as well as Ashley's failure to learn basic reading skills through a phonics approach.

When specifically assessing speech production, the clinician asked Ashley to name the objects in a series of pictures. Ashley correctly produced all the phonemes in the initial, medial, and final word positions up to approximately the developmental level of a four-year-old. He produced substitutions and distortions of certain sounds, such as /ts/, /s/, and /z/ in all positions.

The clinician also tried to determine whether there was a consistency in Ashley's error patterns. She found that he consistently mispronounced the sounds /s/, /th/, /l/ and blended sounds such as /tr/, /pr/, and /cl/. He could not correctly pronounce /th/ and usually substituted an /f/ sound. He also had problems with /r/ sounds and sometimes substituted /w/ for /l/. The clinician was not able to detect a clear /s/ in Ashley's conversational speech.

ability, the setting for intervention, the targeted skills, and the expertise of the teacher. Here we provide only an overview of approaches used with children with mild and moderate disabilities. We return to the topic of intervention for children with severe disorders in Chapter 14.

Medical Intervention

When speech disorders result from structural defects or inadequacies, medical intervention is often the first step in habilitation. Surgery is used for speech disabilities that result directly from defects of the respiratory, oral, and facial musculature involved in speech production. Corrective and plastic surgery can largely prevent the wide-ranging speech problems associated with cleft palate and other orofacial defects.

Clefts of the primary and secondary palates and velopharyngae (lip and palate) inefficiency require special examinations and treatments by a number of different professionals over many years. The lip is typically repaired early in the first year of life. The time for surgical repair of the cleft palate is more variable, but is most commonly performed before the child is two years of age (Moran and Pentz, 1995). When other facial–skeletal anomalies accompany the cleft palate, prostheses designed to facilitate speech are prescribed. Dental surgery may also be necessary.

Therapy

Speech/language pathologists or therapists are concerned with communication, its normal development, and its disorders. They are trained in the evaluation and remedial treatment of speech and language problems in children and adults. In most Canadian provinces, a qualified clinician requires a master's degree in speech pathology and a year of closely supervised clinical work.

Speech therapists/pathologists are employed in hospitals and rehabilitation centres and work as consultants to schools and special education programs. In educational settings, the speech/language pathologist works with teachers to identify potential communication disorders, assesses and diagnoses problems, and plans and recommends intervention activities. While remediation of speech problems specifically is the venue of speech therapists/pathologists, classroom teachers should work proactively with the therapist to reinforce elements the child attains in therapy sessions. At the same time, therapists consider speech and language intervention within the context of the classroom. They will stress the skills that teachers see as essential. These are using appropriate language in a variety of contexts; metacognitive skills; the ability to adjust language to a listener's needs; organizing a message cognitively prior to its verbal presentation; and speaking at a comfortable rate (Elksnin, 1997).

The therapist/pathologist works with individual children to teach them how to speak and listen effectively and how to overcome the effects of communication disorders. To treat articulation disorders, for example, therapists teach children to listen, recognize, and discriminate consonant sounds; to produce articulated speech sounds; and to retain the memory of speech sounds.

Major areas of emphasis in voice therapy include listening and articulatory adjustments and breath-control training. Breath control includes training to relax and reduce laryngeal tension as well as other specialized techniques (Van Osdol and Shane, 1982).

Although the many studies of the symptoms and treatment of stuttering have not revealed all of the possible underlying causes, many effective therapeutic methods have been developed to treat the problem. Psychotherapy, behaviour modification, and biofeedback are used to reduce the intensity of stuttering or eliminate it (Perkins, 1990). Some therapists combine a variety of techniques, including new therapies such as desensitization, parent–child verbal interaction, and fluency shaping. The Research Notes on stuttering in this chapter outline other major treatments.

Technical Aids

One successful use of computers in the classroom is to promote social interaction in children with language difficulties. Studies (e.g., McCormick, 1987; Villaruel, Martin, and Dickson, 1985) have found higher levels of social interaction and social play from delayed children, significantly more turn taking, and cognitively complex and imaginative verbalizations during computer activities.

Technology is a boon for individuals unable to use speech. Elaborate computer-driven devices enable children and adults who have language disorders to communicate more complex and subtle messages. These devices offer multiple outputs, such as print-out, screen, or speech synthesized voice. They are easily activated by a variety of volitional movements, including eye control, finger contact, or sipping and puffing on a blow stick. Further technical devices are described in the section on augmentative communication in Chapter 14.

Educational Intervention

Language is the primary medium through which much classroom learning takes place, and the acquisition of socially and academically appropriate forms of both oral and written language in general is seen as one of the principal goals of education (Reagan, 1997). As efficient speech and language underlie academic success, the goal of any language intervention effort is to enhance a child's ability to use language as an effective means of communication in everyday life and to develop academic skills.

A second goal is bolstering peer acceptance in school-aged children. Training is important because various communication skills have been found to predict social acceptance in middle childhood (Dodge, Pettit, McCloskey, and Boron, 1986). Finally, "Understanding and correcting deficiencies of language can improve behaviour and help a child resolve at least some of his emotional dilemmas" (Gualtieri et al., 1983, p. 169).

Service Delivery Models

The key word in recent language intervention trends is *natural.* Natural procedures take place in naturally occurring situations and pay attention to functional communication and conversational skills. As much as possible, settings should be natural environments and all those close to the child—parents, peers, and teacher—should be involved. This means that the general classroom is the most appropriate setting for children who have speech and language difficulties as their sole impairment.

Several reasons underlie the use of natural environments as the best settings for language assessment and training:

- Much language is learned in a social context. Language production is necessarily the result of an interaction between the skills of the speaker and events in the environment, and language is best taught through social interaction and naturally occurring events.
- The problems of generalizing skills are circumvented. A major problem in language training concerns the transfer of learned language from the training setting to the natural environment. The generalization of language skills appears to be more restricted in children with language disorders, and it is uncertain whether language learned in clinical settings will generalize to other environments (Spradlin and Siegel, 1982).
- Persons in the child's natural environment can be the chief intervenors. Teachers and peers facilitate strategies.
- Because training occurs in natural settings, it is bound to be functional, and this enhances the likelihood that new language will be maintained and generalized.

Educational Approaches

All educational approaches attempt to improve a child's linguistic competence. Although some approaches are designed for special classes or clinics, contemporary intervention, as we have just seen, focuses on natural interaction in natural settings—that is, intervention from the teacher and perhaps a therapist in the general classroom. Ashley's intervention, as described in the case study, is illustrative.

The goal of language intervention efforts for Ashley, as for any child with similar problems, is to enhance his ability to use language as an effective means of communication in everyday life. The goal of training is not absolutely correct grammar or pronunciation. Rather, training should accelerate general communicative development and help Ashley communicate in a way that is understood by others and that seems comfortable for him. There are three main prongs to Ashley's program: individual speech therapy to learn new speech sounds and improve language, much practice in the broader context of academic and social communication, and remediation in academic areas.

Many theoretical explanations of how to teach language have emerged. However, the procedures used in language intervention vary extensively and research has not indicated

Case Study

Ashley (continued)

The speech clinician, Ashley's teacher, the psychologist, and his parent met to discuss a program for Ashley. Ashley's mother explained that he was the baby of the family, the youngest of four children. His parents both work outside the home and are away all day.

The speech therapist explained that phonological speech problems such as Ashley's are developmental rather than physiological and respond well to remedial instruction. She felt that Ashley's problems were caused by a combination of immaturity, lack of opportunity to practise speaking, and self-consciousness. Ashley does not have enough chances to talk at home, and his self-consciousness at school further deprives him of necessary practice. She also noted that Ashley knows he does not speak clearly. He told her that he tries hard, but was bashful about speaking because the children at school made fun of him.

The team agreed that Ashley does not need an Individual Education Plan at this time. The teacher will implement strategies to help him catch up in the language arts, such as placing stress on a sight word vocabulary that will circumvent the articulation problems.

Far more important right now is individual speech training both to improve articulation and to add to self-esteem. The team arranged an hour of speech therapy for Ashley every second day at school. The therapist will teach Ashley how to correctly produce the misarticulated sounds and give him a great deal of speaking practice. As he attains new sounds, the teacher will promote correct use and reinforce use in the classroom. She will also ensure that Ashley has many opportunities to use oral language and will use incidental teaching strategies to improve both his speech and his language. The team hopes that as Ashley gains confidence and improves in oral skills, there will be a positive spillover to areas such as written language.

which strategy for teaching communication is the most effective. In the broadest terms, approaches may be grouped as *grammatical* or *naturalistic*.

Grammatical Approaches

Syntax-based programs may be taught in regular classrooms or special settings. Programs based on syntax teach the child specific language structures, such as subject, verb, and object, and word-order relationships, such as question forms. Syntactic disorders seem to respond best to direct teaching: direct language instruction might be initially used to introduce a new structure that can then be generalized through the use of more interactive techniques.

In these models, specific language skills are identified and then activities are designed so students can use the skills. For example, a child may consistently use "I seen," instead of "I saw." The teacher models, the child imitates the construction, the teacher gives feedback, and then assists the child to use the phrase in other contexts.

Studies have shown that such structured language programs are effective with children who are linguistically delayed. A number of commercial tests and programs support syntax-based programs. For example, the Language Assessment, Remediation and Screening Procedures (LARSP) (Crystal, Fletcher, and Garman, 1976) provide a systematic methodology for the description and treatment of syntactical problems. The Fokes Sentence Builder (1976) is another example of a syntax-based remedial language program.

Naturalistic Approaches

Designed for regular classrooms, performance-oriented approaches attempt to modify, decrease, or increase language behaviours. Since much language is learned through social interaction, imitation, modelling, and expansion of correct communication behaviours are stressed.

Interpersonal–interactive approaches, also used in regular classrooms, are similar to performance approaches. They aim to strengthen a child's ability to use language and to develop communicative competence. Children learn what language is by learning what language can do. Specific objectives include helping the child to interpret contextual clues, strengthening role-taking and role-playing abilities, and increasing the range of verbal and non-verbal communication styles.

incidental

Much of the teaching in these naturalistic approaches is **incidental**: it comes up in normal classroom interactions, rather than in direct instruction. With younger children, teachers use a group of closely interrelated strategies for oral language. Examples are found in Table 4-3.

Curriculum

Apart from the above models (and similar alternatives), no special curriculum exists for children with speech and language disorders. Generally, language teaching for delayed children should be based on normal language acquisition processes. Teachers provide the motivation to communicate, many opportunities for teacher–child and child–child interactions, and much peer and adult modelling. They create realistic conversational atmospheres, focus on children's interests, and help them to use language to promote or regulate social interaction and to develop skills that refine listening, attention, and memory. They also stress the language arts curriculum of listening, expressive language, and reading.

Table 4-3 Examples of strategies to use in a natural approach to language intervention

Strategy	Description	Example
Imitation	Modelling	The teacher may say "Show me," or "You say this now."
Expansion	A restatement of what the child has just said, with the addition of information	The child may say "Car go," and the teacher expands it to, "Yes, the car goes." Or if the child says, "Camera takes pictures," the teacher can expand to, "Yes, he has a camera to take pictures, like your grandma does."
Extension	Similar to expansions; follows the child's statement with different words	The child says "Cat in the Hat," and the adult responds, "Yes, that Cat in the Hat is making a big mess." Or if a child says, "I miss the bus," the teacher may respond with, "You missed the bus. Were you late for the dentist?"
Paraphrasing	Repeat a statement or question to elicit a reply	Responding, for example, to "Want ball," with "You want the ball."
Recast	Repeat or restate a child's words in the correct form	If a child says sentences like, "That boy hitted me," the teacher responds with "That boy hit you."
Open-ended questions	Genuine requests for information requiring more than a "yes" or "no" response	Examples include, "Why could the man be angry?" "Where is my book?" "Why did the man go to the store?" "Where is he going next?" "Who did the cat scratch? Why?" "What is he going to bring when he plays baseball?" "How many clowns rode on the bicycle?"
Indirect	Using third-person commands	For example, "Tell Tommy what you want."
Praise	A statement describing the child's prior verbal or non-verbal communication as correct, acceptable, or good	"I like how you did that." "That's right!"

Sources: McNeill and Fowler, 1996; Winzer, 1997.

Historical Notes

For centuries, parents, scholars, and teachers have been fascinated by the way children acquire and use language. Virtually all the major philosophers since Plato and Aristotle have considered the problems of the origin and role of human language. Debates centred on the role of language in the progressive differentiation of humans from other creatures and the way in which reason, if an original endowment of humans, manifested itself in language.

Eighteenth-century empiricists were particularly intrigued by language development in humans. (See the profile on Victor earlier in this chapter.) In the 19th century, the study of speech and language was known as *philology*; most of the research was in the form of diary studies. These soon gave way to an examination of children's vocabulary, which is perhaps the most traditional approach to the study of language acquisition. In the early 20th century, the study of language development emphasized language form. In general, language forms were identified and classified into categories related to sentence types, parts of speech, and so on (Owens, 1996). By the 1930s and 1940s, data collection was more formalized. Then, when psycholinguistics emerged as a discrete discipline in the early 1950s, language became a favourite research area. Today, the study of how children learn language is like many other academic pursuits in that different theories that attempt to explain the phenomenon compete for acceptance.

Every theory advanced to explain language development has been criticized. The question is fiercely debated and there are champions of every conceivable position. Occasionally one theory predominates, but generally portions of each are used to explain different aspects. Part of the problem in designing an overall theory is the complexity of both language and communication behaviours (Owens, 1996).

Behaviourists consider language a subset of other learned behaviours and stress reinforcement in language acquisition. But even a rich learning environment cannot explain how children learn so much language so quickly and correctly. A social learning view of language extends the behavioural position to include the processes of imitation. Children are believed to learn to speak one language rather than another, and to speak it with particular vocabularies and idioms, because they imitate and are reinforced for imitating the language spoken in their homes and neighbourhoods.

Because children of all cultures learn language at about the same age and tend to learn it in similar ways, others question whether humans are born with a natural innate tendency to acquire language. Piaget believed that language acquisition is a direct result of cognitive development, that language is the handmaiden of thought. To Piaget, children cannot develop language skills until at least the last stage of sensorimotor development, because it is not until then that a child's mental apparatus allows him or her to represent symbolically an object that is no longer present.

Noam Chomsky (1965), also holding a cognitive-biological position, believes that a sense of grammar is innate, or native, to the human brain. Chomsky postulates an innate language acquisition device unique to and present in all humans that enables us to learn language simply by being exposed to it.

Enormously complex and comprehensive research into the nature and acquisition of language continues apace. The more that is discovered about language and language impairments, the greater the number of questions that emerge. Studies throughout the 1980s included all the traditional topics: phonology, morphology, syntax, pragmatics, and semantics. Stress was placed on the acquisition of pragmatics—an individual's ability to use language appropriately in social situations.

Recently, the functional definition of language

has been expanded in important ways. First is the realization that formal language is only one of several forms of communicative behaviour. Second, communicative behaviour is seen as any behaviour that conveys a social message from one person to another. Spoken language, sign language, the use of communication boards, gestures, and actions (reaching, directed eye movements, use of objects) are considered diverse but legitimate modes of language.

SUMMARY

1. As a component of communication, language is a typically human activity. Language is a complex system of symbols and the rules for using these symbols. It is the product of all aspects of development—physical, sensory, social, and neurological. Speech is essentially a mechanical production of language.

   Human language is incredibly complex, bound by structured rules and characteristic patterns of usage that change in different settings—intrapersonal, interpersonal, group, and societal. Communication includes written language and speech as well as a variety of non-speech forms, such as sign language, and many non-verbal forms, such as gestures and body language.
2. Speech and language disabilities interfere with the ease with which a child interacts with the world. Speech disorders are problems in the articulation of language sounds, voice production, and fluency. Language disorders are problems in the acquisition, comprehension, and formulation of language. Youngsters with language disorders may have the rudiments of a language code but show large gaps in linguistic development and display little consistency in their various deficits.
3. Language development is neither random nor capricious. There are developmental milestones, all reached in infancy or early childhood. A linguistic environment, an intact cognitive/perceptual system, and normal social interaction all underlie the development of language. If the child does not hear language, has some impairment of the cognitive/perceptual mechanism, or has a troubled family background, then the child's development of language will reflect these problems.
4. Compared to language during the preschool years, language during the school years is complex and sophisticated. Children have a firm linguistic base, with a grasp of semantic and syntactic rules and an ever-expanding vocabulary.
5. Speech development depends on having something to say (language) and the opportunity to say it (social interaction). It also depends on the development of the speech mechanisms and articulators—the pharynx and larynx, the tongue, the palate, the lips and the teeth, and the production and modulation of breath flow.
6. Speech and language disorders are manifested in a staggering array of distinct forms. Many remain ambiguous in terms of etiology, prevalence, developmental consequences, and intervention.
7. Communication disorders can have painful consequences for all aspects of a child's development. Disorders of speech and language socially isolate those who have them, impoverish their lives, and impact on school success. When children with communication

disorders are considered as a group, it becomes evident that they have an increased prevalence of learning problems and psychiatric disorders.

8. Language develops in the framework of family associations, social interactions, and interpersonal relationships. This belief underlies the use of natural environments (regular classrooms) for almost all children with speech and language differences. To promote communication, skilled teachers use descriptive feedback, directing, telling and explaining, question asking, modelling, and prompt and coaching statements. When necessary, they use teacher-mediated and peer-mediated strategies and direct teaching.

WEBLINKS

Aphasia Hope Foundation **www.aphasiahope.org/**

Canadian Association for People who Stutter **webcon.net/~caps**

Canadian Association of Speech-Language Pathologists and Audiologists **www.caslpa.ca/**

The Canadian Hyperlexia Association **home.ican.net/~cha/**

People with clefts **www.widesmiles.org**

Speak Easy Inc. **www.speakeasycanada.com/**

Chapter 5

Children with Learning Disabilities

Learning Outcomes

After reading this chapter, you should be able to:

- Understand the common elements found in most definitions of learning disabilities;
- Understand the developmental consequences of learning disabilities;
- Understand the diversity of causes and symptoms of learning disabilities;
- Recognize the relationship between learning disabilities and other mild forms of disability;
- Understand the many forms of intervention used with students with learning disabilities.

Introduction

Perhaps more than any other field of exceptionality, learning disabilities have generated controversy, confusion, misconceptions, and polarization among concerned professionals. While some categories in special education can be easily identified by a common trait, such as hearing loss, visual impairment, or speech dysfunction, learning disabilities do not concern a single, easily identifiable disability, and children with learning disabilities do not form a unified homogeneous group. On the contrary. *Learning disabilities* is a syndrome, a group of related and overlapping conditions that includes vastly different populations who reveal a wide variety of behavioural, learning, social, and interpersonal problems.

Although individuals who are learning disabled differ in many critical ways, they do share some common problems. First of all, they show a marked discrepancy between their potential and their performance. These students have average or above-average intelligence but they seem unable to learn through regular channels and cannot reach their full potential when taught through traditional instructional methods. Second, students with learning disabilities show academic lags, often compounded by hyperactivity, inconsistent performances, memory and attention problems, and perceptual deficits.

Many students with learning disabilities appear bright and receptive in all sorts of ways, but they still fail in school. They earn report cards larded with comments such as "Could try harder," or "Should apply herself," or "He is not working up to his potential." But many of these young people *are* applying themselves, and the more they try and fail, the more unhappy and frustrated they become. They are eventually caught up in a cycle of frustration and failure that threatens their entire educational career and engenders lack of motivation, social problems, increasingly less acceptable classroom behaviours, and dropping out, or even being subtly pushed out, of a school system that cannot accommodate their unique needs.

In the past, children with learning disabilities have been described as hyperactive, distractible, inattentive, brain damaged, slow learning, dyslexic, perceptually disabled, aggressive, and emotionally labile. More unsavoury terms have included *dull, lazy, inept,* and *disturbed.* Because of difficulties in identification, youngsters with learning disabilities were often shunted into classes for children either mentally retarded or emotionally disturbed. Others were placed in non-stimulating settings where their problems and progress were improperly evaluated.

Students with learning disabilities are neither emotionally disturbed nor intellectually disabled. They stand in good company with similarly affected historical figures. Thomas Edison's teacher, for example, described him as "addled." Auguste Rodin's father complained that he had "an idiot for a son." Woodrow Wilson had severe problems with reading and writing (Thompson, 1971). Albert Einstein did not speak until age three; he found school so difficult that one teacher predicted that "nothing good" would come of him (Patten, 1973). Nelson Rockefeller, who became vice-president of the United States, encountered great difficulties with reading. Rockefeller later wrote that he "just struggled to understand words that seemed to garble before my eyes, numbers that came out backward, sentences that were hard to grasp" (Rockefeller, 1976). Suspected of having dyslexia, a specific reading disability, are figures such as Hans Andersen, Winston Churchill, George Patton, Leonardo di Vinci, Galileo, Cher, and Tom Cruise (West, 1991; Spafford and Grosser, 1996).

DEFINITIONS OF LEARNING DISABILITIES

As you can see in the accompanying case study about Danny, learning disabilities is a puzzling condition—one of the least understood and the most difficult to deal with. This results from various factors including the field's evolution, its accelerated growth, its interdisciplinary nature, and the varied and contradictory manifestations of learning disabilities themselves.

Although the term *learning disabilities* did not emerge until the early 1960s, practitioners and professionals were well aware of these children by the beginning of the 20th century. The genesis and development of the field is outlined in the Historical Notes feature at the end of this chapter.

From the outset, the most challenging issue in the field of learning disabilities has been the search for an appropriate definition. Yet even after a century of research and discussion, a universally acceptable definition remains elusive. Lack of a clear definition in turn creates confusion when we talk about prevalence, etiology, strategies for intervention, placement, and the design and use of tools and tests for assessment.

Many reasons contribute to the difficulties facing practitioners and professionals at-

Case Study

Danny

School is really hard for eight-year-old Danny. He tries and tries but just can't seem to learn as easily and quickly as his classmates. When he was younger, Danny loved going to school and was always eager and excited. Now he approaches each day with apprehension.

In the classroom, Danny is very passive, rarely responding to questions or participating at all. He attempts seat work but is often distractible and off-task. When he is, he more and more often bothers other children and engages in minor misdemeanours.

In academic work, specifically reading, spelling, and arithmetic, Danny shows serious lags. He is far behind in math and has not yet really mastered rational counting skills, basic place value, or any number facts. He is further ahead in reading, and has quite a broad range of sight word knowledge. However, he needs much work in phonics and phonological awareness. His weaknesses here hinder his reading and make his spelling very much a hit or miss procedure. His printing is poor, as are attempts at creative writing. Here he has problems in generating ideas, in understanding cause and effect relationships, and in using sequential thought processes that are compounded by the poor printing and spelling. Danny's social skill deficits are becoming more prominent; for example, he exhibits discomfort when given a compliment and has poor eye contact.

Early in his school career the teachers suspected that Danny had learning problems, but it was not until the end of his grade two year that he was formally referred and then administered a battery of psycho-educational measures. On the WISC-III, Danny scored a little above the normal range (Full Scale score 112). Other test results are shown on Danny's IEP, presented later in this chapter.

With the assessment results in hand, the school principal called a team meeting that included the classroom teacher, the special education teacher, the psychologist, and Danny's mother. At the team meeting, the psychologist spoke with some certainty about Danny's problems. She described him as a rather typical child with a learning disability. "Danny," she said, "is fairly typical of children with learning disabilities, who often enter into a cycle of frustration and failure." She went on to explain that their production deficiencies, the self-helplessness syndrome, and the inactive characteristics of these children all interact to produce learners who are passive, who are incapacitated with feelings of self-defeat, and who have a fear of learning. Ineffective coping skills include not asking questions, resisting making choices, being poor risk takers, failing to use effective study skills, and failing to use self-monitoring strategies.

The suggestions generated to assist Danny and an extract from his IEP are shown later in this chapter.

tempting to identify and define a child's learning disabilities. Chief among these are the following:

- Learning disabilities are ill defined in the minds of many educators, psychologists, and parents, and the implications of the condition are neither fully understood nor adequately conceptualized. Even today, some people think that there is no such thing as a learning disability. Others use the term to label every learning problem. When this happens, so many behaviours are included as a learning disability that the term is often applied to students who could more accurately be described as slow learners, as children who misbehave in class, or as those who are absent often or who move from school to school.

- One of the most confusing aspects of learning disabilities is the extremely heterogeneous nature of the identified population. Rather than existing as a single condition, learning disabilities is a syndrome of behaviours, although the components of the syndrome itself are varied and confused.
- The disparate characteristics of the learning-disabled population further muddy clarity between categories of exceptionality. Often, these children are confused with those with mild mental retardation, behavioural disorders, or with Attention Deficit Hyperactivity Disorder. The overlap among categories of mild disabilities is shown in Chapter 1.
- Learning disabilities cannot be simply measured by a numerical designation, such as an IQ score or a decibel loss.
- Learning disabilities is often referred to as a socially constructed category. At the outset, it applied to children from middle class backgrounds with no discernible mental or physical anomalies who were nevertheless failing in school (see this chapter's Historical Notes). Recently, there has been much movement among the categories of mild disability, and "Learning disabilities classes appear to be shifting from protective areas for white, middle-class, failing children to remedial classes for students previously classified as retarded or slow" (Sleeter, 1986, p. 46; see also Chapter 6).
- The movement among categories is partly prompted by the greater social desirability of the term *learning disability* as compared to *slow learner* or *intellectually disabled.* As *learning disabilities* generally reflects the notion of an impairment that is specific rather than global in nature, it is therefore less stigmatizing to the image of the child as a whole person (Harry, 1992).
- Learning disabilities are considered the proper and legitimate concern of many disciplines and professions, including education, psychology, neuropsychology, speech and language pathology, neurology, psychiatry, ophthalmology, optometry, and occupational therapy. The professional groups that are most influential have changed over the years, as pointed out in the Historical Notes.

With such confusion about definitions, perhaps no other area of special education has expended so much effort to define itself and its population. Many definitions of learning disabilities have emerged, and all have their advocates and their opponents. (For a full discussion of definitions and their genesis see Hallahan, Kauffman, and Lloyd, 1999, pp. 7–15). Most modern definitions echo Kirk's original model, quoted in the Historical Notes.

Among the current crop, the one proposed by the National Joint Committee on Learning Disabilities (NJCLD) seems to have become the consensus definition. According to the NJCLD,

> Learning disabilities is a general term that refers to a homogeneous group of disorders manifested by significant difficulties in the acquisition and use of listening, speaking, reading, writing, reasoning, or mathematical abilities. These disorders are intrinsic to the individual, presumed to be due to central nervous system dysfunction, and may occur across the life span. Problems in self-regulatory behavior, social perception, and social interaction may exist with learning disabilities but do not by themselves constitute a learning disability. Although learning disabilities may occur concomitantly with other handicapping conditions (for example, sensory impairment, mental retardation, severe emotional disturbance) or with extrinsic influences

(such as cultural differences, insufficient or inappropriate instruction), they are not the result of these conditions or influences. (National Joint Committee on Learning Disabilities, 1988)

This definition stresses that learning disabilities is a syndrome of behaviours that manifests differently in different individuals. The disabilities are intrinsic to the individual, affect learning and behaviour, and are directly related to problems in school learning. Social, emotional, and motor difficulties may accompany the learning disability but do not constitute disabilities by themselves.

Even though the NJCLD definition has much credibility, it is not universally accepted and there is continuing debate on the matter. It therefore makes sense to examine common elements that are found in most definitions of learning disabilities.

Neurological Dysfunction

Much of the theoretical understanding of learning disabilities grew out of work with children described as "brain damaged." In the 1930s and 1940s, Alfred Strauss argued that children with brain injuries are subject to major disorders in perception, thinking, and behaviour that reduce their ability to read, write, spell, and calculate.

Many theorists still attribute learning disabilities to some type of brain impairment or central nervous system (cns) dysfunction. This pathological emphasis is particularly evident among medical professionals; in educational circles, the tendency over the years has been to de-emphasize pathological aspects of the problems and stress behavioural ones.

Many educators today would like to see the concept of presumed neurological impairment dropped entirely. They prefer to focus on each child's particular perceptual, cognitive, learning, and motor problems and skills so that appropriate educational programming can be developed.

Uneven Growth Pattern

Students with learning disabilities are presumed to have irregular or uneven development of the various domains of development. While some of the components mature quickly, others lag behind. Uneven development manifests as peaks and valleys in a student's performance. Some children, for example, are average verbally but far behind in motor and hand skills. While with their age group in the use of oral language, these children may find it hard to hold a pencil or crayon, make shapes, or learn to print.

Difficulty in Academic Tasks

Academic problems are perhaps the clearest indication of a learning disability. A child may encounter difficulties with a wide range of learning tasks. Specific problems may occur in the acquisition of speech and oral language, in reading, in written language, in handwriting, in spelling, or in arithmetic. Depending on the definition, thinking, motor skills, perceptual skills, and psychosocial skills could be added.

Discrepancy between Potential and Performance

The idea of a discrepancy initially arose in order to separate learning disabilities from mental retardation. Today, students with learning disabilities are most often described as those who manifest educationally significant discrepancies. In the United States, about 98 percent of states use a discrepancy notion in their definitions (Gresham, 1997).

There are two main ways of looking at a discrepancy. It can be seen as a discrepancy between age or grade level expectations, such as reading two levels below grade placement. Or it can be seen in terms of differences among achievement areas such as reading comprehension versus listening comprehension.

The most common discrepancy measure is the former—between a child's tested potential for academic tasks and the child's performance in academic and social domains (between what a child is capable of learning and what the child actually achieves). Potential is judged by the mental age obtained on standardized tests of mental ability, which is then compared to performance on achievement tests. A difference of two years between the estimated potential and the performance is frequently used as an indicator of academic retardation.

In theory, the discrepancy conception allows educators to distinguish children who are learning disabled from those who fail because of low intelligence, behavioural disorders, or other disabling conditions. This does not always follow; see the Research Notes in Chapter 1 on the overlap among categories.

Exclusion of Other Causes

Most definitions of learning disabilities exclude children whose exceptionality is primarily the result of other causes. Children who are learning disabled are not intellectually disabled, behaviourally disordered, visually or hearing impaired, or socially or economically disadvantaged. This is not to say that children with other disabilities cannot also be learning disabled. However, by excluding other disabilities, the field of learning disabilities gains clarity regarding its special population of learners.

Often, the exclusionary clauses simply add more confusion. This happens when we simply define learning disabilities by another type of exclusion: if you don't have any other problems, then you must be learning disabled. As we pointed out when discussing definitional problems, today learning disabilities is somewhat a residual category that includes many students who would have been classified differently in the past. For example, the learning disabilities category has come to include language-minority children who are not necessarily disabled at all (see Jacobs, 1991).

Average or Above-Average Intelligence

Inherent in the whole concept of learning disabilities, and closely associated with the exclusionary clause, is the notion that the child who is learning disabled is of average or above-average intelligence.

Social Deficits

Some definitions define learning disabilities strictly in terms of intellect and achievement; others include emotional and social complications that may adversely affect school learning and achievement. Whether to include social deficits in definitions remains controversial. Arguments for the inclusion rest on data that show that social interactions are often difficult for children with learning disabilities, and that social skill deficits are common.

PREVALENCE OF LEARNING DISABILITIES

Estimates of the prevalence of students who are learning disabled are so high (but vary to such a great degree) that it seems that the school system has fallen in love with the notion. Since 1963 the number of students identified and categorized as learning disabled has been astronomical. Between 1976–77 and 1992–93, the number of students in the United States served as learning disabled increased by 198 percent (Gresham, 1997). In Canada, too, students with learning disabilities make up the largest single group of children with disabilities.

Figures depend upon the definition and the procedures used, so definitional problems and inconsistent identification procedures render exact proportions impossible. By definition, though, students who are learning disabled are atypical, so numbers could not be in very high ranges. Generally, the best Canadian estimates place the number of students with disabilities serious enough to hamper their educational progress at from 2 to 4 percent of the school-age population.

Boys far outnumber girls with learning disabilities, with a ratio of at least four to one. The reasons for this are complex and somewhat unclear. It may happen because boys tend to indulge in more overt acting out behaviour, and are therefore more likely to be referred for in-depth diagnosis. More important are the problems that boys more often have in language and reading, as we discuss later in the section on etiology.

CLASSIFICATION OF LEARNING DISABILITIES

Efforts to classify specific subtypes of learning disabilities can be traced back almost as far as the concept itself. But even after years of intense research, a consensus has not been reached about how to define or classify learning disabilities. These children and youth do not fit into any of the traditional categories of disabling conditions. Moreover, learning disabilities is not a unitary concept; it represents a group of students displaying disparate characteristics who fail to learn appropriately for diverse reasons. The problems take a different course in each individual. In some students, the effects are global; in others, they impinge on specific areas of functioning. Certain displayed behaviours may be more apparent in individuals with mild and moderate disabilities, while others are manifested in students with severe problems.

Classification systems have also changed quite dramatically. As we observe in this chapter's Historical Notes, the roots of the field of learning disabilities are embedded in the areas of neurology, ophthalmology, and other medical specialties. When the disabilities were attributed to various types of brain damage, terminology generally reflected a medical orientation. Common terms included *minimal brain dysfunction, brain crippled, cerebral disordered, neurologically impaired, dyslexic,* and *dysphasic.*

Although the terminology drawn from neurology is less popular today, some terms are still in general use and warrant explanation. In the following, the prefix *a-* means an absence of and *dys-* means a disturbance of.

- *Agnosia* is a lack of knowledge, an inability to recognize the significance of sensory stimuli.
- *Dysgraphia* means a disturbance in the ability to express thoughts in writing.
- *Dyscalculia* is a disturbance in the ability to use and remember numbers and do arithmetic.
- Of all these terms, *dyslexia* is the one that has become part of the common language. Dyslexia is an old term, first introduced by a German ophthalmologist, R. Berlin, and later

> referred to as *word blindness*. Currently, precise definitions vary, but generally "dyslexia refers to a severe difficulty in learning to read" (Mercer, 1987, p. 374) or to "an inability to read normally as a result of damage to the brain" (Myers and Hammill, 1990, p. 63).

Prevalence rates for dyslexia as a reading disorder range from 5 to 10 percent of the entire population, although rates as high as 20 to 30 percent are also reported (Pennington, 1990). DSM-IV (APA, 1994) estimates the rate among school-aged children at 4 percent, with 60 to 80 percent of these male.

Dyslexia and *learning disabilities* are not synonymous terms. Many children with reading problems are not categorically identified as learning disabled. And, while up to 80 percent of children who are learning disabled have reading difficulties, learning disabilities is best viewed as a syndrome of a number of behaviours.

Although the general public still clings to the term, North American educators have long wished to dispense with the term *dyslexia* in favour of *reading disability*. As early as 1969, the National Advisory Committee on Dyslexia and Related Reading Disorders in the United States set out to examine its terminology. The next year, the Committee stated: "In view of ... divergencies of opinion, the Committee believes that the use of the term dyslexia serves no useful purpose" (p. 38).

In contemporary special education, terms drawn from neurology are not employed often. But we still classify and categorize learning disabilities in many ways, with some support for each classification scheme. In Canada, the severity classifications of *mild, moderate*, and *serious* learning disabilities are widely employed. Severity classifications are founded on the belief that learning disabilities are less a question of kind than degree and consequences and can occur on a continuum from severely learning disabled to subtle differences in attention and performance (Little, 1980).

Learning disabilities are also classified as general or specific. With *general* learning disabilities, a student's academic progress is lagging behind that of normal peers in most areas. *Specific* learning disabilities may imply that the student has difficulties in particular areas but performs adequately in others. The term is also used to refer to students who have very serious and deep-seated disabilities.

ETIOLOGY OF LEARNING DISABILITIES

Experts do not agree on the causes of learning disabilities any more than they agree on definitions. Complex and varied etiologies have been proposed. Some say that learning disabilities result primarily from physiological factors. Others stress that the school tasks we expect students to accomplish contribute to learning disabilities by making demands on their maturity levels or learning styles that they are unable to meet. Still others blame environmental factors such as inadequate nutrition, inappropriate diet, or allergies. Moreover, various suspected causes interact in subtle ways, rendering etiology even more difficult to determine. In most cases, the cause of a child's learning disability remains unknown.

Minimal Brain Dysfunction

Following the lead of Alfred Strauss and other pioneer neurologists, a presumption of some type of brain injury is still found in many of today's definitions of learning disabilities. It is described as neurological dysfunction, or sometimes minimal brain dysfunction.

Some researchers believe that minimal brain dysfunction is the root cause of all learning disabilities. They suggest that slight damage to the brain hinders its most efficient functioning and point to disruption of neural cell development during early fetal development.

Although the findings from neurological studies are not yet conclusive, a small but increasing amount of data does point to some neurological abnormalities as a cause of learning disabilities (Hynd and Semrud-Clikeman, 1989). But an easily identified pattern of neurological disturbance has not been found.

Biochemical Disturbances

Some researchers hold that children with learning disabilities suffer from physiological problems or biochemical disturbances. Commonly mentioned sources are diet or environment-related allergies that adversely affect learning.

Food allergies were theoretically linked to hyperactivity by Benjamin Feingold (1975, 1976), who noted that artificial flavours, artificial preservatives, and artificial dyes were consumed in increasing quantities by North American children. Feingold argued that approximately 50 percent of hyperactive children can be helped by eliminating from their diet artificial food colourings and dyes and foods such as apples, oranges, tomatoes, and strawberries that contain certain natural salicylates, Aspirin-like compounds found in some fruits and vegetables.

Genetic Factors

Genetic factors are extremely prominent in research directed specifically toward dyslexia. Researchers know that reading disabilities tend to run in families, especially among male members. Their questions: "What is the rate of familial dyslexia?" and "Are familial reading problems due to hereditary factors or to similar learning environments?"

Ongoing research into rates clearly identifies the familial nature of some reading problems. One investigator (Scarborough, 1989, 1990) found that a family history of dyslexia accounted for 30 to 36 percent of the variance in reading. Another large-scale study (Decker and Defries, 1980, 1981), which compared the families of 125 children with reading disorders to a control group of average readers, found common reading problems in the families of the poor readers, especially among the male members, which led the investigators to argue that learning problems were familial in nature. Studies of twins generally show that when one twin has a reading disability, the other twin is also likely to have a reading disability if the twins are monozygotic rather than dizygotic.

Genetic researchers theorize that dyslexia is linked to a glitch in the brain's wiring that interferes with the ability to translate a written word into units of sound (*phonemes*) (Wingert and Kantrowitz, 1997). The problem seems to be inherited and the influence of the genes operates at several levels. But a child is not born reading disabled in the same way that a child is born redheaded or female. Writing, spelling, and reading problems per se are not biological features that can be inherited; nor are they amenable to medical treatment. Yet, if present, they may stem from some underlying cognitive or neurological defect based on genetic transmission.

So far, research shows linkages between chromosome 6 and phonemic awareness and phonological decoding skills ("Reading difficulties ...," 1997). It also appears that a genetic abnormality is found on chromosome 15, although the mechanism of transmission is still in question, as is the strength of the genetic influence (Smith and Pennington, 1987; Wenar, 1994). The B2 microglobulin gene, which is thought to influence the immune system and male sexual development, is also found on chromosome 15, which may help explain the high prevalence of males among the reading-disabled population (Smith and Pennington, 1987).

Maturational Lags

maturational lag

A **maturational lag** means that a child is slow to reach some developmental milestones. Such a developmental lag does not necessarily imply a structural deficiency or limited potential. Some children may simply be progressing at a slower rate in language, motor, cognitive, or socio-emotional development. Most of these children overcome their behaviour and learning problems as they grow older, although some may continue to lag behind their age-mates. For example, developmentally young children who appeared to be reading disabled at grade three but responded by grade five developed into low to average readers by grade eight (Badian, 1988).

It may be that the effects of schooling on children with developmental lags itself creates the appearance of mild disabilities. Schools assign children to a grade level based on their age, assuming that children of the same age possess the same levels of ability. This is simply not true; children reach their developmental milestones at different times, and to expect all children to be ready to learn the same things on the same schedule is clearly not reasonable. When children are behind the expected schedule, they will manifest characteristics of a child with learning disabilities, such as behaviour, reading, and attention-span problems. These developmentally young children are penalized if they are drawn in by procedures intended to find potential problems and then labelled as learning disabled.

Environmental Factors

Children do not "catch" a disability when they enter school. In most cases they bring with them unspecified cognitive, behavioural, linguistic, and affective characteristics that have developed over time, which interact with the academic and social ecology of the classroom (Cooper and Speece, 1990). Nevertheless, when there is a mismatch between children's learning styles and readiness and classroom expectations, some children may indeed catch learning disabilities when they enter school.

Lloyd (1975), who describes this phenomenon as *dyspedagogia* (maleducation), suggests that children in this category do not have learning problems, but their schools do. Coles (1978) went so far as to assert that learning disabilities are a way to blame a group of students for the failure of the schools. In the same vein, Englemann (1977) argued that "Perhaps 90 percent or more of the children who are labelled 'learning disabled' exhibit a disability not because of anything wrong with their perception, synapses or memory, but because they have been seriously mistaught. Learning disabilities are made, not born" (pp. 46–47).

Proponents of the maleducation point of view believe that if teachers were better prepared to handle the special learning problems of children in the early school years, many learning disabilities could be avoided. They point to inappropriate teaching settings, narrow bands of acceptable behaviour, inflexible grouping practices, narrow curricula, and the fact that most reading difficulties stem from factors such as poor instruction, lack of reading readiness, and/or cultural differences ("Reading difficulties...," 1997).

Dyspedagogia implies more than poor teaching and a mismatch between instruction and a child's needs. It also includes poor curricula, poor health in the child, and poor attendance at school. Poor parental and professional attitudes may also function to weaken a child's motivation and hinder learning.

DEVELOPMENTAL CONSEQUENCES OF LEARNING DISABILITIES

Individuals who are learning disabled simply do not seem to learn in the same way as everyone else does—they sometimes do complicated things very well and then amaze and puzzle us with their lack of competence in areas that seem elementary. Sometimes these youngsters seem to remember incongruous items—they know all the words of TV jingles but forget simple spelling words from one day to the next. Their performance is inconsistent; they show great variability in areas of functioning and large differences between skill areas. Often, the energy levels of these students frustrates teachers; they may spend more time out of their seats than in them and have a higher rate of motor activity than other class members.

Learning disabilities represent a constellation of widely varied behaviours and conditions. Some common characteristics are shown in Table 5-1. This list certainly does not cover all of

Table 5-1 Some common characteristics seen in children who are learning disabled

Attitudes and behaviour

- Intelligent but fails at school.
- May be reluctant to try anything new, be frightened by change.
- Lacks flexibility and is upset when routine is different or the schedule changed.
- Has difficulty in changing from one task to another.
- Says "I don't care" or "I won't" and really means "I can't"; would rather be called bad than dumb.
- Impulsive—says what first comes to mind; calls out in class.
- Forgets assignments and homework as well as books, coats, and pencils.

Language

- Hears the dog barking, a truck honking, the scratching of pencils, the sound of the air conditioner, and footsteps outside, but barely hears mother calling and does not hear what the teacher says.
- Forgets names of people, places, things, own address and telephone number, but does remember the ads on television.
- May be an expert strategist in checkers or chess but cannot understand a riddle or joke.
- Many hesitations and repetitions in oral language; blurred pronunciations in speech.
- Poor verbal expression; language is jumbled and shows poor usage of syntax and semantics. Stops and starts in the middle of a sentence or idea, talks about hospitals, animals, and enemies all at once. Has trouble in relating a story or incident.
- Difficulty in concept formation. Calls breakfast lunch and is confused by yesterday, today, and tomorrow.
- Asks the same thing over and over; asks constant questions but does not seem interested in the answers.

Academic performance

- Rushes headlong into work; is the first one finished, and did all the problems wrong.
- May read *on* for *no*, write *41* for *14*, *p* for *d*, or *q* for *b*, and cannot remember the sequence of letters that make up a word.
- May be able to add and multiply but not subtract or divide; or can do math mentally but cannot write it down.
- Skips words, omits them, or adds them when reading aloud.
- Frequently confuses directions, both oral and written.
- Needs instructions explained for each assignment.
- Can't plan studies and assignments.
- Sloppy and disorganized book work.
- Has difficulty beginning or completing tasks.
- Doesn't complete lengthy assignments.

Coordination

- May hug the cat too tightly but can't hold a pencil; may get frostbite in the snow and not feel the hot water until it burns.
- May be a good swimmer but stumbles up the stairs.
- Does not look before walking, bumps into the door, swings lunch boxes into the nearest legs, and trips easily.
- Has trouble lining up, cannot help bothering the child ahead in the line.

Social

- Relates poorly to peers; may be socially inept and always on the fringe of a group.
- Poor self-esteem and self-concept.
- Lacks judgment.
- Does not seem to understand the affective status of others derived from facial expressions, body movements, and tone of voice.
- Cannot keep a friend and prefers to play with younger children.

the behaviours that have been attributed to students with learning disabilities, and it should be regarded with extreme caution. No child with learning disabilities will display all the behaviours, while the disparate characteristics of the population means that additional behaviours may exist in some children. Most importantly, one attribute or behaviour does not a learning disability make; we probably all have at least one or two of the listed behaviours.

Cognitive Development

Cognitive delays are associated with intellectual disabilities. A learning disability is not a cognitive delay. By definition, students with learning disabilities possess average or above-average intelligence. Also by definition, students with learning disabilities do not acquire academic skills at grade expectancy and at a normal rate, and will lag in some or all academic areas. They show a marked discrepancy between potential and performance.

Thinking requires the ability to conceptualize and solve problems. Because children who are learning disabled are of normal intelligence, they are clearly able to think. Yet significant numbers of these students exhibit memory and thinking disorders; they have problems remembering information over long or short periods of time and demonstrate memory deficits for both auditory and visual stimuli (Torgensen, 1988). They have trouble recalling what things sounded like or looked like and forget math facts, spelling words learned only the day before, and directions. These children forget basic personal information, such as their telephone numbers and their addresses. Students are more likely than their non-disabled peers to forget to take their homework home, to forget to bring completed homework to school, to lose homework, not to complete homework, and to make careless mistakes in homework (Hallahan, Kauffman, and Lloyd, 1999).

Many researchers consider the development of memory to be synonymous with the development of memory strategies (Howe and O'Sullivan, 1990), which include strategies for learning and for problem solving. Self-regulated learners are flexible problem solvers who plan, select, correct, and monitor effective strategies for learning, anticipate problems, and reflect on tasks when they are finished. When students monitor and orchestrate their own learning strategies, the processes form part of a cognitive procedure referred to as **metacognition**, the awareness of basic learning strategies and one's own awareness of how one learns.

metacognition

In most cases, students with learning disabilities do not have deficits in the actual ability to learn. They seem to have performance deficits rather than ability deficits; that is, they are weak in the development of learning and problem solving strategies and have deficiencies in metacognitive skills. Their learning strategies—or lack of them—prevent them from using their basic abilities to the best advantage.

Students who organize information poorly tend to be impulsive when solving problems, miss a logical train of thought, and fail to consider appropriate alternatives before embarking on a course of action. Their responses to problem situations indicate an inability to direct and monitor their learning and behaviour and to generalize and apply what they have learned in other situations.

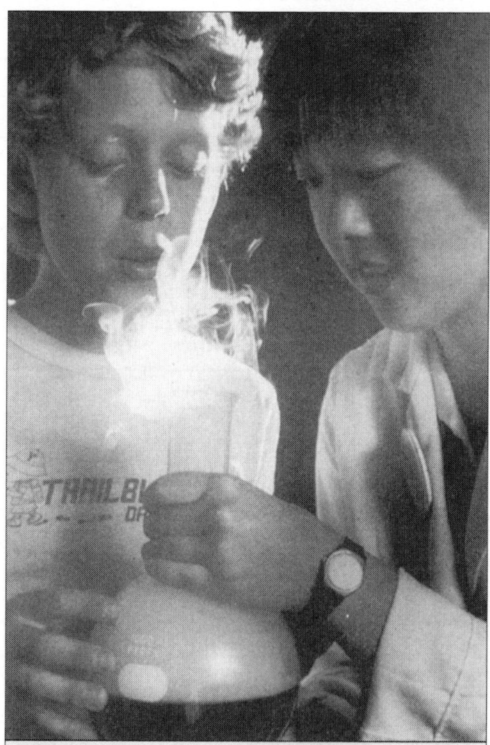

By definition, students with learning disabilities possess average or above average intelligence.

Communication

Language disabilities are closely connected with learning disabilities of all types. So apparent is the connection that some researchers use the term *language learning disabilities* to refer to students with language disorders that adversely affect academic performance. In the classroom, these may be the students who sit at the back and hope that the teacher won't call on them. They rarely volunteer answers and when they are asked to speak they may be hesitant, stumble over words, and use a sparse vocabulary.

Between 65 and 80 percent of school-aged students with learning disabilities have their base deficits in language and reading (Lyon, 1994). They tend to reach a plateau of language abilities in the areas of semantics, syntax, memory, and pragmatics at levels expected of children between eight and ten years old (Wesanko, 1990).

All the elements of language overlap and must develop in tandem if students are to be communicatively competent, so deficits in one area affect the others. In language, students with learning disabilities may show deficits in:

- *Listening.* The teaching–learning process proceeds on the assumption that participants listen to each other. When instructing, teachers use an initiation-reply-evaluate mode. They ask questions, listen, and then evaluate whether or not children have mastered the task through the reply.

  Listening (and therefore responding accurately) is a problematic area for children with learning disabilities. When listening, they tend to misperceive phonemes requiring very fine discrimination such as /m/ and /n/. They also confuse voiced and unvoiced consonants, such as /f/ and /v/ (Wiig and Semel, 1976).
- *Expressive language.* Although they have problems with both expressive and receptive language, students with learning disabilities seem to have greater difficulty using expressive language (Hessler and Kitchen, 1980), particularly semantics and pragmatics. Children with language disabilities may continue to overextend words into inappropriate contexts. For instance, a child may call all liquids that can be poured into a glass "juice," as opposed to milk, water, or soda. Or the child may learn to call all articles of clothing that have sleeves "sleeves," rather than shirts, sweaters, or coats, because something about the sleeve is meaningful to him or her.

  Also often apparent are difficulties with articulation, immature speech patterns, mild speech irregularities, general unintelligibility, and cluttered speech. Students may substitute inappropriate words, repeat the same phrase over and over, or use a monotonous voice.
- *Semantics.* The vocabulary used by these students tends to be small, superficial, and reflective of reductions in the development of underlying concepts. Normally developing children of eight or nine years of age recognize the multiple meanings of frequently used words; adolescents who are learning disabled may not perceive multiple meanings and misinterpret when they read or listen. They often take things very literally, missing the subtle nuances of the language. For example, one adolescent went to a Laundromat for the first time with a small load of washing. On a towel, he read the instruction, "Wash colours separately." He proceeded to do exactly that, using a separate washing machine for each shade of colour. He spent nine dollars and infuriated the other patrons. Another student was handed a tape by a frazzled teacher and asked to "Put it on the video." The boy set it neatly on top of the machine.

  Some children cannot remember the meanings of new words, whether the words are identified by the teacher as necessary for general vocabulary acquisition or discovered by the students when attempting to read English literature, social studies, science, and so on.

Research indicates that 43 percent of students with learning disabilities have word finding problems (Wesanko, 1990). Because of limited vocabulary or the inability to absorb the full significance of words, students with learning disabilities tend to be seriously affected in the areas of generalization, conceptualization, and abstraction.

- *Syntax.* Students with learning disabilities may have problems organizing phrases and words into sentences and are more likely to make syntactical and grammatical errors. They may talk about things out of order, produce rambling and repetitive utterances, and make unrelated statements.
- *Pragmatics.* Pragmatic problems in the social use of language are seen in students who fail to communicate intent, show an inability in turn taking in conversation, and fail to cue their listeners to the topic of discussion. Students with learning disabilities also seem to miss subtle clues in non-verbal communication. One study (Dimitrovsky, Spector, Levy-Shiff, and Vakil, 1998), which investigated students diagnosed as learning disabled in grades three to six, found the children less accurate than a non-disabled group in identifying facial expressions of emotion. No differences related to gender among the students with learning disabilities were found.

Academic Achievement

Academic underachievement is the hallmark of the learning disabled population. Some children show deficits in all subject areas; for others, only a few specific academic skills may be affected. Reading, writing, and mathematics are the three major areas of concern.

Students with learning disabilities appear to reach a plateau at about a fourth- or fifth-grade achievement level (matching their achievement in language). This level is at the point at which basic skill instruction generally ceases and students move on to apply their skills to reading comprehension, math applications, expository writing, and greater use of textbooks in science and social studies. The gap between achievement scores and grade expectancy level widens as students with learning disabilities progress through high school. Even when placed in secondary school resource programs, students do not seem to recoup basic skills. Despite intensive instruction, many adolescents with learning disabilities do not master the higher-level skills involved in reading and written expression (see Chapter 16).

Reading

Among all children, reading problems are the major cause of poor school performance. Reading difficulties affect 15 to 20 percent or more children and adolescents (see Hallahan, Kauffman, and Lloyd, 1999). As well, one in every five children will experience reading difficulty sufficient to make learning and enjoyment of reading a major effort ("Reading Summit...," 1999).

Reading problems translate into poor prospects for later learning. Research suggests that the first-grade readers with the greatest reading difficulties are unlikely to catch up and 90 percent will remain poor readers later in their schooling (Torgesen, 1998). Children behind in reading in kindergarten and first grade are likely to be behind in second and third grade (Juel, 1988). And, if reading is still poor at the end of the third grade, then the prognosis for subsequent rapid gains is bleak (Badian, 1988).

Children not only meet difficulties in the actual reading process, but also they lose motivation and interest. By the middle of elementary school, reading is so aversive to poor readers that they would rather clean their rooms than read (Juel, 1988).

Most children identified for special education are experiencing significant difficulties in learning to read (Bos and Vaughn, 1998), so it is hardly surprising that reading disorders rank high on the list of academic problems of students who are learning disabled. Figures range between 65 and 80 percent.

With reading so problematic for students with learning disabilities, the "History of learning disabilities is full of attempts to identify factors that are key in reading problems" (Hallahan, Kauffman, and Lloyd, 1999, p. 332). Not surprisingly, there is more known about reading disabilities than there is about all the other aspects of learning disabilities put together.

Research findings indicate that students with hard-core reading difficulties manifest a variety of problems. The major difficulties are:

- *Phonological awareness.* Canadian researchers (e.g., Simner, 1997) have demonstrated a strong relationship between early literacy and phonological awareness or phonological processing. **Phonological awareness** is the ability to blend, segment, rhyme, or in other ways manipulate the sounds of spoken words. The better a young child is at segmenting words into their individual sounds, the better the child is likely to read and the faster the reading process. It follows that phonemic awareness weaknesses may underlie children's reading and spelling delays. Too, phonological awareness is almost certainly related to problems in other areas, such as written expression (Lyon, 1995).

phonological awareness

- *Sound–symbol association.* Many young children with learning disabilities have difficulty in understanding the sounds of the letters (Hatcher, Hanline, and Ellis, 1994). Poor readers also have weak sound blending skills (Adams, 1990).
- *Word-attack skills.* Word-attack skills in these students are often deficient; they may be unable to deal with symbols, unable to synthesize parts of a word into a whole, or unable to organize words into meaningful clusters.
- *Miscues.* When reading, students often miss or confuse important details, such as *and* or *but,* resulting in confused interpretation of meanings. Morphology may be critical; some students do not understand morphological variations and meanings.
- *Fluency.* Oral reading may be stilted and full of substitutions, omissions, and additions.
- *Comprehension.* Comprehension is the main purpose of reading. It is a problem in all grades, but at the secondary level the primary reading disability of students who are learning disabled is in the area of reading comprehension. Obviously, comprehension is not possible unless a reader can translate the printed words into the language they represent (*decode*). As comprehension is profoundly influenced by decoding skills, reading is seriously inhibited in the student with decoding problems.
- *Context clues.* Competent readers learn to use multiple sources of information— letters, phonemes, rhymes, past learning, pictures, and context. Individuals with learning disabilities seem to miss context clues and lack sensitivity to various patterns of textual organization and to the relative importance of major and minor ideas (Vallecorsa and Garriss, 1990).

Written Expression

Many students with learning disabilities show marked impairments in all forms of written expression. They cannot meet the multiple challenges of writing that include graphics, syntactic skills, semantics, textual creating sentences, and paragraphing.

Spelling for students who are learning disabled has been described as a "seemingly impossible task" (Leuenberger and Morris, 1990), and their spelling achievement usually lags far behind their grade placement. Poor spelling correlates with reading difficulties; good readers can be deplorable spellers but poor readers are always certain to be bad spellers.

Students with a writing disability tend to write little or laboriously, using incorrect grammar, syntax, and punctuation. They show confused or truncated sentences, with an incorrect sequence of tenses, pronoun reference, and word order. Figure 5-1 shows the written work of an eleven-year-old student with many constraints in his written expression and handwriting.

Good writers devote up to two-thirds of their writing time to planning, focusing on large issues such as the audience and how the final product holds together. They appreciate

story grammar

story grammar—the description of the typical elements frequently found in stories such as theme, characters, and setting.

During the writing process, students with learning disabilities do not have a plan that they consistently refine; instead, they have a less sophisticated approach to composing, one that minimizes the role of planning and operates largely without metacognitive control (De La Paz and Graham, 1997). When composing, they typically convert writing into question-and-

Figure 5-1
Work of an 11-year-old with difficulties in written expression

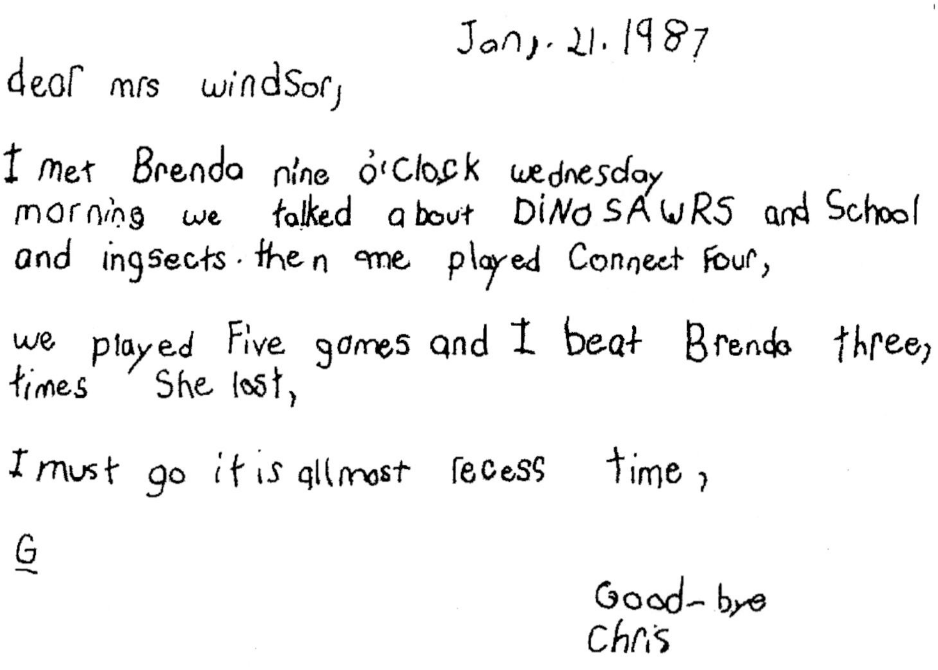

Jan. 21. 1987

dear mrs windsor,

I met Brenda nine o'Clock wednesday morning we talked about DINOSAWRS and School and ingsects. then me played Connect Four,

we played Five games and I beat Brenda three, times She lost,

I must go it is allmost recess time,

G

Good-bye
Chris

answer tasks, quickly telling whatever comes to mind and producing papers with poorly developed ideas (Sexton, Harris, and Graham, 1988).

Writing is characterized by shorter and lower-quality stories than those written by normal students. While students with learning disabilities may have a basic understanding of story structure, their stories often lack organization and coherence and contain relatively few story elements overall (see Montague and Graves, 1993). They generally include basic story elements such as setting, plot, and resolution, but they frequently omit the critical elements of good stories such as the internal responses or plans of the characters (Leavitt and Ioannides, 1993).

Many problems in written expression result from a lack of understanding of linguistic rules. Some students with learning disabilities may be unable to classify and categorize information into coherent sentences; others are unable to produce sentences displaying correct syntactic and grammatical order. One study (Linn, Algozzine, Mann, and Schwartz, 1987) that used standardized competency tests found that adolescents with learning disabilities in general performed poorly, specifically on communication items requiring identification of an irrelevant statement in a selection, use of apostrophes, and use of /s/ to show possessives.

Students with a handwriting disability tend to write laboriously and as little as possible (see Simner and Eidlitz, 2000). They may produce clearly deviant writing, with scrawling letter formations, reversals, transformations, uneven slant, and inability to keep to the lines on the paper. Uncoordinated motor movements and difficulty in judging the writing space are the most common causes of handwriting problems (Gerard and Junkula, 1980).

It follows that areas such as note taking, so important in secondary-level programs, suffer. Students are often unable to identify important information, write fast enough to keep up, or make sense of the notes later. Rather than a record of pertinent information, the notes are often scribbles, single words, and drawings that have little relation to the content covered (Weishaar and Boyle, 1997).

Mathematics

The prevalence of arithmetic disabilities is estimated to be at least 6 percent of the general population (see Miller, Butler, and Lee, 1998). It is higher among students with learning disabilities: about 25 percent have math problems.

Students with learning disabilities experience much greater difficulty in most aspects of math performance than their non-disabled peers. The research points out that:

- Math is typically characterized by high failure;
- Basic skills such as counting, writing numerals, and basic addition and subtraction are deficient;
- Students with learning disabilities progress approximately one year for every two years in school;
- Adolescents with learning disabilities make an average of one year's growth in grades seven through twelve;
- Twelfth-graders with learning disabilities perform at a high fifth-grade level (Carpenter, 1985; Miller, Butler, and Lee, 1998; O'Melia and Rosenberg, 1994).

Perceptual Development

Perceptual and processing difficulties in the auditory and visual modes, together with problems in coordination and motor skills, are part of the traditional conception of learning disabilities. Also included are haptic disorders, which concern the information transmitted through touch, body movement, and position.

perception

Perception involves the use of the senses to recognize, discriminate, and interpret stimuli. Students unable to process perceptions accurately are said to have *perceptual disorders*, sometimes referred to as *psychological processing deficits.* Visual perception problems are most commonly associated with learning disabilities. Many early studies (e.g., Calfee, 1977) indicated that visual perception problems are common and that, as a group, children with learning disabilities perform poorly on tasks designed to assess visual perceptual abilities.

Visual perceptual problems lead to difficulties with oculamotor coordination, with spatial relations, with figure–ground perception, with the discrimination of differences, and with the recognition of likenesses. Children find it difficult to differentiate symbols, and may reverse letters and shapes in their printing and drawing. They have problems in identifying the letters of the alphabet, reading the printed page from left to right, drawing basic shapes, and staying on the line when printing or writing.

Other studies (e.g., Harber, 1980) showed that auditory disorders occur with greater than normal frequency among children who are learning disabled. This problem is often recognized when children attempt to spell words. Their poor spelling results from their inability to discriminate sounds, to blend sounds, and to *encode* (spell) or *decode* (read) words. The child with an auditory dysfunction may have difficulty synthesizing sounds into words, analyzing words into word parts, and associating sounds with symbols.

Motor Development and Coordination

Haptic problems, which encompass touch, body movement, and position in space, are thought to be relatively uncommon. Haptic problems may be important in handwriting, because tactile information dictates the grasp of the pen or pencil. As well, researchers suggest a relationship between visual motor and haptic abilities, and body image and laterality.

laterality
directionality

Laterality refers to an internal knowledge of the differences between left and right; **directionality** is an awareness of left and right in the environment outside the body. Out of an infinite number of motor experiments, children learn the differences between an activity on the right side of the body and the same activity on the left. The pattern thus becomes a skill, and the skill becomes a habit. At approximately five or six years of age, most children establish complete cerebral dominance and consistently prefer to use one side of their bodies in dealing with the world. Laterality is the motor basis for spatial concepts. When children have developed laterality, they can project this to directionality concepts in external space such as up and down, and in front and behind.

The laterality theory maintains that learning is adversely affected if the child does not establish a tendency to perform most functions with one side of the body. The failure to establish laterality, directionality, and dominance may account for many reversals and similar confusions in children's reading and writing. When mixed dominance is encountered with other signs, such as enuresis (bed wetting), preference for play with younger children, or infantile speech patterns, it may suggest a maturational lag or developmental immaturity that can interfere with a child's abilities to function in academic work.

In the past, many left-handed children were considered to be at high risk for learning disabilities. While it is true that among the learning-disabled population (and indeed among nearly all populations of problem learners) there is a far higher proportion of left-handers than in the general population, the hand dominance in itself does not seem to be the problem. The difficulties arise with incomplete or mixed dominance, which translates into confusion in directionality or right and left discrimination.

body image

Body image refers to a person's awareness of the body, its capabilities, the interrelationship of body parts, and the relationship of bodies to the environment. Children with body-image problems may not be able to organize themselves within their environment. They may be clumsy; slow in dressing and undressing and have difficulty in putting on a sweater; unable to walk across the classroom without knocking into chairs and desks; and unable to draw figures.

General uncoordination refers to a lack of muscular control. Motorically disordered children may walk with an awkward gait, are uncoordinated in physical activities, and have difficulties in running, skipping, or throwing and catching a ball. Overflow movements, which occur when the child wants to perform a movement with one hand and the other hand involuntarily follows in a shadow movement, may be present.

Social and Emotional Development

Research since the early 1970s has documented the social difficulties encountered by many students with learning disabilities. It suggests that social interaction and social acceptance re-

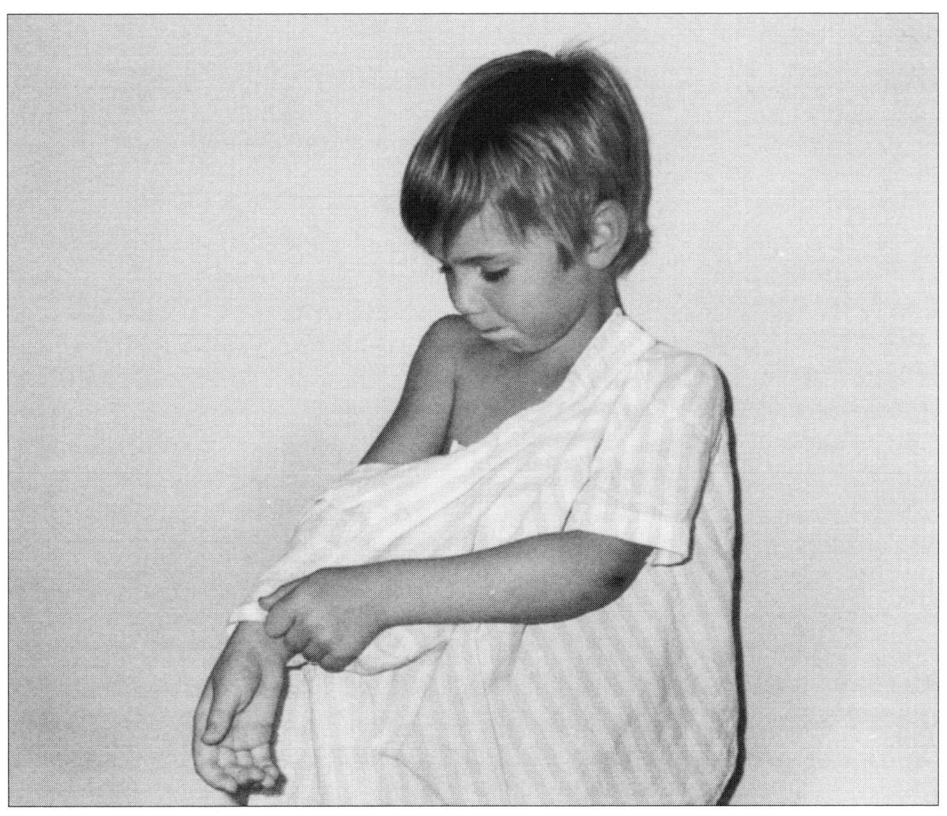

Children with body image problems often have difficulty with tasks such as dressing.

mains deficient in comparison with other children. This seems to be true regardless of whether the judgment of a child's social competence is based on teacher perceptions, parent perceptions, peer perceptions, or the actual behaviour of the child observed in social interaction (Coleman and Minnett, 1992).

Students who are learning disabled in inclusive settings interact with teachers and students at much lower rates than do their non-disabled peers (McIntosh, Vaughn, Schumm, Haager, and Lee, 1994). One study (see Weiner, Harris, and Shirer, 1990) found that approximately 50 percent of a sample of 90 children with learning disabilities in suburban schools had peer relationship problems, with about 35 percent being neglected and 15 percent rejected. Especially problematic for these children are being called names and being laughed at by other students when performing poorly at a game (Conte, Andrews, Loomer, and Hutton, 1995).

The reasons why individuals with learning disabilities inspire negative responses are not clear. Studies have chiefly examined communication, including non-verbal communication, and social perception skills.

It is suggested that inadequate skills in social perception, specifically in skills employing empathy, role taking, and making social inferences, contribute to the difficulties (Holder and Kirkpatrick, 1991). These children perform less well on role taking in interpersonal tasks that require taking an alternative viewpoint (Horowitz, 1981). They tend to ignore interpersonal signals from their peers and have trouble perceiving the moods of others.

Communication difficulties may make satisfying interactions less likely and communication breakdowns more frequent (Poikkurs, Ahoren, Nahri, Lytimen, and Rusku-Puttonen, 1999). An inability to interpret facial expressions is probably central to the problem (Holder and Kirkpatrick, 1991). Students with learning disabilities are less accurate than non-disabled children in interpreting the non-verbal behaviour of others.

It has also been suggested that students with learning disabilities possess the necessary social skills but lack the motivation and cognition to apply them when necessary (Perlmutter, 1986). Or it may be that students with learning disabilities differ along temperamental dimensions and these influence social interactions with teachers. Differences may then influence teachers' management and instructional strategies.

self-concept

With all of this, it seems little wonder that students often develop secondary emotional problems. **Self-concept** is a person's description of him or herself in relation to roles, attributes, or characteristics. Compared to their peers, students who are learning disabled tend to hold lower self-concepts about academic performance, even in areas in which they have had little experience or instruction. They tend not to attribute their learning to their own ability, and develop an external locus of control. When this happens, students view themselves as controlled by outer rather than inner forces. They hold lower expectations for success, credit any successes to luck or the ease of the task rather than their own abilities or efforts, and view failure as further verification of their own persistent lack of ability. Such pessimistic appraisals lead to less optimism about improving their performance in the future, even when they receive special education services, and to reduced levels of effort and negative affect.

Students who retain an outward locus of control may revert to learned helplessness, an important individual difference that appears to affect children's performance in a variety of settings (Fencham, Hokada, and Sanders, 1989). Children who display learned helplessness have no faith that their efforts will result in desired outcomes. Because they expect to fail, they lose their motivation.

emotional overlay

Children with learning disabilities may also develop an **emotional overlay,** an adverse reaction to learning problems and academic failure. In many cases it is extremely difficult to determine whether the learning or the adjustment problem came first, and the exact interaction of these in a child's functioning.

Co-occurring Disabilities

Between 24 and 52 percent of children with learning disabilities are reported to have significant social, emotional, and behavioural problems (Rock, Fessler, and Church, 1997). The two most common co-occurring disabilities are Attention Deficit Hyperactivity Disorder (ADHD) and emotional disturbance/behavioural disorders.

Children show many externalizing behavioural disorders such as aggression, antisocial behaviour, and conduct problems (Richards, Symons, Greene, and Szuskiewicz, 1995). Anxiety and depression are often seen in these students (Kavale and Forness, 1997).

Compared to normally developing students, those with learning disabilities show more problem behaviours, behave in a less appropriate fashion in both regular and special classes, and often display maladaptive styles of responses during instructional activities, possibly as a result of their poor cognitive performance (Bender and Smith, 1990). They are less task oriented. One study found a learning-disabled sample to be on task only 57 percent of the time, as compared to 70 percent for the non-disabled sample (McKinney, McLure, and Feagans, 1982). Others (Roberts, Pratt, and Leach, 1991) reported that a group of students with mild disabilities were off task twice as often as were non-disabled students.

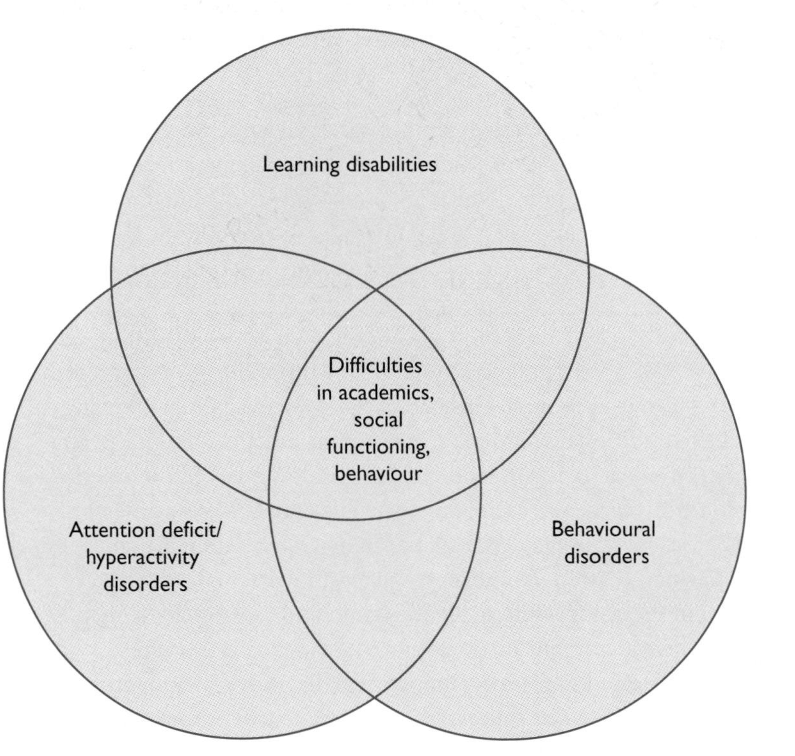

Figure 5-2
Interplay of characteristics

Such attention problems are endemic among youngsters with exceptional conditions, and those with learning disabilities are no exception. There is evidence of considerable overlap between the diagnostic categories of learning disabilities and Attention Deficit Disorder (ADD). Estimates of attention problems and hyperactivity in children identified as learning disabled are broad—from 9 to 80 percent (McKinney, Montague, and Hocutt 1993; Shaywitz and Shaywitz, 1987).

The interplay of learning disabilities and co-occurring conditions is shown in Figure 5-2. As you can see, when off-task behaviour, lowered motivation, and externalizing behaviour come together, they raise further barriers to successful learning. They limit a child's ability to profit from instruction and to have effective interactions with peers and teachers.

Cultural and Linguistic Differences

As we have already cautioned, too often cultural and linguistic differences are mistaken for disabilities in the areas of language, behaviour, social skills, and because of poor exposure to literacy or poor testing. The misrepresentation is observable in the field of learning disabilities where the number of linguistic minority students placed in learning disabilities programs is growing disproportionately (Jacobs, 1991). Limited English proficiency (LEP) is often identified as a learning disability because the characteristics of second-language learners, especially in the early stages of second-language acquisition, are similar to behaviours associated with certain categories of exceptionality, specifically learning disabilities and communication disorders (Winzer and Mazurek, 1998).

ASSESSMENT OF LEARNING DISABILITIES

While there is little agreement on definition, prevalence, or remedial procedures in the field of learning disabilities, there is almost universal agreement on the need for the efficient diagnosis of this population's members. Before setting up remedial programs and deciding on the most appropriate educational placement, it is incumbent on educators to conduct a thorough evaluation of a student in order to pinpoint the kind and degree of specific disabilities present as well as the strengths and weaknesses in each developmental domain.

The identification and assessment of children with possible learning disabilities is anything but easy. Assessment practices are fraught with problems. An acceptable assessment framework is lacking, appropriate instruments are not available, and many of the assumptions that have traditionally underlain assessment practices are under attack. Often, the process suffers from lack of coordination. Many professionals within and outside the school system become involved, and each of these people may hold very different views regarding the nature of learning disabilities. A pediatrician may stress minimal brain dysfunction, a psychiatrist behavioural disorders, and a psychologist intellectual inadequacy.

Even within the school system, identification and assessment is often a rather hit and miss process. There is currently no single procedure to identify learning disabilities. Clinicians use a variety of tests and rely heavily on personal diagnostic judgment. As well, there is little consensus regarding when children should be tested, by whom, and to what purpose.

Children with learning disabilities may show deficits and lags in specific developmental tasks in several or all of the following functions: sensorimotor abilities, language, perception, thought processes, emotions, and social behaviour. A comprehensive and detailed examination of a child's physical and psychological make-up depends upon a battery of psychological and educational tests. Measures are supplemented by observations of the child, a physical examination, an evaluation of hearing and vision, interviews with the child and the parents, and information gathered from other sources. School records and the comments of earlier teachers are potent sources of data.

Generally, identification involves two processes: *screening* and *psycho-educational diagnosis.* The multiple sources of data are shown in the appendix table, Tools for Assessment.

By definition, a learning disability involves a discrepancy between a student's potential and his or her performance. Therefore, one of the first steps in the formal diagnosis is an assessment of intellectual potential to rule out the possibility of mental retardation and simultaneously to establish the fact of normal mental ability. Broad-coverage tests such as the Wechsler Intelligence Scale for Children-III (WISC-III) are usually given first. Although the Wechsler scales have proven both valid and reliable in the assessment of children with learning disabilities, IQ testing is beset with problems. It may, for example, underestimate the scores of children with learning disabilities, and it is difficult with young children not old enough to meet the definitional discrepancy criteria.

Once intelligence is judged to be normal, clinicians use more specific measures in a range of areas: auditory, visual, and motor processing; achievement, most particularly in language arts and mathematics; diagnostic tests to pinpoint specific areas of weakness; and perhaps tests of vocational skills and adaptive behaviour.

Achievement tests, though second in overall importance to intelligence tests, are used because of the IQ/achievement discrepancy measure. Achievement tests examine a spectrum of tasks such as oral reading, reading comprehension, language, spelling, math, and general knowledge. Performance on these measures is often presented as grade equivalents or percentile ranks.

As language problems assume greater importance in learning disabilities, there is a concomitant emphasis on assessing language competencies. Teachers use observations, language samples, and standardized tools. (See Chapter 4.)

Psychological Processing

psychological processing

Psychological processing (more often called *learning styles* today) refers to how an individual processes sensory information and puts it to meaningful intellectual use. Theories about learning disabilities have long taken into account the possibility of processing deficiencies; indeed, this has been a major position in the field for the past forty years.

The use of tests to diagnose underlying processing deficits was introduced at the same time that learning disabilities developed as a category of exceptionality. These measures have generated much concern and controversy. Opponents argue that because psychological processes are not directly observable and must be inferred from a child's performance, it is almost impossible to accurately assess underlying psychological processes. Nevertheless, a wide variety of measures that purport to assess such areas as auditory and visual processing, motor subskills, and kinesthetic functions are available.

Although processing is not considered as fundamental to learning disabilities as previously thought, and although the tests and special instruction based on their results are used far less frequently than in the past, we cannot totally discount these factors. Table 5-2 shows the auditory and visual subskills upon which many of these tools focus.

Table 5-2 Examples of visual and auditory processes

Process	Ability	Implications and problems
Visual perception	The ability to make visual stimuli meaningful	The child may have problems attending to and interpreting visual stimuli.
Visual discrimination	The ability to perceive dominant features in different objects or symbols	The child may confuse letters and words that look alike.
		The child may not see the internal detail, as in rid/red, or may fail to see the general configuration, as in ship/snip.
Visual closure	The ability to identify a common object from an incomplete visual presentation	The child may have difficulty assembling puzzles and objects, identifying missing parts, or completing words by closing spaces between letters, as in rab-bit.
Visual figure–ground	The ability to focus on the foreground and ignore the background visual stimuli	The child may not be able to distinguish words; for example, the child may be unable to point to the first word of the second paragraph.
Visual memory	The ability to recall the dominant features of the stimulus item	The child may not be able to copy patterns or arrange blocks in a series.
Visual sequential memory	The ability to recollect the sequence of a number of items presented visually	The child fails to recognize visually familiar words and forgets the arrangement of letters in a word.
Auditory perception	The ability to recognize and interpret stimuli that are heard	The child may have problems attending to and interpreting auditory stimuli.
Auditory discrimination	The ability to recognize differences between sounds and to identify similarities and differences between words	The child may not hear the similarities in initial or final sounds in words or be able to discriminate short vowels such as pin, pan, pen.
Auditory closure	The ability to identify sounds and words from an incomplete auditory presentation	The child may have problems in sound–symbol association and especially in blending sounds.
Auditory figure–ground	The ability to focus on the foreground sound and ignore other sounds	The child may not focus on the dominant sound; the fan on the overhead projector may be more important than the teacher's voice.
Auditory memory	The ability to recognize and recall previously presented auditory stimuli	The child may have problems retaining and recalling auditory experiences.
Auditory sequential memory	The ability to reproduce from memory sequences presented auditorily	The child may forget or confuse oral directions, the sequence of events, the sequence of letters in a word, and the sequence of words in a sentence.

INTERVENTION WITH CHILDREN WHO HAVE LEARNING DISABILITIES

Since a learning disability can be highly deleterious to a child's academic and social functioning, as well as future success in life, treatment becomes a critical issue. A wide variety of intervention approaches have been employed. Some approaches are controversial; others contradictory. For example, some early studies supported training for visual perceptual functions (e.g., Brod and Hamilton, 1973), but other research suggested that such training is not in the least helpful (e.g., Camp, 1973).

It is the disparate characteristics of students who are learning disabled that confounds intervention. Given the extremely heterogeneous nature of the population, no single approach, method, or technique can be expected to offer a solution to every problem.

Medical Intervention

Historically, medicine and learning disabilities have been closely linked, particularly in the area of diagnosis. Until quite recently, learning disabilities were conceptualized in relation to biophysical disorders —specifically some form of minimal brain dysfunction. Today, the field has moved away from a medical model to a diagnostic and educational model for remediation. However, the medical profession continues its active interest in learning disabilities. The current foci of medical interest are drug therapy and diet management.

Psychopharmacological Management

Drugs were first used in the treatment of hyperactive children in 1937. In the last few decades, synthetic compounds have rendered the effects of drugs more predictable, and today psychopharmacological treatment for children diagnosed as hyperactive and/or with attention deficits is the most frequently used method of management.

A comprehensive discussion of drug therapy for children identified variously as learning disabled, behaviourally disordered, and Attention Deficit Hyperactivity Disordered is found in Chapter 7.

Diets

One theoretical source of biochemical disturbance is allergy to foods, food dyes, artificial flavours, and preservatives. Benjamin Feingold (1975) popularized the notion that some substances in foods are linked to hyperactivity in some children. Feingold hypothesized that artificial colourings and flavourings were pharmacologically active substances that produced or aggravated hyperactive symptoms in children. He proposed a diet (the K-P Diet) to restrict the intake of artificial food colours, flavours, preservatives, and foods with natural salicylates. After a stabilization period, foods would be gradually reintroduced to identify the particular items that affected a child.

Informal clinical evaluations and parent testimony suggested that Feingold's diet relieved hyperactivity in 30 to 40 percent of the children who tried it (Swanson and Kinsbourne, 1980). Results of controlled studies have shown equivocal results. Some studies indicate that Feingold's diet may help only a small percentage of hyperactive children (Spring and Sandoval, 1976); others suggest that claims for the importance of food allergies in causing learning disabilities are exaggerated (Henker and Whalen, 1980).

But while skepticism concerning Feingold's hypothesis persists, concerns about the diet's adverse effects seem unwarranted. Rimland (1983) warned that we must be careful of abandoning something with few, if any, ill effects and the potential for some good results.

Technical Aids

Computer technology has much to offer students with learning disabilities. The computer has infinite patience for daily review. There are program learning packages, voice printers, programs to teach logic, and programs to develop self-concept. Some programs have been designed to provide supplementary drill and practice in academic skills. Others attempt to overcome passivity and help the child take a more active part in the learning process by developing active learning styles and problem-solving strategies.

Educational Intervention

Educators must be deeply concerned about how and what to teach pupils who have demonstrated that they learn differently and not very readily the things with which education is charged with teaching them. The challenge for those involved with students who are learning disabled revolves around how to prevent learning failure, how to individualize education for a particular child, and how to provide special education programs for students who are not responding to traditional instructional approaches.

Intervention in educational settings varies, largely determined by how learning disabilities are defined and understood in a particular school. Disparities in approach, program delivery, procedures, and teaching tactics also occur from situation to situation and from teacher to teacher according to personal preference and training.

Service Delivery Models

Until the 1960s, children with learning disabilities were typically educated in general classrooms. During the mainstreaming period, the regular classroom–resource room combination was the common method of program delivery. Today, a majority of students with learning disabilities are educated in regular classrooms.

Placement is not an easy issue and controversy hounds the field. There is great reluctance to segregate students labelled as learning disabled, and many educators argue that such students can be educated in the general classroom full time with support (e.g., Banarji and Dailey, 1995). Others feel that the move toward full inclusion is not warranted (e.g., Roberts and Mather, 1995; Zigmond, Jenkins, Fuchs, Deno, Fuchs, Baker, Jenkins, and Couthino, 1995), as students with more severe disabilities require intensive services. Advocates of retention of a continuum of services contend that special classes and resource rooms contribute more to the academic achievement of some types of students with special needs, especially those who are learning disabled or emotionally disturbed, than do general classrooms (Fuchs and Fuchs, 1995b).

Some educators and parents fear that a return to full educational services in general classrooms will serve only to resurrect past inequities. They see an uneven balance in the potential for positive social affiliations and the ongoing challenge of passing courses with few or no accommodations or adaptations.

Without a continuum of services, some students who are learning disabled flounder in traditional classrooms. For example, a recent study of settings where students with learning disabilities were included (Zigmond et al., 1995) failed to find academic benefits for students. Rather, they found that the achievement outcomes were "neither desirable nor acceptable" (p. 539). A review of five case studies of inclusive classrooms (Baker and Zigmond, 1995) commented that some elements of effective instruction were missing or infrequent, including adaptations, progress monitoring, and individualized attention.

One major area of concern is the competencies of general classroom teachers. Few teachers in general education classes currently possess the breadth of knowledge or the competencies to meet the individual needs of students with learning disabilities. While teachers recognize the low achievement of such students, they do very little that is different instructionally when these students are assigned to regular-content classes. A study of sixty social studies and science teachers who were seen as effective with students with learning disabilities by peers, principals, and self found that the teachers made few adaptations to meet special learning needs (McIntosh, Vaughn, Schumm, Haager, and Lee, 1994). Another found that 60 percent of students with learning disabilities are not offered accommodations or modifications and yet are expected to meet the same academic standards as other students (Wagner, Newman, D'Amico, Jay, Butler-Nalin, Marder, and Cox, 1991). The one adjustment that is commonly made is to lower grading standards so that students who are learning disabled have a good chance of passing the course (Zigmond, Levine, and Laurie, 1985).

Students themselves are ambivalent. When Klinger and colleagues (1998) examined elementary students' preferences for in-class or pull-out programs, they found that students preferred the pull-out model, although students with learning disabilities were closer to an even split than other groups. Nor did students seem to care one way or the other. The consensus was that inclusion was better for making friends, pull-out for learning.

Full inclusion or some alternate model is not a decisive horse race for students with learning disabilities. There is no research evidence that any one service delivery model meets the needs of all students; indeed, empirical research in the field so far fails to support the efficacy of inclusion for students with learning disabilities (see Heflin and Bullock, 1999).

The current consensus is for responsible and selective inclusion, which translates as the retention of a full continuum of services. For example, a policy statement of the New Jersey Commission on Learning Disabilities stated that, "The regular education classroom is one of many educational program options but is not a substitute for a full continuum necessary to assure the provision of an appropriate education to all students with learning disabilities" (see Maloney, 1995, p. 25).

Educational Approaches

In a field as important as learning disabilities, one would think that the way to teach these students most effectively has been the subject of intense investigation and practice. Such is not the case. Issues of definition, etiology, referral, and identification seem to have taken precedence over issues of actual classroom practice, and research evidence on effective strategies for increasing the academic achievement of students with mild disabilities in inclusion classes is limited (see Keele, Dangel, and Owens, 1999). Few studies have been conducted and results are often meagre and disappointing.

A diverse range of general and specific approaches exists in educational intervention for students with learning disabilities. *General approaches* refer to techniques such as adapting curriculum and grading requirements in the regular classroom or providing resource room assistance in areas of academic lag. *Specific approaches* refer to a great deal more program adaptation and direction, such as teaching to subskill deficits or metacognitive training.

In instructional terms, learning disabilities may be seen in three ways. Programs focus on underlying problems (processing), observable problems (skills), and strategy problems. Twenty years ago, educators stressed process training approaches that sought to remediate processing deficits. Such an emphasis is quite rare today, and the focus is now on behavioural (skills) or cognitive (strategy training) approaches. Modern techniques that stress careful instruction in the academic areas as well as strategy training tend to be more successful than the earlier indirect approaches that attempted to train students in the dysfunctional processes interfering with learning (Lloyd, 1988).

Behavioural (Skills) Approaches

Behavioural approaches, also referred to as a *skill model* or *task-based perspective*, assume that a child's problems are external and result from some gap in instruction. The major focus, therefore, is on the mismatch between school tasks and the unique ability patterns and learning styles of students with learning disabilities and their ability to perform academic tasks. Teachers provide direct instruction in weak academic areas and focus on the skills needed for academic success such as word decoding and basic number facts.

Within each skill subject, a hierarchy of skills is defined. Briefly, teachers would:

1. Determine the student's current repertoire of skills and information through informal and formal testing, school records, and medical data.
2. Determine the skills and informational deficits of the student.
3. Specify the long- and short-term goals of the instructional program for each student.
4. Break these down into small, measurable, and more immediate objectives.
5. Select instructional procedures and techniques.

task analysis

Task analysis—analyzing the behavioural components and prerequisite skills of a task—plays an integral role. When a teacher task-analyzes an objective, the elements of the task that a child must master are clearly identified. For example, reading skills are broken down into the smallest possible steps and taught one step at a time. Instruction begins at the level of the simplest skill not mastered by the child.

Especially for young children, skills approaches can be very successful. In contrast to earlier pessimistic appraisals (e.g. Badian, 1988), recent U.S. studies, for example, show that when students with severe reading problems are given early, intensive instruction, almost 95 percent can reach the national average in reading ability ("Reading difficulties ...," 1997).

Not every curriculum area suits such a structured approach based on specific, building steps. While content subjects such as math and handwriting lend themselves quite nicely to such a model, subjects like social studies are more problematic.

Cognitive Approaches

metacognition

Advances in cognitive psychology have resulted in the development of programs that focus on learning and thinking skills. They focus on **metacognition**, simply defined as an individual's awareness of his or her own cognitive performance and the use of this awareness in altering one's own behaviour. Cognitive approaches are founded on the belief that learning is a mentally active and constructive process that involves the learner's use of strategies to acquire, store, retrieve, and apply knowledge (Andrews and Violato, 1996).

Self-regulated learners have developed metacognitive competence, which begins to develop around ages five to seven and improves throughout school. They own a combination of academic learning skills and self-control— they have both the skill and the will to learn (McCombs and Manzano, 1990).

In contrast to efficient and self-directed learners, poor learners fail to develop efficient metacognition; they simply do not understand the relationship between strategic learning and successful performance. Many students with learning disabilities fit into this group. They have metacognitive deficits; that is, they do not lack the processes entirely, but they seem to use them inefficiently and ineffectively.

What Are Metacognitive Processes?

Before we discuss strategy training, it makes sense to be clear about what metacognition is and the processes involved. Within the general concept of metacognition, there are two types of behaviour. The two behaviours comprising metacognition are *knowledge* and *skill*, alternatively referred to as *cognitive strategies* (control executive strategies) and *learning strategies*. Metacognitive processes are illustrated in Figure 5-3.

Knowledge is the overarching organizing process: the general strategies used in accomplishing a learning goal. It includes how a person thinks and acts when planning, executing,

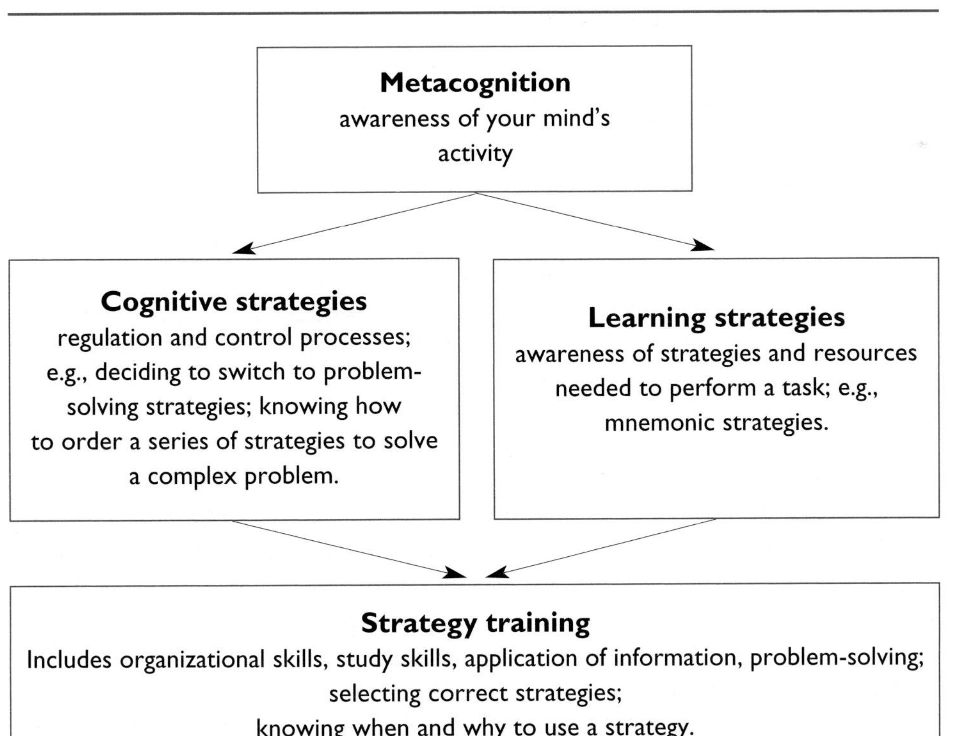

Figure 5-3 *Metacognitive processes*

and evaluating performance on a task. The outcomes of executive strategies are an indicator of how well a person uses methods and strategies to control and promote his or her own learning. The ability is shown, for example, when competent readers reduce their reading speed when they reach a difficult passage (Befring, 1997).

learning strategies

Learning strategies refer to an individual's approach to tasks that are either generic or domain-specific. Generic strategies are problem-solving skills that apply across many areas of the curriculum such as planning, setting goals for studying, skimming information, locating information, generating questions, note taking, and test writing. Included are mechanisms such as tracking attention to task, asking questions such as, "Am I understanding this?" monitoring speed, and assessing the amount of time it takes to learn and understand certain material. Specific strategies are those used in one situation, such as remembering a /sh/ combination in reading or a principle in geometry.

Strategy Training

Effective strategy users constantly monitor their progress to see whether the strategy they're using is as effective as it should be. They also use *conditional knowledge*—knowing when and where to use a strategy (Anderson, 1990). For example, by matching a strategy such as skimming to a goal such as getting an overview of the content.

Research findings indicate that students with learning disabilities in general lack comprehension monitoring skills and efficient task strategies. They fail to maintain and generalize learned strategies, do not understand the relationship between learning strategies and successful performance, and do not apply efficient strategies such as verbal rehearsal and chunking spontaneously (de Bettencourt, 1987).

Metacognition develops over time, but the process can be helped by effective instruction (Hiebert and Raphael, 1996). Individuals with learning disabilities show significant improvement following strategy training, also known as learning–thinking instructional programs, cognitive training, cognitive behaviour modification, or strategic instruction. (Note that the differences in cognitive models are semantic. Each model stresses the importance of students learning systems of action that lead to the solution of problems.)

Strategy training typically provides the learner with a set of self-instructional steps to increase effectiveness in the acquisition, organization, and expression of information. Training teaches the strategies needed for acquiring information from written material, techniques for remembering information, and methods for improving written expression. The ultimate aim is to provide students with tools that will enable them to become autonomous learners and devise their own strategies.

There are several important sequenced areas in strategy training:

- Teaching students to consider the many variables involved in problem solving. Students must analyze the task at hand; identify the steps necessary to complete the task; identify the effective strategies; delineate the necessary steps; and decide how to go about implementing the strategies.
- Teaching students to regulate the processes involved in problem solving, such as planning, checking, testing, revising, and evaluating. Here students reflect on what they already know; they devise a plan for attacking the new problem; they monitor their progress; and they evaluate the outcome of the plan.
- Increasing student effectiveness in the use of specific cognitive skills employed in prob-

lem solving. Simply telling students about effective strategies is not enough; practice is essential.

For math, for example, strategy training is the best intervention (Miller, Butler, and Lee, 1998). One way to teach the procedures is for an adult to first perform the specified task while verbalizing aloud, covering questions about the task, self-guiding instruction on how to do the task, and self-evaluating performance on the task. The student then performs the task while the adult instructs aloud. Following this, the pupil performs the task while verbalizing aloud. The student can now perform the task while using self-verbalization in a whisper and, finally, perform the task using merely subvocalizations. Throughout, the student should be provided with feedback about the utility of the self-instructions for performance.

Another example is POSSE, a strategy to assist reading comprehension. In this strategy, students follow the steps of:

Predict ideas

Organize the ideas

Search for the structure

Summarize the main ideas

Evaluate (Englert and Mariage, 1991).

- Keeping tasks within the learner's repertoire. Metacognitive ability is dependent on the interaction between person, task, and strategy variables. Students must be able to accomplish the tasks they are self-instructing themselves to do; self-instructional support for reading will be of little use if the passage is too difficult for a child.
- Learning appropriate strategy use and generalization. Teachers can explicitly point out other tasks and settings in which self-instruction can be used, and use a variety of trainers, settings, and tasks to increase the chances that the student will learn to use self-instruction successfully outside of training sessions.

Teachers need also to define when certain strategies are used. For example, mnemonic devices can be extremely valuable in aiding student recall of important information because they strengthen the relationship between what is known and what is to be learned. When Scruggs and Mastropieri (1989) taught adolescents with mild disabilities information about the First World War using either a variety of mnemonic strategies or the more traditional drill and practice, students who learned through mnemonics recalled substantially more content than the traditionally taught group and retained the information for a longer period.

While mnemonic strategies have emerged as one of the most powerful instructional techniques in special education for promoting the acquisition of academic content (Scruggs and Mastropieri, 1990), students must know when mnemonics are suitable. They may help with science content but may not be as applicable to learning a passage of Shakespeare.

Strategy instruction is not a quick fix but it does work. For training in the use of learning strategies to have a significant impact on student success, the instruction must be intensive and extensive. Students should be trained in the techniques until a reasonable criteria for performance has been reached, then followed up with booster sessions in order to give a better chance that the trained skills will be maintained. Extensive instruction may be necessary to foster the use and transfer of appropriate strategies.

A number of other techniques have grown from cognitive strategy training. For example, attribution training is relevant to students with learning disabilities who often develop an outward locus of control. **Attributions** are the reasons that people give for what happens to them. Attribution training involves attempting to recognize the relationship between hard work and success (Hallahan, Kauffman, and Lloyd, 1999). Students are guided to think of their success or failure in terms of the use or non-use of a strategy. For example, "I wrote a good paper because I used a writing strategy" (Stevens and Englert, 1993).

attributions

Curriculum

A major characteristic of pupils with learning disabilities is an inability to learn adequately in the general classroom through traditional teaching techniques. Because of the heterogeneous nature of the learning-disabled population, schools must provide different administrative arrangements, varied approaches, and be willing to permit adaptations to the regular curriculum and assessment procedures.

Among the vast range of adaptations are differentiated assignments, focused questions, intermittent tutoring, grouping, and supplementary instruction. If possible, curriculum adaptations should stress changing the format rather than watering down the curriculum. Specific ideas for teaching are found in the In the Classroom feature at the end of Chapter 6. Secondary programming is discussed in Chapter 16. See also the IEP for Danny below.

Case Study

Danny (continued)

At the team meeting, the psychologist explained about learning disabilities. The classroom teacher suggested a skills approach, with much small-group direct teaching for Danny. As in any teaching approach, the skills model should be tailored to Danny's individual needs. The teacher may need to adjust the materials, change the timing, alter the lesson format, or adjust evaluation techniques to help Danny.

Improvements in reading may be accomplished by a word-family approach. This will build on Danny's strong sight-word vocabulary while strengthening his weak phonic skills. Rather than focusing only on sound–symbol association, Danny may benefit from much work in structural analysis of such items as prefixes, suffixes, and compound words. Danny also needs to return to intense instruction in phonological awareness.

Proficiency in writing relies on an expanded experiential and knowledge base and the development of adequate listening, speaking, and reading skills. To improve writing, the teacher must first build Danny's motivation to write and his confidence that his thoughts are worthy of communication. A writing program should include daily writing and sustained writing. As well, peer collaboration will allow Danny to use talk to elaborate writing and to become more familiar with words, ideas, and composing procedures.

Remediation of arithmetic problems requires an individual math program with step by step instruction, beginning at Danny's level of performance and advancing at his rate. Danny must learn the basic skills in which he is deficient. He must master the number facts to nineteen and develop a concept of place value before he can learn the four arithmetic processes. To master the number facts he needs daily oral and written drill as well as many opportunities to generalize these facts to other solutions. In learning math, he needs practical associations. Whenever possible, concrete materials should be used, but Danny will need much practice to translate concrete sums into numerical notation. Place value should be taught with many concrete materials, such as Popsicle sticks, Cuisenaire rods, and a calculator. Later, decimals should be taught as related to money, and integers can be taught with the temperatures on a thermometer.

Danny's social problems appear to rise directly from his academic frustration. Learning tasks should be structured to allow him much success. He must demonstrate mastery of each step before progressing onward. To build his self-esteem, praise should be realistic and consistent. Danny's progress should be charted with some type of graphic display.

EXTRACT FROM DANNY'S IEP

Name Danny
Chronological Age 8-1
Grade 3
Teacher Mrs. Als
School Warren Place

Assessment Results

PPVT 46th percentile TERA 32nd percentile
TEMA 12th percentile Gates-MacGinitie 1.6 GE

Present Levels of Functioning

In arithmetic, Danny exhibits a marked discrepancy between his potential and his performance. He functions more than two years below his grade level in this area. He is also delayed in his reading, though not as severely. By using his extensive sight-word vocabulary, he is able to partly camouflage his deficits in word-attack skills. Danny's academic problems seriously frustrate him, and he is increasingly resorting to overt acting-out behaviour.

Placement

- Regular classroom
- Individualized math program
- Although Danny should try to remain in the same reading program as the rest of his class, his success and attitudes to reading might improve with a special set of high-interest, low-vocabulary readers presented in small-group instruction.

Long-Range Goals

- Danny will improve decoding skills in reading.
- Writing skills will be stimulated through daily and sustained writing with a peer.
- Danny will improve math skills by learning basic facts.
- Danny will learn about days and months, time, and simple money exchange.

Short-Term Objectives

- Using a listening station, Danny will decode 15 to 20 selected words.
- Danny will use the words in his own stories.
- Danny will read the decoded words in short paragraphs.
- In a paragraph, he will capitalize and use periods.
- Daily, Danny and a peer will write together for ten minutes on a teacher-selected topic.
- Using a software program on calendar skills, Danny will recognize the days of the week and say them in order.
- Using concrete objects, he will say and write numbers to 100.
- With a peer tutor, Danny will practise number facts to nineteen to 100-percent accuracy.
- When given short addition and subtraction problems, Danny will align them on the page correctly and solve to 100-percent accuracy using concrete objects.

Historical Notes

It is probably true to say that there have always been people with learning disabilities—if we are referring to persons of average intelligence who suffer some dysfunction that hinders their learning by traditional methods. By definition, however, learning disabilities are tied to academic achievement. Therefore, when pushing a plough was more important than pushing a pen, and when schooling was not a social norm for all children, the unique problems of individuals with learning disabilities would simply not have existed.

It was at the opening of the 20th century, when compulsory school laws propelled all children into some form of education, that the particular difficulties of students with learning disabilities came to the fore. As neurology and ophthalmology developed as medical specialties in the late 19th century, physicians began to describe problems in understanding and using spoken and written language that were associated with damage to specific areas of the brain.

Many different disciplines contributed to the new field. Along with physicians, neurologists, and ophthalmologists, speech therapists, psychologists, and educators all brought their own professional orientation and focus. Early research emphasized clinical investigation rather than practical application in the schools and focused primarily on three disorders: spoken language, written language, and motor and perceptual problems. In 1877, for example, Kaussmaul first described congenital "word blindness." In 1896 James Kerr, a British physician, and W. P. Morgan, an ophthalmologist, also reported cases of word blindness. Eye surgeon James Hinshelwood investigated cases of word blindness, word deafness, and mind blindness. He published *Congenital Word Blindness* (1917), the first true monograph on the unique problems of children we now refer to as *learning disabled.*

In the early 1920s, Samuel Orton, an American psychiatrist, noted that children with learning problems often displayed mixed laterality and suggested that the failure of one hemisphere of the brain to become dominant caused the disorder. Orton coined the term "strephosymbolia" for individuals who saw "mixed symbols" when they tried to read (Orton, 1927).

Although these early researchers made some provocative and relevant findings, it was the work of Alfred Strauss, a neurologist, and Heinz Werner, a developmental psychologist, that established the conceptual base and the research and theories in the field. Strauss and Werner investigated the impact of brain damage on children's behaviour and psychological development. When they began to study children of normal ability who were experiencing learning difficulties, Strauss and Werner were able to delineate a group of common behaviours—a behavioural syndrome—that they believed characterized children suffering from minimal brain damage.

In the 1950s, William Cruickshank cemented the link. Following Strauss' lead, he worked with children with cerebral palsy and showed that persons of normal intelligence could also display inattention, hyperactivity, and poor learning.

Five principal components were delineated— hyperactivity, hyper-emotionalism, impulsiveness, distractibility, and perseveration, which came to be known as the Strauss Syndrome. While these components have been expanded, subdivided, and made more specific over the years, they still describe the core behavioural characteristics of children with learning disabilities.

The actual term *learning disabilities* came into use in 1963 to describe students who experienced continual school failure yet did not fit into the traditional categories of exceptionality. It was first used as a standard description for children of normal intelligence with learning problems by Samuel Kirk, one of the pioneers in the field, at a Chicago parents' meeting in 1963. Kirk defined his term carefully:

> Recently, I have used the term "learning disabilities" to describe a group of children who have disorders in development in language, speech, reading, and associated communication skills needed for social interaction. In this group, I do not include children who have sensory handicaps, such as blindness and deafness, because we have methods of managing and training the deaf and the blind. I also exclude from this group children who have generalized mental retardation (Kirk, 1963, p.3).

Kirk's speech had three major effects. First, it isolated the general characteristics of the population to be subsumed under the label of learning disabilities. Second, it stimulated the growth of the Association for Children with Learning Disabilities (ACLD), renamed the Learning Disabilities Association (LDA) in 1989. Primarily a forum for parents of learning-disabled children, the ACLD expanded rapidly and became a powerful lobby group in both Canada and the United States.

Third, the creation of a new term served as a catalyst to generate interest in the field. Kirk's conception created an entirely new area of special education and set it on the road to an astonishing expansion. Such growth has never been experienced by any other area in special education in such a short time. The massive interest in the area, the number of students identified and served as learning disabled, the development of parent and professional organizations, and the contributions of allied disciplines has been little short of phenomenal. Today, learning disabilities is the largest single focus of special education in many Canadian school districts.

SUMMARY

1. The term *learning disabilities* first appeared in 1963. As it implied an educational rather than a medical orientation and was relatively non-stigmatizing, it appealed greatly to parents and educators.
2. The reasons why students with learning disabilities fail are not easily discerned. The condition is generally regarded as a multifaceted concept in terms of etiology and clinical manifestations. Students with learning disabilities exhibit an entire syndrome, or collection of symptoms. Their problems lie well outside the normal range for their age level and persist despite repeated efforts to correct them. They are hindered by their disabilities and prevented from realizing their full potential.
3. Controversies that continue to plague the field of learning disabilities often revolve around the formulation of a universally acceptable definition. Although the term *learning disabilities* has gained wide recognition among educators and the general public, a precise definition has not yet surfaced. Current definitions fail to reflect any consistency, and this spills over to influence critical areas such as classification, identification, prevalence, and instructional approaches.
4. With the movement toward inclusive classrooms and lacking a universally accepted definition, there is a blurring of categories. Many more children are moving under the learning disabilities umbrella, although the term may not accurately apply to them because their problems are of a different nature. Although misdiagnosis is one culprit in the numbers designated as learning disabled, other factors are at work.
5. Clinicians and teachers generally use tests first to determine traits and eligibility for special services, and then tests of academic achievement. Further tests are sometimes administered to identify the specific psychological processes in which a child is deficient. For

example, a child's reading problems may be the result of a processing problem in auditory discrimination or visual figure–ground processing.

6. The difficulties that students with learning disabilities face in dealing with various types of information may cause them to be less task-oriented, less verbally facile, and less responsive than their peers. Children are likely to show attention problems, be more distractible, and exhibit poor self-esteem, an external locus of control, poor motivation, and learned helplessness. They are often disorganized, uncooperative, slow to adapt to change, and overly active. Many children with learning disabilities experience negative social relations with significant people in their lives—parents, teachers, peers—as well as with strangers.
7. Reading deficits are endemic. It seems there are delays in the development of phonological awareness. Arithmetic problems occur with less frequency than reading disabilities and have traditionally received less attention. Problems in visual perception and visual processing include difficulties with oculamotor coordination, spatial relations, figure–ground perception, the discrimination of differences, and the recognition of likenesses.
8. While general classroom placements are appropriate for most students with learning disabilities, the goal of inclusion for all students is inconsistent with views expressed by many in the special education community. Concerns exist among parents, professionals, and advocacy groups regarding inclusion for students with serious learning disabilities.
9. *Metacognition* refers to higher-order thinking processes. Metacognitive strategies serve to support, guide, and extend the thinking processes of their users. Recently, educators have begun to reconceptualize students who are learning disabled as those who have not developed effective learning strategies. They see a need for strategy training to teach students how to use metacognitive skills, which involve self-monitoring, practising, reality testing, and coordinating the processes of studying and learning.
10. Cognitive instructional programs stress information processing, organizational skills, study skills, application of information, and problem solving. Essentially, the procedures are designed to improve learning effectiveness and social performance in school settings and to teach students to become independent learners.

WEBLINKS

Dyslexia, Learning Disabilities, and Literacy Resource Site **www.greenwood.org/**

Learning Disabilities Association of Canada **www.ldac-taac.ca**

Wechsler Intelligence Scale for Children: III
edcen.ehhs.cmich.edu/~mnesset/wisc2.html

Chapter 6

Children with Intellectual Disabilities

Learning Outcomes

After reading this chapter, you should be able to:

- Understand the definitions of mental retardation and adaptive behaviour;
- Recognize the risk factors that can result in mental retardation;
- Relate the category of mental retardation to other forms of mild or significant disability;
- Recognize the developmental consequences of the different levels of intellectual disability;
- Understand accommodations, adaptations, and modifications that teachers can make to assist learners with special needs.

Introduction

Intellectual disability is not an illness, nor is it a disease. Essentially, the term refers to delayed intellectual growth that is manifested in immature reactions to environmental stimuli and below-average social and academic performance.

As with many areas of special education, the field of intellectual disabilities is characterized by constant change, evolution, and growth in attitudes; in research; in expectations; and in education and training. Compared to even thirty years ago, present attitudes toward individuals who are intellectually disabled are strikingly positive. As a result of new research, professionals now entertain rising, but realistic, expectations for their clients who are intellectually disabled.

A number of issues and dilemmas are apparent in the field of mental retardation. One of the major issues revolves around normalization and deinstitutionalization and the manner in which individuals can be most effectively included in schools, communities, and workplaces. Branching from this is the question of inclusion into general classrooms. There is little question that many students with mild intellectual disabilities can be effectively included, especially at the elementary levels. When the placement of students with significant problems is broached, then dissension arises. The issue is approached here and fully discussed in Chapter 14.

DEFINITIONS OF INTELLECTUAL DISABILITIES

Intellectual disabilities have long been recognized as an exceptional condition, and numerous attempts have been made to define retardation within various disciplines including medicine, psychology, social work, and education. Still, definitions have never been standardized and a universally accepted definition does not exist.

Although recent definitions are very flexible, they remain rooted largely in medical models of disability. (See the Historical Notes in Chapter 3.) Even today, the concept of mental retardation is still captured within intelligence and adaptive behaviour scores used with labels. We can see this in the case of Nicholas. The psychologist began the assessment with a measure of mental ability, used a number of achievement tests to determine Nicholas' present levels of functioning in language and core subject areas, and then administered a scale of adaptive behaviour. With these results, she determined that Nicholas fit within the commonly accepted definition of intellectual disability.

Even the terminology in the field of mental retardation is problematic. Over the centuries, persons with intellectual disabilities have been described by a plethora of labels, many of them decidedly offensive. In 1910, Henry Goddard, an American psychologist, divided retardation into the categories of *feeble-minded, moron, idiot,* and *imbecile.* These descriptors lingered until the 1950s, when the term *mental retardation* became generally accepted. Today, however, that term suffers its own problems. Because it is used for individuals with the most severe disabilities, it suggests a deficit within an individual and evokes the impression of a condition that is always a permanent and comprehensive incapacity. Yet, especially in the case of mild conditions, intellectual disability does not include the expectation of biologically based, permanent, and comprehensive incompetence (Harry, 1992). Mild mental retardation is a condition that can improve as a result of changes in either the individual or the environment.

Because of the negative connotations, some people today prefer the term *intellectually challenged,* which reflects the social aspects of the disability; that is, people find difficulties in meeting the challenges of our highly industrialized, technologically oriented, and fast-paced society. Others in the field prefer to use the more inclusive term *developmental disability.*

Nevertheless, the primary definition used today is that first adopted in 1959 by the interdisciplinary American Association on Mental Deficiency (AAMD) (today known as the American Association on Mental Retardation (AAMR)). The criterion for adaptive behaviour, not in the 1959 version, was added later. Under this widely accepted definition,

> Mental retardation refers to substantial limitations in personal functioning, characterized by significant subaverage intellectual functioning, existing concurrently with related limitations in two or more of the following adaptive skills: communication, self-care, home living, social skills, community use, self-direction, health and safety, functional academics, leisure, and work. Mental retardation is manifested before age 18. (AAMR, 1993)

There are three critical points in the AAMR definition. These refer to subaverage intellectual functioning, deficits in adaptive behaviour, and manifestation during the developmental period.

Case Study

Nicholas

In his grade two classroom, Nicholas is far behind his peers in reading and math. He has a short attention span, poor on-task behaviour, low motivation, negative peer interactions, and generally seems to find school very trying and difficult. His teacher has attempted a number of adaptations, such as peer tutoring in reading and a token economy to improve on-task behaviour, but to little avail. He eventually referred Nicholas to the school principal, asking for an assessment and some assistance in developing an appropriate program.

A school psychologist administered a number of measures to Nicholas, including the WISC-III, a measure of receptive language (Peabody Picture Vocabulary Test, PPVT); a test of language usage (Test of Language Development, Primary TOLD-P); a reading test (Test of Early Reading Ability, TERA); and a measure of math readiness (Test of Early Mathematical Ability, TEMA). She also carefully noted Nicholas' *presenting behaviour*—the way he approached the situation and the measures, and the way he interacted with her.

In some ways, the test results confirmed the teacher's suspicions. Nicholas showed a Full Scale IQ score of 66, with very little difference between the verbal and the performance scales and very little scatter among the subtests. The raw scores on the other measures were all reported as percentiles; the psychologist found that Nicholas scored in the 21st percentile on the PPVT, the 14th on the TOLD-P, the 4th on the TERA, and the 8th on the TEMA.

What surprised the psychologist was Nicholas' interactions during the testing sessions. Although he seems to dislike classroom work, he really enjoyed the one-to-one situation with the psychologist and readily attempted everything presented to him. And he talked throughout. He particularly wanted to tell the psychologist about his hockey and how the night before his team "had just killed those guys from Medicine Hat," and gone on to win the trophy. Nicholas demonstrated adequate vocabulary and sequencing in his stories when talking about hockey, although he showed many problems with syntax.

To round out the assessment, the psychologist used a scale of adaptive behaviour, a series of statements answered by Nicholas' mother. She found that Nicholas had many deficits in this area, but chiefly in the school environment. His performance was far better in sports, which he liked and where he was well accepted by peers.

Subaverage General Intellectual Functioning

Individuals are not considered intellectually disabled unless they score below 70 IQ on a standardized test of mental ability; that is, two or more standard deviations below the mean. This is a relatively recent cut-off point—before the 1970s, children who fell between one and two standard deviations below the norm (IQ 85 and below) were included in the mentally retarded category. The definition adopted by the American Association on Mental Deficiency in 1973 limited the category of mental retardation to those with an IQ of 70 or less. With this change, 80 percent of the mentally retarded population was eliminated (Zetlin and Murtaugh, 1990). Today, students whose IQ scores fall between 85 and 70 are considered borderline or perhaps slow learners, but not mentally retarded.

Adaptive Behaviour

Since the 1950s, changing definitions of intellectual disabilities have given increasing prominence to the concept of *adaptive behaviour*. The construct was first delineated as a component of mental retardation by Edgar Doll in the early 1940s and formally added as a criterion in 1961. With the addition of the adaptive behaviour construct the concept of mental retardation broadened, and adaptive behaviour is crucial to today's definitions.

adaptive behaviour

Nearly all conceptions of adaptive behaviour use the basic definition formulated by the AAMD. In this, **adaptive behaviour** is seen as "the degree and efficiency with which an individual meets the standards of personal independence and social responsibility of his age or cultural group" (Grossman, 1977, p. 11).

Adaptive behaviour is a dynamic construct influenced by cultural norms and age-related expectations: it refers to how well a person is able to adapt to environmental demands, and differs according to the individual's age group and particular situation. The preschooler, for example, needs sensorimotor skills, communication, self-help skills, and socialization to adapt to the environment. We do not expect the preschooler to be interested in vocational prospects and an expanded peer group; these are the adaptive concerns of the adolescent.

The dynamic nature of adaptive behaviour also implies that, over time and with experience, adaptive behaviour can change. Specific adaptive limitations often co-exist with strengths and other personal capabilities; with appropriate supports over a sustained period, therefore, the life functioning of the person with intellectual disabilities will generally improve.

Note that individuals must demonstrate poor adaptive behaviour as well as subaverage intellectual functioning before they can be classified as retarded. Students who manifest deficits in adaptive behaviour but score within the normal range on IQ tests are usually labelled *emotionally disturbed* or *learning disabled.*

Adaptive behaviour has been critical in the identification of mental retardation for more than forty years, yet lively debate about and criticism of the construct remains common. Some researchers (e.g., Zigler, Balla, and Hodapp, 1984) want to disregard adaptive behaviour and focus solely on subaverage intellectual functioning; others (e.g., Barnett, 1986) stress adaptive behaviour and see the interaction between individual characteristics and societal demands as absolutely vital.

Some researchers want definitions that include academic and more cognitively oriented skills. This harks as far back as 1973, when Mercer expanded the phenomenon of adaptive behaviour and described the "six-hour retarded child"; that is, the one who cannot cope with the methods, pace, and materials of the regular educational classroom but functions quite adequately in other environments.

Others intentionally omit these types of cognitive behaviours. Adaptive behaviour is said to include only social functioning and interpersonal relationships, functional academic competencies, and vocational/occupational competencies. The latter position is most prominent today. Competencies related to functional independence are perhaps the most widely accepted component of adaptive behaviour. Skills involved relate to toileting, dressing, feeding, avoiding danger, and maintenance of a minimal level of health and safety (Reschley, 1989).

Developmental Period

Under the AAMR definition, the *developmental period* refers to the time between conception and the eighteenth birthday.

CLASSIFICATION OF INTELLECTUAL DISABILITIES

While many educators prefer the AAMR classification system, we still occasionally hear the more traditional terms *educable* and *trainable*, which educators have used over the years to try to describe the educational needs of children who are intellectually disabled. This terminology reflects the ability of children labelled as *educable mentally retarded* (EMR) to benefit from academic instruction, whereas those called *trainable mentally retarded* (TMR) are presented with a more non-academic program that focuses on training in life skills and skills for independent living.

Most professionals agree that the most useful system to classify retardation is that proposed by the AAMR, which considers the condition along a continuum, or scale, of severity.

Table 6-1 Degrees of intellectual disability and expected developmental and academic characteristics

IQ level	Support needs/degrees	Expectations
70–90		Not classified as intellectually disabled. Capable of competing in school in many areas.
55–70	Mild Intermittent	Capable of basic academic subjects up to advanced elementary levels; will achieve about half to two-thirds of what normally developing peers do. General achievement ranges from second to fifth grade. Gap widens in secondary school.
40–55	Moderate Limited	Capable of attaining self-help skills, communication skills, and social adjustment. Limited academic achievement but can attain many functional skills and basic functional academics. Can achieve economic usefulness later in routine jobs under supervision.
25–40	Severe Extensive	Can attain basic communication and self-help skills. May or may not be ambulatory. Additional disabilities hinder attainments.
Below 25	Profound Pervasive	With intensive training, may learn basic self-help and communication skills. Often not ambulatory; may be medically fragile and/or technology dependent.

The AAMR's categories—mild, moderate, severe, and profound retardation—describe an individual's functioning clearly. The AAMR system carries no negative stereotyping and little stigma. As adjectives, the words *mild, moderate, severe,* and *profound* apply to many other things besides retardation (Hallahan and Kauffman, 1991).

When severity classifications are employed, it is important to remember that there will probably be as much variability within any one group as there is among the groups and among or within groups of normally developing individuals. As well, the cut-off scores leave room for clinical judgment. An IQ of 54 may be judged as moderate or mild mental retardation. Table 6-1 indicates, in broad terms, the educational expectations at each severity level.

Classification by Needs

Recently, a new set of qualifiers arrived in the field of mental retardation. The *Diagnostic and Statistical Manual* of the American Psychiatric Association (DSM) (APA, 1994) still uses severity levels and, as we just saw, they are still used by the AAMR. In 1992, however, the AAMR attempted a change.

Rather than severity, the proposed system changes dependency to support needs, keys terms to the level of services required, and describes them in ways that are prescriptive for programming needs. Specifically, it replaces the levels of *mild* to *profound* with *intermittent, limited, extensive,* and *pervasive,* terms that refer to the supports needed. In this classification based on supports, an individual's needs are classified in several domains; for example, communication (McLean, Brady, and McLean, 1996).

A child needing intermittent supports would require only a little extra assistance in the classroom. In contrast, a child needing pervasive supports would require supports characterized by constancy and high intensity, that are provided across environments, and that are of a potentially life-sustaining nature (Kaplan, 1996).

In Chapter 1 we discussed the use of labels and the controversy that often surrounds labelling. But in this case, the change in classification by the AAMR seems to have passed most people by. These new AAMR terms have been largely ignored by the field (Vergason and Anderegg, 1997).

PREVALENCE OF INTELLECTUAL DISABILITIES

Any attempt to estimate the incidence rate of a relatively common disorder almost invariably fails to take into account some affected individuals. This occurs in the case of intellectual disabilities, where mild conditions prove elusive and difficult to accurately pinpoint and many cases go unreported.

The reasons why it is extremely difficult to obtain true and accurate prevalence figures for intellectual disabilities are outlined below.

- Different IQ cut-off points are used. Whereas the AAMR uses an IQ of 70 as the beginning of the designation of mild mental retardation, a school system may use an IQ of 75.
- Methods of gathering data for prevalence studies differ.
- Different definitions of adaptive behaviour are used.

- Different regions and social classes show different prevalence. The majority of children labelled as intellectually disabled come from a lower socio-economic bracket. As we discussed in Chapter 3, children from lower socio-economic strata have a greater risk of incurring brain damage because of factors such as malnutrition, poor prenatal and postnatal care, and environmental hazards during infancy. Hence, large urban areas with a high lower-class population show a higher proportion of mental retardation.
- There are gender differences within prevalence estimates. A higher percentage of boys than girls are found among the population considered to be mildly intellectually disabled, somewhere between five to ten times as many boys as girls. This may result from a higher probability of adverse biological factors affecting male children. It may also result from the fact that expectations tend to be higher for males, or it may be that the more aggressive behaviour usually found among males can lead to referrals for assessment and to the label of mental retardation.
- With reference to the above two points, the concept of mild mental retardation is particularly controversial since children in this category are drawn almost exclusively from poor families, often of minority origin. Although gender and racial imbalance (more males and ethnic children) continue, there is also a greater hesitancy to label children as EMR.
- Different age groups show different prevalence figures, especially among the group classified as mildly mentally retarded. Prevalence is low in the preschool years (less than one percent in children below the age of five), increases dramatically during the school years, and declines later (Drew, Logan and Hardman, 1992).

  The high rates among school-age children are no doubt a reflection of the environmental demands of school. As a social system, the school has a certain set of expectations, which some of these children fail to meet. In fact, some researchers contend that high-functioning children with delays do not officially become retarded until they enter school and encounter reading, writing, and math. They pass through the school system labelled as intellectually disabled but then go on to occupy normal roles in society.
- There has been a redistribution among categories that is a direct result of the birth of the field of learning disabilities in 1963 and the redefinition of retardation ten years later. This led to a kind of hydraulic relationship among the mild categories of exceptionality, with the most significant movement occurring between learning disabilities and mild mental retardation. Today, many youngsters who previously wore the label of mild mental retardation are being propelled into the classification of learning disabilities. The overlap of categories is discussed in Chapter 1.
- Jurisdictions, too, are developing stricter criteria for diagnosing intellectual disability. As this happens, the number of children identified as learning disabled increases.
- In the United States, there is quite a deal of reluctance to label children as mentally retarded because of court challenges, such as Larry P. vs. Riles (see Winzer and Mazurek, 1998).

One of the major results of the difficulties outlined above is changes in professional perceptions of the field of mental retardation. While the area of intellectual disabilities traditionally held a primary position in the field of special education, today we see an about-face, and mental retardation is a shrinking category. This relates to both the number of children identified and labelled and to the amount of research directed toward it.

Reduction in the rate of intellectual disabilities has not resulted from any significant change in rates for severe and profound—and perhaps moderate—retardation, but from dramatic changes in the way we now define and label the condition, particularly mild retardation. There are stricter criteria and a reluctance to label, together with a preference for the designation of learning disabilities. Given a normal curve, a theoretical 2.27 percent of the population might be expected to fall two or more standard deviations below the mean. In reality, this does not happen. Only about 1 to 1.5 percent of the population meets the AAMR definition of retarded in both intellectual functioning and adaptive behaviour.

More than 75 percent of those identified as intellectually disabled are mildly retarded. For the moderate, severe, and profound levels (IQ of 50 or below), a review of twenty studies found three or four persons per thousand (McLaren and Bryson, 1987). Severe and profound intellectual disabilities are extremely low-incidence conditions. Note, however, that there is evidence of a recent increase in the number of children with severe and profound conditions, as children who may not have survived in the past are now saved by medical advances (Alper, Schloss, and Schloss, 1994). Figure 6-1 shows the prevalence and severity of mental retardation.

What this means for the schools is that the current population of children considered to be mildly intellectually disabled has changed quite dramatically. Today, we find that pupils identified as mildly mentally retarded tend to have greater disabilities than those of previous years and their average ability level is lower than before. Included today are children with

Figure 6-1
Prevalence and severity of mental retardation

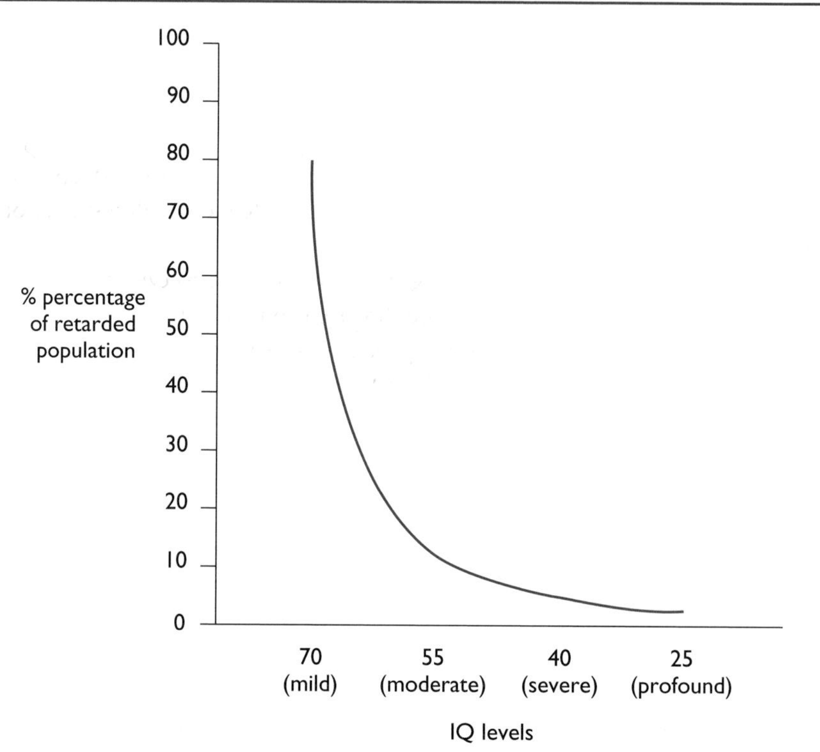

Down syndrome and those previously classified as *trainable mentally retarded* (TMR) (Robinson, Palton, Polloway, and Sargent, 1989).

ETIOLOGY OF INTELLECTUAL DISABILITIES

In both historical and contemporary contexts, etiological considerations have been prominent in the field of mental retardation. Nevertheless, the causes of intellectual disability remain highly controversial. Even though our knowledge has increased a hundredfold, we are still unable to answer some of the most fundamental questions and are frequently powerless to explain the condition of a specific child.

The agents that cause intellectual disabilities are legion and include genetic and chromosomal differences, infections such as maternal rubella, intoxicants such as drugs, postnatal diseases, and childhood accidents. The approximately 50 percent of cases where causes of retardation can actually be specified are almost exclusively of the moderate to profound severity levels. When causes can be pinpointed, they are referred to as *organic* causes, divided into the categories of *genetic factors* and *brain damage.* Children affected by organic causes are usually diagnosed well before school entrance because their conditions are readily apparent. Far more problematic in diagnosis are those children who show no clear-cut evidence of an organic cause. The condition, referred to as *non-specific mental retardation,* is found most often among individuals with mild intellectual disabilities.

The following brief discussion on the etiologies of intellectual disabilities supplements the information presented in Chapter 3. Table 6-2 presents a sample of etiologies, some common and some rare, that can lead to mental retardation. Note that some conditions occur within more than one classification.

Genetic Defects

About 750 genetic disorders are associated with intellectual disability (Hodapp and Fidler, 1999). Even with such a diversity of etiologies, problems due to heredity still account for only a small percentage of mental retardation.

As mentioned in Chapter 3, advances in genetics have sparked renewed interest in the behaviour of people with specific mental retardation syndromes. Many individuals show distinctive behavioural features or behavioural phenotypes (see Dykens and Kasari, 1997). For example, Williams syndrome is a genetic disorder estimated to occur in one in 20 000 live births. (Healey, 1999). Affected individuals show very specific behaviours and physical traits (see Table 3-1).

Chromosomal Problems

Chromosomal abnormalities include too many chromosomes, too few chromosomes, and chromosomes that are attached to one another. Abnormalities in the structure and number of chromosomes can be caused by natural mutation of genes, by radiation, and by a host of other factors that are only partly understood. Apart from Down syndrome, the number of children with intellectual disabilities due to chromosomal abnormality is quite small.

Worldwide, Down is the most common clinical cause of mental retardation (Manfredini,

Table 6-2 Some causes of mental retardation

Infections and intoxicants	Infections: rubella, syphilis, toxoplasmosis, herpes simplex, bacterial infections, viral infections, parasitic infections Intoxicants: drugs, poisons, smoking, caffeine, alcohol, lead
Trauma or physical agents	Anoxia, irradiation, trauma
Metabolism or nutrition	Lipid storage diseases: Tay–Sachs disease, Hurler's, Hunter's Carbohydrate disorders: galactosemia, hypoglycemia Endocrine disorders: hypothyroidism Amino acid disorders: phenylketonuria Other: Prader-Willi syndrome, malnutrition
Gross brain disease	Neurofibromatosis (von Recklinghavsen's disease), Sturge-Weber syndrome, tuberous sclerosis (epiloia), Huntington's chorea
Unknown prenatal influence	Anencephaly, microcephaly, Apert's syndrome, meningomyocele, hydrocephalus
Chromosomal abnormality	Chromosomal aberrations: Down syndrome, Klinefelter's syndrome, cri-du-chat Autosomal dominant gene disorders: neurofibromatisis, tuberous sclerosis, Sturge-Weber syndrome Autosomal recessive gene disorders: phenylketonuria, congenital hypothyroidism, maple syrup urine disease, Tay–Sachs disease, Smith-Lemli-Optiz syndrome X-linked disorders: Lasch-Nyhan syndrome, fragile X syndrome
Gestational disorders	Prematurity, postmaturity, low birth weight
Psychiatric disorders	Psychoses
Environmental influences	Psychosocial disadvantage, sensory deprivation

1988). Intellectually, the child with Down syndrome can fall anywhere in the retardation spectrum, but most tend to be classed as moderately retarded. Down syndrome accounts for approximately 10 percent of all cases of moderate and severe mental retardation (Hallahan and Kauffman, 1991). Individuals with Down syndrome who have normal intellectual development are exclusively those with the mosaic form of the condition.

The fragile X (Fra (X)) syndrome has attracted the interest of health, education, and human service professionals because it is common, its inheritance pattern is unique, and it presents a wide variety of disabilities. Frequency estimates indicate that Fra (X) may be second only to Down syndrome as an etiology of mental retardation in males. Among males with fragile X, approximately 30 percent may be severely or profoundly retarded; the majority are moderately or mildly retarded, and 10 percent have borderline or low–normal IQs (Dykens, Leckman, Paul, and Watson, 1988; Hagerman and Sobesky, 1989).

Lesser degrees of impairment are found in fragile X females. Research indicates that they are usually less cognitively affected than males, although one-third have mental retardation, usually in the mild range (Reiss and Freund, 1990).

Whether they are intellectually disabled or fall into the normal range, a significant number of fragile X children display specific behavioural and learning difficulties (Forness and Kavale, 1994). In addition, fragile X is associated with greater risk for a range of disorders involving social relations (Dykens, 1996). A controversial finding relates to the possibility of a decline in cognitive skills with age. Various studies have reported significant drops in IQ over time, possibly due to progressive neurological degeneration (Simen and Rogers, 1989).

Infections and Intoxications

Infections and intoxications that lead to mental retardation can occur in the pregnant mother, the infant, or the young child. Rubella and syphilis in the mother both cross the placental barrier and can damage the fetus.

Pediatric AIDS is the fastest growing infectious cause of mental retardation and brain damage in children. Of infants born with HIV infection, 78 to 93 percent become developmentally disabled through central nervous system involvement (Gray, 1989).

Intoxicants and poisons in the pregnant mother or the child can also cause intellectual disabilities. One of the most important outcomes in this category is Fetal Alcohol Syndrome (FAS), which joins Down syndrome, fragile X syndrome, and spina bifida as one of the most common currently known causes of mental retardation. Of these conditions, FAS is the most directly preventable, at least in principle.

Mental retardation appears to be associated with the more severe cases of FAS. Researchers report an average IQ of 65, with a range from 16 to 106 (Landesman-Dwyer, Martin, Smith, and Streissguth, 1980). Still others note that although the structural deformities caused by a mother's drinking during pregnancy are permanent, the behavioural problems of alcohol-exposed children seem to increase with age (Vorhees and Mollnow, 1987).

In the developing child, meningitis and encephalitis can lead to mental retardation and other anomalies. More encephalitic children than meningitic children suffer retardation. Childhood accidents involving cerebral assault or prolonged loss of consciousness can also cause brain damage that leads to retardation. Child abuse is increasingly being cited as another cause of brain damage (see Chapter 11).

Environmental Influences

The great majority of children with identified intellectual disabilities are categorized as mildly retarded with the etiology "causes unknown." These are the children we described in Chapter 3 as environmentally at risk. They live in an environment or have experiences that make them more prone to developing some form of disabling condition and/or more likely to fail in school. Children often come from deprived backgrounds and many of their problems spring from psychosocial disadvantage, poverty, inadequate nutrition, family instability, lack of educational opportunity, or an unstimulating infant environment. Subtle genetic factors may interweave with socio-economic deprivation to further affect a child's development. The relative influence of genetic factors to environmental ones is unknown.

DEVELOPMENTAL CONSEQUENCES OF INTELLECTUAL DISABILITIES

Intellectual disabilities cover a variety of physical, intellectual, academic, and behavioural characteristics. Viewing intellectual disability on a continuum, we can place children who are mildly disabled and having trouble with academic subjects at one end and profoundly retarded youngsters who may be non-ambulatory and non-responsive to their surroundings at the other. However, when discussing the population of persons with intellectual disabilities, we must keep in mind that categories of severity often overlap and are subject to change. We must also be aware that, despite their intellectual limitations, youngsters who are intellectually disabled show more similarities to other children than they do differences. They feel, think, hope, play, have fun, and find mischief, just like everyone else.

trait plasticity

Of particular importance is very early intervention, which allows teachers and parents to reduce the impact on child development. When IQ can be changed, this is called **trait plasticity**. Experts say that IQ is malleable by about twenty points. Early intervention with children with Down syndrome, for example, has shown that the condition need not always cause moderate to severe mental retardation. The psychological profile of babies with Down shows that they seem to develop normally in early infancy. The rate of development slows after six months of age, and by ten months these infants receive lower scores than normally developing infants on measures of intellectual development (Kopp, 1983). For children with Down syndrome, early and sustained intervention halts the decline in cognitive development. It also appears to prevent further decreases throughout the remaining early childhood years (see Guralnick and Bricker, 1987; also Chapter 15).

Physical Development

Individuals who are mildly intellectually disabled present few if any divergent physical symptoms that differentiate them from their peers. Minor differences may be seen in measures of health and of physical and motor performance. The range in age at which motor and language milestones are attained is far greater than for normally developing children. In early childhood, children with intellectual disabilities reach developmental milestones later; they may take up to nine months longer to learn to walk, talk, eat, and toilet themselves. These children are also likely to be somewhat below the comparative standards for height, weight, and skeletal maturity. In motor areas, they perform below the standards of non-disabled children (Bruininks, 1977).

Physical impairments become more complex in children with moderate retardation. These children tend to be markedly less able physically and more uncoordinated.

Traditionally, researchers and practitioners have tended to group together people who are severely and profoundly intellectually disabled, although these groups differ in several ways. Of course the categories do overlap, as do severe and moderate disabilities.

Individuals who are severely retarded may show poor speech, inadequate social skills, poor motor development or non-ambulation, incontinence, sensory impairments, seizures, and cerebral palsy.

The population of persons who are profoundly retarded can be divided functionally into two groups. "Relative" profoundly retarded persons have less organic damage and are capable of some degree of ambulation, communication, and self-help skills. "Absolute" profoundly retarded individuals are some of the most seriously impaired of all people with disabilities. The nature and degree of their disability is so great that, without various forms of intensive training and therapy, they exhibit virtually no adaptive behaviour. As well, many of these people exist in a medically fragile state.

Cognitive Development

Cognition is the process of recognizing, identifying, associating, and inferring meaning beyond the figural information provided by the environment that allows an understanding of a concept and application to new conditions (DeRuiter and Wansart, 1982). **Cognitive development** implies orderly changes that occur in the way children understand and cope with their world.

cognition

cognitive development

By definition, intellectual disability equates with deficiencies in cognitive development. Nevertheless, an intellectual disability means only slowing down, not stopping. Individuals with intellectual disabilities have impaired or incomplete mental development; their problems are specifically a retardation in the development of intellectual and adaptive behaviour. Their ability to learn and their capacity for putting learning to use is limited but certainly not non-existent. More and more research evidence indicates that retardation is quantitative rather than qualitative. That is, children who are intellectually disabled pass through the same cognitive developmental stages in the same order and manner as non-disabled children.

In studies of children with Down syndrome compared with non-disabled children of the same developmental level and socio-economic status, for example, investigators have found no differences in the sequence of sensorimotor development (Rogers, 1988). Children with intellectual disabilities simply pass through the stages more slowly and attain lower levels of achievement. On Piaget's periods, those who are mildly intellectually disabled function no higher than concrete operations; those who are moderately disabled do not surpass pre-operational stages, and those who are severely and profoundly disabled are at the sensorimotor stage.

Learning and Memory

The most specific consequences of intellectual disability involve its effects on an individual's potential to learn and to progress academically. Although individuals basically learn in the same fashion as do other people, students have difficulties in all aspects of intellectual functioning including concept learning, attention, and language. Memory, a key aspect of learning, is particularly problematic. Memory efficiency decreases as the level of retardation increases.

Memory is often explained through the constructs of information processing, which holds that we process information in different ways and at various levels of analysis. Essentially, information processing looks at the sensory register where information is perceived and attended to; at short-term memory where information that has been passed through the sensory register is held for about five seconds; and at long-term memory where retained information is stored, probably permanently. We could use the example of a young child hearing a catchy jingle on TV. The child attends to the jingle (sensory register), takes it into short-term memory, and then sings along and repeats the jingle over and over (rehearsal and elaboration) and in this way passes it to long-term memory where it is stored for retrieval later when the child, perhaps, wants to sing it for Daddy.

For information to move from short-term to long-term memory, we must do something to help us retain the information. Memory strategies include such things as rehearsal, subvocalization, and mnemonics. For individuals with disabilities, the greatest difficulty seems to be with short-term memory, which may result from an inefficient use of memory strategies. In addition, students often do not understand why they are memorizing certain information, in what context the information is meaningful, or how to internalize the structure provided by teachers (Gerber, 1988).

Students can be taught to use strategies successfully and thereby improve their memory functioning. (See Chapter 5.) And, once individuals with intellectual disabilities have thoroughly learned information, their long-term memory is comparable to that of non-disabled learners.

Difficulties with memory are compounded by problems with observational learning, organization, selective attention, generalization, and motivation. Students with intellectual disabilities find it very hard to select learning tasks and attend to all of their relevant dimensions. They also have difficulty paying attention and keeping on task. In the classroom, they tend to be less attentive, spend less time on academic tasks, and spend more time out of their seats than non-disabled children (McGee and Richgels, 1990). As well, they are less able to apply the knowledge or the skills they have learned to new tasks, problems, or stimulus situations. They have problems in generalizing and transferring skills.

Concept development, especially at abstract levels, is weak. For example, children with mild disabilities have significant deficits in the understanding of basic concepts such as *above, always, other,* and *different.*

As the degree of retardation increases, problems with learning and memory become more severe. However, learning is both possible and common for children with moderate to profound mental retardation. Using classical and operant conditioning procedures, educators have taught many skills in the domains of adaptive behaviour, simple academics, and vocational skill formation to severely retarded, and some profoundly retarded, individuals. (See Chapter 14.)

Communication Development

Youngsters with intellectual disabilities acquire language more slowly. Typically, their language levels remain below those of non-disabled children and are often below their general mental age.

Children demonstrate delays in sentence length, sentence complexity, and speech-sound discrimination. Their expressive language tends to be less complex than that of peers, and some children meet difficulties in generalizing the rules of grammar. They do not gain as much information from verbal or non-verbal receptive language; both children and adults who are mentally retarded do not decipher affective facial expressions as well as their peers (Adams and Markham, 1991; Maurer and Newbrough, 1987).

It is estimated that speech disorders affect about 55 percent of the total population of persons with intellectual disabilities. Some speech problems are the result of structural differences or malformations.

Language problems are not related to the etiology of the condition, but to its severity. Youngsters who are mildly intellectually disabled may be delayed in talking, but mutism is rare. Individuals who are moderately mentally retarded use stereotypical language, rarely free of defects. Among persons who are profoundly retarded, expressive speech and language skills are extremely limited. Mutism is common among individuals who are severely and profoundly retarded, as are primitive levels of speech such as babbling and jabbering.

Studies of children with Down syndrome suggest that their language acquisition and development is essentially similar to the language development of non-retarded children. They follow the same general path in acquiring language, but their language lags behind their non-verbal cognitive abilities, may proceed at a slower rate, and is often significantly delayed. Babies with Down vocalize less frequently. Many of these children do not acquire two-word phrases until three or four years of age.

Some children with Down syndrome do not acquire functional speech until eight years; some not at all. They often have oral problems that affect articulation—an overly large tongue over which they have less muscle control than other children, or an inability to close the passage from the nose to the mouth, resulting in hypernasal speech.

Academic Achievement

Pupils categorized as mildly intellectually disabled form the largest group of retarded learners and possess the widest range of skills and needs. In general, these students are slower in developing motor and social skills. In the classroom, they tend to underachieve in all academic areas. In fact, they do not achieve in school at a level commensurate with their intellectual potentials.

In elementary school, students who are mildly intellectually disabled accomplish about two-thirds of what other children will accomplish in an academic year (see Figure 6-2). This lag presents challenges to secondary-level educators, as we discuss in Chapter 16.

The cognitive characteristics associated with intellectual disability such as slower learning rates, failure to identify relevant features of tasks, difficulty responding spontaneously to newly learned material, and difficulty regularizing learned skills to new situations makes academic achievement problematic and difficult. Adding to the list of barriers are poor motivation, problems with short-term memory, lowered ability to generalize and transfer skills, and failure to use the strategies needed for successful learning. These students also have short attention spans and frustration with academic tasks. They cannot gain insight easily or reason as well as non-disabled children and find it more difficult to remember abstract ideas than concrete information. They often require more time than their normally achieving peers to attain accuracy and speed of performance.

Reading and all the language arts suffer. Math and arithmetic are not easy for students with mild disabilities. They often have difficulty with such basic skills as counting, writing nu-

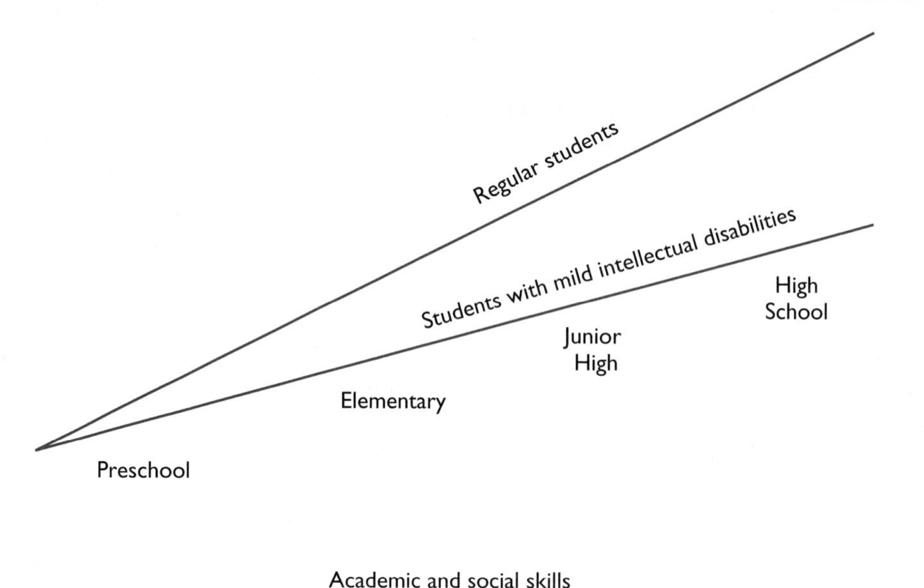

Figure 6-2
Differences in functioning of mildly retarded and non-retarded children in school

merals, and learning basic associations, and may not be competent even in the basic addition and subtraction facts. Students will meet particular difficulties in comprehending arithmetic concepts that involve abstract notions and symbols, and are unlikely to follow systematic strategies for solving word problems.

Individuals who are moderately intellectually disabled have limited intellectual ability, difficulties in working with abstract ideas, and problems in generalizing learning to new situations. They are not ready for much academic work until their early teens.

Children and young adults who are severely or profoundly disabled experience major challenges to successful adaptation. Their intensive instructional and technological needs must be met if they are to overcome the intellectual and adaptive demands of their homes, schools, and communities. Many individuals suffer such serious problems that they will likely require life care and supervision.

Individuals who are severely or profoundly disabled can acquire basic living and self-help skills; they may learn to regulate toilet habits, to eat with a spoon or fork, to throw a ball at a target, to understand simple verbal directions, and to participate in simple play and games. These groups are discussed more fully in Chapter 14.

Social and Emotional Development

In some children with mental retardation, social skill deficits are marked. Students are poorer at interpreting social cues and at generating strategies for solving social problems (see Leffert, Siperstein, and Millikan, 2000). It follows that they often have special personal and social problems and exhibit atypical development patterns in socialization. The more severe the disability, the lower the percentage of social interactions with non-disabled peers (Guralnick, 1981).

Children initiate far fewer social exchanges and tend to engage in shorter sequences of reciprocal interaction than do their normally developing counterparts (Beckman and Lieber, 1994). They may fail to respond readily to initial overtures from others; this lack of response further isolates the child as it serves to discourage interaction.

In general, students with intellectual disabilities are not well accepted by their non-disabled peers and often have trouble making friends (Luftig, 1988; Zetlin and Murtaugh, 1988). These children are frequently the subject of teasing, which serves to diminish their self-concepts and further compounds the problems in self-esteem that accompany low achievement. Children may be rejected because they look different or show unusual behaviour, and then don't try again because of low motivation.

On the other side of the coin, studies of how children with disabilities feel about peers (Wenz-Gross and Siperstein, 1997) find that children with disabilities were less likely to view their peers as a source of support than normally developing children. This is particularly strong in the area of emotional support. In friendships, children reported less intimacy, loyalty, self-esteem, and contact in their friendships than did normally developing peers.

Students who are moderately retarded have rather clear-cut deficits in adaptive behaviour; they have problems with interpersonal relationships, social concepts, emotional instability, and communication. As these children grow older, the progressive widening of their developmental lag tends to make their retardation more obvious. This is in contrast to persons who are mildly disabled whose condition becomes less obvious in adulthood.

Behaviour

Students with intellectual disabilities are at risk for the same types of psychological disorders as are students without cognitive defects (Stough and Baker, 1999). Children with intellectual disorders have a higher rate of behavioural disorders than do other children (Einfield and Tonge, 1995). In a study of the relationship between intellectual deficits and aggression (Huessman, Eron, and Yarmel, 1987), results indicated that childhood aggression was correlated with low intellectual and scholastic aptitude. Children with low intelligence abilities had difficulties learning needed skills for non-aggressive problem solving and probably experienced increased frustration and stress.

As well as behavioural disorders, there exists a significant correlation between the level of retardation and psychiatric processes. The prevalence of mental illness has been estimated to occur in from 14 to 64 percent of the retarded population (see Galligan, 1990). One of the most serious disorders is schizophrenia.

There may be a higher rate of depressive disorders in persons with intellectual disabilities. Studies estimate that as many as ten percent of people with intellectual problems suffer from depression, as compared to one to five percent for children without mental retardation (Stough and Baker, 1999). Many show symptoms of loneliness, sadness, and worry. Note that adults with Down syndrome seem to have more depression and dementia than other adults with mental retardation (Dykens, 1996).

Especially in children, it is extremely difficult, if not impossible, to determine whether the emotional disturbance caused the mental retardation, or vice versa. Children who are emotionally disturbed in early childhood may be deprived of the normal sources of intellectual and social development. A low IQ (especially if below 50) increases the probability that an infant will have problems in perceiving, understanding, and responding to the environment and is therefore associated with the pathology of psychoses. Conversely, the child who is intellectually disabled may withdraw and display the behaviours characteristic of children who are emotionally disturbed.

Maladaptive behaviour, which includes both inappropriate behaviours and self-injurious behaviours, is found across the spectrum of the population of intellectual disabilities but is more common in persons who are severely and profoundly retarded. As with skill development, the frequency of maladaptive behaviours is extremely variable. (See also Chapter 13.)

Inappropriate behaviours include aggression toward other people and objects, tantrums, and such stereotypical (self-stimulating) behaviour as meaningless repetitive movements, rocking, and hand waving. Hand–mouthing (finger and hand sucking) is common. Less prevalent behaviours include vomiting and rumination, disrobing, pica and coprophagy (eating inedible objects, including feces), stealing, and material hoarding (Whitman and Scibak, 1979).

self-injurious behaviour

Self-injurious behaviour, defined as any self-inflicted, repetitive action that leads to laceration, bruising, or abrasions of the client's own body, is common. Persons who are severely and profoundly retarded may engage in head banging, eye gouging, biting, scratching, self-pinching and hitting, and rectal digging. The prevalence of self-injurious behaviour ranges from 8 to 19 percent (Gedye, 1989). Higher frequencies are found among those who are severely retarded and profoundly retarded, as compared to individuals who are mildly intellectually disabled.

Very little is known about the origin of these behaviours, although some are part of normal development and seem to provide sensory feedback. For example, body rocking as self-stimulation is almost universal in babies in the latter part of the first year. But research has not identified the variables that lead to self-stimulation then going on to become an aberrant behaviour.

In fact, researchers have only just begun to study the ubiquitous stereotyped behaviour that is seen in some form among different developmental disabilities. They do not yet know the precursors that lead to abnormal development of self-stimulating and self-destructive behaviours, the mechanisms that cause these behaviours to persist, and the effectiveness of existing prevention programs (Berkson and Tupa, 2000).

Co-occurring Disabilities

Across the spectrum, persons with intellectual disabilities show more co-occurring conditions than do the rest of the population. Epilepsy is the most frequent additional disability in children with mental retardation, with a reported prevalence of 5 to 50 percent in mild cases and 26 to 50 percent in persons with severe retardation.

There exists a strong negative correlation between IQ level and the presence of organic brain pathology, central nervous system impairment, and other disabilities. In other words, as one proceeds down the scale, the incidence of co-occurring disabilities increases, with blindness, deafness, cerebral palsy, epilepsy, and other physical anomalies the rule rather than the exception. One study (Kapell, Nightingale, Rodriguez, Lee, Zigman, and Schupf, 1998) found in a sample of persons with mental retardation a higher percentage of medical and visual disorders than age and gender peers in the general population. A British Columbia study of non-specific retardation (Herbst and Baird, 1983) found that 27 percent of people with mild intellectual disabilities had additional conditions. In contrast, 73.1 percent of profoundly retarded individuals suffered additional conditions.

Survival rates vary with the level of retardation. Herbst and Baird (1983) found the death rate among mildly intellectually disabled persons was twice as high as that of the general population. It was seven times higher among those severely retarded, and thirty-one times higher among those profoundly disabled. Moreover, the mortality rate among people who are profoundly retarded is almost 50 percent higher than among those with severe retardation. Mortality rates for non-ambulant persons are significantly higher than for those who are ambulant (Balakrishnan and Wolf, 1976).

Down Syndrome

In children with Down syndrome, consistent patterns of development have emerged in the research. There seems to be a decline in cognitive scores after about six months, with a slight increase in adolescence.

Children with Down demonstrate particular difficulty with expressive language. Their impairments are relatively less pronounced in social development and in the mastery of adaptive skills associated with daily living, although growth in these domains progresses at a slower rate than that of normal developing children (see Hauser-Cram, Warfield, Shonkoff, Krauss, Lipshur, and Sayer, 1999).

People with Down syndrome are prone to a range of serious health problems. Only within recent years has the life span of children with Down syndrome begun to approach that of the general population. In 1929, these individuals had a life expectancy of nine years; by 1980, it had advanced to more than thirty years; now 25 percent of individuals with Down syndrome live to the age of fifty (Patterson, 1987). The mortality rate is still high, however, especially perinatally and in the first years of life, largely due to congenital heart conditions and increased susceptibility to infections. After age one, mortality is considerably reduced. Between ages five and ten, life expectancy is only 6 percent below normal.

Down Syndrome is a cause of mental retardation, ranging from mild to profound.

About 40 percent of children with Down syndrome have congenital heart defects. Gastrointestinal malformations and reduced resistance to respiratory infections are common. Children are especially susceptible to otitis media and the resultant conductive hearing loss; as many as 75 percent of children with Down syndrome may have significant hearing losses, and the detrimental effects of hearing loss are believed to be greater for these children compared to non-retarded youngsters (Whitman, Simpson, and Compton, 1986).

Children with Down syndrome have biochemical differences. Recent research on chromosome 21 has shown that its genes are linked not only to Down, but also to susceptibility among normal individuals to cancer, Alzheimer's, congenital heart defects, and vision problems (Kolata, 1988).

If individuals with Down syndrome survive to middle age, they are more likely to develop cataracts, leukemia, and Alzheimer's (Patterson, 1987). There is a twenty- to fiftyfold increase in the risk of developing leukemia, probably because of a gene on chromosome 21 that is known to cause leukemia if improperly activated (Patterson, 1987; Siwolop and Mohs, 1985). Adults with Down are predisposed to Alzheimer's, with a prevalence rate of 54.5 percent in the sixth decade (see Prasher, Chowdhury, Rowe, and Bain, 1997).

Cultural and Linguistic Differences

In both historical and contemporary conditions, prejudice has caused individuals to be judged as deviant or disabled on the basis of characteristics that are typical for their minority group or from stereotyping. This is particularly true in the case of mental retardation where the conjunction of disorder (or presumed disorder), ethnicity, and special education has a rather nasty history (see Winzer, 1993).

We have already mentioned that there is an over-representation of students from culturally and linguistically diverse groups in programs for speech and language disabilities and for learning disabilities. This also occurs in the field of mental retardation, although there is far greater reluctance today than in the past to refer students to this category. Caution results from the growth of the field of learning disabilities, the inclusive movement, and the overlap among categories. Especially important are a number of court cases in the United States, such as Larry P. vs. Riles, class actions that have disputed the use of IQ tests and inappropriate placements for minority students.

ASSESSMENT OF INTELLECTUAL DISABILITIES

A complete assessment of a child suspected of intellectual disabilities fulfills several major needs. A first step is a full pediatric medical evaluation of the child in order to pinpoint secondary conditions, recognize and identify the child's strengths, and detail necessary medical treatment regimes.

Within the educational milieu, assessment looks at two broad areas. First, it must be determined if a child's mental ability and adaptive behaviour fulfill the definitional criteria for mental retardation. Second, assessment data provide guidelines for the development of an appropriate program and/or treatment plan and the establishment of objectives and remedial strategies.

There are virtually thousands of tests, measures, inventories, and scales available. Yet assessment remains problematic. Diagnosticians still encounter grave difficulties in arriving at an accurate assessment of the learning potential and adaptive behaviour of many children who are intellectually disabled.

Formal diagnosis is not one short affair. Assessment incorporates a range of medical, formal, and informal processes using a variety of assessment instruments, different types of procedures, and different personnel. In an extreme case, as an example, a child with a severe intellectual impairment and co-occurring disabilities may be seen by a physician for physiological assessment, an audiologist for hearing acuity, an ophthalmologist for visual efficiency, a physical therapist for gross motor functioning, an occupational therapist for fine motor skills, a psychologist for intellectual ability, and a teacher for educational achievement.

Educational procedures may include direct testing, ecological or functional assessment, assessment of adaptive behaviour, achievement tests, social skills assessment, or some other assessment procedure. The tools administered depend on the strengths and needs of an individual. A test that suits a child who is mildly disabled, for example, will likely be inappropriate for one with severe retardation.

Screening

In the school system, educational screening often precedes psycho-educational diagnosis. For children with moderate to profound intellectual disabilities, screening may not take place simply because many of these children will have overt and obvious problems. Such clear-cut organic or psychological signs accompanying severe disabilities make it possible to identify them in infancy. In contrast, many cases of mild intellectual disability are not suspected until children enter school.

Teachers are often the first to recognize that these children have problems and are at the forefront in identifying their needs and referring them for further assessment. Not only can teachers observe students over a period of time and note academic performance in the classroom and social behaviour in and out of the classroom, but also they have access to pertinent school records and to the observations and comments of other teachers who may have encountered the child in earlier grades.

Assessment of Intelligence

Founded on the AAMR definition, the formal assessment of intellectual disabilities has two major areas of concern— IQ and adaptive behaviour. IQ is the pivotal concept: an assessment of intelligence is important in order to meet the definitional criteria of an IQ level two or more standard deviations below the norm. IQ has been around for a long time and a range of measures are in use. A sampling is shown in the appendix table, Tools for Assessment.

Children in the more severe ranges of intellectual disability are often untestable through the usual standardized IQ tests such as the WISC-III. In cases where organic brain pathology and physical disabilities are present, IQ levels are estimated through the use of developmental scales, measures of adaptive behaviour, observations, and other tools. (See Chapters 13 and 14.)

Assessment of Adaptive Behaviour

The inclusion of adaptive behaviour in the definition of intellectual disabilities brought its own set of problems. Lacking consensus on the exact nature of the construct, the question of how to effectively assess adaptive behaviour is beset with difficulties.

Despite this, numerous scales have appeared (see the appendix table, Tools for Assessment, for samples). Still, no single, quantifiable, and reliable assessment procedure exists and almost all of the scales designed to measure adaptive behaviour have been criticized.

Many adaptive skills are very visible, such as using the toilet, feeding oneself, dressing, and peer relations. Adaptive behaviour scales, used with children in all severity ranges, generally consist of lists or inventories of these and other common behaviours, as well as maladaptive behaviours. The scales are completed by someone close to the child—a parent, teacher, or primary caregiver.

INTERVENTION WITH CHILDREN WHO HAVE INTELLECTUAL DISABILITIES

Many different types of intervention are used with individuals who have intellectual disabilities. Medical and pharmacological interventions are especially important for individuals with organic etiologies. Social and early intervention is critical for infants and preschoolers and their families (see Chapter 15). Various therapists may intervene to improve secondary motor, language, or speech disabilities.

It is in the schools, however, where the major focus occurs. Most students with mild disabilities are placed in general classrooms, and the crux of education for students with moderate to profound mental retardation has altered in recent years to greater placement in neighbourhood schools.

Medical Intervention

No surgical procedures or miracle drugs are known to actually improve intellectual ability or adaptive behaviour. In general, medical intervention attempts to prevent or correct the organic causes of retardation rather than alleviate the condition itself. We have already discussed the values of screening in cases such as phenylketonuria. Surgical intervention has been used with children who have Down syndrome in an effort to alleviate speech and eating problems and to render their appearance more normal. Increasing numbers of families are seeking this option, especially for tongue reduction to improve speech and looks.

People with severe disabilities are more likely to receive medication to change their behaviour than most others in society (Kennedy and Meyer, 1998). Some drugs offer great promise for selectively reducing challenging behaviour while improving other forms of adaptive functioning (Kennedy and Meyer, 1998). Nevertheless, there are serious reservations about the overuse of drug therapy.

Technical Aids

Technological advances have resulted in the development of devices designed specifically for persons with developmental disabilities. A range of instructional technology is employed in classrooms, primarily involving microcomputers and innovative software.

Computers seem to promote academic achievement and more positive attitudes about learning, particularly for disadvantaged students and other low achievers (Lepper and Gurtner, 1989). For people with severe disabilities, independent functioning is supplemented with aids for self-help skills and environmental control, for example, a device that produces a signal for a non-toilet-trained child to go to the bathroom, a self-feeding tray for persons who are multiply disabled, and special bathing devices. Adaptive equipment is discussed in Chapter 12.

Educational Intervention

Intellectual disabilities are related to delayed intellectual development in areas considered important for school success. Students classified as intellectually disabled achieve below grade level and usually experience difficulties throughout their school careers. Achievement is related to the degree of disorder, and various settings and strategies are directed toward this population. In Chapter 14 we return to intervention for persons with severe and profound disorders.

Service Delivery Models

Within the school system, the current trend is to include students with intellectual disabilities in the regular classroom, especially those with mild disabilities. A student's success in the classroom depends on a number of additional factors that include support services, curriculum adaptations and modifications, acceptance by the other students, the classroom teacher's experience with and exposure to children who are exceptional, the availability of community resources, and the age of the student.

In the past, children with moderate and severe intellectual disabilities attended special schools. Although these schools provided an appropriate curriculum, a controlled learning environment, and a suitable daily schedule, they had the drawback of segregation. Today, students who need special education arrangements may be in the regular classroom with assistance or perhaps placed part of the time in special classes in the regular school.

There is often much more intervention at elementary than secondary levels. Although services for a majority of students with disabilities have significantly improved and expanded in the years since the passage of Public Law 94-142 in the United States (see this chapter's Historical Notes), the provision of appropriate educational services remains problematic for many secondary-school-aged students with disabilities. Secondary education programs tend to be more explicitly vocationally oriented than those at elementary levels and are directed toward securing employment upon graduation. (See Chapter 16.)

Educational Approaches

There are three major goals in the education of students with intellectual disabilities: productivity, independence, and participation. To accomplish these goals, students are presented with instruction in the areas of academic, social, self-help, community living, and vocational skills. Depending on the extent and severity of the disability, the major goals are not always fully achievable; success may be only fractional for children functioning at the low end of the continuum.

Students Who Have Mild Intellectual Disabilities

The actual curricula objectives are the same for students with mild intellectual disabilities as for their peers. Students require instruction in basic academic skills, particularly basic literacy and numeracy. Teachers must also stress the cognitive, language, and social domains. Each program will be individualized based on a student's unique set of strengths and weaknesses.

In the early grades, children who are mildly disabled are taught readiness skills in such areas as math and reading. At the intermediate school levels, educational emphasis may be placed on activities for everyday life such as functional reading, writing, and math, and areas such as learning about the local environment, transportation, budgeting, peer relationships, personal hygiene, and personal and recreational interests. At the secondary level, the components of transition are critical. This is the focus of Chapter 16.

The In the Classroom feature at the end of Section 2 presents ideas about instruction for students with mild disabilities. You can also see how a child with mild disabilities may be accommodated in the continuing case study of Nicholas, the child we met at the opening of this chapter. The most appropriate placement for Nicholas at this time is the general classroom, with an IEP and adaptations in core areas of weakness.

Case Study

Nicholas (continued)

When the psychologist, the classroom teacher, and the parents met to discuss Nicholas' program, the psychologist asked the parents many questions about Nicholas' activities outside the classroom and how he performed in the home and the neighbourhood. She pointed out that Nicholas' competence outside school, specifically in sports, did not match his obvious lacks in classroom learning—which, even with somewhat restricted ability, should be higher.

It appears that Nicholas has many "street smarts" but is not transferring these to school learning and demonstrated little knowledge of reading and writing in his grade two classroom. To stimulate his interest, a program was built on his personal likes. For example, sports—especially hockey—are of major interest to Nicholas, and the individual reading program was based on this.

In the actual teaching/learning situation, there is much documentation of the success of accomplishing specific academic objectives through direct instruction. For a child who has poor memory, low task commitment, and poor language, this is a necessary component. Nicholas needs structured direct teaching daily, with much repetition.

In all areas, concrete materials should be used. Persons who have mental disabilities will often learn better if the stimuli they encounter are real and not symbolic. For example, money skills should be taught using real money, and social skills with real people.

The program developed for Nicholas focuses very heavily on functional skills and uses materials from his own experiences and interests. An extract from Nicholas' IEP is given below.

EXTRACT FROM NICHOLAS' IEP

Name Nicholas
Teacher Mr. McPhee
CA 8-2
Grade 2
School St. Basil's

Present Levels of Functioning

Nicholas was referred by his classroom teacher for psycho-educational assessment as he is falling further and further behind his classmates, especially in the core areas of reading and math.

Cognitive

On the WISC-III, Nicholas showed a Full Scale score of 66 (+ - 5). This is below the norm.

Language

Nicholas appears to have below-average language ability based on results of the PPVT-R and the TOLD-P. However, the psychologist noted his strong use of appropriate language when talking about things that really interested him, although syntactical lags were obvious.

Reading

Nicholas has barely made a start in formal reading. He is at a beginning grade one level.

Math

All math concepts seem to be difficult for Nicholas. He does not seem to understand place value. However, he knows the names of coins and seemed further advanced and far more interested when using real money.

Placement

Regular classroom

Adaptations

- IEP
- Direct instruction in reading and math
- Peer tutoring
- Promotion of social interactions
- Modified report cards

Long-Range Goals

- Stimulate interest in school activities by building on relatively strong language based on his own experiences.
- Correct syntax and expand language incidentally
- Develop a sight-word vocabulary
- Read very short paragraphs and books (e.g. *Sports Illustrated for Kids*) about sports.
- Use coins as the major manipulative to teach rational counting, place value, addition and subtraction facts, and basic computation.

Short-Term Objectives

- Learn ten sight words related to sports with the teacher, in a small group, or with a peer tutor.
- Read and discuss short paragraphs about sports in a small group.
- Use written exercises (fill-in-the-blank, draw, underline the word) to stress sight words and to teach reading directions.
- Use pennies for rational counting to ninety-nine, forward and backward.
- Use coins for simple equations.

Students Who Have Moderate Intellectual Disabilities

For students with moderate disabilities, the curriculum is less academically oriented than for children who are mildly disabled. In general, children who are moderately disabled do not learn to read beyond the first-grade level. Children are taught to read names, directions, and labels, and to write relevant names and words. They are also introduced to numbers, time, and simple money exchange.

The ultimate goal of education is functional independence. Recent trends in public school curricula for students and young adults who are moderately and severely disabled have seen a movement away from the specification of curricular goals on the basis of developmental age; teachers now direct instruction toward chronological-age-appropriate skills that students need to meet the demands of their community environments (Wiggins and Behrmann, 1988).

When functionality is the core of the curriculum, it is referred to as a *functional ap-*

Case Study

Ben

Ben is in his last year of school. When he was only a preschooler, he was identified as being moderately mentally retarded. Throughout elementary school he was included in the regular classroom with modified programming. However, it was soon apparent that secondary programs are not consistent with Ben's future needs, and almost all of his secondary experience has been in a program that stresses life and occupational skills and functional academics.

Now in his final year in school, Ben's transition plan (see Chapter 16) is more critical than ever. It includes functional academics, community services and agencies, vocational training and work experience, and opportunities to function independently in the community.

At the moment, Ben's teacher is working with Ben and his classmates on living and recreational skills in a thematic topic on communities. They are learning about shopping, restaurants, and other community places. For example, under shopping the lesson areas and activities include making a shopping list; floor plans and aisle signs; the sequence of shopping and shopping in aisle order; locating items, prices, and sizes; and unpacking and storing groceries. The restaurants segment includes areas such as standing in line; selecting a seat; ordering; and table manners. In the section on the post office, Ben learns about buying stamps, addressing envelopes, and sending mail (see Beakley and Yoder, 1998).

proach or *life-skills instruction.* Adaptive behaviour, self-help skills, life skills, and social skills are the important components of this approach, which is fully discussed in Chapter 14. An illustration is given in the brief case study about Ben.

Training in life skills is essential for students with mental handicaps.

Students Who Are Severely and Profoundly Disabled

While almost all students with mild intellectual disabilities will be educated in regular classrooms, and many with moderate disabilities will be in regular classes or schools, the placement of students who are severely and profoundly disabled is more controversial. For these youngsters, there exist conflicting and extreme ideologies that revolve around the issue of inclusive schooling. (See Chapters 13 and 14.)

There is no question that for children who are severely and profoundly disabled we must redefine the term *education* beyond its traditional academic limits. The goals of education are different than those for non-disabled students and for those with milder disabilities. Many more personnel are involved: these children often require a range of other services from professionals such as doctors, speech therapists, social workers, and psychologists.

The major educational goals are to decrease dependence on others, increase awareness of environmental stimulation, teach basic communication and self-help skills, and push achievement levels higher. The training of individuals who are severely and profoundly retarded begins with basic survival and self-help skills, along with the elimination of undesirable behaviour. Repetition and simple conditioning are primary teaching strategies. Training involves imitation, language acquisition, self-feeding, ambulation, dressing skills, toilet training, social and recreational behaviour, and functional academic skills.

Although behaviour modification is used with virtually every type of disability, it is particularly useful in the education and training of children with severe and profound disabilities. Behavioural methods seem to succeed where others fail, and the behavioural emphasis on specific task analysis is particularly well suited to the problems of individuals who are severely disabled. Behaviour modification has been successfully used to teach a diverse array of skills, including self-help skills, eating, toileting, dressing, socialization, and language acquisition. As well, a range of behaviour modification techniques have been employed in the elimination of maladaptive behaviours.

Social Intervention

Advocacy groups of parents and professionals exist for the sole purpose of improving life conditions for the population of persons who are intellectually disabled. The Canadian Association of Community Living (CACL) (formerly the CAMR) is typical. Essentially, the CACL performs the following functions:

- Encourages the acceptance of all people who are intellectually disabled into the life of the community;
- Promotes the enactment and implementation of legislation to improve the welfare of people who are intellectually disabled;
- Promotes improved educational and vocational training for intellectually disabled people;
- Furthers the education and training of personnel for work in the field of intellectual disabilities;
- Provides centres for the gathering and distribution of information about intellectual disabilities;
- Fosters research concerning all aspects of intellectual disability;
- Develops better public understanding of people who are intellectually disabled and their needs (CAMR, 1980).

SUMMARY

1. Under the AAMR definition, three factors must be present before an individual can be considered within the category of mental retardation—subaverage general intellectual functioning, deficits in adaptive behaviour, and manifestation during the developmental period.

Historical Notes

As a human condition, mental retardation has been acknowledged in literature for 2500 years. However, only sparse and scattered information about the actual living and social conditions of persons with mental retardation exists before the 17th century. It does appear that little was done for those in society who appeared different or deviant. Often, they became the focus of society's accumulated fears and myths. Many were treated cruelly. Sometimes they were seen as buffoons, and sometimes as special conversants with higher powers.

Actual teaching of students with mental retardation began in France in the early 1800s. It rapidly translated to the New World, where special facilities were established in Boston in 1848 and Ontario in 1873. In the early 1900s, special classes developed in the public schools to extend schooling to larger numbers and a more varied clientele of students for longer periods.

In the late 19th century, biological theories of degeneracy and repressive theories of heredity ushered in a period of cruel and callous treatment. *Eugenics*, essentially founded on the idea that the future good of society depended on allowing only the average or superior to marry and procreate, developed as an important and influential theory. It determined to a large extent the treatment of persons with mental retardation until the 1930s. During this period, educators and the general public assumed a qualitative difference between normal and abnormal; persons with disabilities were thought to have traits and characteristics of a degree and type that made them fundamentally different from the general run of humanity. Many persons who were disabled were locked away, forbidden to marry and procreate, and viewed as pariahs in society.

Although schooling became the norm for all children in the first half of the 20th century, children with intellectual disabilities were often excluded from the schools for the sake of preserving order, protecting the teacher's time, and assisting the learning of other students. Or students were placed in segregated classes, euphemistically titled "opportunity classes," or "auxiliary classes," or "classes for slow learners."

A clinical model predominated, representing a view in which disability was characterized as stemming from biological defect. Educational goals focused on overcoming or compensating for the disability. Students were trained in manual arts, practical skills, handiwork, and personal and social adjustment skills.

It was not until the 1950s that curriculum for students with mild retardation changed and began to represent an extension of the general school curriculum. At the same time, interest developed in how to train and teach people with more significant deeper disabilities and curricula for those with moderate and severe retardation emerged.

The 1960s were the turning point in the education of persons with retardation. In that decade a matrix of factors persuaded the educational system to embark on a search for more appropriate ways to educate all children with disabilities. One of the most significant events was the 1959 *Manual of Terminology and Classification in Mental Retardation,* which presented a new view of retardation. It reflected sociopolitical changes and departed from previous definitions that considered the condition an incurable trait. At the same time, parent pressure, the philosophy of normalization, legislation, litigation, a panel on mental retardation called by U.S. president John Kennedy, a series of efficacy studies, and exposés of the deplorable conditions in institutions for mentally retarded persons and for juvenile delinquents created a climate for change. Massive funding and research was directed to the area. Special education services for students identified as mildly retarded came to occupy a central role and a large share of fiscal and human resources in the schools.

With the 1975 passage of Public Law 94-142 in the United States, the notion of educating all students in the least restrictive environment emerged. Legislation was joined to litigation, civil rights, parent pressure, normalization, and deinstitutionalization. Soon, mainstreaming and then inclusion in the general classroom became the most common option for the education of children and youth with mental retardation.

2. Adaptive behaviour is a difficult construct to operationalize, define, and measure. In the broadest sense, adaptive behaviour refers to an individual's ability to cope or deal effectively with personal and social demands. The existence of limitations in adaptive skills occurs within the context of community environments typical of the individual's age peers and is indexed to the person's individualized needs for support.
3. In current definitions of mental retardation, there is considerable controversy about terminology, adaptive behaviour, and the use of IQ tests. Today's definitions, especially of mild disability, do not see it as a permanent condition but one that improves with sustained intervention and also one linked to the demands of formal schooling. There is a higher incidence of retardation during the school years, with lower incidence figures during the preschool years and adulthood.
4. The redefining of children labelled as mentally retarded in 1973 to omit those functioning between one and two standard deviations below the mean accompanied increasing numbers of students being categorized as learning disabled. *Learning disabilities* is today the largest focus of special education in many school districts and *mental retardation*, per se, seems to be a category of declining importance.
5. The agents that cause mental retardation are legion and include genetic and chromosomal differences, infections such as maternal rubella, intoxicants such as drugs, postnatal diseases such as meningitis, and childhood accidents.
6. In trying to pinpoint the existence and severity of intellectual disabilities, clinicians are challenged to find a range of observations and measures that are appropriate for individual children. Data on a child's levels of cognitive functioning (IQ tests) are employed as one measure used to determine an individual educational program.
7. Although youngsters with mild intellectual disabilities may consistently lag in academic areas such as reading, math, science, and social studies, they learn in the same way as other pupils. Studies on the learning characteristics of these children show that even if their rate of learning is slower and the level reached not as high, their learning curves approximate those of non-disabled pupils. Individuals who are severely and profoundly retarded must often struggle to achieve ambulation and simple physical activities. For individuals in these two levels of severity, physical development is often impaired and co-occurring conditions are common.
8. Children labelled as mildly intellectually disabled form the greatest proportion of the retarded population. Today, the majority of these students are educated in regular classrooms. Following graduation, many such individuals blend into the social fabric of their

neighbourhoods, holding jobs, marrying, and having families. Once that adjustment is made, they are no longer retarded according to the AAMD definition.

9. Children with moderate levels of intellectual disability are being educated in regular schools, either in regular classrooms or in special self-contained classrooms. Teachers present limited academic curricula with a stress on functional skills in all domains. The inclusion of students who are severely or profoundly retarded is beset by controversy. These children have grave barriers to learning, often demonstrate maladaptive behaviour, and are often multiply disabled. Although structured behavioural programs can impart useful skills, argument rages about the most appropriate placement in which to present these skills.

WEBLINKS

Canadian Down Syndrome Society **www.cdss.ca/**

Fragile X Syndrome **www.fraxa.org**

In the Classroom

Good teaching applies to an integrated class the same way that it applies to any class. For all students, it is the teacher's responsibility to provide warm and accepting learning environments. Still, there is no question that integrating students with exceptional conditions involves a wider range of organizational and instructional materials and alternatives than does regular teaching. Children may need special attention because of limited ability, poor motivation, sensory or physical impairments, or specific learning disabilities.

When students with disabilities are within general environments, their success depends on a matrix of factors. Inclusion cannot work unless these factors, shown in the table below, are in place.

Including students with special needs demands some changes in the standard learning environment. The teacher must be able to meet individual learning needs through appropriate changes in the environment, instruction, and content. The process of change in environment and instruction is diagrammed in the accompanying figure.

While there are many generic strategies and approaches, in at least some cases different adaptations and modifications are needed depending on the child's type and severity of disability. However, the range of adaptations is enormous, there is wide variation in the use of possible instructional arrangements, and styles vary across classrooms. Moreover, changes in teaching methods are often not that obvious or different. In general, specialized competencies and teaching methods are extensions and refinements of core competencies rather than new sets of teaching behaviour and skills (Ysseldyke and Algozzine, 1990).

Teachers will use procedures and techniques that, for purposes of clarity, we arbitrarily refer to as *accommodations, adaptations,* and *modifications* in the physical, instructional, and psychosocial environments. Distinctions between accommodations, adaptations, and modifications are subtle, and there is much overlap. We can say that:

- An *accommodation* is a change that assists a child's functioning in the environment, a technique that eliminates or minimizes the learning differences

Making inclusion work

School	Restructuring to merge special education and regular education to create a more unified educational system School personnel are committed to accepting responsibility Accommodations made to the physical plant and environment Principal is supportive
Teachers	Positive attitudes; believe students can succeed Appropriate expectations Willingness to collaborate, adapt, and modify Tolerant of diverse student levels Real and perceived knowledge of students with disabilities Knowledgeable about and accepting of a child's problems and requirements Willing to plan learning experiences individualized to the child's needs
Team approach	Co-operation and collaboration Develop shared responsibility for students through regular and special education teachers working side by side with heterogeneous groups of students Team planning and teaching
Individualization	IEP Environmental adaptations Specialized devices and equipment
Curriculum	Curricular adaptations Curriculum matched to each student's needs Adapted regular curriculum Modified special curriculum Developmentally and age-appropriate curriculum Many strategies implemented such as co-operative learning and direct instruction Different grouping arrangements and lesson formats used
Evaluation	Appropriate policies for monitoring individual progress Accurate and ongoing assessment Adapted tests and grading practices
Supports	Individual supports for students with disabilities, including materials and personnel Appropriate teacher training Paraprofessional assistance Therapists and other related services
Social	Peer support Social skills training
Parents	Parents support program goals

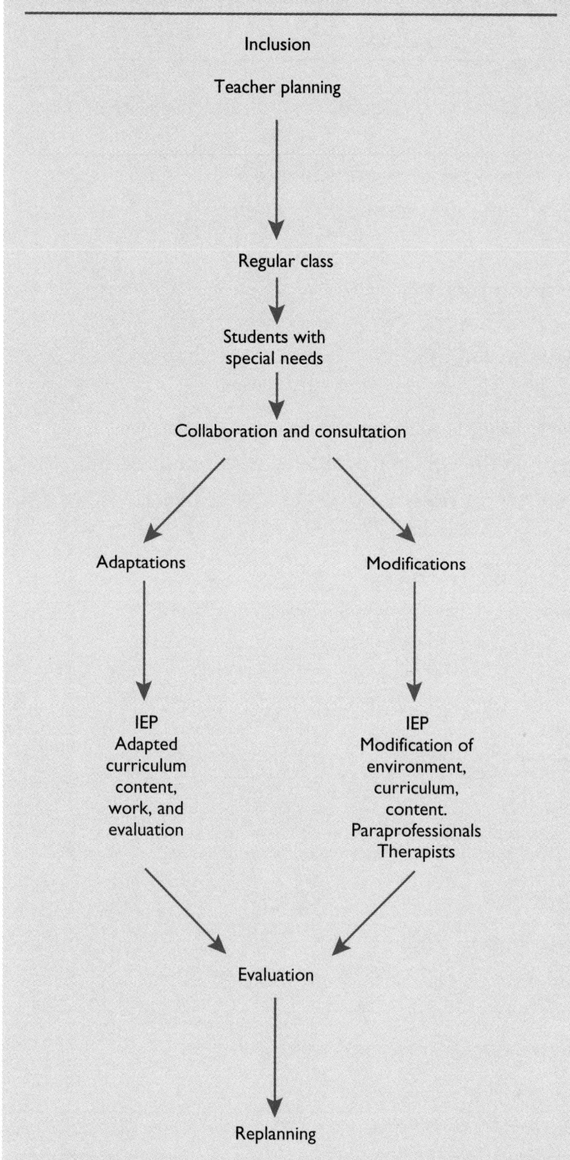

by offering alternate ways of handling a task. For example, an FM system for a child with a hearing impairment; seating close to the teacher for the child with a behavioural disorder; increased lighting, but no glare, for the child with a visual disability; or extra space between desks for the child with a physical disability.

- *Adaptations* are changes to the regular curriculum that retain the same outcomes as those for normally developing children. Adaptations refer to how teachers change instruction. The array of adaptations from which a teacher may choose is broad. Strategies such as precision teaching, cognitive strategy training, co-operative learning, monitoring of children's on-task behaviour, appropriate pacing of instruction, and peer tutoring have been shown to be effective in integrated classes. More specifically, teachers may employ a slower pace with many redundant questions and much drill and practice for children with learning difficulties; many diagrams, visual materials, and media for students who must grasp ideas without depending solely on language; maps, graphs, and so on in string, pasta, or raised glue for students with visual impairments; work sheets with only one type of activity or question for students with learning disabilities; self-tests and checklists so older students can monitor themselves; practice questions before an examination for older students; co-operative learning strategies for average and below-average students; and independent studies for gifted learners.
- *Modifications* step away from the general curriculum and have learning outcomes that are substantially different from the prescribed curriculum. They generally apply to children with significant disabilities for whom the regular curriculum may not be relevant.

Providing appropriate adaptations for students with disabilities entails much more than finding a list of suggested adaptations for various subjects. It requires a great deal of advance planning, assessment of student ability and skill, consideration of resources, and curriculum planning. Particularly important is collaboration and input from a special-education teacher.

A major difficulty is matching appropriate adaptations and modifications to student learning deficits. This is facilitated when planning is individualized and documented in an IEP, as we discuss in Chapter 1. But it is simply not possible to adapt teacher-centred instruction to the diverse needs of every student, so teachers must select adaptations that suit a range of learners. As they make adaptations, teachers should ask the following questions:

- Can I do this in a reasonable amount of time with a reasonable amount of effort? Research shows that the less time and resources required to implement a change, the greater the acceptability to teachers.
- Can I fit this with my general teaching? In presenting instruction, teachers should alter the stress and pacing of lessons, the type and amount of seat work, and grading practices. Changes must often be made in the content of the lesson, which may be adapted to make it more concrete and relevant to children's recent experiences. Teachers can use multilevel instruction. In this, a main lesson is prepared and taught with variations included for individual student needs.
- If we teach this subject this way, will Jane be able to participate and learn the concept? Traditional instructional arrangements and lesson formats include lecture, demonstration, practice, whole class discussion, games and simulations, and experiential learning, and range from large group instruction to co-operative learning groups and peer partners to individual and independent seat work. Since students with disabilities often have problems in large groups and in independent seat work, some type of small group or individual instruction can be an effective adaptation. For example, change a format from an independent research project into an arrangement such as group investigation in order to include Jane.
- If I use this format, will Joe participate? Compared to one-to-one and small-group teaching arrangements, whole-class arrangements are consistently associated with the lowest levels of engaged behaviour (see Logan, Bakeman, and Keefe, 1997). As students with disabilities show lower levels of engagement in tasks than do their normally developing peers, a change to small-group instruction may also be beneficial for Joe.
- Is the adaptation relevant? To be effective, an adaptation or modification must match an evident problem or need of a particular student or group of students.
- How do I make the change? Inclusive practices do not presume that all teachers possess all the expertise needed to include all children; left alone, the solitary teacher cannot possibly know everything required to meet the learning needs of every student. Assistance must be provided in the areas of curriculum modification, participation, and social integration by special education teachers, paraprofessionals (aides), and non-disabled peers.

The range of adaptations is huge. In the accompanying table we point out some generic changes that are suitable for many special learners.

Examples of Generic Adaptations

Content adaptations

- Slow pace, wait time • Teach to learning styles • Use mastery learning

Instructional adaptations

- Use experiential learning that allows students with disabilities to be active rather than passive participants
- Use mnemonic devices
- Shorten directions
- Provide mediators
- Change format; for example, to a small group

- When large-group instruction is used, break the instruction up with an activity that allows all students to participate and move around
- Use advance organizers • Preface all remarks with a title, or the main idea of the lesson
- Use cognitive learning strategies
- Use many instructional scaffolds (types of supports that help students take the step from their current learning to adding new skills or knowledge)

Grouping adaptations

- Use co-operative learning, often recommended as a fundamental strategy in inclusive and multicultural classrooms • Set up learning centres

Adapting materials

- Make materials self-correcting • Highlight critical features • Block out extraneous elements

Cueing, feedback adaptations

- Provide response prompts • Use corrective feedback • Provide visual clues

Involving students

- Students appreciate it when teachers make changes in instructional techniques to allow for individual needs (Vaughn, Schumm, and Kouzekanani, 1993). Give older students some say in the adaptations that will be used.

Management adaptations

- Different delivery of reinforcers
- Use evaluative feedback. For example, "I like the way you formed your letters," rather than "Good work."
- Contingency contracts
- Change seating • Counselling
- Social skills training

Evaluation and grading adaptations

- Modify grades and report cards to reflect an individual student's level of improvement
- Use curriculum-based assessment

Study skills

- Teach study skills
- Note all assignments on a special bulletin board • Use study guides to tell students what to study

Three approaches of great relevance to inclusive classrooms are direct instruction, co-operative learning, and peer tutoring. For learners with special needs, a direct didactic approach has the best track record (Walberg, 1991). As well, there is clear evidence that children with learning and behaviour problems benefit from peer tutoring and co-operative learning. These methods have also been promoted in the education of students with cultural and linguistic differences.

Direct Instruction

One hallmark of an effective learning environment for students with mild disabilities is the degree to which the environment is constructively active. In an effective learning environment, the teacher engages in active teaching and the student is actively engaged in successfully completing academically relevant tasks. The teacher monitors student performance and provides informed feedback. This approach is referred to as *conventional teaching* or *direct instruction.*

Direct instruction is founded on behavioural task analysis. It refers to activity-focused, teacher-directed classroom procedures that are systematic and usually conducted according to an individual plan. The components of direct instruction include explicit step-by-step teacher procedures that account for student mastery, immediate feedback, practice, and gradual fading from teacher direction. Learning is achieved by identifying the specific objective to be attained, arranging appropriate stimuli to elicit the responses, programming learning sequences in small steps, and reinforcing desired behaviours. Procedures include prompting, shaping, or reinforcing implemented in a precise and consistent fashion.

The key elements of direct instruction are:

- *Review and check previous day's work*—daily review, homework check, and, if necessary, re-teaching.
- *Present new content or skills*—rapid presentation of new content and skills in very small steps.
- *Provide guided practice*—guided student practice under close teacher monitoring.
- *Check for understanding*—corrective feedback and reinforcement.
- *Provide independent student practice*—independent practice in seat work and homework.
- *Review frequently*—weekly and monthly review.

Co-operative Learning

Co-operative learning (also referred to as *shared learning, collaborative learning,* or *small-group learning*) is "a generic term for the instructional organization of children into small mixed ability study groups in which participants co-operate with one another to achieve academic goals" (Rich, 1986, p. 339). Within their groups, students know they can reach their goals if, and only if, peers in their group also reach their goals.

There are three basic formats of co-operative learning: peer teaching, in which students explain material to each other, listen to others, and arrive at a joint understanding of the material; a group format, where members pool information; and the jigsaw format, in which each student is assigned a task. Within these three main formats, many different co-operative learning strategies have been developed in laboratory settings and in classrooms. On the formats and procedures for different versions of co-operative learning see Winzer and Mazurek (1998).

Peer Tutoring

Peer tutoring, defined as "a more able child helping a less able child in a co-operative working pair carefully organized by a teacher" (Topping, 1989, p. 489), is an effective instructional alternative for students with learning disabilities and other special needs. The tutoring program should emphasize repetition, incorporate review, and ensure that the tutee reaches mastery level before advancing to the next tasks.

Not every student is suitable as a peer tutor. The optimal tutor is one who has mastered the skill to be taught and can follow the lesson independently of the teacher. A good tutor can reliably and accurately correct the tutee's errors and has the social skills necessary to form a long-term tutorial relationship (Grenwood, Carta, and Hall, 1988).

Behaviour manifestations, needs	Tips
Lags or difficulties in reading	• State a purpose for reading, such as looking for specifics. • Use various models for reading, such as in-class text reading, semantic maps, pre-teaching new vocabulary, silent reading. • Use general materials such as catalogues from Sears or Canadian Tire or high interest materials based on student preferences. • Use daily testing, repeated practice.
Poor comprehension of reading materials	• In order to provide pacing and ensure better understanding, read orally to the class. • Use reciprocal teaching, which involves students and teacher in a dialogue of written material to discover the meaning of a written passage. The steps are: 1. Summarize: identify and paraphrase the main ideas of the text. 2. Question generating: self-questioning about comprehension. 3. Clarifying: discerning where and if there has been a lack of comprehension. 4. Predicting: what will happen next (Palinscar and Brown, 1984).
Difficulty comprehending content area texts.	• Highlight textbooks • Provide supplementary content written to a lower level than the textbook. • Provide outlines of textbook chapters and outlines of lecture presentations for older students. • Teach textbook structure, such as headings, subheadings, differing print, introductory and summary paragraphs.
Expressive language delays or difficulties	• Use directed questioning and responses. Make questions meaningful to activate a child's thinking and promote problem-solving. Wait patiently for an answer. • Respond to the content rather than the correctness of the language; stress the answer, not the grammar. • Follow the child's lead and reply to the child's initiations or comments. Communication is maintained by conversational responses, not "good talking." For example, "I saw monkeys" is related to "Monkeys are funny," not "Good talking" (Owens, 1991). • The function of language depends on its effects on the environment. Focus on making language a part of a child's routine. Set the scene, provide materials, and prompt dialogues that children can use with each other. • Use puppets; young children tend to be braver about poor performance or use of language when they are protected by the puppet.

Behaviour manifestations, needs	Tips
	• Use experiential units in which instruction is modified to focus on tasks such as building things, setting up household tasks, or preparing food. This gives a child constant repetition of specific language. • Avoid placing pressures on the child to use oral language. • Don't speak for the child.
Receptive language delays or differences	• Speak clearly and at a moderate speed to be more easily understood. Use a normal pace and loudness and avoid over-enunciation. • The exception to the above are dysphasic children. Rapid sound changes may cause problems that impair their ability to identify and discriminate consonants. For these children, speak at a slower rate to improve comprehension. • Stress important points in a lesson with "Watch now," or "Listen carefully." • Repeat and reword if the child seems confused. • Give directives that are as explicit as possible. After giving a direction, have the child repeat it to show comprehension.
Speech problems	• Work proactively with the therapist. Find out what sounds the child is stimulable for (ready to learn). Target these sounds in individual sessions and give the child real-life opportunities to produce them. • Recognize and reinforce the child's use of correct forms. • Use formal reinforcement such as praise or stickers. • Create realistic conversational atmospheres where speech is valued. • Let students use response cards (a card they hold up on a Popsicle stick) rather than calling on individual students.
Limited vocabulary	• Focus on the children's interests. • Present new words with incidental teaching. Cazden (1988) suggests that word meanings are most easily learned through interactions and conversations with an adult who introduces new words. • Present new words in many contexts. The likelihood that a child will learn the meaning of a new word from a single exposure in a meaningful context ranges from 5 to 20 percent. • Use "Think, pair, share." After posing a question to the class, ask the students to find a partner, make eye contact, share their responses to the question, and remember their partner's response.
English is a second language	• Know the stages of second language acquisition. • While adding a second language and language culture to the child's repertoire, do not try to replace the first language and culture; retain both.

Behaviour manifestations, needs	Tips
	• Become familiar with features of students' dialects so as to understand better and distinguish miscues from errors. • Try to get trained aides who speak the child's language. • Use much oral language work. Garcia (1988) found that students learn math and literacy skills most effectively when student–student discussions take up to at least 50 percent of instructional time. • Stress oral language and conversational skills before moving to reading and written language. • Adapt English instruction to make it highly contextualized and multisensory, to be more easily understood by students. • Assign students classroom roles that capitalize on their strengths and do not make unrealistic demands on English skills.
Inefficient learning strategies	• Specifically teach learning strategies and strategies to improve memory. • Have students explain concepts and skills in their own words. • Use cognitive frameworks (also called story maps, critical thinking maps, cognitive maps, semantic feature analyses, induction towers, flow charts, study guides, and structured outlines). These highlight the salient points of an academic activity and are anchors for knowledge around which students build new information (Boyle and Yeager, 1997). • Use advance organizers. • Use student self-evaluation where students perform a task such as taking a test and, given a checklist of strategy tips, are then asked to tell which of these they did or did not use. • Use strategic note taking. This procedure involves using special cued note paper in which the student fills in the details during and after a lecture. The cues are: 1. Today's topic. Identify the topic and briefly summarize any knowledge the student has of it before the class 2. Major points of the lecture, given in clusters. 3. New points included in the lecture. 4. Later, write five main points from the lecture and describe each point (Weishaar and Boyle, 1997).
Low or fragmentary achievement	• As a general rule, the more abstract the learning experience, the less these students will be able to experience success. Emphasize concrete, meaningful content, especially in initial instructional presentations. • Present tasks in an uncomplicated, brief, and sequential fashion. • Sequence from the simple to the more complex. • Promote an atmosphere of success.

Behaviour manifestations, needs	Tips
	• Promote transfer of learning by applying learning to other situations, objects, and problems in the learner's environment. • Students with memory problems tend to be passive learners; they learn more easily if good demonstrations and visual aids provide them with a concrete model to watch and imitate.
Needs much repetition	• Ensure mastery of new material through repetition and over-learning. • Provide many opportunities for drill (repeating a task) and practice (applying the task to similar situations). In math, for example, students may be drilled on number facts through rote repetition, work sheets, and games. They may then practise the skills through the actual performance of a task, such as applying the number facts to addition problems. • Use Computer Assisted Instruction (CAI), proven to be particularly effective for children with intellectual disabilities.
Passive learner, outward locus of control	• Motivation increases as competitiveness decreases. Rewarding effort rather than ability is likely to serve as a motivator for all students. • Motivation also involves allowing students opportunities to control and monitor their own learning and behaviour. Allow some degree of freedom in selecting tasks or assignments. • As these students are more limited in their learning, they require more reinforcement. • Arrange cross-age tutoring, where students with special needs tutor younger children.
Off-task behaviour	• Use free-write, free-tell, or write-alongs. • Stop an activity for five minutes and have the students write or tell you about any item that confuses them, what they've learned, and their questions. • Seat students near the front of the room so that distractions are behind them, or use carrels to cut down on distractions • Divide teaching into small modules; teach in small building steps. • Students are led to persist longer if they are given attribution feedback on effort ("You've been working hard") or ability ("You're good at this"), or some blend of the two, particularly ability feedback combined with teaching particular strategies in math and reading comprehension (Dohrn and Bryan, 1994).
Disorganized	• Allow short answers to questions • Use Computer Assisted Instruction. • Define all requirements of a completed activity. For example,

Behaviour manifestations, needs	Tips
	"Your math is complete when all five problems are complete and corrected. • Provide multiple written prompts such as "To answer this question, look on page 12" (Boyle and Yeager, 1997). • On worksheets, use lots of spacing; provide ample space for writing or drawing; avoid crowding and extraneous print; limit the type of questions; provide clear and concise directions; provide examples; use typing or printing in place of handwriting. • Have students keep an assignment notebook. • Use many organizational devices to assist student learning such as dates for assignments written on the board, reminders about homework.
Test anxiety	• Students are at a great disadvantage if they do not understand the format or the instructions of a test. From five to fourteen hours of instruction time spread over five to seven weeks appears to be the effective range of instruction time needed to improve test-taking skills and "test wiseness" (Grossman, 1995; Samson, 1985). • Teach students to focus on the types of questions that are likely to arise, to answer the easy questions first, to allot time properly during a test, to answer all the questions, and to check their work. • Teach how to carefully read all the questions and how to develop an outline before writing an essay. • Allow children to take tests using different formats. For example, a youngster may respond more easily if allowed to tape record test answers. • Allow slow writers extra time to finish tests. • Administer practice tests before the real thing. • Give alternative forms of the test—oral, essay, short answer, multiple choice, fill-in-the-blank. • Use clear, readable, and uncluttered test forms. • Pre-teach and preview major concepts.
Difficulty completing homework	• If homework is important to your program, keep in mind that too much can overwhelm the student who is learning disabled. • Use a homework planner. • Never give homework as a punishment. • Listen to what students say about their homework experiences. • Put smiling, frowning, and neutral faces on the cover of homework assignments. Have students circle the one that describes their feelings about the assignment. Discuss.

Behaviour manifestations, needs	Tips
Behavioural problems	• Be specific, consistent, and systematic in expectations and actions. • Maintain a warm and supportive emotional climate. • Be honest but liberal with praise. • Use consistent reinforcement and provide continuous and immediate feedback.
Needs cultural awareness and cultural sensitivity	• Be familiar with the home and community. • Know the child as an individual. • Be aware of differences in order to understand the behaviours and learning styles of students from diverse cultures.

SECTION 3

Children and Youth with Behavioural Disorders

Just about every parent has, at some time or another, been frustrated and annoyed with the behaviour of his or her child. In the classroom, on an almost daily basis, every teacher confronts minor misdemeanours and unacceptable behaviours from students. Far less often (but with mounting frequency) teachers see students who show behavioural excesses that include physical and verbal aggression, defiance, temper tantrums, lying, swearing, stealing, throwing chairs, spitting, wearing attention-getting T-shirts, and generally disrupting the classroom.

All teachers have to devote some attention to classroom control; typically about 10 percent of their time (Crealock, 1983). But aggressive and non-compliant children can turn a chore into a full-time occupation. Problem behaviours impose a tremendous demand on teachers, often consuming 80 percent of instructional time (Sugai and Horner, 1994). Teachers often feel overwhelmed by misbehaviour in the classroom (Martin, Linfoot, and Stephenson, 1999); they report that challenging behaviours, ranging from physical violence to social withdrawal, are among the most difficult to manage in school settings.

Young people who show behavioural excesses and seem intent on satisfying impulses that are incompatible with the kinds of classroom control and academic activities that the teacher has in mind are likely to be referred to special education. Along with reading difficulties, conduct disorders are "one of the most common forms of exasperating deportment and psychopathology that brings students into special education" (Kauffman, 1997b, p. 338). One study (Phipps, 1982) reported that 82 percent of the boys referred for special education were referred primarily because of their behaviour.

When students exhibit, to a marked and prolonged extent, behaviour that is clearly undesirable, inappropriate, and maladaptive in its social context, they are grouped into the broad category of *behaviourally disordered*. This classification includes conduct disorders, anxiety and withdrawal, immaturity, delinquency, and Attention Deficit Hyperactivity Disorder.

Behavioural disorders are often grouped with learning disabilities and mild mental retardation as mild disorders. We devote a separate section to these students for a number of reasons. These are:

- The category of *behaviourally disordered* is of increasing concern in our schools. Educators must be deeply concerned about children and youth who fail to comply with the demands of the school and the classroom and who may indulge in various forms of criminal and antisocial behaviour outside the school environment.
- It seems that more students are exhibiting violence, aggression, and defiance in the classroom than ever before. Teachers are seeing increasing instances of violent and aggressive behaviour at earlier ages, more children who show defiance, and more aggression toward property and persons. School violence includes those behaviours that seriously disrupt the safe learning environments of classrooms and schools. The youth violence observed in North American communities is increasingly present in Canadian schools (MacDonald, 1997).
- Educators, police, and lawyers agree that youth crime is more sophisticated and more terrorizing than ever before (Campbell, Grange, Cernetig, Ha, and Galt, 1997). For example, a survey of police services and school boards across Canada found that 80 percent of respondents felt that there is more violence in schools now than ten years ago. Dolmage (1999) reports on a Canadian study of the perceptions of seventy-one secondary school administrators in two large districts, which found that 62 percent felt that the prevalence of youth violence had increased significantly in Canadian society at large and 56.4 percent believed it had increased significantly in schools. Note that only 28.1 percent believed it had increased significantly in his or her own school.
- Educators need to understand the behavioural difficulties likely to be seen in children and youth so that they may better appreciate that these children are not in direct control of their deviant behaviours. Among the diversity of symptoms seen in these children runs an undercurrent of anxiety, inhibition, apprehension, depression, and overcontrol (Edelbrock, 1979). As well, understanding the complex and interconnecting issues and variables that underlie and affect behavioural disorders can help educators identify early, formulate expectations, plan assessment strategies, and develop and implement strategic plans for intervening in the context of schooling (see Sprague and Walker, 2000).
- One of the major tasks of teaching is to establish and maintain order in the classroom, and discipline is usually the number-one issue facing individuals who are responsible for any classroom, particularly if they are new teachers. In fact, research has repeatedly found that new teachers list maintaining classroom discipline, motivating students, and interacting with parents as among their greatest concerns. In one survey (Feitler and Tokar, 1982), chronic student misbehaviour was noted as the main source of job stress by 50 percent of the respondents.
- Contemporary schools are caught in the dilemma between creating and sustaining a harmonious inclusive community and the individual student whose behaviour pressures teachers to seek alternative environments. But we cannot dismiss these students out of hand, and many with mild behavioural disorders can indeed function in regular classroom settings.

- Many young teachers are caught unawares by serious behavioural deviations. For example, George and colleagues (1995) indicated that two-thirds of teachers of children with behavioural disorders reported that their college course work was poor preparation for their teaching environments. In tandem, Jack and colleagues (1996) found that only 5 percent of the teachers in their study indicated that they learned about the management strategies they used in their classrooms from course work; most learned them from other teachers.

In this section we discuss a range of behavioural disorders that teachers may encounter in the classroom. The more profound disorders of behaviour, such as childhood schizophrenia, are discussed under the category of pervasive developmental disorders in Chapter 13.

Chapter 7

Children and Youth with Behavioural Disorders

Learning Outcomes

After reading this chapter, you should be able to:

- Recognize that the category of *behavioural disorders* is fluid, increasing, and encompasses many groups;
- Understand the various classifications and sub-groups within the area of behavioural disorders;
- Understand the different conceptual models and how they underlie etiological consideration and direct treatment;
- Understand the developmental consequences of the different categories of behavioural disorders;
- Recognize the varied assessment procedures in the field of behavioural disorders, with particular reference to functional assessment;
- Detail methods of medical, therapeutic, and educational intervention for students with behavioural disorders;
- Discuss the validity of inclusive schooling for all students with behavioural disorders.

Introduction

Children and adolescents with behavioural disorders are not rare, and most of us have come into contact with or observed such young people. These disturbing, different, and disapproving individuals test the limits of our society in ways that challenge the wisdom of convention. They are often harmful and destructive in their actions, they create problems for almost everyone with whom they interact, and they never permit us to rest comfortably in our routines. These troubled children are some of the most difficult to handle, and they lack the appeal that others have. They frequently withdraw from profferred help or reject it outright.

Of all the deviant behaviours exhibited, the two most common are aggressive acting-out behaviour and social withdrawal. In the classroom, aggressive, acting-out, and disruptive children are unlikely to escape attention. Such youngsters challenge and frustrate teachers, disrupt classrooms, and hinder the achievement of everyone in the environment. Children who are anxious and withdrawn are more likely to be overlooked at the outset, but most teachers will quickly respond to their unusual patterns of behaviour.

As the Historical Notes at the end of this chapter show, children and youth with behavioural disorders have long been a societal concern, although special education for such students is a fairly modern development. It was not until the 1950s that services for mildly and moderately disturbed children and youth really emerged. Yet even today this field is in many ways both confused and confusing. Terminology is inconsistent and much dissatisfaction exists with current definitions: there is considerable debate about how to subdivide the various disorders in a reliable and helpful way. Treatment regimes and interventions vary, and few provisions have been made for students at secondary levels. The majority of current intervention practices, administrative arrangements, and teacher training programs have been developed with younger children in mind, and most special programs for behaviourally disordered children are found in elementary schools. Many students are underserved. In 1999, James Kauffman noted that "Far less than half of the population of students with behavioural disorders have been identified for special education and are typically identified only after several years of serious difficulties" (Kauffman, 1999).

DEFINITIONS OF BEHAVIOURAL DISORDERS

After reading the accompanying case study about Andrew, you may think that he is a typical child with a behavioural disorder and that these forms of behaviour are fairly simple to define and classify. Nothing could be further from reality. There is no such thing as a typical child with a behavioural disorder—the only commonality is that the excesses are chronic and extend far beyond the norm. And, given the varied behaviours and the uniqueness of every affected individual, definitions, terminology, and classification is very confused.

The original term for behavioural disorders, *emotionally disturbed*, first appeared in the literature about eighty years ago without being defined (Reinert, 1980). Numerous definitions of this complex condition have emerged in the intervening years, but a universally accepted definition is extremely problematic. No single definition of behavioural disorders exists in Canada. Ten provincial or territorial jurisdictions have official definitions, and there are eight different definitions (Robert, 1995).

The many attempts to define disturbed child populations and to define aberrant behaviour have had only varying degrees of success. Lack of a precise and universally accepted definition of just what a behavioural disorder is then creates problems in estimating prevalence, in identifying characteristics, in assessment, in etiology, in devising treatments, and in educational approaches.

The definitional confusion is all related in some way to the following factors:

- Traditionally, the study and treatment of behavioural disorders has been the domain of clinical psychologists, researchers specializing in abnormal psychology, psychiatrists, and, more recently, educators. It follows that deviant behaviour is defined and concep-

Case Study

Andrew

As a preschooler in nursery school, Andrew aggressively bit, fought, and scratched his way through the program. During the early school years, he became almost a legend at Maple Elementary. From the day he walked into the kindergarten, Andrew's overt, abusive, and aggressive behaviour was obvious. He would physically and verbally harass his peers on the smallest provocation and when restrained or reprimanded by the teacher revert to massive temper tantrums and language that was creative and explicit in its obscenity.

Andrew's excessive behaviours were chronic and far beyond the norm expected at his age. Few interventions seemed to work. The teacher instigated a number of behaviour reduction programs that included daily report cards, time outs, a token economy, and high rates of teacher reinforcement for appropriate behaviour.

In the next two years, Andrew continued to strike out with hostility and aggression. His behaviour affected his own learning and social interactions as well as the equilibrium of those in his environment. He spent much of his time in early elementary school ejected from the classroom or in the principal's office.

By this time, the teachers had given Andrew the de facto label of *behaviourally disordered*, among other less kindly descriptors. But it was not until the close of his second-grade year that Andrew's parents agreed to a formal assessment. The teacher's referral noted that in the classroom Andrew would attend to tasks for only a very short period and often failed to complete work at all. He acted out his anger as well as verbalizing it. Not surprisingly, Andrew had trouble making and keeping friends and seldom participated in play, alone or with classmates. As well, Andrew seemed totally unresponsive to external pressure, whether in the form of a reward or punishment. In fact, it seemed the more he was rewarded, the worse he behaved and the less he learned. Likewise, the more he was punished, the worse he behaved and the less he learned.

At the team meeting, the psychologist's comments confirmed what the school already strongly suspected: Andrew had a serious conduct disorder that was negatively affecting his academic progress and teacher and peer interactions. With the team, the psychologist wrote an IEP, including a behaviour reduction plan, that would be in place for Andrew's grade-three year. An extract from the IEP is shown later in this chapter.

tualized in many ways, and the definitions proposed come from a variety of perspectives and disciplines.

- Abnormal behaviour has an obvious referent in normal behaviour. But there is a continuum that runs from mental health to mental illness, and human emotions and behaviour are so varied that a precise notion of normalcy is difficult to derive. Lack of an adequate definition of mental health or normalcy makes behavioural disorders an open-ended category of deviance rather than an entity. All behavioural disorders are abnormal in the sense that abnormal means "away from the norm," and behavioural disorders are deviations from average or standard behaviour. But problems in identification occur when we try to pinpoint just where on the continuum behaviour becomes aberrant; it is very hard to draw a line between serious behavioural disorders and problematic behaviour that is fairly common in childhood.

- Varying behaviours are exhibited by all children and deviant and unusual behaviours may exist in the repertoires of normally developing children. Such behavioural problems fluctuate and decline as children get older and are not necessarily signs of clinical deviance. Lying, for example, is reported for the majority (53 percent) of six-year-old boys; by the age of ten, lying decreases to 10 percent of boys. In girls, the pattern is more dramatic, with a high rate (about 48 percent) at age six and no lying reported as a problem at age eleven (see Kazdin, 1989).
- To confuse the issue further, children who are disturbed sometimes behave quite normally. Distinctions between normal and disturbed behaviour are generally in the amount or degree rather than in kind. Children with behavioural disorders perform certain behaviours too often or too intensely, or not often or intensely enough, but specifying this amount and degree is difficult.
- There is not a single symptom that is common to all pupils who are behaviourally disordered, or even to a subgroup of these children, because there is no such thing as a typical student who is behaviourally disordered.
- The patterns of behaviour exhibited by children with disorders are often unpredictable and subtle, rendering their conditions even harder to define. Children are versatile in their antisocial behaviour, and are likely to display a wide variety of inappropriate behaviours, which may or may not be associated with particular situations. In some children, for example, a certain subject in school or a specific object will trigger an anxiety attack.
- The behavioural problems change as children grow older. Four-year-olds may disobey their parents; as teenagers, they may engage in vandalism and delinquency.
- Behavioural disorders cannot be measured quantitatively. We have no instruments analogous to the IQ test to determine a mental health quotient.
- Legal and educational terms differ, and while the educational and the legal system are not at odds, their perspectives and their solutions may be different. Delinquency is a legal term applied by the criminal justice system to indicate that a youth has been adjudicated by the courts and found guilty of criminal behaviour. The educational term, *antisocial behaviour*, is less restrictive than delinquency because it includes behaviours that are norm-violating but not necessarily delinquent (Nelson, Rutherford, Center, and Walker, 1991).
- Social and cultural expectations differ. Behavioural disorders occur among the rich, the poor, the gifted, the intellectually disabled, and members of all racial and ethnic groups. There are, however, varying reactions to certain behaviours. Deviance is defined by social groups that recognize some behaviours as infractions of the rules and label as deviant persons who do not conform to these socially defined rules. This is why a disproportionate number of students from culturally and linguistically different groups are labelled as behaviourally disordered.
- Children rarely decide for themselves that they are behaviourally disordered; that determination is made by teachers and parents. But any observers' interpretation of a situation is precariously subjective, and disruptive behaviour is often in the eye of the beholder. Students regarded as disruptive by one teacher may be ignored by another; rules might be enforced by one teacher but not by another.

- Following on the above, it is true that, to some degree at least, behavioural disorders correlate with teacher tolerance levels. Teachers place different demands on students depending on their own behaviour standards and the degree to which they are accepting of specific maladaptive behaviours. Varying teacher tolerance levels of deviant behaviours result in a high degree of variability in the teacher decision-making process about who has a problem and who should be referred to special education.
- There is often a relationship between behavioural disorders and other disabling conditions. For example, some children with intellectual disabilities also manifest behavioural disorders. In an early study of hearing-impaired children (Schlesinger and Meadow, 1972), researchers found five times as many children with severe emotional disturbance and three times as many with moderate disturbance as they found among hearing students. As discussed in Chapter 5, many students who are learning disabled develop an overlay of emotional problems that compound their learning difficulties and conceal their primary disorder.

Of the many definitions of behavioural disorders currently available, the one proposed by James Kauffman (1991a) is particularly relevant from an educational point of view. Kauffman notes that children with behaviour disorders

> are those who chronically and markedly respond to their environments in socially unacceptable and/or personally unsatisfying ways but who can be taught more socially acceptable and personally gratifying behaviour. Children with mild and moderate behavioural disorders can be taught effectively with their normal peers (if their teachers receive appropriate consultative help) or in special resource or self-contained classes with reasonable hope of quick reintegration with their normal peers.

This definition focuses on behaviours that are inconsistent with current societal standards and ones that are personally unsatisfactory. Kauffman recommends specific educational settings and maintains a positive outlook for children's success through appropriate educational intervention.

Kauffman's definition also has much in common with other current definitions that usually include the following statements about behavioural disorders:

- They deviate in an extreme way from the norm.
- They recur chronically. The chronic nature of the behaviour is a differentiating and important item. In children with behavioural disorders, the behaviours are not transient and episodic; rather, they last six months or longer, and interfere with expected age-appropriate functioning (Paul, 1987).
- They violate social or cultural expectations.
- They affect a child's self-esteem, interpersonal relationships, and probably school achievement, and therefore require special education intervention.

PREVALENCE OF BEHAVIOURAL DISORDERS

Based on media reports, official concerns, and educators' reactions, it would seem that the incidence of hyper-aggressive, undercontrolled behaviour and violence in our schools has increased dramatically during the past few decades. There appear to be accelerated rates of juvenile crime, with the age of children committing delinquent acts decreasing.

While incidence rates, especially as reported by the media, should be treated with great caution and some skepticism, it is true that ever-increasing numbers of children are being identified as behaviourally disordered. However, accurate prevalence figures for behavioural disorders are not available, chiefly because of the lack of a clear and precise definitional construct. Estimates vary tremendously. In fact, prevalence estimates change in every revision of DSM.

Prevalence rates for disorders that are mild but require intervention range from 7 to 15 percent (Coleman, 1992; Cotler, 1986). Somewhere between 2 and 10 percent of the school-aged population exhibit serious and persistent behavioural problems (Coleman, 1992; Cotler, 1996; Kauffman, 1991a; Kazdin, 1989).

Boys exhibit more behavioural deviance than girls, including learning difficulties, hyperactivity, bed wetting, and antisocial behaviour (Wicks-Nelson and Israel, 1991). First-born males are more likely than later-borns to exhibit behavioural disorders and to be rated by teachers as anxious and aggressive toward their peers (Lahey, Hammer, Crumrine, and Forehand, 1980).

Many children with behavioural disorders come to the attention of professionals in the middle childhood and early teen years. The prevalence of behavioural disorders is low in the beginning grades, reaches a peak in the middle grades, and begins to fall off in high school. Delinquency, however, peaks during adolescence.

Children from lower socio-economic levels are more likely to be regarded as problems. There is a reported higher prevalence of aggressive behaviours among lower-class children as opposed to those from the middle and upper classes (Hallahan and Kauffman, 1991). And, as we have mentioned with cautions, a higher proportion of those identified as behaviourally disordered are from minority groups.

CLASSIFICATION OF BEHAVIOURAL DISORDERS

As in many areas of special education, the field of behavioural disorders has seen evolving terminology and classification systems over the years. At the outset, a variety of descriptors, largely arising from a psychiatric base, were used: these included *neurotic, psychotic, obsessive,* and *emotionally disturbed.* Current educators prefer to dispense with psychiatric terms, but still debate whether to call these children *emotionally disturbed, behaviourally disordered, socially maladjusted, deviant, psychologically impaired, educationally handicapped, character disordered,* or *delinquent.*

In the past, the general category of behavioural disorders was referred to as *emotional disturbance,* with two severity levels differentiated. Children with milder conditions were referred to as *mildly emotionally disturbed*; those with serious problems, such as infantile autism and childhood schizophrenia, as *seriously* or *profoundly emotionally disturbed.*

Today, the terms *emotionally disturbed* and *behaviourally disordered* are often used interchangeably for those with milder disorders. (The American IDEA uses the former term.) However, most professionals opt for behavioural disorders because this term focuses on the most obvious problems. Some suggest that the term *children in conflict* is more appropriate (Reinert and Huang, 1987).

With the difficulties related to definitions and terminology, it is not surprising that consensus does not exist about the classification of behavioural disorders into types and degrees of deviance. Research is giving some direction, but there are more problems than clarity. Classification difficulties concern not only how and what to classify, but the value of any classification system at all.

Researchers from various disciplines have tried to find meaningful classifications in various ways. The most important are described below.

Clinical Classification

The principal modern clinical classification scheme is that provided by the American Psychiatric Association (APA) in its *Diagnostic and Statistical Manual of Mental Disorders* (DSM). DSM is a clinical manual that describes behavioural symptoms of all disorders currently recognized by the APA and defines the symptoms and signs required for the diagnosis of each disorder.

One problem with the DSM classification is that disorders are judged as either present or absent; they are not defined as deviations from the norm and evaluated on a continuum. Too, although the DSM diagnostic criteria distinguish between child and adolescent onset, they were originally developed for adults and are not school-oriented (except for truancy). Further, there is some evidence that DSM criteria do not identify most preadolescent girls with early onset antisocial behaviour (Zoccolillio, Tremblay, and Vilano, 1996).

Classification by Severity

When severity levels are used, classification is not an either-or proposition; rather, it is based on how much behaviour differs from what is considered normal. Disorders are classified along the traditional severity lines—as mild, moderate, severe, or profound.

Dimensional Classification

Dimensional classification systems see behaviours overlapping to form a syndrome or cluster that contributes to a specific condition. Groupings or clusters of specific behaviours are usually derived from observer descriptions of deviant behaviour, which are then quantified into groupings using the statistical procedure or factor analysis.

Perhaps the most widely used dimensional system is that of Quay and his colleagues (1972, 1986), who used behaviour ratings by teachers and parents, children's life history characteristics, and children's questionnaire responses to statistically derive six behavioural dimensions. These begin with conduct disorders, anxiety and withdrawal, socialized aggression, and immaturity/attention problems. Quay's fifth category, motor excess, refers to states where a child is restless, unable to sit still, tense, unable to relax, and overly talkative. The sixth dimension includes those children who display psychotic behaviour: those who express far-fetched ideas, have repetitive speech, and show bizarre behaviour.

The dimensional classification provides a relatively reliable basis for description. We discuss the first five dimensions later in this chapter when we look at the characteristics of children with behavioural disorders. The sixth dimension, psychotic behaviour, is reserved for Chapter 13.

Classification by Behavioural Type

Definitions of behavioural disorders are based on excesses or deficits of social behaviour. Following this, behaviours are often described as *externalizing* or *internalizing.* This is not a formal classification, but it does provide a useful description. For example, students with conduct disorders and socialized aggression externalize their behaviour through such acts as disobedience, lying, stealing, fighting, sexual delinquency, and destructiveness. In contrast, anxious and withdrawn children internalize their behaviour. They may suffer from nausea, pains, headaches, phobias, fears, obsessions, shyness, nightmares, crying, depression, self-consciousness, and withdrawal.

ETIOLOGY OF BEHAVIOURAL DISORDERS

Psychiatrists, psychologists, and educators have traditionally placed great emphasis on identifying the causes of behavioural disorders in children, hoping that an understanding of the origins of the disorders would lead directly to their treatment and cure. Despite a vast amount of research, investigators still do not fully understand the causes of any type of psychopathology, and there exists no empirical evidence linking behavioural disorders to any specific causes. Deviant behaviour usually involves the interaction of several factors rather than a single cause. Each additional variable increases the risk of behavioural disorders, and the risk is greater when several factors combine.

Most major developmental theories have been used to explain behavioural dysfunctions. They are founded on certain conceptual models that represent the different theoretical orientations of allied disciplines. As etiology is closely linked to conceptual models, there are considerable differences seen in both the presumed causes and in the importance that researchers attach to finding the causes of disturbance. The psychodynamic model, for example, focuses almost exclusively on causation, while the behavioural model is concerned with the outward manifestations of deviancy. Table 7-1 presents an overview of the models and associated treatments.

Table 7-1 Conceptual models and associated treatments in the area of behavioural disorders

Approach	Assumption	Treatment	Sample of methods
Biophysical	Behavioural difficulties represent a physiological flaw. They arise directly from constitutional, genetic, neurological, or biochemical problems. Disease, malnutrition, and substance abuse are included here.	Alter the child's physiology	Drug therapy; change in diet. (The only intervention that has a research base is drug therapy.)

Approach	Assumption	Treatment	Sample of methods
Psychodynamic	Deviant behaviour is determined by past experiences; students with behavioural disorders are suffering inner turmoil; they can be helped by being made aware of their feelings and how to deal with them.	Discover the underlying conflicts that cause problem behaviour	Various therapies and counselling techniques: verbalization and clarification of previously repressed thoughts; corrective emotional experiences resulting from the child's relationship with understanding adults; presentation of alternate modes of behaviour.
Psycho-educational	An eclectic approach that sees behaviour as having various causes.	Create trust while helping the child to meet academic goals	Therapies, crisis intervention, success in academic pursuits. Preventative classroom planning; permitting or sanctioning certain types of behaviour; tolerating behaviour that is beyond the child's control.
Behavioural	Emotional or behavioural deviance is the definable consequence of either mislearning or restricted learning. Normal, healthy, and desirable behaviours may be acquired to supplement or replace undesirable behaviours by consistently applying established behavioural principles of learning.	Rearrange environmental events. Focus on the behaviour, not the underlying causes.	Reinforcers, punishments, time-outs, contracts, and so on. Selecting instructional programs on the basis of objectives to be achieved through practice with reinforcement and measurement until criterion performance is reached.
Ecological	Behaviour disorders are a function of the reciprocity between a child and the environment; problems are the result of agitated transactions between the child and those in the environment.	Change the nature of the interaction between the child and the environment.	Counselling and a team approach. Crisis intervention; environmental modelling; curriculum planning. Identifying whatever norms happen to be used in the class setting; finding means for children to meet classroom goals.

Approach	Assumption	Treatment	Sample of methods
Psychosocial	Can be seen as part of an ecological model, although the focus is on a child's relationship to family, peers, and others in the environment.		
Holistic	Behavioural disorders have diverse etiologies that interact with each other.		

These conceptual models are not just theoretical; they guide and direct interventions. As you examine the models, however, you will notice that the components of some models are compatible, others are not. But teachers know that no one intervention exists for every troubling behaviour that is manifested in the classroom. Because a single cure-all strategy is not out there waiting to be discovered, educators tend to draw ideas from a number of approaches.

Biophysical Model

As the name suggests, a biophysical approach holds that behavioural disorders relate to biological causes. Some evidence suggests that certain biological factors—genetic conditions, constitutional conditions, prenatal and birth factors, and environmental hazards—do increase the risk of behavioural disorders. But, despite accumulating data, researchers remain wary. Information about the relationship between biophysical factors and behavioural disorders is scattered, and it is rarely possible to demonstrate a relationship between a behavioural disorder and a specific biological factor.

Geneticists maintain that no genes directly determine behaviour. Nevertheless, some genes do determine enzymatic and biochemical functions that, in turn, can have both major and subtle behavioural effects. For example, the neurotransmitters serotonin, dopamine, and norepinephrine play important roles in regulating behaviour, and low serotonin levels especially have been linked to such aggressive behaviours as fighting, arson, and suicide (Sylvester, 1997). As well, some very specific genetic defects may cause dramatically disturbed behavioural functioning. Children with untreated PKU, for example, often show deviant behaviour along with mental retardation.

From another line of genetic research, we know that temperaments are inherited, and temperamentally difficult children are more likely to become antisocial adolescents and adults (Baum, 1989). Boys and girls who are moody and ill tempered at age ten tend to be ill-tempered adults whose relations with their spouses and children are generally unpleasant and full of conflict (Caspi, Elder, and Bern, 1987).

Also available are genetic studies on family relationships. Twin studies, for example, suggest that heredity is involved in behavioural disorders, but little is known about the mechanisms. As well, there is a greater risk among biological siblings of children with

Attention Deficit Hyperactivity Disorder (ADHD): approximately 20 to 30 percent have the disorder (Murphy and Barkley, 1996).

Recent work with the biological parents of children with ADHD show that the parents are themselves more likely to have psychiatric disorders and to report greater distress than parents of children in normal and non-clinical groups. Parents of ADHD children seem to have more stressful events and are more likely than other parents to have marital disturbances (Murphy and Barkley, 1996).

Mounting evidence further suggests the possibility of a relationship between behavioural disorders and neurological disturbances. But researchers are baffled by the exact relationship; they point out that "the evidence linking behavioural characteristics to brain dysfunction is circumstantial, speculative, and in most cases clearly not documentable" (Smith and Robinson, 1986, p. 223).

Along with genetic problems and neurological disturbances, disease, malnutrition, and brain trauma may predispose children to develop emotional problems. Substance abuse can also lead to serious emotional and behavioural problems.

Psychodynamic Model

The psychodynamic model and approaches originated with the extremely complex theory first defined by Sigmund Freud in the early 1900s. Today psychodynamic models continue to exert a strong and persuasive influence on the terminology, definitions, and taxonomies of behavioural disorders. Essentially, a psychodynamic approach is concerned with the development of and interaction among the intrapsychic (mental) processes believed to underlie human behaviour. Behavioural disorders are observable symptoms reflecting inner turmoil created by abnormal intrapsychic processes, so psychodynamic approaches attempt to locate the origins of behaviour within the context of psychological development.

Psycho-educational Model

Advocates of the psycho-educational model agree that children with behavioural disorders may have dealt unsuccessfully with developmental problems. Efforts are made to discover why children demonstrate deviant behaviour; there is a simultaneous stress on the acquisition of academic and daily living skills.

Behavioural Model

Early 20th-century investigations of reflexive and voluntary behaviour, arising particularly from the work of Ivan Pavlov and John B. Watson, laid the groundwork for modern behavioural psychology. Bolstered by B. F. Skinner's principles of operant conditioning, the behavioural model has exerted a profound influence on psychotherapy, counselling, education, and special education.

While the behavioural model includes a number of theories and points of view about human behaviour, two points most clearly define it. First is the assumption that behaviour—including deviant behaviour—is acquired and is regulated by certain identifiable principles of learning. Second, the behavioural model has a commitment to scientific methods of studying behaviour and behaviour change.

Behaviourists believe that all behaviour is learned and that behavioural disorders represent inappropriate learning. In general, behaviourists do not define and classify behavioural disorders. Instead, they try to understand their origins by observing, describing, and measuring deviant behaviour, by noting the conditions under which it occurs, and by detailing the relationship among the complex environmental factors that elicit and support deviant behaviour. By changing these conditions, behaviourists attempt to extinguish the undesirable behaviours and shape appropriate responses.

Ecological Model

Ecology refers to the overall pattern of relationships involving an organism and its environment (ecosystem). From an ecological point of view, an individual's behaviour is the product of the interaction between the individual and all the variables in his or her environment.

Problem behaviour does not simply reflect inappropriate action by a student; rather, it is influenced by undesirable interactions and transactions between the student and others. That is, "Many emotional or behavioral disorders, though not all, originate or are made worse by the child or youth's social interactions" (Kauffman, 1997b, p. 7).

Classrooms are ecological systems where students and teachers are constantly interacting. Behavioural disorders arise when there are disturbances in the "goodness-of-fit" between a child and this ecosystem. Some characteristics of a child (usually the behaviour) agitate the ecosystem, and the ecosystem responds in ways that lead the child to provoke further agitation. For example, a student's temper tantrums in school might be the problem, but from an ecological perspective, the behaviour of the student's teachers, peers, and parents—their expectations, demands, and reactions to the tantrums—must also be taken into consideration.

The *ecological approach* reduces the danger of assuming that behavioural problems reside wholly within the child. It may be that the environment is not providing the necessary supports to enable the child to progress in adaptive development. To overcome the disturbance in the interaction between child and environment, changes may need to be made in both.

Psychosocial Model

The *psychosocial model* focuses both on the family and on extra-familial influences, those agencies outside the family that influence a child's cognitive, social, and emotional development. Three important extra-familial agents of socialization are schools, peer groups, and television.

Research and theory that focus on family patterns as possible sources of behavioural disorders find that family conditions may predispose a child to develop behavioural disorders or precipitate maladaptive behaviours. Predisposing conditions include families characterized by harsh discipline, little parental involvement with the child, and poor monitoring and supervision of a child's activities. Precipitating factors are an immediate stress or incident such as divorce, separation, or the chronic illness of one or both parents.

Parental attitudes and child-rearing techniques are often critical in the development of aggressive behaviour. As a predictor of an antisocial adult personality, having an antisocial parent places the child at significant risk for antisocial behaviour; having two antisocial parents puts the child at even greater risk (Robins and Earls, 1985). There seems to be a high degree of intergenerational similarity for antisocial behaviour: children in aggressive families are more likely to be aggressive and, in turn, their children are more likely to be aggressive (Farrington, 1987).

Research has also concluded that there is a significant cause-and-effect relationship between television violence and aggressive behaviour.

Holistic Model

The *holistic approach* attempts to encompass the other models by viewing behavioural disorders as essentially indivisible phenomena that are more than just the sum of separate parts (Cullinan, Epstein, and Lloyd, 1991). The holistic model therefore acknowledges that the etiology of inappropriate behaviours may be illness, childhood traumas, poor relations with others, inappropriate learning, problems in socialization, any combination of these, and many other factors.

CHARACTERISTICS OF CHILDREN AND YOUTH WITH BEHAVIOURAL DISORDERS

Children and youth with behavioural disorders exhibit a spectrum of behaviours ranging from disruptive and cantankerous outbursts to severe withdrawal from social interaction. More than a hundred different characteristics have been attributed to children and youth who are behaviourally disordered. In very general terms, students

- Show an inability to learn that cannot be explained by intellectual, sensory, or health problems;
- Demonstrate behaviours that do not compare favourably with those manifested by normally developing children;
- Exhibit inappropriate types of behaviours or feelings under normal conditions;
- Exhibit behaviours that are generally unacceptable to the child, to normal peers, and to adults;
- Exhibit a comparatively high number of problem behaviours;
- Show behaviours that interfere with their expected performance relative to chronological age;
- Continue and even increase the behaviours unless structured and systematic intervention occurs;
- Show an inability to build or maintain satisfactory interpersonal relationships with peers and teachers;
- Show a tendency to develop physical symptoms, pains, or fears associated with personal or school problems.

Table 7-2 expands these common characteristics and behaviours, grouped within the dimensional classification system. Keep in mind that all children demonstrate some of these traits at one time or another; they only become problems when they occur chronically,

Table 7-2 Some behaviours seen in children and youth with behavioural disorders

Conduct disordered

- Fighting, hitting, assaults
- Destructive behaviour
- Impertinence and impudence
- Attention seeking
- Uncooperative and negative behaviour
- Hyperactivity
- Poor relationships with others
- Distractible, short attention span, and less task oriented than other children
- Lags in all academic areas, especially reading

Socialized aggressive

- Assaultive
- Delinquent activity
- Gang vandalism
- Destructive, disobedient, hostile, truant
- Lying
- Substance abuse
- Verbally abusive
- Sexually precocious

Anxious and withdrawn

- Anxious, fearful, shy, timid, tense, and withdrawn
- Depressed and sad
- Self-conscious and hypersensitive
- Cries frequently
- Short attention span
- Poor self-esteem that affects interpersonal relationships and academic achievement

Immature

- Clumsy
- Easily frustrated
- Lacks initiative
- Passive
- Messy
- Short attention span
- Socially inadequate

Motor excess

- Overtalkative
- Unable to relax
- Accelerated rates of motor movement
- Short attention span
- Impulsivity
- Distractibility

acutely, and in tandem. Also note that even though these children are categorized on different dimensions, there is considerable overlap between groupings, especially between conduct disorders and socialized aggression and between immaturity and anxiety and withdrawal. In addition, the problems of attention deficits may be seen in a number of populations of learners who are disabled.

Conduct Disorders

Conduct disorder is the term used to describe hyper-aggressive and highly disruptive children who form the major portion of those identified in the schools as behaviourally disordered. Estimates of the prevalence of conduct disorders range from 6 to 16 percent in boys and 2 to 9 percent in girls under age eighteen (see Kauffman, 1997b).

Students who are conduct disordered exhibit antisocial behaviour, which refers to overt, aggressive, disruptive behaviour, or to covert antisocial acts that are repeated infractions of socially prescribed behavioural patterns and that violate social norms and the rights of others (Kauffman, 1991a; Loeber, 1985). DSM-IV (APA, 1994) groups conduct disorders into four headings: aggressive to people and animals, such as bullying, threatening, or forcing sex on someone; destruction of property, such as setting fires or destroying others' property in some way; deceitfulness or theft, such as breaking and entering or shoplifting; and serious violations of rules, such as running away or being truant.

Because children with conduct disorders have failed to develop reliable internal controls, their behaviour is impulsive, distractible, hyperactive, and disruptive. They have short attention spans and sometimes seem not to know right from wrong. Their behaviour is not age-appropriate. For example, temper tantrums are common among two- and three-year-

While temper tantrums in preschoolers are expected, the same type of behaviour in an older child may indicate a conduct disorder.

olds, as these young children strive toward independence. Among normally developing children, unfocused temper tantrums diminish during the preschool period and are uncommon after age four (Hartup, 1974). In children who are behaviourally disordered, tantrums are more likely to continue; a twelve-year-old throwing a temper tantrum is demonstrating clearly inappropriate behaviour.

oppositional defiant disorder

Aggressive behaviour refers to "those behaviors—verbal, nonverbal, or physical—that injure another indirectly or directly and/or result in extraneous gains for the aggressor" (Zirpoli and Melloy, 1997, p. 332). Aggression is of more concern to teachers than any other aspect of behavioural disorders. In DSM-IV, two specific disorders involving aggression are mentioned. **Oppositional defiant disorder** is a condition in which children argue repeatedly with authority figures, show resentment, and often throw temper tantrums, although physical aggression is limited. The other condition is called *conduct disorder*, of which aggression is one of the most overt manifestations. The precursors, development, and outcomes of childhood aggression are discussed in the Research Notes feature below.

Research Notes

Childhood Aggression

Among all human emotions, aggression is probably the most studied; it was a favourite topic for psychologists throughout the 20th century. Explanations for aggression have come from evolution (no group in the animal kingdom is free of aggression), social learning (aggressive behaviour is learned and often rewarded), and modelling (children do what they see). All theories agree that although aggression in moderation is a useful survival tool, it becomes a problem when it is prolonged, frequent, and severe.

Aggression seems to be one of the true differences between the sexes. It is found more strongly in males and is also more tolerated in boys. As well, aggression is developmental in nature and becomes more acceptable with age. Older children (eighth graders) judge aggression to be less reprehensible than do younger children.

The major influences on aggression are temperament, the family, peers, and television. In relation to temperament, the temperamental traits that make infants difficult may be related to behaviour problems of aggression and anxiety (Bates, 1987), but infancy is at best a modest predictor of later problems. Parents' attitudes and child-rearing strategies play a more important role. Cold and rejecting parents and those who are hostile and punitive often apply physical punishment erratically and permit their children to express frequent aggressive impulses. In early life, stress and constant threats seem to rewire emotional circuits, as in the mother who screams at a child who falls down, "It's your own fault," as opposed to the soothing parent (Begley, 1996).

Aversive behaviour and physical punishment provide models and a partial sanctioning of aggressive responses. It may reinforce a child's aggressive behaviour toward others and teach patterns of attack and counter-attack so well that children become blind to alternative ways of solving conflicts.

Eventually, children who live in highly coercive family settings may become resistant to punishment. The use of arbitrary, high-intensity tactics elicits defiance from young children, rather than the compliance that parents want (Crockenberg and Litman, 1990). Children learn to fight coercion with coercion, often defying their parents by repeating the same acts for which they are punished. If they are spanked, for example, the spanking serves as a model of the very aggressive behaviour that the parents are trying to suppress. One study (Herronkohl, Egolf, Ellen, and Herrenkohl, 1997) found the severity of physical discipline in the preschool years to be related to assaultive behaviour in late adolescence. Males were more assaultive than females; people with higher intelligence and women are more likely to break the violence cycle (Kaplan, 1996).

To be aggressive, children must know that they can get others to do what they want by causing them distress. The early part of life is a particularly critical time, when techniques for controlling others by aggressive means are rapidly acquired. The knowledge that other people can serve as obstacles that block one's intended course of action probably comes very early, and between the ages of one and two this knowledge seems to be extended (Maccoby, 1980). Patterns of aggressive behaviour frequently seem to be well established before age nine (Patterson, 1982).

Once established, antisocial behaviours show relatively high continuity, and there is substantial stability of aggression over time. And, the more extreme the antisocial behaviour in young children, the more stable it tends to be throughout childhood and adolescence. Antisocial or non-compliant behaviour is particularly likely to be stable over time when the first antisocial behaviour appears at a young age, is frequent, appears in more than one setting, and consists of several distinct forms of antisocial behaviour (Loeber, 1990).

The correlations between early aggression and later antisocial behaviour may be as high as .92 (see Loeber and Stouthamer-Loeber, 1996, 1998). Highly aggressive three-year-olds are likely to become aggressive five-year-olds. Children's level of physical and verbal aggression at ages six through twelve are fairly good predictors of their tendency to threaten, insult, tease, and compete with peers at ages ten to fourteen. Olweus (1987) found that children described as aggressive at thirteen and fifteen years of age were more likely at twenty-four to be engaged in criminal and antisocial activities. There are different manifestations of later violence including frequent fighting by age eighteen, partner abuse, and conviction for violent offences by age thirty-two.

Normally developing children learn to use aggressive behaviour to overcome resistance and tend to become more aggressive as they develop. Normal aggressive behaviour does not approach the degree seen in children with conduct disorders. For these youngsters, aggression becomes a dominant theme in their social interactions. In today's schools, childhood aggression, as manifested in classroom and schoolyard bullying, is a mounting problem. See more on bullying in the Research Notes feature.

Socialized Aggression

At-risk children and youth who show major discipline problems in school appear to substantially overlap with those who offend outside school. These youths, characterized as *socialized aggressive*, are chronic violators of broad cultural mores and social values. They are hostile, destructive, disobedient, and often verbally and physically abusive. They tend to lie, steal, and vandalize, sometimes assaulting people as well as property. They view social problems in hostile terms, do not seek explanations, generate few solutions, anticipate few consequences for aggression, and see violence as a legitimate way to solve problems (Guerra and Slaby, 1990).

These traits match those of children characterized as conduct disordered, except in one area. The difference is that students who are socialized aggressive are active in delinquent

Research Notes

Schoolyard Bullying

Think back to your own school days. Were you ever intimidated and frightened by the school bully? Perhaps you were. But even though bullying has been around for a long time, it has only recently been recognized as an enduring and underrated problem in today's schools. Today educators, parents, and society recognize that what has been a historically misunderstood problem in our schools and families is serious.

By 1996 a nationwide poll revealed that 88 percent of adults believe that school violence, including bullying, is a serious problem in Canadian schools (Hutchinson, 1997). In a survey of Edmonton-area junior high school students (MacDonald, 1995), over 50 percent considered bullying to be a "very big" or a "big" problem. A Saskatchewan study (Bidwell, 1997) found that about one-third of teachers surveyed considered bullying a serious problem in their classrooms.

Bullying is a form of aggression. It is a type of social interaction in which a more dominant individual, the bully, exhibits aggressive behaviour intended to cause distress to the less dominant individual, the victim (Smith and Thompson, 1991).

There are different kinds of bullying, and bullying behaviour differs among individuals. However, most common definitions of bullying show three things in common: bullying is a repeated action that occurs over a prolonged period of time; there is an imbalance of power; and the verbal, psychological, and/or physical negative actions of bullying are unprovoked (see Bentley and Li, 1995).

Manifestations include threatening to injure another person for no apparent reason, requesting tasks to be performed that are undesirable to the other individual, and threatening negative consequences to individuals if their requests are not met by the victim. Additionally, the bully may intimidate the victim by initiating acts such as name calling, teasing, pushing or shoving, and using physical dominance for intimidation (Craig and Peplar, 1997).

Name calling and other types of verbal harassment represent some of the most prevalent forms of bullying. They frequently develop into physical forms. Much of the bullying in school—coercion, intimidation, and threats that often start as mean-spirited teasing—progresses to extortion and physical attack. In adolescents, bullying may diversify into more sophisticated forms of verbal and social aggression, as well as sexually focused aggression.

More boys than girls bully (Craig and Peplar, 1997; Marano, 1995). It may be, however, that the acts of girls are underestimated because they take a different form. Girls display more subtle and complex forms of meanness than do boys (Marano, 1995), and female bullying may be more difficult to detect.

While many adults claim that bullying is simply part of the school experience, there are complex problems related to both bullying and victimization: bullying can have long- and short-term negative consequences for both bully and victim. Donaldson (1999) pointed out that "Students participating in bullying activities either as bullies or as victims were more likely to be isolated, to feel less accepted by others, and to perpetuate the cycle of abuse" (p. 203).

For the bully, the actions may be part of a cluster of behavioural problems. Bullies themselves may be depressed, tend more to serious thoughts of suicide than their victims, seem to be more prone to dislike school, and are more likely to engage in behaviours that compromise their health, such as smoking (Evenson, 1999). The prognosis for chronically violent individuals is generally poor (Guetzloe, 1999b). Without corrective intervention, bullies are at risk for antisocial behaviour in adult life and unstable relationships. Bullies tend to become antisocial adults, and some studies indicate that they may commit more serious crimes and be more likely to indulge in abuse of spouse and children (Marano, 1995).

groups and loyal to delinquent friends. Delinquent behaviours are rewarded by peer attention at the same time as they attract some form of punishment from adult society. Thus a vicious circle is set in motion: more delinquent behaviour and more reward from the peer group, catalyzed by more punishment from the adult community and more anger on the part of the adolescent.

The classification of socialized aggressive is often equated with socially maladjusted rather than emotionally disturbed or behaviourally disordered. This is because the United States Public Law 94-142 and its recent amendments specifically exclude "children who are socially maladjusted, unless it is determined that they are seriously emotionally disturbed" (U.S. Dept. of Health, Education and Welfare, 1977, p. 42478). The distinction is subtle and depends upon the effect of the condition on the student. It is felt that behavioural disorders are persistently distressing to the child, while social maladjustment may not be. Within their gangs, socialized aggressive youths may enjoy considerable prestige as a result of their aggressive and norm-violating behaviours. Nevertheless, scholarly opinion holds this exclusionary clause in the U.S. federal definition of emotional disturbance (behavioural disorders) to be ill-founded (Kauffman, 1991a; Nelson et al., 1991). The ways of acting exhibited by these youths are clearly indicative of problems in socialization and ethics development that fall within the scope of the broader concept of behavioural disorders.

Socially maladjusted students take part in antisocial and violent behaviours. Antisocial behaviour includes aggression, noncompliance, bullying, intimidation, gang vandalism, stealing, fighting, truancy, and sexual harassment. Violence includes assault, rape, and property destruction. Often, these actions fall under the rubric of *delinquent behaviour*, which implies any illegal act by a juvenile regardless of whether the perpetrators are apprehended (Nelson et al., 1991). Once children and youth come to the attention of the courts they gain a new label: *juvenile delinquents* or *young offenders*.

The problems surrounding delinquency are of grave concern to parents, the juvenile justice system, and law enforcement agencies, as we explain in the Research Notes feature.

Juvenile Delinquency

The term *juvenile delinquency* has a legal connotation, not an educational one. Nevertheless, even though primarily a social and a legal concern, the problems are relevant to schooling. Students at risk for juvenile delinquency have well-developed patterns of antisocial and aggressive behaviour, are rejected by normal peers, and have low academic performance, poor grades, and substandard achievement.

Few human behaviours have been subject to as many varied and contradictory explanations as juvenile delinquency. All the possible etiologies we have presented for behavioural disorders, plus quite a few more, have been proposed. Some researchers believe that delinquent youth have a character trait known as *social anomie*, a lack of entrenched societal norms and values; students do not appear to internalize a coherent set of values and standards for regulating their own behaviour. Others adhere to the appealing theory of an innate criminal personality type.

Although the nature of the relationship between

the constructs is not clear, one theory links learning disabilities with juvenile delinquency. Support for the link comes from the continual school failure that characterizes both conditions; the fact that students with learning disabilities are more at risk for adjudication regardless of race or socio-economic level (Keilitz and Dunivant, 1986); and the significantly greater prevalence of learning disabilities reported in delinquent youth populations than in non-delinquent populations. In Canada, a review of the prevalence of learning disabilities among adolescents in trouble with the law and young offenders with academic problems indicates a range of 4 to 36 percent (Crealock, 1984, 1986; Murphy, 1986).

Overall, however, the two best predictors of delinquency seem to be measures of parental family management techniques and child problem behaviour. The paths that children at risk follow in their acquisition of delinquency seem to begin with negative, harsh, and incompetent parenting and, in some cases, awareness of the commission of criminal acts by family members. An antisocial behaviour pattern develops that can become associated with school failure, peer rejection, membership in a deviant peer group, and ultimate socialization into a delinquency subculture.

Incompetent and harsh parenting also gives birth to childhood aggression, recognized as a strong predictor of behavioural difficulty in adolescence and early adulthood. Early forms of antisocial behaviour are linked to the early onset of official juvenile offences (see the Research Notes on childhood aggression earlier in this chapter). About half of antisocial children become adolescent delinquents and roughly half to three-quarters of these individuals become adult offenders (Blumstein, Cohen and Farrington, 1988; Farrington, 1987).

The course of chronic delinquency follows an anticipated path, a progression from less serious to more serious incidents. Boys starting their criminal careers in late childhood or early adolescence are at the greatest risk for becoming chronic offenders (Farrington, 1983; Loeber, 1982). There is some evidence that early onset is linked to more physical aggression and more violent crime (Moffitt, 1993).

Much less risk attaches to the late starter—someone committing his or her first offence in middle to late adolescence. Late starters are often not as extreme in their aggression as early onset youth. Lacking the early training for antisocial behaviours, this individual has not experienced the dual failure of rejection by normal peers and academic failure (Patterson, De Baryshe, and Ramsey, 1989). Boys first arrested between ten and twelve years of age average twice as many convictions as later starters (Farrington, Gallagher, Morley, St. Ledger, and West, 1986).

In Canada, youths are adjudicated under the Young Offenders Act (1984), amended in 1995. Corrections are the responsibility of the federal government, which enacts legislation outlining juvenile offences, age limits, and court procedures and penalties. Provincial governments administer the legislation, supply containment facilities, provide probation officers, and carry out court judgments. Correctional programs extend along a continuum of levels of intervention, with diversion at one end and containment at the other. Programs may be open, residential, or community-based, and are located wherever there is a substantial population of young people (see Reist, 1991).

Anxiety and Withdrawal

Anxiety is a fairly recent addition to the catalogue of childhood behavioural disorders; it did not appear in DSM until 1980. Currently, DSM recognizes generalized anxiety disorder and social phobia.

The problems of anxiety and withdrawal are estimated to affect 2 to 5 percent of the child and youth population at some time (Kauffman, 1997b). There is not nearly as much literature on children who are anxious and withdrawn as there is on those with conduct disorders, and much is inconclusive, especially in regard to later outcomes.

anxiety

Anxiety can be described as a fear with a future reference. It is vague, undifferentiated, and uncertain, relating to futuristic events that have not yet occurred. Feelings of anxiety include distress, tension, uneasiness, worries, and fears.

In some instances, anxiety may be an adaptive response to threats from the environment. Many people, for example, are anxious and apprehensive about entering a new situation and meeting new people. Most anxieties are mild or short-lived, and most people are able to deal with them after some initial worry. Anxiety becomes abnormal when it happens in situations that most people can handle with little difficulty. In generalized anxiety, symptoms are present most of the time and not directly related to a specific situation.

Anxious children tend to develop a pattern of adjustment to cope with anxiety. In doing so, they forgo assertive, independent behaviour; become excessively withdrawn, fearful, secretive, and apathetic; and often spend large amounts of time fantasizing and daydreaming instead of interacting with those around them. Because they have low self-concept and little self-esteem, and are self-conscious, hypersensitive, and sad much of the time, they may be so shy that they find it painful even to go to school.

Once in school, anxious and withdrawn children have acceptance problems (Siperstein and Leffert, 1997), but outcomes for students with anxiety and withdrawal are not as clear as they are for the conduct-disordered population. Some (e.g., Coie, 1985) conclude that withdrawn children are not at any greater risk for the development of maladjustment than are other children.

phobias

Severe anxiety may include **phobias**, persistent and irrational fears of a specific object, activity, or situation with no rational basis. Of the host of possible phobias, some of the most common are fear of the dark, of animals, of vehicles, and of school.

Some anxious children become extremely withdrawn.

Among children, school phobia is one of the most common. Although phobias in general are found more often in girls than in boys, (Erickson, 1992), school phobia affects about two percent of the school-aged population and has the same incidence in boys and girls (Wolman, 1978).

School phobia seems to be more than simply an irrational fear of school. Children not only fear school but also suffer nausea, abdominal pain, and other physical difficulties associated with tension and extreme agitation. Children with severe school phobia may simply refuse to attend school. If forced, they may spend most of the time either mute or crying. Sadness and deep depression are not uncommon. Symptoms subside if the child is allowed to stay home and on weekends.

Some children who are withdrawn regress to earlier stages of development and demand constant help and attention; others become depressed for no apparent reason (Klien and Last, 1989; Kovacs, 1989). Their depression is similar to that seen in adults.

The depression is more than just a feeling; it is accompanied by cognitive, motivational, and physical symptoms. The most extreme manifestation is suicide. Severe behavioural disorders, in fact, are by far the most prevalent conditions associated with suicidal behaviour, and many studies have confirmed the link between suicidal behaviour and emotional instability (e.g., Pfeffer, 1986).

Adolescents are a generally healthy group. Although they face such hazards as substance abuse and teenage pregnancy, they have survived childhood diseases and not yet encountered the complaints of adulthood. Suicide, however, has become the second leading cause of death for young people (Cole, 1992) (accidents are the first). Worse, for every successful suicide it is estimated that there are 50 to 100 attempts (Pagliaro, 1995).

The problem is not new; the first symposium on adolescent suicide was held in Vienna in 1910 (McBride and Siegel, 1997). But numbers are on the rise: the Suicide Information and Education Centre in Calgary documented a 60-percent increase in adolescent suicides between 1970 and 1985 (McBride and Siegel, 1997).

Suicide rates are higher in Canada than in the United States. Canada ranks third behind Norway and Australia for the fifteen- to twenty-four-year-old group. Highest rates are in the Yukon and Northwest Territories (Cole, 1992; McBride and Siegel, 1997).

Immaturity

Not much is known about the special nature of children who are characterized as *immature.* While similar in many ways to those who are withdrawn, immature children seem even less able to function in the regular classroom. They demonstrate many of the characteristics that we discuss in the chapter on learning disabilities in relation to maturational lags and attention deficits. They appear to be very clumsy, socially inadequate, passive, easily frustrated, messy, and lacking in initiative. They have short attention spans and frequently fail to finish assignments. Often they show a preference for younger playmates.

Attention Problems and Motor Excess

Two very similar (and very controversial) conditions fall into this category: Attention Deficit Disorder (ADD) and Attention Deficit Hyperactivity Disorder (ADHD). Together they have become the most popular disabilities of the past decade. Writers observe that "not since the establishment of learning disabilities as a special education category has a condition so captivated both the professional community and general public as has attention deficit hyperactivity disorder" (Reid, Maag, and Vasa, 1993, p. 198).

While the terminology and interest is fresh, the condition is not new to the fields of education, psychology, and pediatrics. There have always been children who couldn't sit still, who wriggled and fidgeted, and seemed not to concentrate on anything for longer than a few seconds. In the past, teachers and parents might have called them Fidgety Phils; psychologists and other health professionals used terms such as *neurological dysfunction, anatomical dysfunction of the right cerebral hemisphere, cognitive memory deficit, soft neurological signs,* and *minimum brain dysfunction syndrome* (Campbell, 1997; Meents, 1989).

Hyperactivity was first described in 1845 by a German physician, Henrich Hoffman. In the following decades, hyperactivity became one of the most deeply investigated and controversial disorders within the fields of pediatric medicine, clinical psychology, and education. Hyperactivity was identified as the most common childhood behavioural disorder presented to doctors, psychiatrists, teachers, and other related professionals, not to mention parents (Weiss and Hechtman, 1979).

In 1968, the second edition of the *Diagnostic and Statistical Manual of the American Psychiatric Association* (DSM-II) provided the first official diagnostic classification of hyperactivity, which DSM characterized as hyperkinetic reactions of childhood. The disorder was given a specific name in 1980, and since then every new version of DSM has presented a revision of the ADD/ADHD criteria. The term Attention Deficit Disorder was first used in DSM-III in 1982. In 1987, DSM-III-R used the term Attention Deficit Hyperactivity Disorder.

Initial research defined two conditions: Attention Deficit Disorder and Attention Deficit Hyperactivity Disorder. Recent studies indicate that ADD without hyperactivity is uncommon, and today there is more use of the composite syndrome, ADHD. There are suggestions, however, that ADD occurs more often with students who are learning disabled, while ADHD may be more frequent among children with disruptive behavioural disorders (Barkley, Du Paul, and McMurray, 1990; Lahey and Carlson, 1991).

Following its introduction as a diagnostic category, research and interest in ADHD increased dramatically. Nevertheless, the procedures for identification, assessment, and especially treatment remain embroiled in controversy. There are numerous definitional and diagnostic problems, not the least being a lack of consensus about an exact name for the condition, the characteristics that accompany it, and its prevalence rates. There are also criticisms of the distinction between ADD and ADHD, controversy over which version of the DSM criteria is preferable, and recurring concerns about teachers' wholesale adoption of the category.

While teachers make many referrals of ADHD, and many are familiar with the primary symptoms, studies of teachers' knowledge have consistently revealed specific misconceptions. Teachers' knowledge about diet and sugar intake, the effects of medication, children outgrowing their symptoms, and the prognosis of ADHD is problematic (Sciutto, Terjesen, and Bender Frank, 2000).

There is little doubt that the diagnosis is popular among educators and parents, more so in North America than anywhere else. Increasing numbers of children are reported as ADHD. Up to 3.5 million children in the United States are said to have Attention Deficit Disorder or its cousin, Attention Deficit Hyperactivity Disorder ("New developments ...," 1995). In Canada, the growth in diagnosis of ADHD has been staggering. An estimated half-million Canadians, most of them school children, have been diagnosed. However, in Britain, the diagnosis is only about 0.03 percent for the same age group (Campbell, 1997). Australia is currently experiencing local epidemic outbreaks of ADHD. But in Victoria, an Australian state, an average school of a thousand children would not have one receiving treatment for ADHD. In two other states, Western Australia and New South Wales, approximately ten students in every thousand would be treated for ADHD (Slee, 1997).

Many people look askance at the high number of children being diagnosed as ADHD. Child misbehaviour is changed into child pathology and, as one psychologist chides, "The diagnosis has become a wastebasket into which any misbehaving child can be tossed" (in Campbell, 1997, p. 30).

Within the special education community, critics of the role of clinical diagnosis of ADHD have pointed out that it does not lead to special placement and does not predict response to instruction. ADHD is not included among the thirteen categories in the American IDEA (1997), and many hold that adding ADHD as a disability category is unnecessary because students diagnosed as ADHD who manifest symptoms severe enough to impair educational performance currently are eligible for educational services under existing categories such as learning disabilities or behavioural disorders (e.g., Ysseldyke, Algozzine, and Thurlow, 2000). Other educators object to ADHD because it may divert resources away from children with serious disabilities and it is difficult to define and identify (Aleman, 1991).

ADHD is characterized by three primary features: inattention, impulsivity, and hyperactivity. These three major criteria for ADHD are not situation-specific; rather, they are displayed by affected children at all times. It is important to understand the behaviours that make up each component. In brief:

attention

- Attention disorders are characterized by difficulty in concentrating. The child has problems with **attention**: the process of tuning in to sensory information, and with engagement or active participation.

  Attention and engagement are developmental: the younger the child, the lower the rates of engagement. Very young children cannot discriminate between what is and what is not important. They flit from activity to activity, show high rates of movement, and are easily distracted by visual and auditory stimuli. The parts of the brain that allow the child to sustain attention and screen out distractions become increasingly myelinated between the ages of about four and seven.

impulsivity

- **Impulsivity** represents a child's difficulty in withholding active responses, such as blurting out statements or grabbing materials (Zentall, 1993). Impulsive students do things without thinking and do not learn from experience. They have difficulty organizing themselves, need much supervision, speak out of turn, and don't wait their turns in games or groups. They may show angry outbursts, be social isolates, blame others for their problems, fight with others quickly, and be very sensitive to criticism (Alderson, 1993). They are poorer at tasks requiring sustained attention and meet difficulties in problem solving and planning.

  perseverate

  Impulsive students do not double-check their work. They ignore details, write before thinking and planning, leave off word endings, do not organize compositions, copy sloppily from the board, and do not self-correct. These students (and others with ADHD) may **perseverate**: they purposelessly and sometimes disadvantageously repeat an activity. For example, a child may finish addition problems on page one and continue to add on page two, even though the instructions clearly indicate a switch to subtraction.

hyperactive children

- **Hyperactive children** display rates of motor behaviour that are too high for their age groups. They seem unable to restrain their activity, to sustain attention, to resist distracting influences, and to inhibit impulsive responses. Boys are more prone than girls. It is estimated that hyperactivity occurs in 3 to 20 percent of all elementary school children, with a sex ratio of three or more boys with the disorder to every girl (Wicks-Nelson and Israel, 1991).

The accelerated rates of activity and the excessive, non-purposeful movement disturb others, worry teachers, and cause their families discomfort and even despair. Young hyperactive children are constantly on the move, pushing, poking, asking questions, but never waiting for answers. In the classroom, they are unable to sit still. When confined to a seat, they translate their need to be active into finger and foot tapping, as well as other disruptive activities. Hyperactive teenagers may drum their fingers, shuffle their feet, open and close their desks, and continually visit the pencil sharpener, other desks, and other areas of distraction. Even when asleep, the child shows excessive activity and other sleep problems (Alderson, 1993).

Children with generalized hyperactivity have a very early onset of problems. Typically, signs are evident in early childhood, often by the age of three and even in infancy. There is a mean onset age of four years (Alderson, 1993; Barkley, Fisher, Newby, and Breen, 1988).

ADHD is a medical diagnosis. The prevalent opinion about causes is that ADHD is an invisible function with a basis in the central nervous system that involves a faulty regulation of a particular neurotransmitter, norepinephrine (Alderson, 1993). Some researchers have documented a genetic factor in ADHD; they report findings of similar characteristics for anywhere between 60 and 75 percent of the relatives of children with ADHD and for 30 to 50 percent of their siblings (Goodman and Sevenson, 1989). Nevertheless, the efforts expended to find a biological etiology of ADHD have been generally inconclusive and often contradictory.

Note that an opposite theory is emerging. Some hold that ADHD is epidemic because of the modern acceleration of life. Investigators posit that environmental causes include family breakdowns, both parents working, and the growing influence of television, movies, and video games (Ecklund, 2000).

Typically, ADHD has been the domain of active prepubescent males. Females are often unidentified, for they express the disorder through talking or being busier, which is more socially acceptable than the gross motor activity often seen in boys. This means that girls are less likely to be hyperactive and also less likely to receive special education services for the condition. Only very recently have researchers begun to study girls with ADHD.

DEVELOPMENTAL CONSEQUENCES OF BEHAVIOURAL DISORDERS

Children and adolescents with behavioural disorders deviate significantly from their peers in the quantity, quality, and modes of their emotional expression. As you have seen, apart from this overarching trait there is no symptom common to all pupils who are behaviourally disordered, or even to a subgroup of these children. There is no such thing as a typical behaviourally disordered or disturbed student: behavioural disorders may take one or many specific forms, can be manifested in various ways, and the severity of disturbance ranges from mild to serious and debilitating.

Cognitive Development

Studies show that intelligence and scholastic achievement are negatively correlated with aggression and delinquency for both boys and girls. Compared to the normal distribution of intelligence, many children with behavioural disorders fall into the slow learner or mildly intellectually disabled category. Most have IQs in the dull normal range—around 90—and very few score above the bright normal range (Hallahan and Kauffman, 1991).

Academic Performance

Only rarely is a child who is behaviourally disturbed academically advanced; the few children who do seem competent academically are seldom able to apply their skills to everyday problems (Hallahan and Kauffman, 1991). Many of these youngsters are underachievers at school, as measured by standardized tests. They often experience difficulty with basic school skills and do not achieve academically at the expected level for their mental or chronological ages. They are usually behind in reading, arithmetic, and spelling (Lewis and Doorlag, 1991).

Research supports a relationship between underachievement and externalizing behaviour (Richards, Symons, Greene, and Szuskiewicz, 1995), as well as reading disabilities and aggression (Cornwell and Bawden, 1992). This is not surprising, as students with conduct disorders tend to be non-compliant and uncontrolled, alienating teachers and other students. Because they create such problems in classroom management, teachers tend to instruct children who have conduct disorders with fewer academic questions, less extended feedback, and fewer dyadic work interactions. With non-compliant behaviour and less instruction, students may rapidly enter a pattern of severe academic failure that quickly becomes cyclical. When children do not learn the skills needed for coping with academic pressures, they react by withdrawing or lashing out in angry frustration. They soon learn to dislike the learning process, resent the school experience, and often resort to truancy.

At first glance, anxiety may not seem as academically and socially debilitating as aggression. But timid, passive behaviour, dependency, isolation, and withdrawal interfere with the development of potential. Children tend to develop a defeatist attitude along with feelings of worthlessness and excessive self-criticism.

Different problem behaviours evoke different attitudes among teachers, and some writers contend that acting-out behaviours are viewed more negatively than withdrawn ones (Li, 1985). Others find that teachers consider socially withdrawn behaviours and non-communication (negative aggression and poor peer co-operation) to be the most difficult type of behaviour to manage (Safran and Safran, 1987).

Whether considered the most difficult or not, it does seem that children who are anxious and withdrawn may be ignored in the classroom. One study (Finn, Pannozzo, and Voelkl, 1995) that measured the academic achievement of compliant, disruptive, and withdrawn fourth graders found that the withdrawn children scored considerably lower than the other two groups. Investigators surmised that the attention that teachers must give to disruptive children actually helps these youngsters, but withdrawn children do not disturb the classroom and therefore tend to be more ignored.

The general characteristics of ADHD—inattention, distractibility, impulsivity, and hyperactivity—can cause or compound academic problems. Obviously, children who are easily distracted from learning tasks learn less than those who pay attention—and, by definition, children diagnosed as ADHD are easily distracted, don't stay on task, and have short attention spans.

When compared to normally developing students, students with ADHD are more likely to receive lower grades in academic subjects and lower scores on standard measures of reading and math (Zentall, 1993). More than eighty percent of eleven-year-old students with ADHD are reported to be at least two years behind in reading, spelling, math, or written language.

Communication

Speech and language disorders cut across all areas of exceptionality and are likely to be found among children with behavioural disorders. A higher prevalence of behavioural disorders are found among seriously language-delayed children and, conversely, the most frequent secondary special education service provided for students with behavioural disorders is speech and language intervention.

Sometimes the communication problems come first. Children who are not successful in communication often demonstrate negative, resistant, or attention-getting behaviour and are at risk for both psychiatric and learning disorders (Baker and Cantwell 1987; Owens, 1991). Sometimes it is the initial emotional disorders that seem to cause the difficulties. Of psychiatric outpatients, 24 to 65 percent may suffer speech and language problems (Giddan, Melling, and Campbell, 1996). When investigators (Gualtieri et al., 1983) surveyed forty consecutive admissions to a child psychiatric inpatient facility, they found—after in-depth speech, language, and intelligence testing—that 20 of the 40 had moderate to severe language disorders.

Yet teachers sometimes feel that children who are behaviourally disordered communicate *too* well. They interrupt in class, swear, use aggressive language, speak defiantly to adults, and indiscriminately vent their emotions. They often use language to disrupt and control social situations. This excessive use of language may not be a communication disorder, but it is certainly a social problem.

Social Development

The terms related to social development in normal and deviant individuals are notoriously difficult to define. Researchers in the area use a plethora of related terms and concepts that arise from the general idea of socialization. In brief:

- **Socialization** is the means by which individuals become reasonably acceptable and competent members of their society. Through socialization, children acquire the discipline and the skills, the knowledge, the ambitions, and the empathy for those around them that allow them to participate in the life of the family and later the school and the community.

socialization

- **Social cognition** is the knowledge and cognitive activities employed by people in dealing with the social world (Pearl, 1987).

social cognition

- **Social competence**, "the ability of children to successfully and appropriately select and carry out their interpersonal goals" (Guralnick, 1990, p. 4), includes the development of meaningful and productive relationships with peers, social and communication development, degrees of independence, and other factors that may contribute to becoming socially acceptable.

social competence

- **Socially competent individuals** perform behaviours that they believe will effect rewarding outcomes and avoid acting in ways that might cause negative outcomes (Schunk, 1987).

socially competent individuals

- Social skills, though entwined with cognition, are a distinct area of learning and development. **Social skills** are "those responses which within a given situation prove effective;

social skills

or ... maximize the probability of producing, maintaining, or enhancing the positive effects for the interactor" (Foster and Ritchey, 1979, p. 626).

sociability

- **Sociability** is a term that describes a child's willingness to engage others in social interaction and to seek their attention or approval.

prosocial behaviour

- **Prosocial behaviour** is voluntary behaviour intended to aid or benefit others (Holmgren, Eisenberg, and Fokes, 1998).

All of these concepts are relevant to students with behavioural disorders in the sense that such students exhibit deficits in socialization, social cognition, social competence, and social skills. Instead of being sociable, these children show excessive aggression and defiance and develop intense and far-ranging interpersonal problems with teachers, peers, parents, and others in their environments. Compared to samples of normally developing children, those with conduct disorders are usually less responsive to social reinforcement, less empathetic, and less sophisticated in their understanding of and responses to their peers' behaviour (Baum, 1989). Those who are anxious and withdrawn fail to respond appropriately to those in their environments.

At both elementary and secondary levels students with behavioural disorders are seldom socially accepted; they are often actively rejected, not just neglected. This is especially true for highly aggressive children, who are less likely to make friends, are disliked by most of their peers, and are more likely than others to be attacked by peers.

Accepted children display high frequencies of sociable behaviour, whereas rejected children show aggressive and disruptive behaviour (Siperstein and Leffert, 1997). Aggressive children provoke a large number of fights, and are also more likely to become the targets of aggression. Non-aggressive children who are harmed under ambiguous circumstances are much more likely to retaliate if the harm-doer has a reputation as an aggressive child (Sancilio, Plumment, and Hartup, 1989).

When aggressive children do make friends, they tend to gravitate toward peers with more equal levels of aggressive, disruptive, antisocial behaviour. As early as middle childhood, antisocial children tend to associate with other antisocial and/or rejected peers either by choice or default (Dishion, Andrews, and Crosby, 1995; Farmer and Hollowell, 1994).

Social problems also affect children with ADHD. In fact, the time periods required for peers to notice and disapprove of children with ADHD are distressingly brief, measurable in minutes or hours (Bickett and Milich, 1990).

Cultural and Linguistic Differences

A potent factor that places children at risk for a range of adverse educational outcomes is minority/ethnic group identity with or without limited English proficiency due to residence, immigration, or community norms. Today, a high proportion of students served under the categories of behavioural disorders or serious emotional disturbances are from culturally and linguistically diverse groups. Misdiagnosis is often a culprit here. When a student's linguistic and cultural background is perceived as a disability, he or she can then be diagnosed and treated as learning disabled or behaviourally disordered.

Equally important are the ideologies and expectations of school systems, which can have an immediate and profound effect on behaviour. Behaviour considered normal and adaptive in a subculture may be looked upon as deviant or inadequate by members of the dominant group. When minority-group children bring to school different skills, different expectations, and different competencies than those valued by the dominant culture, they may be misconstrued as having problems that require special education. Or when classroom management procedures do not match cultural mores, students are less likely to change their behaviours, teachers become more frustrated, and a cycle is set in motion.

Co-occurring Disabilities

Co-occurring problems that compound academic underachievement are common. We have already mentioned speech and language problems found among the population of students who are behaviourally disordered. As well, about 38 to 75 percent of children and adolescents with serious behavioural disorders are also identified as having learning disabilities or severe learning problems (Rock, Fessler, and Church, 1997).

Approximately 50 percent of children with ADD/ADHD qualify for some other diagnosis. They have a higher incidence of anxiety, depression, mood disorder, and Tourette syndrome than do children not so diagnosed ("New developments ...," 1996). Probably 25 percent have learning disabilities and 20 to 60 percent are diagnosed with oppositional defiant disorder or conduct disorder (Tyler and Colson, 1994).

ASSESSMENT OF CHILDREN AND YOUTH WITH BEHAVIOURAL DISORDERS

Behavioural disorders are easier to identify than to define or classify. Children with conduct disorders attract attention with their overtly disruptive behaviours. Immature and withdrawn children are a little harder to identify but are still fairly recognizable. Indeed, within the educational system, children with behavioural disorders are so readily identified by school personnel that systematic screening procedures become redundant.

Teachers are fairly accurate in identifying behavioural disorders; both experienced and inexperienced teachers can accurately perceive difficulties among children on the basis of behavioural deviations (Schwartz, Wolfe, and Cassar, 1997). Teachers' informal judgments have therefore served as a fairly reliable means of screening these children.

When it comes to referral for diagnosis and additional assistance, teachers tend to over-refer children showing conduct disorders. Childhood aggression accounts for a disproportionate number of referrals to special education programs and to mental health and child guidance centres (Epanchin and Paul, 1987). On the other hand, teachers tend to under-refer children with internalizing problems such as anxiety and withdrawn behaviour (Hallahan and Kauffman, 1991).

In any form of assessment used with these pupils, there are some rules of thumb. In general:

- Past and present behaviour is the best predictor of future behaviour (Sprague and Walker, 2000).
- Assessment is an ongoing process, not a one-shot procedure. It is a "dynamic, self-

correcting process" that is "ongoing, exploratory, hypothesis-testing" (Ollendick and King, 1999, p. 427.)

- Assessment is intimately linked to treatment. For example, if an assessment shows that misbehaviour repeatedly results in teacher attention, then a behaviour reduction plan will focus on behaviour that allows a child to access teacher attention in more appropriate ways.
- When assessing because a student is disruptive, teachers need to consider the motivating forces, whether it is an isolated event or part of a predictable pattern, and whether or not the student is motivated to change.
- Assessment is broad and must include cognitive, affective, social, and academic domains.
- Assessment must be carefully planned and systematic so that behaviour and environmental conditions are defined precisely, appropriate samples of activity are obtained, and results are presented coherently (see Kerr and Nelson, 1998).
- Particular facets of behaviour must be included. A teacher or assessor should consider frequency (how often the behaviour occurs); intention (how damaging or disruptive the behaviour is); duration (how long); and versatility (the number of different types of behaviours).

There are many processes and tools available for assessing behaviour. (A sampling is shown in the appendix table, Tools for Assessment. See also the measures outlined in Section 2.) A complete assessment includes clinical interviews (with the child and parents); observations; rating scales (teacher ratings, peer ratings, and self-ratings by the target child); personality tests; and formal and informal tools to assess a child's mental ability, academic achievement, oral language development, perceptual–motor development, and auditory and visual acuity.

Functional Assessment

As we point out in Chapter 2, functional assessment or analysis is often used with students with behavioural disorders and those with severe disabilities. Functional assessment relies on the systematic administration and interpretation of quite a range of indirect and direct measures of student behaviour—for example, parent and child interviews, observation, direct observation, plotting the identified behaviour, and experimental modification of a student's environment. The focus is on the function of a behaviour—what purpose does that behaviour serve for a student, how to reduce or eliminate the behaviour, and how to replace it with a more acceptable alternate behaviour.

Observation

One facet of functional assessment is the variety of procedures devised to help teachers identify youngsters who deviate significantly in intra- and interpersonal learning and social behaviours. One of the most potent processes, teacher observation, tries to answer the following question: When is a behavioural disorder a behavioural disorder? Teachers look for form—the form or shape of a behaviour that involves a description of the behaviour itself, such as a temper tantrum. They also look for chronicity and frequency. It is important also that observations take into account a variety of settings and circumstances, such as different times and subject areas in the classroom, the playground, and other school activities.

Direct Observation

Direct observation, a more structured behavioural analysis technique, is a cornerstone of behavioural functional assessment (Ollendick and King, 1999), particularly important for externalizing behaviour. Observers record instances of specific behaviours to establish the frequency, durability, and age-appropriateness of a behaviour. Data recording may be as simple as a narrative system, or it may be more sophisticated with codes to score behavioural deviations, language skills, motor behaviour, and so on.

There are limitations on the amount of behaviour that can be documented, and students are often versatile in the types of behavioural deviations they display. As we cannot observe all behaviour, we must sometimes be content with a sample to make observations more manageable. There are different sampling techniques; in each, systematic observations of a child are undertaken over a period of not less than a week, and preferably longer.

event sampling

Event sampling is used to determine the frequency or length of a specific behaviour. The procedure includes two types: frequency counts and duration recording. A frequency count is used for behaviour that is of relatively short duration, such as the number of times a child hits another child. A duration measure (duration sampling) is an indication of how long something occurs and is used for behaviours that vary considerably in length, such as negative or positive peer interaction or self-stimulating behaviour.

From the case study about Andrew introduced at the beginning of this chapter, we know that his teachers are particularly worried about the physically aggressive behaviours he shows. The procedures used to observe Andrew's overt physical behaviours are shown in the continuation of the case study.

Rating Scales

When more formal procedures are used, teacher judgment measures (teacher ratings of behaviour) are the most widely used tools for diagnosing conduct disorders in a classroom setting (Hoge and Andrews, 1992). These tools have been found to be quite accurate. (See the appendix table, Tools for Assessment.)

Formal Assessment

An estimation of potential based on an IQ test, assessment of communication skills, and pupil performance in academic, social, psychomotor, and self-help skills provides a basis for sound instructional decisions. Do keep in mind that although a formal psycho-educational diagnosis will contain components that assess a child's potential and performance, the overall assessment remains subjective. No measure of behavioural disorders can parallel the IQ; emotions are simply not defined by objective parameters.

Once teachers have identified and referred a child, it is not a simple task to find out what is wrong, what is not connecting. Nor is it easy to determine whether a behavioural problem is serious enough to warrant further diagnosis. As pointed out, many temporary behavioural disorders occur in normally developing children, and we do not want to identify a child incorrectly any more than we want to overlook a child who needs help.

Case Study

Andrew (continued)

In the course of a school day Andrew slaps, punches, and generally annoys the other children in the room. On any number of occasions, he has thrown books, pencils, and trash cans. When restrained, a tirade of foul language often followed by a violent temper tantrum ensues.

In using direct observation techniques, Andrew's teacher would begin by measuring his behaviour and comparing it to that of three other somewhat problematic children in the class. Over a period of at least five days, the teacher would enter a checkmark on a tally sheet each time Andrew and the other three children exhibited physical aggression. The average number of aggressive behaviours in the five days provides a baseline. The teacher can profile Andrew's baseline, compare it to those of the other children, and decide whether to refer him for intensive assessment. In addition, when a behaviour reduction program is begun for Andrew, the teacher can quickly measure his progress by comparing his current status to the baseline. Figure 7-1 shows the baseline for Andrew and the three other children.

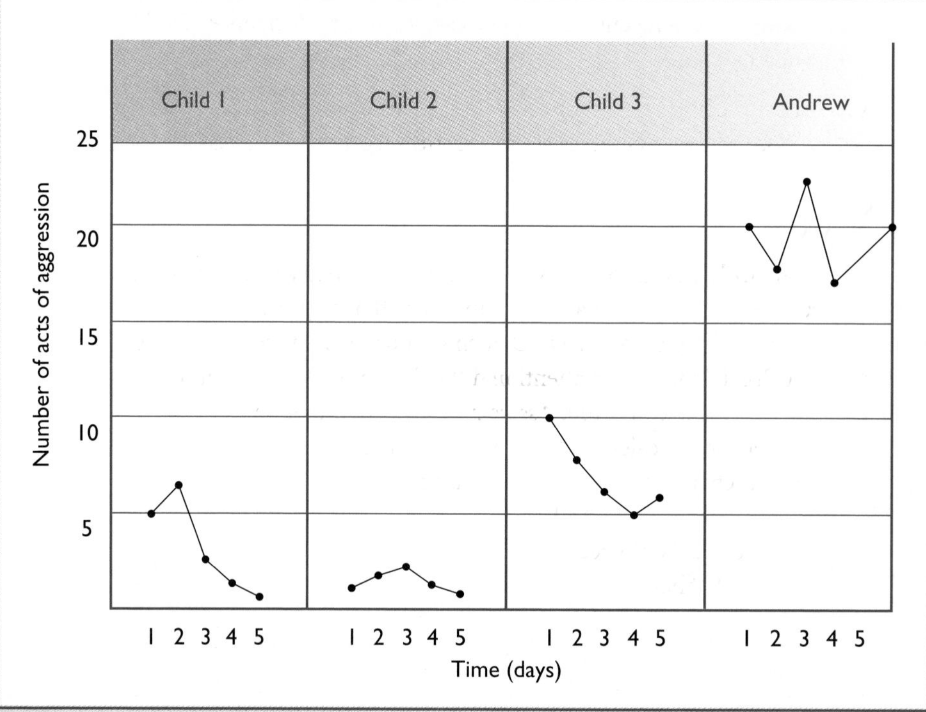

Figure 7-1
Baseline graph for charting physical aggression in children

Ecological Assessment

Ecological assessment views an individual's behaviour as a function of the values of the social system within which he or she is being evaluated, and includes the child's total ecological system (the various environments in which the child functions). Assessment includes an examination of the materials, methods, and curriculum, as well as teacher expectations, discipline, cultural and social factors, and so on. For example, it may examine whether methods of presentation of content and classroom grouping match the learning style of an individual learner. A child from a Native culture will probably be far happier in co-operative learning groups than in competitive independent seat work (Winzer and Mazurek, 1998).

Social Skills Assessment

Socially competent individuals possess certain groups of skills: interpersonal and self-related behaviour, academically related skills, skills related to peer acceptance, communication skills, and assertiveness skills. The purpose of social skills assessment is to ascertain whether or not children possess these skills. It attempts to answer certain questions, to wit:

- What is the child's social status?
- What are the child's social/behavioural deficits?
- What, if any, behaviours interfere with the acquisition or performance of social skills?
- What are the antecedents preceding and consequences following performance of a skill? (Elksnin and Elksnin, 1997).

Once teachers have answered these questions by assessing the extent to which particular skills are being used, or not used, by a child, they can identify target skills to teach.

Assessing ADHD

ADHD is classified as a neurological disorder. Measurement is particularly difficult, with few well-defined markers to separate normal behaviour from that requiring professional help (Campbell, 1997). To be diagnosed as ADHD, a child must exhibit eight of fourteen symptoms appearing in DSM-IV that reflect attention difficulties, impulsivity, or motor hyperactivity, with onset before the age of seven. Assessment requires parent and teacher interviews, parent and teacher rating scales, and direct observation. Diagnosis is conducted by matching parents' and teachers' descriptions of a child's behaviour with the inventory of behavioural descriptions provided in DSM-IV.

The American Academy of Pediatrics recently released guidelines for the diagnosis and evaluation of children suspected of having ADHD. They noted that the assessment should include information from parents, teachers, and other school personnel about the core symptoms, including settings, age of onset, duration of symptoms, and degree of functional impairment. DSM-IV criteria should then be used. The ADHD should be present in more than two of the child's settings and adversely affect social and academic functioning for at least six months ("New developments ...," 2000).

Obviously, a proper diagnosis requires more than six hours of interviews with the child, the family, and teachers. But today, with many family doctors making the diagnosis, a child may be labelled as ADHD after a twenty-minute examination (see Campbell, 1997), which means that a child may be superficially evaluated and prematurely placed on a medication trial.

INTERVENTION WITH CHILDREN AND YOUTH WHO HAVE BEHAVIOURAL DISORDERS

The problems created by and for children and youth with behavioural disorders should not be underestimated. Nor should the challenges these students create for educational systems and teachers be seen as anything less than serious. In recent years methods of intervention for students with behavioural disorders have been largely developed according to various theoretical perspectives. Distinctly different conceptual models have developed to guide intervention. Each conceptual model contains a set of assumptions about why children behave as they do and what must be done to correct disorders.

Keep in mind, however, that many students with severe behavioural disorders need a complete emotional overhaul—a restructuring of their emotional development. This process requires intervention from many agencies, not just the school.

Medical Intervention

Medical intervention for students with behavioural disorders rests almost entirely on psychopharmacology (drug therapy). In recent years, drugs have become the standard treatment regimen, and an increasing number of children are being prescribed drugs for use at school.

Drugs administered to children vary widely in purpose and pharmacological action. Generally, the drugs fall into three major categories: stimulants, major tranquilizers, and anti-depressants. For children with ADHD, stimulants are the drugs of choice among physicians. Stimulant medication seems to be the least complicated of the possible medications and seems to produce the fewest side effects. Tranquilizers and anti-depressants are reserved for a smaller group of patients. The major tranquilizers such as thioridazine (Mellaril), chloropromazine (Thorazine), and haloperidol (Haldol, Serenace) may be prescribed for children with very serious behavioural disorders. Antidepressants, such as imipramine (Tofranil) and amitriptyline (Taroxyle, Tryptant, Elevil) may be administered for problems such as enuresis (bed wetting) and childhood depression. Antihistamines such as diphenhydramine (Bendryl) and hydroxyzine (Atarax and Vistaril) are the two most commonly used in treating childhood anxiety disorders.

Of the stimulant drugs prescribed to control hyperactivity and inattentive behaviour, the most commonly recommended are the psychostimulants: methylphenidate hydrochloride (Ritalin) and dextroamphetamine (Dexedrine, Deanol, and Cylert). Ritalin, originally patented in 1950 by the CIBA Pharmaceutical Company, is the first choice of doctors, probably because it seems to produce fewer side effects. Ritalin is prescribed about ten times more than the other two combined (Gadow, 1986). Pemoline (Cylert) and Adderall (a combination of various amphetamines) are used for nonrespondents to Ritalin.

Perhaps 60 to 90 percent of children diagnosed with attention deficits and/or hyperactivity receive stimulant therapy for prolonged periods during their school careers (Safer and Krager, 1988). And the numbers are increasing. In the United States, numbers increased 2.5 to 5 times between 1990 and 1996 (Diller, 1996; Hancock, 1996). By 1996, American youngsters were consuming 90 percent of the world's Ritalin (Will, 1999). Health Canada estimates that the amount of Ritalin consumed in Canada in 1996 was 4.6 times more than in 1990 (Campbell, 1997). Across Canada, prescriptions for Ritalin jumped 500 percent throughout the 1990s (Van Rijn, 2000). In Alberta from 1992 to 1993, there was a 40-percent jump (Bell, Fisher, and Rodriguez, 1994). A more recent report on Alberta from the Federal Thereupeutic Products Program found a 37-percent increase in usage in 1999 over 1995 (Ecklund, 2000).

Psychotropic drugs affect the neuron cells of the central nervous system either by increasing or decreasing their excitability. They are prescribed to control hyperactive and inattentive behaviour in the hope that their effect will produce better peer relationships, improved self-image, and pleasure in acquiring competencies.

There are different dosages of Ritalin. Short-acting Ritalin comes in three sizes—5 mg, 10 mg, and 20 mg. Also available are long-acting, sustained-release 20 mg tablets, called Rital SR, that last seven to ten hours, but this product has not been as successful as the short-term tablet (Copeland, 1994). Concerta, a new single-dosage extended-release form, lasts twelve hours and can be taken before the child leaves for school ("New developments...," 2000).

Most children respond positively to the medication—about 70 to 80 percent in various studies (Elliott and Worthington, 1995; Neuwirth, 1994). Two conditions that respond particularly well to psychopharmacology are poor selective attention and concentration and impulsivity. When the medication is used in carefully controlled dosages, the majority of youngsters show medication-related improvements that facilitate academic functioning and are often successful in reducing hyperactive behaviour and increasing attention skills.

While chemical treatment is celebrated in the professional literature as successful, we should also consider possible adverse affects, specifically the ethics and advisability of wide drug use with children. Ethical problems revolve around the drugs and their illegal use in our society. Some deplore psychopharmocology "employed to relieve burdensome aspects of temperament" (Will, 1999, p. C6). Others see drug therapy as a ready remedy for teachers who blur the distinction between education and therapy.

There is no evidence that taking stimulant medication causes addiction or an increase in taking medication as an adult (Elliott and Worthington, 1995). Do note, however, that some students prescribed Ritalin refuse the medication, but others sell it. The move from therapeutic to recreational use of the medication is common. Ritalin can then be a health risk when crushed or injected into the body (Bailey, 1996).

Other concerns focus on the short- and long-term effects of drug therapy. Many children show an appetite loss that gradually decreases after a few weeks of use (Elliott and Worthington, 1995). There may be headaches and stomachaches initially in some children. Long-term effects may include growth inhibition, sleep and diet disturbances, and persistent tics.

The effects of the stimulants are apparent after thirty minutes and they last for three to four hours. But because any beneficial effects dissipate rapidly upon discontinuation of the medication, researchers are concerned about what they refer to as "short-term efficacy."

About one-third of children suffer a rebound effect from the medication: as the pill wears off, they show behaviour that may be worse than was present before the medication was taken (DuPaul and Stoner, 1994).

Medication is best viewed as one component of a comprehensive treatment program; an adjunct to other interventions such as special education and behaviour management. The Canadian Pediatric Society (1988) advocates a thorough interdisciplinary approach, with teachers playing a major role in the entire process. The teacher has an essential role in monitoring the effects of the therapy.

Therapy and Counselling

The developmental histories of many students with serious emotional and behavioural disorders have often been characterized by turmoil, uncertainty, abuse, neglect, unclear family communication, abandonment, and ineffective modelling (Jones, 1996). Because many students suffer a serious lack of self-esteem, depression, or anxiety impairment, the importance of interventions in the affective domain, which help students understand themselves and their environment, cannot be overestimated.

As providing students with an understanding of their own dysfunctional perceptions and clarifying their own reality lays the basis for healthy self-esteem and productive self-talk (Jones, 1996), there is created a need for various therapies and counselling techniques. Many occur in clinical settings; some are applicable to the classroom.

Individual psychotherapy implies a transaction between a child and a therapist. Techniques rely heavily on discussion and the probing of feelings and attitudes. Simply because young children may not realize that what they are experiencing is different from what other people feel, traditional therapeutic approaches have not been entirely successful with children. Children do not have adequate labels for internal experiences, and so they are unable to properly describe their feelings of anxiety, depression, or resentment.

As children have a difficult time with traditional "talk" therapy, indirect methods such as music, art, and storytelling are used instead to help children to communicate about therapeutic issues. Young children communicate more easily through play than through words, so various forms of play therapy have also evolved.

In play therapy, the therapist creates an atmosphere where a child can freely express feelings, concerns, and conflicts. The therapist, who assumes the role of co-player, model, or observer, then interprets the child's play to find the source of fears and problems, or tries to reflect back the feelings expressed by the child.

In addition to different therapies, counselling is often employed with children and youth with behavioural disorders and their families. The major goal is to help the child eliminate unacceptable behaviours and learn more appropriate ways of responding to people and the environment.

group therapy

Individual, group, family, guidance, and career and vocational counselling are used. Although individual counselling is popular, many counsellors suggest that **group therapy**—the simultaneous treatment of several clients, usually in the same age range—is a more natural way to work with children. By treating children in a group, the therapist can use group processes and face-to-face peer interactions as primary vehicles for change.

Group techniques make use of modelling, play, verbal interactions, peer influence, socialization, experience, and mutual support. Within the context of the group, children can unlearn inappropriate behaviours and learn new ways of relating more easily through the interaction and feedback in a safe practice situation with peers. At the same time, children learn to help other people, to accept help from others, and to talk openly about themselves and abandon facades. They take more risks and accept responsibility for their growth and the growth of others (Ohlsen, 1977).

Educational Intervention

As we point out in the Historical Notes at the end of this chapter, the how and where for educating students with behavioural disorders is a long-standing dilemma in special education. Today, with the thrust toward inclusive schooling, students with behavioural disorders are often cited as exemplars of the times when inclusion is not appropriate. For example, in the United States, as compared to the total of all students with disabilities, almost four times as many students with behavioural disorders are educated in segregated settings and only half as many in general classrooms (Cheney and Muscott, 1996).

Service Delivery Models

For most if not all school-aged children with mild behavioural disorders, the general classroom is the common milieu. With support, appropriate programming, and individualization, regular teachers can teach and manage these students.

But what about students with serious and violent behaviour? For these children, there is "a murky picture as to the future of inclusive education" (Bassett, Jackson, Ferrel, Luckner, Hagerty, Bussen, and MacIsan, 1996, p. 365). Whether they belong in the regular classroom is an ongoing argument, as shown in the Debate box below. You will notice that the arguments for the inclusion of students with serious behavioural disorders are very sparse compared with those for special programming. It seems that accommodation for problem behaviour may be less feasible than accommodation for instructional needs.

If prevalence figures are correct, all schools will have to confront this issue at some time. When doing so, a number of interrelated factors must be considered. Placement decisions must take into account the needs of the child as well as the boundary conditions: the classroom teacher and the other children in the class. Educators must determine the extent to which a student's learning or behaviour deviates from what is considered typical for age and grade; they must then address the teacher's tolerance and ability to deal with the child's difficulties.

The possibility of violent and dangerous behaviours must be considered when deciding on the least restrictive environment for a child. Some children with behavioural disorders exhibit behaviours "so severe that they require comprehensive and intensive intervention" (Kauffman, Lloyd, Baker, and Riedel, 1995, p. 543). They need classroom situations that provide a structured environment, individualized attention, and behaviour management practices and reward systems that allow them to learn new and positive behaviours.

Placement decisions must also address the consequences for other class members. Some students are so violent that it is best for them and the other students if they are served in alternate settings. As well, when teachers take excessive time to respond to behavioural problems, valuable classroom instructional time is lost.

One of the great fears of teachers is increased behaviour problems from special education

A Matter of Debate

The Educational Placement of Students with Serious Behavioural Disorders

For students with behavioural disorders, inclusionary practices are contentious and unresolved. At issue is not only the learning of the individual child, but also the progress of other class members and the safety of the teacher and others in the environment. Many writers assert that we may be glorifying the mainstream to the detriment of some children, especially those considered to be behaviourally disordered. Certainly, as the following debate indicates, there is ample evidence suggesting the need for great caution in including these students.

Arguments for inclusion	**Cautions about inclusion**
All students should receive their education in a general classroom setting.	For students with behavioural disorders, teachers strongly promote special class placement (Kauffman and Wong, 1991; Kazdin, 1987).
Studies (e.g., Farmer and Farmer, 1996; Glassberg, 1994; Meadows, Neel, Scott, and Parker, 1994) on the effectiveness of traditional pull-out and self-contained classes for children with behavioural disorders tend to support the use of general education settings and cast doubt on the utility of self-contained settings as catalysts for critical socialization processes.	Efficacy studies on the inclusion of students with serious behavioural disorders suggest that such placements are not as successful as special education classes.
One of the assumptions of inclusion is that children will benefit from social modelling of non-disabled peers in the regular classroom. Disabled students are provided with appropriate models of behaviour and will naturally model appropriate behaviours.	There may be too much disparity between these children and their peers for effective modelling to take place. Most students with serious behavioural disorders need to learn specific new skills if they are to function successfully in the mainstream.
The interaction improves children's self-image.	Students with conduct disorders are far from ideal classroom participants. They are disruptive and defiant, deficient in social skills, and do not fit either the teacher's or the peers' expectations for classroom behaviour. They are likely to be rejected.
Children will be accepted because of contact and familiarity.	Children elicit dislike and rejection. General classrooms are not safe havens if children are disliked and rejected.
Mainstreamed students with behavioural disorders have higher academic skills, better work habits, and higher grades (Meadows et al., 1994).	Students may show frustration due to task difficulty or boring curriculum, both associated with disruptive behaviour.

Arguments for inclusion	Cautions about inclusion
Students show less aggression, and less extreme behaviour, than those in self-contained classes (Meadows et al., 1994).	Violent students are more likely to erupt in inclusive or crowded classes where they may not receive a small teacher-student ratio, a structured setting, and individualized curriculum ("The discipline ...," 1996).
All teachers can and should accommodate difficult-to-teach students.	Traditional approaches to managing problem behaviours have not been responsive to the behavioural and learning characteristics of students with chronic behavioural problems (Carpenter and McKee-Higgins, 1996). Effective teaching of these students almost certainly requires a more extensive repertoire of instructional and management procedures than that exhibited by good teachers, in addition to greater perseverance in the face of failure.
Effective teachers are distinguished by different ways of instructing and managing students. They tend to be characterized by high standards for students and low tolerance for behavioural excesses and can therefore handle behavioural problems.	The needs of students with behavioural disorders may fall outside the limits of most effective general education teachers. Teaching of students with behavioural disorders may require skills, attitudes, and beliefs that are different from those of teachers who work effectively with more ordinary students.
All teachers should possess competency in classroom management, which is the major competency necessary to be successful.	Aggressive students show behaviour that fails to respond to known behaviour-management strategies and persists in spite of other supports provided.
With collaboration and support, teachers can accommodate these students.	Many of the practices known to be effective with children who are difficult to teach are not accepted by general educators (Lloyd, Keller, Kauffman, and Hallahan, 1988). "It is only with great effort that teachers are induced to learn and practice the positive, supportive procedures emananting from 3 decades of scientific research on behavior management" (Kauffman, 1999, p. 455).
The extent to which accommodations and interventions are provided can determine success or failure for students with behavioural disorders (Lewis, Chard, and Scott, 1994; Meadows et al., 1994).	When students with behavioural disorders are integrated into general classrooms, teachers provide little academic support or modifications and almost no behavioural support and adaptations (Meadows et al., 1994).
Classes that contain even one violent student should have at least two adults in attendance, whether it be another teacher, an aide, or an adult volunteer.	The energy and resources needed for success in the regular classroom may not be commensurate with the questionable gains achieved (see MacMillan, Gresham, and Forness, 1996).

students in general; particularly, there is considerable resistance among teachers to including students with behavioural disorders. Both prospective and experienced teachers report more positive attitudes toward students who can learn and who do not inhibit the learning of their peers (Wilczenski, 1992). Many general education teachers specifically disagree with the placement of students with intellectual disabilities and behavioural or emotional difficulties in the general classroom (Taylor, Richards, Goldstein, and Schilit, 1997). In a recent survey (Heflin and Bullock, 1999), teachers responded to accepting students with behavioural disorders with varying degrees of fear and skepticism.

It may be that when a child raises classroom management from a chore to an obsession, disrupts the learning of other students, and demands too much teacher time, we must confront alternative programming for that child. More restrictive placements run a gamut from general classroom with a full-time or part-time aide; to a regular classroom on a part-time basis with some special class placement; to placement in a special classroom with some regular classroom integration. Some students with severe and chronic disorders may need to be in special classes or a special school where teaching can be more precise and consistent (Brigham and Kauffman, 1998). These should be considered temporary placements. The ultimate goal of segregation is rapid return to a regular classroom once the child has learned to behave less aggressively and less disruptively.

Case Study

Andrew (continued)

As Andrew grew older, the character of his aggression changed. His achievement and academic interests were minimal, and he developed a more pronounced pattern of physical assault, swearing, truancy, and smoking. His achievement was at a very low level, hardly surprising given his behavioural problems, his apparent lack of academic interests, and his resentment of school and authority. Andrew had large gaps in reading skills, both for word attack and comprehension. His spelling was poor and creative writing exercises were beyond him. Only in math did he show any interest or potential.

By the middle of Andrew's first year in junior high school, his disruptive behaviour, fighting, and irrational conduct led to a number of suspensions. After he lit a fire on the school bus, he was transferred to a special class for children with problems. Even among this smaller group, Andrew's behaviour continued to be outlandish.

Andrew requires structured and consistent behavioural intervention in a supportive environment that offers much opportunity for success. However, developing successful behavioural interventions for a student such as Andrew is a complex process that must take into account the child's motivation for misbehaving, his or her likes and interests, and positive as well as negative reinforcements. Too, the match between teacher characteristics, including standards and tolerances, and a student's behavioural and learning needs must become a priority; mismatches between teacher expectations and standards and child behaviour may result in teacher resistance.

When devising an intervention program (behaviour reduction plan), it is critical that educators develop realistic goals for student behaviour. Initially, teachers may need to accept behaviours that would ordinarily be deemed inappropriate. For example, when a student exhibits explosive anger, a realistic first step might be to accept screaming or cursing as long as the child is not physically aggressive.

In the special placement, observations by Andrew's teacher showed that his behaviour during math was calm, while his behaviour during reading or language was at its most violent. In light of this, the teacher mounted a two-pronged program to alter Andrew's behaviour and improve his academic functioning.

Andrew's classroom environment was changed so that students worked in cubicles on individual programs for the first half of the morning. At the same time, a token economy was established with the co-operation of all students in the class. The teacher also decided to stress Andrew's strengths in order to help his weaknesses. Reading, as a specific remedial subject area, was eliminated from his timetable. Math became the fulcrum of Andrew's education. For example, as Andrew tackled math word problems, his reading comprehension improved; he later enjoyed writing math problems for the class. Math concepts, such as distance and scale, were extended to other areas, such as social studies.

EXTRACT FROM ANDREW'S IEP

Name Andrew S.
Age 12
Grade 7
School Green Middle
Teacher Mrs. Potts

Placement

At this time, Andrew will be placed in a special class. He can return to the regular classroom when his aggressive and violent behaviour decreases.

Needs/Adaptations

No physical adaptations. Needs warm, supportive environment with structured program and much reinforcement. Intervention by counsellor.

Long-Range Goals

- To decrease/eliminate violent behaviour.
- To decrease aggressive behaviour and learn alternate responses to frustration.
- To follow reasonable adult requests.
- To decrease time required to begin assigned academic tasks.
- To implement a social skills program.

Short-Term Objectives

- To learn alternate responses to aggression, such as ignoring, through role playing.
- To role play on following adult requests; to use token economy with daily child and teacher evaluation.
- To use a commercial social training package for social skills.
- To use a timer for beginning work on time.
- To learn to set goals for himself for each set of tasks.

Educational Models

As we have pointed out, the conceptual models from various disciplines are used to explain and treat behavioural disorders. Many programs relate to one specific model; studies support the belief that programs with a solid philosophical base and with staff who believe in that philosophy are the most likely to be effective (Beare, 1991). On the other hand, no single method has proven adequate in the management of all children who are behaviourally disordered, and teachers select strategies from various models. Refer to Table 7-1 for an outline of common interventions related to the various conceptual models.

Psychotherapeutic Intervention (Psychodynamic Approach)

The psychotherapeutic approach holds that the guiding principles of psychoanalysis should be employed in educational intervention with children who have behavioural disorders. The essential element among the numerous theoretical orientations and practical approaches to psychotherapy is an attempt to relieve a child's distress and encourage development. Underlying this approach is the belief that traditional psychoanalytic concepts can be used to find the underlying causes of behavioural disorders and emotional disturbance.

There is little value in changing a person's overt behaviour; instead, intervention should alter the underlying psychopathology by helping the person remember unfortunate experiences from infancy and early childhood. These memories provide insight, allowing the patient to come to grips with the causes of disturbed behaviour.

When translated into educational settings and intervention, therapists focus on uncovering the underlying psychology to improve a child's psychological functioning through revealing and relieving the child's unconscious psychic emotions and inner conflicts. The teacher's major concern is to help the child overcome inner turmoil rather than to alter behaviours or focus specifically on academic skills.

Psycho-educational Approaches

When approaches are termed *psycho-educational*, the supportive atmosphere, concern for underlying problems, and therapies match psychotherapeutic models. But a far greater emphasis is placed on educational success; teachers focus on academic skills and work closely with therapists to come to the root of a child's problems through counselling, life space interviews, bibliotherapy, and so on.

Teachers are trained to focus on their students' positive learning goals rather than on their defects and problems. This philosophical framework leads to a more positive, learning-directed approach than many other forms of mental health treatment.

Behavioural Approaches

During the 1960s, behavioural psychology was systematically incorporated into work with students with behavioural disorders. Today, behavioural approaches are the preferred intervention of many educators.

Behaviourists do not concern themselves with the deep-rooted probing of psychodynamic approaches. Nor do behaviourists categorize children's behaviour as abnormal, evil, mysterious, or deviant. Rather, they assume that the same principles that guide the development of normal behaviour are involved in the development of inappropriate behaviour. All behaviour is caused and controlled by environmental events outside the child and all behaviour is therefore observable, measurable, and subject to change through a change in the environment. With this in mind, behaviourists attempt to use the principles of behaviour therapy (behaviour modification) to alter the inappropriate behaviour. Examples of behaviours that can be modified include hyperactivity, aggressiveness, distractibility, bed wetting, excessive fearfulness, and harmful anxiety.

Three basic interrelated forms of treatment characterize the behavioural approach. The first uses teaching and training techniques to create behaviours that do not already exist. The second uses a number of techniques to maintain and generalize behaviours that are already established. The third uses other techniques to confine, reduce, or eliminate problem behaviour. Typically, all three modes of treatment are undertaken simultaneously. Behavioural techniques can be simply conceptualized on the *ABC rule.* The procedures attempt to change the events (antecedents) that precede problems (behaviours), as well as the events that follow (consequences).

Compliance is not the sole goal of a child's socialization. Changing antecedents and consequences means bringing about more appropriate behaviour, not just eliminating poor behaviour. This is referred to as the *fair-pair rule*, which states that when a behaviour is decreased teachers should select a desirable behaviour to increase at the same time. Under the fair-pair rule two questions need to be addressed in developing a procedure for behavioural changes: "What do I want the student to do instead?" and "What is the most effective and efficient means to help the student reach his or her goals?"

Regardless of whether the student is withdrawn or aggressive, the first objective is to exhibit a positive response instead of the current behaviour; that is, give students a repertoire of appropriate responses rather than merely eliminating behaviours. For example, we may want a student to play with peers on the playground instead of playing alone, and to play appropriately with groups instead of hitting peers during games. For both behaviour patterns, we have identified what we want the child to do instead of the current problem behaviour. Providing reinforcement for playing in a group may result in an increase in this behaviour along with a simultaneous and connected decrease in the inappropriate behaviour of hitting others. Reinforcers (rewards) are used to increase desirable behaviour, and aversion techniques are used to decrease or extinguish undesirable behaviour.

Reinforcement can be provided by anything that a child finds pleasurable. Reinforcers are usually divided into three types: *primary reinforcers* are things like candy and food; *secondary reinforcers* include objects that have no intrinsic value of their own, such as tokens and stars. Whether a child receives a primary or a secondary reinforcer, it is always accompanied by a *social reinforcer* such as a smile, a hug, or a pat on the back. Reinforcement is represented in Figure 7-2.

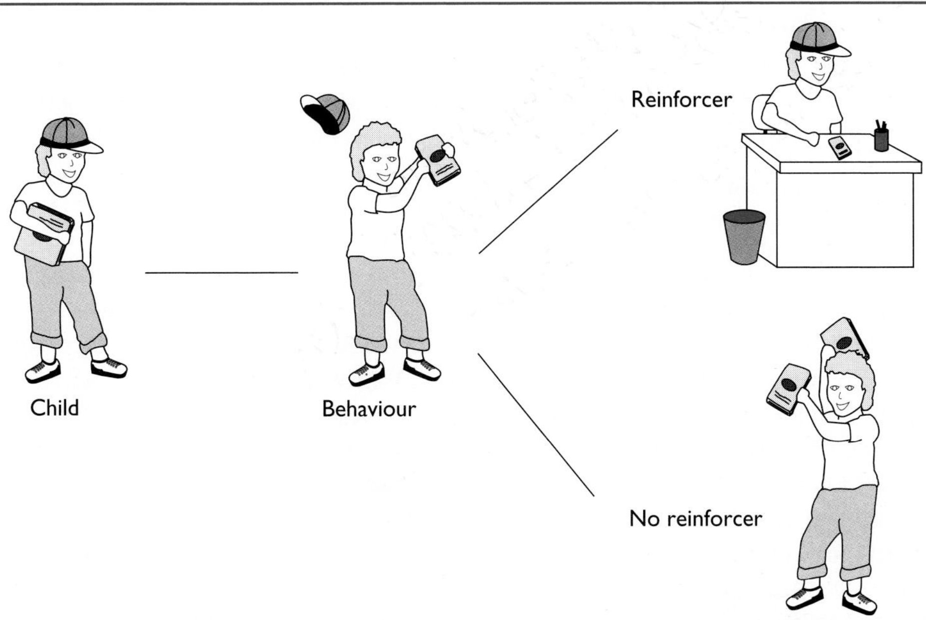

Figure 7-2
How reinforcement works

Selecting and using reinforcers is not as simple as it seems. As Mossish (1997) points out, the Achilles heel of the reward and consequences system is that it works only if children care about the rewards and the consequences. If children develop an immunity they can defeat the system, as in, "Send me to the office. I don't care."

Still, positive reinforcement is far more effective than punishment, which is a poor deterrent to unwanted behaviour and should be used sparingly. Punishment generates students' anger, bringing greater conflict. Punishment does not answer the "why" of poor behaviour, does not teach appropriate behaviour, and does not suppress behaviour. In fact, it may lead to the emergence of other unacceptable behaviours, and may be used by children as a negative means of gaining attention from adults.

Some forms of behaviour modification are more suitable for general classrooms; others work better in self-contained settings. Token economies are widely used. The following case study, a look at Class 7B, describes a token-economy system employed with an entire class. Such systems are equally applicable to individual class members.

Ecological Approaches

The usual positive aspects of life in school and community are not present for students with behavioural disorders. Ecological approaches acknowledge that each environment has mul-

Case Study

Class 7B

The grade seven class at the end of the hall was well known to all the students and teachers in the school. Any trouble, vandalism, or disruptive behaviour could generally be traced to that group of nine children. Although each child in the class was unique, they all behaved in ways that were unacceptable to the school and the community. The children in this class had been punished so often that such disciplinary measures as detentions, time outs, and suspensions had little meaning for them. Indeed, such punishments usually resulted in increased resentment toward school personnel and an even more active dislike of learning.

Rather than using further aversive measures, the grade seven teacher decided to institute a token-economy behavioural program. Because of her students' age, the teacher invited and incorporated their suggestions for every step of the program. From some students, she won immediate co-operation. Because the students' problems were so diverse, she decided to focus only on on-task behaviour.

During the first weeks of the program, the children were told exactly how much seat work would earn a token. For example, three math problems earned a poker chip. On Friday afternoon, students with ten chips could trade them in for a reinforcer, such as the viewing of a special film.

As the program continued, the teacher shaped her students' behaviour by making them work longer to earn tokens and by raising the token price of reinforcers. Wisely, she changed tokens and reinforcers often. She soon saw positive changes in behaviour, more on-task behaviour, increased learning, and a new sense of pride and achievement in the class.

tiple dimensions, as does each pupil. Approaches focus on how a student functions in the classroom environment and on altering the match between the child and the environment. They use group processes such as discussion groups, class meetings, and role playing, and may also include the teaching of the social skills and adaptive interpersonal behaviours.

Role playing involves both emotional and cognitive components. Participants assume a specific role in a demonstration or simulation. It is important to let the students be deeply involved in specifying the details of each role playing sequence, such as a fight at school. Participation increases the similarity between the role play in the instructional session and what the student has experienced outside the classroom.

role playing

Some students may perform better with a social script that structures the role playing. Scripts show the roles played by the members, the sequence of activities, and the reward structure. *Social autopsies* are discussion oriented—they analyze behaviour by dissecting and discussing social mistakes, discussing who was harmed, and planning for the future.

Teachers may use **bibliotherapy**, a procedure based on the concept that books serve a therapeutic purpose, especially for children with disabilities (Pardeck, 1990), and that reading stories with positive role models can affect an individual's attitudes and behavioural responses. Not only are books relaxing, but they also can help children work through a crisis and they can help children see how others have confronted problems and gain insight into alternative solutions (see Sridhar and Vaughn, 2000).

bibliotherapy

Promoting Social Skills

Social skills are specific behaviours that people perform when interacting with others. Training in social skills was popularized in the 1980s and has since become an important academic feature for children with behavioural disorders. Instruction is intended to help them make and keep friends, get along with adults, and modify their behaviour.

In the classroom, a teacher can promote communication skills, prosocial skills, collaborative skills, and group maintenance skills. These include:

- Greeting behaviours;
- Ways to extend and receive invitations;
- Positive listening skills, such as listening attentively, sharing and encouraging, and engaging in verbal and non-verbal interaction with others;
- Conversational skills, such as asking about other people's interests, responding to others' questions, and maintaining an extended conversation by taking turns to comment on a topic;
- Giving verbal and non-verbal compliments and positive feedback;
- Using positive methods of gaining teacher attention (for example, when asking about a work assignment);
- Acceptable habits of cleanliness, grooming, and health;
- The ability to inhibit reactions to stimuli to stem inappropriate outbursts;
- Self-management skills which enable children to select appropriate choices based on probable consequences.

When teachers are asked to rate social skills, they assign most importance to skills such as following rules and directions, volunteering answers, and interacting with teachers and peers about schoolwork. Less important to teachers are skills involving conversation, initiating social contact with peers, and assertiveness. The type of social skills that teachers perceive as critical for classroom success has implications for their selection of skills for intervention.

As the range of social skills needs to be addressed, the best way for teachers to determine which social skills to teach is to conduct informal natural observations. One way to promote social skills is to introduce a social interaction program within the context of the entire classroom. Alternatively, training can be directed solely at children who show deficits, with the training taking place in settings where the social behaviour would most naturally occur.

Lessons are best implemented in groups of three to five students, which optimally include socially competent peers to serve as models. The first group lesson should focus on three things: an explanation of why the group is meeting, a definition of what social skills are, and an explanation of what is expected of each student during the lesson. It may also be helpful to implement behaviour management procedures for the group, such as contingencies for compliance and non-compliance. As lessons continue, it is important to prompt the students to use newly learned skills throughout the day and across settings to promote maintenance and generalization, and to reinforce the students when they use new skills (Lewis, Heflin, and DiGangi, 1991).

Quite a number of commercial programs have been developed for children and adolescents that incorporate effective methods of behaviour modification, modelling, role playing, feedback, and transfer of training. Skills range from how to have a conversation to learning to resist peer pressure. The Early Childhood Social Skills Program (Odom, Kohler, and Strain, 1987) is a well-validated procedure for normally developing children and those with developmental delays for classroom implementation. Skills include making offers and requests to share, offering play suggestions, making offers and requests to give assistance, showing affection, and giving compliments. There are two phases in the program: formal teacher instruction, and practice. For instruction, the teacher places children in groups during play and teaches a skill. Sharing is the first skill taught. To teach, the teacher demonstrates the strategy and then monitors as all children perform. For adolescents, the ASSET program (Hazel, Schumaker, Sherman, and Sheldon-Wildgren, 1981), developed at the Kansas Institute for Research in Learning Disabilities, provides a set of training procedures to help students gain social interaction skills. (See the Historical Notes at the end of this chapter for some critical elements of social skills instruction and curricula.)

Curriculum

Coherent, comprehensive descriptions of educational programs for students with behavioural disorders are relatively rare in the professional literature. The curriculum for students with mild disorders will generally parallel that for normal youngsters, although alternate methods for basic academic skills development may be required. To the extent that the curriculum is not a powerful enough tool for motivation and reinforcement, the teacher needs to compensate with other methods. That is, academic curricula must have affective components. Besides academic success, disturbed children need a warm, supportive atmosphere that promotes an increase in self-esteem, self-concept, and social skills.

ADHD is an emerging field with exploratory methodologies and a growing number of projects contributing to more effective educational practices. Almost every type of instruction attempted with every type of deviant behaviour had been tried with students with ADHD. Research into behaviour management for students with ADHD has focused on increasing on-task behaviour, task completion, compliance, impulse control, and social skills, while reducing hyperactivity, off-task behaviour, and disruptive behaviour and aggression.

Some classroom ideas are found in the In the Classroom feature at the end of this section.

Programs Addressing School Violence

A substantial portion of all juvenile crime happens in school buildings or on school grounds—included are bullying, truancy, and gangs. Educators are naturally concerned with children and youth who are aggressive and bullying, and those who add to violence in the schools. Keep in mind, however, that records show that most students who are violent are not special education students.

The rising tide of antisocial and violent behaviour in our schools has captured the country's attention, and in recent years a great deal of research and writing has been directed toward the areas of school violence and serious learning disruptive behaviour (see Carter, Janzen, and Paterson, 1999). U.S. figures suggest continuing growth in the rates of juvenile violence; similarly in Canada. Since 1986, the number of young people charged with violent crimes has increased 131 percent.

Do note, however, that it was in 1986 that sixteen- and seventeen-year-olds began to be charged under the Young Offenders Act, which meant that previously adult crimes became juvenile charges. As well, Canadian youth court statistics show no increase in the severity of youth violence in the past five years (Dolmage, 1999). Finally, serious school violence must be kept in perspective: the incidents are infrequent considering the huge numbers of students in school.

In the United States, "The prevention of violence is a leading priority for most public school systems" (Mehas, Boling, Sobieniak, Sprague, Burke, and Hagan, 1998, p. 20). In Canada, too, there is a growing professional interest among educators in establishing better learning environments. These have led to multifaceted prevention and intervention efforts combining parents, schools, communities, and the health and criminal justice systems. Provinces have introduced various models and programs, such as the Safe and Caring Schools initiative in Alberta, the "zero tolerance for violence" in Ontario, and the Second Step program in Saskatchewan school divisions.

Common features of school-wide behavioural management systems include:

- A total staff commitment to managing behaviour, whatever approach is taken;
- Clearly defined and communicated expectations and rules;
- Consequences and clearly stated procedures for correcting rule-breaking behaviours;
- An instructional component for teaching students self-control and/or social skill strategies;
- A support plan to address the needs of students with chronic, challenging behaviours ("School-wide ...," 1997, p. 2).

Social Intervention

Social intervention encompasses a variety of methods and services to help children with behavioural disorders and their families. Children's mental health centres provide a range of treatment programs. Foster care may also be used to remove a child from home for a period of time; this can be done if the family is unable to cope with a child's behaviour or if the home atmosphere is considered to be damaging for a child.

Historical Notes

Children and youth with mild behavioural disorders gained the attention of reformers and educators in the middle decades of the 19th century, becoming a part of what was referred to as the *child rescue movement.* Child rescue advanced in tandem with the stress on free and compulsory education for all students that began in Canada in the late 1840s and became law in the 1870s. At the same time, legislation was gradually passed in the areas of child labour, family courts, juvenile courts, and children's aid societies. The first Juvenile Delinquency Act was passed in 1905.

When compulsory school laws sent all children to school, the schools were forced to find ways to accommodate students who were unruly, recalcitrant, or truant. School exclusion, expulsion, or suspension was one solution to a behaviourally disordered pupil. Another was the establishment of segregated classrooms, where such children could obtain special instruction and where they would not disrupt other pupils or take a teacher's time.

The first segregated classes in the public schools, called *unruly classes*, opened in 1879. By 1910, segregated special classes were a permanent feature of most urban school systems. Along with segregated classes, there were also placements in reformatories and industrial (later, training) schools.

For decades, segregated placements remained the most important vehicle for providing services to children and youth with behavioural disorders. But self-contained programs, even those identified as model programs, were often instructionally sterile and relied primarily on a curriculum of control (Knitzer, Steinberg, and Fleish, 1990).

In the 1950s, the preferred treatment for behavioural disorders became psychiatric in nature. Treatment was based on the development of a therapeutic relationship between therapist and child; education required changes in the child's total living environment, which often meant placement in a residential setting.

After students with behavioural disorders had experienced a hundred-year legacy of educational services that relied heavily on segregated settings, including not only special education but also services connected with hospitals and orphanages, the early 1970s witnessed positive changes. Strong attacks on the legitimacy of a medical paradigm in the treatment of childhood emotional disorders emerged, as well as discontent with settings and educational intervention. In Canada, a number of provincial and national reports on education stressed the need for expanded and more effective educational services for children with behavioural disorders. They urged the federal and provincial governments to assume educational responsibility, and asked local education authorities to provide educational services for all children within their jurisdictions (Csapo, 1981a).

After that, service for students with behavioural disorders developed rapidly. Nevertheless, students remain underserved. Writers chided that Canadian children with serious emotional or behavioural problems were receiving less attention in 1988 than in 1981 (Dworet and Rathberger, 1990). In 1994, a cross-Canada survey of educational programs for behavioural disorders (Shantz, 1994) found that 85 percent of school districts surveyed provided programming.

Today, a pall of pessimism is increasingly apparent in the field. Writers observe that educating students with behavioural problems will continue to be "one of the most stressful, complex and difficult challenges facing public education today, and perhaps one of our greatest failures" (Osher, Osher, and Smith, 1994, p. 7).

Despite more than 150 years of various solutions that have emerged and decayed, the prognosis for children and youth with behavioural disorders is anything but serene. To date, no instruction has been devised that permanently alters this condition and that successfully diverts children and youth from a trajectory leading to a host of long-term negative developmental outcomes (Walker, Colvin, and Ramsey, 1995). Students show excessive dropout rates, high rates of academic failure, poor achievement, low graduation rates, high numbers of institutional placements, and poor post-school adjustment (Eber, Nelson, and Miles, 1997).

Varied models and approaches are used both because of the myriad nature of the disorders and because no one method has proven effective for all behavioural disorders. But, as James Kauffman (1997b) points out, "The education of children and youth with emotional or behavioral disorders is not now governed by a consistent philosophy or conceptual model that is linked to instructional methodology" (p. 121).

Educational programs have not shown particularly positive outcomes. For example, the teaching of social skills and fostering of children's social competence has become a major curriculum emphasis in both general and special education (Rutherford, 1997). Yet there is scant evidence that teaching social skills has been an effective strategy (Kavale and Forness, 1995). The effectiveness of social skills training has been modest at best, and the long-term generalized effectiveness remains uncertain (Rutherford, 1997).

When inclusion is discussed, educators are forced to consider carefully the most enabling environments for those with serious behavioural disorders. More than 55 percent of these students continue to be educated in separate settings (Bassett et al., 1996).

SUMMARY

1. We use the term *behaviourally disordered* to describe children and youth who are meeting difficulties in adjusting to normal behavioural expectations. Classroom behavioural problems are one of the most common reasons children are referred to special education.
2. In the field of behavioural disorders, the most fundamental and pressing question involves how to find precise definitions. Many disciplines work with children who are behaviourally disordered so that varying professional perspectives exist, each with its own theories concerning the causes, definitions, and treatment of the disabilities. But, while deviant behaviour has been conceptualized in many ways and definitions have been proposed from a variety of perspectives and disciplines, a universally accepted definition does not exist.
3. Classification systems may use the severity system or the classification proposed in DSM-IV, but it is most common today to establish clusters or dimensions of behaviour. Behaviour can also be seen as internalizing or externalizing.
4. Of the many variables contributing to human experience, none has been conclusively shown to underlie emotional problems, and many factors can lead young people to act out in ways that are unacceptable and reprehensible. Causes may be genetic, biophysical, disturbed family climate, deleterious environment, academic difficulties, faulty learning, and other school factors, to mention only a few. A combination of risks has far more negative effects on children than any single source of risk.
5. It would seem that the overt behavioural disorders would be easy to identify and assess. This is not true. In assessment, a major problem when evaluating behaviour centres on what is normal behaviour as opposed to what is abnormal in the classroom. The expectations of teachers and other observers play a key role in defining behavioural disorders.
6. The types of behaviours that most clearly signal elevated risk for behavioural disorders

are aggression, peer rejection, academic failure, and affiliation with deviant peers, with family, school, and environment contributing to the risk.

7. The characteristics of children and youth with behavioural disorders are so varied that no single measure or tool can pinpoint all of the symptoms or all of the causes of the behavioural and learning deficits. Multiple assessment tools are available. Promising contributions come from teacher nominations and observations, teacher ratings of maladjusted behaviour, and functional analysis.
8. Children with conduct disorders attract attention with their overtly disruptive behaviours. Delinquency refers to a set of antisocial behaviours acquired over time; delinquent youth are shaped through contact with a variety of social and emotional factors that increase the likelihood that they will become or continue to be adjudicated offenders. Those who are anxious and withdrawn internalize their behaviour: they may exhibit nausea, pains, headaches, fears, obsessions, shyness, nightmares, crying, depression, self-consciousness, and withdrawal. Phobias—specific, out-of-proportion anxiety—can be but are not a necessary concomitant of anxiety and withdrawal. ADHD refers to a cluster of related behavioural characteristics that are usually most evident in the classroom. Children with ADHD tend to be distractible and to spend more time in off-task behaviour than do their peers.
9. Both negative aggression and poor peer co-operation are outer-directed (externalizing) behaviours that can disrupt others. In contrast, anxiety is inner-directed (internalizing) and typically not disruptive to other students. For these youngsters, the greatest threats are to themselves, not to those around them; for example, they may be overlooked in the classroom.
10. ADHD is a new focus for special education. With mounting research interest more children are being diagnosed, the term has entered educational parlance, and researchers are directing considerable attention to the condition. It is now generally agreed that ADHD is a biomedical disorder with possible genetic links in some cases.
11. Bullying is a form of aggression, a particular kind of violence to which children are exposed. In general, bullying is a school problem that starts early and thrives in the middle school years.
12. Faced with rambunctious, contrary, or unfocused children, some people leap to the conclusion that drugs can solve the problem. The use of psychotropic drugs to control behaviour and increase academic functioning is a matter of deep concern and considerable controversy. In the short term, drug therapy seems effective for many children.
13. Many students with behavioural disorders can be well served in regular classrooms provided teachers are given assistance regarding how to manage misbehaviour. Considerations include the individual child and the types of behaviours manifested, the learning and comfort of other class members, the teacher and his or her effectiveness in handling deviant behaviours, and the supports available to teacher and child. No student should be removed from the regular class until it is clear that effective programming cannot be provided there.
14. Successful behaviour change is related to the additive effects of multiple interventions based on diversified treatment modalities. No single approach suits each child with a behavioural disorder, and the approach that works today may not work tomorrow.

Those intervening with students who are behaviourally disordered require a spectrum of different approaches and techniques and should be familiar with the components of all models.

15. All psychotherapeutic approaches search for the child's inner conflicts and motivations while trying to explain current or past events. *Behavioural* approaches are more concerned with producing desirable behaviour. The *ecological* approach to behavioural disorders emphasizes the need to look at the total interaction of the child with the social environment to know how the youngster's ecological system functions and how his or her behaviours fit or do not fit these ecosystems.
16. Teachers' belief systems determine the standards they maintain for students, what behaviour they will tolerate, and how they expect individual students to behave. Teachers employ various methods of discipline and management. They combine these with teaching children specific prosocial behaviours through methods such as modelling, shaping, coaching, and cognitive problem-solving skill development, and prompt children to engage in interactions and role playing. Teachers also attempt to change the attitudes of normally developing children toward their peers with disabilities through role playing, peer tutoring, and reinforcement.
17. ADHD requires multimodality treatment that may include psychopharmacology, psychosocial intervention, and special academic assistance and accommodations.
18. The development of social skills has important implications for children's academic and vocational success as well as for long-term mental health adjustment. The use of skill-streaming instruction can increase prosocial and positive behaviour. While there is no ideal curriculum for teaching social skills, areas usually incorporate skill identification, modelling, role playing, reinforcement, and generalization.

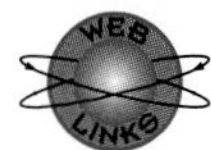

WEBLINKS

Attention Deficit Disorder Library **qlink.queensu.ca/~3dw18/add.htm**

Behavioural intervention **www.cec.sped.org/bk/focus/specfoc.htm**

Bibliotherapy **www.storiestogrowby.com**

Canadian Journal of Behavioural Science **www.cpa.ca/ac-main.html**

Canadian Professionals' ADD Centre
www.usask.ca/psychiatry/CPADDC.html

The Challenge of Difficult Children **www.smu.edu/~egibson/**

Diagnostic and Statistics Manual Criteria for ADHD
www.chadd.org/dsm_iv.htm

Guidance and discipline **www.nncc.org/guidance/guide.disc.page.html**

Responding to school crises **smhp.psych.ucla.edu/resource.htm**

In the Classroom

Managing children of any age, any grade, and any functional level can be a challenging and often frustrating task. No matter how well teachers manage their classrooms or how conscientious, consistent, and fair they are, there will inevitably be some children who fail to respond as positively as others and who consistently test the teacher's authority.

Controlling behaviour and teaching discipline and self-control are aspects of the broader construct referred to as *classroom management.* In general terms, classroom management refers to "the way in which teachers manipulate the classroom environment to minimize disruptions and give all children the optimum opportunity to engage in appropriate behaviour and reach learning and social goals" (Winzer, 1995, p. 627).

Classroom management includes curriculum planning, organizational procedures, resources, arranging the environment, maintaining child progress, and anticipating potential problems. Within the construct of classroom management, behaviour management refers to all the ways in which teachers control inappropriate and disruptive behaviour, as well as ways in which children are taught discipline and to control their own behaviour.

The word *discipline* derives from *disciple,* a follower of the master's teaching. Discipline means helping children to learn to guide their own behaviour in a way that shows respect and caring for themselves, other people, and the physical environment. Self-discipline involves being able to consider an outcome and select the behaviour that will achieve it (Glenn and Nelson, 1987).

Discipline must be taught, learned, and internalized, because discipline is necessary if the classroom and the children it contains are to function properly. In classroom situations, approaches to behaviour management can be seen in three ways—*prevention, defusion,* and *follow-up.*

The best way to handle inappropriate behaviours is to prevent them from happening in the first place. **Preventative discipline** refers to strategies and procedures that militate against any discipline problems arising. Good preventative discipline includes providing a warm and interesting environment, logical routines, clear rules, much positive reinforcement, children's knowledge of consequences for misdemeanours, and a curriculum matched to the needs of the child. When the curriculum is meaningful and well presented, students are less inclined to engage in disruptive behaviour.

When preventative measures fail, *defusion* is a necessary approach. When students are continually confrontational, teachers need strategies that defuse the behaviour, rather than increasing it. They must not allow the student to pull them in the direction of confrontation or a cycle will be set in motion (Colvin, Ainge, and Nelson, 1997). Defusing strategies lessen the likelihood that the situation will escalate.

There seem to be several stages through which students pass on the way to major behavioural outbursts (see Johns and Carr, 1995). Non-verbal behaviour, such as sighs and putting the head down on the desk, characterize the anxiety stage. Here, teachers can respond with active listening and nonjudgmental talk.

In the *stress* stage, a student can show frustration through actions such as tearing paper or tapping pencils. Teachers can use proximity control, boost interest, ignore, redirect the student, or give a choice between behaviour and the loss of a privilege.

The *defensive* or *verbal aggression* stage is characterized by the student arguing and complaining. Here, teachers can state the rule or expectation, request explicitly that the student "Take care of the problem," or encourage the student to ask for help.

By the *physical aggression* stage, a student has lost control and begins to throw objects or threaten or hit others. In the presence of serious threatening behaviour, a teacher should disengage and break the cycle of successive interactions by delaying responding. *Delay*—briefly look at the student, look at the floor, look detached, pause. *Disengage*—for example, say "Excuse me," and move to your desk and pick something up. Return to the student, redirect, and withdraw. Alternatively, the teacher can remind the student that he or she still has choices, escort the student from the class, or get help from other staff members.

In the final stage, *tension reduction*, the student releases tension through crying or verbal venting. Teachers should try to help the student gain insights into the behaviour.

Defusion is not all that is needed; there must be later follow-up. Follow-up provides consequences for the behaviour and helps the student to find alternate ways of behaving. When following up, forgive and forget the past; do not allow past misdeeds to form the basis for present interactions. Convey the idea that you like the child even if you do not find the behaviour acceptable.

Behavioural manifestations, needs	**Tips**
Needs supportive environments	• Establish supportive interpersonal relationships with students. • Try to create a warm atmosphere characterized by acceptance without permissiveness • Bear in mind that each child is unique. • Children must be treated as individuals regardless of their behaviour patterns. • Involve the child's parents: make daily communication with the home or issue daily report cards. • Allow older students to be involved in setting up reinforcement systems, such as a token economy.
Needs consistent expectations	• The need for consistency is very high; whatever system of classroom management is used, it can be successful only if it is implemented in a systematic and consistent fashion. Provide clear expectations: students need to know what to expect of the teacher, what is expected of them, and what the consequences are for success and failure. When teachers are consistent in enforcing rules, children learn self-control. • Establish routines; set clear limits to behaviour. • Make class rules sparingly. • Remind students of the rules often. The younger the students, the more often the rules should be reviewed. • Levy mild penalties following inappropriate behaviour to promote consistent behaviour change.
Needs monitoring of behaviour and learning	• Determine why the student is acting in a certain way. • If you can discover what a child is trying to get with a behaviour, then you can find an alternative behaviour that meets the needs. • Keep rigorous documentation of behavioural interventions.
Commits chronic classroom misdemeanours	• Keep a sense of humour. • Share your problem students with a buddy: When you reach the breaking point, send the student to the buddy with something to do. Return the favour.

Behavioural manifestations, needs	**Tips**
	• Seat disruptive children among others who are well behaved. • Remove objects or toys that cause problems. • Keep a careful eye on scissors, pencils, and other potentially dangerous objects. • Immediately remove the results of poor behaviour. • Consider the timetable: if a certain time or subject seems to cause disruption, alter the scheduling. • To eliminate aggression, eliminate the payoff for aggression; model and coach, create non-aggressive environments, and teach social skills.
Is confrontational or makes threats of violence	• Develop the ability to show a flat face (no emotion). • Give the student a chance to save face and cool down. For example, "It's your call. Take a minute to think about it." • Send for help; get the names of participants and witnesses. • Make the office aware of the incident. • If in doubt, do nothing. • Take a minute to think over the options. • Provide models of non-aggressive responses to aggression-provoking behaviour. • Provide reinforcement for non-aggressive behaviour; do not allow positive reinforcement for aggressive behaviour. For example, reward students when they are doing something well, even in the middle of misbehaving. For example, you might say "You're very angry and I appreciate that none of those books are going in the direction of people." • If you step into an aggressive act, devote as much attention as possible to the victim and ignore the perpetrator as much as possible.
Hyperactive	• Be organized and consistent. Disorganized and chaotic classrooms can elevate hyperactivity in children, as can unpredictable classroom schedules. • Allow the child to move, doodle, or squeeze a small ball while in class. This can actually increase concentration.
Attention problems, distractibility	• Children with ADHD are driven by their interests. Increase interest in what they are working on. • Provide high levels of feedback, praise, and reinforcement. • Remove clutter in the classroom. • Seat away from high stimuli such as bulletin boards. • Allow to move when appropriate • Cover desk with brightly coloured paper to draw attention to work.

Behavioural manifestations, needs	Tips
	• Define student workspace when in large group activities; for example, on the floor with masking tape of carpet squares. • Have different coloured book coverings for each class. • Establish a signal to silence students and gain attention, such as clapping or dimming lights. • Frequently use student names. • Use study carrels. • Allow stand-up desks and table. • Present short tasks. • Provide self-correcting materials. • Use response cost programs rather than token economy.
Off-task behaviour	• Set a beeper to go off at various intervals. Every time the beeper sounds, students earn points if they are on task. • Break up long lessons by changing the pace and allowing some physical movement. • Hold attention for longer periods by facing the student and establishing eye contact. • Use concrete aids such as flow charts, flip charts, and overhead projectors. • Students may attend more closely if they are provided with a lesson outline or a glossary of key terms prior to the lesson. • Children with intrinsic attention problems are difficult to handle in groups, and teachers may consider reducing the amount of time these students spend in group settings. • Proximity control—seating the student near the teacher—may also help to sustain attention.
Anxiety and withdrawal	• For anxiety, peer mediated interventions are most promising. • Do not call on withdrawn students to answer questions unless they volunteer. • When an anxious student does answer and makes a mistake, be supportive with "That's a good try," or "You almost made it," and move onto another student immediately.
Poor academic skills	• Focus on academic skills. • Provide children with experiences in which they can succeed. • Use organizational folders. • Use thematic projects that allow children to pursue their interests and be active participants.
Needs training in social skills	• Teach social interaction skills. • Ensure that students participate, as far as possible, in all aspects of school programs at the elementary and secondary levels.

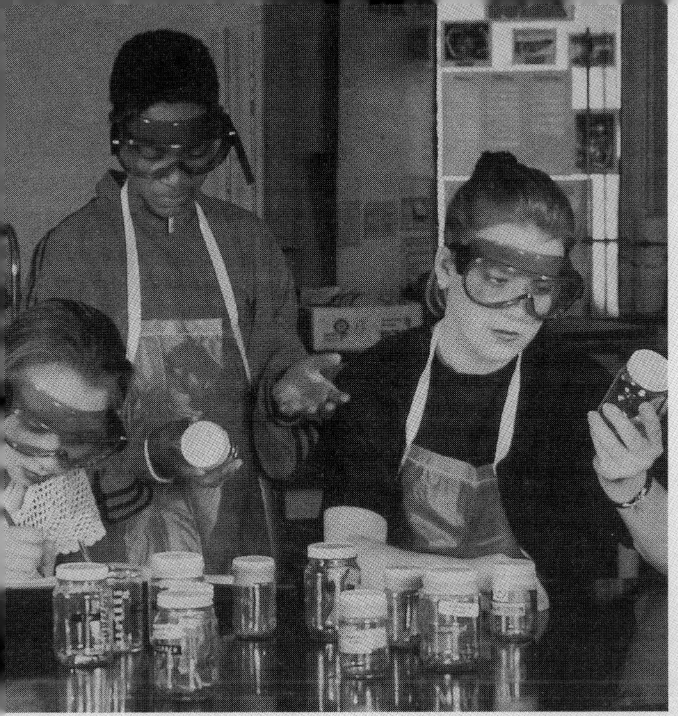

SECTION 4

Children Who Are Gifted, Talented, and Creative

After reading about the children and youth with disabilities in this text, you may think that educating students with gifts and talents is a facile process, easy for teachers, well-accepted in the educational community, and underlain by enabling legislation and appropriate funding. Nothing could be further from the truth.

It is a given that students who are gifted learn more, faster, and more thoroughly than their peers. It is not as well accepted that children with gifts and talents should be considered exceptional and provided special education services to develop their full potential.

Canadian provinces and territories address the education of students with gifts and talents in different ways. As examples, Alberta Education has outlined a vision of schooling that emphasizes challenging students who are gifted and talented to the fullest in specialized school settings. In Saskatchewan, an Educational Development Fund is designed to finance educational innovations and may provide funding for approved programs for gifted students. There is an absence of educational resources and special programs for students who are gifted in the eastern provinces of Newfoundland, Nova Scotia, New Brunswick, and Quebec, a reflection in part of changing paradigms about inclusive schooling. Manitoba and British Columbia have adopted a non-categorical approach to the provision of services to students who are gifted and talented, endeavouring to meet the needs of all students within the regular education framework (see McFadden and Ellis, 2000).

Many issues circulate in the education of students with gifts. While identification, placement, and teacher training are prominent, the major issue is whether a public education system that is philosophically and administratively egalitarian in nature should provide special services for children who are already well endowed.

The restrictions placed on programs for students who are gifted are both academic and attitudinal. All are associated, to a greater or lesser extent, with the notion that "the cream will rise to the top." Many people still believe that children who are gifted are smart enough to make it on their own. They see these students typically doing well in school, easily meeting age and grade levels for achievement, and tending to be well behaved. They therefore rationalize that pupils who are gifted will develop their abilities even if not provided with special education: If students don't do well, then they're not gifted, anyway.

Myths about students who are gifted being able to do well regardless of environment and the amount of stimulation and opportunity are compounded by the fact that most of these children demonstrate no immediate problems that can serve as a basis for an emotional appeal for special services. Traditionally, special education has been viewed as a way to help children who perform poorly in school, and children with outstanding abilities rarely arouse the same level of concern as do youngsters who are disabled. Children with gifts and talents are not perceived as suffering from social stigma or unhappiness; rather, giftedness is considered highly desirable and a boon to social status.

Many educators feel that although we are morally obliged to help children with disabilities, there is no moral necessity to assist those children who are already advantaged. They question the ethics of a society that labels a select few, that provides special opportunities for the elite, and that attends "to the exclusive needs of only a small segment of learners" (Sapon-Shevin, 1984, p. 79). It is not desirable to identify some students as gifted and the rest as ungifted, they argue. All students at all ages have relative talents and strengths and schools should help all students identify and understand their own special abilities.

The underlying concern is that special education for the gifted might subvert our commitment to egalitarianism and jeopardize the principle of democratic education by creating an overadvantaged elite or meritocracy within the school population. Because of this attitude, we direct our special education programs, and the taxes that support them, largely into programs for students who are disabled. Our regular education programs serve the needs of average children. The gifted we leave to fend for themselves, even when this involves a waste of their potential.

Most thinking individuals would agree that Canada's youth who have gifts and talents form one of the country's greatest undeveloped resources. Many of the leaders, scientists, and artists of the next generation are likely to emerge from the current crop of children who are gifted and talented. Nevertheless, debates surround the issue of egalitarianism versus special programs and are germane to today's education of these students. In fact, it is this single issue that will determine ultimately the fate of education for students with special gifts and talents.

Chapter 8

Children Who Are Gifted, Talented, and Creative

Learning Outcomes

After reading this chapter, you should be able to:

- Differentiate between giftedness, creativity, and talent;
- Appreciate why students who are gifted require special education;
- Understand the measures used to identify and assess students who are gifted;
- Explain the various approaches to accommodating giftedness employed in schools and the pros and cons of each approach.

Introduction

Gifted is a somewhat abstract term applied to people who, by virtue of outstanding abilities, are capable of high performance (Clark, 1988). Gifted individuals have greater ability in some areas than most of us. Generally, we admire such people, but occasionally we are a little envious of their talents and achievements. We seem to have to work much harder than they do to achieve only mediocre results.

A variety of variables figure in the scenario of giftedness, including talent, aptitude, creativity, personality, and motivation. Some individuals soar to great heights in the talent domain, others in intellectual ability, and still others in creative endeavours. A few individuals achieve remarkably high levels across several domains.

Special education attempts to provide for any child markedly different from the average, even if this difference is a positive one. Gifted, creative, and talented students have special educational needs—they may learn in ways different from other students; they are more curious; and they think more abstractly. At the same time, students who are gifted are vulnerable to the same forces that affect other children and youth and can become frustrated and bored in unstimulating learning environments.

To reach their full potential, children who are gifted, creative, and talented must be confronted with suitable challenges and stimulating educational experiences. The provision of these special services to the gifted population has always been a difficult undertaking that poses many complex issues and problems for educators. A great deal of professional skill and sensitivity is required to identify the special needs of gifted students, while the development of appropriate programs taxes the skill, resourcefulness, and empathy of teachers as they walk a tightrope between equity and excellence. Administrators must balance economics with pedagogy.

Yet an increasing number of educators, administrators, legislators, parents, and researchers support the idea that giftedness needs to be fostered and nurtured. They argue that children who are gifted have the same right as other children to develop to their full potential and therefore require special education and appropriate related services. Without educational opportunities and challenges, children who are gifted may hide their abilities or bury them in underachievement. In fact, probably half of the gifted population do not match their tested ability with comparable achievement in school.

Case Study

William, Troy, and Richard

The Jones School is an elementary school in a pleasant neighbourhood in a large Canadian city. In the school's three grade five classes, there are three students considered to have gifts and talents. Each of these children is unique and each is posing different challenges to the school and teachers.

William's giftedness was identified early and as a result he was accelerated and skipped grade four. In the classroom, William reveals outstanding abilities in verbal tasks and abstract thinking, particularly shown in written classroom assignments. He is an "easy" child, good at games, and well accepted by his peers. He works far above the classroom norm but does not seem to resent the drill and practice that is part of the day.

In his first years in school, most of the teachers saw Troy as an almost perfect student. He always finished his work, performed at a high level, and was well behaved, compliant, polite, and helpful.

Troy was identified during second grade as a gifted child. After that, each teacher attempted to put in place different types of enrichment activities for Troy. That he was sometimes bored and a little frustrated was masked by his good behaviour and happy nature.

This situation changed once Troy was in grade five. Mr. Jane, Troy's teacher, did "not believe in giftedness" and insisted that Troy do exactly the same work as everyone else. The teacher was surprised to then see mounting behavioural problems, acting-out behaviour, and poor peer relations, chiefly attributable to Troy's bossy and directive attitude. There was a concomitant significant drop in Troy's achievement, all compounded by his inability or unwillingness to comply with expected school behaviour in matters of dress and personal hygiene.

Troy frustrated and angered the teacher, especially when he contested the information being presented. This happened so often that Mr. Jane finally referred Troy for special assistance as a student with a behavioural disorder. As part of the referral, Troy was reassessed. The assessment showed Troy to be functioning well above the norm (Full Scale IQ 144). During the testing sessions, however, Troy was resentful and manipulative, and stated that he "did not appreciate having his brain examined." He eventually complied with the examiner's requests and finally confided that "When I was five I was an optimist; at seven a pessimist. Now I'm a cynicist."

When another grade five teacher used a nomination scale, the results gave no indications of gifted potential in Richard. However, the teacher was puzzled by the peaks and valleys in performance that emerged as she filled out the scale. Richard has excellent reasoning ability but difficulties in memorizing, paying attention, and following several directions at once. Solving oral math story problems is often easier for him than remembering multiplication facts. He frequently talks about complex ideas but writes slowly and illegibly. He seems to have difficulty in managing time and is slow in processing information.

Similar ups and downs were indicated by his parents. They agreed, for example, that Richard suffered serious lags in reading but judged him highly in his oral language abilities, his commitment to projects once started, and his interest in a range of hobbies and collections. Richard did not rate himself highly, but his peers did. In the peer nominations, they agreed overwhelmingly that Richard was the student who could think up unusual and interesting stories and games.

With such contradictory evidence, the teacher asked if the school psychologist could present Richard with an assessment. On the WISC-R he scored 142 on the Verbal Scale and 138 on the Performance Scale, for a Full Scale of 140. Achievement testing showed his reading to be at second grade level, although his math was at about his grade level.

DEFINITIONS OF GIFTEDNESS

To be gifted is to be superior in some way to the average. But beyond this almost meaningless statement, no universally accepted definition of giftedness exists and no set of traits adequately defines any gifted child. The uniqueness of each student with gifts and talents is shown in the case study. William is compliant and helpful; Troy is resentful and outspoken; and Richard's other problems mask his potential.

This does not mean that the field has not been on a constant search for a universally accepted definition. In fact, the importance of adequately defining giftedness as a precursor to identification and as an indicator of prevalence has led to a multiplicity of definitions. In one publication, seventeen different conceptions of giftedness were identified (Sternberg and Davidson, 1986).

Many factors underlie the definitional problems found in the field. These can be summarized as follows:

- There is no such thing as a typical child who is gifted; particular talents and social environments give rise to varying personality patterns. Some students who are gifted in language and the arts may have only average aptitude in math; some students who are mathematically gifted may not do well on tests of verbal abilities.
- Although many different gifts and talents have been identified and creativity can be, at least partly, explained and measured, gifted, talented, and creative individuals are typically lumped together as a single category.
- Identification of signs of giftedness, of potential for high-quality creative achievement, remains a relatively inexact science (Feldhusen, 1989). There is no consensus on how to measure superiority or how to recognize potential giftedness.
- There are two quite different views about the definitions of giftedness. One looks at giftedness as potential; the other looks at it as the actual production of outstanding work.

The giftedness-as-potential view often uses an IQ cut-off between 120 and 140 or restricts giftedness to a percentage of the population, ranging from the top 1 to the top 20 percent. Some school districts (for example, in Pennsylvania and the East York Board of Education in Ontario) make an IQ score of 130 and above the cut-off for a child to be identified as gifted (Mark, Beal, and Dumont, 1998).

When giftedness-as-product is used, definitions dismiss the idea that IQ alone determines giftedness; they focus on the attributes of identified individuals who are gifted and their potential value to society. Product definitions base giftedness on an individual's consistently remarkable performance in some socially useful area, and assign the term "gifted" only to people who have attained outstanding achievements.

Although confusion currently reigns about definitions, one thing is clear—the definitions of giftedness have changed. When the roots of the field of gifted education were laid down by pioneers such as Francis Galton and Lewis Terman, high IQ was viewed as the critical dimension of giftedness. Two threads emerged from this perception.

First, children with high IQs were the most deeply investigated, and early definitions tended to be narrow and restricted. They relied on psychometric measures and limited giftedness to specific performance on an intelligence test. This is discussed in the Historical Notes at the end of this chapter and in the Research Notes on Terman's studies on p.292. Second, the focus was on "school-house giftedness," connoted by high test scores and good grades.

Since Terman's day, perceptions of giftedness and beliefs about what abilities should be recognized and developed in Canadian schools have changed dramatically. Newer defini-

Figure 8-1 *Interaction of Renzulli's characteristics*

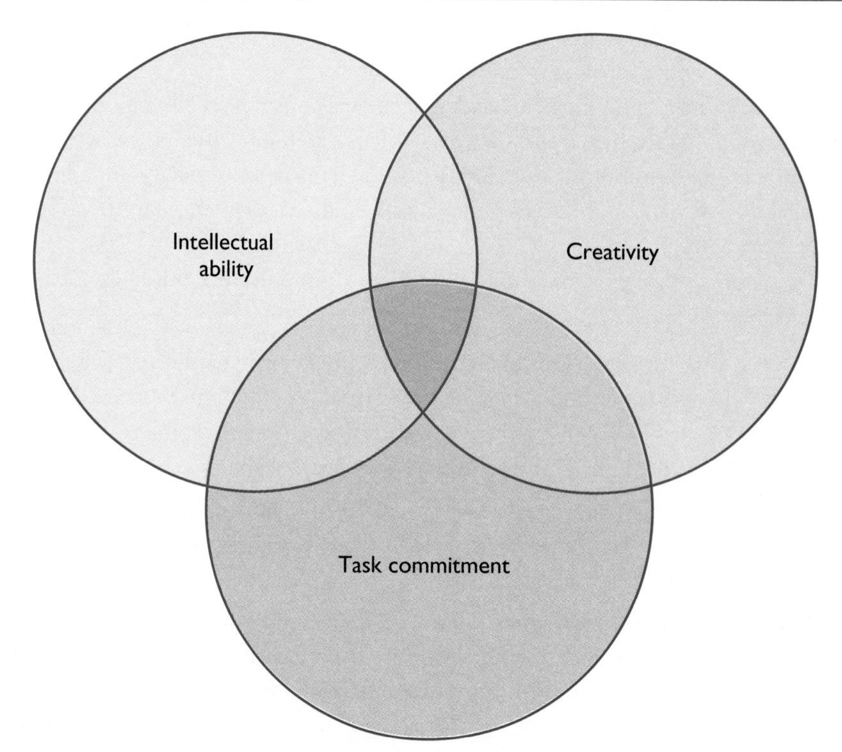

tions of gifted and talented give a broader view of the concept. They have become much more liberal in terms of both the types of behaviours attributed to individuals who are gifted and the degree of behaviour that must be elicited before the label gifted is applied. Current perceptions overthrow the notion that giftedness is merely manifested through outstanding academic performance, because "school-house giftedness" is only weakly associated with adult eminence or creative contribution (Siegler and Kotovsky, 1985; Sternberg, 1987).

A widely employed definition, originally adopted by the United States Office of Education in 1977 and revised in 1981, states that

> children who are gifted are those who give evidence of high performance capability in areas such as intellectual, creative, artistic, leadership capacity, or specific academic fields, and who require services or activities not ordinarily provided by the school in order to develop such capabilities. (PL 97-35, sec. 572)

This definition manages to be inclusive, specific, and practical. It encompasses a wide range of gifts, talents, and creative aptitudes; stresses the necessity for special education provisions for students identified as gifted; and ties identification to the necessity for programming.

Another widely accepted notion comes from Joseph Renzulli, who believes in defining giftedness largely as product because he holds that, in the end, giftedness is determined by the contributions an individual makes to humanity. Renzulli studied adults known to be gifted and concluded that three characteristics were required for remarkable achievement: high intellectual ability, high creativity, and the ability to carry tasks through to completion. The interaction is shown in Figure 8-1.

It is not enough to possess only one of these traits; as the figure shows, it is only where the circles intersect and the three traits come together that, according to Renzulli, true giftedness is found (Renzulli and Reis, 1991). Renzulli (1978) feels that children who are gifted and talented "are those possessing or capable of developing this composite of traits and applying them to any potentially valuable area of human performance" (p. 261).

PREVALENCE OF GIFTEDNESS

The lack of a universally accepted definition of giftedness makes it very difficult to estimate its prevalence in the population at large and in school-aged children. However, we can reasonably assume that only a small percentage of a school population will require special programming for the gifted. In this general sense, giftedness is said to occur in 2 to 5 percent of school-aged children. Highly gifted are probably one in 10 000 of these, and the superior gifted are perhaps less than one percent of the gifted population (1:50 000 or fewer).

CLASSIFICATION OF GIFTEDNESS

To compound definitional problems, a host of other terms and varied classification systems have emerged. However, the classification systems are quite different from those found in fields such as intellectual ability. Severity levels would not make much sense. We could perhaps call a person *mildly* or *moderately* gifted, but not *severely* or *profoundly* gifted. Any classification, therefore, revolves around the varied components that contribute to giftedness.

Terms used to describe individuals who are gifted include words such as *precocious, tal-*

ented, creative, and *genius.* The terms *gifted* and *talented* are frequently used interchangeably. As the Historical Notes point out, *genius* was the original term used to indicate a particular aptitude or capacity. Today, we reserve the word for those persons who demonstrate extremely rare intellectual powers.

Gifted Children

In the early 1920s, the term *gifted* appeared to describe high-achieving individuals. Gifted implies the possession of special abilities in diverse areas.

Many researchers are critical of the concept of school-house giftedness that we explained in the previous section. Nevertheless, the term *gifted* is still most often used to refer to students with above-average academic endowment. This happens because, educationally speaking, the most important components of giftedness are those defined relative to the school in which an individual finds himself or herself. **Academic ability** refers to intellectual ability measured by performance on IQ tests and other standardized tests of academic achievement (Marland, 1972). **Academically talented students** are generally considered to be those scoring at the 95th percentile or higher on these measures.

academic ability

academically talented students

To differentiate the heterogeneous population of persons who are gifted, new terms are emerging. Writers speak to modestly gifted, highly gifted, and superior, with arbitrary thresholds of IQ 130, 150, and 180. Most will be modestly gifted. Highly gifted persons are "Those whose advancement is significantly beyond the norm of the gifted" (Silverman, 1989, p. 71). Only a few rare individuals are superior, with IQs beyond 180.

Sometimes, young gifted children are said to be *precocious.* This word comes from the Latin *preacox,* meaning to precook or to boil beforehand. **Precocity** refers to remarkable early development. Many children who are highly gifted show precocity in particular areas of development such as language, music, or mathematical ability. The fields that have produced the most prodigies are music and chess (Feldman, 1993).

precocity

Creative Children

During the 1960s, definitions began to add components of creativity. But defining creativity is fraught with difficulties. As Barbara Clark (1988) observes, "creativity is a very special condition, attitude, or state of being that nearly defies description" (p. 46).

Paul Torrance, a pioneer in the study of creativity, defines it as the process of sensing problems or gaps in information, forming ideas or hypotheses about such gaps, and communicating the results (1966). Others note that creativity may be seen as the "activities and products invented in the interest of solving a problem" (Cole and Sarnoff, 1980, p. 6). Howard Gardner (1983) pursues a similar route and sees a creative person as one "who regularly solves problems, fashions products, or defines new questions in a domain in a way that is initially considered novel but that ultimately becomes accepted" (p. 35).

The components of creativity are perhaps less elusive than an exact definition. Torrance elaborated on four characteristics—fluency of ideas, or producing a number of responses to a given stimulus; flexibility, or shifts in thinking from one category to another; originality, or unusual and clever responses; and elaboration, or the addition of details to basic ideas or thoughts (Torrance, 1969). Later researchers have followed Torrance's lead and see several dispositions working together to foster creativity—curiosity, flexibility, insightfulness, optimism, and the ability to blend divergent and convergent thinking. Divergent thinking is the type of thinking in which considerable searching about is done and a number of answers are produced. It seems to be only a component of creativity, however, as divergent thinking in childhood is not highly correlated with creative abilities in adulthood (Feldhusen and Clinkenbeard, 1987). Divergent thinking is in some ways the opposite of convergent thinking, which focuses on one right answer, or toward a relatively determined answer. This relationship is diagrammed in Figure 8-2.

The link between intelligence and creativity is difficult to pinpoint. Above a threshold score of about 120 IQ, the correlation between giftedness and creativity disappears. Nevertheless, June Maker (1993) postulated that creativity and intelligence are two components of the same construct because the key element in giftedness is the ability to solve complex problems in the "most efficient, effective, or economical ways"(p. 71). Other research suggests that creativity uses three kinds of intelligence (Sternberg and Lubart, 1995). *Synthetic intelligence* allows a creative person to see a problem in a new way. *Analytic intelligence* allows the individual to recognize which new ideas are productive and allocate resources to solve the problem. In using *practical intelligence*, a creative person promotes an idea by using feedback from others.

Creativity may very well be an innate trait that can be stimulated or quashed. Creativity seems generally to decrease as children get older, a tendency that may be accounted for by both age and culture. As well, creativity tends to occur in spurts. During the first three years of school, most children increase their creativity, perhaps because teachers in these grades allow much freedom of expression. After grade three, a sharp drop in creativity occurs, followed by a gradual decrease during the remaining elementary and middle-school years (Bernard, 1973).

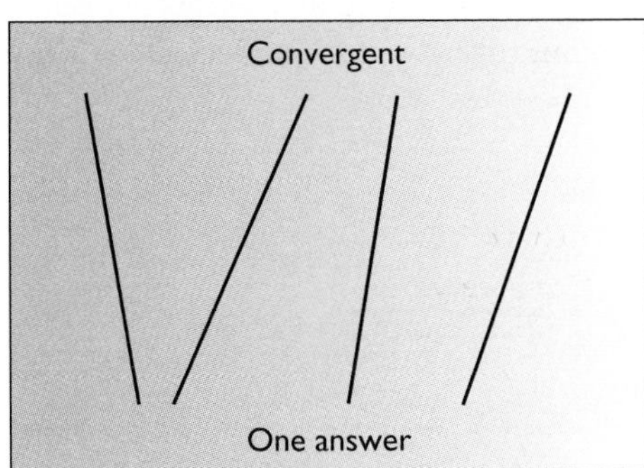

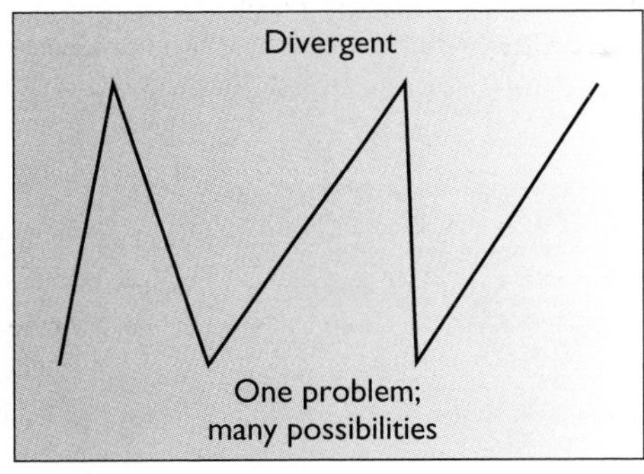

Figure 8-2 *Convergent and divergent thinking*

Talented Children

talent

If giftedness is above-average competence, then **talent** is above-average performance. Talent refers to a specific dimension of a skill in areas such as music, visual arts, drama, athletics, and particular academic domains. Canadian psychologist François Gagné calls talent "the developmental product of an interaction between aptitudes and intrapersonal and environmental catalysts" (1991, p. 66). Some children have unusual talents in one field and limited abilities in other areas. Talented children begin to nurture their special traits early, and children are often encouraged by their parents and extensively tutored or coached by experts.

But there seems to be more to talent than that. Some of us may practise our pitches and putts forever but will never play with Tiger Woods. Why? It seems that certain aptitudes make it easier to learn certain skills and genetic factors may influence one's abilities in a particular area (Gagné, 1991). As well, the direction of an individual's talent depends on many factors such as experience, motivation, interest, emotional stability, hero worship, parental urging, and even chance.

There seem to be three phases in talent development. First there is playful exploration, which entices the learner into further involvement. Then there is acquisition of skills and attention to detail, with rigorous practice. Finally, a commitment to excellence is made (Bloom, 1985).

Just as the link between creativity and giftedness is complex and confusing, so research has also not yet shown the relationship of talent to giftedness. Gagné (1985) presented one of the first major attempts to delineate talent as distinct from giftedness. He suggested that talent is an ability focus that emerges out of general ability. Therefore, giftedness is a prerequisite for talent, but an individual who is gifted is not necessarily talented.

Leaders

Leadership is a neglected area. It is defined as the ability to effect positive and productive changes that are self-enhancing or group-enhancing. Plowman (1981) described leaders in these terms: *charismatic, intuitive, generative, analytical, evaluative,* and *synergistic.* Those with high leadership abilities demonstrate empathy and sensitivity, personality and proficiency, and possess charisma, the ability to actualize values to the extent that dynamic group change is effected.

Children who display early leadership qualities will interact easily with a variety of people; be sought out by others; possess confidence; establish the mood of the group; be sensitive to the feelings of others; show others how to improve on a task; and generate many ideas and solutions (Karnes and Strong, 1978).

The relative contribution of genetic and environmental factors with respect to giftedness is not clearly understood.

FACTORS CONTRIBUTING TO GIFTEDNESS

Children with gifts and talents are found at every economic level and in every stratum of society, throughout all ethnic, cultural, and racial groups. However, we do not yet understand what contributes most to giftedness, or why some gifted people achieve eminence and others fade into obscurity. The multiplicity of factors that bring a Tiger Woods or a Margaret Atwood to prominence have not yet been untangled and identified.

The effects of heredity and environment are both important in the development of children who are gifted and talented, but the relative contribution of genetic and environmental factors is not clearly understood. Genes carry potential for various characteristics from parent to child down through the generations, but the genes alone cannot produce a human being. Each of us is born in a unique environment in which conditions act and react with one another. The individual human being is the total expression of all these complex and constantly interacting forces.

Genetic Factors

Francis Galton and other early researchers maintained that most human traits were passed down through the generations on "germ plasm." When the dangers of a purely genetic view of development became obvious, the pendulum swung toward a strong emphasis on environmental conditions, especially after the 1930s.

Although the proposition that intelligence and abilities are inherited is not popular in our egalitarian society, it is now abundantly clear from the field of behavioural genetics that there is a significant role played by genetic transmission in the development of intelligence. Most authorities in the area of behavioural genetics hold that genetic factors are at least as important as environmental factors in determining intelligence (e.g., Bouchard and McGue, 1981; Scarr-Salapatek, 1975). Among Caucasian children in North America and Europe, it is estimated that half to three-quarters of intelligence variation is due to genetic factors (Scarr-Salapatek, 1975). There is also no doubt that some of us have more inborn capabilities in music or visual perception or linguistic ability than others (Plomin, 1989).

Environmental Factors

The complex study of genetics has not yet revealed how genes influence giftedness. Moreover, even the strongest hereditarians acknowledge the great influence of environment on the development of intelligence. Giftedness is not just a condition bestowed on some and denied to others. Rather, it is a set of traits that must be nurtured in order to reach their full development (see Gagné, 1985).

The unique development of gifted traits can occur only through specific interactions within family units and later with appropriate training and education. The importance of nurturing is clearly evidenced by the many deprivation studies that have demonstrated the negative effects of malnutrition and lack of stimulation on infant functioning. The high proportion of first-borns among the gifted population further suggests the importance of environment to the full development of intellectual potential. Unlike younger siblings, first-borns receive full attention and much stimulation from their parents, even if only for a short time.

No race, ethnic group, or culture holds a monopoly on giftedness. Yet the statistical probability of giftedness increases when a child's parents have higher than average intelligence and provide a better than average home environment. Bright children are more likely to be born to bright parents, although some children who are gifted are born to slow learners. Other factors in the environment that seem most clearly to affect the development of giftedness are the values and expectations of the culture; the socio-economic level of the family with accompanying nutritional and other health variables, attitudes, and values; the number of children in the family; and the presence of environmental stimulation.

Using the family as a starting point, many investigators have attempted to unravel the specific family variables associated with gifted-level abilities in children. What they find are many favourable qualities in these families, particularly parental interest in child-rearing and a strong commitment to the development of the child's talents and abilities. When Benjamin Bloom and his colleagues (Bloom, 1985; Bloom and Sosniak, 1981) examined the home environments and the early training of exceptional people in the arts, in athletics, and in cognitive skill areas, they found that the home environment and the person's parents were almost entirely responsible for nurturing the child's early interests and the development of his or her skills.

Highly educated parents are more likely to produce children who are gifted and to provide them with enriching environments. On the Stanford-Binet Individual Intelligence Test, the average score for children of college graduates is more than ten points above the mean, whereas for children of parents with less than high school education it is about six points below the mean (Kaplan and Saccuzzo, 1993). In a Canadian study of gifted kindergarten children, Barbara Perks (1984) found that 59.5 percent of their fathers and 50 percent of their mothers had post-secondary education. This compared to 30.9 percent of fathers and 27 percent of mothers for non-gifted children. Perks compared the reading material available in the children's homes and found that 61.9 percent of the families of children who were gifted had more than 300 books, as compared to 18.4 percent of families of non-gifted children.

Certainly, bright children come from lower socio-economic homes, but not as often as we would expect. Intervening factors may include lack of motivation, family expectations, neighbourhood aspirations, and financial pressures.

DEVELOPMENTAL CONSEQUENCES OF GIFTEDNESS

Like every population, individuals who are gifted form a heterogeneous group. Differences run the gamut of possibilities; among persons who are gifted will be found the active, the lethargic, the healthy, the infirm, high achievers, low achievers, the painstakingly patient, and the lightning quick. The single thing that people who are gifted have in common is "the ability to absorb abstract concepts, to organize them more effectively, and to apply them more appropriately than the average youngster" (Gallagher, 1975, p. 19).

Table 8-1 outlines some of the common characteristics of students who are gifted, talented, and creative. View this list with caution; probably no child displays all of these traits. Rather, each child possesses a unique subset of descriptors, which come from, but do not include, all the behaviours of the larger set. As well, attach no credence to the notion that these are *wunderkind*, adept in all areas of functioning. Like everyone else, children who are gifted have their warts, and teachers must accommodate problems as well as potentials. Also be aware of the great variance in the gifted population that renders many

Table 8-1 Some common characteristics of children who are gifted, creative, and talented

Traits common in children who are gifted

- Wide range of ability
- High academic achievement
- Insatiable curiosity
- Good observational skills, with a willingness to observe both the usual and the unusual
- Verbal fluency and a large vocabulary; may talk a lot and have many ideas; often use metaphors and abstract ideas and enjoy debating issues
- Ask a lot of questions; inquisitive about the world and want to know the why and how as well as the what
- Committed to finding out what happens if something is done, as in a science experiment
- High motivation with persistent goal-directed behaviour and high task commitment; stick to a topic to completion
- Long attention span; become absorbed in self-selected tasks
- High energy level, with an intense concentration of activity
- Organizational and planning skills
- Innovative, creative, divergent responses
- Ability to synthesize large amounts of diverse information; ability to think and perform in an interdisciplinary manner
- Superior reading ability
- Ability to grasp and retain knowledge
- Ability to convey ideas effectively
- Ability to work independently, with little or no need for adult monitoring
- Ability to assume and discharge responsibility; possess decision-making capabilities and leadership qualities
- Avid collectors and hobbyists; join many clubs
- Easy adjustment to new situations
- Mature sense of humour
- Appreciation of social values; show advanced ethical thinking; often prize integrity, independent judgment and social values and ideals; are interested in political and social issues
- Tend to be task- and contribution-oriented more than recognition-oriented
- Superior in height, weight, health, energy, and vitality
- Establishment of favourable relationships

Traits common in children who are creative

- Tendency to ask many questions that may be embarrassing, advanced, or controversial, often challenging the teacher and the textbook
- Production of work that is off the beaten track, with much humour and playfulness
- Boredom with recitation and memorization of facts; preference for talking about ideas and problems
- Good problem-solving ability with new and unusual ways of solving problems; show a variety of approaches to problem solving; are resourceful and can solve problems through ingenious methods
- Keen sense of humour and a fine sense of the absurd; reputation among teachers and students for wild and silly ideas
- Skill in abstract thinking

- Use a wide variety of resources
- Considerable energy
- Unexpected answers on examinations
- Pleasure in working alone
- Apparent lack of hard work, coupled with good performance in examinations
- Unusual capacity for originality, concentration, and hard work on special projects
- Imagination and inventiveness; show playfulness in experimentation
- Versatility and diversity of interests
- See associations and innovations

Traits common in children who are talented

- Persistent goal-directed behaviour and high task commitment
- Imaginative and inventive; acute observational skills
- Perceptive and imaginative in the interpretation of stimuli
- Pronounced intuitive sense combined with a high degree of artistic integrity
- Ability to interpret and interconnect to a refined degree
- Attack drawing, painting, or sculpting in non-prescribed ways, often not taught by the teacher
- Use of technical ability as a foundation for reinterpretation, refocusing, and retranslating, chiefly for personal satisfaction
- Ability to detach oneself from the surroundings and focus intently on the task at hand. This is especially true of auditory attention in musicians.

other characteristics possible. The true extent of that variance is not even known, because of our inability to identify all children who are gifted.

Physical Development

Throughout history, there has been a persistent stereotype of the individual who is gifted as an "egghead." The person with gifts was viewed as physically weak, homely, socially inept, narrow in interests, and prone to emotional instability. Such stereotypes were shattered by Lewis Terman, who found that, as a group, individuals who are gifted exhibit superior physical traits. The children in Terman's study were larger at birth, walked sooner, went through puberty earlier, had fewer diseases and operations, and reported less nervousness than average persons (Terman and Oden, 1959).

Although children who are gifted may physically outstrip their agemates later on, their superiority is seldom detectable at birth or even during the first year. Nor do children who are gifted show advanced motor skills as a general trait. Teachers are very likely to find young children who can read far above level yet are unable to write their own names legibly, referred to as *dyssynchrony.*

Academic Development

Three general characteristics seem typical of the learning behaviour of students who are gifted—an internal locus of control, independence, and self-motivation. In fact, one of the most ubiquitous traits of both productive students who are gifted and eminent adults is high motivation and persistence.

Students like learning, enjoy difficult subjects, and are willing to spend extra time on projects that stimulate their interest. They learn more, faster, and more easily than do their agemates. They also learn to read sooner and continue to read at a consistently more advanced level. Children at this level of functioning are also more adept at critically evaluating facts and arguments. Because they more readily recognize relationships and comprehend meanings, they can reason out problems more effectively.

All these factors place children who are gifted far ahead in academic achievement. They can master the curriculum content of a grade two or three times faster than the average child. One study of curriculum compacting (Reis and Purcell, 1992) found that gifted students had already mastered from 25 to 75 percent of the math and language arts curriculum before it was taught. In elementary mathematics a good rule of thumb for students who are gifted is that two years of standard content can be covered in one year (Van Tassel-Baska, Landau, and Olszewski, 1985).

Social and Emotional Development

One common and persistent myth regarding individuals with gifts, especially those in the arts, is that they are prone to mental disease. The question of whether individuals who are gifted are more emotionally stable, self-sufficient, and less prone to neurotic and psychotic disorders than average people has been the subject of intense research, which offers modest support for the superior adjustment of persons who are gifted. The consensus now is that persons who are gifted are at least as well, if not better, adjusted than their peers (see Neihart, 1999). In a study of gifted students in grades five, eight, and ten, Ottawa researchers (Schneider, Clegg, Byrne, Ledingham, and Crombie, 1992) found that the children who were gifted were relatively well-adjusted individuals.

This relates to students who are moderately gifted. Those who are extremely precocious may be at greater risk for social problems than their modestly gifted peers. Students with very high IQs are less popular and have more difficulty with peer relations than their agemates. Possibly their unusually high intelligence makes it difficult for their peers to relate to them intellectually or socially. One study (Dauber and Benbow, 1990) discovered that extremely gifted students viewed themselves as more introverted, less socially adept, and more inhibited. The extremely gifted adolescents also reported that their peers saw them as much less popular, less socially active, less athletic, and less active in the crowd.

Modestly gifted children tend to be well liked by their peers, although popularity may taper off in secondary school settings. Sometimes they alienate peers simply by the discrepancy between them or by their eagerness to demonstrate their unusual talents. Tannenbaum (1962) reported that bright students most favoured by peers were intelligent, athletic, and nonstudious. The least-favoured gifted students were intelligent, studious, and non-athletic. In the Tannenbaum studies, boys rated more highly than girls. A later study (Cramond and Martin, 1987) of teachers and preservice teachers found much the same. Respondents valued not academic brilliance but athleticism as a critical determinant in a person's likeability. Males were rated more highly than females.

Behaviour

Like other children, students who are gifted are not always well behaved. They may interrupt others, fail to listen, be argumentative, refuse to comply with requests they view as trivial, be excessively critical, teasing, or bossy, or display a high energy level that results in perpetual motion and disorganized work habits (Whitmore, 1979). Perfectionism is a common trait in children with gifts and talents (Parker, 1997). Students are often too critical of others and of themselves and need help in accepting failure.

Research has not found significant differences in the attitudes of gifted and non-gifted students toward school. However, students who are gifted are often impatient with the routines in a regular classroom: chalk and talk, endless drill and practice, and repetition, along with a concomitant lack of stimulation and challenge, can bore and frustrate advanced learners. In fact, children who are gifted and talented complain a great deal about the boredom of their classroom experiences. They say they are forced to spend a lot of time being taught things they already know, doing repetitive drill sheets and activities, and receiving instruction on new material at too slow a pace (Feldhusen, 1989).

Creativity leads to a set of personality traits characterized by a strong self-concept that gives little credence to outside academic and social sanctions. Creative children tend to have high independence and be less conforming than their peers. This is especially true of boys. In junior high school classrooms of students with gifts, creative boys are eight times as likely to quarrel with the opinions of peers and teachers as are creative girls.

Ethical Development

Students who are gifted develop steadfast values quite early, with strong concerns for right and wrong. They wrestle with problems that we often associate with adults. When Derevensky and Coleman (1989) asked seventy children aged seven to thirteen in a Toronto school for the gifted, "What are the things to be afraid of?" the students gave fears generally expressed by chronologically older students, such as death and nuclear war. Nicholas Colangelo (1989) asked 125 gifted children to define problems that were important to them. More than 50 percent chose typical teenage dilemmas of friendships and love relationships. However, they also identified thirty-six issues dealing with more adult themes such as public welfare and life and death scenarios.

Cultural and Linguistic Differences

Two of the most troubling issues in special education are the persistent over-representation of minority and economically disadvantaged populations in special education and their under-representation in programming for gifted students. Many students who are non-white, non-middle-class, or from language minority groups are not identified and taught as gifted learners.

A major reason accounting for under-representation is an implicit demand that children always manifest giftedness in the same way—the same equating with the majority culture's definitions of giftedness. The demand is not reasonable, as children from other cultures are shaped by different value systems and certain traits that define giftedness in the dominant culture may not even be allowed to appear because culturally different children show different interests and attitudes.

For example, definitions of giftedness in a First Nations context are quite different from those usually used by psychologists and educators who primarily function in the institutions of dominant society (Friesen, 1997). What is clever and creative for the child on a reserve, where different value systems are in operation, will not be the same as for the child growing up in a suburb.

Minority students may not understand the classroom game as well as other students, which teachers then interpret as a lack of ability or potential (Subsotnik, 1997). White, middle-class gifted children tend to display a high level of verbal ability; in contrast, Native children raised on reserves are normally very quiet and verbal precocity would not be an indicator for Native gifted children. But knowing about spirituality—the sacred traditional ways—is a manifestation of giftedness (Friesen, 1997).

ASSESSMENT OF GIFTEDNESS

At first glance, the identification of gifted and talented children and youth may seem to be a relatively simple task. Nothing could be further from the truth. From the outset, one of the major concerns in gifted education has been the problem of identification and its measurement correlates. Even today there is much confusion, and the issue of identification and assessment remains highly problematic. So much so that Borland (1989) suggested that the process of selecting students and placing them in appropriate programs is the most difficult, controversial, and thankless of all the tasks involved in developing and implementing programs for the gifted.

Even though much of the success of programs for students who are gifted is contingent upon sound identification procedures, an ideal identification system has not been developed. Identification of signs of giftedness and of potential for high-quality creative achievement "remains a relatively inexact science" (Feldhusen, 1989, p. 8). Multiple reasons account for the difficulties. For example:

- Part of the difficulty lies in the wide range of areas to be assessed. Outstanding ability comes in a number of different forms and requires a variety of ongoing identification procedures. Yet there exists no single adequate identification procedure or combination of procedures that addresses all important areas and therefore effectively taps a high proportion of students who are gifted.
- All forms of identification systems are less than perfect. The younger the child, the less confidence can be placed in the reliability and validity of the measures. So when the term *gifted* is used to describe young children, it essentially applies to potential rather than accomplishment and is making guesses about the future with limited information (Colangelo and Fleuridas, 1986).
- The selection of students for gifted programs should be a recurring activity, not a one-shot affair. Both IQ and interests can change and specific abilities can emerge. The correlation of the IQ of a child at age six or seven with the same person's IQ at age seventeen is approximately +0.7 (Bloom, 1964).
- In the past, giftedness was viewed as a univariate construct, basically consisting of those traits that were measured by IQ tests. Children with high IQ scores formed the bulk of the population identified as gifted. Today, it is rare that giftedness is identified only through IQ scores.

As mentioned earlier in this chapter, conceptions of giftedness as IQ were established by Lewis Terman, who conducted an important longitudinal study into giftedness. (See the Research Notes for more on the Terman studies.) Terman's work represented the first full-scale longitudinal study of the nature of giftedness; it legitimized the field, and the serious inception of a gifted movement began with Terman. Many of Terman's findings remain remarkably relevant; so far, his study is unsurpassed in the field of giftedness. The one area that has been disputed and altered is Terman's establishment of IQ tests as the sole measure of giftedness. Psychologists are no longer satisfied with intelligence defined simply as what IQ tests measure.

Contemporary researchers are finding evidence of multiple intelligences rather than a single general intelligence. J. P. Guilford (1988) and Howard Gardner (1983) are the modern proponents of the concept of multiple cognitive abilities.

Research Notes

The Terman Studies

Lewis Terman, an American educator and psychologist, expanded the concepts and procedures related to IQ developed by Alfred Binet in France at the beginning of the 20th century. Terman believed the Binet scale assessed a wide range of performance and could be adapted for use with high-functioning children. In 1916, he published the Stanford-Binet Individual Intelligence Test in conjunction with Stanford University.

Terman held that intelligence was manifested essentially in the ability to acquire and manipulate concepts. He defined the gifted as those who scored in the top 1 percent of general intellectual ability as measured by the Stanford-Binet Scale or a comparable instrument (Terman, 1926). Terman carefully distinguished giftedness from talent and creativity. He viewed talent as the potential for unusual achievement, but only when combined with high IQ scores. Creativity, he believed, was a personality factor, and thus differed from both giftedness and talent.

In 1922, armed with the Stanford-Binet tests and a single-measure concept of intelligence, Terman embarked on a massive study of giftedness among California school children. This study, which included 1528 children, "was designed to discover what physical, mental, and personality traits are characteristic of gifted children as a class, and what sort of adult the typical gifted child becomes" (Terman and Oden, 1951, p. 21).

To determine his population, Terman relied on teacher nominations and group intelligence tests. He then identified the gifted children from those scoring at or above 140 points on the Stanford-Binet Individual Intelligence Test.

Although Terman died in 1956, the study continues today. The remaining "Terman kids" are now in their eighties. Longitudinal research found the following:

- Most students in the sample came from a middle or higher socio-economic group, with a low incidence of broken homes.
- Nearly half of the children could read before entering kindergarten.
- One in five children skipped part or all of the first grade.
- On average, the children finished school 14 percent faster than normal students.
- The children averaged 40 percent higher than their agemates on achievement tests.
- They preferred abstract subjects, such as literary

debate and ancient history, and were less interested in such practical concerns as penmanship and manual training.

- They read more and better books, made numerous collections, and had many hobbies.
- When retested as adults, they were found to have retained their intellectual superiority.
- As adults, they were ahead in terms of occupational status, incomes, publications, and patents. They earned more money, had more managerial jobs, and made more literary and scientific contributions than the average adult. When checked in 1959, Terman's group had published over 2000 scientific papers and 33 novels and taken out 230 patents (Sprinthall and Sprinthall, 1990).
- Middle-aged people in Terman's sample maintained their superior physical characteristics. They were far above their agemates in general health, physique, mental health, and emotional adjustment. Fewer than 5 percent of Terman's population were rated as seriously maladjusted, and the incidence of problems such as ill health, psychiatric disturbance, alcoholism, and delinquent behaviour was but a fraction of that normally observed in the general population.
- Although reaching college age just before the Great Depression, when college attendance was not common for women, over 67 percent of the Terman women earned at least a bachelor's degree.
- The female sample contained more childless women than normative samples of similar ages and as a group had relatively higher incomes and levels of employment than women of comparable ages (Holahan, 1991).

Multiple Intelligences

Psychologist J. P. Guilford of the University of Southern California was one of the first to propose a multidimensional theory of intelligence. Guilford's Structure of Intellect analyzes intelligence in terms of its specific skills and divides intellectual performance into three dimensions: operations, contents, and products. Each of these dimensions encompasses several abilities. The first, *operations*, stresses the methods people use to process information. *Contents* has to do with how a learner classifies processed information; *products* refers to the forms and structures that people use to organize information.

Guilford's novel and distinctive approach was widely influential within the psychological field. It prompted researchers to reconsider intelligence as a diverse range of intellectual and creative abilities. Within gifted education, Guilford was the impetus behind creativity research. He inspired interest in the characteristics of creative thought processes, in tests of creativity, and in other psychometric measures based on the 120 factors of the Structure of Intellect. For example, a test called the Structure of Intellect–Learning Abilities (SOI–LA), is classified as an intelligence test. There is also a Gifted Screening Form (GSF), which consists of ten areas that Guilford determined to be most related to the characteristics of individuals who are gifted (Meeker, 1979).

When Howard Gardner (1983) proposed an alternate theory of multiple intelligence, he departed from Guilford's more traditional psychometric approach. In essence, Gardner holds that many forms of thinking are prominent both inside and outside of school. He sees intelligence as involving the use of problem-solving skills that enable people to resolve genuine problems, create effective products, and find or create new problems. Both the problems and the products must be relevant to the particular cultural context (Maker, Neilson, and Rogers, 1994). That is, individuals develop competence in different domains that are independent of each other, and society plays a role in shaping and defining the competencies through its value system.

Gardner originally postulated that the capabilities that people develop fall into seven areas: linguistic, logical–mathematical, spatial, bodily, kinesthetic, musical, and interpersonal–intrapersonal. He recently developed an eighth form called naturalist intelligence.

Most people are not gifted or even highly competent in all areas. However, Gardner holds that children evidence strengths in many domains of development that have not been traditionally identified with intelligence, such as art, music, and movement. In his view, if a child's intellectual profile is identified at an early age, it should be possible to channel specific talents in ways that enhance a child's educational opportunities. Gardner believes that the development of high-level competence requires innate capacity, motivation, and opportunity. Environment, cultural context, and language may also influence all of these important factors (Maker, Neilson, and Rogers, 1994).

Although research on multiple intelligences is in its infancy, Gardner's work, like Guilford's before him, has had an impact on the education of students who are gifted. Today, those involved in the identification and assessment of children who are gifted are strongly persuaded to look not only for children with high IQs but also for those who are gifted in other dimensions as well.

Assessment Measures

Recently, the process of identifying learners with gifts and talents has become more diversified, especially in terms of the instruments used. A sampling of procedures and instruments is shown in the appendix table, Tools for Assessment.

When educators define giftedness in terms of potential, they use identification procedures that emphasize IQ tests and other predictive measures such as academic achievement, creative products, and critical thinking. When giftedness is seen as current achievements, identification procedures stress observations and nominations, performance in academic subjects, performance assessment, or a review of a portfolio.

There is little evidence to indicate that any one identification procedure is better than another. For example, when researchers (Shore and Tsiamis, 1986) compared two groups of children either on the basis of traditional measures of achievement or on that of parent and teacher identification, they found that the groups were not distinguishable and concluded that formal selection by testing was not necessary for a substantial number of students who are gifted.

In any procedure some special populations tend to be overlooked—and then these children pass through school unidentified, their gifts and talents uncultivated. Especially open to non-identification are gifted underachievers; gifted females; atypical children who are gifted, a population that includes children who are disabled and children with learning disabilities; and those who are from minority backgrounds and/or are culturally different from the majority population.

Tests of Mental Ability

IQ tests may be used in identification; they are a legal requirement in some areas. The Stanford-Binet Individual Intelligence Test and the Wechsler Intelligence Scale for Children (WISC-R or WISC-III) are the most commonly used measures.

Often, a shortened measure of an IQ test is highly desirable. There are two types of shortened intelligence tests—those created independently and marketed as short tests and those that exist as short forms of already well established, more involved IQ scales. Mark, Beal, and Dumont (1988) recommend a short form of the WISC-III because an "unusually high performance on a number of subtests would indicate, with a high degree of predictability, that a score well within the gifted range could be expected" (p. 2).

In many ways, individual IQ tests appear to be the best single method for identification of children with superior cognitive abilities. They possess high validity as predictors of success in academic settings and their scores are relatively stable over time. Assuming that motivation remains constant, these tests can reveal not only a child's present abilities, but also those that will develop in the future. IQ tests can also identify those children who are gifted but still underachieving.

Even with these finer points the tests are not a panacea, and a number of problems exist. IQ measures may reflect a racial or a socio-economic bias and reinforce existing inequalities in selection of children for special programs. As well, giftedness seems to be characterized by qualitative differences in thinking and insightfulness, which may not be clearly reflected by performance or intelligence tests (Reis, 1989). The tests may fail to measure some traits, behaviours, and potentials that are significant indicators of giftedness and thereby fail to identify some of our most promising and potentially capable students.

Group Tests

Because giftedness has traditionally been defined on the basis of intelligence, identification procedures have typically involved some measures of intellectual ability. Some schools begin by screening students with standardized group intelligence tests. However, all currently available group intelligence tests have a high prevalence of underidentification and overidentification of exceptional children, particularly with reference to creative divergent thinkers and very young children. It is not unusual for scores on group intelligence tests and individual IQ tests to vary as much as 30 points (Martinson, 1975). In addition, group intelligence tests may identify proficient test takers at the expense of those who may score somewhat lower but who are highly creative and original thinkers (Renzulli, 1979). Group intelligence tests also appear to penalize children from lower socio-economic and minority groups.

Achievement Tests

Achievement tests can be employed systematically to identify children with gifts and talents who are already achieving at a high level academically. These tests have been used very successfully to identify school children who are performing extremely well in specific fields, such as mathematics.

Portfolios

As we explain in Chapter 2, a portfolio is a type of performance test made up of continual collections of a student's work. Portfolios are emerging as a promising measure in the assessment of learners who are gifted.

Observation

Especially for young children, observation is a potent method to identify those who are potentially gifted. A three-year-old may be observed to tackle mathematical problems that are taught in grade three. A four-year-old may be able to read at a high-school level. High verbal ability with early and extensive vocabulary development is a good indicator of IQ. A child may say the first words at seven months; an eighteen-month-old may use language like most children at thirty months; older children ask many questions and have good memories.

Many children with advanced vocabularies have an intense interest in books. They learn to read relatively early and easily and carry out the task fluently. One-half to three-quarters of verbally talented children are reading by the age of five (Piirto, 1994). (Parenthetically, very advanced reading in the early grades does not guarantee that students will still be outstanding years later [Mills and Jackson, 1990].)

dyssynchrony

Parents and teachers should not expect very young children to be gifted in everything. Especially in preschool children who are potentially gifted, we see **dyssynchrony**; that is, uneven development. This applies particularly to motor skills. Some children learn their letters from some combination of teaching by parents, older siblings, and preschool teachers and try to write early. But even if children know the letters, they probably do not possess the fine motor skills to form them well.

Teacher Nomination

Teacher nomination has traditionally been, and remains today, a major method for identifying youngsters who may be gifted, talented, and creative. It is an inexpensive screening method founded on the premise that teachers know their students well enough to spot those with strong abilities. But even as teacher nominations are appreciated for their apparent relevance to children's educational experiences and functioning, they are criticized for their ineffectiveness in accurately identifying children with gifts.

Teacher nominations are suspect because they may result in few correct identifications. Teachers, who are fairly efficient in rating students' academic levels and identifying students requiring special help, are relatively poor in identifying youngsters who may be gifted, talented, and creative (Perks, 1984).

Teacher nomination proves no better than conventional group screening. One early study (Renzulli, 1979) found that teachers were only 50 percent successful when requested to identify those students whom they considered to be gifted and talented. Others (Haywood Gear, 1976; Perks, 1984) discovered effectiveness rates of between 10 and 57 percent, with effectiveness measured as the number of pupils correctly identified as gifted.

Why are teachers, who know their students well, so poor at identification procedures? Teachers may look for the wrong things. Some tend to choose one sex over the other; others tend to choose conformist high achievers and overlook creative or divergent thinkers. Or teachers may not understand giftedness. One study found that 61 percent of public school teachers and 54 percent of private school elementary teachers reported that they had never had any training in teaching students who are gifted (see Reis and Westberg, 1994).

Training programs, questionnaires, and rating scales not only improve accuracy in identification by up to 40 percent but also simultaneously improve attitudes and teaching strategies (Haywood Gear, 1976; Perks, 1984; Reis and Westberg, 1994). Rating scales are particularly helpful in objectifying teacher judgment because they identify children on the basis of clearly defined characteristics such as learning, motivation, creativity, leadership, communication, and the arts.

Parent Nomination

Parent nomination questionnaires are another economical means of identifying children who are gifted and talented. Parents see their children make up games and stories, invent and build things, solve problems, and create all sorts of products. From these observations, parents may identify high performance. One study found that parents' implicit beliefs about their children's ability levels closely related to the children's actual tested IQ. Parents were especially accurate in their assessment of creative thinking, abstract thinking, and memory abilities (Louis and Lewis, 1992). In another survey in the United States of 1039 parents of gifted children, 70 percent of the children were identified accurately by age three. Of all the characteristics that caused parents to suspect giftedness, "early verbal expression" was mentioned most frequently (Gogel, McCumsey, and Hewitt, 1985).

Parent accuracy varies from 11 to 76 percent (Khoury and Appel, 1979), which still tends to be better than teacher nomination. Nonetheless, problems do exist. Parents from lower socio-economic neighbourhoods are more likely to report their child as gifted than parents from higher socio-economic locales, partly because well-educated parents tend to set higher intellectual standards for their children. Other parents may be unaware of their child's outstanding abilities, especially if they have little chance to compare his or her accomplishments with those of other children of a similar age.

Peer Nomination

Peer nominations have been judged very favourably by experts in the field and are growing in popularity as a screening technique for giftedness (Gagné, 1989). Davis and Rimm (1985) wrote that, "peers are extraordinarily good at nominating gifted and talented students" (p. 78), while others (Richert, Alvino, and McDonnell, 1972) have judged peer nominations to be the most adequate technique for screening leaders and creative individuals. Peer nomination may be especially helpful in identifying rural gifted and minority children, as well as those who are disadvantaged or disabled (Banbury and Wellington, 1989).

Self-Nomination

Self-nomination forms have been used with students who have strong artistic, creative, scientific, or other interests and talents. They are especially recommended at the junior and senior high-school levels, where peer pressure may cause youths to mask special talents (Davis and Rimm, 1994).

Measuring Creativity

Children who are gifted, especially academically gifted, may be identified by their high levels of achievement and motivation. Omitted from the equation here is creativity, which is difficult, if not impossible, to measure accurately.

An instrument that yields a single score or index of children's creativity or creative giftedness simply does not exist. This is hardly surprising. First, creativity is so varied and shown in so many ways that it is not reasonable to try to use a standard measure to assess what is in reality such a nonstandard trait. Second, there is still no unifying theory of creativity embraced by all researchers and practitioners, and it seems unlikely that a general theory will ever emerge.

Despite these difficulties, more than sixty instruments for measuring or assessing creativity exist (Treffinger, 1986). Many are based on Guilford's work (refer to Table 8-1).

Leadership

Leadership does not describe inborn characteristics but cumulative capabilities that result from an intermixing of the child's innate abilities and experience. To assess leadership, observation of performance together with some rating checklist is most appropriate.

Visual and Performing Arts

In this field, talent is still most often assessed by expert judges in an audition setting. Experts in the arts are not enthusiastic about the use of tests to determine artistic ability and prefer exhibitions, performances, auditions, and interviews. Nevertheless, a range of measures are available to assess potential and aptitude, especially in the areas of music and visual art (Khatena, 1982).

Problems in Identification

As we pointed out at the beginning of this section, identification problems abound in the field of gifted education. Not only are there questions about how and what to identify, but also certain groups tend to be overlooked. Because of this, one of the major initiatives in current gifted education is attempts to locate and nurture hidden talent (Gallagher, 2000).

Gifted Underachievers

To some people, the phrase *gifted underachiever* is an oxymoron. Yet we cannot contradict the body of research data that shows that many children with gifts and talents do not develop to their full potential. Intellectually gifted students especially, in contrast to those gifted in athletics, arts, or leadership, may be at risk for learning difficulties in school (Whitmore, 1988).

Academic underachievers are those about whom we can make a reasonable prediction of academic potential that is not fulfilled. These are children who are gifted on IQ tests but whose academic achievement is grade level or less (Yewchuk, 1984). Such performance does not necessarily equate with failure or underproduction; children may indeed work at an average level but not at one commensurate with their ability. Others, of course, do not attain even average levels.

A complex of factors contributes to the high proportion of underachievers among the population of persons who are gifted. These include:

- Impossible expectations. Pervasive misunderstandings of the nature of giftedness may result in inappropriate expectations and consequent adult responses that place students at risk (Whitmore, 1988). For example, when parents and teachers believe that learning and school achievement are easy for all students who are gifted, they tend to demand more effort and tolerate little error or imperfection. Or, when adults believe that such children are so much more mature than their peers developmentally, they tend to expect more mature behaviour than is reasonable and forget the childishness that is necessarily present in all children.

- Conflict between giftedness and creativity and the typically rigid classroom. Children who are gifted are turned off by conformity to precise directions, excessive repetition, memorization and drill, uniformity of assignments, and the lack of opportunity to pursue interests and work independently. In a classroom that requires a high degree of conformity and achievement on schedule with a restricted and often dull curriculum, these children may feel stifled and frustrated. They can't or don't conform to classroom mores, feel that there is nothing to learn that is interesting and challenging, and gradually sink into underachievement.
- Learning not to learn. In the early years, a child may need to make little, if any, effort to make good grades. Consequently, when academic demands become greater, the student does not know how to apply effort. Such children may then lack confidence, have poor study habits, and do inconsistent work.
- Social and emotional factors. Some students may underachieve because it is socially safe. If they feel that peer relationships are jeopardized by expectations of superior performance, they may not want to be singled out as different. Other students may have unfavourable self-concepts that distort their perceptions of the world and undermine their motivation and goal orientation. One father described his underachieving son as "an emperor and a Renaissance man at age four, dethroned by age six, and a behaviour problem and underachiever thereafter" (in Rimm and Lowe, 1988, p. 358).

Females Who Are Gifted

Both in school and in the working world, more males than females are considered gifted and talented. By an overwhelming margin, men achieve high status and recognition more frequently than do women of the same age. There is no conclusive evidence that this disparity is the result of biological differences; rather, available research points far more clearly to social and cultural expectations as an explanation for the disproportionate number of males recognized as gifted. Society encourages narrow role definitions and behaviour options for women and broader ones for men. It is considered neither proper nor advantageous for girls to be too superior. Girls who insist on their giftedness are encouraged to become musicians or artists, rather than physicists or engineers.

Females have not been encouraged to enter academic disciplines and careers historically dominated by males. Certainly, more women are entering such non-traditional professions as chemistry, engineering, dentistry, and physics, but the numbers are still small.

Elementary school gifted and talented programs identify girls in equal or greater numbers than boys. However, by tenth grade, girls begin to drop out of these programs at a greater rate than boys. Boys are more likely to take math and science gifted programs, whereas girls populate gifted programs that focus on language arts (Sadker, 1999). Talented girls are then less likely than talented boys to pursue a career in the sciences.

Why do women tend not to pursue math to the same extent as mathematically gifted

Gifted females should be encouraged to participate in traditionally male-dominated activities.

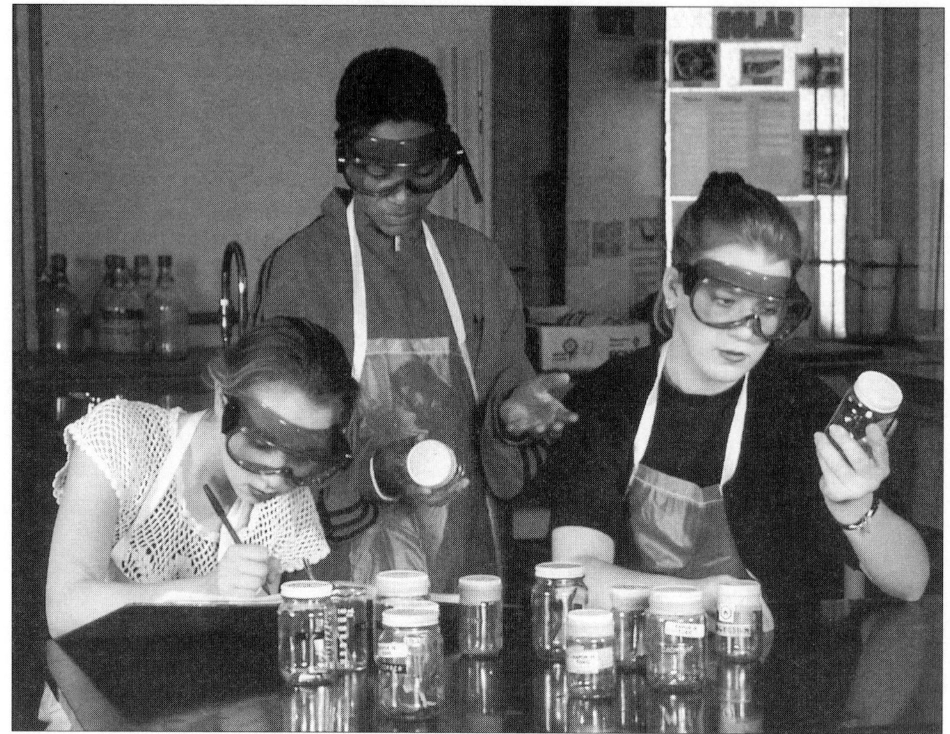

males? Kerr (1988) argues that girls who are gifted are rewarded for intellectual achievement at early ages but by adolescence they are rewarded for social conformity, which may include seeing math as masculine. Others contend that girls who are gifted find it difficult to reconcile their academic interests with the areas of excellence traditionally seen by society as sex-role-appropriate for women (Schwartz, 1980). As high achievers, girls who are gifted are expected to be active, assertive, and exploratory; as females, they are encouraged to be nurturing, passive, and dependent (Handel, 1983).

It is during early adolescence, the age when sex roles are heavily reinforced by parents and peers, that girls generally begin to encounter problems that obscure their giftedness. Often, parents of girls who are gifted are more concerned about their daughters' social adjustment than their academic boredom. Teachers tend to reinforce quiet, non-aggressive, and noncompetitive behaviour among girls.

Perfectionism is common among gifted students, and girls may fear failure. Perceived academic competence is an important factor in global self-worth of children, especially girls, who are gifted from grade four to grade eight (Hoge and McSheffrey, 1991). By the age of thirteen or fourteen, some of these youngsters have a motivation to avoid failure at any cost rather than a motivation to succeed.

Gifted Students Who Are Disabled

A child who is both gifted and disabled may be described as one who demonstrates at least one attribute of educational, emotional, or physical/sensory impairment. The spread of intelligence in the population of persons with disabilities matches that of the general population, so the prevalence of giftedness is about the same. It is estimated that 2 percent of all children with disabilities are gifted (Whitmore and Maker, 1985), although some authorities argue that a 5-percent cut-off is probably more realistic (Davis and Rimm, 1994).

Why, then, are so many children with disabilities overlooked in identification procedures? The answer is entwined with common perceptions, the traits of disability, and the identification procedures themselves.

A gifted child who is also disabled fails to meet stereotyped expectations of giftedness. Many teachers, administrators, students, and parents have trouble accepting that a child with a disability may also have outstanding abilities: they focus entirely on the child's disability to the exclusion of his or her individual potential and capabilities.

Individual students probably exhibit many contradictions by deviating substantially both above and below the norm, showing both strengths and weaknesses that are very pronounced. This means that a major portion of their classroom time is spent in remediation of learning to circumvent the effects of the disability, which in turn may preclude the recognition and development of cognitive abilities (Willard-Holt, 1998).

Not only may gifted children who also have disabilities lack the opportunity to reveal superior mental or creative ability, but also no one instrument or checklist is capable of identifying the range of characteristics and conditions that may be present in a gifted child with a disability. Teacher observations of a child's behaviour are critical in identifying those who are both gifted and disabled. Observations must be made over time rather than in isolation.

Gifted Students Who Have Learning Disabilities

Empirical research on gifted students with learning disabilities is limited. Some aspects are quite clear, however. In general, there are three groups: mild under-achievers; severe learning disabled with no giftedness recognized; and the largest group—learning disabilities that mask giftedness (Brody and Mills, 1997).

All of these students have talents and strengths in some areas and disabling weaknesses in others. They have unique characteristics related to persistence and individual interests but possess lower academic and self-efficacy than their peers who are not gifted and also learning disabled (Baum, 1995; Baum and Owen, 1988).

In children who are both gifted and learning disabled, the giftedness is often not identified. The reasons parallel those we mentioned for children with disabilities, with an added glitch. Sometimes, when giftedness and learning disabilities co-exist, they tend to mask one another so that neither the giftedness nor the disability is immediately evident. The disability may depress the IQ and achievement scores so that these students are not eligible for gifted programs, yet their giftedness allows them to compensate well enough for their weaknesses to maintain grade-level expectations, which prevents detection of their learning difficulty (Silverman, 1989). The result is that they frequently do not qualify for special education services. At other times, a child may be receiving special education services, and the giftedness is completely overlooked.

Gifted Children Who Are Culturally Different

Standardized tests are inappropriate in the identification of most culturally diverse students, including those with giftedness. Instead, teachers should use a collection of instruments and procedures that include observations, nomination forms, dynamic assessment, and rating scales. Assessment and identification procedures should measure how a child meaningfully manipulates a symbol system held valuable in the culture; thinks logically when given appropriate data; uses stored knowledge to solve problems; reasons by analogy; and extends or extrapolates knowledge to new situations or unique applications (Clark, 1988).

INTERVENTION WITH STUDENTS WHO ARE GIFTED, CREATIVE, AND TALENTED

The basic educational goals for children with gifts and talents are the same as for all other students: to develop their abilities in ways that are consistent with their personal needs and the best interests of society. At the same time, schools must develop mechanisms to identify children who are gifted and provide them with appropriate educational programs.

Technical Aids

For most children who are gifted, technical aids, in the sense of hearing aids and wheelchairs, are not relevant. Children who are gifted should, however, be able to take advantage of the new advances in information and communication technology. For students who are gifted, computers and the Internet can become idea engines, their tool to discovery, exploration, and collaboration. They can do research, apply thinking skills by working with real problems and computer simulations, and master languages such as Logo.

Educational Intervention

Inevitably, educational models and approaches are a function of definition, be they implicit or explicit. Reflecting the difficulties in pinpointing the most effective definition of giftedness and gifted individuals is the wide variety of practices and programs that have been devised over the years to cater to these students.

Nobody is sure of the best way to educate students with gifts, and it is true to say that there is a lack of systematically developed models and systematic experimental evaluation of programs and program models with explicit goals, objectives, and specified outcomes. Numerous models and programs have been attempted, all intended to come to grips with three major problems: the balance between the quest for excellence and a zeal for equality; the wide range of abilities among the gifted population; and teachers' lack of special instructional methods. The four most common types of educational provisions used in Canada are *acceleration, ability grouping, mentoring programs,* and *enrichment.*

Service Delivery Models

As in every area of contemporary special education, debates about placement rage in the field of giftedness. Many educators promote general class placements with additional accommodations. They argue that special programs for the gifted run counter to the spirit of the inclusive classroom. Others stress separate placements at least part of the time. They detail the countervailing forces that grew in strength in the late 1980s and 1990s and that may prove disadvantageous for students with gifts and talents. These are the inclusion movement, the promotion of detracking, heterogeneous groupings by age and grade level, and the serving of precocious youngsters in regular classrooms. This means, detractors argue, that many precocious and highly talented young people get no specialized instruction whatsoever even though the goals and practices of existing programs are often ineffectual for them.

While many current educators disagree with competition in the classroom and have moved toward a greater emphasis on co-operative learning strategies, promoters of special placements contend that "gifted education and gifted students are in deep trouble without grouping practices" (Davis and Rimm, 1994, p. 10). The value of co-operative learning is questionable when heterogeneous groups are used for highly able students (see Feldhusen and Moon, 1992). A study of the preferred learning styles of 169 gifted high school students showed that both males and females preferred individualistic learning styles over co-operative learning for all subjects (Li and Adamson, 1992).

Teachers' voices are important in this debate, as are their attitudes about and perceptions of students who are gifted. In fact, so critical are teachers' attitudes that some researchers argue that children who are gifted should be placed in regular classrooms only if the teacher is prepared to assist them (see McCarthy, 1994).

A review of the literature (Cramond and Martin, 1987) found that teachers hold conflicting attitudes toward students with gifts. Some studies saw teachers viewing students with gifts positively and giving them preferential treatment; others found teacher discomfort and resentment that could lead to apathy toward gifted education. Other research has found "disturbing evidence of neglect" in regular classrooms (Culross, 1997, p. 24). Finally, in a sample of ninety-eight parents of gifted children, Kaufman and Sexton (1983) found that 45 percent had encountered a teacher who they felt was unsympathetic to the special needs of the child who was gifted.

Some teachers disagree with special programming on both philosophical and pragmatic grounds. Bransky (1987) found negative attitudes among classroom teachers, which she attributed to a poor foundation of knowledge about the pull-out programs for students who are gifted. Some teachers argue that the classroom that loses children who are gifted is robbed of leadership. Others express concern about the fragmentation of their programs or the need to reschedule lessons (Meyers, 1984). Occasionally, teachers are averse to designing programs for learners who are gifted. Others realize that teachers of students who are gifted need special traits, but are unaware of the traits or have little confidence in their ability to develop them (see the accompanying Research Notes on teachers). Archambault and Hallmark (1992) found that 42 to 62 percent of the 7000 teachers in their studies had absolutely no exposure to methods for teaching the gifted.

Educational Approaches

The education of students who are gifted is replete with different models offered in varied settings. Typically, more program options are available in urban and suburban areas and in the elementary schools. Of the models below, only enrichment is always offered in the general classroom. Mentoring and ability grouping have traditionally been mainly pull-out models, and settings for acceleration vary.

The research literature is quite unhelpful about the best approach. For example, it does not provide clear evidence for or against ability grouping in terms of academic achievement. When Goldring (1990) analyzed twenty-three studies on delivery methods, he found that students who were gifted in special classes achieved more than students of high ability in regular classrooms, but the benefits of the special classes depended on the subject. The largest effects were in science and social studies, with smaller effects in math, reading, and writing.

Research Notes

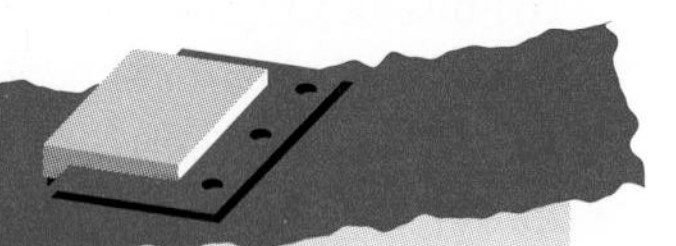

Teachers of Students Who Are Gifted, Creative, and Talented

Should gifted children be taught by gifted teachers? This is one of the controversial questions that exist in the field of education of gifted students. If it is decided that gifted children should be taught by gifted teachers, then what exactly is a gifted teacher? Is it the teacher who possesses gifted traits? Or is it the teacher who is gifted at the profession of teaching?

Research on gifted teachers has generally looked at three areas: the personal characteristics of outstanding teachers of the gifted; their competencies; and those behaviours that set outstanding teachers apart (Whitlock and Du Cette, 1989).

An early study (Bishop, 1968) found that gifted students opt for teachers who are older and experienced and well above average in intellectual pursuits, who enjoy their profession, and who are respectful to students and other teachers. Later research bolstered these findings, showing that gifted students preferred teachers with creative and positive personalities and high intelligence (e.g., Webb, Meckstroth, and Tolan, 1982).

The characteristic most often described as desirable is that of being a facilitator of learning. Additionally, traits such as flexibility, creativity, good self-concept, depth and breadth of knowledge, sense of humour, counselling ability, maturity, teaching experience, and resourcefulness are deemed important (Story, 1985). These characteristics, of course, are the mark of any good teacher.

Certainly, teachers of gifted children should possess all the traits common to good teachers. But they should also possess knowledge, understanding, and empathy for the gifted population. These teachers should have a high level of creativity and energy to meet the special demands of gifted children. As well, teachers of gifted students need to be lifelong learners; to possess superior mental abilities; to be divergent thinkers; to be well educated in the liberal arts; to demonstrate competence in effectively individualizing instruction; to demonstrate skills in teaching science and arts; to have excellent skills in communication; and to have a healthy self-concept (Bell, 1986; Whitmore, 1985). Teachers also need a broad knowledge of subject areas, an eagerness to be with bright children, and dedication to students, and they must believe in the importance of enhancing pupils' self-image and maturity (Whitlock and Du Cette, 1989).

The higher the grade level, the stronger the advantage of special classes. Similarly, Vaughn and colleagues (1991) analyzed the research and found small to medium positive effects on academic achievement and critical and creative thinking.

Whether grouping and special programs affect children's self-esteem is unknown. Grouping, once popular, was criticized in the 1970s and '80s on the grounds that ability grouping lowers self-esteem and motivation, restricts friendship choices, and often widens the gap between high and low achievers (see Elbaum, Vaughn, Hughes, and Moody, 1999). However, it has been shown that children of medium and low ability are either not affected or are negatively affected by ability grouping, but that the achievement of high-ability students is positively affected by ability grouping that includes curriculum modifications directed to their learning characteristics (Kulik, 1992; Kulik and Kulik, 1991, 1992). On this theme, it may be that gifted programs are most justifiable when the content of the special program is truly an accelerated curriculum, not just add-ons. The most popular subject for acceleration is math. (Language arts or social studies are usually the focus of enrichment programs.)

Further on self-esteem is a Calgary study (Bourque and Li, 1987) in which the investigators assessed sixty students with gifts between the ages of nine and eleven who were placed in regular and segregated settings to see if they differed in perceived competence, social adjustment, and peer relations. As rated by teachers, educational setting did not appear to have any differential impact on social adjustment, on peer relations, or on socio-metric nominations, and was not an important factor for self-esteem, social adjustment, or peer relations. Note that what students liked most about being in a special program was freedom of choice and self-directedness.

Finally, research on the enrichment programs we discuss below does not yield clear evidence that they adequately stimulate children who are gifted. It generally does not find achievement benefits. Inclusive schooling is likely to accommodate the needs of only the mildly gifted students who are talented in specific domains (see McFadden and Ellis, 2000).

Advocates of enrichment maintain that the programs allow a child to remain in the regular classroom with age-level peers. Detractors point out the difficulty of meeting individual needs with a few extra activities in a generally inadequate learning environment. They contend that enrichment often promotes the false impression that something substantial is being done for the gifted. In fact, enrichment has been referred to as "busywork and irrelevant" (Stanley and Benbow, 1986).

Acceleration

Acceleration means moving faster through academic content. Students speed up their progress through the existing curriculum to complete a prescribed program in a shorter time period. Included within acceleration models are early school beginning, grade skipping, ungraded classes, continuous progress, self-paced instruction, telescoping the curriculum, mentorships, extracurricular programs, concurrent or dual enrolment, credit by examination, correspondence courses, high-school courses for credit, extra load, seminars for college credit, early admittance to post-secondary programs, and honours programs.

Two general characteristics define acceleration models. First, acceleration is one of the most time-honoured options in gifted education and has been practised throughout the history of providing educational provisions for this population. Second, there is probably no other area in the education of students who are gifted that is more controversial.

Supporting acceleration practices is a body of data that "are unanimous in their support of the benefit of accelerative alternatives, both academically and socio-emotionally" (Keating, 1980, p. 56). From the point of view of its proponents, even the word *acceleration* is a misnomer; the process is really one of bringing youth who are gifted and talented up to a suitable level of instruction commensurate with their achievement levels and readiness so that they are properly challenged to learn new material (Feldhusen, 1989).

Opponents of acceleration marshal an impressive array of arguments that focus on psychosocial rather than academic reasons. They view the practice of allowing students who are gifted to progress through the educational system at their own rate as potentially hazardous to social and emotional adjustment.

Hence, we have a situation where the literature on the academic acceleration of students who are gifted consistently demonstrates a lack of harmful effects, but many educators and administrators resist the implementation of the model in their schools (Feldhusen, 1989; Southern, Jones, and Fiscus, 1989). The major arguments from both sides of the debate are presented in the Debate feature.

A Matter of Debate

Acceleration for Students Who Are Gifted

There is no argument more contentious in gifted education than that revolving around acceleration. Opponents of acceleration have marshalled an impressive array of arguments. On the other hand, advocates cite eighty years of positive research findings.

The psychosocial reasons for hesitation in implementing acceleration programs are more numerous than the academic reasons (Swiatek and Benbow, 1991). However, a body of literature spanning five decades has consistently associated the acceleration of precocious children with positive change in their academic achievement and a lack of negative effects on social and emotional growth. Studies do not indicate that acceleration is harmful, and many indicate that it is beneficial (Southern, Jones, and Fiscus, 1989).

Arguments in favour of acceleration	Cautions about acceleration
Accelerated students perform as well as older students with whom they are placed and exceed the achievement of non-accelerated students of the same age and ability by almost a year (Kulik and Kulik, 1984).	Children cannot escape the physical and emotional limits imposed by chronology.
Not one study exists showing that acceleration is harmful to social or emotional development (Benbow, 1991).	Acceleration programs emphasize the differences between gifted and average students, thereby jeopardizing the social acceptance of gifted students.
Highly talented young people suffer boredom and negative peer pressure in heterogeneous classrooms.	Those enrolled in special classes will lose the ability to function in the larger world of average people (Swiatek and Benbow, 1991).
Students are entitled to challenging and appropriate instruction. The one size fits all mentality that is an outgrowth of the inclusion movement reflects a mistaken view of human development.	Acceleration violates the concepts and principles of the inclusionary movement.
With acceleration, boredom, restlessness, frustration, underachievement, and disruptiveness can be replaced by enhanced motivation, improved self-concepts, and improved study habits and productivity (Davis and Rimm, 1994).	Acceleration conflicts with the school's perceived role to socialize students and make them good workers.
Gifted youth may have self-concepts that clearly relate to and recognize giftedness, and their self-concepts may be influenced positively by partici-	Special opportunities lead gifted students to become conceited and self-centred; children will become contemptuous of their age peers and

Arguments in favour of acceleration	Cautions about acceleration
pation in a gifted program (Feldhusen and Hoover, 1986).	may suffer negative emotional and social consequences (Southern, Jones, and Fiscus, 1989).
Empirical research indicates that acceleration provides academic settings that are well suited to the needs of high-ability students (Benbow, 1991).	Children will not fit in with more mature classmates.
Most gifted children are psychosocially mature. Evidence does not link forms of acceleration to socio-emotional adjustment problems (Cornell, Callahan, and Loyd, 1991).	Gifted children may show deficient or retarded psychosocial development.
Literature reviews (Swiatek and Benbow, 1991) show that no studies yield evidence that accelerated students exhibit deficits in knowledge or achievement.	Acceleration may lead to gaps in knowledge of the participants or poor retention of material learned at an accelerated pace (Van Tassel Baska, 1989).
A meta-analysis of the results of 314 studies of the academic, social, and psychological effects of acceleration at the elementary and secondary levels (Rogers, 1990, cited in Davis and Rimm, 1994) found that no form of acceleration led to a decrease in any area of performance academic, social, or emotional, and that there appear to be generally positive effects from most forms of acceleration.	The self-concepts of gifted students will suffer if they are set apart from their average counterparts. Accelerated pupils will not socialize with older children, will have fewer friends, will not be happy, and will miss important social interactions (Southern, Jones, and Fiscus, 1989).
Acceleration programs reduce the time that students need to complete the curriculum. Students can maximize their intellectual potential, maintain their interest and motivation, enter high school, post-secondary, and graduate studies earlier, and get a faster start on their careers.	Students may burn out if they are placed in classes that are advanced for their chronological ages.

Ability Grouping

Students who are gifted need interaction with peers who share their interests and concerns. The general tenor of research indicates that they require social and emotional support from a group of true peers—simultaneously a student's intellectual and chronological equals—to maintain a positive self-concept and intellectual interaction and to transform abilities into productive reality.

As the name suggests, ability groupings (pull-out programs) refer to changing the environment to bring students who are gifted into contact with each other. Students are removed from heterogeneous settings and placed in special groups; in some cases, they go to special classrooms. In others, independent groups of students progress at different rates within the same classroom. Special groups may meet full-time or only part-time. They may be made up of students from a single school or from several schools within a district. Groups may meet during regular school hours or on an extra-curricular basis.

Certain criteria ensure the success of pull-out programs. These include integration with the regular curriculum; daily program experience; placement with intellectual peers; pace of program matched with the student's learning rate; a complex and higher level curriculum; and excellent teachers (Belcostas, 1987).

As with acceleration, pull-out programs are far from universally accepted. Opponents claim that the practice is undemocratic because it fosters intellectual elitism and limits contacts between gifted and normal children. Pragmatically, they contend that pull-out programs are often frivolous. Programs often diverge from the regular school curriculum, do not give grades, do not have instruction in traditional subject matter, focus on the affective rather than the academic, and do not have written curricula (Van Tassel Baska, 1987).

In contrast, advocates argue that only when children who are gifted are grouped together can they be provided with truly effective instruction. As far as curriculum is concerned, they believe that since separate gifted programs provide for students who differ from the norm, the programs also should differ in their adherence to the conventional structures associated with education.

Mentor Programs

Mentorships have been recognized as one of the most effective organizational configurations to help students who are gifted to realize their potential. Three common but interrelated types of mentorship programs include career exploration, guidance, and development; content-based programs that focus on enrichment in an area of interest to a student; and personal growth programs that stress self awareness leading to higher aspirations (McFadden and Ellis, 2000).

Mentor programs are cost-effective and serve as a liaison between the school and the community. Students work, at a specified time, with adults in the community with whom they share a special interest. Usually the teacher, the mentor, and the student set up a project with the final results to be presented to the class in some form.

Mentoring can play a catalytic role in helping students negotiate the major transitions of academic life. Benefits include career and interest advancement; an increase in knowledge and skills; the development of talent; enhancement of self-esteem and self-confidence; development of a personal ethic or set of standards; establishment of long-term friendships; and enhancement of creativity (Edlind and Heansly, 1985).

Enrichment

In many situations it is impossible and perhaps unnecessary to take children who are gifted from their assigned classrooms. Enrichment programs provided by regular classroom teachers are the solution.

enrichment

Enrichment involves providing special activities in the regular classroom setting. Rather than increasing the pace of progression through the regular education curriculum, enriched experiences focus on adjusting the breadth and depth of the curriculum, the tempo and pace at which the curriculum is introduced, and the kind and content of material that is presented.

Activities involve a broader range of skills and deeper understanding than the regular curriculum, and are designed to challenge and interest children while focusing on their

Case Study

William, Troy, and Richard (continued)

In the education of students who are gifted, a deeper examination of the regular curriculum cannot be achieved by adding a few tasks. Rather, it needs a consistent and structured curriculum expansion founded on broad goals directed at their specific needs. Curricula should be designed to allow children of high ability such as Troy, William, and Richard to master important conceptual systems that are at the level of their abilities in various content fields.

After the reassessment of Troy, the psychologist recommended that enrichment activities be available for him in the regular classroom and that he spend some time with the resource room teacher, who would put a special program in place for him. An extract from Troy's IEP is found below.

EXTRACT FROM TROY'S IEP

Name Troy
Teacher Mr. Jane
Date November 12, 1999
Grade 5
School Jones

Results from Formal Assessment Administered 21 October, 1999

Test

WISC-III: Full Scale 93rd percentile, Performance 91st percentile, Verbal 95th percentile
Key Math Diagnostic Arithmetic Test: 91st percentile
Test of Adolescent Language Development: 98th percentile

Strengths

Works well alone
High achiever
Strong oral language
Is popular
Is inquisitive
Searches for significance
Seeks to organize
Enjoys problem solving
Exhibits intense concentration
Has high energy, alertness, eagerness
Diverse interests and abilities
Independent

Weaknesses

Perfectionist
Bored with classroom work
Constantly argues with teacher on things and people
Won't conform to school rules

Major Needs

- Opportunities to make use of high level thinking skills
- Activities that build on logical and thinking skills
- Research skills
- Self-selected projects

Setting

- Regular classroom/resource room

Long-Range Goals in Pull-Out Program

- Learn basic research skills
- Explore a topic of own choosing in depth
- Communicate findings to grade seven class

In-Class Goals

- Complete general classroom work before moving to own projects
- Adhere to a contract for an independent project prepared with the teacher

Special Program

- Take part in debating club

unique patterns of strengths and weaknesses. Of course, enrichment activities are good for all students, but it must be kept in mind that for students who are gifted there must be higher-order objectives outlined within enrichment.

We can see this in the sample enrichment unit presented here. This example examines seeds and plants and is loosely based on Benjamin Bloom's taxonomy of educational objectives (1956). This type of unit can be used effectively with students who are gifted as a group assignment or as independent study.

Sample Enrichment Unit

Plants and Seeds

Knowledge

- List all the parts of a seed plant you can find.
- Define the following terms (related to seed plants): bulb germination, dormancy, dicotyledon, dissemule, root hair.
- List the many methods of seed dispersal.
- Name the conditions necessary for germination and development in a plant.
- List the enemies of plants (as many as you can find).
- Look at several beauty magazines to see how plants are used in make-up and other beauty aids.

Comprehension

- Why do leaves change colour in the fall?
- Explain how a plant takes water from the earth and uses it in its living processes.
- Explain the difference between coniferous and deciduous.
- Describe how a plant grows, from fertilization through to maturity. If you like, you can use an example to help you.
- Describe the role of chlorophyll in photosynthesis, explaining why green plants turn yellow and die if they do not get enough sunlight.
- Describe the role of a seed plant in the ability for life to exist on earth.

Application

- Using a microscope, diagram the cell structure of a leaf.
- Diagram the different parts of a seed plant.
- Show how you can tell how old, and how tall, a tree is.
- Make your own perfume, using the leaves of flowers.
- Show how a seed plant takes root and begins to grow.

Analysis

- Conduct an experiment to see how far seeds can travel.
- Compare and contrast coniferous and deciduous trees, and the way they grow.
- Conduct an experiment to see what happens when seeds are crowded too close together.
- Compare past and present uses of plants in the field of medicine. Are there any similarities?
- Conduct an experiment to see what will happen to a leaf when it is coated with Vaseline. Why does this happen?

- Conduct an experiment to determine the lengths to which plants will go so that they can get sunlight?

Synthesis

- Design an environment possessing ideal conditions for the growth of seed plants.
- Choose two plants and, using your knowledge about genetics and plant breeding, predict the outcome of a cross between them. Describe the new creation. What are its strength and weaknesses, if any?
- Grow several bean seeds, controlling different environmental conditions in each instance. Predict the outcome in each case, and compare it with the actual results.

Evaluation

- Decide whether or not the commercial use of greenhouses can be beneficial to people in the long run.
- Acid rain has a great effect on plants. What exactly is that effect, and what can we do about it? Are we doing all we can right now?
- Assess the value of gardens in space. Are they worth the trouble?

Source: Hicks, 1987

Curriculum

The difference between the regular program and the program for students who are gifted is one of degree. Some classroom practices currently being studied include independent projects, creative writing on self-selected topics, teaching thinking skills, encouraging discovery, and using classroom questioning that encourages reasoning and logical thinking (Gubbins, 1991).

There are quite a number of recognized and validated instructional models and enrichment activities that apply to the whole class, groups, or individuals. For example, the Revolving Door model (Renzulli and Smith, 1984) is essentially a resource room adjunct program. It is designed to identify giftedness, to provide enrichment activities, and to overcome many of the problems related to student selection, motivation, and interests. Tannenbaum's (1986) Enrichment Matrix Model includes techniques for differentiating the curriculum, supplementary content areas (anthropology, leadership, psychology), and interdisciplinary content areas (aesthetics, humanities). The Integrated Curriculum Model (Van Tassel Baska, 1994, 1995) incorporates interdisciplinary themes in advanced content areas as well as higher-order thinking and processing skills.

The Enrichment Triad approach delineates three types of enrichment activities for students. Type I, General Exploratory Activities, is appropriate for all students. Type I activities expose pupils to exciting topics, ideas, and fields of knowledge not ordinarily covered by the regular curriculum, and include visiting speakers, field trips, demonstrations, interest development centres, and the use of many different kinds of audio-visual materials. Type II, Group Training Activities, is also appropriate for all children. It consists of methods, materials, and instructional techniques designed to develop thinking processes, research and reference skills, and personal and social skills. Type III activities, Small Group Investigations, are very rigorous and challenging. Students self-select areas of study and take responsibility for initiating, conceptualizing, and planning the activity or project. They investigate real problems and topics using appropriate methods of enquiry (Reis and O'Shea, 1984).

The Autonomous Learner Model (ALM) (Betts, 1985) is designed for secondary-level special classrooms but can also be used at elementary levels. It is usually presented during one period at specified times throughout the week. While not a total program, ALM meets the socio-emotional needs of learners who are gifted and encourages independence in the learning setting. In a three-year sequence, students move through five major dimensions:

- *Orientation:* understanding giftedness and group building activities;
- *Individual development:* learning skills and career involvement;
- *Enrichment activities:* exploration and investigation;
- *Seminars:* general interest and advanced knowledge;
- *In-depth study:* independent projects and mentorships.

independent studies

For individual students, teachers can use **independent studies**, individualized learning experiences that allow students to select a topic, define problems or questions, gather and analyze information, apply skills, and create a product to show what has been learned.

Individual studies individualize and extend classroom learning experiences in ways that incorporate interdisciplinary skills and higher-level thinking skills. Students can go beyond the confines of the classroom, pursue personal interests, develop self-directness, explore the world of work, and develop research and other skills.

Students do not necessarily work alone. Committee studies allow collaboration based on shared interests and abilities. Whether by committee or truly independent, the steps are:

- Select and delimit a subject or topic;
- Formulate key questions to pursue and answer;
- Develop a plan and time sequence;
- Locate and use multiple resources;
- Create a product;
- Share the findings of the study.

Historical Notes

Cultural values have always determined the attitudes of society towards its outstanding members. Different eras have valued achievement in different fields of endeavour. Ancient Greece admired the philosopher, Rome the soldier and orator, and Renaissance Italy the artist. In the modern age, remarkable early development, or precocity, was seen in many major historical figures. Beethoven performed in public at age seven, Thomas Jefferson began serious study at five, and Pablo Picasso drew before he could walk. Others who contributed significantly to our cultures bloomed later and only after surviving hardships or overcoming disabilities. Winston Churchill was a sickly child with a speech impediment; Edison's teachers described him as "addled"; and Auguste Rodin had a learning disability. Vincent van Gogh suffered crippling bouts of depression that eventually led to his suicide.

Before the mid-19th century, giftedness was a visible, yet poorly defined and understood, phenomenon. Even as much honour was paid to individuals who made significant contributions to their own or succeeding cultures, genius was often misunderstood and popularly viewed as directly related to insanity.

Francis Galton, an English scientist and eugenics advocate, was one of the first to research and write about giftedness. Galton proposed that motivation to achieve was innate and inborn and claimed that genius would actualize itself despite external circumstances (Galton, 1869), a position that led to the enduring and dangerous myth that "the cream will rise to the top" regardless of difficulties or lack of environmental support.

As a descriptive term for a specific group of individuals who are highly intelligent and strong academic achievers, *gifted* was first used in the literature by Guy M. Henry in 1920. In the following years, behavioural scientists used *gifted* as the sole designation to describe people with high intelligence. As a wider conception of the array of human potential developed, the constructs *talented* and *creative* came into use in the 1960s.

Special day classes for gifted pupils emerged in the United States during the 1890s, but the movement was small and the classes scattered. By the mid-1930s, there were still only seventy-five such classrooms in the country. Canada also established classes, but again the movement, compared to that for children with disabilities, was small. Community-based gifted education was founded in London, Ontario, in the late 1920s, when concerned teachers and parents worked together to design an enrichment program for the elementary grades (Bain, 1980). On the Prairies, the Enterprise Method developed and trained students in learning and community-oriented group activities. The Major Work Program, first adopted in Alberta, flourished briefly across the country. It offered selected children greater intellectual stimulation, along with training in advanced creativity and problem solving (Bain, 1980). Other programs have developed in Canada, many of them based on the philosophy of Samuel Laycock of Saskatchewan. From the 1930s to the late 1960s, Laycock championed the cause of those exceptional children who were capable of creativity and leadership but were too often ignored by society. Saskatchewan, in fact, has had a continuous program since the 1930s for very gifted learners (Lipp, 1988).

In the 1970s, concern for the special needs of children who were gifted was reawakened, in large measure by the evidence that many of these youngsters were bored with the lockstep of mass education and were turning into chronic underachievers and dropouts. Another major spur was the mounting pessimism of North American educators as they saw their educational standards drop far below those of the Japanese and the Europeans. Another was an offshoot of the women's movement that began to open avenues for females to enter less traditional roles.

But even today, attempts to provide appropriate programs are undermined by popularly held stereotypes and myths. Galton's myth that "the cream will rise to the top" has been perpetuated as educators have persistently argued about whether special programming for individuals already well endowed violates the ethics of a democratic school system. Funding, willingly ceded to children functioning below the norm, has been only grudgingly allowed to those with superior abilities. Compared to that for children who are disabled, education provided for those who are gifted and talented has been a very small-scale enterprise.

SUMMARY

1. Giftedness is considered as a component of special education because students who are gifted require appropriate educational opportunities and challenges if they are to develop to their full potential. However, there is not another category in special education as fraught with political, emotional, and educational issues as that of giftedness. Difficulties revolve around just who is gifted, how to identify gifts and talents, how to offer

special programming, and how to balance the needs of students who are gifted within the parameters of an egalitarian school system.

2. Not the least of the problems that plague the field of gifted education is the lack of a universally accepted definition. It is very difficult to find a definition that encompasses all children and youth who are gifted, talented, and creative because these students demonstrate such a broad array of characteristics and behaviours. As well, a consensus has not been reached on whether to define giftedness as performance or potential.
3. *Giftedness* may be defined as a combination of above-average general ability, a high level of creativity, and a high level of task commitment. Essentially, *creativity* is a capacity to restructure the world in unusual or useful conceptual terms by bringing unusual and unexpected responses to bear on given situations. Research has looked at creativity both as a type of giftedness and as a subtype.
4. Although we no longer claim that giftedness springs entirely from the genes, it is only reasonable to assume that genetics have some effect. Environment is important, but, beyond the obvious general advantages, it is not known what specific factors in upper- and middle-class homes encourage giftedness.
5. For a long time, the study of giftedness was dominated by a single variable—a child's tested IQ. Today, the most prevalent identification models used call for multiple means of identification. The heterogeneity of the population, the plethora of available definitions, and the administrative problems make identification particularly difficult and uncertain. Problems can and do occur at various points in the process.
6. Within identification procedures, many children with gifts go undiscovered, particularly those who are culturally, ethnically, linguistically, socially, or economically different from the norm; gifted females; and gifted children with disabilities. Children who are disabled in one way may be exceptionally gifted in another. When the child has a learning disability, his or her superior intellectual ability is working overtime to compensate for the weaknesses caused by the disability. Culturally different children should not be expected to demonstrate the same strengths as white, middle-class children.
7. The provision of programs for students who are gifted is one of the most controversial issues in special education. With the exception of classroom enrichment, all of the practices recommended for academic achievement of students with gifts and talents focus on separate programs or different curricula. This, of course, is the opposite of inclusionary practices. Although advocates of education for gifted students have traditionally recommended alternative settings, they also lean toward inclusive programs when specialized instruction is not available.
8. Various methods of acceleration entail progress through an educational program at rates faster or ages younger than considered the norm. Research on the efficacy of any particular administrative model is somewhat inconclusive, but acceleration appears to have a strong edge. However, practitioners seem to regard acceleration in general, and early entrance in particular, as risky approaches in serving the needs of children who are gifted.
9. Enrichment in the classroom implies more than tacking on a few activities to the existing curriculum. Many strategies and models are available for raising the level of challenge for students who are gifted.

WEBLINKS

College of William and Mary, Center for Gifted Education
www.wm.edu/education/publicat.htmCommunity/NLAGC/nlagc.html

Structure of Intellect (J. P. Guilford) **www.gwu.edu/~tip/guilford.html**

Council for Exceptional Children ERIC Clearing House on Gifted Education **www.cec.sped.org/index.html**

Edmonton Catholic Schools Gifted and Enrichment Home Page
abccalgary.org/localinfo.html

Gifted and Talented Education Council of the Alberta Teachers Association
www.perpetual.net/gtec

Gifted Education: A Resource Guide for Teachers
www.bced.gov.bc.ca/specialed/gifted/toc.htm

Gifted Education in Alberta **www.educ.ucalgary.ca/altagift**

Gifted Programs and Services from the Centre for Gifted Education at the University of Calgary **www.ucalgary.ca/~gifteduc/**

Gifted Resources Page **www.eskimo.com/~user/kids.html**

National Research Center on the Gifted and Talented
www.gifted.uconn.edu/nrcgt.html

Newfoundland and Labrador Association for Gifted Children
calvin.stemnet.nf.ca/

In the Classroom

To educate students who are gifted, a school can make changes in the learning environment, in the content of lessons, and in the skills taught. Environmental changes include acceleration and ability grouping. Content includes what students study and the rate at which they study it. Skills relate both to process—how the students work with information—and to products—how they represent what they know.

Various processes that encompass content and skills are used to provide enrichment in the regular classroom:

- *Curriculum compacting* (telescoping) is used to bring the content up to the level of the child (Reis, 1995) and to move students through the curriculum far more rapidly. It is designed to adapt the regular curriculum to meet the needs of above-average students by either eliminating work that has been mastered previously or streamlining work that may be mastered at a pace commensurate with the student's ability. A major goal of curriculum compacting is that students' time is used more efficiently on appropriate topics or activities rather than completing tasks they already know.
- *Horizontal enrichment* involves examining a certain curriculum area in greater depth. Students

who are gifted don't need more work, but rather different work that is challenging and interesting. They should do the regular curriculum, but may delve into it in deeper ways. For example, a child in grade three may do all the addition problems set for the other students but then go on to do another set in Roman numerals.

- *Vertical enrichment* refers to students doing additional independent work of their own choosing in the classroom such as the individual studies discussed earlier.
- *Research skills.* For students who are gifted, we need to add a fourth process—research skills—to the curriculum. Students must be assisted in developing skills and strategies that enable them to become more independent, creative, and self-sufficient seekers after knowledge. Lacking research skills, students cannot undertake self-directed learning (also called autonomous learning, self-teaching, individualized education, independent learning, and personalized teaching).
- *Self-directed learning.* There are almost as many conceptualizations of self-directed learning as there are researchers and theorists. Essentially, self-directed learning means that students are given autonomous control of their own instruction. Included are library research projects, scientific research projects, and independent study in art, music, and drama; learning centres; and field trips.

Behavioural manifestations, needs	**Tips**
Independent, with high internal locus of control	• The degree of conformity in the classroom should be reasonable and flexible. Mary, for example, may not listen intently when you read to the class, but neither should she be permitted to divert the attention of others. • Make assignments that allow some choice. • Provide opportunities for choices in assignments. • Try to find mentors.
High self-motivation	• Individualize as much as possible. • Provide time for students to do their own work at school. • Teach methods by which the children can discover knowledge for themselves. • Let students teach each other through small-group work and cluster groups. • Have students regularly share with the class what they are doing. • To stimulate creative students, allow learning by exploring, testing the limits, searching, manipulating, and playing. • Tell students you appreciate their creativity.
Demonstrates high-level skills	• Use written expression for a variety of purposes—informative and persuasive as well as narrative. • Use individual reading assignments with self-selection of materials. • Introduce important ideas as early as possible. • Teach to the highest cognitive level possible. • Design a curriculum that facilitates the movement from teacher-directed to self-directed learning styles.

Behavioural manifestations, needs	Tips
	• Teach students to utilize all of their thinking processes.
Works quickly, needs more rapid pace	• Pace is one of the most important variables in teaching: present material more rapidly and with less practice than for average learners. • Do not work in a qualitatively different way than for other children; just present more advanced material. First teach the basic structure of a discipline, but then try to have the students approach it as a specialist would approach it. • Provide an appropriate time span for learning activities that are consistent with a child's style.
Needs research skills	• Stress technical writing. For example, teach how to phrase research questions. • Teach how to write proposals and how to present primary research data in graph, table, diagram, and statistical form. • Stress the processes of problem solving as well as the products of work.
Needs interaction with intellectual peers	• Use cluster rather than co-operative learning.
Underachieves	• Provide support and respect for the child's efforts. • Establish standards and provide instruction, guidance, and support, with encouragement and co-operation rather than competition (Whitmore, 1980).
Female students	• Provide early entry into stimulating and challenging programs. • Provide models that contradict sex-role stereotypes. • Provide information about scholastic requirements for career alternatives to stereotypical disciplines.
Has a disability	• Provide a nurturing environment that values individual differences. • Use strategies such as advance organizers, developing test-taking skills, and special notes that help to compensate for the disability.
Culturally diverse students	• Gain parental involvement and support and develop program models, goals, and objectives that are meaningful for the local culture.

SECTION 5

Children with Sensory Impairments

Hearing and vision connect us profoundly with our environment. Because of this, they are known as the distant senses. Even when we are not aware of it, and even when we are asleep, these two senses, especially hearing, keep us connected and in touch with the world. With this in mind, it is easy to realize how the loss of hearing or vision isolates an individual from family, friends, the community, and the physical environment. Nor is it surprising that such isolation has the potential to damage a person psychologically, socially, emotionally, and educationally. The greater the loss, the greater the potential isolation for the affected individual.

Blindness and deafness are low-incidence conditions, and although teachers may encounter some of these children it is far more likely they will meet students who see poorly or who are hard of hearing. As these hearing and vision problems are mild, many go undetected until children reach school age. Some children's problems are never identified, which places children at risk for being mislabelled as learning disabled or dismissed as dull, stupid, or lazy.

In concert with much of contemporary special education, the education of students who are visually impaired or hearing disabled is beset with issues. For example, whether or not to stress braille in the education of students who are blind, the issue of bilingual education for those who are deaf, and the problems of curriculum and setting for those who are deaf-blind (see Chapter 14).

Of all the contentious issues, placements stand first and foremost. Many students with sensory impairments have moved from special classes and residential schools to integrated programs within public schools where they may be supported by resource-room and itinerant-teacher programs. Nevertheless, the debate on inclusive schooling remains prominent. Integrating students with sensory disabilities is challenging to teachers, especially when the student has a hearing impairment.

Techniques and approaches to include hearing impaired or visually impaired students are, of course, quite different. The main difference is in language and communication: children with visual impairments use language to keep in contact with their environments; those with hearing impairments use visual means that usually include speech reading and sign language.

Chapter 9

Children with Hearing Impairments

Learning Outcomes

After reading this chapter, you should be able to:

- Differentiate between the categories of deaf and hard of hearing;
- Understand the developmental consequences of hearing loss, especially in relation to language and speech acquisition;
- Recognize some of the technical aids that assist persons who are deaf;
- Identify the variety of communication modes used in the education of students with hearing impairments;
- Understand the nature of deaf culture and the deaf community and how it impacts on contemporary education for students who are deaf.

Introduction

If you were to take a casual survey of a hundred people and ask who had had a medical checkup, dental checkup, eye examination, or hearing assessment in the past twelve months, only a very few would mention a hearing test. Why? Because in North America we pay less attention to hearing loss than to almost any other medical condition.

Hearing loss is silent, painless, and invisible, one of the least recognized and most misunderstood disabilities. Severe and profound hearing loss (deafness) is a low-incidence condition; however, milder forms of hearing impairment (hard of hearing) are far more prevalent.

Most people think of deafness as simply a lack of sound, but this is one of the least of the problems. The greatest single result of serious hearing impairment is the concomitant impairment in communication skills. Hearing loss, a physical ailment, spills over to affect the development of speech and language, the most important components of interpersonal communication. As Helen Keller (1933) pointed out, deafness also means "the loss of the most vital stimulus—the sound of the voice that brings language, sets thoughts astir, and keeps us in the intellectual company of men" (p. 68). When Beethoven became hearing impaired, he wrote that he was "soon obliged to seclude myself and live in solitude" (Freeland, 1989, p. 1).

For children, hearing impairment poses a serious threat because hearing is so critical for learning. In normal child development, speech and language are acquired spontaneously and almost effortlessly. From their earliest days, normally hearing infants process language, preparing to become competent communicators. They have intact auditory processes on which to build an early mastery of the sound, shape, and sense of language. Babies do not merely listen passively to the language around them; they take in, process, and organize the language they hear and, like miniature linguists, they recreate for themselves the language of their culture.

For babies who are deaf, life is devoid of sound effects and spoken script. Children who are hearing impaired do not hear the sounds made by themselves and others. They are isolated from the human voice, and this inevitably hinders or halts their acquisition of speech and language.

In the past, few children with serious hearing impairments were admitted to general classrooms. However, the vigorous advocacy of the past twenty years on behalf of all children who are exceptional has wrought profound and fundamental changes in the particular area of the education of students with hearing impairments. Although provincially funded residential/day schools remain an important instructional vehicle, the current emphasis on appropriate integration with support services has meant shifts in program locations, student placements, and greater possibilities for general class participation for youngsters who are hearing impaired.

Nevertheless, educational integration is an issue (only one of many) that remains beset

Students with hearing impairments have special needs in the classroom.

with controversy. Many deaf people, advocacy groups, and some professionals working with students who are deaf reject the practice and see little benefit within the present inclusive practices (see Rodda, Grove, and Finch, 1986). The issue is intertwined with the continuing viability of deaf culture and the deaf community, as well as with the mode of communication and bilingual education for children and youth who are deaf.

THE HUMAN EAR

The human ear, a truly marvellous instrument, is designed to collect sound, process it, and transmit it to be decoded in the brain. The ear is one of the most complex organs in the body, a triumph of miniaturization, fitting into a space not much larger than a hazelnut. It can detect sounds much softer than the dropping of a pin but still filter sounds a million times louder.

Hearing impairments are caused by interference with any part of the ear's transmission system. Impairment may take the form of restriction in the range of frequencies received, distortions along the frequency spectrum, or a failure to perceive sounds.

The ear's anatomy is usually discussed in terms of the external, the middle, and the inner ear. Figure 9-1 illustrates the major parts of the human hearing mechanism.

The External Ear

The outer ear is the visible cartilage structure on the side of the head, referred to as the pinna. This is the least complex part of the hearing mechanism and the least important for hearing. An external canal, or *meatus*, runs obliquely from the pinna to the ear drum. The ear drum, or tympanic membrane, is a tough, tightly stretched tissue that separates

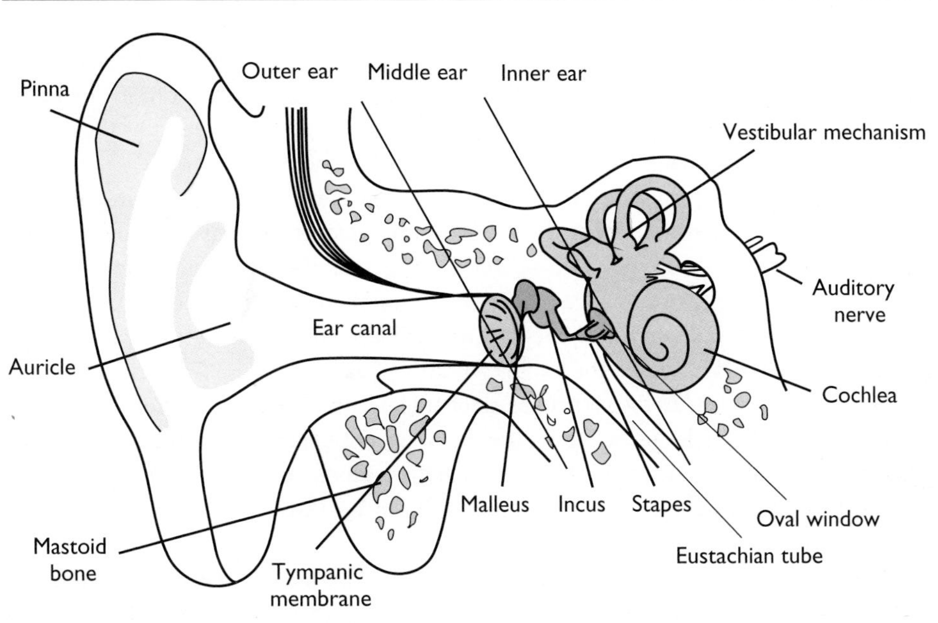

Figure 9-1
Anatomy of the human ear

the outer from the middle ear. It is at the ear drum that hearing really begins.

The pinna serves to collect sound waves and filter them into the meatus. The external canal is lined with coarse hairs and 4000 wax glands that secrete cerumen. The wax traps insects, dust, and other irritants, guards against infection, and lubricates the canal and the ear drum.

ear drum

The **ear drum** is a concave mechanism that vibrates freely when struck by sound waves. Even the faint vibrations of a whisper cause it to vibrate, but perhaps only a millionth of a centimetre.

The Middle Ear

The inner surface of the ear drum is located in the air-filled cavity of the middle ear. The middle ear drum surface holds three small bones, the malleus, the incus, and the stapes, also called the hammer, the anvil, and the stirrup. These tiny bones, the smallest in the human body, form a bridge, the *ossicular chain*, between the ear drum and the inner ear entrance at another drum called the *oval window*. There are two muscles in the middle ear, one joined to the stapes and the other to the ear drum. The Eustachian tube connects the middle ear to the nasopharynx.

In the middle ear, the transmission of sound becomes more sophisticated. When sound waves strike the ear drum, it vibrates and moves the three small bones. These bones transmit the vibrations across the middle ear cavity to the inner ear through the oval window. The middle ear amplifies the sound about twenty-two times, and also protects the inner ear from very loud noise.

The Eustachian tube serves to equalize the pressure on both sides of the ear drum. You may have experienced the discomfort of unequal pressure in an airplane descent. To clear the Eustachian tube, and to make the ears "pop," passengers yawn deeply, suck on hard candy, blow their noses, or swallow.

The Inner Ear

The inner ear, the real organ of hearing, is located in a cavern of the skull. It is about the size of a pea, an intricate mechanism with thousands of moving parts. Because it looks like a complex maze of passages, the inner ear is called the **labyrinth**. It contains the cochlea and the vestibular mechanism, which are independent in their functioning.

labyrinth

cochlea

The **cochlea** is a tiny, snail-shaped structure filled with a fluid similar to cerebrospinal fluid. Its twisting interior is studded with thousands of microscopic hair cells, each one tuned to a particular vibration that responds to a particular fragment of sound. Within the cochlea are highly specialized structures, such as the organ of Corti and Reissner's membrane. The auditory nerve, which is about the diameter of a pencil lead and consists of more than 31 000 nerve fibres, relays messages to the brain.

vestibular mechanism

Behind the cochlea lies the **vestibular mechanism**, composed of three fluid-filled semicircular canals. These loops of tubing are the organs of balance. Information regarding movement and balance is fed to the brain through the vestibular mechanism. Other nerve endings in the body also contribute to the sense of balance—those in the eyes, feet, muscles, and joints.

The intricacy of the inner ear structure is matched by the complexity of its function. When air-carried (conducted) sound pushes on the ear drum, it causes the stapes to vibrate on the oval window leading to the inner ear, which makes the fluid in the cochlea begin to move. A low-pitched sound pushes at the top of the cochlea and a high-pitched sound at the base. For example, if middle C is sounded, then the cochlea's middle C hair cells vibrate, waving in the fluid. The waving produces a wisp of electricity that feeds into the auditory nerve and is transmitted to the brain. There the signal is unscrambled and converted into meaningful sound. An overview of the sequence is provided in Table 9-1.

Most sound travels on air (air conduction). With bone conduction of sound, sound travels directly through the jawbone and the mastoid bone to the inner ear fluid. Because we hear our own voices by bone conduction, we hear ourselves quite differently from how our listeners hear us and often have trouble recognizing our own voices on a tape recorder.

Table 9-1 The sequence of hearing

1. Sound waves enter the ear, travel through the external canal, and vibrate the ear drum.
2. The vibrations of the ear drum move the bones of the middle ear.
3. The footplate of the stapes moves the oval window and sets the cochlear fluid in motion.
4. The movement causes the hairs immersed in the cochlear fluid to move. This stimulates the attached cells to send a tiny electrical impulse along the fibres of the auditory nerve to the brain.
5. In the brain, impulses are translated into meaningful sound.

Case Study

Steven

There does not seem to be any identifiable reason for Steven's severe hearing loss. Mrs. J. was healthy throughout her third pregnancy. She was a little, but not overly, concerned when her infant arrived nearly a month before term. Labour was normal, lasting about fourteen hours. The infant cried lustily, and Mrs. J. readily accepted the explanation that he was in neonatal intensive care only because he was of slightly low birth-weight.

Steven spent only a month in the neonatal unit. Once at home, he proved an easy baby who smiled and cooed at everyone. He began to babble early, but at about ten or eleven months of age stopped making many sounds at all.

His mother was aware quite early that something was amiss with Steven. She suspected a hearing impairment by about eight months when Steven seemed impervious to cleaning, vacuuming, or telephone sounds. At this time, his mother took him to a pediatrician, who simply told her that the child would grow out of whatever she thought was ailing him—or alternatively, she was simply an overprotective parent. When Steven was twelve months of age, another doctor suggested that perhaps he was developmentally delayed or even mentally retarded.

As Steven grew, he reached all the physical developmental milestones and became a sociable, gregarious child. His mother knew that a diagnosis of a significant cognitive disability did not suit her outgoing little toddler. But it was not until Steven and his mother saw two other physicians when Steven was almost a year and a half old that a diagnosis of profound hearing impairment was made.

Almost immediately, Steven was fitted with hearing aids, which, to everyone's surprise, he readily accepted. He was placed on a home-visiting program where a teacher came to the family's home weekly and taught him language, including sign language, and promoted speech. She showed Mrs. J. how to stimulate vocalizations, and gave her some tips on receptive language development.

Mrs. J. behaved toward Steven and disciplined him just as she did the older children. She accepted his disability but held appropriate expectations for his development. He became an integral part of the family circle. Sibling resentment was not directed at any special treatment Steven received; it surfaced only when he got into the same type of mischief that any preschooler does.

By age two-and-a-half, Steven's expressive language was restricted to two words—*ma* for all his wants, and *moo* for a special toy car. Receptively, he responded consistently to his own name and "No." Steven also began to develop his own unique set of gestures and actions to convey meaning to his listeners.

When he was three, his mother enrolled Steven in a total communication preschool program. This decision had more to do with geography than to adherence to any one philosophy of communication. Although his parents would desperately like Steven to speak and not sign, a total communication program was in the area. As well, the parents realized that language acquisition is the important goal, whatever the mode.

DEFINITIONS OF HEARING IMPAIRMENT

The broad category of *hearing impairment* stretches from marginal hearing losses that may be a real concern only in noisy situations to profound deafness where individuals cannot hear voiced sounds, even with amplification (hearing aids), and must resort to speech reading and, often, sign language. Steven, the child in the case study, has a severe to profound hearing loss. He cannot hear language or speech and has resorted to his own idiosyncratic home signs for basic communication.

A number of definition and classification systems are used in the field of hearing impairment. A general definition states that:

hearing impairment

- **Hearing impairment** is a generic term indicating a hearing disability that may range in severity from mild to profound. It includes the subsets of deaf and hard of hearing.

deaf person

- A **deaf person** is one whose hearing disability precludes successful processing of linguistic information through audition, with or without a hearing aid.

hard-of-hearing person

- A **hard-of-hearing person** is one who, generally with the use of a hearing aid, has residual hearing sufficient to enable successful processing of linguistic information through audition.

PREVALENCE OF HEARING IMPAIRMENTS

Approximately one in ten Canadians, or about two million people, have some form of hearing impairment. Perhaps one in forty has an impairment serious enough to affect daily life and communication, and one in 400, or about 50 000 people, suffers from profound deafness.

Hearing loss is most tragic when it strikes the very young. Its incidence at birth is quite low, however. About one infant in every 1000 is born profoundly deaf, or is deaf before the age of three. But when infants with mild losses are included, the numbers go as high as one in 750 (Ruppert and Buhrer, 1992).

It is difficult to arrive at an exact determination of the prevalence of hearing impairment, and estimates vary considerably. One widely accepted estimate holds that 5 percent of school-aged children have hearing outside the normal limits. Of this number, 10 to 20 percent require some type of special education ("Children with communication ...," 1995).

Of the many factors that hinder researchers from arriving at accurate prevalence and incidence figures for hearing loss, the most important are

- Inconsistent definitional data.
- Confusion regarding identification and reporting.
- Methodological problems in surveys. For example, after comparing surveys in Canada and the United States, Jerome Schein (1994) found that hearing impairment in the United States has a prevalence rate of 86 per 1000, as compared to 41 per 1000 in Canada, which reflects the younger overall age of the Canadian population. Schein also found that rates vary considerably across the Canadian provinces, from a low of 34 per 1000 in the Northwest Territories to 61 per 1000 in Prince Edward Island and Manitoba.
- Difficulties in accurate early identification of hearing loss. The average age of identifying childhood hearing loss is quite late—between 17.5 and 25 months (Mayne, Yoshinaga-Itano, Seday, and Carey, 2000).
- Increasing prevalence of hearing impairment with age. Hearing loss among elderly persons is especially common. Serious hearing problems affect one in 10 people over 65 years of age, and 4 out of every 10 over 75 (Ontario, Ministry of Health, 1978).
- Difficulties in estimating hearing impairments among individuals with multiple disabilities, who are often reported according to their primary disability.
- A shortage of research in some areas. An extensive body of research deals with deafness; much less exists in relation to hard-of-hearing individuals. While hard-of-hearing children are much more common, their true numbers are unknown, as many cases are misdiagnosed or simply overlooked.

CLASSIFICATION OF HEARING IMPAIRMENTS

The distinction between deaf and hard of hearing is not as clear-cut as the above definitions imply. Both groups are heterogeneous, and subcategories of each are often used. The classifier's orientation often determines the system of classification. Those with a strictly physiological perspective are interested primarily in the measurable degree of hearing loss. On the other hand, educators want to know how hearing impairment will affect a child's functioning. Because hearing loss is closely linked to language delay, educators tend to categorize chiefly on the basis of language ability.

Four major, though closely interrelated, classification systems for hearing impairment are in use. These are founded on the degree of hearing impairment, the cause, the site of the deficit, and the age at which the impairment developed. Table 9-2 shows the main classification of systems.

Table 9-2 Classification of hearing impairment

Severity	Time of onset	Etiology	Site
Mild	Prelingual	Congenital	Conductive
Moderate	Post-lingual	Adventitious (deafened)	Sensorineural
Severe			
Profound			

Classification by Severity Level

Severity levels classify hearing loss according to the amount of hearing (acuity) in a person's better ear. Acuity is measured by the subject's response to loudness across a range of frequencies. *Decibels* and *hertz* are used to measure loudness and frequency, respectively. Individuals are classed as deaf or hard of hearing depending on whether they hear sounds at certain intensities of loudness across a range of frequencies.

This classification is further structured by designation as *mild, moderate, severe,* or *profound* hearing loss. Table 9-3 illustrates the levels of hearing impairment.

decibel

A *bel*, named after Alexander Graham Bell, is the unit of loudness intensity. Each bel is broken down into ten parts, known as *decibels* (dB). A **decibel** represents the smallest difference in loudness intensity that can be perceived. Hearing loss is measured on a decibel scale, beginning with 0 dB, a figure that designates the point at which people with normal hearing can detect the faintest sound. Inability to hear sounds of 25 to 30 dB or more is considered to be a hearing loss. However, a loss of 60 dB is not merely six times greater than a loss of 10 dB. The figures are logarithmic, not arithmetic, so that 60dB is 10^6 times louder than 10 dB. Figure 9-2 shows the decibel (dB) level of some common sounds on an audiogram, a chart on which hearing is recorded.

hertz

Sound waves are produced by the to-and-fro waving movement of molecules. One complete to-and-fro movement makes a cycle; the number of cycles per second determines the *frequency* of a sound. Cycles per second are measured in **hertz** (Hz)—a frequency of 1000 Hz indicates 1000 cycles per second. As the frequency increases, the pitch of the sound becomes higher.

speech range

Although the human ear is sensitive to frequencies between 50 Hz and 20 000 Hz, most human speech falls between 500 and 2000 Hz. This range of pitch is known as the **speech range**. Middle C on a piano is about 500 Hz.

Table 9-3 Levels of hearing impairment

Range	Severity	Implications
0–25 dB	Insignificant	
25–40 dB	Mild hearing loss; hard of hearing	May have difficulty with faint or distant sounds. May have problems in conversations, groups, or settings with much ambient noise.
40–60 dB	Moderate hearing loss; hard of hearing	Frequent difficulty with normal speech, especially in conversations, groups, and class discussions.
60–90 dB	Severe hearing loss; hard of hearing	Great difficulty with even loud or amplified speech, which seems faint and distorted. Requires amplification and intense speech and language training.
90 dB+	Profound hearing loss; deaf	May be aware of loud sounds and vibrations, but generally cannot understand even amplified speech.

Classification by Site of Loss

Hearing impairment is also classified according to the part of the hearing mechanism that is affected. Problems in the mechanical transmission of sound waves through the outer and middle ear are called **conductive hearing losses** because something stops the air conduction of sound. Conductive losses generally affect the intensity of sound reception but do not distort the sound. Conductive losses, affecting the outer and middle ear only, usually respond favourably to medical or surgical intervention.

conductive hearing losses

Impairment in the inner ear is caused by abnormal sense organs (sensory) or defective auditory nerves (neural). These **sensorineural hearing impairments** interfere with the conversion of sound waves into neural impulses for the brain. Not only is sound intensity hampered, but any sound received may also be distorted. Sensorineural hearing loss is the common type among children with serious losses.

sensorineural hearing impairments

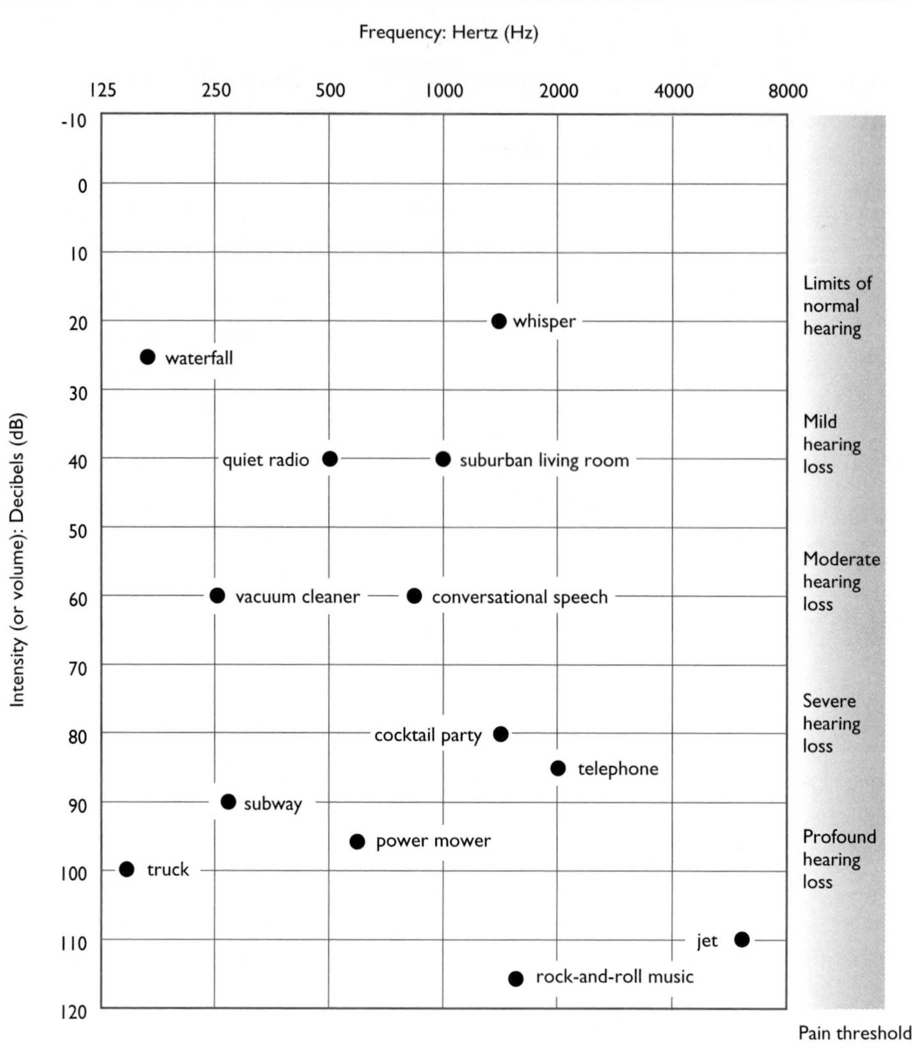

Figure 9-2 *Chart showing the hearing level of some common sounds*

Classification by Etiology

congenital hearing impairment
adventitious hearing losses

A **congenital hearing impairment** is one that is present at birth; an *adventitious* hearing impairment is acquired some time after birth through accident or disease. People with **adventitious hearing losses** are sometimes described as *deafened.*

Classification by Age of Onset

prelingual deafness
post-lingual deafness

Closely connected to the classification of adventitious and congenital hearing impairment is that concerned with age of onset. Children with **prelingual deafness** are those who were deaf prior to the development of speech and language. Children with **post-lingual deafness** became deaf after the development of speech and language. The cut-off point is often set at two years of age (Meadow, 1980). Note that fewer than one child in ten loses hearing after the age of two.

Children with prelingual (congenital) hearing losses do not have the opportunity to practise the listening skills essential to developing speech and language. Inevitably, prelingual impairment affects every aspect of communication development from birth onwards. Children who acquire hearing impairments after they develop speech and language usually find it easier to develop communication skills. The later in life an impairment occurs, the greater the child's linguistic capabilities are likely to be.

The case study of Steven is illustrative here. Although the medical profession could not pinpoint a reason, Steven had a severe to profound sensironeural bilateral congenital hearing loss. Audiometric assessment showed a loss of 95 dB in the right ear and 100 dB in the left. Even with amplification, Steven found speech acquisition extremely difficult. By the time he arrived at school, he had very little intelligible speech.

ETIOLOGY OF HEARING IMPAIRMENTS

Etiological and diagnostic considerations in hearing impairment are the venue of medical and paramedical personnel. *Audiologists* are chiefly involved in the assessment of hearing and in recommending and fitting amplification equipment. *Otolaryngologists* are medical personnel concerned with the problems of the ear, nose, and throat that affect hearing and speech. They also handle voice disorders through medication and surgery.

Impairments of the Outer Ear

External otitis, or swimmer's ear, is an infection of the skin of the external auditory canal. Also in the canal, an excessive build-up of wax can result in decreased hearing acuity. Infrequently, a child is born with missing or undeveloped auditory canals. This condition, known as **auditory atresia,** interferes with the air conduction of sound and requires medical or surgical intervention before it impedes a child's education. *Microtia* refers to a misshapen or extremely small pinna. Perforation of the ear drum, resulting from any number of causes, can also produce hearing impairment.

auditory atresia

The problem of foreign objects in the ear has always existed and probably always will. Nature designed the ear to clean itself. An old saying claims that if a finger were intended to go in the ear, it would have been made small enough to fit. Unfortunately, many other things do fit—the ends of pencils, beads, carrots, peanuts, and bobby pins. Even cotton swabs can do enormous damage, either by puncturing the paper-thin ear drum or pushing accumulations of wax further into the ear.

Impairments of the Middle Ear

Middle ear hearing impairments are more serious than those affecting the outer ear, but most are surgically correctable. The great majority of middle ear conditions are conductive hearing losses, meaning that the conduction of sound by air is hindered. The result is a loss of intensity of sound, though not usually a distorted pattern. Conductive losses do not exceed 65 dB.

The most common form of ear infection in children is **otitis media,** a condition in which the mucosal lining of the middle ear becomes inflamed and the cavity filled with fluid. Infections use the Eustachian tube to reach the middle ear from the nose or throat. Otitis media is most extreme in infancy, when the Eustachian tube is shorter, wider, and in a more

otitis media

horizontal position. It is estimated that 50 to 75 percent of children have one episode of otitis media in the first year of life (Roberts, 1997). The peak prevalence for otitis media is between six and thirty-six months (Bluestone, 1982). After six years of age, the incidence steadily decreases. However, in the normal school environment, 20 to 30 percent of children between the ages of five and twelve will have at least one bout of middle ear effusion.

Otitis media affects males more often than females. The prevalence is higher among lower socio-economic groups, in children with cleft palates, and in those with other craniofacial anomalies. Children with Down syndrome are especially susceptible to otitis media and its resulting conductive hearing loss.

Researchers have also found a higher prevalence among Native children, but a lower prevalence among Blacks (Robinson, Allen, and Root, 1988). When Scaldwell and Frame (1985) examined children in six Ontario Native communities, they found a higher incidence of otitis media among school-aged children. The reason for the higher prevalence among Natives is unclear, but it may be a combination of genetic, socio-cultural, environmental, and economic factors.

otosclerosis

Otosclerosis is a hereditary condition characterized by the destruction of the capsular bone in the middle ear and the growth of a weblike bone that attaches to and restricts the stapes. Otosclerosis, which is twice as common in females as in males, affects 2 percent of the population and is clinically active in more than 0.5 percent ("Hearing loss ... ," 1982). The condition is rare in children and is not usually noticed until adolescence or the early twenties. Resultant hearing losses can be at the 50 or 60 dB level, necessitating the use of a hearing aid or corrective surgery.

Other middle ear problems can be caused by blows to the head or a fall. They can also result from congenital defects.

Impairments of the Inner Ear

The most devastating hearing impairments are caused by sensorineural problems of the inner ear. A great many childhood sensorineural impairments are attributed to "causes unknown." Identifiable causes include the traditional villains, with the most profound losses stemming from meningitis, maternal rubella, and hereditary factors.

Today, rubella and Rh factor are well controlled, if not eliminated, and there are inoculations against forms of meningitis. Heredity factors remain prominent; estimates range from 30 to 60 percent (Moores, 1982). There are about sixty-five types of hereditary deafness. Hearing problems may be inherited on a dominant trait (14 percent), a recessive trait (44 percent), or as a sex-linked disorder (2 percent) (Lowenbraun and Thompson, 1982).

Prematurity itself does not cause deafness. However, premature and low-birth-weight babies are at higher risk for hearing disorders. Deafness can also result from birth complications such as prolonged labour, abrupt birth, or the use of obstetrical instruments. Failure to breathe immediately after birth—**apnea**—is another commonly reported cause of hearing problems.

apnea

presbycusis

Among adults, progressive nerve deterioration, known as **presbycusis** (deafness of age), is the most common cause of auditory defect. The older one gets, the more one is prone to presbycusis. As well, intracranial tumours, cerebral hemorrhages, inner ear fistula (a build-up of inner ear fluid), acoustic neuroma (tumour on the auditory nerve), and viral infections and vascular spasms in the inner ear can cause permanent or temporary Sudden Hearing Loss Syndrome.

Prolonged exposure to tones of high intensity are increasingly recognized as causes of sensorineural hearing loss. For example, a power lawnmower emits 100 dB, a subway train 90, a riveting gun 130, and a jet take-off 105 or more. Modern music also causes hearing impairments: rock bands often reach 115 dB. Muscles in the middle ear protect the inner ear from excessively loud low-pitched sounds, but no such action protects the ear from the new high-pitched sounds.

Ménière's disease, a condition characterized by nausea, vertigo—a spinning sensation—and tinnitus, is a particularly devastating problem for adults. Ménière's is caused by a buildup of endolymphatic (inner ear) fluid that creates increased pressure on the inner ear. The pressure increases ruptures in the inner ear compartments, which causes the vertigo.

Ménière's disease

The tinnitus that accompanies Ménière's disease can also occur as a sole condition in both deaf and hearing individuals. The word *tinnitus* derives from Latin, meaning to "tinkle or ring like a bell." For some sufferers it may be hearing a ringing or a hiss, but for others it is living constantly with the noise of a squeaking door hinge, the squealing of an unoiled metal bearing, or the sound of fingernails being dragged across a blackboard (Agnew, 1986). The chronic nature of the condition causes great distress and becomes the central issue in the lives of some affected people.

Tinnitus is not an audiological phenomenon but a medical condition. The actual mechanism is not known. Tinnitus does not have a specific site of origin; it can be produced anywhere along the auditory mechanism, or it may not be generated by the auditory system at all. Anything that can go wrong with the ear may have tinnitus associated with it as a symptom—wax against the drum, tumours on the nerve, otosclerosis, Ménière's disease, and exposure to excessively loud sounds (Agnew, 1986).

Syndromes

Hearing loss can be inherited alone or in combination with other abnormalities in a syndrome. Impairments of hearing accompany skeletal deformities in Treacher-Collins syndrome and abnormal skin pigmentation in Waardenburg's syndrome, and are sometimes part of the multiple disabilities of Down syndrome. Approximately four to five percent of congenitally hearing-impaired individuals suffer from Usher's syndrome, which results in hearing impairment and a progressive deterioration in the visual field through retinitis pigmentosa (see Chapter 14). Pendred's syndrome and Jervell and Lang-Neilson syndrome are also associated with hearing impairment. There are six types of Alport's syndrome, an X chromosome–related condition that results in progressive bilateral sensironeural hearing loss associated with bilateral kidney disease.

DEVELOPMENTAL CONSEQUENCES OF HEARING IMPAIRMENTS

The major disability associated with hearing impairment is the impact on the development of speech and language. This can, and often does, spill over to adversely affect other developmental domains.

Cognitive Development

The cognitive development of individuals who are hearing impaired is a provocative and challenging area of research. Studies dating back to the 19th century have considered IQ levels, the relationship between language and thought, concept acquisition and development, perceptual processes, and memory function. As 150 years of research findings accumulated, ideas about the cognitive development of individuals with hearing impairments changed, sometimes quite dramatically.

Studies before 1950 showed school children who were deaf to be three or four years behind hearing children and about ten IQ points below the norm (Meadow, 1980). However, the reason for past perceptions of poorer intellectual development lay not within the child but in the testing procedures used. When assessment is matched to linguistic capabilities, students with deafness score within the normal range of the performance scales on tests of mental ability. In general, the hearing-impaired population fits on the same curve for intelligence as does the rest of the population (Quinsland and Vanginkel, 1990).

The relationship between cognitive development and how linguistic deficits affect thought has been an area of investigation. In general, research has found that children who are deaf consistently demonstrate the same thinking processes as hearing children, with language as the mediating factor. The latter point here means that students who are deaf but who have acquired some language consistently outperform those with less language ability.

Children who are deaf can think logically without a linguistic system, but problems still emerge in the development of perceptual and conceptual processes. Comparisons of concept formation and abstract thinking skills between hearing-impaired and normally hearing children yield somewhat inconsistent results, but some (e.g., Braden, 1987) assert that all children who are deaf suffer metacognitive deficits. These may result in part from the memorization, drill, and rote learning so characteristic of traditional programs for the education of students who are deaf.

Studies of the performance of children who are deaf on memory tasks also show conflicting results. For example, children are more likely to retain words that have a sign equivalent than words that do not, and they are more likely than hearing children to remember geometric forms better than digits.

Communication

If you look back to the case study about Steven, you will see that he is a normal, outgoing, sometimes mischievous little boy. The way in which he differs from his siblings and peers is in his acquisition and development of speech and language. For Steven and all other children with hearing impairments, speech and language are the areas of development most severely affected by a hearing impairment. Deficits vary considerably as a result of many factors including the degree of hearing loss, the training and use of residual hearing, the child's age at the impairment's onset, the etiology of the impairment, the family climate, the early mode of communication, and the educational setting.

For children with mild or moderate hearing losses, the effect on speech and language may be minimal. Communication for the child who is hard of hearing has more in common with that of the normally hearing child than with that of the child who is deaf, because both hearing and hard-of-hearing individuals use audition rather than vision as the primary mode for speech and language development.

Children who are hard of hearing use their residual hearing to develop speech and language, and they use spoken language adequately to transmit and receive information, although they may speech read as a supplement to auditory skills. Even so, children who are hard of hearing may be at risk for educational failure. Some research suggests that a mild to moderate hearing loss (10 to 40 dB) impairs the listening performance of a young child to the extent of becoming an auditory handicap (Gdowski, Sanger, and Decker, 1986). Moreover, environmental variables such as extraneous noise and the distance from the speaker can adversely affect a child's auditory comprehension.

Otitis media causes temporary to chronic mild conductive hearing losses that may fluctuate under certain conditions, such as when the child has a heavy cold, and in certain environments, such as a noisy classroom. This will impede speech and language development to some extent. The accumulated effects are usually felt in about the third or fourth grade.

Early otitis media may be implicated in later speech disorders (e.g., Roberts, Burchind, Koch, Fodto, Henderson, 1988). Children may show inefficient listening skills and sporadic misunderstandings in speech; they may, for example, confuse the markers -ed and -ing and misunderstand small words in connected speech such as *are, to,* and *in.* In addition, children with recurrent middle ear disease are at considerable risk for losing high-frequency auditory sensitivity; psycho-acoustic studies have found that intensity discrimination is adversely affected by the presence of high-frequency hearing losses (Fausti, [1987]).

For children who are deaf, the impact on communication is far more devastating. Most loud speech is inaudible to the child, even with the most sophisticated hearing aids. This means that children face major difficulties in learning language, as well as significant articulation, voice quality, and tone discrimination problems.

Because children who are deaf cannot hear the words of people around them, they have no language models. Even with optimal intervention, their language levels are seriously retarded. Every element of language is affected—semantics, syntax, morphology, pragmatics, and phonology.

One study of 132 deaf and hard of hearing children who used a variety of communication modes found an average of 300 signed or spoken words at three to four years of age, and 514 words at five to six years of age (Yoshinaga-Itano, 1994). That must be compared to the 10 000 to 14 000 or so we would expect to find in a hearing child of six years. (See Chapter 4.) Not only is vocabulary in any mode restricted, but students who are deaf plateau in vocabulary development when they are about twelve or thirteen years of age (Mayne, Yoshinaga-Itano, Seday, and Carey, 2000).

Constructions such as phrasal verbs (*turn off, run in*) pose great difficulties. Similarly, figurative language (idioms, similes, metaphors, proverbs, and so on) involves every area of comprehension and semantics and is beyond most students who are deaf (see Arnold and Hornett, 1990). An idiom such as "hit the road" transgresses the laws of logic and is almost impossible to justify for a literal-thinking deaf person. One teacher tells how a young child who was deaf looked bewildered when she signed to him, "Your nose is running." To the child, running was something done on the playground and not something that noses did.

Individuals who are hearing impaired have specific voice and speech characteristics and vary in their speech intelligibility. In general, however, speech is an area of great difficulty. In an early study (Jensema, Karchmer, and Trybus, 1978) teachers rated the intelligibility of the speech of their students who were hearing impaired; more than 42 percent of the children were rated as unintelligible or barely intelligible. According to the survey, approximately 13 percent of the children would not even try to use their voices for speech. Later reports put the average speech intelligibility of children with severe to profound losses who wear aids at about 20 percent, although there is wide variability in reported figures (Carney, 1986).

In young hearing children, close parallels exist between the development of pretend play and the development of language. Whether this is true when it comes to children with hearing impairments is moot. For example, Canadian researcher Mary Lyon (1997) studied symbolic play and language development in thirty-nine severely to profoundly deaf children who were twelve to thirty months of age. Lyon found that play and language were not as linked as they are in hearing children. Deaf children develop play and play at the same levels as other children, even with low language, although higher language levels did equate with higher and more mature levels of play. Other researchers (e.g., Higginbotham, Baker, and Neill, 1980) studying play find that communication deficits interfere with normal play development; children who are hearing impaired tend to engage in less complex and less social play than do normally hearing children. One study (Higginbotham and Baker, 1981) found that preschoolers with hearing impairment between forty-seven and sixty-six months of age preferred solitary constructive play, whereas hearing children of the same age preferred co-operative dramatic play.

Academic Achievement

The academic achievement of students with hearing disabilities is closely aligned to their acquisition of language. With the difficulties that most of these students meet in acquiring language, it is perhaps not surprising that their academic performance compares poorly with documented potential.

Those pupils who are hard of hearing and rely primarily on residual hearing and speech for communication sometimes have language deficiencies that limit their reading comprehension as well as their oral communication skills. Students who are deaf uniformly appear to lag educationally by three to five years.

Numerous studies of reading achievement have shown that the mean reading scores of children who are deaf are well below those of hearing children; there is a lag of two to eight years. According to data published by the Center for Assessment and Demographic Studies at Gallaudet University (1991), the average eighteen-year-old with a severe to profound hearing loss reads with the comprehension of a normally hearing child in the early months of third grade. This is below or barely at literacy level. Only three percent of deaf eighteen-year-olds read at the same level as the average hearing reader of the same age.

There is some evidence that readers who are deaf use many of the same metacognitive strategies to comprehend print as do hearing readers (Andrews and Mason, 1991). Case studies of the reading process show that children who are deaf use contextual information to reconstruct the text using their semantic knowledge. But many of these students have very restricted vocabularies (LaSasso and Davey, 1987). Most can't comprehend even the most commonly used words, and children with limited vocabularies are likely to experience great difficulties in language and reading. These will be especially noticeable if reading words are removed from context, creating an unnaturally difficult situation. To add to the language and semantic difficulties, many readers who are deaf are deficient in world knowledge—the general background knowledge and prior experience of many of the topics found in commercial texts.

Children who are deaf are less educationally behind in more mechanical skills such as arithmetic and spelling. But while they seem to achieve well in mathematical computation, they are less successful at mathematical problem solving, which is predicated on a language base.

Social and Emotional Development

Because severe hearing loss so dramatically affects language and communication, it may produce barriers to normal social interaction that appear impossible to overcome. The severity of social maladjustment patterns often depends on the depth of the hearing loss and the type of impairment. Severe and profound hearing losses are more likely to result in social isolation.

Students who are hard of hearing represent an unaddressed population often misunderstood and underserved (David, 1990). In these cases, the hearing impairment may be misdiagnosed and a child's inappropriate responses may be erroneously seen as behaviour problems or learning disorders. When this happens, the child's self-sufficiency, social maturity, and personality development are placed at risk.

Children who are deaf show a higher degree of emotional instability, neurosis, and maladjustment than hearing children. Estimates of the rates of emotional disturbance among students who are hearing impaired range from 8 to 22 percent. Although the range is broad, there is also sufficient evidence to conclude that the frequency of behavioural disorders is higher than for the general population of school-age children (Adams and Tidwell, 1989).

Abnormal social development in children who are hearing impaired is often manifested by impulsive, irresponsible, and dependent behaviour. Frequently, children seem to disregard the feelings and misunderstand the actions of others. They typically exhibit a high degree of egocentricity and a low frustration threshold. These traits cause them to make inordinate demands and to act out their frustrations if demands are not met.

Co-occurring Disabilities

An estimated 25 to 33 percent of students who are deaf or hard of hearing have secondary learning problems (Schildroth and Hotto, 1996). Emotional disorders, mental retardation, and learning disabilities are the most common (Meadow, 1980). As well, all studies on vision screening indicate a higher incidence of visual deficits than among normally hearing children (Silberman, 1981).

Family Variables

The way in which the parents and the family react to and accept a disabling condition profoundly influences the development of the child with the disability. This is even more true in the area of hearing impairment, where the hearing status of the parents is a significant variable and where parental child-rearing attitudes appear to be the best predictors of the self-concept of children who are severely to profoundly hearing impaired (Warren and Hasenstab, 1986).

Approximately 10 percent of babies who are hearing impaired are born to deaf parents. These children form a distinct subgroup within the hearing-impaired population. Children deafened by genetic factors tend to have far more positive outcomes than do children who are deaf and born to hearing parents.

Emotional and behavioural disturbance is about half as prevalent among deaf children with deaf parents as among children who are deaf with hearing parents (Stokoe and Battiston, 1975). Children who have deaf parents outperform children with hearing parents on measures of language skills. In school, deaf children of deaf parents consistently perform at a higher level on tests of academic achievement than do deaf children of hearing parents.

The reasons that underlie the differences between children who are deaf who have hearing parents and those who have deaf parents are not difficult to pinpoint, but they are important to understand in light of our upcoming discussions on bilingual-bicultural education and the deaf community. The prominent factors that emerge are:

- Early identification. It is during infancy that children who are born deaf most closely resemble their hearing peers. Deaf infants follow the normal patterns of visual exploration and motor development. They also cry and coo and vocalize like other children during the first few months of life. Not until they reach the babbling stage at about six months do their sound patterns become differentiated from those of hearing infants. By the age of ten months, infants who are deaf show a significant decrease in babbling behaviour. This happens because they cannot hear their own babbling and do not receive reinforcement from the speech of adults.

  For a child of parents who are deaf, hearing loss may be anticipated and identified in the first months of life, allowing early language input and intervention to begin. In contrast, it is typical of children of hearing parents to be identified much later—between 17.5 and 25 months—and much prime intervention time is lost.
- Acceptance of the diagnosis. Deaf children who have deaf parents are born into families that already have experience with deafness. Parents who are deaf understand the child's condition and seem better able to cope with any negative feelings that accompany diagnosis.
- Language use. Parents who are deaf are fluent in sign language, so their children usually experience language acquisition and family interaction earlier and at a greater rate than do other children who are deaf. Mothers who are deaf help their infants acquire language in the same way that hearing mothers do with hearing babies. Deaf mothers of infants who are deaf seem to sign more slowly and modify the location of the sign so that the child can see it more easily, and use more repetitions (Erting, Prezioso, and Hynes, 1990).
- The deaf community. Children who are deaf with parents who are also deaf have closer exposure to other deaf people and to the discrete culture of the deaf community. Such cultural awareness and identity enhances the self-concept of children who are deaf (Innes, 1994). Identity with deafness seems important because anecdotal reports suggest that some students do not realize that they will be deaf adults when they grow up because they have never seen a deaf adult. One study found that one-third of young people had, as children, thought they would grow up to be hearing (Gregory, Bishop, and Sheldon, 1995).
- Co-occurring disabilities. Deafness in families is genetic and children rarely suffer additional injuries to the nervous system before birth. As a result, their incidence of secondary disabilities is no greater than for the population at large.

Hearing Children of Deaf Parents

We must also give a passing glance at another subgroup with potential language, speech, and social and emotional difficulties. Although not hearing impaired, the communication and emotional prognosis for hearing children of deaf parents can be problematic.

Research in this area is fairly scattered. One study (Schiff and Ventry, 1976) of fifty-two hearing children of parents who were deaf found that only twenty-three had developed normal language. The other twenty-nine showed speech and language problems, including defective articulation, deviant stress and intonational patterns, and fluency disorders, problems that did not disappear after the children entered school. In another study of six preschool hearing children of deaf parents (Murphy and Slorach, 1983), three of the children showed delayed and deviant language development and three had other language problems. Finally, a British study (Flaxbeard and Toomey, 1987) of ten hearing children of parents who were deaf found that the children exhibited conversational difficulties, memory problems, reasoning difficulties, and poor language comprehension.

Socially, young children may take on unexpected burdens simply because of the parents' deafness. Hearing children feel a strong responsibility to help parents make decisions, to explain deafness to hearing people, and to be an advocate for the deaf community.

Cultural Differences

Cultural and linguistic differences take on a somewhat different meaning when applied to persons who are deaf. As linguistic differences are the major effect of deafness, it is not speaking a language different from the majority that may be difficult in school, but having no language at all.

The notion of cultural difference must also be expanded. On the one hand, there are many students who are recent immigrants or refugees and are also hearing impaired. These children have their own unique set of problems (see Akamatsu and Cole, 2000).

On the other hand, we must look to the deafness as culture. A number of times we have mentioned the **deaf community**. This term refers those hearing-impaired people who share common attitudes, experiences, language, and participate in social institutions run for and by the deaf. (Note that in this context *deaf community* and *the deaf* are acceptable descriptors.)

deaf community

Obviously, like any other group, the deaf population is extremely heterogeneous, comprising people of varying levels of auditory capabilities, linguistic skills, cognitive abilities, social skills, and emotional development, as well as varying in ethnicity, socio-economic status, geographic location, and so on. This disparate and heterogeneous population has one defining commonality—people in it use sign language and so find that their lives are defined by unique experiences and communication modalities that differ from those of an oral-language-based hearing society.

As a discrete group with a common language binding it, the deaf community in Canada can be traced back to the formation of the first residential schools in the mid-19th century. Today the deaf community is growing both in numbers and in political and social activism.

In the past few decades, the fertility of deaf adults has rapidly approached that of the general population. Moreover, a deaf person typically marries someone else with a hearing loss. Today, in-group marriages are estimated at between 86 and 90 percent of all marriages involving deaf people (see Reagan, 1988).

Socially and politically, many deaf adults describe themselves as a cultural or minority group and use the term *deaf* to designate cultural group membership (Brubacher, 1994; Dolnick, 1993) in the same way that others use, say, Canadian or Italian. This cultural view of the deaf community "views deaf people as a group that shares a common language and a common means of communication" (Stewart and Akamatsu, 1988, p. 238). It provides a huge variety of organizations at the local, regional, national, and global levels. Choices include such general categories as religion and sports as well as more specialized groups such as deaf rock climbers and the International World Games for the Deaf.

Deafness as culture is also an overarching concern in educational placement and curriculum. The deaf community promotes segregated schooling, preferably in residential settings. As the child who is deaf is a member of a unique linguistic and cultural group, "Forcing deaf children to be part of the hearing world denies them the right to themselves" (Elliott, 1993, p. 11).

ASSESSMENT OF CHILDREN WHO HAVE HEARING IMPAIRMENTS

Measuring a hearing impairment and its effects is quite complicated because measurement must incorporate the physical, psychological, and educational aspects as well as the impact on speech and language acquisition and development (see the appendix table, Tools for Assessment).

To assess the various domains, a number of professionals and paraprofessionals need to be involved—physicians, audiologists, psychologists, educators, and speech and language therapists.

Measurement of Hearing Loss

audiology

Audiology is the science of detecting and correcting hearing impairment. The major purposes of audiology are to assist in medical diagnosis; to provide an overall assessment of hearing in order to ascertain the need for supportive services; and to detect changes in hearing that may have resulted from exposure to hazards. Audiologists use many sophisticated methods to assess hearing. In general, three major categories of hearing tests are used—pure tone audiometry, speech audiometry, and specialized tests for very young and difficult-to-assess children.

Pure Tone Audiometry

Almost all children with severe or profound hearing losses will be identified well before the school years. Detection of those with milder losses is far more problematic. It is estimated that 80 percent of children with hearing impairments are identified through informal means, usually observations by parents or teachers (Barringer, Strong, Blair, Clark, and Watkins, 1993). Table 9-4 outlines some of the behaviours that suggest mild hearing loss. Teachers and parents should be alert to these behaviours and send children with suspected problems for audiological evaluation.

School systems provide screening at set intervals. The most common screening procedure is the sweep test, a procedure that uses pure tone audiometry to establish an individual's threshold of hearing at different frequencies. The **threshold of hearing** is the level at which a person first detects a sound.

threshold of hearing

A sweep test uses a portable audiometer to present tones at 20 to 25 dB across a range of frequencies. Children who show problems at the screening level are then referred for in-depth audiological testing.

Screening may not identify all children requiring in-depth assessment. School screening has been known to fail to identify at least half of children with otitis media (Gdowski, Sanger,

Table 9-4 Possible signs of mild hearing loss in children

- There appears to be a physical problem associated with the ears, such as buzzing, earaches, discharge, or frequent colds and sore throats.
- The child has poor articulation, particularly missing some of the consonant sounds.
- The child cocks the head or turns the body toward the speaker in an obvious effort to hear more accurately.
- The child has more than usual trouble in following directions.
- The child frequently asks for information to be repeated.
- The child appears to be inattentive when spoken to in a normal voice.
- The child speaks or sings too loudly or too softly.
- The child talks too much and appears not to want to relinquish control of the conversation.
- The child is withdrawn and unwilling to mingle with classmates or neighbours.
- The child gives incorrect answers to simple questions.
- The child is functioning below potential ability in school.
- The child is becoming a behaviour problem at school or at home.

and Decker, 1986), and especially children who suffer a recurrent "on-again, off-again" otitis media and therefore present inconsistent responses. Screening may also fail to detect students with high-frequency losses.

When an individual requires in-depth pure tone testing, the procedure is relatively simple. The audiologist presents a variety of tones at levels from 0 to 110 dB across a range of frequencies, usually 125 Hz to 8000 Hz, testing each ear individually. The person being tested responds by raising a hand when a sound is detected, and the data for each ear are plotted on a chart of hearing called an *audiogram.* Figure 9-3 shows an audiogram on which is plotted the average loss (both ears) of three individuals.

Person A has a flat loss of about 70 dB. This person begins to detect sounds only at the level of 70 dB and would be regarded as moderately hearing impaired. Because of the amount of residual hearing, especially across the speech range (500 to 2000 Hz), a hearing aid would help this individual.

Person B suffers a hearing loss described as a "ski slope loss" because of its shape. This person, with little usable hearing above 90 dB and none across the speech range, would be categorized as profoundly deaf. Person C displays a saucer-shaped audiological pattern and is also profoundly deaf but with some hearing at the very low and very high frequencies.

Speech Audiometry

Speech audiometry is designed to assess an individual's ability to detect and understand speech. The speech detection threshold refers to the intensity level at which a person can hear, but not necessarily understand, speech. Much more important is the **speech reception threshold** (SRT), the level at which an individual actually understands speech.

speech reception threshold

To ascertain the speech reception threshold, the tester presents the person with a list of two-syllable words (called *spondees*) that have equal stress on each syllable—*baseball* or *ice*

Figure 9-3
Audiogram

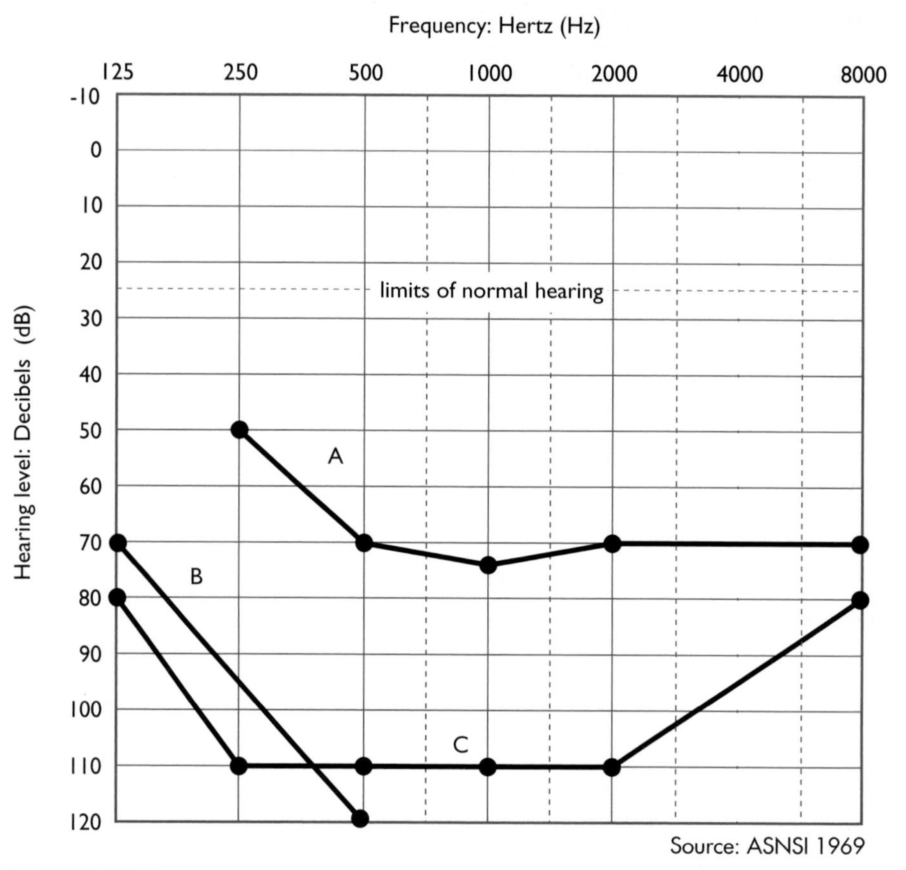

cream are examples. Each ear is tested separately, and the level at which half of the words are understood is the speech reception threshold.

Tests for Young Children

Pure tone audiometry can be used only with people who understand what is expected of them; that is, who can discriminate among sounds of different intensity and tone and then communicate their discriminations. For a child under the age of about four, the process is too complicated.

So that hearing impairment can be identified as early as possible, a number of special tests have been devised for very young children. Special tests have also been developed for those whose disabilities do not suit standard pure tone audiometric testing. The two most common forms of specialized hearing tests are *electrophysiological* and *behavioural.* (See also Chapter 14.)

Electrophysiological Assessment

Electrophysiological procedures include electroencephalography-evoked (EEG) response audiometry (also known as *auditory brainstem evoked response*) and impedance audiometry. EEG assessment measures responses to auditory stimuli but requires no active participation on the part of the child. Electrodes are attached to the scalp, sounds of varying intensities are delivered through an earphone placed over the infant's ear, and brainwave activity is recorded. By evaluating the brainwave patterns, an estimate of hearing, or hearing loss, can be made. Note that although these tests help to detect whether a child in fact hears sound, they do not provide information about the child's ability to interpret the auditory stimuli.

Acoustic impedance audiometry assesses conductive hearing losses by measuring the movement of the ear drum and middle ear muscles and bones in response to auditory stimulation. The audiologist can detect fluid in the middle ear, a sign of otitis media, for example.

Behavioural Assessment

Behavioural testing includes observation of behaviour, reflex audiometry, and play audiometry. Observations focus on the orienting responses infants show when they turn their heads toward the source of a sound. Diagnosticians can gain a crude measure of hearing status by observing infants' reactions to loud sounds.

Under the age of five or six months, infants also display reflexive behaviours that are useful for testing hearing (reflex audiometry). A startle movement, a reflex that affects face, arms, trunk, legs, and eyes, is present at birth and elicited by loud sound.

Play audiometry is used with children over two years of age. It involves an audiometer and a game in which the child performs an activity in response to the sound. The child may respond by building a stacking toy, dropping blocks into a box, or putting pieces into a puzzle.

Psycho-educational Assessment

A range of measures is needed to assess the psychological and educational functioning of students with hearing impairments. The one commonality among tools and procedures is that they circumvent the effects of the hearing loss and match the linguistic deficits of the child.

Non-verbal tests are the most appropriate for children who are deaf. The most widely used IQ test is the Performance Scale of the Wechsler Intelligence Scale for Children (WISC-III), which is believed to yield fairly valid IQ scores for children who are deaf aged nine to sixteen. The Verbal Scale is usually omitted from the battery, and an IQ score is calculated on the basis of the Performance Scale alone to assess cognitive functioning.

Assessment of the English skills of students who are deaf has a large literature. A sample of critical educational measures for assessing speech and language are shown in the appendix table, Tools for Assessment. Assessment tools for American Sign Language (ASL) are being developed, but currently there are no widely available standards or norms against which to measure the development of ASL (Singleton, Supalla, Lotchfield, and Schley, 1998).

INTERVENTION WITH CHILDREN WHO HAVE HEARING IMPAIRMENTS

Children and youth who are deaf or hard of hearing require considerable intervention to provide health care, rehabilitation, therapy, and education. Generally, intervention involves two major components. The first is medical intervention to try to correct the physical causes of hearing loss and to provide amplification. The second form of intervention focuses on minimizing the educational and psychological consequences of hearing loss through counselling, special education, and support services.

Medical Intervention

Most conductive hearing losses can be medically corrected. Chronic otitis media is alleviated by antibiotics in the early stages or by a myringotomy, a procedure in which ventilating tubes are placed in the eardrums to provide proper ventilation between the middle ear cavity and the outside environment via the external ear canal.

Otological surgeons can free the stapes in the case of otosclerosis; surgically reconstruct the middle ear (tympanoplasty); rebuild the three tiny bones of the ossicular chain; repair, shift, or rebuild an ear drum; and construct new membranous windows into the inner ear. When infants are born with an atresia, surgeons make a bony canal into the middle ear.

Ménière's disease is treated with diet and varying surgical approaches. Surgery exposes or decompresses the endolymphatic sac from its surrounding bony structures behind the mastoid bone and a shunt then drains excess fluid.

Cochlear Implants

There are no prosthetic devices capable of restoring normal hearing. However, some lost function of the cochlea may be replaced through the use of a prosthesis called a cochlear implant.

Cochlear implants were developed in Australia in the late 1970s. They have become much more sophisticated since then, and an enormous range of rehabilitative devices are now available. There are intra- and extra-cochlear implants, and single and multichannel systems used with pre- and post-lingually deafened individuals. In 1993, implants were approved by the Ontario Ministry of Health.

The term *cochlear implant* is somewhat misleading, as it implies surgical reconstruction of the cochlea by repair or transplant. In actual fact, the implant is a device that converts sound into mild electrical currents to stimulate the cochlea and allow for some recognition of speech. In persons with profound deafness, the specialized hair cells in the cochlea that stimulate the nerve endings no longer work. In essence, the cochlear implants replace the function of these hair cells.

All cochlear implants consist of basically the same components and work essentially the same way. The device picks up sound, creates the sensation of sound in the inner ear, then sends it to the brain for interpretation. Specifically, each implant has a microphone that looks like a behind-the-ear hearing aid and is connected to the speech processor and transmitter by two cords. An encoder (speech processor), which is a tiny computer that changes the sound to electrical impulses, is worn on the person's belt. It looks like a pocket calculator and weighs about 3.5 ounces. There is an electrode driver that transmits the signal to the electrode either across the skin or by direct connection, and an electrode that transmits the impulses to the nerve through the cochlea. The entire process takes milliseconds; there is virtually no delay between the presence of sound and its coding by the processor and interpretation by the brain.

Implants provide more and better sound cues to the person than do hearing aids. Individuals who prior to the implantation relied entirely on speech reading can carry on a conversation more adequately because they can hear at least some of their own voice and are able to recognize the words of others.

In general, these devices are designed for persons over age two with a profound loss in both ears, who receive little or no benefit from hearing aids or vibrotactile devices, and who are motivated to persevere through the necessary auditory training (Clark, Tong and Patrick, 1990). Not all people who are deaf are suitable recipients for implants; those with tinnitus, for example, may actually suffer an increase of head noises with the devices. Nevertheless, for many people who are hearing impaired, cochlear implants bring speech into a world that was previously silent.

Technical Aids

In the classroom, it is seldom necessary to find special materials or equipment for the child with a hearing impairment other than their particular prosthetic equipment. Such equipment involves amplification or tactile methods to improve auditory comprehension. In addition, computers and information technology hold promise for the education of students who are hearing impaired.

Amplification

Hearing aids are primarily sound amplifiers. As such, they can help children to develop residual hearing, to improve the audition of their own voices, to use speech in a purposeful way, and to expand their vocabulary and language abilities. Even for those who are profoundly deaf, the few distorted fragments of amplified sound that reach them may assist in the development of speech and language.

Aids differ in size, cost, and efficiency. While the various types can provide equivalent amounts of amplification (technically called *gain*), certain aids are designed to provide more amplification than others. This means that there can be a close match between the type of aid and the user's unique needs.

Massive research has brought new digital hearing aids that operate in a fundamentally different way from the previous generation of analog hearing aids. Digital aids operate in ways similar to a mini-computer. The sound waves that strike the microphone are digitally encoded, processed, and manipulated with each manipulation capable of producing a different acoustical output; for example, different amounts of amplification and different degrees at different speech frequencies.

Despite the proven effectiveness of hearing aids, only one hearing impaired person in three or four actually owns and uses one (see Schein, 1994). A review of the literature (Stone and Adam, 1986) indicates that most children who are hearing impaired are wearing inadequate aids. The most important of the many reasons for non-use and incorrect use are outlined below.

- Many children resist wearing a hearing aid because the awkwardness of the strange appliance outweighs their awareness of any benefits. After children are fitted with hearing aids, they still have much work to do before they can use or understand speech. They must learn to interpret the sounds they hear and to duplicate the sounds of speech.
- There is a widespread belief that persons with sensorineural hearing losses cannot benefit at all from an aid.
- Another belief holds that hearing aids are not appropriate for persons with mild hearing losses. However, some mild losses can be alleviated successfully with amplification.

- Some people cannot get used to the noise of the hearing aid. Amplification is indiscriminate, and hearing aids pick up extraneous reverberations. This can distort what is heard and may flood the individual with disconcerting auditory stimulation.
- Some people refuse to wear a hearing aid out of vanity or self-consciousness.
- Economic considerations are a factor. Not only are the aids expensive, but batteries, ear moulds, and receivers need to be replaced periodically.

In classroom situations, group amplification systems may be used. The FM (frequency modulation) system is the most popular. With a classroom FM system, the carrier wave is transmitted through the air via frequency modulation from a teacher-worn microphone to a student-worn FM receiver. FM transmission allows students who are hearing impaired to hear the teacher clearly from any location in the classroom, whereas an individual hearing aid has a restricted range of about six feet.

One of the biggest difficulties facing all hearing aid users is background noise. When the signal-to-noise ratio is poor, an auditory signal may be audible to the child who is hearing impaired but may not be intelligible. With direct audio input systems, an FM system is joined to the child's individual aid. This means that the hearing aid can be adapted for a wide variety of difficult listening situations and can cut out at least some extraneous classroom noise.

Vibrotactile Devices

Vibrotactile devices are tactile aids that help individuals to feel sound using the tactile/kinesthetic senses. They aid in speech development by vibrating to sounds so that users can feel and imitate the differences in duration, intensity, rhythmic pattern, pitch, and voice control. They also differentiate look-alike consonants, such as p/b/m, t/d/n/l/, and sh/ch. Children hold the device in their hands or strap it to an arm.

Telephone Devices

The telecommunication device (TTD), sometimes called the TTY (tele-typewriter), offers persons who are deaf direct telephone access to each other and to community services. Instead of listening to a message and responding orally, the person with a TTD communicates by reading and typing. Typed messages are changed to electrical signals and then translated back to print on a TTD at the other end of the telephone connection.

Household Devices

To aid deaf adults in the home, a number of tools have been developed. These devices visually signal through flashing lights when, for example, the baby is crying, the telephone or doorbell is ringing, or a wake-up alarm, smoke alarm, or fire alarm has sounded.

Captioned Films

Captioned television shows have been a boon to the hearing-impaired population. Closed captioning is an electronic process that converts the audio portion of a television program into written words that appear at the bottom of the TV screen. In some programs, captioned messages also describe sound effects or off-screen nuances that are vital to the storyline (Hysert, 1993a).

Educational Intervention

Students who are seriously hearing impaired may require extensive curricular modifications to compensate for the educational handicaps that accompany severe and profound hearing impairments. Modification of educational objectives may also be necessary to address the child's actual functional level rather than chronological age or grade placement.

Service Delivery Models

Severe and profound hearing impairment equates with potential classroom communication difficulties, so much so that placement decisions are fraught with both practical and political problems. Political overtones arise because many deaf people and professionals working with students who are deaf do not accept educational integration as it is now conceptualized. They describe the integration of students who are deaf as "forced assimilation"—an "unnatural attempt to make deaf persons hearing" (Elliott, 1993, p. 11). Advocates for students who are deaf, such as the Commission on the Education of the Deaf, have issued statements supporting a strong separate special education system (Fuchs and Fuchs, 1994).

On a more practical level, placement decisions must address the complex, difficult, and often frustrating task of including students with severe hearing losses, especially if adequate communication and social supports are lacking (see Jones, Clark, and Soltz, 1997). In the matter of supports, or lack of them, an American manual providing guidelines for services states clearly that "[D]irect instruction from a certified teacher of children who are deaf, who is competent and adept at the child's language or communication mode, is preferable to placement in an environment where communication depends upon the use of interpreters and other support personnel" (Easterbrooks and Baker-Hawkins, 1995, p. 54).

It is not unusual for teachers to express anxiety about working with a student with hearing impairment in a regular setting (Chorost, 1988). Experts contend that "Deafness is arguably, ..., the most difficult for teachers to deal with, since in its severe form it is not so much the deprivation of sound but the deprivation of language which creates a barrier to learning" (Palmer and Sellars, 1993, p. 37).

Many general classroom teachers are not very knowledgeable about hearing impairment and related considerations. Rittenhouse (1987) found that only about 25 percent of the high school teachers he sampled felt that the information made available to them equipped them adequately for the task of developing IEPs. In Nova Scotia and New Brunswick, surveys revealed that the primary areas of concern for teachers are information on hearing loss in general, techniques for attaining comprehension, expectation levels for students with hearing impairment, effective techniques for teaching and managing behaviour, and the effective use of amplification (French and MacDonnell, 1985).

In addition, no clear picture of inclusion for students with severe hearing losses has yet emerged. University of Alberta researcher Michael Rodda and his colleagues (1986) found that only about 10 to 15 percent of all deaf children can be successfully included.

Taking note of the above, there must be various educational settings available for students with hearing impairments. In general, the educational setting for a specific child is determined by linguistic needs; the severity of the loss and the potential for using residual hearing with or without amplification; academic level; social, emotional, and cultural needs, including appropriate interaction and communication with peers; and communication needs, including the child and the family's preferred mode of communication (Marschark, 1993).

In 1995, approximately one-third of students who were deaf attended residential schools, the most traditional setting. The other two-thirds of students with severe hearing impairments attended programs in residential/day schools or day classes located in regular schools ("Children with communication ...," 1995).

Residential/Day Schools

Supporters of segregated settings marshal arguments that centre on deafness defined as a distinct culture—a deaf community. They argue that deaf persons "constitute a legitimate cultural and linguistic group and that they are entitled to educational programs which take this into account" (Reagan, 1988, p. 1). Viewing themselves in this fashion, people who are deaf tend to see the residential schools as a cultural component vital in creating group solidarity.

In specialized settings, multiple social supports are in place. Graduates of residential high school programs have described their social experiences more positively than graduates of mainstream programs.

Special Classes

Self-contained special classes, located within regular elementary or secondary schools, offer separate programs for students who are hearing impaired. Teachers are especially trained.

General Classroom

Many people view inclusion in the general classroom as a viable option on the continuum of services available for students with severe hearing losses. They disagree with schools for the deaf and special class placements, tending to equate them with settings for mainstreaming failures, not as appropriate settings catering to the individual needs of many students who are deaf. They argue that regular classroom placement exposes students to excellent language models and that there they must learn to use speech in order to interact with teachers and peers. In the psycho-social domain, students' perceptions of themselves are based on comparisons with hearing peers, preparing them to cope in an integrated society. Offering support are studies that find that integrated students who are hearing impaired are more successful academically than those not integrated (Bunch, 1994; Holt, 1994).

The social domain is somewhat more problematic, although the findings on whether or not inadequate communication affects peer interaction are equivocal. For example, Aplin (1987), who studied forty-two children aged seven to sixteen with sensorineural losses attending ordinary schools, found them significantly better adjusted than their peers in special schools. Other research leans toward the conclusion that social integration may be more difficult to achieve than academic inclusion. In general education, students may be isolated, lonely, or socially rejected. Students who are hearing impaired demonstrate only minimal self-initiated interaction with normally hearing teachers and peers; many are permanent outsiders and never really become an integral part of their mainstream classes (e.g., Jaussi, 1991). Since there may be only one hearing impaired student in a school, students are frequently on their own when trying to initiate or sustain friendships with peers (Foster, 1988). This stretches right across the school years and into college. (See the case study on Christopher in Chapter 16.)

Early intervention with support for social interactions may circumvent some difficulties. As you can see from the case study that continues to discuss Steven, he began school in a regular preschool program with an adapted IEP. In transitioning to the general school system, he remained with his peers and was provided support through an IEP, an interpreter, and additional assistance in the areas of speech and language.

Case Study

Steven (continued)

Steven's preschool teachers set him several long-range goals. These included the introduction of simple nouns, verbs, and colour signs; some awareness of gross sounds through play activities and listening exercises; and increased vocalizations. They also structured many activities to expose Steven to language, such as story telling, "dress up," and art and craft activities. Steven's teachers showed his parents how to stimulate home communication and use home-making activities to present language. Steven's parents were encouraged to learn more sign language so that they could communicate more effectively with their son.

When Steven reached age five, his mother went to enroll him in the local kindergarten. The principal listened to her explanation of Steven's problem and agreed to place the child in a regular classroom for kindergarten, although no special aide or interpreter would be available. The principal did not seem to think this would be a problem, as she said that "Socialization was far more important than learning at this age, especially for a handicapped child." How surprised she was when Steven's mother explained carefully that she was placing Steven in the regular classroom not for socialization but for learning. She expected him to learn everything that other children did, and she also expected the school to provide assistance to ensure that he could.

What finally happened was that Steven remained in nursery school for the kindergarten year and then went to the local school for grade one. He was provided with an interpreter in the classroom. The home visiting teacher and later an itinerant teacher collaborated with the regular classroom teacher on his IEP, although the teacher was somewhat reluctant to make special adaptations. She felt that having an interpreter in the classroom was the only change that would be needed for Steven.

Once Steven's needs were explained to the classroom teacher, she did meet with the school's special education consultant, the interpreter, and Steven's mother to plan an IEP (an extract is shown below). While the curriculum would parallel that taught to the other children, there would be a greater stress on speech and language using a natural approach. For example, Steven would receive extra classroom assistance in learning new vocabulary, and would be provided with many opportunities to interact in small groups with other children. Reading would be taught through a whole-word method rather than through a phonics approach, although Steven would participate in all of the many literacy activities offered, with an emphasis on storytelling and language experience approaches.

A speech therapist would work with Steven weekly and, as new sounds or words were acquired, the teacher would stress these in classroom activities and reinforce correct usage. As well, the ongoing assessment of communication development would be a feature of Steven's program.

During the IEP planning process, the special education consultant provided the teacher with many teaching tips and techniques. Throughout the school year, the two teachers collaborated closely. The teacher also used a few signs, such as "Good morning," and "Nice work, Steven."

EXTRACT FROM STEVEN'S IEP

Child Steven
Teacher Ms. Smith
School Sunny Heights
Grade 1
Birthdate June 12, 1995

Medical Information

Audiological assessment shows Steven to have a bilateral hearing loss in the severe to profound range.

Adaptive Equipment

- Individual hearing aid
- Special seating—middle row, front
- Interpreter

Areas of Need

Speech training, auditory training, language, and communication (both oral and sign mode).

Areas of Strength

Normal cognitive functioning, good motivation, strong social skills.

Assessment/Performance Information

Date October 1999
Test Informal observations
Result Restricted receptive and expressive language; limited vocabulary; little speech use with many deviations. Uses sign for most communication; also speech reads to some extent

Date October 1999
Test Test of Early Developing Reading Ability (TERA)
Result Very basic literacy skills; understands the use of print and conventions of language such as reading from left to right. Barely started on formal reading. Only a small sight vocabulary—logos, own name, McDonald's, and so on.

Date October 1999
Test WISC-III, Performance Scale only
Result Normal cognitive functioning.

Persons Responsible

Teacher, Ms. Smith: Stress oral skills; include in all activities; work with interpreter. Reinforce therapy sessions.
Interpreter, peer tutors, speech therapist (weekly): Auditory training, speech acquisition, language, sign vocabulary.

Long-Range Goals

- Steven's program will target speech and language development within the regular curriculum and with specialized assistance from an interpreter to assist classroom interactions. In the classroom, the teacher will stimulate language and communication skills through promoting interaction with other children; incidental teaching that includes expansions, paraphrasing, and open-ended questions (see Chapter 4); specific language intervention such as stressing therapy goals and correction where appropriate; and group learning.
- A second long-term goal is to begin to teach literacy skills. The teacher will use a word-recognition approach to circumvent the problems caused by the hearing loss, joined to the more holistic, experience-based method that is in place for other class members.

Short-Term Objectives

- When presented with words on flashcards, Steven will say the word, say it in a sentence, and write the word.
- Steven will read short sentences containing new words.

- Steven will write/draw in his journal daily with encouragement to use new reading words.
- Steven will be placed in small learning groups as much as possible for socialization and language development.
- To further promote peer interaction, peer tutoring (twenty minutes daily) will be arranged for oral reading. Cross-age tutoring will also be arranged.

Itinerant Programs

When students are included in regular classrooms they should be supported by interpreters, resource rooms, or itinerant teachers. Resource rooms offer hearing-impaired students from regular classes a chance to obtain tutorial assistance in a special class from a trained teacher of the deaf.

Itinerant programs provide specialist teachers who offer tutorial assistance to hearing-impaired students who are included into regular classrooms. The itinerant teacher assists the child and the regular classroom teacher, and also acts as a facilitator or liaison with other support personnel, parents, and school administrators.

Educational Interpreters

The great majority of classroom teachers do not have proficiency in sign language and finger spelling. Enabling students to attend regular classes requires special assistance, and teachers may have to work with an interpreter in the classroom.

The interpreter, sometimes called a *transliterator*, is a normally hearing person who facilitates the transmission of information between individuals who do not communicate with a common language or code. Educational interpreters translate directions, content, and assignments presented orally by teachers, relay the comments of peers, and share the student's responses and questions with teachers and peers (Salend and Longo, 1994).

ASL has its own semantic and syntactic structure. This deaf sign-language user is talking about his work. Literally, the signs translate as (a) boring, (b) work, (c) a lot.

There are different types of interpreters. A *signed system interpreter* makes speech visible and, in turn, converts manual communication to speech. The *interpreter* translates spoken language directed toward a student with a hearing impairment into a signed system such as ASL or a school-based system. An *oral interpreter* facilitates the student's understanding of verbal messages by subtly mouthing the complete verbal message or its paraphrased equivalent.

There is little extant research on educational interpreting in kindergarten to grade twelve classrooms. We do know two things. First, interpreters can function most effectively as an instructional resource in the classroom only when they carefully coordinate their efforts with teachers (Salend and Longo, 1994). Second, the tasks undertaken by interpreters are complex. For example, the interpreter must not be controlling, must know when to talk and when to pause, must sustain the child's attention, must explain and clarify concepts, and must prompt on-task behaviour (see Monkman and Baskind, 1998).

In general, the interpreter should be seated in a glare-free, well-lit location with a solid coloured background free of visual and auditory distractions. Interpreters should sit in front of the student without blocking the view of the chalkboard, overhead projector, or the teacher. However, the positioning of the interpreter depends on the nature of the instructional activity. When the teacher is using a lecture format, it may be better for the interpreter to stand or sit to the side and slightly in front of the teacher, with the student's desk located three to five feet away. In a one-to-one instruction setting, the interpreter should be placed facing the student from a distance of about four to six feet. During group activities, the group should be seated in a circular fashion with the interpreter located across from the student (Salend and Longo, 1994).

Educational Approaches

Authenticated evidence of the education of students with deafness can be traced back to the late 16th century. Almost since that time, teachers divided themselves into two irreconcilable camps. The "oralists" viewed deafness as a human handicap to be overcome through the development of speech and speech reading. The "manualists" argued that deafness is a human difference that requires its own language, the language of signs.

Rampant conflicts in expert opinion about the use of sense modalities in the education of hearing-impaired children still exist. The stances are not as irreconcilable as they once were, but educators still hold quite different philosophies about the most effective means to impart language, promote academic development, and whether or not to stress speech.

Communication mode is the fulcrum. Many modes developed over the centuries and are still possible. The most important are described below, moving from unisensory to multi-sensory approaches.

acoupedic

- *Acoupedic methods.* The **acoupedic** (a unisensory approach) is an oral method that aims to develop intelligible speech through the maximum development of listening skills. It is founded on the belief that children in the first year of life have hearing abilities that, if activated sufficiently, play a functional role in determining speech development. On the other hand, auditory deprivation during this time diminishes these abilities and obstructs speech development. Evidence suggests that the process is irreversible (Brokx, 1987).

  The acoupedic approach requires early intervention, early amplification, a normal listening environment, the use of auditory feedback mechanisms, and the preparation of parents to act as first models of communication (Pollack, 1980). This method excludes all visual clues, such as speech reading, thus the term *unisensory*. It encourages a child to use residual hearing to the greatest extent possible.

- *The oral/aural method.* Like other processes in special education, the oral/aural method used with children who are deaf today evolved through a number of stages. Beginning about 1867, teachers employed a pure oral method that placed stress on speech reading and writing but forbade the natural gestures that we all use as part of our communication.

  The pure oral method evolved into the oral method of speech and speech reading along with amplification through hearing aids, which were invented in the 1920s. This method downplayed the importance of writing and permitted natural gestures. From this grew the current oral method, more correctly called the oral/aural approach. It places stress on speech and speech reading and uses amplification and auditory training as integral components of speech and language development.

  speech reading

  Lip reading or **speech reading** is the skill of understanding speech through watching the lips and face. The latter term is more accurate because facial expressions impart to spoken words a whole spectrum of feelings, attitudes, and visual clues.

  Speech reading is a difficult skill to acquire because only about 30 percent of English sounds are visible on the lips (Stewart, 1984). For example, the colour words *red*, *white*, and *green* all look pretty much the same on the lips, as do *bat* and *mat*, *manic* and *panic*, and *measure* and *pleasure*. The difficulties with such look-alike words are almost insurmountable. Imagine a child trying to distinguish between "a red bat" and "a green mat." When words look the same, speech readers must anticipate them and fill them in, but this takes sophisticated language knowledge—an area of deficit for most people who are deaf. To add to the problems, the average speaker makes about thirteen articulatory movements a second during normal conversation. The average observer, however, can only visually record eight or nine movements a second (Sanders, 1971).

- *Cued speech.* Originated by Orin Cornett at Gallaudet University, cued speech is another primarily oral method of communication, though rarely used today. The system uses eight hand configurations and four hand positions to supplement the visible manifestations of speech. The hand cues add information to the speech reading process so that all single sounds can be identified by the child with a hearing impairment.

- *The Rochester Method.* This method was named after the Rochester School for the Deaf in New York, where it was first used in 1877. It employs finger spelling in conjunction with speech, speech reading, and amplification. Ontario schools experimented with this method in the 1980s but today there are no programs that use finger spelling alone (Luetke-Stahlman and Luckner, 1991).

- *Total Communication.* By the early 1970s the benefits of using some manual components in the education of children with hearing impairments were apparent, and many educators turned from an oral emphasis to one that stresses a combination of methods. Total Communication uses speech, speech reading, and amplification, along with a school-based manual system.

  The school-based manual systems of Total Communication are a marriage of necessity between American Sign Language (ASL) and English. In systems such as *Signing Essential English* and *Manual English*, signs are presented in the order of English and with correct morphological structures.

- *American Sign Language.* Unlike school-based manual systems, American Sign Language (ASL or Ameslan) does not follow the semantic and syntactic structure of spoken language. ASL has its own rule-governed syntactic system, a rich system of morphological processes, and a large lexicon of vocabulary.

  Since the 1960s there has been a veritable explosion of research into ASL from the fields of linguistics, psycholinguistics, and socio-linguistics. This has led to a recognition that ASL is a true language; it is not related to or in any way derived from spoken English but is more accurately viewed as a distinct and genetically unrelated language (Reagan, 1988).

  ASL is founded on a combination of symbolic gestures produced by the shape, the location, and the movement of the hands. Many of the signs symbolize concepts rather than individual words. Most have an arbitrary tie to the referent. Some are iconic in that they represent an object or action for which they stand; some are *metonymic*—they take a relatively small aspect or feature of the referent and use that as the basis of the sign. For example, the sign for *dog* is snapping the fingers. ASL has no signs for the grammatical markers, such as -ed or -ing endings, that express verb tense and condition. Rather, users depend on facial expressions and body language to replace voice intonation and enhance meaning (Meadow, 1980).

  Deaf people see ASL as their natural mode of expression and show great attachment to their "beloved language" (Schein, 1989, p. 29). In 1988 Manitoba recognized ASL as a heritage language of the deaf; Alberta followed in 1990.

  Although sign language is typically associated with people who are deaf, some has crept into everyday usage. For example, the football huddle was invented by a deaf player in the 1890s. Similarly, a deaf athlete was responsible for the ball and strike hand signals used in baseball. These were devised in 1888 by a deaf baseball player in Washington (Pirro, 1993).

  Sign systems around the world essentially evolved from the sign language systemized by de l'Épée in France in the mid-1700s. However, these systems are no longer universal. They were quickly adapted to local needs and, like spoken language, each country has its own unique version. In North America ASL is used as an almost generic term. There is also CSL (Canadian Sign Language) and LSQ (Langue de Signes Québécoise).

Bilingual-Bicultural Programs

Among deaf adults, the common mode of communication is American Sign Language (ASL or Ameslan). Because they hold that ASL is the natural language of the deaf community throughout anglophone North America, deaf adults favour bilingualism for all children who are deaf.

Currently, educators and deaf adults are using the terms *bilingual* and *bilingual-bicultural* to refer to educational innovations. These refer to the classroom use of two languages—ASL and English, and to two cultures, deaf culture and hearing culture.

Bilingual-bicultural (bi-bi) education was first developed by researchers Bienvenu and Colombos and explored at Gallaudet University in the 1970s (Swanwick, 1998). The approach is still in its seminal stages and formal curricula for teaching American Sign Language (ASL) are only now being developed. However, an increasing number of schools for the deaf are utilizing the practices of bi-bi education (Easterbrooks, 1999). In the United States, Miller and Moores (2000) present data that concludes that bilingual education is already a reality in 75 percent of the largest programs for deaf students.

In 1993 Ontario became one of the first places to authorize the use of ASL as the language of instruction for students who are deaf. Ontario schools for the deaf now use ASL and written English and allow students opportunities to develop their auditory and speech potential. There are five key principles to Ontario's bilingual/bicultural policy: child-centred education, development of literacy skills in ASL and English, understanding and appreciation of deaf culture, appreciation of cultural diversity, and the development of a positive self-image ("Statement ...," 1993, p. 1).

Bilingual education uses ASL and English. Children use ASL as the major medium of instruction in preschool through the primary grades, with a major focus on sign production and comprehension. Development of English literacy begins in third grade and from then on ASL and English are used fairly equally for instructional purposes (McAnally, Rose, and Quigley, 1987).

Compelling arguments underlie the use of bi-bi educational approaches, the two most important centring around deaf culture and language acquisition. We have already explored deaf culture and the perceptions of the deaf community.

Language studies are varied. They point to an array of meaningful research that clearly shows ASL to be a viable, rich language. Another strand shows that young children without any contact with sign language invent their own "home sign," a kind of communication through pantomime. Home signs progress from simple single signs to real "sentences" (see Mayberry, Woodlinger, Cohen, and Goldwin-Meadow, 1987). This indicates the tenacity of visual manual modes for children who are deaf who develop their own idiosyncratic systems without instruction.

When young children are exposed to the more formal language of ASL, they show an earlier onset of the first sign than would normally be expected for a child's first spoken word, and they typically acquire a sign language vocabulary more rapidly than a hearing child does a spoken one (Bonvillian, Orlansky, and Novack, 1983). First signs tend to emerge earlier than first words. Human infants, whether deaf or hearing, typically initiate their symbolic communication in the gestural mode rather than the vocal mode because control of the hands matures more rapidly than the speech areas of the brain. According to Bay (1975), the visual cortex matures prior to the auditory cortex, facilitating the onset of a visual language system before an oral/aural system.

Finally, a strong base in one language facilitates learning another language. With ASL, children who are deaf come to school with a firm linguistic base. The mastery of a language system is of enormous benefit in problem solving and academic performance.

Many hold reservations about bilingual education for students who are deaf. The major arguments contend that English is crucial for functioning in our society because the language of the majority culture is English, not ASL. Speech is important for students who are deaf in their efforts to negotiate the hearing world and whatever aptitude a child may have to develop speech may be jeopardized by a practice that fosters ASL to the exclusion of speech.

Many other arguments for and cautions about bi-bi education exist. These are outlined in the Debate box.

A Matter of Debate

Bi-Bi Education

Many deaf parents and educators support the idea of bilingual education for students who are deaf. In this approach, very young children first learn sign language and then build English onto this linguistic base. As might be expected, the educational use of ASL is a matter of controversy and confusion, compounded by a lack of definitions of key terms and a scarcity of relevant data (Miller and Moores, 2000).

Arguments for bi-bi education	Cautions about bi-bi education
Language is commonly taken as central to group identity, as its most important marker. The deaf community stresses the role of deaf persons in determining their own destiny and denotes sign language as essential to their identity.	Ninety percent of deaf children are born to hearing parents who are not part of the deaf community.
The similarities between the development of spoken language and sign suggest a biological foundation for language learning. Deaf children are preprogrammed to learn sign.	The language of the majority culture is English, not ASL.
The absence of meaningful, satisfying communication between a child and parent may result in disturbed and fragmented communication, isolation from the family, poor school achievement, and higher rates of psychiatric disturbance. A common mode of communication prevents frustration and assists a child's emotional development.	Hearing parents use spoken language as their primary mode of communication.
Parents and other hearing people involved with a deaf child can learn ASL or a manually coded system.	Kemp (1998) has documented that the learning of ASL is equivalent in difficulty to the learning of any spoken language.
Young deaf children who are taught a conventional sign system, such as ASL or signed English, develop language in sign that is comparable in content and form to the language that young hearing children develop in speech (Goldwin-Meadow and Morford, 1985).	English is crucial for functioning in our society.
The various manual codes are awkward, artificial, do not really map English grammatical components accurately, and have not really	Sign may be more natural for deaf children, but a sign system does not have to be ASL—it can be an English-based system.

Arguments for bi-bi education	Cautions about bi-bi education
improved the academic achievement of students with serious hearing disabilities.	
School-based systems are unpopular with deaf adults, and the claim that they improve English remains unproven (Reagan, 1988).	English should be signed as it is spoken so that the linguistic input results in mastery of English.
When researchers (Schick and Moeller, 1989) examined the expressive English language usage of deaf children using manually coded systems, they found that students produced English to a high degree and that they had internalized the rules of English.	After studying a class of elementary deaf children, Supalla (1992) reported that children instructed through manual codes had basic problems expressing English syntax.
Early manual communication helps rather than hinders the development of oral language.	Whatever aptitude a child may have to develop speech might be jeopardized by a practice that fosters ASL to the exclusion of speech.
Intelligible speech for a deaf person is a mark of success by oralists, not by deaf persons who have other criteria for success.	Children who use signs will not be motivated to learn to speak, use their residual hearing, or speech read.
Deaf adult communication uses ASL as the common language of discourse; English is the written language and the means of access to the hearing world.	Speech is important to deaf students in their efforts to negotiate the hearing world.
Deaf children rarely develop functional oral communication skills, so little is lost by the absence of spoken language in their environments. Only about 17 percent of students taught by oral methods ever become orally fluent, but nearly 75 percent become fluent manually.	Speech proficiency is of undeniable value to the individual who is deaf.
Reviews of research suggest that the use of signs can facilitate literacy but has no effect, either positive or negative, on vocal skills (see Miller and Moores, 2000).	The use of English codes and spoken language offer access to the phonological system, a requirement for literacy.
The use of signing has led to a general improvement in the academic achievement of deaf students (see Miller and Moores, 2000).	There is some minimum threshold level of English proficiency needed before a deaf student can productively read and write (Mayer, 1999).
Deaf parents prefer to see their children intellectually challenged rather than constantly taught language.	The needs of deaf children to learn English must be carefully balanced with their need to develop intellectually.

Arguments for bi-bi education	Cautions about bi-bi education
The mastery of a language system is of enormous benefit to academic performance.	Children who are deaf are often learning to read at the same time they are learning English. ASL may impact on reading because it is structurally different from English and deaf readers must re-code print into their own language.
Deaf adults hold that the bilingual approach is feasible and can be beneficial to students.	The field is not clear on its goals on using ASL in the classroom. We do not know how deaf children learn ASL or how to teach it to them (Bowe, 1992).

Curriculum

In the education of students with hearing impairments, the content is similar to that presented to hearing children. Differences are chiefly a matter of degree. For hearing students, teachers build a mastery of reading and written language upon a child's intact linguistic base of listening and speaking. In contrast, students who are hearing impaired must learn an entire language system. For example, to learn the single word *mother*, a child who is deaf must:

- Learn the concept.
- Learn to say the word.
- Learn to speech read the word.
- Learn the sound of the word through the hearing aid.
- Learn to recognize the printed word.
- Learn to recognize the written word.
- Learn to spell the word.
- Learn to print or write the word.
- Learn to sign the word.
- Learn to read the sign.
- Learn to finger-spell the word.
- Learn to read the finger-spelled word.
- Learn to use the word in context.
- Learn to use the word in different contexts. (After Levine, 1981, p. 100)

As you can see, the process of developing language skills is long, arduous, and often tedious. Two major strategies for the teaching of language have evolved—the formal or grammatical approach and the informal or natural approach. All other methods essentially hark back to these two traditional approaches.

The grammatical approach focuses the student's attention on the structural aspects of language. (See Chapter 4.) Armed with structural information, students learn to generate language deductively. The natural approach (performance) attempts to parallel the ways in which hearing children acquire language. The content and sequence of instruction are determined by the needs of individual children. Experienced learners respond better to the grammatical approach, younger children to the communicative. This is illustrated in the In the Classroom feature that closes Section 5.

Historical Notes

It is to the Abbé Michel Charles de l'Épée (1712–1789), a French cleric, that people who are deaf owe their education and their sign language. In 1760, de l'Épée opened a school for deaf students in his own home in Paris. At the outset, the Abbé knew little about deaf people, their education, their language, or the impact of deafness. But as he studied his pupils closely, de l'Épée noticed that without any teaching or guidance, they evolved a language of simple signs by which to communicate.

Building on these basic signs, he developed a system of what he called "natural signs." Then, to teach his students metaphysical and abstract concepts, as well as the grammar of French, the Abbé also created a system of "methodological signs." With this structure, de l'Épée systemized a language of signs for persons who were deaf.

The first American teacher of students who were deaf, Thomas Hopkins Gallaudet (1787–1851), trained at de l'Épée's school and then established the American Asylum for the Education and Instruction of Deaf and Dumb Persons in Hartford, Connecticut in 1819. In 1857, Gallaudet's youngest son, Edward, became president of the National Deaf Mute College in Washington, D.C. In 1864, the college, with Abraham Lincoln as patron, became a degree-granting institution. In 1893 its name was changed to Gallaudet College in memory of Thomas Hopkins Gallaudet. Now called Gallaudet University, the facility remains the world's foremost degree-granting institution for students who are hearing impaired.

The education of students who were deaf was the first form of special education to be undertaken in Canada. In 1829, one Ronald McDonald, a reporter with the *Montreal Gazette*, was sent by the government of Lower Canada to train with Gallaudet in Hartford. McDonald opened a school for deaf children in Champlain, Quebec, in 1831, which operated for five years. Later, the Catholic Church in Quebec opened schools for deaf boys in 1848 and deaf girls in 1851.

The most prominent pioneer in the early history of Canadian special education was John Barrett McGann (1810–1880), who arrived in Toronto from Ireland in 1855. With assistance from Egerton Ryerson, McGann's work culminated with the Ontario Institution for the Education and Instruction of the Deaf and Dumb, established at Belleville in 1870, and the Ontario Institution for the Education and Instruction of the Blind, at Brantford in 1872.

Residential schools to serve the needs of students with serious hearing impairments were eventually established in all provinces, and most remain today. At the outset, the mode of instruction was sign. Then from 1905 to 1975, oralism (speech and speech reading) took precedence and sign language was virtually outlawed. Schools allowed no sign language in classrooms and deaf teachers were not generally employed.

By the 1970s, the failure of the oral system was glaringly apparent and by 1975 a remarkable shift had taken place in communication modes. Approximately two-thirds of deaf children were taught through some form of manual communication and one-third orally (Miller and Moores, 2000).

Today, sign language is well accepted as a mode of instruction, especially in residential schools. Deaf adults regard sign language as a defining characteristic of a recognizable minority group and often prefer to send their children to residential schools as these facilities foster the concept of a deaf community and a deaf culture.

SUMMARY

1. Hearing loss (or hearing impairment) is a generic term that encompasses two major groups—those who are deaf and those who are hard of hearing. The difference lies in the intensity of the hearing loss and the amount of auditory input that the individual can use. People who are deaf cannot, even with the use of a hearing aid, hear speech; those who are hard of hearing can hear speech with or without amplification (hearing aids).
2. A hearing impairment is not the deprivation of sound but the deprivation of language. Because hearing loss interferes with both the reception and the production of language, the greatest single handicap of defective hearing is its effect on the development of communication skills. Children who are hearing impaired are isolated from the human voice and therefore isolated from language. As teaching is essentially a linguistic activity, hearing impairment poses a serious threat to children's learning.
3. Children who are deaf are likely to be identified during the preschool years. In contrast, the auditory problems of hard-of-hearing children may not be detected until they undergo a routine school screening, and perhaps not even then. Apart from the immediate problems for children, non-identification means that incidence and prevalence rates are extremely difficult to determine.
4. As long as the sounds of conversational speech remain audible, effective communication skills are possible. However, even mild losses can be educationally devastating.
5. Individuals who are hearing impaired are usually deficient in the language of the majority culture even when expert in the language of signs. Although they possess the same intellectual potential as the rest of the population, their deprivation in language can cause problems in every aspect of functioning. Academically, most deaf graduates today can barely read the daily newspaper. Emotionally, deaf students are prone to a greater number of emotional and psychological problems. Socially, many deaf persons turn for acceptance to the deaf community, where sign language is the accepted mode of communication.
6. Many deaf adults see themselves as a distinct culture, a deaf community.
7. Many of the etiologies responsible for hearing losses affect many domains of development. It is estimated that up to 33 percent of children with hearing impairments suffer co-occurring disabilities.
8. Once a child's medical and audiological data have been gathered, he or she should receive and wear a personal hearing aid as soon as possible. All infants, children, and adults who are hearing impaired can benefit from an aid. Cochlear implants are now considered viable alternatives to hearing aids for some children to improve speech perception abilities.
9. As in many areas of special education, inclusive schooling is controversial, with ardent advocates and cautious watchers. Educational setting is more than a matter of location. For students who are deaf, setting makes differences in the communication mode used, the type and amount of support services, the stress of the curriculum, and the possibility of identification with the deaf community and deaf culture.
10. One essential service that many students with hearing impairments attending regular classes need is an educational interpreter. The importance of classroom interpreters is ob-

vious as a support service for students to allow access to the same curriculum that is afforded hearing students.

11. Over the years, many approaches to teach communication have evolved. In the past, communication modes attempted to overcome the spoken language communication barrier with hearing aids, auditory trainers, and the like. In recent decades, the education of students who are deaf has undergone major changes. There has been a movement toward inclusion, a widespread adoption of total communication, and the initiation of bilingual-bicultural education.
12. Although the deaf community wants children to use what they see as their natural language and wants educators to accept bilingual education that includes ASL, bilingual education for students who are deaf is founded as much on political arguments as it is on educational considerations, and the idea is far from universally accepted.

WEBLINKS

The Canadian Hearing Society **www.chs.ca/**

Deaf Canada Web **dww.deafworldweb.org/int/ca/**

The Deaf Education Option Web **www2.pair.com/options/**

Students with Hearing Loss
www.bced.gov.bc.ca/specialed/hearimpair/toc.htm

Canadaian Cultural Society of the Deaf **www.ccsdeaf.com**

Silent News (a deaf newspaper) **www.silentnews.org**

Chapter 10

Children with Visual Impairments

Learning Outcomes

After reading this chapter, you should be able to:

Understand the various types of visual impairments, with their causes and developmental consequences;

Differentiate between legal and educational blindness;

Identify the various devices used for reading and mobility;

Understand the types of adaptations, modifications, and support necessary to successfully include a child with a severe visual impairment in the regular classroom.

Introduction

It is difficult for most of us to imagine life without sight. Vision and hearing are the senses that most connect us with our world. Well over half of the information our brains receive about the world comes through our eyes (Immen, 1995). In fact, the visual system is so dominant that many of us close our eyes to think more clearly and concentrate.

To many people, a world without images would seem bleak, frightening, and virtually impossible to navigate. It would seem socially cold; through expression and eye contact, our eyes play a crucial role in social interaction. Sight also affects our other senses; seeing something good to eat, for example, can trigger hunger pangs.

Most of us have a special fear of blindness. A 1988 survey found that blindness was the most feared disability for 42 percent of the 1072 adults surveyed. In the same survey, blindness was listed the fourth most feared disease, after AIDS, cancer, and Alzheimer's disease (Augusto and McGraw, 1990).

Sighted people tend to react to blindness on an emotional level and see persons who are blind as either dependent or heroic. These long-standing perceptions are documented in the Historical Notes at the end of this chapter. Despite these common images, visual disabilities are not as daunting as they first seem. Many persons who are blind have contributed significantly to our culture, and many other thousands who did not achieve fame lived normal and successful lives in spite of their disability.

Of course, this is not to deny that visual impairments can be among the most severe of all physical disabilities. Severe visual impairment can interfere with learning, social growth, adjustment, and mobility. In children, visual impairments cause complex developmental problems that make special education a necessity. Unique education needs include, but are not restricted to, early intervention; concept development; listening, study, and research skills; alternative methods for reading, writing, and mathematical computation; sensory training; daily living, socialization, and recreational skills; sexuality, career, and vocational training; utilization of low vision; accessibility to technology; orientation and mobility training; and meaningful transition programs (Huebner, 1985).

In recent years, many changes have occurred in the education of students who are visually impaired. Among the most dramatic is the inclusion of many children into public school classes. As well, greater attention is directed toward the functional rather than the legal definitions of sight handicaps, which has broadened the category of students who can benefit from special education. Children with borderline problems now qualify for services, as do children with visual impairments and co-occurring disabilities.

Educators have also learned a great deal more about the effects of visual impairments on learning, and there is increased emphasis on the development of residual vision. It is now re-

Many individuals overcome visual impairments.

alized that residual sight is enhanced, rather than diminished, with use, and children who were formerly classified as blind are now classified as *low vision* or *visually impaired.* At the same time, braille literacy is being reaffirmed by many in the field as an educational priority for children with severely limited vision. The ability to read and write braille maximizes students' chances of educational and vocational success and lays the foundation they need to benefit from many new technological advances (Stephens, 1989).

New advances have also occurred in the diagnosis and treatment of visual disorders, particularly in the fields of ophthalmology and optometry. Vastly improved optical aids have been developed to enable children with severe sight impairments to read print materials. Advanced computer technology has brought many sophisticated devices that compensate for lack of vision.

THE VISUAL SYSTEM

The visual system consists of the eye, which receives the light image; the nerve pathways, which transmit the image to the optical centres of the brain; and the brain itself, which interprets the image. Visual impairments can result from any interference with the passage of light as it travels from the outer surface of the eye along the nerve pathways to the brain.

The Eye

The eye is probably the most precious square inch in the human body. It is only 2.5 centimetres in diameter but its functions are extraordinarily complex and precise. It is composed of the eyeball and the accessory structures, such as the eyelids and muscles, that protect and move it. The eyeball is held in place by connective tissue in the orbit and is protected in front by the upper and lower eyelids. Figure 10-1 shows the structure of the eyeball.

The eyeball is a sphere wrapped in three layers of tissue. The outermost layer consists of the *sclera* and the *cornea.* The middle layer contains the *iris* and the *lens,* the muscles that support them, and the fluids that fill the eye's two chambers. The inner layer is the *retina,* the actual seeing part of the eye.

Light is essential for sight. A close look at the eye reveals that behind the black pupil and coloured iris there is a clear lens that serves to focus light gathered from the environment onto the retina. On reaching the cornea, the rays of light are refracted to pass through the anterior chamber of the eye. As the rays pass through the crystalline lens, they are further refracted. The lens is capable of changing its shape to accommodate light from objects at various distances. From the lens, the light makes its way through the *vitreous humour* and comes to focus on the *fovea,* the most sensitive spot of the retina. Images received by the fovea are here inverted, making the bottom appear like the top and vice versa. The refraction and inversion of an object are illustrated in Figure 10-2.

The fovea possesses a rich supply of light-sensitive nerve cells, the rods and cones, which convert the light into electrochemical impulses. These impulses are transmitted to the brain from the back of the eye through the bundles of nerve fibres that form the optic nerve. Immen (1995) describes the nerves that connect the eye to the brain as "the original information highway." The data are sent digitally, in a steady stream of electrical impulses, along

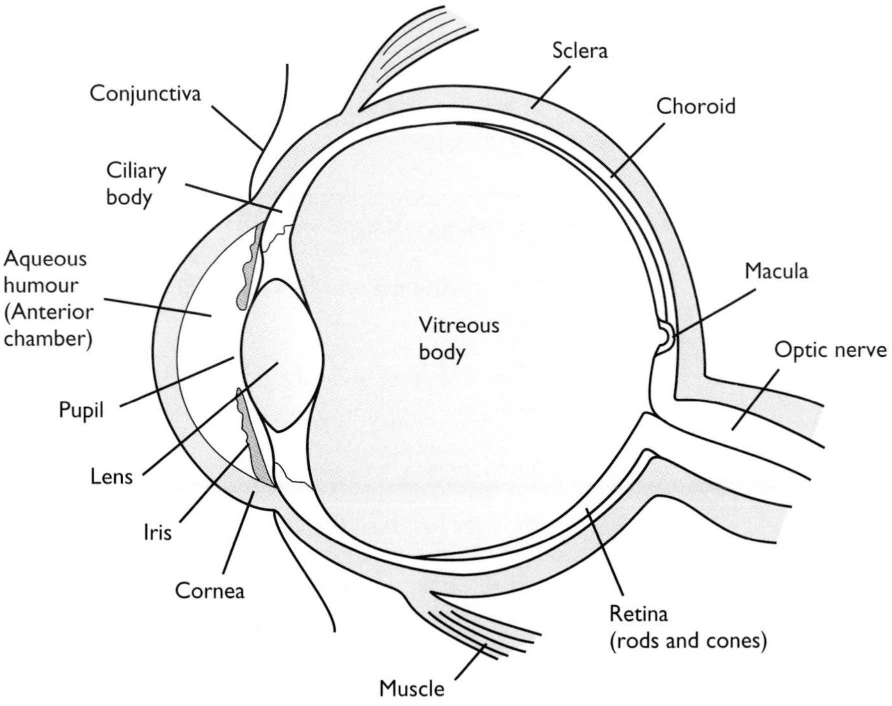

Figure 10-1
Anatomy of the eye

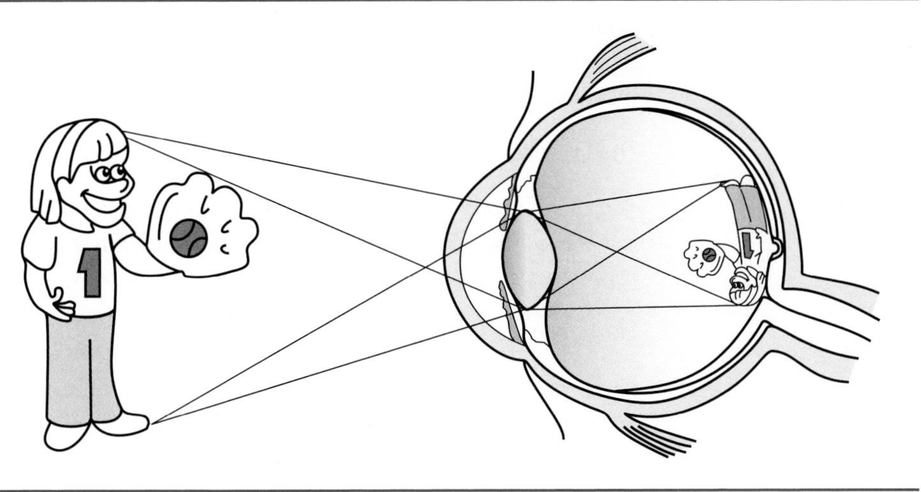

Figure 10-2
Refraction and inversion of an object

a chain of nerve endings. Images are received and interpreted in the occipital lobe of the brain. Hence, vision is a function of the brain, not the eye.

Table 10-1 outlines the important parts of the eye. The sequence of vision is shown in Table 10-2.

Table 10-1 Parts of the eye

Sclera	Tough, flexible, white outer covering of the posterior portion of the eye. Its front part is commonly recognized as the white of the eye.
Cornea	A transparent window covering the front of the eye, continuous with the sclera.
Lacrimal apparatus	Glands that provide the tear film essential to the health of the cornea.
Iris	A circle of muscles that gives the eye its colour and adapts the size of the pupil aperture in response to light intensity.
Lens	A crystalline lens held in suspension by the iris.
Choroid	A vascular layer in which the blood supply to the retina is embedded.
Retina	A tissue-thin, intricate, and sensitive layer that consists of up to a quarter of a billion photo receptors and other nerve cells. Lines the back of the eye.
Ocular muscles	The six muscles connected to the outside of the eyeball that allow the eye to focus on an object, follow a moving target, and rotate. The muscles of one eye work in perfect synchrony with one another and with those of the other eye to enable the two eyes to coordinate. They are among the most rapidly responding muscles in the body.
Fovea	The most sensitive spot on the retina.
Macula	A crater-shaped yellow area of the retina in the centre of our focus. The point of clearest vision even though it represents only one-thousandth of our field of vision.
Cones	Photoreceptors that collect bright light.
Rods	Photoreceptors that work in teams to collect low light.

DEFINITIONS OF VISUAL IMPAIRMENT

If you have been reading carefully, you will remember that we have already used a number of terms in this chapter—*visual impairment, severe limited vision, low vision,* and *blindness.* Abu, the child in the case study, was described as *severely visually impaired.* He has some

Table 10-2 The sequence of vision

1. When light reflected from an object hits our eye, the light rays pass through the cornea where they are refracted.
2. From the cornea, the light rays pass through the aqueous humour and proceed on their journey to the lens and the vitreous humour.
3. The rays are then directed to the central part of the retina. This contains rods and cones, which are light receptor cells. These are then stimulated by the light rays and consequently converted to electro-chemical energy.
4. The energy is further transmitted through the optic nerve to the visual centre of the brain, where the visual information is interpreted (Abang, 1980).

Case Study

Abu

Abu's parents were very excited about their first child. They talked and planned and organized as they got ready for the baby's arrival. When Abu was born, his disability was almost immediately noticeable to the attending physicians. Within twenty-four hours the parents were informed that their new baby was severely visually impaired. Abu's grandparents did not live in Canada, so his mother and father had almost no one to turn to for support.

The infant years were particularly difficult for Abu's mother. Many of her expectations for the child did not materialize. Certainly, he seemed to reach developmental milestones almost on target and by two years of age was developing language and some intelligible speech. Abu's mother tried to hide her fears, and played and talked with her child as much as possible. When he was three she asked, with little optimism, if he could attend the local nursery school. To her surprise, the school personnel willingly accepted Abu and were pleased to allow her to work as a volunteer on the condition that she intervene with all the children, not just Abu.

The nursery school experience proved an enormous success for Abu and for his mother. The teachers modified activities where necessary for Abu. For example, they added sand to the finger paints so that he had greater tactile experiences. An extract from Abu's IEP is shown later in this chapter.

Abu's mother is enthusiastic about integration and holds more positive attitudes about his future. She knows that his inability to perceive through the use of his eyes changes the way he learns, understands, and relates to the world, and that he will require additional assistance to overcome the deficits imposed by severe visual impairment. But she now realizes that Abu can learn and interact, and that he may achieve some of the goals his parents so hopefully set for him.

residual vision but will need many aids and will not attain normal visual functioning and acuity, even with correction.

Given the above, you can see that there are many terms in the broad category of visual impairment. These terms are difficult for a number of reasons. First, various terms are used to describe degrees and severity of visual impairment. Second, both legal and educational definitions are in place. And third, definitions often reflect the different agencies interested in visual impairment.

Visual impairment is the most generic term and can include people reading this text who have very mild visual impairments as well as those with low vision and those who are totally blind. We are interested in serious visual problems that affect living and learning. These problems are divided into two general categories, low vision and blindness.

low vision

blindness

- **Low vision** means that a person's corrected vision is lower than normal.
- **Blindness** means that individuals have no sight, or so little that learning takes place through the other senses. Only 10 to 15 percent of the entire population of persons with visual impairments are totally blind.

Together with generic definitions of visual impairment, two other types are used—medical/legal definitions and functional/educational definitions. For educational purposes, medical/legal definitions are not as appropriate as the latter because they do not adequately describe a child's visual functioning.

Legal Definitions

Legal definitions are founded on *visual acuity*, the measure of the smallest image distinguishable by the eye, and on *visual field*, the entire area that can be seen when staring straight ahead, reported in degrees. Normal individuals can see 180 degrees.

Acuity measures begin with the 20/20 normal vision with which we are all familiar. This derives from the Snellen chart (often seen hanging on the back of your doctor's examining-room door), which consists of a series of letters, numbers, or symbols that must be read from a distance of twenty feet. Each line is a different size that corresponds to a standard distance at which it can be distinguished by a person with normal vision. This gives the measure 20/20 vision, which should not be read as a fraction. Snellen's equation was $V = d/D$, where V is visual acuity, d is distance, and D is the distance at which letters are clearly read. Normal vision is 20/20.

In Canada, legal blindness is defined as an acuity measure of 20/200 (6/600) or less in the better eye with the best correction; or visual acuity of more than 20/200 if the widest diameter of the field of vision subtends an angle of no greater than 20 degrees (CNIB, 1980). Visual acuity of 20/200 means that a normally sighted person can see at 200 feet (approximately 60 m) what the visually impaired person can see at 20 feet (6 m).

There is also a legal definition of *partial sight* (low vision). A partially sighted individual has a visual acuity greater than 20/200 but not greater than 20/70 in the better eye after correction (CNIB, 1980).

Educational Definitions

visual functioning

Visual functioning (visual efficiency) refers to what a visually impaired person does with his or her residual vision; it is the way in which an individual uses vision for purposeful behaviour in the various activities of daily life. There is no correlation between the amount of residual vision a person has and the way in which vision is used. Two people with the same etiology and visual acuity may be very different in the way they use their residual vision.

Some people may be able to discern light, colours, or shapes. Some may be able to read by seeing clearly through one small area but have trouble getting around. Others may be able to see the whole work area but have difficulty reading. In others, fatigue, lighting, and emotions may affect the manner in which residual vision is utilized.

For these reasons, functional/educational definitions that indicate how well the child can use vision for learning are more useful than legal ones for educational purposes. Under a functional definition, a **child with a visual impairment** is one whose visual impairment interferes with his or her learning and achievement and requires adaptations in the presentation of learning experiences and/or the nature of the materials used in the learning environment.

child with a visual impairment

PREVALENCE OF VISUAL IMPAIRMENTS

Severe visual impairment, including total blindness, is a low-incidence condition. It is primarily an adult disability, probably one-tenth as prevalent in children as in adults. Only about one in 1000 children under the age of eighteen have severe visual impairments (Hatton, Bailey, Burchinal, and Ferrell, 1997).

People with low vision far outnumber totally or functionally blind people, who have no usable sight at all. In fact, students with low vision comprise between 75 and 80 percent of the school-aged population that is visually impaired (Bryan and Jeffrey, 1982).

In 1986, Statistics Canada conducted a special post-census disability survey. While this survey provided only estimates, it did indicate that the prevalence of visual impairment in the general population was 2.6 percent. Among the population of persons with other established disabilities, the prevalence of visual impairment was 15.9 percent (Naeyaert and Grace, 1990).

It should be noted that although severe visual impairment is a low-incidence condition in the western world it is of particularly high prevalence in many countries of the Third World, where blindness affects millions of children and adults. In Asia, Africa, and South America, conditions such as water-borne blindness and vitamin A deficiency join to poverty and lack of sanitation to allow severe visual impairments to thrive. There are probably ten million blind people living in the world today (Mazurek and Winzer, 1994).

CLASSIFICATION OF VISUAL IMPAIRMENTS

There are many kinds of visual disabilities attributable to diverse causes and defined slightly differently. As a result, there are a number of ways to classify the conditions. One classification system is not necessarily better than another; they just describe different things and are used for different purposes.

Classification by Degree

Following the generic definitions discussed earlier, individuals with visual impairments may be classified in terms of the type and degree of disability—as *mild, moderate,* or *severe.* General severity classifications are as follows:

- Near-normal vision. Many people reading this text will have mild impairments that are correctable through prescription glasses. These individuals are able to function without special training regardless of the strength of corrective lenses or reading aids they may need.
- Moderate visual disability (moderate functional impairment). People in this group have a moderate reduction of acuity, but no significant visual field loss. Specialized aids and lighting are needed, but sight is comparable to normal vision with correction.
- Low vision refers to a person "who is still severely visually impaired after correction, but who may increase visual functioning through the use of optical aids, non-optical aids, environmental modifications and/or techniques" (Corn, 1980, p. 3). A person with low vision can read with special aids such as magnifying glasses or large-print books.
- Blindness (profound visual disability). Individuals in this group are the most visually impaired; they require education, habilitation, or rehabilitation to function at an independent level.

Classification by Age of Onset

congenital low vision

adventitious low vision

Children with visual impairments are often classified by age of onset of the problems. **Congenital low vision** refers to conditions that are diagnosable at birth or shortly thereafter. **Adventitious low vision** refers to conditions caused by accident or disease some time after birth.

Because many eye conditions change over time, age of onset can be critical in adjustment and learning, particularly in the development of concepts such as colour. Teresa Abang (1980) tells of a congenitally blind man who, when asked what he saw, said, "I see nothing." An adventitiously blind man responded to the same question with "I see darkness all around me." While the first man did not realize that he was experiencing darkness, the other had a memory of light and darkness.

ETIOLOGY OF VISUAL IMPAIRMENTS

Visual problems arise from any interference with the formation of images on the retina or the transmission of retinal images to the brain. Optical errors, defects of the eyes, diseases, syndromes, and associated conditions all affect vision to a greater or lesser extent. An outline of some conditions, their consequences, and their etiologies is shown in Table 10-3.

In the last century, the major causes of visual impairment included such things as ophthalmia neonatorum (inflammation of the eyes of the newborn); syphilis and smallpox; and massive epidemics of meningitis and scarlet fever. Measures such as washing the eyes of the newborn, vaccinations, and vastly improved sanitary conditions have eliminated most of these causes. During the past decade, retinopathy of prematurity, optic nerve hypoplasia, and cortical visual impairment have been among the most prevalent types of eye disorders in young children (Teplin, 1995).

Heredity is another leading cause of blindness in children under one year of age, with cataracts and retinoblastoma significant causes in terms of the number of children affected. Metabolic and vascular diseases, which include diabetes in the mother and disturbances in the metabolism of the infant, form an additional etiology.

Table 10-3 Examples of types of visual impairment and their etiologies

Category	Example	Manifestation	Etiology
Refractive errors	Myopia	Near-sightedness	
	Hyperopia	Long-sightedness	
	Astigmatism	Distorted or blurred vision	
	Cataracts	Growth over lens	Aging, heredity, disease, and infection
Eye pathologies	Glaucoma	Impaired outflow of vitreous fluid causes pressure on eyeball	Congenital, heredity
	Retinopathy of prematurity	Fibrous mass that destroys the retina	Prematurity; oxygen in incubator
	Retinoblastoma	Malignant tumour on the retina	Genetic
	Albinism	Lack of skin pigmentation	Genetic, error of metabolism
	Optic nerve atrophy	Nerve degeneration	Damage to the optic nerve
	Retinitis pigmentosa	Narrowing of field of vision	Hereditary
Ocular-motor problems	Strabismus	Seeing double	
	Nystagmus	Rapidly moving eyeballs	
	Amblyopia	Lazy-eye blindness; lack of depth perception	Arises from strabismus
Other problems	Colour blindness	Deficient in colour vision	
	Photophobia	Extreme sensitivity to light	Genetic
Syndromes	Usher's syndrome	Retinitis pigmentosa and progressive hearing loss	Genetic
	Joubert syndrome	Ataxia, slow motor activity, nystagmus	Neurological disorder

In general, the etiologies and consequent conditions in visual impairments may be grouped as follows:

- Refractive errors, caused by irregularities in the shape or size of the eyeball, the cornea, or the lens. Errors of refraction may also occur in association with diseases of the eye or with oculomotor disturbances.

- Oculomotor (ocular motility) problems, caused by disturbances in eye movement.
- Eye pathologies, caused by damage or disease before or after birth to one or more of the structures of the eye.
- Additional defects and causes, which include albinism and abnormalities of the central nervous system that may result in faulty eye–muscle coordination.
- Various syndromes that have visual impairment as one manifestation.

Refractive Errors

myopia

Many people reading this book probably have minor visual losses caused by one of the four common types of refractive errors—*myopia, hyperopia, astigmatism,* and *presbyopia.* **Myopia** (nearsightedness) is the greatest single cause of defective vision in children and young adults. The myopic eye is unable to focus the image precisely on the retina; the length of the eye or the shape of the cornea cause light rays to focus in front of the retina. In most cases, myopia can be corrected with concave optical lenses.

hyperopia
astigmatism

Hyperopia (farsightedness) is caused by too short an eye or too flat a corneal surface. The image is focused behind the retina. Corrective lenses aid hyperopic people. **Astigmatism** is the result of an irregularity in the curvature of the cornea or lens of the eye. The rays of light are refracted unevenly so that horizontal and vertical rays are focused at different points on the retina. In most cases, astigmatism is correctable.

presbyopia

With advancing age, numerous body changes occur. Some of these natural developments relate to changes in the eye's muscle tone and other tissues. **Presbyopia**, from the Greek word meaning "sight of age," is a condition in which the lens of the eye loses its ability to accommodate to near objects. The lens changes shape and lets us concentrate on a particular spot. To focus on distant objects, it flattens somewhat; when moving in close, it gets rounder. As we get older, the lens loses some of its adaptability and up-close focus becomes more difficult. In addition to blurring and difficulty with reading at normal distances, persons with presbyopia will usually experience "tired eyes" or headaches while doing close work. Most people at the age of forty or thereabouts develop some degree of presbyopia and need glasses for reading and other close work.

Disturbances of Ocular Motility

Normal vision requires the coordinated use of two eyes. Images from each eye are fused in the vision centres of the brain so that only one image is perceived. To achieve a synchronized image, the ocular muscles in both eyes must work in perfect harmony. *Oculomotor disturbances* occur when the eyes cannot control their direction of focus.

strabismus

Strabismus, one of the most common oculomotor problems, results from inefficient ocular motor mobility. It can affect one or both eyes. Strabismus may be evident at birth or may not appear until the child begins to look at objects close up. Divergent strabismus causes what is called a "wall eye." *Amblyopia*, sometimes called "lazy-eye blindness," results from strabismus. The brain will not tolerate double vision and eventually suppresses the image coming from the weaker eye.

Surgery, eye exercises, patches, or prescription lenses are used for strabismus. Treatment becomes less effective the longer it is postponed, and the longer suppression goes untreated, the more difficult it becomes to restore normal visual functioning.

Diplopia, or double vision, is another result of lack of coordination between the two eyes. **Nystagmus**, a rhythmic involuntary movement of the eyes, is often found in conjunction with other disabilities, such as Down syndrome. Ocular motility problems are common in children with cerebral palsy and other neurological disorders.

nystagmus

Eye Pathologies

The most common eye diseases found in children cause clouding of the cornea and lens and dysfunctions of the retina and optic nerves. These diseases may be congenital or adventitious.

A **cataract** is an opacity of the lens or its capsule that restricts the eye's ability to receive light and therefore interferes with central and peripheral visual acuity. If the lens becomes cloudy, the light rays are blocked or distorted when they reach the retina, making things look hazy or dull, or dazzlingly bright.

cataract

Cataracts are caused by a chemical change in the lens itself. The exact reasons for the change are not understood, although there may be a hereditary tendency to develop cataracts. For the most part, cataracts are associated with aging and almost half the population over the age of sixty-five will suffer some degree of cataract formation ("Cataracts ...," 1990). Younger people may be affected in association with conditions such as diabetes.

Some babies are born with cataracts, often the result of maternal rubella. In rare cases, cataracts result from a blow to the eye or from exposure to radiation, toxic chemicals, or intense heat ("Cataracts ...," 1990).

Glaucoma, a condition responsible for 12 percent of the blindness in Canada and the United States, has been called "the sneak-thief of sight" because its onset is slow and insidious. Glaucoma is caused by the increased intra-ocular pressure that occurs when the eye fluid that should be continually drained backs up along the outflow route. The increased pressure destroys intricate, sensitive structures in the retina, which then loses its ability to transmit pictures to the brain.

glaucoma

Congenital glaucoma is a baffling and mysterious hereditary condition that is a major cause of severe visual defects in children. Untreated glaucoma can cause total blindness in both children and adults.

Retinopathy of prematurity (ROP), until recently called *retrolental fibroplasia* (RLF), describes a condition affecting the retina and the vitreous humour. ROP, first described in 1942, is seen in low-birth-weight babies (under 1.5 kg), and was first attributed to high levels of oxygen in incubators. After its cause was discovered, there was a drop in the incidence of ROP. Since the mid-60s, the incidence of milder ROP has been rising, and the 1980s saw a further resurgence of ROP as babies with even lower birth weights survived (Trief, Duckman, Morse, and Silberman, 1989).

retinopathy of prematurity

Current research indicates that oxygen alone does not account for all cases of ROP, and ROP is not always restricted to premature infants (Teplin, 1995). It is birth-weight, gestation age, and duration of administration of oxygen together that are the most important factors in the development of ROP (Trief et al., 1989). Today, ROP primarily affects babies with a birth weight of less than 1000 grams. About 20 percent of infants born weighing less than 1500 grams also show evidence of ROP (Trief et al., 1989).

The problems of ROP begin as a distortion and outgrowth of the blood vessels of the retina. This is followed by the separation of the retina and the formation of an opaque mass behind the lens composed of detached retina, blood vessels, and fibrous tissue. There is bleeding, scarring, and detachment of the retina; the extent of visual impairment depends on the amount of scarring.

retinitis pigmentosa

Retinitis pigmentosa affects about one in 4000 people worldwide. It is a hereditary condition that is actually a collection of diseases caused by as many as 150 different genes. The condition causes degeneration of retinal tissues and loss of peripheral vision. The age of onset of retinitis pigmentosa may vary from childhood to early adulthood. Other abnormalities, such as cataracts and glaucoma, may also be present.

Damage to the blood vessels that supply the retina can cause *macular retinal degeneration.* The macula is the small area in the central portion of the retina that is responsible for fine or distinct vision, such as is required for reading. Macular degeneration may be inherited, but it is also associated with injuries such as contusions and concussions. The condition results in extremely poor central vision and may be undetected in young children.

Another type of retinal degeneration is associated with a high degree of myopia. Abnormal growth in the length of the eye causes a thinning of the retina and destruction of the retinal cells.

diabetic retinopathy

Diabetes is a major cause of retinal disease in young adults. **Diabetic retinopathy** is a disease of the retina's blood vessels. Not all diabetics develop retinopathy; generally, however, the longer the diabetes is present, the more likely that changes in the retina will occur. People who have had diabetes for more than fifteen years are at greatest risk, and as medical technology and synthetic insulin prolong the life expectancies of people with diabetes retinopathy is becoming more common. The type of diabetes affecting a person does not seem to be the critical factor; some people with mild diabetes that is completely controlled by diet lose their sight, while others with severe forms of the disease do not experience any visual loss ("Diabetic...," 1990).

In the early stages of diabetic retinopathy, the blood vessels in the retina start to weaken and break. The leaked fluid distorts the light rays entering the eyes, and the person's vision blurs and fluctuates; or the person may see floating spots and a reddish haze. In the later stages, the blood vessels may shut down completely, which causes the retinal nerves that transmit sight images to the brain to die from loss of nourishment.

This kind of vision loss is gradual but permanent. New abnormal blood vessels may replace the old ones but they are unable to nourish the retina properly. They may start to grow into the normally transparent inner chamber of the eye, further interfering with the person's vision. If scar tissue forms it can pull on the retina, tearing or detaching it completely. The result is total blindness ("Diabetic ...," 1990).

Retinal detachment occurs when a hole or rip in the retina allows the inner retina layer to separate from the back portion. Eye fluid can then enter through the break, seep between the layers, and further pressure the inner layer to peel or detach. Total blindness may result if the detached retina is not promptly reattached.

Optic nerve atrophy results from damage to the fibres of the optic nerve. Degeneration of the nerve may be partial or complete; its onset may be gradual or abrupt. Optic nerve atrophy may result from inadequate blood supply to the nerve or from optical diseases such as glaucoma or retinal degeneration.

Optic nerve hypoplasia (ONH) seems to be a relatively new type of visual impairment in which the optic nerve fails to develop fully during fetal development. Vision can range from normal to total blindness. ONH is associated with other neurological and endocrine abnormalities (Hatton, et al., 1997).

retinoblastoma

Retinoblastoma results from a malignant tumour on the retina that may spread to the optic nerve and other areas. The condition usually arises in infancy or early childhood. It can be inherited as a Mendelian dominant trait with incomplete penetrance, which means that the person carrying the condition may not manifest the lesion but can still pass it on to offspring. In the past, surgical removal of the eyes was necessary. Today, the malignancy can be arrested without removal of the eyes. Still, blindness inevitably ensues and even a cured patient can transmit the condition to offspring.

Other Defects

colour blindness

Colour blindness is a rare, sex-linked, hereditary disorder found almost always in males. Defects of colour vision arise from the absence or malfunctioning of the cone cells of the retina. Cones come in three varieties, sensitive to the wavelengths of either blue, green, or red light. In some people, one of the three types of cones is missing, making them colour blind for that range of the spectrum (Immen, 1995). Persons with colour defects are likely to confuse colours, most commonly red and green.

True colour blindness (seeing everything in shades of grey) is very rare. Although colour blindness is common among those with central vision problems, the condition is not necessarily associated with visual impairments.

albinism

photophobia

Albinism is a condition carried as an inherited autosomal recessive trait. It is not sex-linked and the gene must be inherited from both parents, each of whom either has albinism or is a carrier of the trait. Albinism affects the production of melanin, the pigment contained in hair and skin. A pigment deficiency in the retina, iris, and choroid causes the pupil to take on a deep reddish colour and the iris to appear greyish, light blue, or pink. In visual terms, albinism is characterized by decreased acuity, astigmatism, nystagmus, and **photophobia**, a condition in which very bright light blinds the individual and thus decreases acuity (Abang, 1980).

Some central nervous system disorders may manifest as a lack of response to light stimulus in the cortex. *Cortical blindness* sometimes refers to blindness caused by swelling in the brain tissue due to trauma or congenital malformations (Hammer, 1984). At other times, the term describes blindness that cannot be medically explained. Most often, children who are congenitally cortically blind have other problems that are serious enough to affect several body systems. The visual functioning of children with cortical visual impairment has been shown to fluctuate from day to day and may improve in some cases (Good, 1992).

Syndromes

Usher's syndrome

A number of syndromes have associated visual impairment. For example, when deafness is associated with retinitis pigmentosa, the condition is known as **Usher's syndrome**, named after the British ophthalmologist who in 1918 stressed the link between visual and auditory impairments. Usher's syndrome is a leading cause of deaf-blindness. (See Chapter 14.) Joubert syndrome is a rare neurological disorder. Individuals show ataxia, slow motor activity, and often abnormal eye movements, including nystagmus.

DEVELOPMENTAL CONSEQUENCES OF VISUAL IMPAIRMENTS

Obviously, the developmental consequences of total blindness differ from those related to low vision. Reading, other academic areas, socialization, life skills, and orientation and mobility are all affected by the severity of the visual loss. The correlation is certainly not clear-cut, but as a broad generalization, we can say that the greater the degree of visual impairment, the more sharply reduced will be the range and variety of a child's experiences and the greater will be the restrictions placed on the child's ability to move freely within an environment.

We can also say that visual impairment is linked to altered developmental pathways in young children. The global development of young children who are visually impaired tends to be delayed when compared to the development of sighted children. As well, development is influenced by the type of eye condition.

Motor Development

Social, exploratory, and manipulative experiences lay the foundation for competence in communication, concept development, motor development, and self-reliance. Vision plays a leading role in an infant's first efforts to independently explore the environment. As the new world comes into sharper visual focus, the developing neuromuscular system sparks a push toward motor exploration and the infant reaches out to touch, feel, taste, and probe. Without vision, infants find it more difficult to explore their environment, to reach out into space, and to become aware of their bodies in space.

Very young children who are blind have no natural motivation to lift their heads or roll, and they are less able to orient themselves to the external environment through such skills as reaching, crawling, and walking (Warren, 1984). Restricted experiences mean that congenitally blind children may be delayed in motor development. Certainly, infants who are blind acquire early motor skills such as sitting and standing at about the same time as other children, but they may be slower in crawling and walking. Delays in walking until sixteen to nineteen months are common, and even children with sufficient vision for orientation and mobility purposes may show a lack of confidence and a delay in ambulation.

Cognitive Development

The intelligence levels of persons who are visually impaired parallel those of the general population. How children learn and whether lags in learning are attributable to visual impairment is, however, a subject of intense debate.

Researchers debate whether or not children who are blind do more poorly on tasks involving abstract thinking and whether they are much more likely to deal with their environment in concrete terms. Because these children rely far more on non-visual perceptions, the notions they form may differ from the notions of sighted children. However, many current researchers argue that the assumption that children who are blind experience problems of sensory reference has little basis in truth (Landau, 1983).

Another area of contention revolves around whether or not children with severe visual impairments lag significantly behind their sighted peers in the development of Piagetian tasks such as classification and conservation. Research is equivocal because much traditional testing of classification and conservation is based on visual information, and, even when traditional visual tasks are adapted into a tactual mode, they cannot be considered comparable.

Early play behaviour, so critical in all domains of development, differs from that of sighted children. Of all disabilities, infantile autism and blindness seem to be the ones that affect the development of sensorimotor and symbolic play the most significantly.

Although functioning at expected developmental levels in other domains such as receptive language and cognition, children with severe visual impairments may be substantially delayed in sensorimotor play and exhibit delays or deficiencies in symbolic and social play. They may be at least two years behind in cognitive play as compared to sighted children (Hughes, Dote-Kwan, and Dolendo, 1998). Abnormalities in symbolic play seem to be related to the limitations imposed by visual impairments.

Perceptual Development

For children who are blind, the world is one of smells, sounds, and textures uninformed by the visual information that offers such a rich variety of colour, shape, and size detail to sighted persons. Hearing is the only distance sense available, and individuals who are blind must build their knowledge from auditory experiences joined to those that are olfactory, tactile, and kinesthetic.

It takes effort and concentration to learn to use the touch and auditory senses to compensate for lack of sight. There is no magical sensory compensation of the remaining senses; blind persons must learn to pay more attention to auditory and tactual clues that sighted people can afford to ignore.

For the person who is blind, texture, weight, temperature, shape, and size merge into a sequence of touch sensations to permit identification of an object. An individual uses synthetic touch—the tactual exploration of objects small enough to be enclosed by one or both hands. For larger objects, the person employs analytic touch, exploring the various parts of an object and then mentally reconstructing the parts (Hallahan and Kauffman, 1991).

Communication

Verbal language is critical in information-gathering functions for children who are blind. Even before they develop speech, infants with visual impairments use vocalizations to achieve and maintain social contact. They learn a great deal about people in their environment from voices, learn to measure personal attention by the nearness of the speaker and the touch gestures that accompany speech, and become adept at interpreting meaning from nuances or variations in voice tone.

Studies of the speech and language development of children who are visually impaired have provoked as much controversy as those on abstract thinking and Piagetian tasks. Whether language development parallels that of sighted children or whether it is delayed or different is not clear.

There seem to be language differences in the types of words acquired and in reciprocity and pragmatics (see Hatton et al., 1997). Bigelow (1987) found that very young children who were blind acquire vocabulary in the same way as sighted children, although some differences emerged in the percentage of words in each classification. Others have studied verbalisms where a child uses words inappropriately and without an experiential base. For example, "a shirt as red as an apple" is a verbalism.

A different line of research has looked at the increased numbers of questions that children who are visually impaired tend to ask as part of their information gathering. As sight decreases, so questioning increases, but children who are blind tend to ask fewer open-ended questions than do sighted children (Fichten, Judd, Tagalikis, Amsel, Robillard, 1991).

It may very well be that any speech and language difficulties in children who are visually impaired are more closely related to social and emotional factors than to low vision or blindness. Delays in speech and language development may result from restricted interaction with the people around them.

Academic Achievement

The educational achievement of children who are visually impaired is as variable as the population itself. One general trait, however, is that students who are visually impaired tend to achieve more highly in some areas than others. For example, arithmetic is problematic; students who are blind do not perform well and tend to be from 8 to 27 percent below average-sighted children in basic arithmetic performance (Weiss and Weiss, 1981). On the other hand, the work of students who are blind in literary subjects is about the same as that of their sighted peers.

Reading can be a problem, primarily because of the slower rate of reading large print or braille. As well, students who use braille often have problems with spelling because the contractions in braille do not conform to English spelling usage. Braille is discussed later in this chapter.

Social and Emotional Development

Vision has a neuron growth spurt at the age of two to four months that corresponds with the time that babies really begin to notice the world, and peaks at eight months (Begley, 1996). During this period, sighted infants typically respond to attentive social initiations from their parents by visually focusing on their parents' eyes, smiling, and occasionally shifting their gaze to scan their parents' faces and the environment. In contrast, infants who are visually impaired demonstrate a flat, solemn affect characterized by bland facial expressions and the absence of expressive behaviour. Smiling is difficult to elicit (Baird, Mayfield, and Baker, 1997). All this can adversely affect parent–child relationships.

As they grow, children who are visually impaired often demonstrate special needs in relation to self-awareness, self-esteem, and social skills. This happens because severe visual impairments tend to interfere with spontaneous social activity and with social interaction and communication. The visual impairment affects the child's ability to utilize visual clues, which are needed for the modelling and feedback that underlie social skill acquisition. For example, children do not possess built-in feedback for appropriate head and facial movements once they are engaged in conversation.

Therefore, children who are blind face obstacles in obtaining the full benefits of peer interaction and may have trouble in acquiring an adequate repertoire of interpersonal skills. They often behave in ways that decrease their effective interaction with peers: research indicates that children with visual impairments initiate interactions less frequently than do their peers, have difficulty extending appropriate conversation, and are more likely to be rejected by peers (Mar and Sall, 1995).

Because of their visual limitations, children miss many important non-verbal cues given by their teachers and peers through facial expressions, gestures, and body language. As they fail to make expected eye contact with peers and typically will not smile, communication with sighted people may be harmed by lack of eye contact (Fichten, et al., 1991). The failure to look at people may be interpreted as disinterest rather than as a manifestation of the disability itself.

Co-occurring Disabilities

Between 33 percent and 70 percent of children with visual impairments have co-occurring disabilities, the most frequent being mental retardation (Hatton et al., 1997), followed by emotional disorders and learning disabilities. The existing literature also points to a relatively high incidence of autism among children who are congenitally blind.

The literature on the dual occurrence of learning disabilities and visual impairment is scarce, and educational research almost non-existent. Existing studies suggest that between 14 and 65 percent of students who are visually impaired also have learning disabilities. This is much higher than expected with a typical cross section of school-age students, probably because of the original etiology such as neurological problems or prematurity (Erin and Koenig, 1997).

Young children who are blind often engage in self-stimulating behaviours such as body rocking, side to side head rolling, and eye poking or eye pressing. This is somewhat different from the self-stimulation often seen in students with developmental disabilities and should not be taken as a necessary signal of problem behaviour.

ASSESSMENT OF CHILDREN WHO HAVE VISUAL IMPAIRMENTS

Most children with severe visual impairments either are born with the disability or acquire it at an early age. Therefore, it is important that children be assessed early so that intervention can begin. If detected soon enough, at least some visual impairments can be corrected through the use of lenses, medication, and surgery.

A comprehensive assessment of a child with a visual impairment takes into account two areas—medical diagnosis and treatment of the problem, and psycho-educational assessment that leads to efficient educational planning. Both areas often begin with screening.

Screening

Screening procedures assess large numbers of children in order to identify those needing additional diagnosis. In Manitoba, Rathegerber (1981) reported on screening procedures for visual impairments that identified 21 to 34 percent of children on the first screening and 11 to 24 percent on the second. When the identified children were sent for professional examinations, more than two-thirds required some care, either as an immediate prescription or for some incipient condition noted by the eye practitioner.

The most common screening procedure used in the measurement of central vision acuity is the Snellen chart, developed in 1862 by Herman Snellen, a Dutch ophthalmologist. This standard letter chart, familiar to most adults, may not suit young children and those who cannot read. Children are screened with the symbol E chart, which has Es pointing in different directions. Or the chart may have an outline of common objects rather than letters.

Many children with visual problems are not identified until after they are enrolled in school and expected to read. In the identification of milder visual disorders, teachers are often on the front line when they observe children who have no outward appearance of anything wrong with the eyes but who exhibit abnormal behaviour. This includes frequent rubbing of the eyes, excessive blinking, crossing one eye when reading, or holding a book abnormally close or far away.

Children who are suspected to have a visual problem should be referred for comprehensive eye examinations. Signs of visual problems that teachers can observe are presented in Table 10-4, below.

Diagnosis

As in the field of hearing impairment, both electrophysiological and behavioural measures are available for intensive diagnosis, used depending on both the needs and the condition (ability to respond) of the child. (See the appendix table, Tools for Assessment.)

In infants, diagnosis relies on observations of the child's responses to visual stimuli, such as a light or a moving object. Clinicians look for reactions of the pupils of the eyes to light,

Table 10-4 Some signs of visual problems
One eye turns in or out.
In near work, the child squints, closes, or covers one eye.
The child rubs the eyes, squints, or shakes the head while looking at near or far objects.
The child tilts the head or closes one eye.
The child is fearful of walking down stairs or running freely.
The child frequently falls or bumps into objects.
The child holds objects very close to—or far away from—the eyes.
The child appears to have abnormal eye movements.
The child complains of fuzzy vision.
The child has frequent eye infections, swollen eyelids, watery eyes, or reddened eyes or lids.
The eyes tear excessively.
The child has encrusted eyelids or frequent styes on the lids.
The child is poor or slow in reading.
The child is inattentive during reading class.
The child often loses the place when reading or persistently skips lines and confuses letters.
The child often stops to rest after brief periods of reading.
The head turns when the child is reading.
Pages in notebooks are poorly organized.
The child misaligns both horizontal and vertical series of numbers.
The child has difficulty in focusing on the blackboard.
The child can't remember things he or she has seen.

blinking in response to light presentation, eye movements in response to objects moving in the visual field, and eye fixation on stationary objects. In one test, the child is held over the parent's shoulder facing the examiner while a toy or other familiar object is moved into the temporal field. The child is tested for each eye separately and for both eyes together, and the child's reaction is observed.

Eye examinations, used with older children, consider physical aspects—visual acuity, visual field, oculomotor control, and the effects of specific diseases or injuries and prenatal factors and functional aspects—the extent to which residual vision is being utilized and whether the child has opportunity, incentive, or optical aids to enable him or her to use residual vision. Also determined is a child's maximum potential for achieving acuity and the type of optical aids the child needs to reach the maximum acuity level (Abang, 1980).

Psycho-educational Assessment

When a child is deficient in a sense modality, assessment is fraught with problems. For students with visual impairments, many interlocking factors contribute to the difficulties met in the assessment process. These factors are outlined briefly below.

- The intelligence levels of blind and sighted children cannot be easily compared (Warren, 1984);
- We do not have intelligence tests that are equally meaningful for both sighted and visually impaired children. IQ tests for individuals who are blind do not evaluate them in a way comparable to the evaluation of sighted children (Warren, 1984).
- There is a lack of viable effective or standardized procedures for testing both the totally and partially blind populations (Johnson, 1989).
- The test formats may disadvantage pupils with visual impairments since most existing tests depend to a large extent on printed stimuli (Johnson, 1989).

To circumvent the visual disabilities, much IQ testing of children who are blind has been conducted using the non-visual verbal portions of common IQ tests. For children who are blind, tests use tactile or auditory modes; for those partially sighted, aural modes, large type, or magnified materials are used.

Several tools have been designed for visually impaired populations or specially adapted from other measures. Samuel Hayes, a psychologist involved with the Perkins School for the Blind, reasoned that children who are blind would be disadvantaged in using tests developed for sighted children. His modification of the Stanford-Binet Individual Intelligence Test, the Interim Hayes Stanford-Binet, eliminated items requiring sight. Following Hayes, various versions of the Binet tests have been commonly used with children who are blind, such as the Perkins-Binet and the verbal scales of the WISC-R (Warren, 1984). The Stanford Achievement Tests have been adapted and are available in both braille and large print for levels from second grade to college. Further examples are shown in the appendix table, Tools for Assessment.

INTERVENTION WITH CHILDREN WHO HAVE VISUAL IMPAIRMENTS

Intervention with the population of students who are visually impaired serves different purposes, depending on the nature and degree of the visual loss, as well as the unique goals of differing professional disciplines. Generally, the major areas of intervention are habilitation (therapy) and education, which includes reading and optical enhancement, learning to use alternate modalities, and orientation and mobility training.

Medical Intervention

Preventative medical intervention begins immediately after birth, when the eyes of newborns are routinely washed with a one-percent silver nitrate solution to prevent infection. Later, children are inoculated to prevent diseases that may result in visual impairments.

To identify and treat serious visual impairments, medical intervention is provided by an *ophthalmologist* (a medical doctor); an *optometrist* (a specialist in vision problems); and an *optician* (a technician who makes lenses). Protocols include medication, surgery, technical aids, and prescriptive lenses to control and maximize visual function. In the surgical area, laser-beam techniques are used to reattach damaged retinas, and there are sophisticated techniques for corneal transplants, artificial lens transplants, and the removal of cataracts. Various types of drug therapies and medications reduce the risk of blindness from glaucoma and diabetes.

Therapy

When children have severe visual impairments, special attention must be directed toward the efficient use of residual vision, gross motor skills for mobility, and fine motor skills for independent functioning, including compensatory hand skills. These children tend to use their hands in broad, sweeping motions and fail to acquire precise search and grasp skills.

Occupational therapists evaluate the effect of a child's visual impairment on daily living, play, and motor skills, and then design programs to improve these. For example, because young children with visual impairments may have weak hands and fingers and need hand skills, the program may incorporate manipulation of clay and Plasticine, squeeze toys, pegboards, and puzzles.

Technical Aids

There is not another field of special education that has benefited as much from technological advances as has the field of visual impairment. More than 2000 technical aids, accessories, and devices exist for reading, mobility and orientation, and magnification.

In the classroom, a student may use adaptive computer peripherals such as a voice output system, specialized keyboard, or a screen-enlarging device. There is also a four-track tape recorder/player, a Perkins brailler, a print enlarger machine, a talking calculator, and different types of reading aids.

For everyday living, an example of an exciting innovation is Voiceprint, a 24-hour reading service telecast specifically for persons who are blind, which is broadcast on television to an estimated five million Canadian households that have cable systems. Supported mainly by Communications Canada and Rogers Communications, Voiceprint is a non-profit organization providing time-sensitive news, current affairs, and topical information from all major English daily newspapers, plus over 100 Canadian and international newspapers, magazines, and periodicals (Hysert, 1993b).

We address technology again later in this chapter under the relevant headings.

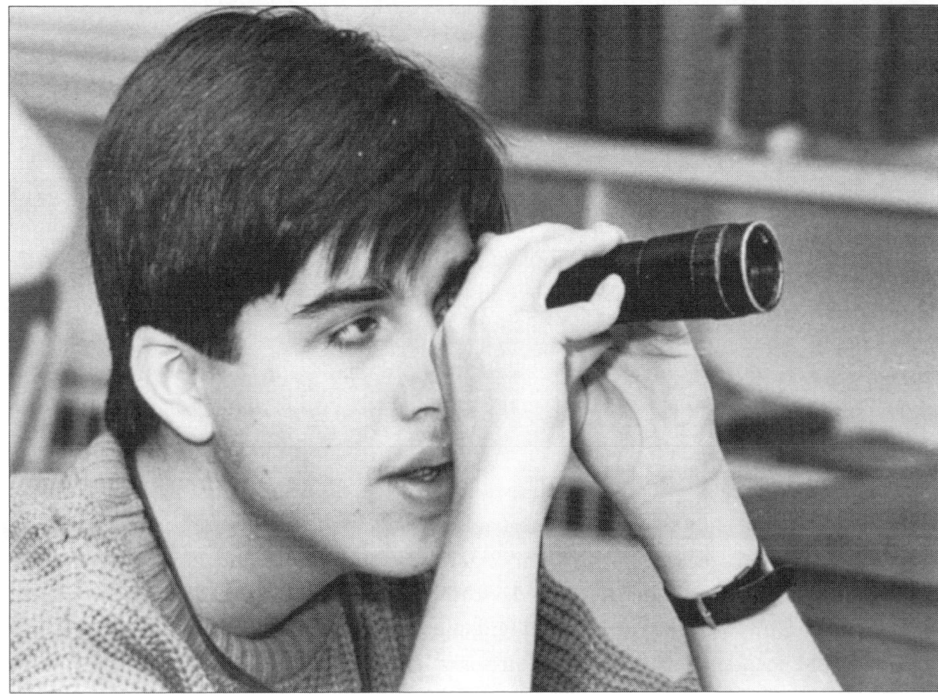

A variety of technical aids have been developed to assist children with visual impairments.

Educational Intervention

We point out in the Historical Notes that end this chapter that different options have long been available for the education of students with visual impairments. Integration into general classrooms is a long-standing tradition, and so are residential schools and special classes. The needs of an individual student at a particular point in his or her educational career have been, and are, the deciding factors.

Service Delivery Models

In recent years, the emphasis on inclusion has meant a shift from segregated residential school education for students with severe visual disabilities to education in neighbourhood schools. Nevertheless, residential schools still play a role in Canada. Some educators contend that short-term placement in residential schools may be a feasible solution to the difficulties experienced by some children with visual impairments (MacCuspie, 1993).

Many school districts make available a continuum of placement options. This continuum could include:

- Self-contained programs designed mainly for younger children or students with special learning difficulties. The special class permits intensive individualization of instruction and concentrated attention to a child's problems.
- The general classroom and a resource room that functions as a part-time classroom staffed by a specialist teacher who provides individual instruction as required, administers special tests, and adapts regular classroom materials.
- The general classroom and itinerant teacher assistance. An itinerant program makes it pos-

sible for most children with visual disabilities to be integrated into regular classes. A specialist teacher travels from school to school within a district to offer special instruction to children at all school levels, including those in special programs. Specialist teachers design and provide instructional programs in braille reading, braille math, and other academic subjects; teach the use of visual aids and electronic reading devices; may assess braille-reading readiness, visual perception, mobility, and social development; and design and provide instruction in self-help skills. They work closely with school personnel who are involved with students who are visually impaired. Itinerant teachers also interpret the medical, educational, and social implications of visual impairments and help teachers to adapt learning materials.

- The general classroom with accommodations and adaptations. Today, many students who are totally blind or severely visually impaired are enrolled in regular schools in all grades from kindergarten to secondary school.

Successful integration depends on five components—the availability of specialist teachers; access to special equipment and optical aids; a braille transcription service; co-operation among principals, regular teachers, and special education teachers; and access to alternative programs for students who need them. Classroom needs include a flexible teacher and peer acceptance and interaction. Personal student characteristics include social skills, a positive self-image, independence, family acceptance, and inner motivation (Bishop, 1986).

Inclusive programming may be more successful for students with visual impairments without additional disabilities if started in the early years. This is certainly true about Abu, the child we met in the case study at the opening of this chapter.

Case Study

Abu (continued)

Early intervention is important for very young children with visual impairments and their families. From infancy on, children may be trained in motor skills, locomotion and mobility, self-help skills, and communication. When they are integrated into nursery schools or day-care centres, adaptations to the environment and modifications to the program enhance their progress.

Researchers have identified specific program variables likely to influence intervention outcomes significantly and positively. These include the physical and cognitive adaptation of the classroom to accommodate children with disabilities; the provision of multi-sensory learning stimuli and experiences; incorporation of the child's strengths and weaknesses in the development of curricula; promotion of peer tolerance; a focus on independence and exploration of the environment; and the promotion of social interaction (see Guralnick, 1988).

The staff at the nursery school that was Abu's first educational experience were cognizant of his special needs. They designed a program that focused on his needs in classroom interactions, activities, and additional assistance, especially for orientation and mobility. This is shown in the extract from Abu's IEP below.

EXTRACT FROM ABU'S IEP

Name Abu
Age 4 years, 7 months
Centre Daycrest
Supervisor Ms. Teacher
Report number 2

Abu has been attending the centre for almost a year. During this time, he has been working on individual goals and objectives embedded within the daily routines and activities of the centre. A specialist teacher assists with orientation and mobility training (white cane) on a biweekly basis.

Adaptations

No particular environmental adaptations are necessary. Additional lighting is provided in the reading corner. Some special materials are provided; for example, large and sturdy toys. There are books that provide alternative sensory information and pictures that are clear and uncluttered. Some toys are adapted. For example, some have bases that are covered in textures such as sandpaper. Abu wears his glasses quite readily.

Assessment

At the outset, an assessment of Abu's potential and progress was undertaken. The full assessment included a psychological report as well as observations and informal checklists used by the teachers.

Present Levels of Functioning

Cognitive: The report of the psychologist confirms the teachers' observations that Abu is a child functioning at the norm. His language, problem-solving skills, and the activities he undertakes in the centre are normal for a child of his chronological age, taking into account the visual disability. Play behaviour lags somewhat. Abu is still into the stage of constructive activities and is not yet involved in symbolic play alone or with peers.
Language: Abu shows good language skills, although he requires more experience in some areas. He asks many questions and shows a natural curiosity.
Behaviour: At first Abu was very shy with his peers. As he becomes more confident, he is increasingly accepted by the other children. He is beginning to participate in group work.
Motor: Abu's gross motor skills are developing. Fine motor skills are lagging a little, probably the result of the visual impairment.

Long-Range Goals

- To develop security in the environment and in moving about in it.
- To strengthen the other sense modalities, especially audition and touch.
- To stimulate peer interactions.
- To introduce and practise orientation and mobility with the white cane

Objectives

- Improve auditory skills through identification and localization of sound. Use games with entire class.
- Improve tactile discrimination, especially in painting corner.
- Improve taste and smell awareness.
- Encourage the use of residual vision.
- Improve social interaction through teaching appropriate smiling behaviour in a small-group situation.

There are cautions about inclusion for all students with visual impairments but, possibly because of a history of successful integration, these do not approach the clamour of, say, hearing impairments or behavioural disorders. Most arguments centre on balancing the needs of students.

Those with cautions point out that as children are given opportunities to learn more skills associated with general educational expectations they are likewise restricted in the attainment of special skills such as braille and orientation and mobility. Social interaction, the activities of daily living, and incidental learning are difficult in inclusive settings.

Other critics worry about social isolation. During the adolescent period, many students who are visually impaired encounter difficulties in establishing relationships with peers. Even in integrated settings, they often do not interact. Competition with sighted peers can also cause difficulty, even with training and education.

Educational Approaches

Education for students who are visually impaired can be clustered into seven major areas to form a curriculum that combines the general curriculum goals of the child's grade level with specialized instruction. Areas of focus are the regular curriculum; use of special aids and equipment; communication skills; visual stimulation; orientation and mobility; personal competence, such as self-help skills and daily living skills; and vocational guidance and career education.

Curriculum

Students who are visually impaired can participate in practically all aspects of school activities. Reading is one potential area of difficulty, often because of slower reading speeds. For students who use braille, extra attention must be also paid to English spelling forms. Mathematics may be problematic. To master mathematical concepts, students need to explore the dimensions of shape and build up a vocabulary of meaningful mathematical terms. Physical education and creative activities are a particular focus in a well-rounded curriculum. Students who are visually impaired need daily opportunities for vigorous exercise. Older children may need to correct body posture and movement. They may hold their heads down, droop their shoulders forward, or walk with a shuffling gait.

Special Aids and Equipment

The greatest challenge facing people with visual impairments is the overwhelming mass of printed material in our world. Students are usually unable to use standard printed materials such as textbooks, classroom handouts, reference materials, and schedules; cannot access material written on the board or on an overhead projector; and cannot participate when media such as slides are used.

low-vision aids

Low-vision aids augment residual vision by increasing the size of the retinal image (Zammitt, Hare, Mason, and Elliott, 1999). For the majority of students classified as severely visually impaired, large print materials form the major reading medium. In large print, eighteen-point is the most popular type size. Large-print readers will generally use normal handwriting in their work; the size of the writing is likely to conform to their type-size preference.

Closed-circuit-television reading aids resemble regular television sets. They have a camera that scans reading material and conveys it to a monitor for enlargement. Users can regulate the size of the image to their own needs. Some machines are powerful enough to use with microfiche. Variable speech tape recorders are the most commonly used speech compressors.

For persons who are blind, braille is the traditional medium of literacy. After its acceptance in North America in the 1890s, braille was widely used (see the Research Notes). Then, during the 1960s and much of the '70s, a strong emphasis on the use of vision for individuals with visual impairments meant that the use of braille declined dramatically. Some people even felt that high-tech advances would eliminate the need for braille completely.

The percentages of braille users are telling. In 1955, more than 50 percent of all persons

Research Notes

Braille

Braille originally arose from the work of Charles Barbier, engineer, inventor, philanthropist, and officer in Napoleon's army, who devised a code which he called *criture nocturne*—night writing. These were not tracings of the ordinary alphabet but a secret code based on a twelve-dot unit, or cell, two dots wide and six high. Each dot or combination of dots stood for a letter or a phonetic sound.

When Barbier's system was presented to the French Academy of Sciences in 1808 it was hailed as a brilliant invention. Various adaptations of the system were undertaken by Barbier and duly submitted to the Academy. One report found its way to the school for the blind in Paris. However, the twelve-dot system was tried but rejected in 1820 as impractical: the cells were simply too large to be read by a single fingertip.

Louis Braille (1809–1852), the son of a harness maker, was born in Coupvray, a French town about forty-five kilometres from Paris. He had slit an eye at age three while playing with a sharp knife in his father's workshop, and the resulting infection destroyed the vision in his other eye. Louis first attended the village school where he did very well even without the advantage of schoolbooks. Then, in 1819, his father sent him to the Paris Institute for the Blind. Louis proved an outstanding student and eventually became a teacher at the school.

Frustrated with the methods of teaching reading to blind pupils, usually raised print or embossed regular print, Braille embarked on a search for a more efficient means and soon discovered Barbier's military code. When Braille undertook the adaptation of the Barbier system, he first solved the problem of the size of the cell by cutting the number of dots in half. He then devised a new code, alphabetic rather than phonetic, employing combinations of six dots. Because the new code was arbitrary, the symbols could stand for anything the users wanted to code. With his new system, Braille taught his students to read with more efficiency than was possible with embossed letters.

Braille's alphabetic code was published in 1834, his music notations in 1839. The braille system for reading and writing was officially adopted at the Paris School for the Blind in 1854. Dr. Simon Pollak, one of the founders of the Missouri School for the Blind, brought braille from Europe in the 1850s, but the braille code failed for many decades to find a niche in North America. Educators preferred systems closer to regular written language. Schools for the blind used typefaces such as Moon print, New York print, and raised print.

It was not until 1892 that resistance to braille was finally overcome. Once accepted as a means to assist blind persons with reading and writing, braille evolved into a well-established system that employs many abbreviated signs and symbols.

with severe visual impairments used braille. In 1963, about 55 percent of legally blind children used braille. By 1978, the rate dropped to 18 percent, and in 1989 only 12 percent used braille. By 1994, only 9.45 percent were braille users; in 1995, the number was 9.62 percent (De Witt, 1991; Schroeder, 1996).

Today there is an increased emphasis on braille as both educators and adult blind persons recognize that it is important to have more than one literacy medium. Further, data suggest that braille is not only a tool of literacy but an identity mechanism for adults who are blind, a symbol of independence and competence, even group identity (Schroeder, 1996).

Learning braille is complex and time-consuming.

The braille alphabet uses six dots arranged in two rows of three dots each. Each dot is numbered. (Figure 10-3 shows the braille alphabet.) Numbers and punctuation signs are also represented in braille; numbers use dots 3 to 6, and the use of dot 6 just before a letter indicates a capital. Braille has been adapted to many written languages, including those that do not use Roman letters. As well, a scientific and mathematical code has been developed.

For literacy, there are two braille alphabets. Grade 1, or alphabetic braille, is referred to as the simplified braille code. Grade 2, or abbreviated braille, is more common and much faster. There is also a Grade 3 braille.

Because of the complex rules underlying Grade 2 braille structure and the many abbreviations, teaching braille reading is more complex and time-consuming than teaching print reading. For the reader, the process is slower than reading print because the reading range of the fingers is much narrower than that of the eye. Reading efficiency is more difficult to achieve: readers must develop tactile tracking skills, a light touch, good reading posture, and smooth coordination of both hands.

A skilled two-handed reader begins by placing both hands at the beginning of a line. When the middle of the line is reached, the right hand continues across the line while the left hand locates the beginning of the next line. The left hand begins to read the first several words of the new line while the right hand moves to its new reading position.

Blind braille-reading students require braille textbooks. Traditional braille transcription was expensive and facilities were sparse. Computerized braille has almost superseded the slow and tedious manual versions and made the process both rapid and compact. Today, computer braille transcription centres are available in both Canada and the United States.

The Optacon (Optic to Tactile Converter), which converts printed material to braille, is the most widely used reading device. By passing a scanning device over the printed material, the microprocessor converts the words to braille via a small electronic braille-writing

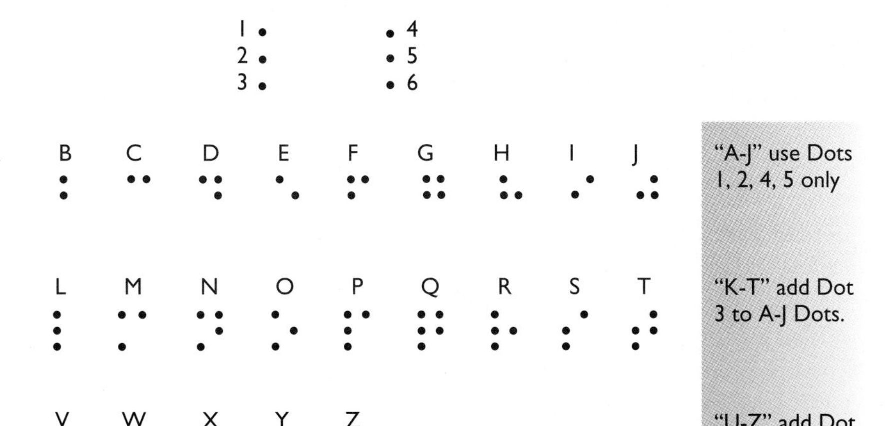

Figure 10-3 *The Roman alphabet in braille*

device that permits a person who is blind to "read along" as the viewer passes over the written words. Young children as well as adults can use the Optacon to gain immediate access to print materials.

Reading with the Optacon is not the same as reading with braille. With the Optacon, the user holds a small camera in one hand to read printed material and convert it into impulses. With the index finger of the other hand, the user can feel the letters and numbers through a tactile array of 144 small vibrating rods contained in a portable battery-operated electronic section about the size and weight of a portable cassette tape recorder. For example, if the camera moves across the letter H, the user of the Optacon feels two vertical lines and one horizontal line moving beneath his or her fingers and tries to recognize the letter shape (Abang, 1980). Recognition of letter shapes requires a great deal of skill and practice.

Raymond Kurzweil's reading machine, first introduced in 1976, is designed to convert printed materials to an audio output. Its camera picks up printed letters, which are then converted into synthesized speech.

For writing, the slate and stylus are the braille version of pen and paper. The user presses the stylus through openings in the slate that holds the paper. Since the material must be read from the underside of the paper, it must be written in reverse by starting at the right margin and moving toward the left.

In the first decade of the 20th century, Frank Hall invented a machine, the brailler, that allowed a person to type braille. Although less portable than a slate and stylus, the brailler is easier to use. Paperless braillers, such as the Cranmer Modified Perkins Brailler, allow students to feed information into a computer and receive a braille printout. The user can also write in braille, store material, and correct or amend material as on a standard computer.

Visual Stimulation

Until the 1960s it was believed that children should conserve their vision so as not to "wear it out." Today's educators believe that if residual sight is used rather than saved, most children with visual disabilities can actually improve their visual functioning. The more children use their vision, particularly at close range, the more they stimulate the pathways to the brain. The brain accumulates a variety of visual images and stores them as memories. This process enables children to function more as visual learners.

A range of visual skills are targeted—attention to lights and objects; tracing and scanning; and figure–ground discrimination. Visual perception takes in object discrimination, the use of pictures, sorting and classification, and sequencing.

Vision is further stimulated with the use of prescription devices and low-vision aids, which can considerably increase a child's ability to maximize near-vision potential. Children do not naturally use this equipment; they need training in how to use special aids and equipment, including aids for magnification. There are three main types of magnification and telescopic aids: hand-held magnifiers and telescopes; stand magnifiers, fixed focus or focusable; and headband aids—spectacles, clip-on loupes, and telescopes.

Orientation and Mobility

To move freely and confidently, individuals who are visually impaired must know where they want to go, how, and in what direction. They must be able to move at a reasonable rate and with grace, comfort, and safety along existing routes between an origin and a destination.

orientation
mobility

Teaching independent travel is referred to as *orientation and mobility* (O and M) training. **Orientation** refers to an individual's knowledge of his or her position in space; **mobility** refers to negotiating that space. Training means learning to use a travel aid, such as a cane or a dog. Also stressed are the use of auditory, tactual, and kinesthetic senses together with any residual vision.

An orientation and mobility instructor (pripatologist) teaches mobility skills. Traditional O and M follows a sequence of skill building beginning in an uncomplicated controlled setting and extending slowly to functional tasks. O and M has usually been reserved for persons who are blind. Today some experts recommend it also for individuals with low vision (Smith, Del'aunne, and Geruschat, 1992).

Orientation (cognitive mapping) involves knowing the spatial relations among objects or landmarks and one's own position in relation to the relevant objects or landmarks. Sighted persons use their visual system for orientation. Vision provides information as to where a seen object is in relation to the body, stimulating other senses so that they can determine whether or not the object is moving. Vision also maintains accurate functioning and position in space in spite of changes in the position of the eyes, head, and body, and judges relative direction (Howard and Templeton, 1966). These orientation tasks involve the retina, eye movements, visual direction, kinesthetic judgments, the vestibular apparatus, and auditory location.

Persons who are blind have little or no access to the visual information needed to construct cognitive maps. They acquire knowledge of the spatial relations among objects through tactile, proprioceptive, or auditory modes. Whereas a sighted person relies on visual representation and visual angle of perspective, persons who are blind must rely on sound distance to judge their relationship to an object. A person learns to detect subtle changes in the pitch of high-frequency echoes as he or she moves toward objects. This is the *Doppler ef-*

fect, a physical principle that says the pitch of a sound rises as a person moves toward the source (Hallahan and Kauffman, 1991).

When guides are used, human guides are probably the most efficient (called the sighted guide technique). But human guides are not always available, and a constant human guide would inevitably lead to a decrease in independence.

Teaming a properly trained dog with a person who is blind helps in the achievement of independent mobility. Only a small proportion of the blind population actually use a dog guide. To qualify, the individual must be over sixteen, emotionally mature, responsible, and selected by an O and M specialist for dog training.

Children do not use guide dogs. The most usual breeds used for guiding are German shepherds, Labrador retrievers, golden retrievers, and sometimes setters, and these dogs are too big for young children to handle. As well, the dogs are not pets and need constant grooming and care, and children are not mature enough to keep from playing with the animal or to competently care for its needs.

Ideally, all guide dogs are placid, steady, precise animals of constant concentration, oblivious to people around them as they work with their blind owner to whom their responses are exclusively directed. But such dogs are rare, and all have idiosyncrasies that must be taken into account when matching a dog with a master. Some dogs are too fast for the owner; others are too slow. The case study on Pete and his dog illustrates what can happen when there is a mismatch between dog and owner.

Case Study

Pete

Pete is now twenty-seven years old. He lost his vision as the result of an accident when he was only three years of age. Pete was sent to a residential school for the elementary years but attended the local high school near his home. He is now taking his master's degree at university.

At school, Pete was taught to use the Hoover cane and developed excellent mobility and orientation skills. But he wanted a guide dog and as soon as he was old enough applied to a centre for one. When Pete's application was accepted, he went to the centre and worked for nearly a month with the dog selected for him, under the guidance of a highly qualified trainer. Not only did Pete learn about how the dog could assist his own mobility, but he learned how to care for the dog—to feed it properly, to groom it regularly, and to provide it with lots of exercise. After Pete brought his dog home, workers checked on both his progress and the dog's care and health.

Pete's first dog eventually grew too old to work and Pete keeps him as a beloved pet. He now has a second dog, a young Irish setter. He is, however, finding this experience a little different. The dog is young and more skittish than the first one. When people, not realizing that the dog is working, play with and pet it, the dog responds. The dog loves the snow and, as they live in St. John's, has plenty of opportunity to go bounding over snowbanks and icy sidewalks. When this happens, the dog seems to be in control of Pete, rather than Pete being in control of the dog. Pete is not sure he can overcome these problems and is thinking that the white cane may be more suitable for him at the moment.

The prescription cane, also called the *long cane*, the *white cane*, and the *Hoover cane*, is the most common travel aid used by children and adults. It essentially came from the long staff that has been the symbol of blindness at least since Roman times. The cane is made of aluminum or fibreglass; its length is determined by the user's height and comfort level. The traveller holds the cane in front, swinging it in small arcs to detect obstacles.

A wide variety of other travel aids exist. Many work on a radar principle, sending out beams of ultrasound which cannot be heard by the human ear. If the beam hits an object, some of the ultrasound is reflected back to the device and converted into audible tones. For example, the Sonicguide supplies three kinds of information about an object—direction, distance, and general characteristics. The Sonicguide may be used with a long cane or a dog guide, and can be fitted into eyeglass frames.

The laser cane transmits invisible infrared light. When it detects an obstacle, some of the light beam is reflected back to the cane, vibrating a pin beneath the user's index finger. The Mowat Sensor is a small hand-held device, light enough to be carried in a pocket or purse. It can be used to locate fallen objects, doorways, or even mailboxes.

The age of onset of a visual impairment does not predict an individual's ability with mobility skills. Canes are used with young children who are blind to increase mobility, early exploration of the environment, and self-confidence, and to decrease dependence on others. Young children can also be taught to use specially adapted sensing devices; these can improve the locomotion and mobility of children as young as one year.

The infant's Sonicguide uses a headband mounting and permits obstacle detection as close as fifty centimetres. The Canterbury Child's Aid is a binaural spatial sensor that reflects objects sensed from two receiving transductors mounted a small distance apart on an adjustable headband. Echoes are transduced into audible sounds that are presented to the ears through small speakers or earphones. The distance of an object is coded primarily in frequency; high frequencies signify faraway objects. The lower the frequency, the nearer the object.

A tactual map is a raised map that is used by blind persons as a supplemental aid for travel, navigation, and mobility. Maps portray immediate indoor and outdoor environments, providing just enough information to support the specific movement requirements of the person who is visually impaired (Golledge, 1991).

Personal Competence

Young children who are visually impaired often need help in acquiring self-help skills such as dressing, feeding, and toileting. In older children, personal competence revolves around social skills. Adolescents often need assistance to balance their interests, to tackle new areas of learning, to take risks, and to overcome a fear of failure. (See Chapter 16.)

Social Intervention

The care and training of persons who were blind made rapid advances with the return of blinded soldiers from Europe after the First World War. In 1917, a representative group of blinded soldiers and civilians met with women's organizations and businessmen and set about forming the Canadian National Institute for the Blind (CNIB). Since that time, the

Historical Notes

Over the centuries, common perceptions of blindness have been surrounded by fear, myth, and superstition, all interwoven into two contradictory themes. One common thread has blindness associated with darkness, despair, loneliness, and punishment—"one of those instruments by which a mysterious Providence has chosen to afflict man" ("Address...," 1836). The opposing theme held that blind persons were compensated for their lack of sight by both psychological and physical factors. Their condition was associated with superhuman and spiritual powers, uncanny memory ability, and musicality.

Perhaps because blindness is such an obvious disability and one that is so feared by many people, blind persons were early granted special privileges, albeit ones that confirmed their deviant and different status in society. In ancient Rome, only those who were blind were allowed to beg on the steps of the temples, and throughout the centuries this privilege extended to the steps of churches in many places. Beginning in the 4th century, hospices for the blind were established. In the 13th century, one of the first hospitals was founded in Paris for blinded soldiers returning from the crusades.

Formal schooling for persons who were blind began in Paris in 1784, in Boston in 1832, and in Halifax in 1870. As well, many positive changes were wrought by dedicated educators such as Samuel Gridley Howe, by slowly evolving legislation, and by advocacy groups such as the Canadian National Institute for the Blind (CNIB), which was formed by blinded veterans after the First World War.

John Barrett McGann was the first person in Canada to undertake the education of students who were blind. Beginning in 1861, he admitted blind children to his Toronto school for the deaf, where they were taught by his fifteen-year-old daughter, Effie. In 1866, the Grey Nuns founded the Nazareth Institution in Montreal.

Publicly supported institutions opened in Halifax in 1870 and in Ontario in 1872. By 1875 there were three institutions for pupils who were blind in Canada, which gathered pupils from all across the Dominion. It was common practice, for example, for Alberta students with visual disabilities to be sent to the Ontario institution as late as the 1970s (Conn-Blowers and McLeod, 1989).

Educational integration came quickly for students with severe visual impairments. As early as 1839 Samuel Gridley Howe argued that blind children deserved "an equal participation in the blessing of education with seeing children" (Perkins Institution, 1839, p. 80). Chicago in 1900 witnessed the establishment of the first special class for blind students. After that, classes for children who were blind and sight-saving classes for those with visual impairments who were able to read print opened in most urban school districts. In sight-saving classes, children with poor sight were encouraged to "save" or reduce demands on their vision.

As early as 1911 there are reports of children who were blind being integrated into regular classrooms, and some educators were wont to argue that children with visual impairments were easily assimilated and taught in regular classrooms. In 1949, the year that the first children with retrolental fibroplasia reached school, the total number of visually impaired students in the public schools began to increase, and their population grew faster than that of the residential schools. By 1956, 25 percent of children with visual impairments attended regular schools; by 1980, the numbers had risen to 95 percent.

CNIB has developed as a national voluntary service that serves more than 39 000 blind and visually impaired Canadians. The CNIB has two major objectives: to foster the integration of visually impaired Canadians into the mainstream of society and to prevent visual disabilities.

The Canadian Council of the Blind is a national organization made up of and run entirely by blind people. It is concerned with the welfare of individuals who are blind and maintains active committees on legislation, recreation, employment, and other matters of concern to blind Canadians. The Council works in close liaison with the CNIB.

SUMMARY

1. Visual impairments vary widely in both degree and type. At one end of the spectrum are people who are totally blind and have no sight at all. At the other end are those with near-normal vision.
2. Mild visual impairments are a high-incidence condition; the incidence of severe visual impairment and blindness is very low. Severe visual impairment accounts for only about one percent of all children who are disabled.
3. At the simplest level, the human eye can be seen as consisting of three parts—the eye itself, which picks up visual messages; the optic nerve, which transfers the messages; and the brain, which interprets the messages. Images are passed through the eye and along the optic nerve to the brain by light. If anything stops or hinders the correct passage of the light, visual problems occur.
4. Because people categorized as visually impaired have vision problems that range from mild disability to total blindness, a number of terms and definitions are used that cover this wide spectrum.
5. All children should be screened and observed in the classroom for behavioural and physical symptoms of visual impairment. Complete eye examinations are necessary to diagnose visual acuity and functioning and to determine optical needs. In psycho-educational assessment, children with severe visual impairments are particularly difficult to assess using standard measures and procedures.
6. A severe impairment in one of the most important of the human senses affects many other areas of a child's functioning, most particularly motor and mobility skills. Children also miss imitation and social reciprocity.
7. Surgery and correction are the most common forms of medical intervention.
8. Provided there are appropriate supports for both the student and the classroom teacher, many students with severe visual impairments are included into general classrooms. Ideally, specialists in the area of visual impairment collaborate with classroom teachers in assessing and developing instructional programs for children who are visually impaired and those with co-occurring disabilities.
9. Training in orientation and mobility enables children who are blind to move with confidence and independence within their environment. Along with travel aids, children learn to gauge distance and direction from variations in sound.

WEBLINKS

Canadian Braille Authority **www.langara.bc.ca/cba/**

The Canadian National Institute for the Blind **www.cnib.ca/**

Guide dogs **www.guidedogs.ca**

Materials Resource Centre for the Visually Impaired **www.lrdc.edc.gov.ab.ca/scripts/cgiip-exe/mrc/mrc.htm**

National Braille Press **www.nbp.org**

Retinopathy of Prematurity **www.ropard.org**

Students with Visual Impairments **www.bced.gov.bc.ca/specialed/visimpair/toc.htm**

In the Classroom

The consequences of hearing impairment and visual impairment are quite different. Students with severe hearing losses learn visually, often with a manual system of communication such as ASL. Those who are visually impaired use language to anchor them to their environments; they learn through audition and often through tactile means such as with braille or an Optacon. Students with hearing impairments range from those who are hard of hearing to those with profound hearing losses. For all of these students, the commonality is difficulty with language and speech to some degree. As well as the ideas presented below, readers should also take into account the tips on language presented in Section 2 of this text.

Given the many types of visual impairment, the range of severity levels, and the unique ways that individuals use residual vision, it is not surprising that children with visual impairments also form an extremely heterogeneous population. In a classroom, teachers may meet students with restricted vision who cannot see at a distance; those who are unable to see near images clearly; and those who need special lighting and optical aids to learn visually.

Behavioural manifestations, needs associated with hearing impairment	**Tips**
Cannot learn through audition	• Allow students to make full use of the visual clues they rely on so heavily. • Seat the child near the front of the room and a little to one side; the second seat from the front allows an optimal distance of about two metres for speech reading and the detection of visual clues

Behavioural manifestations, needs associated with hearing impairment	Tips
	• Ensure good lighting, especially on the speaker's face. Teacher should face the light source. Natural light is better than fluorescent lighting.
Cannot hear classroom dialogue	• Allow children to turn in their seats when other students are talking or to move their seats when they need a better view. • Point or move your head to cue children in to the person who is talking or the object under discussion.
Uses speech reading to understand messages and information.	• Speak naturally. Do not overenunciate; this makes speech reading more difficult. • Try not to smile or whisper while speaking; this distorts the shape of the lips. • Try to stand still while talking. • Remember that children cannot speech read if the teacher talks to the chalkboard or speaks in the dark during a movie or filmstrip. • Keep the book low while reading aloud to allow children a good view of your face. • Be in close proximity when speaking. Speech reading is best at about two metres; hearing aids function best within the same distance. • Use many visual aids. These are helpful for hearing children as well.
Wears a hearing aid or uses an FM system	• Provide an environment as quiet as possible so the child can listen to the best auditory message. • Environmental noises are a problem for children with hearing aids because all sounds are amplified. Keep auditory and visual distractions in the classroom to a minimum. • Check daily that hearing aids are working. • Keep a supply of extra batteries.
Has poor language knowledge	• Repeat and rephrase information and directions. • Encourage children to ask questions if they are not sure.
Needs an interpreter	• For older students, provide the interpreter with class routines, projects, and long-term assignments to help students understand and prepare for assignments.
Experiences social isolation	• Especially for older students, use techniques such as co-operative learning to promote peer interaction and communication skills.

Behavioural manifestations, needs, associated with visual impairment	Tips
Learns auditorily	• Provide direct learning experiences through a distance sense. Use a multi-sensory approach. • Especially in the elementary years, students need concrete experiences, unifying experiences, and to learn by doing. • Enhance communication skills through language arts, conversational practice, social skill instruction, and role playing. • Use words such as "look" and "see" but avoid "this," "that" and other intangibles. • Take care with statements that require visualization, such as "Pick up the papers." • When using the chalkboard, give much verbal information. • Explain, using concrete terms. • Don't raise your voice. • In teaching reading, a phonics approach may prove helpful for students who cannot see whole words.
Slower reading rate with braille or large print	• Allow longer time for tasks that require reading. • Tapes or records are helpful teaching devices, giving the student a break from visual fatigue. • Scores on standardized achievement tests may be depressed by slow responses due to a slower reading or writing rate. • Allow more time for tests.
Needs adapted materials	• On application worksheets, blacken the print. • Use buff rather than white paper. • Assign a variety of types of seat work. • For older students, use graphs made of sandpaper, yarn, spaghetti, and other materials.
Needs large-size print	• Low-vision students write in a size compatible with their own visual capacity. Stress legibility, not size. • Students work under extra pressure and will be tired at the end of the day. Large amounts of homework should not be assigned.
Needs social skill assistance	• Point out classroom rules to which the student must adhere. • Expect the same quality of work as from other students. • Try to emphasize the child's strengths without denying the special needs.
Needs orientation and mobility training	• If necessary, use a buddy at first but do not allow the student to grow too dependent. • Don't move furniture in the classroom without informing the student.

Behavioural manifestations, needs, associated with visual impairment	**Tips**
Needs adapted/adaptive equipment	• Cut down glare on glass, desks, and chalkboards in the classroom. • Provide tilt-top desks. • Try to have classroom displays at the student's eye level. • Provide adequate storage space for materials while still keeping the student physically integrated.
Needs different lighting	• Check the lighting needs of the child. In children who are sensitive to light, acuity increases with decreasing illumination.
Needs visual stimulation	• If the child wears glasses, be sure that they are clean.
Needs to stress visual functioning	• Know how, when, and under what circumstances students can use their vision most effectively. Students with central field defects may benefit from eccentric viewing techniques. Those who have nystagmus need to discover the best posture for reading. Those with poor peripheral vision can turn their heads, rather than move their eyes for scanning. • Become familiar with the optical aids, large print, and reading aids.

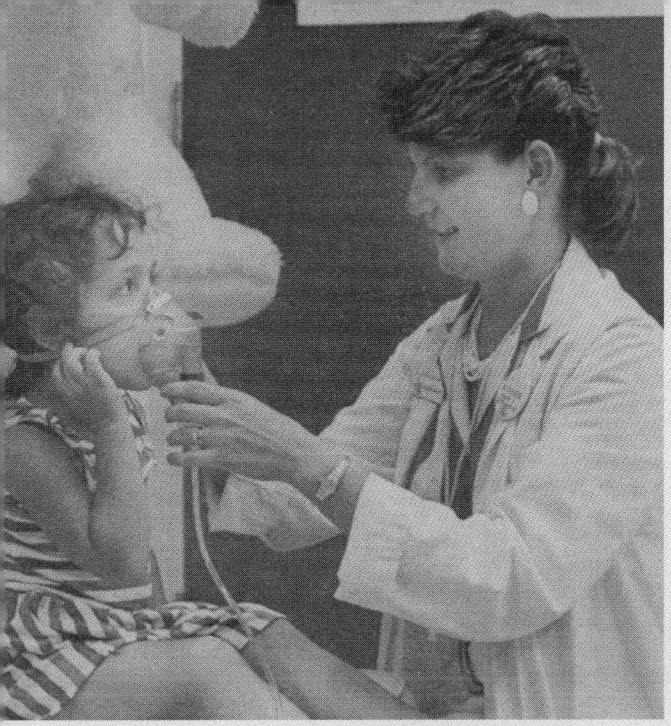

SECTION 6

Children with Low-Incidence Disabilities

Nowhere in the study of exceptionality or special education is the spectrum of possible disorders more apparent than in the area of children with special health care needs, neurological disabilities, and orthopedic and physical disabilities. Of youngsters with these disabilities, almost half have cerebral palsy. Children with asthma and allergies make up almost all the remainder of the population. Children with other conditions, such as cystic fibrosis or spina bifida, form only a tiny percentage of those with physical and health disabilities.

Given such a diverse population, the medical, social, technical, and educational needs of these children vary dramatically. Some students require intense intervention; others need only minor adjustments to classroom physical layout or scheduling. Some children use adaptive equipment, including orthotic and prosthetic devices, to assist their functioning. Much adaptive equipment is used for support, for mobility, and for positioning.

Physical, neurological, and health disorders are low-incidence conditions; pervasive developmental disorders and multiple disabilities are conditions of even lower incidence. These disorders, though relatively rare, have devastating effects on children's development and potential. These children present such a tremendous challenge to the school system and so test the ingenuity of teachers and diagnosticians that they have been the subject of intense research activity that has spawned a variety of treatment approaches.

Pervasive developmental disorders are severe qualitative subnormalities that are not normal for any stage of development. Subsumed within the broad category of pervasive developmental disorders are *childhood psychoses* that affect many basic areas of psychological development at the same time and to a severe degree. Children with psychoses display severe abnormalities and disturbances that are seen as distortions of development. For example, *schizophrenia* is a condition characterized by qualitative changes in functioning such as association disturbances, delusions, hallucinations, attention deficits, and inappropriate social interaction.

Included among pervasive developmental disorders are children with infantile autism. They differ markedly from those whose psychoses begin later, and most researchers today hold that *autism* is a developmental disorder that is distinct from childhood psychoses such as schizophrenia. Children who are autistic present a shifting array of behaviours that seem to defy analysis; they indulge in repetitive, ritualistic, and solitary activities, responding to those in the environment with aloofness and indifference.

Children who are psychotic and autistic show extreme variability in intellectual functioning; many, however, function at pre-academic levels. Especially in children with autism, language development is often so poor as to render verbal communication impossible; language is either non-existent or bizarre in nature. Deficits range from phonological to syntactic and pragmatic defects. Many children do not speak at all, nor do they appear to comprehend language. Others show echolalia, parroting, meaningless jargon, and the incessant repetition of questions and statements.

Children with severe or multiple disabilities have a range of impairments. While innumerable combinations of disabilities are possible, some appear more often than others and some are more difficult to cope with than others. Within the population with multiple disabilities, children who are deaf-blind are among the most studied.

Definitions are particularly untidy in the fields of health disorders and physical disabilities and there are many ways of categorizing the conditions for purposes of discussion. In this section, we arbitrarily discuss children with specific health care needs in one chapter and then look at children with neurological difficulties in Chapter 12.

Under pervasive developmental disorders, we discuss children with childhood schizophrenia and those with infantile autism. A chapter is reserved for children with severe and multiple disabilities. The reader must remain aware that much overlap exists in all the conditions mentioned in this section. Many children with autism, for example, are actually multiply disabled, and many children with multiple disabilities exhibit autistic behaviours. Pediatric AIDS can be discussed as a health problem, as a neurological difficulty or, depending on the course of the disease, as a multiply disabling condition.

Chapter 11

Children with Special Health Care Needs

Learning Outcomes

After reading this chapter, you should be able to:

- Identify some of the more common health disabilities and their developmental consequences;
- Understand the special needs of children with health problems in educational settings;
- Prepare an emergency protocol.

Introduction

Special health care needs are diseases and conditions that affect the lives and functioning of children and adults. The category includes a huge range such as cancer, diabetes, asthma and allergies, and genetic problems such as cystic fibrosis and muscular dystrophy.

Many health problems result from a variety of genetic and environmental causes; others are associated with prenatal problems, prematurity, and problems of gestation. Some conditions are transient, others are lifelong; some occur more frequently in children than in adults. When found in children, the majority of chronic illnesses manifest themselves during the first three years of life.

Essentially, special health care needs are medical problems that are handled within medical parameters. Because medical concerns are the major factors affecting learning for these children, their medical needs and technological dependence must be met before they can benefit from the classroom experience.

With today's medical and technological advances, we are seeing more and more students who need some type of medical assistance in our classrooms. Some children are technologically dependent; a child who in the recent past would never have left the hospital may now attend a neighbourhood school in a wheelchair with a ventilator or a gastrotomy tube. So while today's classrooms still have the traditional educational accoutrements—pencils, books, and pull-down maps—there may also be an oxygen tank, a box of latex gloves, or a wheelchair.

It is predicted that most classroom teachers will meet a child with special health needs at least once in their careers ("Growing challenge ...," 1998). On average, for example, there are two children in every classroom with asthma at any given time (Getch and Newharth-Pritchett, 1999). This fact makes it imperative that contemporary teachers possess at least some knowledge of health maintenance; they must be familiar with the appropriate medical procedures and interventions that are part of the regular care of students with special health care needs as well as those required in emergency situations. Teachers should recognize too that children with special health needs are often on a roller coaster of changing needs that is unlike any other disability. These students are subject to unpredictable ups and downs due to the changing course of some illnesses. Other conditions result in a different sort of roller coaster of changing needs as children are in remission or in acute periods or are recovering from surgery or serious bouts. Teachers must be aware of changing treatments, new medications and treatment regimens, and accompanying side effects.

Regardless of the diagnostic category, children with special health care needs have the same wants as other youngsters, and the basic goals of education are the same for these youngsters as they are for all other students. But while the challenges presented by children with health care needs are more environmental and attitudinal than educational, educators must be aware of the factors that put students at risk for learning difficulties. These include fatigue, limited vitality, short attention span, and limited mobility.

While children with special health care needs require additional monitoring by school personnel, most will be placed in regular classrooms and will not require special education services. Special education may be warranted only because the condition or illness results in loss of school time and the child is consequently falling behind in school work. We can see this cogently in the case of Czeslov, a child of average ability who is lagging badly in academic domains not because of any deficits in ability or behaviour but because his illness keeps him away from school so often.

While the number of health problems involving other body systems is staggering, in this chapter we restrict discussion to a few specific and sometimes life-threatening conditions most often seen in our classrooms. We also discuss child abuse and neglect and musculoskeletal impairments.

Abnormalities of the bony structures include limb deficiencies and a number of congenital conditions such as muscular dystrophy, spinal curvature, and osteogenesis imperfecta.

DEFINITIONS OF SPECIAL HEALTH CARE NEEDS

One of the major difficulties in discussing health care needs (and neurological disorders) is the diversity of conditions and their sequelae. This diversity leads to a range of overlapping descriptors. For example, orthopedic and neurological impairments, while two distinct types of disabilities, may nevertheless cause similar limitations in movement. This means that a single child can be described in a number of ways. A child with muscular dystrophy, for example, can be said to have a health disorder, a musculoskeletal impairment, a physical disability, an orthopedic problem, or a motor impairment. Similarly, cerebral palsy can be categorized as a neurological impairment, a significant motor disability, a physical disability, and an orthopedic disability. The conditions discussed in this chapter and in Chapter 12 (excluding child abuse) are shown in Table 11-1 with their possible descriptors.

Case Study

Czeslov

When Ms. Day, a psychologist in private practice, was asked by the local school board to test Czeslov, she was somewhat reluctant. The school described the child as suffering from cystic fibrosis, a chronic and life-threatening disorder. Ms. Day was unfamiliar with the condition and its consequences and did not quite know what types of educational and psychological tests to use with such a child.

During the assessment process, Ms. Day did not need to make any adaptations to the formats or procedures. Czeslov was a little shy but performed well, and the psychologist was confident that she obtained valid and usable results.

On the WISC-III all of Czeslov's scores were within the average range; he presented a Full Scale IQ score of 124. It was when Ms. Day began to present some educational measures that problems emerged. Although this child obviously had good potential to learn in school, he was now nine years old and showed little progress beyond beginning level in reading and the other language arts. He had developed some basic numeracy skills but his arithmetic was very poor in computation and in using basic addition, subtraction, and multiplication. Division problems were completely beyond him.

Ms. Day could see the school's dilemma. Here was a child with good intellectual potential who was lagging far behind his peers simply because he had missed so many days of school due to illness. Yet the school was loath to designate the child as a special education candidate without some sort of classification that would ensure funding. Nor did anyone really believe that special education was truly necessary for Czeslov, and he certainly did not need a paraprofessional in the classroom.

When Ms. Day, the classroom teacher, the school principal, and the mother met to discuss Czeslov's performance, Ms. Day explained that she found a child of average or above-average ability who was functioning academically two or three years below his classmates. The reasons were easy to discern. The principal found that Czeslov had missed about fifty days of school each year; that is, about one third of classroom time. His medical needs and the intense therapy, plus the changing nature of his condition, meant that on many days he simply could not handle school.

Special education, per se, was not necessary. What was critical was intense remediation in core areas, always taking into account Czeslov's limited vitality and current health status. The main focus was to develop a support system that provided assistance to Czeslov in the classroom and adapted the curriculum and instructional environment to his specific needs.

Reading skills are the first and most important area to consider. To assist Czeslov, the teacher will use direct-instruction techniques. She or a paraprofessional will work with Czeslov in a small group of five or six students for half an hour each day. During the session, all instruction will be focused on reading, writing, and print. The process will generally follow the following scheme: give the children some easy reading; teach new skills with a stress on phonological awareness and phonics; present some challenging reading. Children will also do some writing to focus their attention on print.

A second important area is the social domain. When a child has a serious health disorder and is absent a great deal the attitudes of other class members are critical. It is the teacher's task to ensure that a child is accepted by his or her peers. As well, an understanding and tactful teacher can minimize potentially uncomfortable situations and model accepting attitudes for students.

Table 11-1 Conditions and possible descriptors

Chronic health problems	Neurological dysfunction	Musculoskeletal impairment	Orthopedic impairment	Physical/motor disability	Technology dependent/ medically fragile
Allergies	x				
Arthritis	x		x		x
Asthma	x				
Cancer	x				
Cerebral palsy		x	x	x	x
Clubfoot			x	x	x
Cystic fibrosis	x				
Diabetes	x				
Epilepsy	x	x			
Hydrocephalus					x
Limb deficiencies			x	x	x
Multiple sclerosis	x	x		x	x
Muscular dystrophy			x	x	x
Pediatric AIDS	x	x			
Scoliosis		x	x	x	x
Sickle cell anemia	x				
Spina bifida with myelomening-ocele		x	x	x	x
Traumatic brain injury		x			

Commonly used descriptors are discussed below.

- According to a generic U.S. definition, *health impairment* refers to "having limited strength, vitality, or alertness, due to chronic or acute health problems such as heart condition, tuberculosis, rheumatic fever, nephritis, asthma, sickle cell anemia, hemophilia, epilepsy, lead poisoning, leukemia, or disabilities that adversely affects a child's educational performance" (cited in Heller, Frederick, Dykes, Best, and Cohen, 1999, p. 220).
- *Physical disabilities* are those that affect body systems; they include health disorders and problems related to mobility and motor skills. Physical disabilities that have associated motor disabilities and deviations include cerebral palsy, muscular dystrophy, and spina bifida.

- *Orthopedic conditions* are those that arise from any cause and affect mobility and those "that adversely affects a child's educational performance. The term includes impairments caused by congenital anomalies (e.g., club foot, absence of some member, etc.), impairments caused by disease (e.g. poliomyelytis, bone tuberculosis, etc.) and impairments from other causes (e.g. cerebral palsy, amputations, and fractures or burns that cause contactures" (cited in Heller et al., 1999, p. 220).
- *Musculoskeletal impairments* are specific disorders involving bones or muscles that impede bodily movements in the absence of damage to the central nervous system. Causes range from inherited diseases and congenital malformations to infections and accidents.
- *Neuromuscular diseases* are acquired or inherited conditions that affect cells in the spinal cord, the peripheral motor nerves, the myoneural functions between the nerves and muscles, and the muscles themselves (Sandoval, 1998). Neurological dysfunctions occur before, during, or after birth and include cerebral palsy and head traumas.
- *Technology dependent* refers to conditions that require technological intervention. Children need "a medical device to compensate for the loss of vital bodily function and substantial ongoing nursing care to avert death or further disability" (OTA, 1987, p. 3). For example, a child may be ventilator dependent, oxygen dependent, or nutritional supplement dependent. Or a child may need heart monitoring, apnea monitoring, or kidney dialysis.
- *Medically fragile* is a term that overlaps the above category. Medically fragile children require specialized technological health care procedures for life support during the school day. These students may or may not require special education.

In this chapter we restrict our discussion to health problems and musculoskeletal impairments that do not have neurological involvement. Impairments directly related to damage of the central nervous system are discussed in Chapter 12.

PREVALENCE OF SPECIAL HEALTH CARE NEEDS

The number of students with physical and health disabilities is increasing (Heller et al., 1999). Beyond this general statement, the prevalence of chronic health problems is very difficult to determine. This is primarily because:

- There is such a variety of conditions, and there exist inconsistencies in defining various disabilities;
- Different provinces use different methods for gathering data, producing very different results;
- Nation-wide health statistics tend to rely on a limited number of categories, which means that many health problems go uncounted;
- In both provincial and national surveys, individuals with multiple disabilities may be counted twice;
- Reported increases in certain physical disabilities over the past three decades, especially allergies and asthma, skew numbers;
- Physical disabilities are often found co-occurring with other disabling conditions.

Although it is difficult to obtain exact prevalence and incidence figures for specific conditions, we can say that most are very low-incidence problems. The major exceptions are asthma and allergies, with asthma both a high-incidence and an increasing condition in most developed nations. In fact, asthma severe enough to restrict childhood activities rose approximately 65 percent between 1970 and 1990 (Newacheck and Taylor, 1992). The increased prevalence of asthma now makes it the most common chronic disease in children.

Within Canada, the prevalence of asthma in children is slightly higher than in the United States (Pfeuti, 1997). It affects about 7 to 10 percent of the Canadian pediatric population, as opposed to 5 to 10 percent of children in most industrialized countries (Canadian Lung Association, 1997).

CLASSIFICATION OF SPECIAL HEALTH CARE NEEDS

Health disorders are essentially medical conditions requiring a complex and sophisticated range of interventions that include surgical procedures, prosthetic devices, drug therapy, diet management, and ongoing medical treatment. There is no necessary correlation between health disorders and impairments in other domains of functioning.

Generally, children with health problems show normal development in cognitive, communication, and socio-emotional skills. However, there may be disruptions attributable to the condition, such as long periods of illness, hospitalization, and missed school and peer interactions. These mean that special accommodations and programs are sometimes required.

It is not unusual for a teacher to have a student in the classroom who has a terminal illness. When this occurs, the inevitability of death has to be faced by the teacher and the other children on some level. Teachers may need special training in managing their own and other students' attitudes toward death and dying. When a child with AIDS is in the classroom, for example, children fare best when honest discussions about terminal illness occur right from the beginning (Weiner and Septimus, 1991). Children need to know they had no part in causing the illness and that it is not catching.

Cystic Fibrosis

Cystic fibrosis (CF) is a genetically determined inborn error of metabolism characterized by pervasive dysfunction of the exocrine glands (glands in which secretions are passed through ducts). The condition seems to be both ethnically and geographically variable—it is very rare among Swedes and among African Americans and virtually non-existent among Asians. Among Caucasians, cystic fibrosis is the most frequently occurring genetic disorder in North America and many European countries. One out of every twenty Caucasians is a carrier of the gene for cystic fibrosis, and approximately one birth in every 1600 to 2000 among North American Caucasians is affected (Brinthaupt, 1991). In a family with an affected child, two out of three siblings are likely to be carriers, and one out of five is likely to have the disease.

Cystic fibrosis is transmitted through an autosomal recessive gene, but it appears that more than one genetic defect can cause the disease. The main malformation in the CF gene's twisted double chain of DNA is the absence of a few chemicals. However, some 15 000 DNA samples taken from patients around the world with cystic fibrosis indicate that there are at least sixty, and probably a good many more, additional malformations that produce the symptoms that are classically lumped together as cystic fibrosis. Cystic fibrosis is therefore an extremely complex and involved disorder, quite variable in its manifestation.

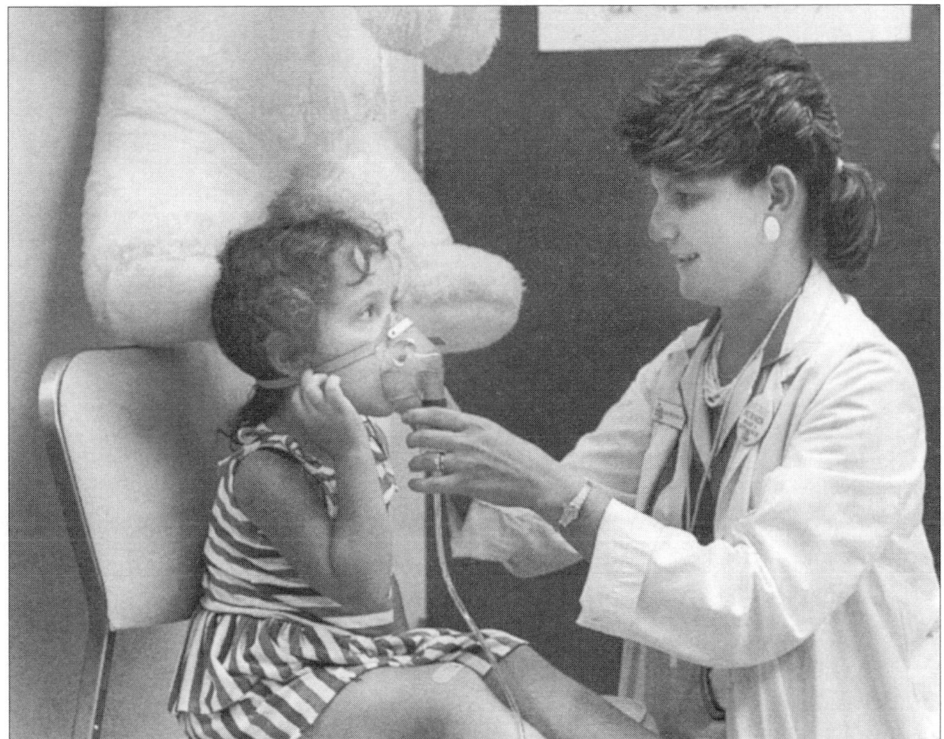

Treatment for cystic fibrosis is extensive. It involves diet management, respiratory disease management, and drug therapy.

The condition primarily affects the respiratory and digestive systems, although there are varied degrees of system involvement. Fully manifested cases present a triad of chronic pulmonary disease, pancreatic enzyme deficiency, and inordinately high sweat electrolytes. Symptoms include high salt concentration in the sweat glands and the production of thick sticky mucus that clogs breathing and digestion. The mucus obstruction disrupts the functions of the lungs and other vital organs. In the lungs it creates pockets of infection and pulmonary dysfunction, which frequently results in chronic episodes of pneumonia and bronchitis. With repeated infection, the lungs are gradually destroyed. As lung deterioration occurs, the heart is also burdened, and heart failure is a common by-product of cystic fibrosis.

Excessive mucous secretions also interfere with or prevent digestion and other intestinal processes. Cystic fibrosis affects virtually every part of the digestive system. The pancreas, gall bladder, liver, and intestines often function abnormally and show changes in the tissues. Children often fail to gain weight despite increased appetite. They grow very slowly and never appear to thrive.

Intervention for cystic fibrosis is as varied and complex as the disease, requiring diet management, therapy and management of respiratory disorders, and various regimes of drug therapy. Before antibiotics were available, approximately 75 percent of children with cystic fibrosis died before age ten. Life expectancy has been greatly extended and at present many older patients are being treated. Recently, surgical transplants have become an option.

Today's primary treatment procedures are medication and therapy. Antibiotics are prescribed when lung infections are present. With medication, percussion therapy serves to dislodge mucus as the chest is vigorously clapped and vibrated. Diet can be quite effective in the management of disorders of the digestive system. The special diet is high in protein, high in calories, and low in fat. This is combined with dosages of an enzyme needed to compensate for the insufficiency of the pancreas.

Developmental Consequences of Cystic Fibrosis

Children with cystic fibrosis do not suffer any form of intellectual impairment and should be educated in general classrooms. However, they will probably miss many days of school because of respiratory infections or intestinal disorders. They may have a chronic cough and may need extra snacks during the day.

It is on the family that a child with cystic fibrosis seems to have the greatest impact. For many families, everyday activities are dependent on the current health status of the ill child. Regimens of treatment, medication, feeding, positioning, and medical care can take up most of the day. Parents must learn the therapeutic techniques to assist in their child's treatment. This usually consists of twice daily half-hour sessions involving chest percussion and postural draining. The purpose of pounding the chest is to elicit coughing, which encourages the elimination of mucus. The changes in posture also aid in the draining process.

When the child is young, meal times can be a recurrent problem, with hours spent feeding the child. As well, medical decisions become an ongoing part of family life. Parents spend much time searching out information and becoming fluent in the medical terms related to their child's illness.

Diabetes Mellitus

Diabetes mellitus is an autoimmune illness, similar to rheumatoid arthritis or multiple sclerosis. The disorder involves sugar metabolism and is caused by a pancreatic disorder in the production of insulin, a hormone needed to metabolize glucose. In diabetes, the white blood cells target the cells that produce insulin.

Unlike many chronic health disorders, diabetes is a high-incidence condition. In Canada, it affects one in every 600 children under the age of ten.

Diabetes is divided into two major types. Type I, or insulin-dependent diabetes, is usually associated with early onset (under twenty-five years of age and as early as six months) and includes juvenile diabetes. Type II, non-insulin-dependent diabetes, ordinarily occurs after age forty. Type II diabetics produce quantities of insulin but they do not use it efficiently.

Type I diabetes brews silently for several years. The onset of the disease is signalled by thirst, hunger, weight loss, fatigue or weakness, excessive urination, and sometimes blurred vision. Onset may occur several months after the outbreak of specific viruses (Rodger and Hunt, 1980). For example, there may be sequelae resulting from maternal rubella. One study of rubella-deafened children discovered that 2 percent had overt diabetes and a total of 20 percent had abnormalities of glucose metabolism (Shaver, Boughman, and Nance, 1985).

Young people stricken with insulin-dependent (Type I) diabetes once faced certain death within a year of diagnosis. As the pancreas lost its ability to make the insulin required for normal metabolism, glucose accumulated in the blood stream and urine. The body then drew on other sources of energy until it literally starved, and death ensued.

In 1921, isolation of the insulin hormone from animals made it possible to control diabetes with daily insulin injections and has since meant survival for millions of diabetics.

Note that neither animal insulin nor the more modern human form offers a cure. Injections must be taken once or more a day for life. Many diabetics eventually suffer from devastating complications. As the disease persists, blood vessels can be damaged, leading to heart disease, stroke, blindness, or kidney failure. Nerve damage is also common (Atkinson and MacLaren, 1990).

The treatment of Type I diabetes involves a diet low in carbohydrates and fats accompanied by regular injections of insulin. Food intake, insulin, and exercise must be carefully balanced and monitored throughout the diabetic's life to prevent immediate and long-term complications associated with **hyperglycemia** (high blood sugar) or **hypoglycemia** (low blood sugar).

hyperglycemia
hypoglycemia

Hyperglycemia leads to *ketoacidosis*, a chemical imbalance that produces acute and serious illness, unconsciousness, coma, and ultimately death. Although moderate but chronic hyperglycemia is thought to cause the long-term complications associated with diabetes in adulthood (such as retinopathy and microvascular disease), the specific effects of a moderate elevation of blood glucose on children's brain functioning is not known. Severe hypoglycemia, caused by an excess of insulin intake, produces unconsciousness and seizures. Both hypoglycemic convulsions and ketoacidosis have been associated with abnormalities in brain functioning (Rovet, Erlich, and Hoppe, 1988).

The symptoms of non-insulin-dependent diabetes, a disease caused by an entirely different mechanism that is not fully understood, are more subtle than Type I diabetes. Type II diabetics are usually older than forty and overweight; susceptibility may be genetically transmitted. These patients produce various quantities of insulin but they typically use it inefficiently. Some are treated with insulin to control blood glucose levels, but they do not require the drug for day-to-day survival (Atkinson and MacLaren, 1990).

Developmental Consequences of Diabetes Mellitus

Children who are diabetic can participate in all school activities unless otherwise advised by a physician. In addition to regular education, children must be taught to manage their condition. Parents and medical personnel teach older children to inject their own insulin, monitor their blood sugar and urine sugar levels, and maintain a balance among nutrition, exercise, and insulin levels.

In young children, this critical balance is often difficult to maintain, particularly in the presence of illness or infection. It is therefore imperative that teachers understand a child's condition and recognize signs of imbalance. Health personnel should provide appropriate guidelines regarding the timing of school meals and school exercise.

Children with diabetes have an average range of intelligence, although those who develop their diabetes early in life are at risk for subsequent neuro-cognitive impairments and often show specific skill deficits. The earlier the onset, the more difficulties are experienced. Researchers who explored the effects on children's cognitive development of insulin-dependent diabetes mellitus concluded that those who develop diabetes before the age of four are at greatest risk for subsequent intellectual impairment (Rovet, Erlich, and Hoppe, 1988). Particularly affected are skills in the visio-spatial area of cognitive functioning and mathematical ability. These findings correlate with a poorer academic history and a greater need for special education. Girls appear to be somewhat more affected than boys.

Diabetes is more than simply a matter of diet, insulin, and urine testing. It also involves an individual's emotional and physical development, which largely depend upon the reaction of others to the condition. The environment affects diabetic control, and diabetic control, in turn, affects the environment. This is particularly true of the school environment, since children spend so much time in school. Students who are diabetic may experience embarrassment over their unusual diets, the urine testing, and any symptoms of diabetic shock that may be displayed. Peers may ridicule them and treat them differently.

Bob's story is illustrative. Here is a ten-year-old lad who was struck suddenly with a chronic and somewhat mysterious disease. It changed his entire life, bringing in its wake medical interventions, constant physical monitoring, and daily injections. Bob is now different from his peers and his life is more restricted.

Cancer

Cancer is a general term used to describe about a hundred conditions characterized by abnormal and uncontrolled cell growth. Although more children recover from cancer than do adults, cancer is the chief cause of death by disease in children aged three to fourteen. Childhood cancer affects about one in every 600 children (Granowelter, 1994).

Case Study

Bob

Bob is entering his first year of high school this year. While many students worry about the move to a large, somewhat impersonal school plant with many teachers and different responsibilities, Bob's reactions are far beyond the usual. He has told his parents over and over that he does not wish to attend high school and that if they force him to go he'll run away from home. His parents, deeply concerned, nevertheless understand Bob's reluctance.

Two years ago Bob was stricken with juvenile diabetes. For a healthy, active, and outgoing child, the effects were devastating. Bob was old enough to understand the chronic nature of the disease and to realize the restraints it would place on his life in terms of insulin injections and diet. He abandoned many of his usual pursuits, ignored his friends, and began to fall seriously behind in school work.

Although Bob is old enough to administer his own insulin, monitor his urine, and adapt his diet, he tacitly refused to do any of these things. It took a psychologist many months to help Bob to realize the necessity of attending to his own health care needs.

Even though he now looks after his own needs, Bob is resentful of the disease and embarrassed about it in front of his friends. His reluctance to attend high school centres on his fear of acute embarrassment in the case of an insulin coma (of which he has suffered a few) as well as his dislike of anyone knowing of his condition.

To help Bob, his parents have again contacted the psychologist and hope that counselling will help overcome some of his deep-seated resentment about the diabetes. The child who is diabetic often experiences feelings of being punished (injections and no sweets) and of being different and inadequate. The child is likely to lack in self-confidence and self-esteem and may avoid activities for fear of failure. Additional praise and encouragement for accomplishments may be necessary.

In adults, the most common cancers are lung, colon, and skin cancers. The most common cancers in children are of the blood, bone, brain, nervous system, and kidney. Acute lymphocytic leukemia (ALL) is the most common of the childhood cancers: approximately one-third of all cancers diagnosed in children are leukemias (Peckham, 1993), and leukemia is responsible for two-thirds of the deaths of children with cancer.

Survival rates for children with cancer have increased dramatically in the past three decades. For example, a child diagnosed in 1960 with acute lymphocytic leukemia had only a 1 percent chance of survival. Today 70 percent of children treated for ALL can expect long-term survival and cure (Bearison and Muhern, 1994). Wilms' tumour (a kidney cancer) has a survival rate of more than 90 percent. Long-term survival rates of children with brain tumours is approaching 50 percent.

Major treatments for cancer are surgery, chemotherapy, and/or radiation. After diagnosis, a four-week treatment period begins with intensive therapy. When remission is confirmed, oral drugs are introduced. Children respond in a variety of ways to current radiotherapy and chemotherapy, which may result in short- and long-term effects.

Developmental Consequences of Cancer

Apart from the condition itself, one of the major outcomes of cancer is the physical and emotional problems arising from treatment. Each child will have a unique experience at the hospital and in the diagnosis and treatment of a particular kind of childhood cancer.

For many children, chemotherapy drugs cause plumpness and hair loss. Other physical results include amputation, disturbances in normal growth patterns, mood swings, difficulties in concentration, muscle weakness, fatigue, nausea, and dramatic weight gain or weight loss.

School is a major part of each child's life, and children with cancer gain special benefits from education at all stages of their illness. They need the satisfaction of being normal, productive learners and should attend school even in the terminal stages of the illness, if possible. School attendance provides peer contact and opportunities for maintaining self-esteem and competence by completing short-term goals. School helps in distracting children from their physical concerns, assists in their long-term emotional and physical rehabilitation, and helps them reach optimal social and psychological development.

Children with cancer are told of the problem to enlist their help in treatment. Teachers too must understand the illness and how it affects the child at each maturational stage. They should be aware, for example, that after a period of hospitalization a youngster may be less energetic and very likely to hold deep concerns about the nature of the illness. A child's anger about forced dependency on parents and frustration at having to submit to the disruptions of therapy can cause withdrawal and regression. All this can result in decreased educational motivation, poor self-concept, social isolation, and an abnormally close relationship with one parent.

While the teacher is a valuable link in the total care of the child, research has not shown promising outcomes. In a survey of eleven parents of children with cancer (Goreau, Kennedy, and Sawalzty, 1996) researchers found that parents felt that schools, on the whole, are not prepared to deal with children who are cancer survivors. Most parents were disappointed with the schools' responses; teachers were not informed about childhood cancer and its effects.

When a teacher is informed, he or she can help by communicating with and supporting parents, by being a liaison between them and other professionals, and by helping the child to interact with others. Teachers can prepare other class members for their classmate's physical changes—loss of hair, weight gain, and the like.

Sickle Cell Anemia

The defective recessive gene involved in sickle cell anemia results in the production of defective hemoglobin. Affected individuals produce abnormal hemoglobin, which then causes distortions in blood cells; under certain conditions, the red blood cells "sickle" (change shape). Sickle-shaped cells tend to clot together; the shape causes the cells to pile up and block small blood vessels, causing pain and tissue destruction (Pierce, 1990). The intensity of the effects varies widely.

Because the sickle cell trait protects against death from malaria, it is common in populations from malaria-prone parts of the world, which include areas of Africa and the Mediterranean countries. Sickle cell anemia is carried by about two million African Americans (about one in ten). Among Hispanic Americans, about one in twenty is a carrier. Sickle cell is therefore thought to affect about 500 000 people in the United States. Of the 10 percent of African Americans with sickle cell, most are *heterozygous* (one normal and one abnormal gene). Only about 0.25 percent are *homozygous* (two defective genes).

Individuals who are homozygous often have long bouts of illness and die in childhood. Because sickle cell impairs circulation, sufferers experience severe pains in their abdomen, back, head, and limbs. The deformed blood cells rupture easily. The disease also causes the heart to enlarge and deprives the brain cells of blood. People with severe cases may suffer heart and kidney problems and pneumonia, which can be fatal.

Those who are heterozygous (carriers) suffer fewer effects; intensity varies widely. Sickling occurs under certain conditions such as exposure to low oxygen levels. In carriers, forty percent of the red blood cells may assume a sickle shape when the supply of oxygen to the blood is reduced. Treatment of a crisis usually involves rest, medication for pain, blood transfusions, and oxygen inhalation therapy.

In older children and adults, it appears that the sickle cell trait is generally benign and does not shorten life, although it may bring danger with exercise and increased altitude. The situation seems to be more serious for infants. In the United States, investigators have reported a mortality rate of 13 to 14 percent among sickle cell children under the age of two (Grover, Shahidi, Fisher, Goldberg, and Wethers, 1983). The spleen, the most efficient blood filter in the body, is vulnerable.

Allergies

allergy

Allergy, a term coined by Clemens von Pirquet in 1906, means "altered reaction" (Hay, 1990). The term is used interchangeably with *hypersensitivity*. It is an abnormal and varied reaction that occurs following a contact with substances or agents that normally do not cause symptoms in other individuals.

Allergies (which include asthma) are the most common chronic disease in pediatrics. Allergic conditions are estimated to occur in 6.6 to 33 percent of children and adolescents (Crawford, 1982). In Canada, recent studies have shown that one in every five school children has a major allergy (Alberta Response, 1989).

There are two major categories of allergies. **Atopic allergies** are associated with hereditary and/or familial factors. The risk to children when both parents have a positive history of allergy is 30 to 40 percent, while the risk to children when one parent has a positive history is 20 to 30 percent (Kuzemko, 1978). **Non-atopic allergies** do not have a hereditary component but result from antibodies produced in response to allergens in the environment.

atopic allergies

non-atopic allergies

A huge range of substances create allergic reactions in humans. Generally, substances are divided into four categories: inhalants, contactants, ingestants, and injectants. *Inhalants* include dust, pollen, mould, aerosol sprays, and strong odours. *Contactants* are substances that come into contact with the skin, including fabrics, metals, cosmetics, and chemicals. *Ingestants* are foods and drugs; *injectants* are agents or substances that enter the body through the skin, including insect bites, bee stings, and some drugs (Voignier and Bridgewater, 1980).

There are a number of types of allergic reaction. One of the most common is *allergic rhinitis*, which may be either seasonal or perennial. The seasonal type—hay fever—is induced by windborne pollens; the perennial form is present throughout the year. Both forms involve nasal congestion, itching of the nose, or repetitive sneezing. *Urticaria* and *eczema* are skin reactions resulting in rashes, itching, swelling, and seeping of body fluids through the skin. *Physical allergy* is a response to cold, heat, or sunlight. *Allergic conjunctivitis* involves itching of the eyes and excessive tears. *Gastro-intestinal allergy* is a response to specific foods or drugs. *Allergic pulmonary disease* is usually referred to as *bronchial asthma*. The major symptom is narrowing of the bronchial tubes resulting in diminished air flow.

Asthma

The word **asthma** derives from the Greek, meaning panting or difficulty in breathing. The condition is defined as a "variable, reversible obstruction of the airways characterized by the narrowing of bronchial tubes, swelling of tissues, and clogging of mucus" (Smith, 1978, p. 48). Asthma should never be considered anything less than a serious condition. Approximately 20 children and 500 adults die as a result of asthma each year in Canada. Of all provinces, Alberta has the highest asthma mortality rate: compared to Saskatchewan and Manitoba, for example, Alberta's death rate is three times higher (Canadian Lung Association, 1997).

asthma

An individual's asthma can be a continuous state of frequent attacks ranging in severity, or an intermittent state consisting of occasional attacks ranging from mild to severe (Howse, 1988). Episodes may be brief or can last for a few hours or weeks at a time. In young children, boys are twice as likely as girls to exhibit the condition. Many children improve or go into remission in adolescence. At the same time, a levelling occurs so that the male–female ratio is one to one after the age of fifteen.

Asthmatic attacks are characterized by wheezing, paroxysmal coughing, and shortness of breath. While a wide variety of stimuli are associated with bronchospasms, there may also be an inherited susceptibility. Many modern researchers believe that asthma is caused by the interactions of heredity and environment (Isabell and Barber, 1993).

Different stimuli account for asthmatic attacks. The first group, *known factors*, include allergens, drugs, exercise, industrial exposure, infections, and reflexes. A second category, *probable causes*, includes things such as air pollutants, chemical irritants, sinusitis, and vasculitis. A final group, classed as *possible triggers*, includes emotions, hormonal imbalance, and weather. Nevertheless, it is extremely difficult to pinpoint exactly which factor or factors trigger an individual asthma attack because the same factors are not always responsible for subsequent attacks (Howse, 1988).

The condition can require immediate medical intervention; children with severe attacks need attention in a matter of minutes or second. Various medications, of which drugs are the most common, are employed in treatment. Since Adrenalin, the first drug treatment of asthma, was introduced, a wide number of drugs have emerged. These include drugs that act on the airways directly, drugs that halt the production of antigens, and corticosteroids that also hinder antigen production (Howse, 1988).

Bronchodilators are used to relieve obstruction of airflow. In severe cases, corticosteroids are useful. Both have side effects. Bronchodilators may overstimulate the child and cause hyperactive behaviour; excessive use of corticosteroids may result in abnormal hair growth, excessive appetite, and slowed growth. Common-sense factors in treatment, other than medications, include rest, sufficient fluids, play and work to tolerance, avoidance of the allergens that cause attacks, and regular exercise to improve postural drainage, strengthen the diaphragm muscles, and expand lung capacity (Pilecka, 1995).

Developmental Consequences of Asthma

Children with asthma do not differ in their school performance from children without asthma but they may experience a greater degree of absenteeism. In fact, school absenteeism is the major problem, especially in the first three years of school. Asthma is estimated to account for as much as 20 to 25 percent of all school absences (Pituch and Bruggeman, 1982).

Despite the fact that children who are asthmatic tend to have IQs slightly higher than average, they are likely to be underachievers and to be behind in schoolwork, especially as adolescents. Children with asthma also have more emotional difficulties, but the nature of the relationship between psychological problems and asthmatic episodes is poorly understood (Pilecka, 1995).

Children Who Are Abused and Neglected

The history of humanity is rife with examples of cruelty to children, ranging from infanticide in early societies to child factory labour in the 19th and 20th centuries. (This is discussed in the Research Notes on child abuse.) So although some researchers feel that child abuse is on the increase, it is more likely that abuse, under modern definitional constructs, is simply more open to identification and reporting.

Child mistreatment is a major problem in our society. As examples, in 1996 there were 3500 cases of physical or sexual maltreatment investigated by Metro Toronto police (Gadd, 1997). In that same year, children under eighteen represented 22 percent of victims of assaults reported to a sample of 154 police agencies; children represented 60 percent of all victims of sexual assault and 18 percent of all victims of physical assault (Fitzgerald, 1999). An earlier report of sexual assaults by family members reported to police found that girls represented 79 percent of cases while boys were victims in 21 percent of cases (Fitzgerald, 1996).

Still, it is not possible to assess the exact dimensions of child abuse and neglect, and there is a general consensus that the actual rate is underestimated by official reports. Various reasons contribute; some of these reasons are outlined below.

- There are no national statistics for child abuse in Canada.

Research Notes

Child Abuse

Child abuse is not new in our modern Western society. As Lloyd de Mause points out, "The human track record of child raising is bloody, dirty and mean" (1975, p. 85). For many centuries, maltreatment was justified in the belief that severe physical punishment was necessary to maintain discipline, to transmit educational ideas, to please certain gods, or to expel evil spirits.

In tracing the history of child abuse, de Mause placed common societal reactions to children within six major, though overlapping and intertwined, stages: infanticidal, abandoning, ambivalent, intrusive, socializing, and helping. Infanticide existed in very early societies. It was not until the 4th century that the church halted the practice. After that, many children were abandoned to wander, beg, or die by the wayside. The ambivalent mode appeared first in the late Middle Ages. Parents still displayed aggressive tendencies toward their children but generally kept them at home. Intrusive parenting, characterized by draconian authoritarianism, arose in the early 18th century.

The need for children to be socialized and helped paralleled the full blossoming of the notion of childhood as a discrete stage of development and children as separate beings, not miniature adults. Children were then provided with special environments, such as schools, and child labour laws brought them out of the mines and the factories.

Overt forms of child abuse prominent in earlier periods may have disappeared. Nevertheless, child abuse remains an endemic problem in modern society. In its modern garb, the problems of child abuse were first brought to the forefront by Caffey (1946), who suggested that ill treatment of children might be an intentional act on the part of parents. This caused a wave of concern, and throughout the 1950s research increased. In the early 1960s, a seminar on child abuse led to the identification of what became known as the Battered Child Syndrome (Kempe, Silverman, Steele, Droegemueller, and Silver, 1962). Following this, there was a flurry of articles, books, and research papers reflecting a heightened interest on the part of educators, social workers, welfare agencies, and politicians. By the 1970s, policies were established and laws enacted that recognized and protected abused children.

In Canada the awareness of child neglect and abuse has increased dramatically. A plethora of child protection laws have led to the development of policies and programs for intervention, education, and prevention. The law now requires the reporting of possible instances of abuse to the authorities. Teachers, neighbours, physicians, and anyone else who suspects child abuse are required to seek assistance for the child.

- Although it is a heavily researched area, scientific studies of the actual prevalence of sexual abuse are rare.
- There is social stigma attached to child beating.
- There are cultural variations in expectations concerning the roles of parents and children.
- Only a portion of children are taken for medical intervention.
- Parents make up believable stories and children are too young or too frightened to disclose what actually happened.
- Some physicians would rather attribute the symptoms to an accident than confront the awful truth.

- With sexual abuse there are severe consequences of disclosure—public retribution, family disruption, unemployment and subsequent economic disaster, loss of friends, and incarceration (Csapo, 1988).

Child abuse exists in all forms of relationships regardless of occupation, educational attainment, religion, marital status, and family configuration. Abuse occurs at every socioeconomic level, although it is more frequently reported among poorer families. The frequency of child abuse appears to vary across cultures (Korbin, 1987).

Definitions of Abuse and Neglect

There have been many thoughtful discussions about appropriate definitions of child abuse and neglect, psychological maltreatment of children, child sexual abuse, and spouse abuse. No consensus has been reached, and one of the most critical issues in research remains the lack of clear and reliable definitions of maltreatment.

In a general sense, child abuse is defined as "any interaction or lack of interaction...which results in non-accidental harm to the individual's physical and/or emotional state" (Helfer, 1987, p. 61). Within the broad definition, subcategories have developed to describe specific aspects of abuse and neglect.

Physical abuse is a non-accidental physical injury to a child. Overt and consistent signs indicate physical abuse. For example, children acquire many strange bruises in the course of normal activities; it is the frequency of such bruising that arouses the suspicion of abuse. Further indications of physical abuse include bald spots, burns from cigarettes or hot water, and marks from a strap or rope. Behavioural indicators of physical abuse include intolerance of physical contact and wearing inappropriate clothing that covers the body. Abused children may arrive at school early and stay late, suggesting a fear of going home.

Sexual abuse is one of the most studied areas. Sexual abuse is defined as "the sexual exploitation of a child who is not developmentally capable of understanding or resisting the contact, and a child or adolescent who may be psychologically and socially dependent upon the perpetrator" (Csapo, 1988, p. 121). Sexual involvement imposed upon a child by an adult includes pedophilia, rape, and all forms of incest. Incest, the most common type of sexual abuse, refers to any kind of sexual activity between a child and relatives, either blood or legal, including fathers, mothers, step-parents, siblings, and so on.

Victims of sexual abuse display a number of manifestations. Children may have difficulty walking or sitting, or may cry without provocation. They may show sudden drops in school performance or sudden non-participation in school activities accompanied by unusually infantile or withdrawn behaviour.

Neglect is the failure to provide adequate supervision, hygiene, nutrition, medical care, or the basic love and nurturing that children need to grow and develop. *Emotional neglect* refers to the failure of caretakers to provide the loving positive emotional atmosphere necessary to the development of self-esteem in a child.

Experts now believe that strong and recurrent psychological abuse and neglect can be as damaging psychologically as overt physical or sexual abuse and may prove to be even more harmful to children in the long run (Hart and Brassard, 1987). Neglect has been cited as the most common form of abuse as well as the most destructive, causing more deaths, injuries, and long-term problems than other types.

Neglected children tend to be ill-clothed and poorly fed. They may have untreated physical or medical problems and appear to be tired and listless. Possible behavioural responses include stealing food, falling asleep in class, frequent school absences, and pugnacious and destructive activity.

Indicators of emotional maltreatment are varied. Many children develop emotional or behavioural disorders for no apparent reason. Many of these cases could be the result of the caregiver failing to meet the child's basic emotional needs. In these children, observers may note delayed development, neurotic traits, or antisocial behaviour.

The Family and Child Abuse

Essentially, abuse is not a fixed single incident but an ongoing interaction between parents and children associated with dysfunctional parent–child relations. When looked at in this way, abuse becomes a complex combination of parent variables and child behaviours.

Studies attempting to define the typical abusive family or parent draw only one definite conclusion—there is no real prototype of an abusive parent. Myriad descriptions have emerged.

Abusive parents have been described as immature, impulsive, self-centred, hypersensitive, quick to react with poorly controlled aggression, and tending to show extremely inconsistent patterns of interaction with the child (Steele, 1986). Abusive parents have little knowledge of good parenting and tend to hold unrealistic expectations; they ascribe adult functions to children and cannot understand that children possess limited control, capabilities, and comprehension. They expect children to be good, loving, and obedient at all times, and when their child's disobedience or inattention threatens their perceptions of themselves as good parents, they use excessive discipline because they see it as their duty to make children behave. Many abusing parents are unable to cope with the complex problems of life. They tend to be isolated or their lifestyle may be chaotic. There seems to be a significant overrepresentation of alcoholism in severe cases of child maltreatment (Famularo, Stone, Barnum, and Wharton, 1986).

Although unable to pinpoint the exact characteristics of abusive parents, much of the literature points to a *cycle of abuse* theory. That is, abusive parents were abused children themselves, and patterns of maltreatment can often be traced back three or four generations (Steele, 1986). Spousal violence also intrudes. Violent men are almost three times as likely as non-violent men to have witnessed spousal violence in childhood, and women who were raised in similar circumstances are twice as likely to be victims of spousal violence (Fitzgerald, 1999). Not only do parents who were abused mistreat their own children, but they tend to repeat the same types of abuse to which they were subjected, be it physical, sexual, or neglect (Steele, 1986).

The *cyclic* theory posits that children learn parenting techniques from their own experiences in the family. A loving, cared-for child learns to become a good parent. A child who is unloved, neglected, and abused learns poor parenting behaviours. If a parent who was abused has a healthy, docile child, abusive tendencies may be held in check. However, if the child is ill or difficult to manage or if other stresses occur, the parent may well harm the child. Abuse and neglect may occur from conception (alcoholic mothers) to adolescence.

Other researchers feel that the assumptions underlying a cyclical theory are not supported by available data, and that the majority of abused parents do not abuse their own children (e.g., Widom, 1989). Anywhere between 25 and 33 percent of all children who are abused grow up and abuse their own children (Kaufman and Zigler, 1989; Widom, 1989), and whether parents continue the cycle of abuse is influenced by many aspects of their developmental history, not just the abuse.

In some families, only one of several children is abused. This child may be different by virtue of sex, by resembling a disliked family member, or by failing to meet the parent's expectations. There is a correlation between excessive crying and child abuse, although which is the cause and which is the effect is a matter of debate.

When children with exceptionalities are considered, research has looked in two directions—abuse of children with disabilities, and abuse as an antecedent of disability. Children with disabilities, sick children, and premature and low-birth-weight children who require special attention or costly treatment and who fail to respond to the caregivers' efforts in ways the parents can appreciate appear to be at greater risk for abuse (Augoustinos, 1987; Frodi, 1981). Abuse seems very common among children with behavioural disorders (Zirpoli, 1990).

When abuse is examined as an antecedent of behavioural and learning problems, there is sufficient empirical evidence to support the widely held assumption that child abuse and neglect have detrimental developmental effects. The data strongly suggest that systematic abuse causes significant dysfunction in intellectual, neurological, emotional, and motoric ability.

Intellectual development has been found to be delayed among some abused and neglected children with no evidence of neurological impairment (Augoustinos, 1987). One major study (Lynch and Roberts, 1982) found verbal scores to be more depressed than performance scores. For academic performance, child abuse directly affects the amount of time children are in the classroom and their ability and interest in learning while in school.

Social and emotional difficulties are endemic. Abused toddlers often respond to agemates' distress with fear, anger, or physical attacks (Main and George, 1985). Abused elementary-aged children tend to be highly aggressive and are often rejected by their peers (Downey and Walker, 1989). Among adolescents, systematic abuse creates substantial at-risk conditions for psychological, interpersonal, academic, medical, and legal problems. Self-image, motivation, personal satisfaction, and success in the workplace are negatively affected (Fink and Janssen, 1992). Adolescents frequently respond to abuse through depression, suicide attempts, explosive anger, alcohol, drug abuse, self-mutilation, running away, or prostitution (see Destad, 1987).

Child maltreatment is destructive to the child who experiences it, to the caregiver who commits it, and to the society that allows it. Teachers hold both a moral and a legal responsibility for reporting suspected cases of abuse. They must know how to recognize the signs of abuse, how and where to report it, and what the school can do to offer support. When considering the significance of symptoms or behaviours, consultation with a public health nurse will prove to be very helpful.

Musculoskeletal Impairments

Musculoskeletal impairments are those that affect body movement and functioning but are not caused by neurological damage. These include a wide range of impairments; some are listed in Table 11-2 and a few are discussed in more detail below. Depending on the type and severity of the conditions, physical and motor development is affected.

Table 11-2 Some examples of orthopedic conditions that affect children

Clubfoot	Congenital malpositioning of one or both feet
Osteomyelitis	Bacterial infection of the bones
Osteogenesis imperfecta	Congenital abnormality of the bony cells resulting in frequent fractures causing deformities
Scoliosis	Congenital or acquired curvature of the spine, often caused by muscle weakness, dystrophy, or atrophy
Hip dislocation	Congenital misplacement of the thigh bone in the hip socket
Legg-Calvé-Perthes	Flattening of the head of a long bone, usually the thigh
Muscular atrophy	Degeneration of muscle tissue due to neural damage

Source: David, 1987

Note that when discussing physical and motor development, we are referring to the acquisition of postural control and the necessary movement patterns to produce functional motor acts. **Motor** is a term used to denote muscular movement; **motor development** is the process through which a child acquires movement patterns and skills.

motor

motor development

Limb Deficiencies

Limb deficiencies include the loss or absence of entire limbs or parts of limbs. A child born with such a condition is said to have a **congenital amputation**. Congenital amputations of unusually large proportions occurred in the late 1950s and early 1960s due to Thalidomide, an anti-nausea drug prescribed to pregnant women for morning sickness. In Canada, the United States, and Europe, thousands of children were born with missing or deformed limbs. This specific condition is called *phocomelia*, a congenital deformity in which parts of limbs or entire limbs are missing or very short.

congenital amputation

Congenital amputations are much less prevalent than acquired amputations. Many children lose limbs in mishaps involving vehicles, contact with high-voltage power lines, burns, and other accidents. In some instances, surgical amputations may be performed to prevent the spread of bone cancer or massive infections. Defective limbs or parts of limbs may also be amputated to permit the use of *prostheses*, functional devices that substitute for missing body parts.

Spinal Problems

There are three types of curvature of the spine: lordosis, kyphosis, and scoliosis. *Lordosis* is an anterior (forward) curvature when viewed from the side. *Kyphosis* is a posterior (backward) curvature when viewed from the side. *Scoliosis*, which refers to a lateral (side to side) curve in the spine that is absent in normal spines, is the most common form of curvature. It is associated with prominent shoulder blades, poor posture, uneven shoulders, and a flattening of the back (Bauer and Shea, 1989). Scoliosis can impair motor functions.

Muscular Dystrophy

A number of conditions are characterized by a weakening and wasting away of muscular tissue. If there has been neurological damage or if the muscles are weakened due to nerve degeneration, the condition is known as *atrophy. Myopathy* occurs when there is no evidence of neurological disease or impairment. When the myopathy is progressive and hereditary, the condition is referred to as *dystrophy* (Hallahan and Kauffman, 1991).

muscular dystrophy

The conditions are rare and most have adult onset. Some are related neuro-muscular disorders, such as *Friedreich's ataxia.* All result in weakness and fatigue, but the predicted life span varies from one type to another. The most common types are forms of **muscular dystrophy,** which refers to a group of inherited conditions characterized by degeneration of muscle fibres without neurological deficit. The condition occurs in different forms, all characterized by progressive muscle weakness. The types differ with regard to age of onset, the site of initial muscle involvement, and the kinds of hereditary transmission. Included are Duchenne's muscular dystrophy, Becker's muscular dystrophy, myotonic muscular dystrophy, and Charot Marie Tooth Syndrome (Strong and Sandoval, 1999).

The most common type of the disorder is Duchenne's muscular dystrophy, often called *pseudohypertonic muscular dystrophy.* The term *pseudohypertonic,* meaning "false growth," describes an enlargement of the calves and sometimes other muscles. This enlargement occurs as a result of fatty deposits in the muscle along with degeneration of the muscle fibres.

As Duchenne's muscular dystrophy is inherited through a sex-linked recessive gene, this form typically occurs in boys. At birth, the child appears normal. In the early stages, the condition is painless and the symptoms unnoticeable. But onset is early and may be evident when the child is learning to walk. Gradually, muscle fibres waste away, to be replaced by fatty tissue. The child's pelvic area is affected first and then the shoulder girdle. By the age of four to seven years, the child exhibits a waddling gait and frequent falls, and has difficulty in climbing stairs and in standing up from a sitting position (Berkow, 1982).

In the second stage of the condition, the child suffers difficulty in muscle movement; by the age of five, many affected children require ambulation aids. The condition worsens so that by the third stage, somewhere about eight years of age, the child is confined to a wheelchair. Finally, the individual is bedridden and totally dependent.

For children with Duchenne's muscular dystrophy, the progressive muscle weakness equates with an abbreviated life span. Before the advent of antibiotics, the life expectancy for children with Duchenne's was even shorter than today's twenty to thirty years. Death usually occurred in adolescence as a result of exhaustion, respiratory infection, heart failure, or, most often, pneumonia. Although life expectancy has been extended and recent investigations have located the gene for muscular dystrophy, no treatment has yet been found to halt muscle decline.

Another form of the condition is *Landouzy-Dejerine muscular dystrophy,* also known as *facioscapulohumeral muscular dystrophy,* reflecting the fact that the facial and shoulder-girdle muscles are the areas first affected. The shoulder girdle is weakened but the forearms are spared. As well, the facial features of affected children show drooping of the eyelids and thickening of the lips. Landouzy-Dejerine muscular dystrophy is inherited through dominant genes but is not sex-linked (Berkow, 1982), and is therefore found in both sexes. The condition commonly manifests itself in adolescence, although onset may occur any time between childhood and late adulthood. The progression of the condition alternates with prolonged periods of apparent arrest. Landouzy-Dejerine muscular dystrophy is not life threatening; life expectancy for affected individuals is normal.

Arthritis

Arthritis is a common term for a variety of chronic systemic conditions involving inflammation of the joints. Many people assume that arthritis is a condition exclusive to adults, especially the aged. In reality, it occurs frequently in children and is then called *juvenile arthritis* or *Still's disease.*

Juvenile arthritis is similar in some respects to the adult type. It affects the large joints, sometimes to the extent of interfering with growth in the bony structures. Joint pain is a common feature, and destruction of the joints may ensue. Other complications of juvenile arthritis include eye and respiratory infections, enlarged spleen, and inflammation of the tissue covering the heart.

The most severe form is *juvenile rheumatoid arthritis,* which affects the heart muscles and can be fatal. More girls than boys suffer from this condition. Among children with other disabilities, *osteoarthritis* is the most common form of arthritis. The cartilage around the joint is damaged, the space between the bones becomes smaller and loses its lubrication, and movement becomes painful or impossible. Osteoarthritis is especially likely to occur when the child has a condition in which a joint has been dislocated. Children with cerebral palsy, for example, may have recurring dislocation and suffer from painful arthritis (Hallahan and Kauffman, 1991).

The causes of both adult and juvenile arthritis are unknown and there is no cure. Aspirin seems to be the most effective medication. In children the prognosis is more favourable than it is for adults; about 75 percent of children with arthritis experience remission of the disease (Berkow, 1982).

ASSESSMENT OF CHILDREN WHO HAVE SPECIAL HEALTH CARE NEEDS

Given the enormous range of conditions, malformations, and diseases encompassed in this category, it is well nigh impossible to make definitive statements regarding assessment. Nor is it necessary. Generally, health disorders and skeletal malformations do not impinge on cognitive and intellectual development, and assessment employs the same range of tools and tests as would be used with regular-class children. However, adaptations in test materials and procedures may be necessary to circumvent a physical disability that impedes movement or mobility, such as muscular dystrophy. (See Chapters 12 and 14.)

INTERVENTION WITH CHILDREN WHO HAVE SPECIAL HEALTH CARE NEEDS

Health disorders and physical disabilities affect children's learning and progress in a number of ways. Learning will be hindered when a child has experienced a great many medical pro-

Medical management for health problems can be a significant part of a child's daily life.

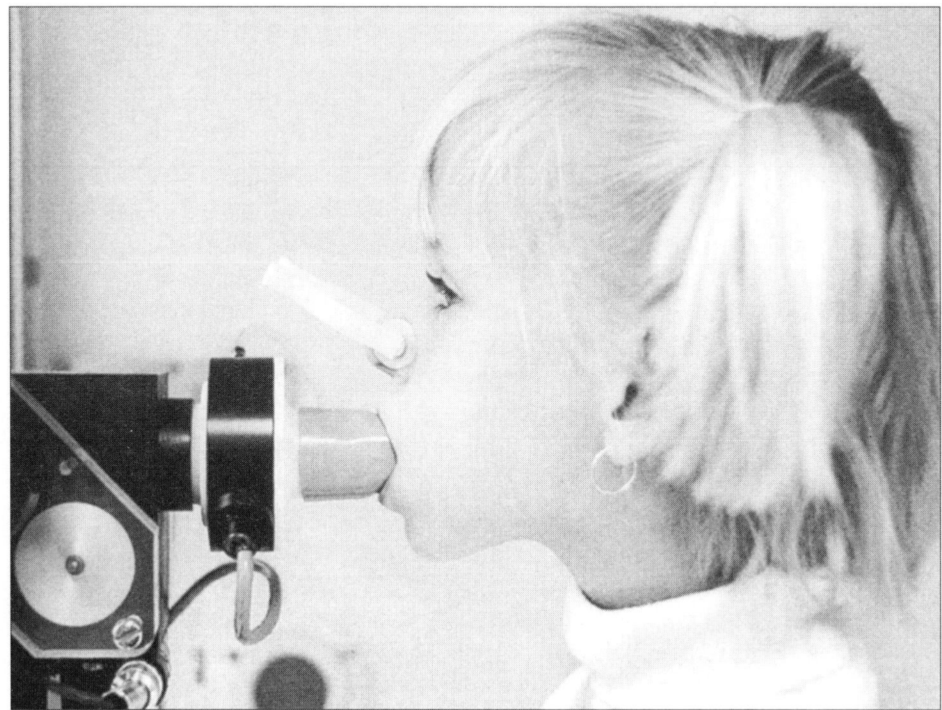

cedures that lead to long periods of recuperation as well as missed time in the classroom. Once in school, children may tire easily, have limited vitality, short attention spans, and limited mobility. A physical impairment can affect a child's range of motion, physical strength, communication, interaction with materials, independence, and daily living skills.

The children discussed in this chapter require a variety of medical, psychological, and educational interventions. Social service agencies frequently become involved with them and their families. As they grow older, students may require counselling and other support for independent living. (See also Chapter 16.)

Medical Intervention

As they are essentially medical conditions, health disabilities require a complex and sophisticated range of interventions, which include surgical procedures, prosthetic devices, drug therapy, diet management, and ongoing medical treatment. The medical management of these children is intensive, far beyond the scope of this text.

Health-related procedures include gastrostomy tube feeding, administration of oxygen, nebulizer treatments, and suctioning (Lowman, 1998). Children with AIDS need medications several times a day (Roberts, 2000).

One of the issues in this field relates to who should provide medical aid to children. Just as we provide a quality education for students with disabilities, we must also ensure that they receive quality medical services that enhance their school experience ("Growing challenge ...," 1998). At the same time, school districts must develop policies that protect both students and teachers.

When a child with a health impairment is in a school, two related documents are necessary. First is a *health services plan*—a document that outlines the child's specific needs, the strategies needed to support the child, the responsibility of staff, and training and resources needed (see Lowman, 1998). Second, teachers should keep an *emergency protocol* that contains information on emergency practices and strategies developed by parents, school personnel, and medical personnel. The protocol includes names, addresses, and telephone numbers of parents or guardians, emergency contacts, and family physicians. An example procedure for planning for a child with complex health care needs is shown in Table 11-3.

Table 11-3 Planning for a child with complex health care needs

1. Form a planning team to gather all necessary information. For example, information on the condition or understanding the intervention procedures.
2. Plan strategies to support a child's needs, note the responsibilities of staff, and the training and resources needed.
3. Prepare the environment. This could include special seating or accommodations for medical equipment such as a ventilator.
4. Prepare other children.
5. Develop a *health services plan* that outlines a child's specific needs. For example, note a child's schedule for drug dosages and for special diet considerations, or how to monitor the status of a diabetic child, the symptoms of insulin reaction, and the immediate remedies. Note the warning signs and symptoms of an asthma attack—the child may wheeze, show retractions where the tissue of the chest wall is sucked in as he or she breathes, prolonged exhalation, rapid breathing, or cold symptoms. Or if a child is wearing braces, teachers must be alert to circulation problems that may show up as swelling, coldness, change of colour, evidence of infection, or other skin problems. In a child with hydrocephalus, a shunt malfunction can be seen in a child's behaviour and physical functioning; for example, the child has a headache or pain in the neck area. Drug-exposed children are often stressed and distressed: some of the most common stressors are transitions, classroom interruptions, and school disruptions such as field trips and fire drills.
6. Prepare an *emergency protocol*. This should contain:
   - Parents or guardian: name, address, telephone numbers
   - Any other relevant parties: name, address, telephone numbers
   - School assistance: name, telephone numbers
   - Family physician: name, address, telephone numbers
   - Emergency contacts: name, address, telephone numbers
   - Local hospital: telephone numbers
   - Ambulance services: telephone numbers
   - Emergency practices based on the needs of a particular child. For example, what to do in an asthma attack or an epileptic seizure.
7. Prepare a medication log if necessary.

Therapy

Students may need rehabilitation training and therapy from a range of therapists—physical, occupational, and speech and language. Counselling assumes importance to help students understand and deal with the stresses of the disability and the treatment. Serious psychological and emotional correlates of physical and health problems are the rightful concern of professionals within the discipline of pediatric psychology.

The level of knowledge children have about their own orthopedic disabilities is related to age. Generally, children move from a broad understanding of the disability at age six to a more acute realization of the implications by age eight (Dunn, McCartan, and Fugura, 1988). By adolescence, most students will have gained a realistic appreciation of their health condition and the manner in which it affects their lives. (See also Chapter 16.)

Technical Aids

Many technical devices are designed to increase personal independence. Compensatory (assistive, adaptive, prosthetic, and orthotic) devices and equipment allow individuals to compensate for or minimize the effects of a disability. These devices are addressed in Chapter 12.

Educational Intervention

Education is a social norm in the lives of children, and the presence of a physical or health problem should not be seen as a reason to halt schooling. Educational intervention for children with special health care needs represents a critical aspect of the child's total health planning. Lacking school experiences, the child's psychosocial development would be seriously jeopardized. Special education assistance may be necessary simply because students are likely to be absent from school often.

Service Delivery Models

Historically, educational services for children with chronic illnesses were developed to address specific diseases such as polio and tuberculosis. These services typically followed a medical model and were offered in special schools or centres that segregated students from their peers (see the Historical Notes at the end of this chapter).

While the great majority of children now attend the regular public school, the needs of children who are technology dependent and/or medically fragile present great challenges to the school system. These youngsters may be placed in a variety of educational settings, depending upon the type and severity of the condition, the related services available, and the prognosis of the disability (see also Chapter 14).

Students themselves seem to prefer general environments. In a study of 106 graduates of a school for students with severe physical disabilities, investigators (Liebert, Lutsky, and Gottlieb, 1990) found that many graduates felt they would have benefited from a less sheltered environment as well as more exposure to peers without disabilities.

Some chronically ill students are in hospital schools found in facilities that specialize in providing long-term care for children. In these, the classroom setting is designed to provide the children with familiar surroundings and continued interaction with other students. Academic involvement helps the child to keep abreast of schoolwork and aids in self-development. Special education teachers provide regular organized instruction in a classroom setting where possible or on a tutorial basis.

For the child who is no longer hospitalized but still unready for school attendance, homebound instruction is a valuable option. A home-visiting or itinerant teacher provides individual tutorials on a regular basis, following the curriculum of the child's classroom.

Curriculum

No special curricula exist or are necessary for students with health problems. They follow the regular curriculum.

Historical Notes

It is reasonable to assume that health disorders have plagued humanity from its beginnings. For example, archeology provides evidence that the ancient Egyptians were aware of asthma and its effects. They treated it by "administering camel or crocodile dung, or by burning herbs on hot bricks and having the asthma patient inhale the fumes" (Isabell and Barber, 1993, p. 247).

In ancient Greece, Hippocrates (ca. 460–377 B.C.) intervened with a variety of conditions. Ancient Rome saw physicians such as Aulus Cornelius Celsus (25 B.C.–A.D. 50) and Galen (A.D. 130–200), an anatomist, physiologist, and neurologist, produce a body of writing that influenced medical progress until the Renaissance. With the Renaissance came the development of more sophisticated surgery and medical practices. An age-old fear of dissecting the human body dissolved, and a huge spurt in anatomy and physiology was witnessed.

In the following centuries, medical advances continued apace. Franz Gall's discovery of the hemispheres of the brain, the discovery of vaccination and anesthesia, and the first glimmerings of the hereditary aspects of certain conditions lent light to medical diagnosis and prognosis. Amputation became feasible and safe in the 19th century with the use of anesthetic (Lowey, 1993).

However, the conditions we discuss in this chapter were often lethal—and indeed, still are. Before the very recent advent of sophisticated medical intervention and technical assistance and devices, affected individuals could anticipate only an abbreviated life span.

Causes, prevention, and cures are still, to a greater or lesser extent, baffling. While, for example, cystic fibrosis and muscular dystrophy are known to result from identifiable defective genes, cures are not yet available. Since the discovery of insulin in the early 1920s, diabetes is controlled, but not yet prevented or cured. Intense medical research has not yet established precise causes and cures for cancer and AIDS.

SUMMARY

1. *Special health care needs* and *physical impairments* encompass an enormous variety of conditions and diseases. Some, such as cancer, are life threatening; others, such as muscular dystrophy, bring an abbreviated life span; still others mean that the child must carefully monitor activities, diet, or drugs.
2. *Health impairments* (chronic health problems) refer to the presence of a disease or medical condition that interferes with school attendance and learning and hinders the ability to lead a normal life. The majority of chronic illnesses occur during the first three years of life. *Musculoskeletal impairments* are disabilities that relate primarily to disorders of the skeleton, joints, and muscles including clubfoot, the absence of some members, or other congenital anomalies; impairments caused by diseases such as poliomyelytis or

bone tuberculosis; impairments caused by cerebral palsy; amputations; and contractures caused by fractures or burns.

3. Health disorders are so heterogeneous that no commonality can be found in students' behavioural, intellectual, and psychological functioning. Even with the same conditions, no two youngsters are affected in exactly the same way. The impact of a health or physical disorder depends upon a number of variables: the age of onset of the condition, the degree of disability, the visibility of the condition, family and social support, the attitudes toward the individual, and the individual's social status with peers.
4. Many illnesses that are chronic were fatal in the past; with current medical intervention, they are no longer life-threatening. As these children enter the school system, they bring with them a range of challenges that extend from simply monitoring drug usage, to watching for fatigue, to classroom adaptations that accommodate neurological dysfunctions, to adaptive equipment for mobility and communication. Probably the greatest challenge for teachers is handling a terminally ill child in the classroom. Many students need pharmacological management; others may require supplemental assistance from support personnel such as physical and occupational therapists, nurses, and teachers' aides.
5. *Cystic fibrosis* is no longer attributed to the action of one deviant gene; there may be as many as sixty different genetic differences that finally manifest as cystic fibrosis.
6. With child abuse, there remain many questions about the prevalence, type and severity, duration of harm, and mediators of damage for causing disabilities. Child abuse actually consists of two problems—the abused child and the abusive parents. Among parents, child abuse and neglect cannot be attributed to any single cause or to any particular class of people. Parents often feel overwhelmed by stress, isolated, incapable of coping, and lacking in resources. More often than not, high stress is the common denominator in abusive families.
7. Child abuse and neglect have developmental effects on the physical, neurological, intellectual, and emotional development of children. Sexually abused children often carry emotional scars for life, while the experiential deprivation that is part of neglect affects every aspect of a child's development. Children can be more open to abuse because of the mental, physical, and behavioural anomalies that increase their vulnerability to abuse, or because they have developed characteristics that increase the likelihood of abuse. Preschoolers, boys, children with disabilities, sick children, and premature and low-birth-weight children appear to be at greater risk for abuse.
8. Forms of *muscular dystrophy* are characterized by progressive muscle weakness and tissue change.
9. Because the conditions are primarily medical, there is no reason that children should require special intervention. Nearly all children with health and musculoskeletal conditions will be educated within regular classrooms. Special education should be available to accommodate lags resulting from lost school time. And, with the chronic nature of the conditions, special attention must be directed toward social and emotional growth and adaptive behaviour.

WEBLINKS

Calgary Allergy Network **www.aaia.ca**

Canadian Cystic Fibrosis Foundation **www.ccff.ca/**

Canadian Diabetes Association **www.diabetes.ca/**

Canadian Lung Association **www.lung.ca/**

Canadian Society for the Investigation of Child Abuse (CSICA) **www.csica.zener.com/**

National Clearing House on Family Violence **www.hc-sc.gc.ca/hppb/familyviolence/**

Chapter 12

Children with Neurological Disabilities

Learning Outcomes

After reading this chapter, you should be able to:

Demonstrate a working knowledge of the human brain and its function;

Identify the major types of neurological disabilities, their etiology, and their developmental consequences;

Understand the special classroom needs of children with neurological disabilities;

Understand that different types of disabilities in this area mean different types of classroom environments and interventions;

Identify a range of devices used for mobility by children with neurological and other motor disorders.

Introduction

Normal development of the central nervous system is the outcome of a carefully timed and precisely regulated combination of structural and chemical events. Something amiss in these events can lead to damage to, or deterioration of, the central nervous system, which in turn is one of the most common causes of physical and neurological disabilities in children.

As in the case of health and musculoskeletal impairments, there exists a huge range of neurological disorders. Some are associated with impairments of the nervous system; others result from diseases and accidents. For many children, the decreased range of motion, the reduced strength of movement, or the addition of unwanted or uncontrolled movement can dramatically affect the way they perform. Many youngsters in this category also suffer co-occurring disabilities such as seizures or diabetes, and can therefore be viewed as multiply disabled.

As the Historical Notes at the end of this chapter show, school placements have altered dramatically in recent years. Depending on the severity of the condition, the related services available, and the prognosis, students with neurological disabilities are served in general classrooms, general classroom and resource room combinations, or very occasionally in special classes. But, as the conditions are not in themselves inherently intellectually disabling, we should soon see almost all children with physical and neurological impairments integrated into regular classrooms.

Table 12-1 presents some causes and effects of damage to the central nervous system. In a short chapter we could not possibly catalogue and describe the range of neurological disorders that can affect individuals. Therefore, we focus on disabilities that teachers are most likely to encounter. The discussion begins with an overview of the human central nervous system.

Table 12-1 Some causes of damage to the central nervous system, with examples

Causes	Examples
Neoplasms	Brain tumour
Oxygen deprivation	Carbon monoxide poisoning, anoxia
Maternal infection	Rubella, syphilis
Maternal intoxication	Fetal Alcohol Syndrome
Child intoxication	Lead poisoning
Child infection	Encephalitis
Malnutrition	Inadequate protein to fetus or young child
Vascular accidents	Brain hemorrhage
Radiation	Excessive x-rays
Genetic defects	Errors of metabolism
Developmental errors	Absence of brain substance
Trauma	Automobile accidents resulting in direct head injury
Chromosomal abnormalities	Down syndrome
Gestational problems	Prematurity

THE CENTRAL NERVOUS SYSTEM

Structurally, the human nervous system consists of the brain, the spinal cord, and all associated nerves and sense organs. *Structures* are the fixed anatomical and physiological features of the central nervous system and are similar across the healthy brains of most individuals. How these structures respond to, organize, analyze, and synthesize incoming information varies with individuals and with the task involved. The way information is processed represents the problem-solving strategies of each person.

The spinal cord and the brain, the two major components of the central nervous system, are each composed of neurons and *glial cells* (the latter name is derived from the Greek *glia*, meaning glue). The number of glial cells is probably ten times the number of neurons (Groves and Rebec, 1988). Glial cells serve in a supportive role for the neurons—they transmit food (glucose and amino acids) from the blood supply to the neurons; some probably serve as scaffolding, and others manufacture a substance called *myelin.* The glial cells develop later than the neurons. They start to form at about thirteen weeks after conception, reach their peak of cell division from eighteen weeks after conception to four months after birth, and cease to form new cells by fifteen to twenty-four months after birth.

Neurons (nerve cells) are the basic units of neurological function; they undoubtedly hold the secrets of how the brain works. Researchers know their role in the transmission of nerve impulses and they know how the neural circuits work, but they are just beginning to unravel their more complex functioning in memory, emotion, and thought. See Figure 12-1 for an illustration of the human brain.

Neurons differ markedly in size and appearance, but they do possess some common characteristics. In common with nearly all cells, neurons have a cell body, a cell membrane, a nucleus, and a cytoplasm. Each neuron consists of three parts—the *cell body*, a simple long

Figure 12-1
The human brain

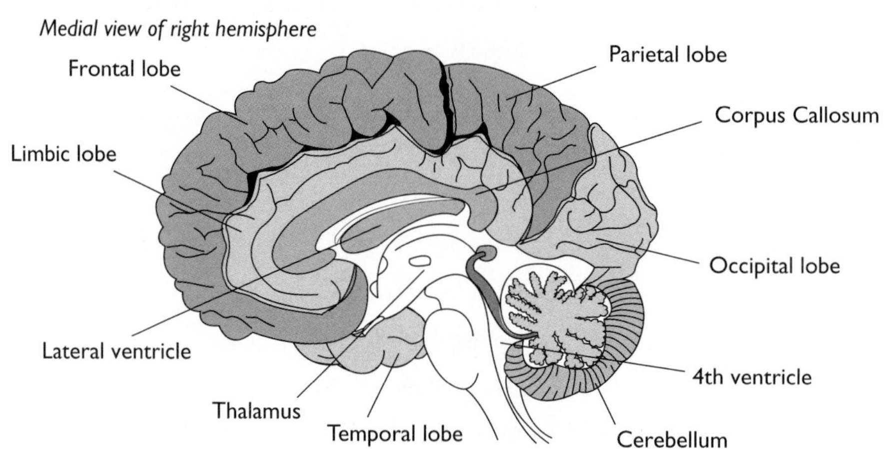

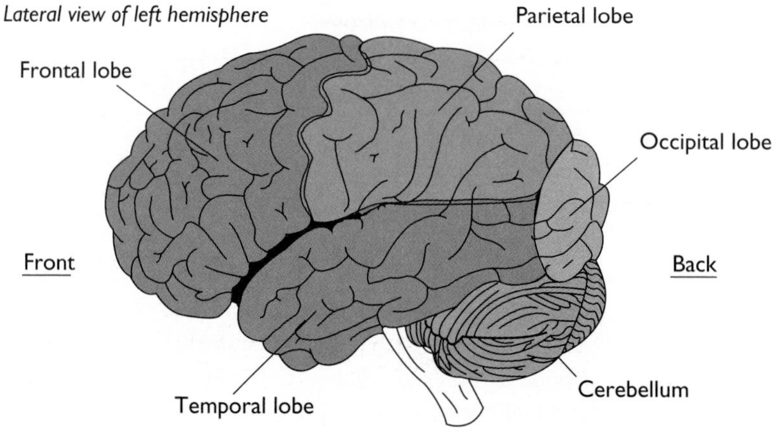

axon that transmits impulses away from the cell body, and several branching *dendrites* that receive impulses from other cells and transmit them toward the cell body. Neurons do not actually touch each other but are close enough to enable chemical electrical impulses to jump the minuscule space (synapse) between the axon of one neuron and the dendrites of the next. In short, the electrical charge of the neuron is changed by the release of *neurotransmitters* at its axon, which in turn effects the release of other neurotransmitters at the dendrite end of the second neuron. It is estimated that there are 60 trillion synapses in the human brain.

Half of the genes—50 000—are involved in the central nervous system in some way (Begley, 1996). There are approximately 12 billion neurons in the human nervous system. According to Cowan (1979), during the time the brain is growing in utero it must be generating neurons at a rate of more than 250 000 neurons per minute. Once the neurons are generated in germinal sites, they migrate to terminal locations where they are differentiated into appropriate neuron types. They are myelinated, form synapses with other neurons, and undergo some selective attrition.

What makes the nervous system work is a process in which the nerve fibres become sheathed with myelin in a process called *myelinization.* The myelin sheaths around individual nerves insulate them from one another and make it easier for messages to pass along the nerve pathways; they help speed up neural transmission and make the brain more efficient.

The Brain

It is something of a paradox that the human brain is so complex that many scientists believe it is beyond its own ability to comprehend. The brain is a densely packed, incredibly complex organ that weighs about 1.4 kilograms and contains billions of neurons.

The *cerebrum* of the human brain—the grey matter that controls higher-level intellectual functioning—is subdivided into two hemispheres. Joining the two cerebral hemispheres is the *corpus callosum,* a thick, boomerang-shaped band of fibres. The corpus callosum contains approximately 200 million neurons and is the massive midline conduit for processing and relaying information between the two hemispheres (Phillips, 1990).

Each hemisphere is divided into four lobes—occipital, parietal, frontal, and temporal. The *occipital* lobe is associated with vision; the *parietal* lobe is involved in spatial orientation. The *frontal* lobe appears to be necessary in anticipatory activity; the *temporal* lobe has an auditory function. A fifth lobe, which is apparent only in a medial view of the brain, appears to be associated with sexual and emotional functions. The lobes may also perform other functions besides these primary ones. Indeed, researchers are finding that many parts of the brain contribute to functions hitherto associated with only one specific area. The brain also contains four *ventricles.* At these sites, cerebrospinal fluid, the fluid that circulates around the brain and the spinal cord, is manufactured.

On casual examination, the two halves of the human brain look like mirror images of each other. However, there are both structural and functional differences. The left half is almost always larger. The right hemisphere contains many long neural fibres that connect widely separated areas of the brain, whereas the left hemisphere contains many shorter fibres that provide rich interconnections within a limited area (Geschwund and Galaburda, 1978).

In humans, the right hemisphere is specialized for holistic processing through the simultaneous integration of information. It primarily houses areas such as visio-spatial organization; orientation in space; perception; and recognition of faces, pictures, and photographs. The left hemisphere controls verbal function and the linear logical thinking associated with verbalization.

A hemisphere is said to be dominant if one process is primarily housed there. Yet overall, neither hemisphere is dominant over the other since each possesses specialized talents and brings different skills to a given task—neither hemisphere is competent to analyze data and program a response alone. Although they are responsible for specialized separate functions, the two hemispheres of the human brain are complementary and information passes readily between them through the corpus callosum and other subcortical bodies.

One of the wonders of human development is the manner in which the human brain, which consists of over 100 billion neurons, can develop so quickly from just a few initial neural cells. Cell differentiation within the brain of the fetus begins during the sixteenth week of gestation. Brain cells begin to multiply most rapidly after the first two months of fetal development, and progressively more slowly after birth. The last three months of fetal life and the first two months after birth are characterized by a spurt in brain growth.

When a baby comes into the world, the brain is a jumble of neurons, all waiting to be woven into the tapestry of the mind (Begley, 1996). At birth the parts of the brain most fully developed are those contained in what is usually called the *midbrain*. The *cortex*, the sophisticated part of the brain, is present at birth but considerably less developed than it will be later.

New connections continue to be built up by the process of myelinization, which occurs in different parts of the brain at different times and parallels brain development. For example, the part of the brain that controls gross motor skills is myelinated long before the parts that control fine motor skills. Four-year-olds can run, jump, and skip, but they must work endlessly to tie a bow or spread butter with a knife. By adulthood, the brain is crisscrossed with more than 100 million neurons that, in reaching out to others, create more than 100 trillion connections (Begley, 1996).

The Spinal Cord

Hemispheres rest on the brain stem, which serves as the connection to the spinal cord, a pencil-thin, segmented collection of neurons that are related to specific parts of the body. Each segment contains both sensory and motor neurons. As damage to a particular portion of the brain will result in disability in the area of the body controlled by that part of the brain, so damage to the sensory cells in the spinal cord results in loss of sensation to the parts of the body affected by those cells.

DEFINITIONS OF NEUROLOGICAL DISABILITIES

neurological impairments

Neurological impairments is one of the subcategories of physical disabilities that we describe in Chapter 11. Essentially, we can say that **neurological impairments** result from damage or dysfunction of the brain and/or the spinal cord. Such damage may occur before, during, or after birth. Potential risks include severe deprivation of oxygen before birth, especially during the first trimester when various important neural structures and interconnections between the brain cells are developing. Other risks are damage incurred during the birth process and damage directly caused by diseases, especially those that attack the central nervous system.

The effects of the damage vary greatly and wide differences are seen in the onset of symptoms, the parts of the body involved, the nature of the symptoms, the degree of severity, and the possible multiplicity of impairments. Injury to the brain may result in a relatively limited specific disorder. For example, one of the traditional etiologies of learning disabilities is minimal brain dysfunction. On the other hand, generalized and diffuse brain damage may cause very wide-ranging effects, including motor disturbances, sensory loss, speech and language disorders, and emotional and behavioural disorders. Diffuse damage will result in mental retardation; damage to the motor areas will cause cerebral palsy.

Injury to the spinal cord alone tends to result in motor and sensory disabilities without affecting intellectual function and special sensory functions (vision, hearing, and speech). Damage to the motor cells of the spinal cord results in **flaccid paralysis**, an inability to move the muscles because the neural impulses needed for muscle contractions are lacking.

flaccid paralysis

How physical and neurological disabilities affect an individual's development and lifestyle also varies dramatically. Some people are devastated by the condition and never achieve their optimal development. On the other hand, Canadians remember with special pride young people like Rick Hanson and Terry Fox who worked through their physical disabilities in efforts to help others.

Children who are physically disabled can participate in many activities with their non-disabled classmates.

PREVALENCE OF NEUROLOGICAL DISABILITIES

While neurological conditions are extremely varied, they are low-incidence disabilities. The prevalence is only about 0.2 to 1.5 percent, or about 2 per 1000 of the school-aged population (Jones, 1983), although rates vary from locale to locale and from decade to decade.

CEREBRAL PALSY

Kent, the child described in the case study, has cerebral palsy, a condition characterized by damage to the brain before, during, or after birth. The damage has left Kent with a range of disabilities. Not only does he have *hypertonia* (spasticity), but there are further co-occurring conditions that place him in the category of *multiple disabilities.* This is not always the case, but many children with cerebral palsy do indeed have additional conditions that place further barriers to successful learning.

Though often accompanied by other disabilities, cerebral palsy is chiefly a motor disorder. It is one of the most common crippling conditions in children. The most commonly cited incidence of cerebral palsy is 1.5 to 2 cases per 1000 live births (Pope and Tarlov, 1991). About 50 000 Canadians have cerebral palsy. More boys than girls are affected, and the condition occurs more often among children born to mothers in poor socio-economic cir-

Case Study

Kent

Kent suffers from a number of disabilities that affect every aspect of his life and development. He has spastic cerebral palsy that restricts his movement; he uses leg braces and a walker for mobility and a wheelchair in the classroom in which he consistently needs repositioning.

The motor impairment has affected Kent's speech, and, at eight years of age, he has developed very little communication. He has a constant drool. Kent has also a moderate to severe bilateral hearing loss and the audiologist has fitted him with two hearing aids. The loss seems to fluctuate as Kent is prone to otitis media in the winter months.

Psycho-educational assessment has shown Kent to be functioning in the low area of the mildly retarded range. With somewhat limited ability and his other problems, Kent's academic achievement is relatively low. He can recognize his own name and a few words and perform simple counting.

Kent has always been placed in a regular classroom, primarily to stimulate his social functioning. The teacher presents a modified curriculum based on his unique strengths and weaknesses and directed by his IEP. The focus is on communication development and functional skills. In her planning for Kent, the teacher considers many factors such as stamina levels; present levels of academic achievement; intellectual ability; independence in mobility and ambulation; and personal motivation. A paraprofessional provides special help with the braces and walker, the wheelchair, with toileting, and with dressing.

cumstances (Hallahan and Kauffman, 1991). An extensive study of children with cerebral palsy (Nelson and Ellenberg, 1986) found that the most likely associated factors were mental retardation of the mother, premature birth, low birth-weight, and a delay of five minutes or more before the baby's first cry. However, about 25 percent of cases have no definable cause (Tyler and Colson, 1994).

In more than two-thirds of cases, cerebral palsy is present at birth (Verhaaren and Connor, 1981). Cerebral palsy is sometimes referred to as *Little's disease*, after the surgeon who first described it. An alternative label is *significant developmental motor disability*.

Classification of Cerebral Palsy

Cerebral palsy may be classified by topography or by type. The topographical classification system, as shown in Table 12-2, refers to parts of the body and is not limited to cerebral palsy. In the topographical system, the suffix *plegia* refers to paralysis.

When classified by the type of brain damage and consequent motor disability, cerebral palsy can be differentiated according to specific motor patterns, as outlined in Table 12-3.

Spastic or *pyramidal* cerebral palsy (more correctly referred to as *hypertonia*) affects approximately 50 percent of children with cerebral palsy. Individuals have suffered damage (lesions) to the motor cortex or to the pyramidal tracts of the brain (Batshaw and Perrett, 1986). Pyramidal cerebral palsy results in problems with voluntary movements. Spasticity, therefore, refers to slow, laborious, poorly coordinated voluntary movements related to the continued presence of a number of primitive reflexes.

reflexes

Reflexes are automatic, involuntary motor patterns that are triggered by specific stimuli. *Simple* reflexes (stretch or spinal reflexes) involve the spinal cord. Above the spinal cord is the brain stem, the seat of tonic reflexes. *Spinal* and *tonic* reflexes contribute to muscle tone, posture, and allow a child to prepare for movement.

Most of the primitive reflexes present in all newborns disappear by about six months of age (see the accompanying Research Notes). If these reflexes persist, as they do in spastic cerebral palsy, they act as impediments to the development of smooth, coordinated movement.

Types of abnormal reflex movements seen in children with cerebral palsy include the rooting reflex, startle reaction, stretch reflex, asymmetrical and symmetrical tonic neck re-

Table 12-2 Topographical classification of cerebral palsy

Monoplegia	One limb impaired
Diplegia	Four limbs involved, with legs most impaired
Hemiplegia	One side of the body impaired
Paraplegia	Lower limbs of the body impaired
Triplegia	Three limbs impaired
Double hemiplegia	Both sides of the body impaired, with each side affected differently
Quadriplegia	All four limbs impaired

Table 12-3 Classification of cerebral palsy

	Pyramidal cerebral palsy (spasticity)	Extrapyramidal cerebral palsy dyskinesia (five types)				
		Athetosis	Rigidity	Hypotonia	Tremor	Ataxia
Movement	Slow and difficult	Consistent, involuntary, writhing	More severe than spasticity	May develop into spastic or athetoid type	Involuntary, rhythmic	Clumsy
Coordination	Poor	Poor	Poor	Varied	Depends upon affected limbs	Poor
Muscle tone	Weak, hypertonic	Fluctuating	Continuous tension	Low	Varied	Varied

flex, protective extensive reactions, and righting reactions. In the presence of the stretch reflex, for example, a muscle contracts involuntarily when suddenly stretched. Thus, when the arm is bent suddenly, the biceps contract but the reflex causes contractions in the opposing triceps as well. A mini-war results, rendering movements impossible to control. This means that children with spastic cerebral palsy cannot move when and how they choose.

Extrapyramidal cerebral palsy differs from spasticity in that the damage is outside the pyramidal tracts. The conditions include athetosis, tremor, rigidity, and ataxia.

Athetoid cerebral palsy, found in approximately 25 percent of individuals with cerebral palsy, is caused by lesions of the basal ganglia. The condition is characterized by constant, involuntary writhing movements, especially in the hands and wrists. Contractions occur in successive groups of muscles, creating extraneous movement that interferes with purposive action. Children with athetoid cerebral palsy show abrupt involuntary movements, difficulty in maintaining posture, and are unable to stop moving when they want to. Athetosis stops during sleep.

Rigidity occurs when there is a low level of motor stiffness that never relaxes. The condition is rare, as is *tremor*, an involuntary movement in one extremity, usually one hand or arm. In constant tremor, the movement is continuous; in intention tremor, the involuntary movement happens only when the child undertakes to do something.

Ataxic cerebral palsy occurs in approximately 15 percent of individuals with cerebral palsy. Ataxia is characterized by poor coordination of the movements associated with balance, posture, and spatial orientation. Children with ataxia tend to walk with a wide gait, their legs well apart to compensate for poor equilibrium. They also exhibit a generalized lack of coordination of both fine and gross motor movements. The eyes are often uncoordinated (Jones, 1987).

Research Notes

Reflexes in Infants

Newborns are unable to control their motor behaviour smoothly and voluntarily. Instead, behaviour consists of twitches, jerks, and random movements, most of which involve reflexes—natural responses with which children are born. They are stereotyped movements produced in response to a particular sensory input.

Some reflexes, such as the various feeding reflexes, are necessary for survival. Others are interesting because they are controlled by the midbrain, that part of the brain that develops first. As the more advanced parts of the brain develop, these primitive reflexes disappear. Infants come equipped with a rooting reflex. If babies are touched on the cheek anywhere near the mouth, they will turn their heads and root around to put their mouths on the object that touched them. There is also the Moro reflex, described by Ernst Moro in 1918. If a loud noise is made near an infant, or if the infant's position is changed suddenly, the baby will throw both arms outwards and then bring them in to the body. This reflex disappears at about three months of age as the neurological system matures. With the Babinski reflex, babies splay out their toes and then curl them in if stroked on the bottom of the foot. In an adult or older child, only the curling occurs.

The reflex actions of babies allow them to react to things in their world as they are learning to control their own bodies. Reflexes also help to ensure survival by protecting vital systems. As well, the presence of reflexes in infants and their eventual disappearance offers insights into the process of neurological development and organization, together with information about the results of damage to discrete areas of the brain. A number of reactions appear to be the precursors of later development and can be used to diagnose certain kinds of brain damage.

When there is damage to both the pyramidal and the extrapyramidal regions of the brain, the child may show mixed effects, such as spasticity of the legs and rigidity of the arms. About 25 percent of cases are classified as *mixed cerebral palsy* (Batshaw and Perrett, 1986).

Developmental Consequences of Cerebral Palsy

The consequences of cerebral palsy vary in relation to many factors that relate chiefly to the type of cerebral palsy, the severity of the condition, and the presence or absence of co-occurring conditions. While no two children with cerebral palsy develop in exactly the same way, the presence of extensive motor disorders alone is sufficient to interfere with normal development.

In normally developing children, each stage of motor development causes a shift in the child's interaction with the environment. Within twelve to fourteen weeks of birth, for example, normally developing children achieve control of head movements. Within six months, they pull to a sitting position. At about twelve months they begin to walk unaided. These milestones offer children increased opportunities to make better use of sensory experience, to gain greater perceptual awareness, and to learn to manipulate objects and their own bodies.

Damage to the motor system impedes this normal developmental course. Children with cerebral palsy have little control of the musculature necessary to reach developmental milestones.

Early diagnosis is difficult; cerebral palsy is generally not diagnosed right at birth because there are few abnormal neurological signs at this time. In fact, a brain-damaged neonate may appear to be perfectly normal for the first several weeks of life. Clues to neuromotor disturbance in infants include irritability, excessive listlessness, pallor, stiffening, arching, excessive startle, nystagmus, and jaundice. In addition, infants with cerebral palsy behave differently. They tend to sleep excessively, have a weak cry, a poor suck, and show little interest in their surroundings. They rest differently, lying in a floppy extended position instead of a semi-flexed one (Batshaw and Perrett, 1986). Note that not all of these signs are found in all infants with cerebral palsy, and not all infants who manifest these signs have cerebral palsy.

As the child develops, predictions can be made on overall progress. If the child can sit by two years of age, for example, he or she will probably walk. About 80 percent of children with cerebral palsy are capable of learning to walk, although many need to use braces and other assistive devices. If the child is able to utter recognizable sounds by age two, that child will probably learn to speak (Bleck and Nagel, 1982).

The brain damage that results in cerebral palsy is not always limited to motor areas. Indeed, as the case of Kent indicates, cerebral palsy can generally be seen as a multi-disabling condition. A high percentage of children exhibit one or more additional impairments. These include mental retardation, learning disabilities, sensory loss, epilepsy, and emotional and behavioural disorders. As well, disorders of posture, listening, breathing, voice, articulation, and language are all found in association with cerebral palsy.

Many people assume, given the external appearance of the condition, that all children with cerebral palsy are intellectually disabled. As a blanket assumption, this is incorrect. However, it is true that the incidence of intellectual disability is significantly higher than average. Estimates of the number of children who are cerebral palsied who have some degree of intellectual impairment range from 25 to 75 percent (Gersh, 1991b; Nelson and Ellenberg, 1986). Little evidence exists to link the severity of intellectual impairment with any particular type of cerebral palsy, although hemiplegia seems to be associated with the best mental development (Batshaw and Perrett, 1986).

The speech and language problems of children with cerebral palsy reflect the complexity of the condition. Estimates of co-occurring speech and language problems range from 50 to 83 percent. Language problems are less common than speech disorders. In some cases damage, usually to certain areas of the left cerebral hemisphere, results in language delays and disorders.

Motor dysfunctions that affect the organs of speech may make intelligible speech impossible (see Jones, 1987). The errors of articulation that accompany cerebral palsy are known as *dysarthria*, a condition discussed in Chapter 4. The speech characteristics of children with spastic forms of cerebral palsy may include articulatory defects, laboured speech with distortions of sound, uncontrolled pitch changes, and husky voice quality.

Visual and auditory problems are the most prevalent and serious of the associated sensory difficulties. It is estimated that more than 50 percent of children with cerebral palsy have visual defects of some type (Lefebrue, 1983); often these are related to loss of control of the ocular muscles. There is also a high incidence of middle ear problems; approximately 25 to 30 percent of individuals with cerebral palsy have hearing defects (Jones, 1983). Other sensory problems include deficits in tactile sensation and the determination of pain, pressure, and temperature.

Children with cerebral palsy may also show learning disorders such as short attention span and distractibility. It is estimated that from 15 to 20 percent are likely to have some type of specific learning disability (Telford and Sawrey, 1981).

An additional problem is some form of convulsive disorder. It is estimated that 25 to 50 percent suffer epileptic seizures (Gersh, 1991a; Jones, 1987). These are most common in hemiplegics and quadriplegics. As well, children who are cerebral palsied with normal IQs are three times more prone to psychiatric disorders (Seidel, Chadwick, and Rutter, 1975).

As the number of accompanying disorders indicates, cerebral palsy is a very complex multi-disabling condition. However, not every affected child faces all or even most of these disorders. Usually children with limited and localized brain injuries face fewer limitations than children with diffuse, extensive brain damage.

For children with orthopedic and motor disabilities such as cerebral palsy, a key factor is the extent to which the disability affects movement potential. Motor skills are integral to almost everything that a child does or wants to do in the environment, and physical and motor problems affect educational and social progress in other ways than mobility. Deficient motor skills can affect cognitive development because they hinder a child's manipulation and exploration.

Children with motor impairments have different first-hand knowledge and experiences than their peers because they cannot explore the environment as other children can. At the sensorimotor stage, for example, children with cerebral palsy have been found to include more visual exploration and less tactile exploration of toys than is seen among children developing normally (see Rogers, 1988).

Similarly, social skills may suffer because efficient motor skills are necessary for many forms of play with peers. Play depends on experience and opportunity, and this alone places restraints on children with severe physical disabilities. Children with motor disorders cannot manipulate toys and other objects, join in dramatic and pretend play or rough and tumble play, or engage in games in which children run and jump and skip.

SPINA BIFIDA

Midline defects, often referred to as *clefts*, result from the failure of parts of the embryo to fuse completely. Such defects may occur in many parts of the body, including the lip, the palate, the eye, and the spine. *Spina bifida* is a congenital midline defect of the spinal column.

spina bifida

Technically, the term **spina bifida** refers to a defect in the bony arch of the vertebrae protecting the spinal cord. In the early weeks of pregnancy, the neural tube of the embryo fails to develop normally. The bony arches of one or more spinal vertebrae do not fuse to protect the spinal cord, which leaves part of the nerve fibres of the cord exposed. The spinal defect may be found anywhere between the skull and the lowest segments of the vertebrae. Generally, spina bifida is evident by the end of the fourth week of gestation, and the severity of the problem is apparent at birth.

Although the process is fairly well understood, the actual cause of spina bifida is unknown. Etiologically, it is believed that both heredity and environment are interweaving factors.

Spina bifida can be detected prenatally by a test that looks at the level of alpha-fetoprotein in the mother's blood. Higher concentrations than usual indicate the necessity for ultrasound or fetoscopy.

The prevalence of spina bifida varies widely from country to country, from area to area, and even within the limits of a particular city. Worldwide, spina bifida occurs in from 0.1 to 4.13 live births per 1000 (Bleck and Nagel, 1982). The incidence in Ireland is about 4 or 5 children per 1000 live births, while in parts of Nigeria it is 0.2 per 1000 live births. In Canada, the highest rate of spina bifida is found in Newfoundland.

There is a slight tendency for the condition to run in families. If one baby is born with spina bifida, there is a four to five percent chance of siblings having the same defect (Myers, Cerone, and Olson, 1981). As with cerebral palsy, spina bifida is found more often in lower socio-economic groups and occurs more frequently in males (Bowley and Gardner, 1980).

Classification of Spina Bifida

The problems associated with spina bifida range from few or no adverse effects to severely disabling depending on the form. Spina bifida is divided into two main forms: *spina bifida occulta* and *spina bifida cystica.* Of the affected population, about 40 percent suffer from spina bifida occulta and the remainder from cystica. This latter form is divided into two types—*spina bifida with meningocele* and *spina bifida with myelomeningocele.* The former accounts for 4 percent of individuals suffering the cystica form; the latter for 96 percent. (See Figure 12-2.)

Spina bifida occulta is the mildest form of the condition and has few or no negative effects. The only visible sign of the condition, if any, is a clump of hair on the skin covering the

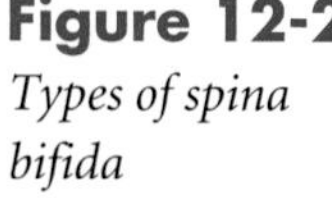

Figure 12-2
Types of spina bifida

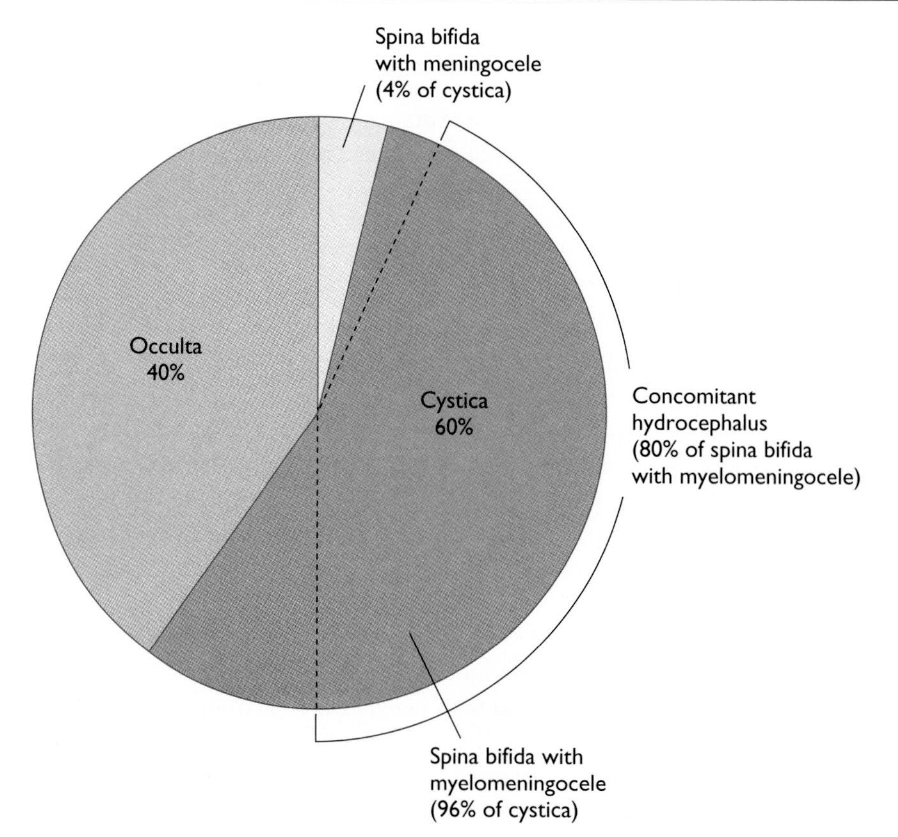

area of the cleft. In fact, this variety of spina bifida may affect up to 20 percent of North Americans; because symptoms are rare, people may not even know they have it (Moore and Persaud, 1993).

The two forms of spina bifida cystica—with meningocele and with myelomeningocele—have different results. In spina bifida with meningocele, the *meninges*, the membranes surrounding the spinal cord, protrude from the plane of the spine and form a sac containing cerebrospinal fluid. Surgery is usually performed in the first days of life to restore the sac within the spinal column. Following treatment, this condition does not usually create any major difficulties, although children must be wary of being hit directly on the area.

Spina bifida with myelomeningocele, the most severe type, results in a protruding sac that contains parts of the spinal cord as well as cerebrospinal fluid. The spinal cord not only enters the sac but also is itself abnormal. Surgical treatment is necessary to deal with the sac, but the neurological damage is irreversible.

The effects of myelomeningocele vary considerably depending on the location of the cleft. The higher the cleft, the greater the damage. Clefts in the lower part of the spine may result in incontinence without paralysis. Clefts in the higher spinal regions produce paralysis and loss of sensation in the lower limbs, incontinence, and kidney problems. In addition to the cleft of the vertebral arches associated with spina bifida, other vertebrae unusual in slope or connection can occur, resulting in an uneven growth of the spine.

Twenty-five years ago, more than 90 percent of children with spina bifida died within a few years of birth from urinary infection or infection of the sac. Today, 90 percent live an average life span (Kaplan, 1996).

Developmental Consequences of Spina Bifida

Children with spina bifida occulta or with meningocele are likely to develop normally. In the absence of co-occurring conditions, spina bifida does not preclude adequate learning ability. Children with spina bifida occulta exhibit a normal range of intelligence; those with meningocele are also likely to have normal intelligence.

Children with myelomeningocele suffer neurological damage that interferes with growth and development. The most obvious neurological damage is the flaccid paralysis of the lower part of the body, which makes braces, crutches, walkers, or wheelchairs necessary.

Children with myelomeningocele lack sensation and control of their bladders and bowel sphincters. Incontinence in itself does not create learning difficulties, but it may create social and psychological barriers for children in school. Non-disabled children usually view incontinence as a sign of immaturity or infantile behaviour and react accordingly.

As incontinent children mature, they learn to cope with their condition. Using a procedure called clean intermittent catheterization, they catheterize themselves every three or four hours (Myers, Cerone, and Olson, 1981). Although it may not create problems, it has been found that children with spina bifida experience very early puberty, with menstruation occurring as early as eight years of age (Allum, 1975). Researchers are uncertain of the cause of this phenomenon.

Children with spina bifida with myelomenigocele may show intellectual disabilities. Perceptual and cognitive dysfunction is prevalent, especially in children with accompanying hydrocephalus. While children show poorer general performance in reading, spelling, and arithmetic, most have good verbal ability, which may tend to mask the cognitive defects.

Although spina bifida may occur as a solitary condition, nearly 80 percent of children who have spina bifida with myelomeningocele have accompanying hydrocephalus. The combination of the two conditions dramatically increases the number of disabilities. The damage to the brain from hydrocephalus and to the spinal cord from spina bifida is likely to render a child multiply disabled.

HYDROCEPHALUS

hydrocephalus

Hydrocephalus is a condition characterized by an excessive accumulation in the brain of cerebrospinal fluid due to an obstruction of its flow. Normally, cerebrospinal fluid is constantly manufactured in the ventricles of the brain, circulates through the ventricles and the space between the two layers of meninges, and is absorbed into the circulatory system. Since fluids are largely non-compressible, a blockage of the flow results in the accumulation of cerebrospinal fluid in an enclosed area, placing pressure on the brain and the skull. The pressure against the skull creates thinning of the bone and separation of the *sutures* (the seams between the plates of the skull). The fluid also presses on the brain tissue, causing distortion of brain substance and damage and death to the neurons.

In some instances, hydrocephalus arrests itself spontaneously. In other cases, the condition progresses and creates increasing pressure on the skull. The progressive accumulation of cerebrospinal fluid results in a range of disorders. Because mental retardation is a primary result, hydrocephalus is included among the clinical forms of mental retardation. Other sequelae include motor disorders, seizures, and even death.

Before the 1950s, no effective treatment existed for hydrocephalus. Children developed marked symptoms; by the age of three months, their heads became too large and heavy for them to lift, and their condition often ended in death. In 1952 an engineer named Holter developed an effective shunt (tube) to drain off excess cerebrospinal fluid and reduce the pressure on the brain. Since Holter's invention, many children with hydrocephalus have been spared extensive impairments.

Developmental Consequences of Hydrocephalus

In persons affected by hydrocephalus, consequences vary with the degree of severity of the conditions, the presence or absence of co-occurring conditions, and the success or failure of treatment. Evidence about cognitive functioning is contradictory. Some researchers have found no correlation between the degree of severity of hydrocephalus and IQ levels (e.g., Soare and Raimondi, 1977); others note that the average IQ of shunted children is 70 to 83 (Tew and Lawrence, 1975). It has also been found that many children who are hydrocephalic have particular learning problems that result in uneven intellectual functioning. Aspects of verbal ability, such as syntax and vocabulary, may be well developed, while comprehension and language usage are defective (Spain, 1972).

EPILEPSY

The word *epilepsy* is derived from the Greek meaning "to be seized," and we still describe epilepsy in terms of seizures. During the 1800s Hughlings Jackson, a pioneer neurologist, defined epilepsy as a condition produced by a sudden violent electrical discharge of brain cells. Echoing Jackson's definition, epilepsy is today defined as

> a convulsive disorder [that] is the expression of a sudden, excessive, disorderly discharge of neurons in either a structurally normal or diseased cortex. The discharge results in an almost instantaneous disturbance of sensation, loss of consciousness, convulsive movement, or some combination thereof. (Harrison, 1980, p. 131)

Implicit in this definition is the idea that epilepsy is not a disease but a symptom of a brain disorder that may be caused by any condition that results in damage to the brain. This does not imply that brain damage necessarily results in epileptic seizures, although it may. The definition further stresses the chronic and recurring nature of epilepsy.

Chronicity is important because it is estimated that between 2 and 3 percent of the population have had, or will have, some form of epileptic seizure in their lifetime (B.C. Ministry of Health, 1978). However, such a single symptom might reflect some transient event, such as a high fever, heat exhaustion, ingestion of certain chemicals, or interference with the normal supply of oxygen to the brain.

The causes of epilepsy are varied and often unclear. Perinatal conditions, early childhood infection, and head trauma are identified as known causative factors. Heredity rarely plays a role: unless both parents have a strong family history of epilepsy, the chances that their children will inherit a tendency to have seizures is very slight.

For about 75 percent of persons with epilepsy, a specific cause cannot be found. In this case, the condition is referred to as *idiopathic epilepsy*, or *epilepsy of unknown origin.* If an individual shows strong evidence of brain damage, the condition is known as *symptomatic epilepsy.* The most common causes are brain tumour and stroke; head trauma of any type; injury, infection, or systemic illness of the mother during pregnancy that affects fetal brain growth; brain injury to the infant during delivery; the aftermath of an infection such as meningitis; and poisoning from substance abuse or alcoholism (Epilepsy Canada, [1994]).

Epilepsy affects more than one percent of the population—more than 280 000 Canadians. No one is immune; epilepsy can strike anyone at any age. However, from 70 to 80 percent of patients develop epilepsy before the age of 18. About 55 percent develop epilepsy before the age of 10, and 44 percent before the age of 5. One of every 2000 people is diagnosed with epilepsy each year; about 14 000 new cases are reported annually (Epilepsy Canada, [1994]. Too, the recognized incidence of epilepsy is greater today than in the past due to a higher survival rate among infants and persons with brain injuries.

Classification of Epilepsy

As a term, *epilepsy* describes two things—the conditions of seizure and the convulsions accompanying some types of seizures. Seizures occur as a result of a temporary breakdown in the brain's communication system caused by disorderly cell activity. There are many types of seizures, some fairly well understood and some still confusing to researchers. The type of seizure depends on the region of the brain where it originates and, to some extent, on the brain's maturation and its ability to spread the electrical discharge to other parts of the body.

The three main classifications of epilepsy are generalized seizures, partial seizures, and unclassified seizures. Seizure types and their progress are described in the accompanying Research Notes.

Research Notes

Types of Seizures

Generalized seizures are bilateral and symmetrical without local onset in the brain. They are often accompanied by loss of consciousness and most have motor components. Generalized seizures include *petit mal* (absence seizures), *myoclonic seizures, grand mal* (tonic-clonic seizures), and *atonic seizures,* which include infantile spasm convulsions. The most common forms of generalized seizures are grand mal and petit mal. Many individuals experience both these forms, which may be either idiopathic or symptomatic.

The grand mal seizure proceeds through relatively distinct stages. Some epileptics consistently experience an aura just before the seizure's onset. This aura may be a subjective sensory or memory experience, such as an odour that is not present in reality. It may take the form of an odd internal sensation, or even a memory phenomenon in which the person actually experiences a scene from the past (Krupp and Chatton, 1983).

Shortly after the aura appears, the individual loses consciousness, falls, and develops generalized stiffness of the body. During this *tonic* phase, the arms are flexed (bent) and the legs extended. The trunk muscles are also in spasm so that breathing ceases. After a short but varying period of tonic activity, the *clonic* stage follows. In this phase, the person exhibits alternate relaxations and contractions of the skeletal musculature, which produce what is often referred to as *thrashing movements.* In the throes of the clonic state, the person may lose bladder and bowel control, bite the tongue, and froth at the mouth. After two to five minutes, convulsive movements diminish and finally stop.

This is followed by a gradual regaining of consciousness. During this time, the person may experience confusion, headache, or other symptoms. A period of deep sleep marks the end of the seizure. If a child suffers a grand mal seizure and then immediately passes into another seizure, the condition is known as *status epilepticus.* This is potentially life-threatening and medical aid should be sought immediately.

Grand mal seizures can occur at any time and in a school setting can be frightening for the beholders and distressing for the victim. Teachers can ease the situation by trying to provide privacy during and after a seizure. If a child begins to have a seizure, the teacher should allow or help the child to lie down, move away furniture, loosen restrictive clothing, and tilt the head to one side to drain saliva. Teachers should never try to hold the child, stop the seizure, or force anything into the mouth.

The petit mal or absence seizure is most frequently seen in children. Some children suffer up to 200 absence seizures a day. These often occur when the child is sedentary, and infrequently during exercise (Berkow, 1982). In more than 70 percent of all cases, petit mal seizures cease altogether by age 18 (Nealis, 1983).

Petit mal is considerably less dramatic than grand mal; the classic absence seizure lasts only fifteen to thirty seconds and is so brief that it is often overlooked or misinterpreted. The child ceases all activity and appears to stare vacantly, as though daydreaming. During this period, there is a loss or clouding of consciousness. The return of consciousness is abrupt and the child immediately resumes interrupted activities.

There are other forms of petit mal seizures. During these, the child's eyes may blink or shift and the hands may move aimlessly. On some occasions, the seizure may be prolonged, lasting for minutes or hours. During these long seizures, the child may simply appear confused and dazed.

Minor motor seizures, often called Lennox-Gastaug seizures, are similar to petit mal. They can be characterized by loss of muscle tone for a moment.

Myoclonic seizures are so called because they are characterized by a single repetitive contracture of a muscle or group of muscles.

Partial seizures begin locally (in a specific area of the brain) and may or may not cause loss of consciousness. They occur in many forms, but the common feature in all is the localized origin of brain irritability. Because they affect very local motor or sensory areas, partial seizures are sometimes referred to as *focal seizures*.

One form of partial seizure is the Jacksonian seizure, which occurs only in cases of symptomatic epilepsy. This type of seizure is characterized by motor symptoms without impaired consciousness. Spasmodic (clonic) movements might start in the peripheral portion of a limb, such as the left thumb. These movements might then progress in an orderly fashion toward the central portion of the body and down into the left leg. Sometimes the violent electrical discharge that begins in one hemisphere of the brain spreads to the other. If this happens, the individual loses consciousness and undergoes a grand mal convulsion.

Another type of partial seizure is the *psychomotor seizure*, sometimes called the *psychomotor equivalent* or *temporal lobe seizure*. It is most characteristically associated with lesions of the temporal lobe of the brain.

Psychomotor seizures are poorly understood. They often include a clouding of consciousness and amnesia (loss of memory of the event). Along with altered consciousness, other manifestations include a change of body position or limbs, confused activity, a dazed expression, nausea, vomiting, drooling, muttering, mumbling, wandering, pallor or flushing, incoherent or irrelevant speech, and inappropriate emotional disturbances. Sometimes these symptoms are accompanied by relatively complex, well-organized movements, such as plucking clothing or any other patterned activity.

The category of *unclassified seizures* includes all other types.

Developmental Consequences of Epilepsy

The effects on learning resulting from epilepsy can be chronic, with permanent impairment in the ability to process information. In other cases, the influence on learning is relatively short-lived, and includes brief transient disturbances in attention and short-term deficits in cognitive functioning. Effects chiefly depend on factors such as the nature of the seizure disorders and the medications used. Even with varied effects, however, a recent study found that retention in grade and placement in special education was twice as frequent for children with epilepsy as for normally developing children (see Williams, Sharp, Bates, Griebel, Lange, Spence, and Thomas, 1996).

Children with idiopathic epilepsy are more likely to develop normally than those with symptomatic epilepsy. Most children with idiopathic epilepsy function normally between attacks, and approximately 70 percent have normal or higher intelligence (Dikmen, Matthews, and Harley, 1975). Symptomatic epilepsy is often seen in children who experience seizures before age two. The early onset of seizures that are unremitting or persistent for several years are more likely to be related to learning problems than is later onset or lower seizure frequency (Rodin, 1989). These children are usually suffering the effects of developmental defects, birth injuries, or a metabolic disease affecting the brain, and are more likely to exhibit multiple disorders that can include mental retardation, sensory loss, or motor disability. As well, generalized seizures are more likely than partial epilepsy to be associated with learning problems. Individuals with more generalized seizures are usually expected to suffer greater disability than those whose seizures are more focused and partial.

Together with possible learning problems, a range of psychological and social adjustment difficulties have been associated with epilepsy, with boys consistently showing problem outcomes with greater frequency than girls (Williams et al., 1996). Students show, for example, increased psychiatric and behavioural disturbances, poor self-esteem, and excessive dependency.

This happens because, in many ways, epilepsy is unique among chronic illnesses. For the individual child, the chronic nature of the disorder and the unpredictability of seizures are disturbing. Although the majority of children with epilepsy are well controlled with medication, and although some may outgrow seizures, none can look forward to a cure and must learn to live with the possibility of lifelong seizures. In addition, no one can predict when a seizure will occur; for this reason, there is little chance to adjust to epilepsy. Children may feel powerless at the prospect of losing control: the ambiguous nature of epilepsy can increase a child's apprehension at not knowing when and under what circumstances his or her behaviour will become visible to others.

Society's reaction to epilepsy remains problematic. Despite the success of modern treatment, confusion and misunderstanding still surround the condition. Some people continue to equate epilepsy with mental retardation or mental illness. This is not correct. Some persons with symptomatic epilepsy may exhibit mental retardation, but they are a minority in the population with epilepsy. Among persons with idiopathic epilepsy, mental illness or intellectual disability do not occur more frequently than in the general population.

TOURETTE SYNDROME

Tourette syndrome is a condition characterized by multiple, involuntary muscular and cerebral tics that wax and wane, remit, and change. The onset is between the ages of two and fifteen, with six to seven years of age the most common time. The disorder results from a chemical imbalance in the brain. About 50 percent of those affected show hyperactivity, short attention spans, restlessness, and poor impulse control (Lemon and Barber, 1991).

Probably 1.6 percent of the entire population is affected with Tourette syndrome. There are about three times as many males as females affected. Only about 30 to 50 percent of persons with Tourette syndrome have *caprolia*, the verbal tic that results in uncontrollable uttering of obscenities (Lemon and Barber, 1991).

Tourette syndrome is often treated with a combination of medication and cognitive behavioural approaches that involve changes in the social environment.

HEAD TRAUMA

In the United States, injuries, usually accidents, are the leading cause of death among children aged one to fourteen; almost half of these deaths occur among children aged one to four. Boys are involved in injuries twice as often as girls. The same is true in Canada, where injuries are the leading cause of death for children and youth after the age of one. For example, in 1990 injuries accounted for 40 percent of all preschool deaths; 50 percent of deaths among five- to nine-year-olds; and almost 66 percent among ten- to fourteen-year-olds ("Injuries...," 1994).

Rates vary greatly across the country and among groups. The preschool rates of injury in the territories are generally much higher than the national average. Injuries are more likely to occur among poor children, boys, and among aboriginal children and youth ("Injuries ...," 1994). Among injuries in general, head injuries are on the rise.

Traumatic Brain Injury

Traumatic Brain Injury (TBI) is defined as

> an insult to the brain, not of a degenerative or congenital nature but caused by an external physical force, that may produce a diminished or altered state of consciousness, which results in impairment of cognitive abilities or physical functioning. It can also result in the disturbance of behaviour or emotional functioning. These impairments may be either temporary or cause potential or total functional disability or psychosocial maladjustment. (Savage, 1988, p. 13)

In the past, as noted, head injuries occurred most often in the fifteen- to twenty-four-year-old range. Today, Traumatic Brain Injury is almost as frequent in children under age fifteen. In the United States, it is estimated that one out of every 500 school-aged children will be hospitalized for traumatic head injuries (Kraus, Fife, and Conroy, 1987). Among adolescents, vehicle accidents —involving either pedestrian or passenger vehicles including automobiles, motorcycles, and bicycles—are the most common cause of head injuries. Among young children, head injuries result from falls (the most frequent cause), bicycle accidents, other recreational activities, assaults, and child abuse.

TBI is unique in several ways, which are explained below.

- TBI is characterized by sudden onset (usually from motor vehicle accidents and falls).
- In some individuals, the effects are not always immediately seen; they may not become apparent for months or even years.
- Advances in acute medical treatment technology have increased survival rates for individuals with TBI. However, about 20 percent are left with some degree of disability.
- TBI is not selective in its damage. It can cause diffuse cerebral swelling due to increased cerebral blood volume, and several areas of the brain can therefore be affected. Because of this, children and adolescents who suffer head injuries can be expected to present concomitant physical and perceptual motor defects and organically based behaviour and emotional disorders (De Pompei and Blosser, 1987).
- The age at which the injury is sustained has a significant impact on the ultimate extent of recovery.
- Each child with a traumatic brain injury progresses through the recovery process in a unique way. Recovery is influenced by the site and extent of the injuries to the brain, the child's age, and other injuries or complications. Children are often in a coma and may at first show a state of confusion, as well as memory, attention, or speech and language impairments.
- TBI in children disrupts the normal developmental processes and sets into motion a parallel process—recovery from injury.
- TBI results in a loss of previous levels of personal, academic, and social functioning. Changes in behaviour and self-management can affect a student's performance, self-esteem, and social relationships (Berglund and Hoffbauer, 1996).
- Behaviour may be different than before the accident. In one study (Scaringi, 1994) parents reported that, in general, their children's behaviour tended to be more volatile; they

were more short tempered and their tolerance level with frustrating tasks was lower. In addition, they had become quite stubborn. These children would often adamantly refuse to perform chores at home, complete homework assignments, and so on. During therapy sessions, they were highly distractible. They played with pencils, erasers, and tried to engage the reporting clinician in conversation that had nothing to do with the task at hand.

- Many children manifest long-term behavioural problems, despite apparent recovery (Wade, Taylor, Drotar, Stancin, and Yeates, 1996).
- Frontal lobe damage is the most common form of injury and ensures diminished cognitive capacity. Other insults to the brain also compromise cognitive functioning. Associated cognitive or information-processing deficits, particularly memory losses, impair a student's ability to learn new information and, consequently, compromise academic performance.
- Although TBI can result in learning disabilities of varying degrees, students show more variability in performance than do those with other learning disabilities (Smith and Luckasson, 1995).
- Language difficulties, the aphasia we discussed in Chapter 4, are common. In acquired aphasia, the age of onset is a critical factor. In children as young as four, evidence exists that the hemispheres of the brain process symbolic communication differently, with left-hemisphere dominance in speech and language. With age, the brain becomes fixed and the various functions cannot be easily assumed by the other related segment of the brain. It is assumed that by about school age the brain has lost much of the organic plasticity found in young children. In adults, functional locational phenomena are even more pronounced, and adults are less able to recover functions lost through brain injury than are children. Nevertheless, many adults recover completely when they suffer serious brain damage of the left hemisphere (Snow, 1987).
- Children who sustain injuries before the age of three may become temporarily mute and show a general inability to respond to the speech of others. However, very young children often make rapid improvement. They seem to relearn language in the same sequence as children acquiring language for the first time. In children more than three years old, symptoms of aphasia are usually different. These children may find it hard to retrieve words they used only moments earlier. Recovery is slower and residual problems are likely to remain.
- Severe TBI is a significant family burden and source of stress during acute hospitalization and in the early weeks following discharge. Stress is multidimensional and affects siblings and the nuclear family. The long-term impact is the greatest concern (Wade et al., 1996).

Developmental Consequences of Head Trauma

On a personal level, TBI often shatters an individual's sense of self. Recovering identity may require a long period of habilitation and multidisciplinary efforts (see Kauffman, 1997b).

Teachers familiar with students with TBI often report classroom difficulties (Savage and Wolcott, 1994). Children who have suffered a head injury may show chronic fatigue for up to a year. Whereas obvious motor problems may be resolved relatively quickly, problems with the execution of refined and complex psychomotor movements, particularly when speed is involved, may persist.

Children may show problems in attention, retention, and auditory and recent memory.

These deficits have implications for the child in the classroom because they influence the degree to which the child can keep up with class procedures such as copying, organizing material, and producing significant amounts of work.

Language problems may persist. When deficits such as lack of speech, restricted expressive output, and problems of breath control are present right after a trauma, they may subside rapidly, but as part of a global disorganization process more subtle and long-standing difficulties with language comprehension and expression may persist. These include problems of word finding, organization of sequenced utterances, and comprehension breakdown as instructional complexity increases (Mira and Tyler, 1991; Ylvisaker, 1986).

It is estimated that among children with mild head injuries, about 25 percent will require special classes; of children with serious injuries, about 50 percent will need special education. For special education intervention, however, there are no particular tested techniques or educational modifications in place (see Tyler and Mira, 1993).

DRUG-EXPOSED CHILDREN

In Chapter 3 of this text, we pointed to the range of possible physical and behavioural difficulties that can affect a child exposed prenatally to drugs. It is important to keep in mind that there is a continuum of casualty risk. That is, the popular notion that all drug-exposed babies are severely affected is a myth; the effects vary dramatically and are moderated or exacerbated by social factors such as poverty, neglect, or drug use by others in the home.

For children who do suffer effects, there are problems in classroom participation. Such children may perceive as stressful some events that teachers view as normal or routine (Evans, Tickle, Toppel, and Nichols, 1997). They are often overwhelmed by the ordinary experiences of a classroom—the classroom and environmental noises, the instructions, questions, interactions, and general business. Some children may withdraw; others may become wild and difficult to control (Rest, 1990).

FETAL ALCOHOL SYNDROME (FAS)

About one in every 500 babies in Canada is thought to suffer from FAS/FAE (Phelp, 2000). The disabilities resulting from FAS or FAE may be the least diagnosed and most misunderstood of all those affecting students today ("Fetal Alcohol...," 1997). Students with FAS experience behavioural difficulties that are long-lasting and varied. They have problems communicating their needs, are easily frustrated, and have little control over their impulses. In the classroom, they often find it difficult to stay on task, to refrain from constant motion, to be non-disruptive, and to work independently for long periods. Children often do not use good judgment and do not learn from their mistakes. Even in individuals with normal IQs, there are academic problems (Kerms, Don, Mateer, and Streissguth, 1997).

ACQUIRED IMMUNODEFICIENCY SYNDROME (AIDS)

Acquired Immunodeficiency Syndrome (AIDS) is caused by the virus HIV (human immunodeficiency virus) that attacks and seriously disrupts the body's immune system, its defence against disease. Without the protection of the immune system, AIDS sufferers are prone to fatal infections and cancers.

Today, there are really only two major populations of children with HIV infection. The first is children with congenital or birth-acquired infection. This group forms the vast majority of children with pediatric AIDS; they have obtained their infection during birth from the mother, who used intravenous drugs or was sexually active with infected partners (Baumeister, Kupstas, and Klindworth, 1990). About 30 percent of infants of HIV-infected mothers will acquire the virus. Almost all of these infected children will develop AIDS before the age of two. The second group of HIV-infected students is adolescents who acquire the virus sexually or through intravenous drug use. A very small third group is those infected by transfusions.

The typical course of AIDS depends upon how the infection was transmitted. For children who are affected before birth, the median incubation period is twelve months. For children infected as a result of transfusion, the median incubation period is three to five years (Simonds and Rogers, 1992). This means that many young children who have transfusion-transmitted AIDS (and some infected adolescents) will be in the school system.

Developmental Consequences of AIDS

Pediatric AIDS is a severe medical condition as well as a potential neurological disability. In some cases, HIV systematically attacks the brain and nervous system. It is estimated that symptomatic pediatric HIV cases involve central nervous system (cns) damage in as many as 78 to 93 percent of cases (Diamond and Cohen, 1987). Some studies show that language deterioration often occurs and is frequently seen before other cognitive and cns abnormalities are detected (Roberts, 2000).

AIDS carries a heavy weight of social and ethical concerns. Public ignorance and fear is dissipating, but the issue of AIDS in school children still evokes passionately held opinions and deep fears. Schools have been among the key North American institutions in which the meaning of AIDS has been debated and deciphered, and schools are still facing problems in trying to accommodate children with AIDS and coming to grips with fears and misunderstandings. Scientists may have demonstrated that HIV is not transmitted by casual contact, but parents and teachers remain concerned about the devastating nature of AIDS.

For parents, AIDS balances their interest in protecting the health and safety of their children against the public's interest in providing non-discriminatory schooling for all children. At the same time, AIDS poses a number of special challenges to teachers who are being forced to confront the issues of risk, relationships, and education and to deal with personal uncertainties and fears. Having a child in the classroom who has AIDS means facing many unknowns. Teachers ask, "How will the other students react?" "What will parents say?" "Can I handle it?" "What type of support can I expect?" and "What should I be concerned about?"

First and foremost, anyone working with or planning for children with AIDS must understand the nature and course of HIV infection in children. They should realize that affected children show typical associated symptoms that include attention difficulties; cardiac disease; cognitive deficits; cold sores; coughing; diarrhea that can be acute and chronic; emotional problems; fine and gross motor difficulties; hearing problems; infections that include frequent bacterial and viral infections and middle ear, eye, and joint infections; seizures;

shortness of breath; speech and language delays; visual problems; weakness; and weight loss (Le Roy, Powell, and Kelber, 1994). There will be progressive neurological defects, including speech, motor, and cognitive regressions. Children may also have to cope with social isolation, long-term hospitalization, parental illness and death, family problems, and lack of understanding.

School transmission of HIV is unlikely. The major health risk is to the child who has the virus, because that child will be more susceptible to and seriously affected by common childhood illnesses or may develop life-threatening complications.

The second challenge for teachers is to be consistently sympathetic and compassionate toward students and colleagues who may be infected with HIV. Excluding a child with AIDS teaches all children the wrong lessons about tolerance and about community.

Third, teachers must help other class members to understand and tolerate the condition. Children need accurate information. For example, a study (Schvaneveldt, Lindauer, and Young, 1990) showed that some third graders believed that AIDS could be contracted from toilet seats or people's clothing, and many held that cigarettes caused the disease.

While children with pediatric AIDS are not necessarily special education candidates, many qualify because of limited strength and vitality and acute health problems. When provided with special education services, the most successful programs for them parallel those for other special learners. Instruction should be designed for success, based on concrete experiences, and broken down into small, manageable steps.

ASSESSMENT OF CHILDREN WHO HAVE NEUROLOGICAL DISABILITIES

Many of the conditions characterized as neurological disabilities require intensive medical diagnosis and management. Vision and hearing assessment are crucial; specific measures are discussed in Chapters 9, 10, and 14. Some children may meet a neuropsychologist—a specialist in understanding and treating the problems that occur following damage to the brain.

There is general agreement that psycho-educational assessment for many children who are neurologically impaired is beset with difficulties that relate to the depth of physical and mental disabilities. Educators also agree that the standard diagnostic and evaluation tools currently used with children who are mildly disabled will often be of little use to those involved with individuals with physical and neurological disabilities, but no consensus exists as to the types of alternate measures to use.

Ways must be found to circumvent the disabilities in order to provide accurate assessment results. The information gathered in the screening and diagnostic processes must allow the formulation of a hypothesis that will take into account all the relevant factors so that intelligent decisions can be made regarding placement and academic planning.

Diagnosticians usually incorporate a battery of measures that range from developmental scales through communication and language tools to tests of mental ability. They use different test procedures and incorporate various adaptations to tests and to responses.

The problems associated with the use of standardized tests with this population are well nigh insurmountable. For one thing, norm-referenced tests are largely standardized on the physically normal population; measures have generally not been specifically developed for those with physical and neurological disabilities. Just as importantly, using standardized tests as the sole measure with children with physical or neurological disabilities places serious limitations on the child and may result in depressed scores that simply confirm the impairment without providing any functional information regarding potential for achievement.

Testing should reflect a child's knowledge and skills, not disabilities, and problems with standardized measures most frequently occur when a child's performance on a particular item is inappropriately influenced by the disabling condition. If standardized tests are used at all, they must be used with a high degree of sophistication and form only one component of a test battery. Many of the tasks that are used in such tests must be eliminated because of motor difficulties, sensory impairments, and special problems.

It is appropriate for testers to modify administrative procedures. For example, eliminate verbal tests from a battery; adapt the way a test is presented, such as holding a picture closer to the child's eyes; or modify procedures, allowing more time for timed tasks. Or, testers can alter the test stimuli by providing larger pictures or speaking more slowly. As well, a physical or occupational therapist may be on hand to assist in handling and positioning techniques so as to maximize a child's performance.

When altering response requirements, there are three general techniques. First, a support adaptation is used when the child must be placed in a certain position or provided some general form of support before being able to pass an item. A prosthetic adaptation is provided for the child who needs a specific piece of equipment, such as braces or a hearing aid, to demonstrate a skill. A general adaptation is one that does not require support or a piece of equipment but still represents a change in the basic requirements of the task or that changes the utility of the skill. For example, a child who is hearing impaired may need to perform communication tasks with sign language. Or a child with a physical disability may be allowed to look toward the response rather than pointing manually.

For children with physical or neurological disabilities, data regarding communication skills (see Chapters 4 and 14), adaptive behaviour (see Chapter 6), and mobility are particularly important. Regular and periodic assessment of development in communication and motor movement provides data about how many skills a child has developed, what type of skills they are, and how they are used. To conduct motor assessments teachers should rely on the expertise of physical or occupational therapists who have in-depth knowledge of the neurobiological system and can recognize the impact of specific impairments on movement and stability. The therapist will conduct an assessment of the physical domains that considers physical status, mobility, and functional aspects (how the child uses motor skills).

INTERVENTION WITH STUDENTS WHO HAVE NEUROLOGICAL DISABILITIES

Physical and neurological disabilities are primarily medical and therapeutic conditions, and intervention stretches far beyond the academic and educational. No single professional can effectively fill the multiple needs of all these children; they receive help from educators, physicians and medical specialists, occupational and physical therapists, speech and language pathologists, counsellors, and others. It is the secondary difficulties in such areas as communication, mobility, and cognitive functioning that are of most concern to educators.

Medical Intervention

Medical interventions cover a broad spectrum of treatments. For example, the hip dislocations, contractures, spinal defects, fractures, and osteoporosis that are common among children with spina bifida require medical assistance.

Although cerebral palsy is neither progressive nor curable, various medical techniques improve functioning. Children with cerebral palsy (and spina bifida) often suffer from **contractures**—a permanent shortening of the muscles, tendons, and ligaments that results in postural distortion and decreased joint mobility. Surgery can ease contractures and correct dislocations, and may also involve repair of the joints to reduce the risk of arthritis (Batshaw and Perrett, 1986).

contractures

Another medical procedure—*selective position rhizotomy*—sees the surgeon cut selected nerve roots below the spinal cord that cause plasticity in the leg muscles (Hallahan and Kauffman, 1991). The treatment allows some spastic persons better control of certain muscles, lets some non-ambulatory children walk, and helps others to move more normally.

Medical treatment for epilepsy focuses primarily on seizure control. Anti-convulsants can control about 50 percent of grand mal, 40 percent of petit mal, and 35 percent of psychomotor seizures. Drugs can also reduce the frequency of grand mal and petit mal seizures in 35 percent of cases, and of psychomotor attacks in 50 percent of cases (Berkow, 1982). The choice of drugs is related to the type of seizure pattern and the presence of side effects from other drugs. The primary goal of anticonvulsant therapy is to achieve maximum control with the fewest possible drugs and side effects.

In the case of head trauma injuries (TBI), immediate medical attention may help to reduce the extent of damage. Trauma medicine has made a great deal of progress in recent years; new brain scan techniques can pinpoint sites of injury in the brain.

Therapy

Physical, occupational, and speech and language therapies are indicated for many children with neurological and orthopedic disabilities. Spina bifida children with myelomeningocele, for example, frequently have other orthopedic complications and problems requiring extensive physical and occupational therapies. In children with cerebral palsy, physical therapy can ease contractures.

For children with orthopedic and neurological impairments, therapies are most commonly associated with sensorimotor development, postural control, activities for daily living, and environmental adaptations. The need for occupational or physical therapy is determined by an absence of robust righting, protective extension, and equilibrium reactions; inefficient sitting and standing posture; limited ability to perform sensorimotor tasks; and inadequate physical fitness for daily living activities (Dunner, Connor-Kuntz, and Goodway, 1995).

Occupational therapists focus on motor development, attention to aspects of the sensory environment, and the achievement of functional daily tasks. They work to enhance a child's potential for learning and try to develop vestibular balance; tactile, kinesthetic, and perceptual motor coordination; and self-help skills.

Physical therapists work with children needing prosthetic management training, wheelchair mobility training, and gross-motor-skill exercises. Physical therapy is directed toward preventing disability; for example, developing, improving, or restoring more efficient muscular functioning and maintaining maximum motor functioning for each child. The physical therapist also provides teachers with information concerning positioning and handling of students and the use of adaptive equipment.

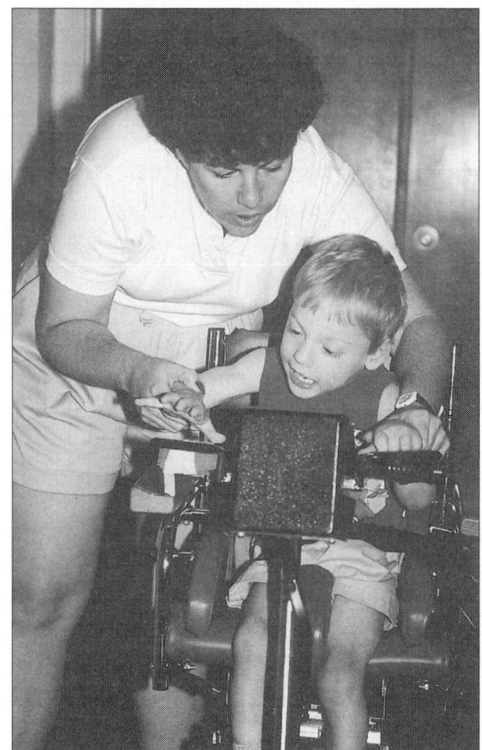

Teachers should know how to position children in wheelchairs.

Promoting optimal postures and movement patterns for functional activities is an important objective for children with physical and motor disabilities. Areas of special concern are positioning and carrying. **Carrying** refers to the way that a child with a physical or motor disability is moved; **positioning** refers to how the child is seated or otherwise positioned.

carrying

positioning

Children must be handled in ways that normalize muscle tone and prevent the development of secondary muscular and structural disorders. Proper positioning can facilitate normal muscle tone and symmetry, provide stable and aligned posture, inhibit primitive reflexes, facilitate normal movement patterns, stabilize head and trunk control, and compensate for the lack of sitting balance (Copeland and Kimmel, 1989). Individual positioning is prescribed for each child.

Technical Aids

The huge range of equipment now available for individuals with disabilities is making a significant difference in the quality of their lives by allowing them more control of events in their environment. Devices and equipment range from the very simple, such as adapted spoons and switch-adapted battery-operated toys, to the very complex, such as computerized environmental control systems.

adaptive (assistive) equipment

Adaptive (assistive) equipment is an umbrella term for these devices. The term refers to any device designed or modified to lead individuals with disabilities to independence. Within the broad category of adaptive equipment are prosthetic, orthotic, and adaptive devices, chiefly used to assist children with physical and motor disabilities and those with sensory impairments. There is quite a lot of overlap in these categories.

Much adaptive equipment is individualized for a child. When individually adapted equipment is used, children demonstrate improved motor, self-care, and social skills (see Dunn, 1989).

Prosthetic Devices

Prosthetic devices are used to replace lost functions and/or provide support. They duplicate normal body movements as nearly as possible while restraining normal functions as little as possible. For example, an artificial leg is a prosthesis for a child missing a leg.

prosthetic devices

Much special equipment is used for mobility and standing. Included are leg casts and braces, ankle–foot equipment, crutches, walkers, and wheelchairs. The most common mobility devices are braces, crutches, and wheelchairs.

Wheelchairs are designed for people who are unable to ambulate or whose ambulation is unsafe and unsteady, or for those for whom ambulation is too strenuous. Wheelchairs are almost as varied as the people who use them. A good wheelchair is tailored to the individual's needs. The main types are self-propelled wheelchairs, attendant-operated chairs, transit chairs, and electric or battery-powered chairs. An electronically controlled wheelchair can provide movement through voice activated commands for a person who is severely disabled; it is programmed to respond to the owner's voice and requires no muscle control.

Orthopedic braces are for the lower extremities. Braces do not prevent contractures or develop walking skills but serve to control and support. There are three main types—short leg braces, long leg braces, and hip braces. A short brace would be used on the ankle joint; a long leg brace from the knee to the ankle. For children with cerebral palsy, braces are used chiefly for control. They help in ambulation, control involuntary movements, and serve to prevent or correct deformities. In spina bifida and muscular dystrophy, the braces are used chiefly for support. Support braces weigh less than control braces.

Crutches are used during periods of temporary disability to help with balance and locomotion, and to reduce weight on the lower extremities. When the disability is of long duration or permanent, crutches have to be designed to reduce the weight the legs must bear and provide stability and support. The surface on which the crutch may operate is important. If it is slippery, rubber-tipped ends, spiked ends, or tripod legs should be provided.

Walkers are upright devices used to provide support and movement. There are various types of walkers that can be modified in various ways to assist the individual but all provide standing support with forward inclined standing. Supported standing forces weight-bearing that is necessary for the normal formation of the hip joints.

Prosthetic equipment may assist in the therapeutic techniques of positioning and carrying. Positioning equipment and strategies allow children with motor problems to achieve postures and movement that might otherwise be impossible or non-functional. Some children need support in a lying position and use adaptive boards, wedges, and bolsters. Positioning equipment is typically designed to place the child in one or more basic postures in as normal a body alignment as possible.

Sitting may be difficult for children with motor disorders. Because children spend a lot of time sitting, it is important that they sit in the most beneficial position. They need to find positions that allow the best hand use, that are easiest for eye–hand coordination, and that present the least difficulties for balance. Modified chairs are for children who have difficulty sitting well or those who have abnormal hip and leg patterns. A special chair aligns the body, limbs, and head; flexes the hips, knees, and ankles; and brings the head and shoulders slightly forward. Adapted chairs include corner chairs and bolster chairs. Both usually have removable trays.

Dangling feet are harmful to children with motor problems, so an abduction block—a chunk of something that the child's legs can straddle—is usually used to prevent the child from sliding to the floor, while a footstool ensures that the child's feet reach a flat solid surface. Straps and other props are sometimes used to improve posture.

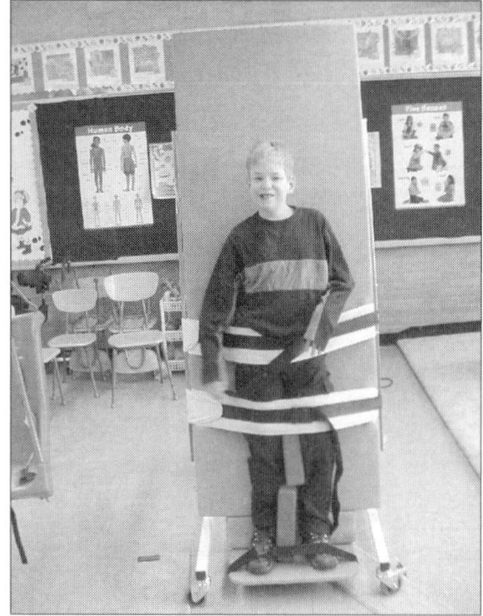

Standing frame.

Boston jackets, AFOs, and hand splints.

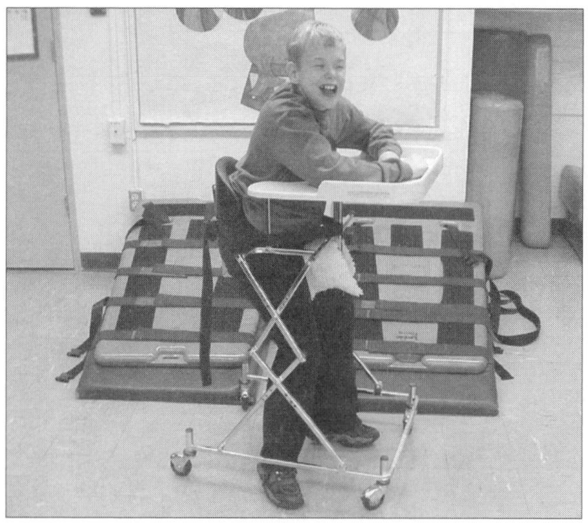

Pommel walker.

Tilt table.

Orthotic Devices

orthotic devices

Orthotic devices assist a limb's action. For example, special utensils (spoons, forks, and dishes) make eating and drinking easier for a child with a movement dysfunction. Some eating implements have Velcro straps to make them easier for the child to handle and control. Adapted spoons have a built-up handle or swivel so that gravity can right the spoon and prevent spillage. A hand splint to support wrist extension can also be used to allow greater finger movements for manipulative tasks.

In the classroom, children may require specialized equipment. Page turners and book stands assist in reading. Magnetized pencils and equipment are helpful for writing and drawing; there are specially adapted scissors for cutting.

Adaptive Devices

Much of the current technology requires pre-academic readiness skills, and most of today's technological devices operate through one dominant modality (for example, touch for keyboards, vision for monitors). However, devices are increasingly allowing for alternative modalities, such as voice-activated computers and television captioning.

The availability of instrumentation that permits persons with disabilities whose cognitive level is less than two years to control devices in their environment is also increasing. As well, many technologies are becoming more transparent (less noticeable and obtrusive) because of miniaturization, the use of lighter materials, and higher capacities for information processing.

Some children with physical disabilities have difficult or unintelligible speech. However, their receptive language is probably far ahead of their expressive language, and they may know and understand far more words than they can express. These students require augmentative communication devices that act as substitutes for speech (see Chapters 4 and 14).

Microswitches are adaptations of particular use to people with motor impairments. Switches—including push switches, pull switches, grasp switches, wobble switches (activated by bending in any direction), pneumatic switches (activated by puffing or sucking on a straw), and sensor switches (activated by very small movements) can be set to operate under the control of almost any muscle in the body. They can be set to operate lights, appliances, or a computer.

Educational Intervention

In the past, non-educational considerations would have taken priority when considering placements for students with physical and neurological disabilities, and many students would have been taught in separate classrooms or special schools. Progress in medical science, improved technology, and changing attitudes have dramatically altered service delivery for these students, and today most are placed in general classrooms.

Service Delivery Models

Inclusion in the general classroom is appropriate for almost the full range of students with neurological disabilities. Special class placement may still be provided for students who have additional severe problems with perception, cognition, or language. Children with recent TBI may require a more structured and quiet environment (Rempel, 1992).

Other children may miss numerous days in school for surgery, medical appointments, and therapy. If school-time lost is extensive, students may be provided hospital or home instruction.

Curriculum

In general, no special curriculum exists for students with physical and neurological disabilities. Many of the needed accommodations are environmental, such as space for a wheelchair or using adaptive equipment.

When a child has severe or multiple disabilities, he or she may require a modified program. With his cerebral palsy, hearing loss, and low intellectual ability, Kent, the child we met in the earlier case study, can be categorized as a child with multiple disabilities. The combination of disabilities makes Kent's condition unique and a challenge for educators. An excerpt from his IEP is provided in the Case Study feature.

For all children with cerebral palsy and other severe motor impairments, additions to the regular curriculum may be necessary to provide ambulation training and to teach certain self-help skills, leisure skills, prevocational skills, and articulation.

Conductive Education

One special curriculum worth mentioning is conductive education, a type of therapy that was developed in Hungary by Dr. Andras Peto in 1945 at the Peto Institute for Motor Disorder. The concept is *orthofunctional*—an individual is able to adapt and cope, to find a way around a problem (Coles and Zsargo, 1998).

The major aims of conductive education are to promote personal development and educational and social fulfillment for children with motor difficulties related to brain and spinal problems and to include children as early as possible in the mainstream.

Care and education of an individual child rests with one person who is with the child twenty-four hours a day. This person is the conductor, thus the name of the program. The conductor attempts to challenge the child. Mobility is stressed and challenges consistently heighten. Children learn through games and music, which strengthen limbs and posture. (For more on conductive education, see Beattie, 1993.)

Case Study

Kent (continued)

Kent's communication has improved; he waves to friends, smiles appropriately, and seems to enjoy stories, singing, and other oral activities in the classroom. But he still has minimal linguistic skills.

For Kent particularly, the individual program must include a potential mode of communication. The development of a system by which to communicate at some level with those in the environment is a first priority.

The language taught using the system and other related activities will build on what have been identified as Kent's interests. He is, for example, very interested in his classmates, so his language will stress names and simple actions such as "See Joe," or "Peter draws." Kent also enjoys books—both being read to and turning the pages himself—so much exposure to highly coloured print materials will be important. He also seems to enjoy music, so he will learn to listen to simple songs on a tape recorder that he will operate himself.

A language therapist works with Kent in a one-to-one situation. After consultation with the teacher and the parents, she decided to introduce Kent to a new language system.

In the past, both Blissymbolics and American Sign Language were tried, but these seemed to be too conceptually difficult for Kent. Because Kent's hand use is quite good, the therapist suggested that the teacher introduce some basic signs from the Amerind system and also teach these to the children in the class. Once Kent learns some simple signs and combinations, he may advance to American Sign Language.

EXTRACT FROM KENT'S IEP

Name Kent
Age 8

Present Levels of Functioning

Kent has cerebral palsy. There may be some language, but so far there is no speech development.

Placement

Kent is in a regular setting. The object is to expose him to language and social models.

Adaptive Equipment

Wheelchair; behind-the-ear aids in both ears; magnetized equipment for writing; large implements.

Additional Assistance

Physical therapy, speech therapy, individual aide in regular classroom.

Long-Range Goals

- During therapy, Kent will learn a simple manual communication system, Amerind. Signs will be used in the regular classroom by the aide.
- Kent will be provided many opportunities to read books either alone or with a peer.
- Kent will operate a tape recorder to listen to simple songs.

Short-Term Objectives

- Within classroom activities, the aide will sign to Kent and prompt him to use known signs.
- Kent will join in small groups with assigned tasks to improve language and social skills.
- Kent will use greeting behaviour—waving—when requested.
- Kent will maintain a supported sitting position in the carpeted reading area.
- Kent will use page turners, with support.
- Kent will look at the book as a peer reads a story.
- When given a tape recorder, Kent will depress the special switch to turn the recorder on and off.

Historical Notes

When institutional settings for students with special needs were first established in the 19th century, they served discrete categories of students, specifically those who were deaf, blind, and mentally retarded. Significant disabilities were seen as potential hindrances to programs because of the individual care they needed, so children who were seriously crippled, not toilet-trained, or considered to be uneducable were not provided with schooling in the institutions or in the public system.

The one major exception was epilepsy. Probably no other 19th-century exceptional group was as misunderstood and inappropriately handled. In that period, no drugs to control the condition or technical devices to assess its etiology existed, and seizures engendered such fear in beholders that they held that epilepsy and insanity were inextricably joined. Institutionalization was imperative, either with those mentally retarded or with those mentally ill.

There are reports of a class in Boston in 1866 for crippled children. But compared to schooling for deaf or blind children, intervention for children described as crippled was a very late development. In Montreal, the world's first organized movement on behalf of crippled children was started in 1906 by a group of educators at the Children's Memorial Hospital.

From the outset, facilities for these youngsters were generally not within the purview of the school system. When they eventually were, segregation was the mode. Despite the fact that these students presented a wide range of abilities, potential, and educational need, and that there was little or no difference between their classroom performance and that of non-disabled students, the majority of pupils who were physically disabled were restricted to special schools or special classes.

Among other reasons, teachers felt that youngsters with physical disabilities would be too difficult to handle and would take a disproportionate amount of time. There was also the traditional predisposition that stereotyped these children and focused on their disabilities while ignoring their strengths. Too, many school plants were not equipped with the physical structures, the modifications, the technical equipment, and the support personnel to handle and teach such students. It was seen as more economical to construct one barrier-free building than to alter all the plants in a school district and to transport children to one central location and then bring the therapists, the teachers, and the other intervenors to the students.

The history of another entire field feeds into the development of education for students with physical disabilities. *Prosthetics* is the field of science concerned with the artificial replacement of body parts, and includes designing, manufacturing, and fitting artificial limbs (Tiessen, 1996).

Prostheses have been used probably since the beginning of humankind. Artificial limbs and braces appear in ancient frescoes, mosaics, and pottery. The first written account is 2200 years old and concerns one Marcus Sergius, a Roman general who lost his right hand in battle and had it replaced with a metal one. Ambroise Paré, the surgeon general from the French army in the 16th century, is considered to be the modern father of prosthetics and orthotics. He made advances in surgical techniques and had many devices made for wounded soldiers. Many other people, from pirates to panhandlers, were leg amputees who used crude peg legs to replace a limb severed by sword or saw. These were fashioned out of forked sticks or tree branches, and fit was forsaken for function (Tiessen, 1996).

Artificial limbs have come a long way. With miniaturized power sources such as motors with sophisticated sensory control and hydraulic and pneumatic components, artificial limbs and braces are extremely functional today. Child amputees, whose residual limbs continue to grow, are the most susceptible to poor fit (Lowey, 1993).

SUMMARY

1. Of the many physical disabilities, the conditions described in this chapter all stem from some form of neurological damage. In this sense, the conditions are not curable, although they can be ameliorated by medical intervention, therapy, drugs, and education.
2. In one sense, the nervous system is complete at birth. The central nervous system of newborn children contains the full complement of neurons, but comparatively few of the axons are covered with myelin. Hence, all the structures are present and the number of nerve cells does not increase, but the size of these cells does.
3. *Physical and neurological disabilities* include a huge range of conditions. Because of the

diverse nature of physical and neurological disabilities, their varied severity, and co-occurring conditions, it is impossible to draw a profile of a typical affected child. In general, physical problems may limit mobility, socialization, independence, learning, and educational opportunities. Children may be further handicapped by their lack of ability to explore the environment adequately.

4. *Cerebral palsy* is the most common neurological difficulty seen in children. Over half the children with cerebral palsy have spasticity in which the muscles don't work in harmony—some muscles are too tight, some too loose. Children with athetosis show jerky, uncontrolled, and writhing movements; those with ataxia show uncoordinated movement and difficulties with positions in space. Together with motor problems, cerebral palsy can include any number of intellectual, sensory, and behavioural disorders.
5. *Spina bifida* comes in a number of forms and may be the precursor of multiple disabilities. Damage to the developing nervous system will leave varying degrees of paralysis, sensory loss, bowel and bladder incontinence, and hydrocephalus.
6. *Epilepsy* is a condition in which the smooth functioning of the brain's electrical system is briefly disturbed, causing a seizure, an electrical storm in the brain. Manifestations depend upon the location, severity, and type of short circuit coming from the brain. The most frightening for the observer is the grand mal seizure, in which a child loses consciousness. Children may also suffer from petit mal seizures—an extremely brief loss of consciousness. Other seizure types include Jacksonian and psychomotor. The developmental consequences of epilepsy are extremely varied; children have more learning and behavioural problems than their peers, and have higher rates of psychiatric disorders.
7. *Traumatic Brain Injury* (TBI) is an insult to the brain caused by an external physical force. Associated problems include cognitive, behavioural/psychological, sensory/motor, and language disorders. Students may experience problems with physical, cognitive, or psychosocial functioning well past their initial physical recovery and rehabilitation.
8. *AIDS* is a complex bio-ecological problem. The disease decimates both the immune system and the nervous system. As increasing numbers of children are being infected with pediatric AIDS, schools must accommodate their special health and learning problems. Children with AIDS have periods of weakness and intermittent bouts of illness. They suffer chronic and frequent illnesses, failure to thrive, and a range of neurological and developmental problems.
9. Accommodations for assessing students with neurological and physical disabilities tend to cluster into four categories—*presentation, response, setting,* and *timing.*
10. Depending on the extent and nature of a condition, a child may require the services of many disciplines, including psychology, physiotherapy, occupational therapy, speech pathology, audiology, and medicine. Occupational and physical therapists work in close collaboration with teachers and parents to assist the child in different functions.
11. *Adaptive (assistive) technical devices* are pieces of equipment used to increase, maintain, or improve the fundamental capabilities of students with disabilities. Adaptive devices serve to make living easier, aiding mobility and ambulation, seating, classroom interaction, and daily living.
12. A physical or neurological disability, by itself, is not a reason for special education services. Students benefit from the same instructional practices and curriculum as others.

WEBLINKS

The Arc's Fetal Alcohol Syndrome Resource and Materials Guide **http://thearc.org/misc/faslist.html**

The Association for the Neurologically Disabled of Canada **www.and.ca**

Cerebral Palsy Canada **www.cerebralpalsycanada.com**

Multiple Sclerosis Society of Canada **www.mssociety.ca**

An Encounter with Tourette Syndrome **http://cec.wustl.edu/~jpk1/tourettes.html**

Epilepsy Canada **www.epilepsy.ca**

FAE Information Service **www.ccsa.ca/fasgen.htm**

Spina Bifida and Hydrocephalus Association of Nova Scotia **www.chebucto.ns.ca/Health/SBANS/**

Chapter 13

Children with Pervasive Developmental Disorders

Learning Outcomes

After reading this chapter, you should be able to:

Differentiate between infantile autism and childhood schizophrenia;

Understand the array of etiologies proposed to account for these conditions;

Appreciate the developmental consequences of psychosis and infantile autism;

Identify the range of service delivery models that are available;

Identify tactics that will support these children in inclusive classrooms.

Introduction

Different types of conditions, including childhood psychoses, childhood schizophrenia, infantile autism, and severe and profound mental retardation, are found under the *developmental disorder* umbrella. As children with pervasive developmental disorders very often exhibit co-occurring disabilities such as epilepsy, perceptual motor dysfunctions, and communication disorders, these conditions can also often be viewed as *multiple disabilities.*

Childhood psychoses and infantile autism represent the most extreme forms of emotional and behavioural disorders. Probably no other conditions are so hard to understand and so far removed from the range of normal experience. They strike at the very essence of human relatedness and human communication, and must therefore be considered the most devastating disorders that affect a child's learning and behaviour. Every aspect of functioning is affected.

Children who are psychotic and autistic frequently exhibit strange and inappropriate behaviour. They may display bizarre body movements and sometimes suffer inordinate fears. Or they may indulge in repetitive motor activity, self-stimulation, and self-mutilation. Many children are completely withdrawn; they never speak at all but pirouette in a silent internal dance, impervious to all around them. Their world may consist of touch sensations, of familiar routines, and rigidly obsessive behaviour. Still, such children may fly into tantrums at the smallest change in their surroundings, from a parent's new hairstyle to a door left slightly ajar.

Because childhood psychoses and infantile autism are so spectacular and bizarre, they have elicited an enormous amount of interest, concern, and research. The importance of the study of pervasive developmental disorders is not related to the incidence and prevalence of the conditions; childhood schizophrenia and autism are rare. However, researchers believe that if they can develop an understanding of psychoses and autism, they will have made a giant step in the direction of unravelling the triple helix of brain, behaviour, and environment.

A number of forms of psychoses, due to multiple etiologies, affect children. Heller's disease, for example, is due to disintegrative brain disease. Asperger's syndrome is rare and the symptoms overlap with autism although there is relatively normal development in cognition and language. In Rhett's syndrome, there is normal development in infancy and early childhood, followed by regression and mental retardation and childhood disintegrative disorder. As well, psychiatric disorders subsequent to brain injuries in older children have also been reported (see Chapter 12).

In this chapter we restrict our discussion of childhood psychoses to schizophrenia. We also delve into the complexities of infantile autism. The manifestations of autism are similar enough to those of childhood psychoses to discuss them together. Children who are psychotic or autistic show a pattern of behaviour characterized by a failure to recognize, understand, or respond appropriately to people in their environment. They demonstrate withdrawal and a high frequency of problematic and bizarre behaviour. Keep in mind, though, that etiology, treatment, and prognosis for autism and for schizophrenia differ quite radically. We also look briefly at Asperger's syndrome.

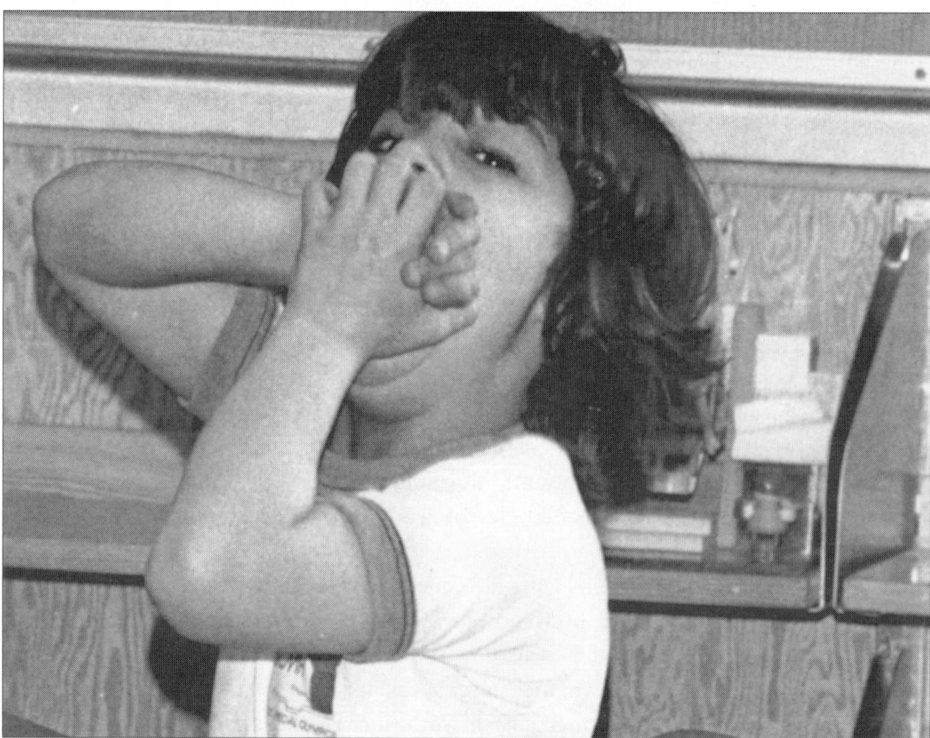

Bizarre behaviour is characteristic of children with childhood psychoses and infantile autism.

Case Study

David

David is our third child. Although the pregnancy was uneventful, he was born nearly a month early after a prolonged and arduous labour. When we brought David home he was fussy and distractible, and he cried almost constantly. He had feeding problems with breast and bottle, and he could not be comforted by holding or rocking.

Even with his feeding problems, David gained weight and developed into a beautiful child. However, his crying continued and worried the entire family. By the time David was a year old, we were sure he had some problem or disorder. Most of the time, David lay in his crib. He never seemed to notice when anyone walked into the room. He never smiled and never liked to be picked up and held. Except for crying, he made almost no sounds, especially not the babbling sounds his two older sisters had made.

At first, we suspected David was deaf. For nearly a year, we went from doctor to doctor seeking help. One doctor said David might be hearing impaired, and told us to come back in six months. Another suggested he was severely mentally retarded, and another said he was simply slow in developing.

One evening, a friend who taught special children was visiting the house. He tried to play with David, but could garner no responses. We discussed our frustration and growing sense of hopelessness. The teacher suggested we get in touch with a local society that helped the parents of troubled children. At this time, the word *autism* had still never been mentioned.

Within a month of being directed to the right facilities, David was diagnosed as autistic. In a way, the diagnosis was a relief. Although we had hoped that David was only slow to mature, we knew in our hearts that something was truly amiss. Professionals may rail against labels, but we badly needed a starting point, a direction in which to find help.

As a family, we now understand David's problems, although we sometimes find it very difficult to cope with them. He has developed only a few words of speech. His baby crying has given way to a high-pitched whine that goes on and on. David is extremely rigid in his attitudes. He has massive temper tantrums that frighten his sisters at home and embarrass us all in public. He is just beginning to be toilet-trained, and still has eating problems. He has great difficulty dressing himself, although he is better at taking his clothes off. Another worry is the continuing effect of David's behaviour on his older sisters. Teenagers have their own wants and needs. We cannot let David disrupt their lives too seriously. Nor can we impose too heavily on them for babysitting.

DEFINITIONS OF PERVASIVE DEVELOPMENTAL DISORDERS

Children with *pervasive developmental disorders* suffer from conditions that affect every aspect of their present and probably future functioning. The adjective *pervasive* means that the conditions affect all developmental domains and will probably be extremely long-lasting, if not lifelong.

To reiterate the definitions given in Chapter 1, a *developmental delay* (pervasive developmental disorder)

> is a condition that represents a significant delay in the process of development. As the process of development is significantly affected, the term does not refer to a maturational lag or an at-risk child. Individuals who are developmentally disabled are those who suffer from chronic disabilities, attributable to mental or physical impairments, or a combination of these, that are manifested before age twenty-two and that result in functional limitations in major life activities requiring special services and treatment that are of extended duration or lifelong.

Childhood psychoses and infantile autism fit under the broad category of pervasive developmental disorders.

Childhood Schizophrenia

childhood psychoses

In general terms, *psychoses* are serious mental disorders in which the behavioural and thought processes of an individual become so disturbed that the person is out of touch with reality. The more specific term, **childhood psychoses**, refers to a heterogeneous group of clinical syndromes characterized by any number of maladaptive behaviours or clusters of behaviours including severe disturbances in ego functioning. Such disturbances affect various aspects of adaptive behaviour, including the perception and ordering of experience, the assessment of reality, the control and channelling of impulses, and the success of interpersonal relations (Cummings and Finger, 1980).

childhood schizophrenia

Childhood schizophrenia is one of the childhood psychoses. To many people, schizophrenia brings to mind the condition of split personalities depicted in movies such as *The Three Faces of Eve.* In reality, adult schizophrenia is not commensurate with split personality. Nor are adult schizophrenia and childhood schizophrenia parallel conditions with only developmentally determined variations in symptomology. Early findings that presumed the childhood condition and the adult disorder to be the same have been replaced by research that sees childhood schizophrenia as a separate and identifiable condition. Today, **childhood schizophrenia** is defined as

> a pervasive psychotic disorder involving a decline or arrest of ego development following a period of relatively normal development, occurring in children who demonstrate some degree of useful language and relatedness to others. Among children characterized as schizophrenic, there are wide variations in personality organization, clinical course, intellectual functioning, and identifiable etiological conditions. (Cummings and Finger, 1980, p. 510)

This definition points out that childhood schizophrenia occurs late in childhood, often around the beginning of puberty. Before its onset, the child has usually developed according to normal patterns. It stresses the wide range of behaviours seen in children characterized as schizophrenic and focuses on particular domains of deviation.

Infantile Autism

The word *autism* comes from the Greek *autos*, meaning “self.” It is fitting, because the most prominent feature of children with infantile autism is their apparent self-absorption and socially withdrawn behaviour. But despite being the subject of more research than any other child psychiatric disorder, autism remains difficult to understand. A precise definition does not exist, the boundaries of autism remain vague and undifferentiated, and so much remains unknown about the condition that it has been described as “the quintessential disability enigma” (Simpson and Myles, 1995, p. 7).

According to recent American legislation (IDEA, 1990)

> Autism means a developmental disability significantly affecting verbal and non-verbal communication and social interaction, generally evident before age three, that adversely affects educational performance. Characteristics of autism include irregularities and impairments in communication, engagement in repetitive activities and stereotyped movements, resistance to environmental change or change in daily routines, and unusual responses to sensory experiences. The term does not include children with characteristics of the disability serious emotional disturbance. (National Association, 1991, p. 2)

This definition is both inclusive and specific. It stresses the age of onset (manifestation is before age three, hence the common adjective *infantile*). It also focuses on the characteristics, behaviours that affect educational performance, the groups excluded, and implies that autism should be viewed as a spectrum disorder; that is, it ranges from mild to severe.

The IDEA definition stresses that infantile autism is a developmental disability, not an emotional disturbance. This is a recent classification. The first changes in classification came when autism was removed from the area of severe emotional disturbance to the area of "other health impaired." With IDEA (1990) it again moved to become a separate category.

PREVALENCE OF PERVASIVE DEVELOPMENTAL DISORDERS

Although pervasive developmental disorders are extremely low-incidence conditions, the changing terminology and classification make prevalence figures precarious. Most estimates allow 5 cases of pervasive developmental disorders per 10 000 children (Treffert, 1970). Infantile autism occurs less frequently than childhood schizophrenia, but prevalence figures for autism tend to vary more widely.

Schizophrenia affects about one in every 100 adults, but is rare in children under the age of eighteen. In most cases, the first symptoms are observed in people ranging from fifteen to forty-five years of age (Kauffman, 1997b). When it does occur in childhood, there are an estimated 3.1 cases per 10 000 children (Treffert, 1970). Among children, twice as many boys as girls are schizophrenic. By adolescence, the ratio is equal between boys and girls (Wicks-Nelson and Israel, 1991).

Prevalence estimates for autism range from 0.4 to 0.5 of the school-aged children population (Kauffman, 2001). The condition is three to four times more common in males (Bryson, 1996).

CLASSIFICATION OF PERVASIVE DEVELOPMENTAL DISORDERS

Dissension and controversy surround the classification of pervasive developmental disorders and the subcategories of psychoses and infantile autism. Many of these problems stem from the historical antecedents of the field (see the Historical Notes at the end of this chapter) as well as the rapid alterations brought to the field by new genetic, psychological, and educational research.

Currently, the most commonly cited classification system is that appearing in the *Diagnostic and Statistical Manual of Mental Disorders* (DSM IV) (American Psychiatric Association, 1994), which identifies several categories of adult, adolescent, and childhood severe and profound disorders. In DSM, the category of *pervasive developmental disorders* refers directly to childhood conditions and includes four subcategories: infantile autism; disintegrative psychoses; other specific early childhood psychoses, including childhood schizophrenia; and unspecified psychoses.

Of these four groupings, we will discuss only infantile autism and childhood schizophrenia. When these two conditions are compared, infantile autism is clearly distinguishable from childhood schizophrenia on a number of variables. These include

- Etiology, which we discuss later in this chapter.
- Age of onset. This is one of the primary characteristics that distinguish autism from psychoses. Infantile autism occurs before thirty months of age and is usually preceded by markedly abnormal behaviour patterns. Childhood schizophrenia is of later onset; children show a normal early pattern of development, followed by severe regression as the condition takes hold.
- Behavioural manifestations. Behavioural patterns in autism are pervasive; those in schizophrenia may be episodic. Children with schizophrenia exhibit a wide variety of symptoms and send very mixed messages to the outside world: their extremes of activity, sudden mood changes, and verbal disturbances bewilder observers. In this way, schizophrenic children are unlike those affected by infantile autism, who tend to exhibit repetitive behaviour. As well, children with schizophrenia may develop delusions and experience hallucinations, whereas those with autism do not. One child with schizophrenia, for example, reported that a kitchen light said to do things and said to "Shut up" (Russell, Bott, and Sammons, 1989).
- Prognosis. Researchers in the area of childhood pervasive developmental disorders agree on only one thing: the dismal prognosis. In terms of future functioning, children who are autistic differ markedly from those whose difficulties begin later. Depending on the age of onset, the course of the condition, and the intensity of intervention, children who are schizophrenic may be returned to somewhat normal functioning; many children never lose the symptoms completely, although some do (Kauffman, 1997b). Encouraging results are certainly emerging in the area of autism, but the prognosis for the whole population remains relatively poor. Table 13-1 shows the major behavioural symptoms of infantile autism and childhood schizophrenia.

Asperger's Syndrome

We need to mention Asperger's syndrome, a subcategory of pervasive developmental disorders. The disorder was first discussed by a Viennese psychiatrist, Hans Asperger, in 1944, although the condition has been recognized in the United States only since 1994.

The profiles of individuals with Asperger's syndrome differ from classic autism although the same domains of communication, socialization, behaviour, and activities are affected. Individuals are often quite verbal, but still struggle with pragmatic language in everyday environments and are confused about the appropriateness of conversational topics. Voices are often monotone, and different from normal in rhythm, rate, and inflection. People with Asperger's often display hypersensitivity to noises and sometimes smells, which may impair social functioning.

Cognitive abilities are broad but fall into the average range. Students often meet difficulties with inferential reasoning, abstract concepts, problem solving, and social judgment. There may be fine motor problems and gross motor clumsiness (Simpson and Myles, 1998; Wagner, 1999).

Table 13-1 Behavioural characteristics of psychotic and autistic children

Behavioural symptoms	Infantile autism	Childhood schizophrenia
Social development		
Emotional responsiveness	–	x
Lack of anticipatory response	+	–
Social imitation	–	+
Looks and walks "through" people	+	–
Extreme aloneness	+	–
Talks to, not with	+	–
Strong attachment to inanimate objects	+	–
Insistence on sameness	+	–
Delusions and hallucinations	–	+
Motor and sensory functions		
Not physically pliable	+	–
Overly sensitive to stimuli	+	–
Often graceful motor performance	+	x
Unusual motor behaviours, such as repetitive movements	+	+
Self-stimulation	+	+
Self-mutilation	+	x
Odd movements and grimaces	+	+
Language and communication		
Delayed acquisition	+	–
Deficient, deviant babble	+	–
Sometimes thought to be deaf	+	–
Overly sensitive to sound	+	–
Non-verbal communication	–	+
Echolalia	+	–
Pronominal reversal	+	–
Spontaneous speech	–	+
Expressive-intonational features	–	+

– seldom occurs x may occur + commonly occurs

ETIOLOGY OF PERVASIVE DEVELOPMENTAL DISORDERS

The etiology of pervasive developmental disorders is a broadly researched area. It is also widely disputed, and etiological data are best described as inconclusive.

Many of the theories concerning the causes of developmental disorders can be categorized as either nature or nurture. Nature theories stress biological dysfunction; in contrast, the nurture approach views the environment as the vital developmental factor. Until the late 1960s, theoretical constructs of childhood psychoses and autism focused on psychosocial (nurture) origins. Compelling recent research increasingly leans toward biological interpretations.

The best approach may be multifactorial, viewing these disorders not as a single entity but rather as the final common pathway of multiple etiologies: that is, attributing developmental disorders to a combination of biological and environmental factors. Infantile autism, for example, is probably a final expression of multiple determinants and may be the result of metabolic, infectious, developmental, environmental, and genetic insults.

Childhood Schizophrenia

If a multifactorial etiology is indeed the best approach to causation in childhood schizophrenia, then it is hardly surprising that the contributing factors are the subject of considerable debate. Children who are schizophrenic display such a wide variety of symptom patterns and respond to so many different treatment modes that no one etiology seems sufficient to account for the disorder.

Early investigations pinpointed environmental factors: maternal overprotection, maternal rejection, stimulus deprivation during infancy, inconsistent parenting, and severe and repeated emotional trauma. However, many children exposed to these factors do not develop schizophrenia, and it is moot whether family forces alone are enough to produce such a devastating condition.

While the significance of environmental factors has not been completely discounted, the weight of accumulating evidence points toward biology as the primary factor in childhood schizophrenia. One consistent finding in support of biological factors is the high frequency of prenatal and perinatal complications among infants later diagnosed as schizophrenic. Pregnancy and birth complications include toxemias, vaginal bleeding, and maternal illness during pregnancy.

Investigators have also found a higher incidence of neurological symptoms in children who are schizophrenic, which leads to the suspicion that the condition may be a manifestation of subtle neurological damage, similar in origin to such disorders as minimal brain dysfunction. Moreover, neurological dysfunction is highly correlated with birth and pregnancy complications, further evidence that biological factors are responsible, at least to some degree, for childhood schizophrenia.

There is also convincing evidence for a hereditary predisposition (Plomin, 1989). Studies of monozygotic twins (e.g., Gottesman and Shields, 1976) have found that if one twin is affected, the other, regardless of environmental variables, is more prone to the condition. Because fraternal twins do not correlate nearly as highly, a genetic determinant is indicated. But along with a genetic component in schizophrenia, the evidence also indicates a strong environmental effect. What appears to be transmitted is not the disorder itself but a predisposition to acquire the disorder.

Infantile Autism

In 1906, Eugen Blueler, a Swiss psychiatrist, used the term *autistic* to describe the withdrawn behaviours he observed among adult schizophrenics. As a discrete syndrome, autism was first identified by Leo Kanner in 1943. Kanner described a number of symptoms that he found among a group of eleven children. In particular, he stressed the subjects' profound withdrawal from human contact and their obsessive desire for sameness in their environment. Kanner also identified similarities in the families of the eleven children. He found the parents to be highly intelligent and unusually high achievers, but also emotionally cold, aloof, and reserved in their interaction with their children.

Kanner himself did not reject biological factors as contributive causes of infantile autism. However, the researchers who followed him chose to focus almost exclusively on psychogenic properties. They speculated that lack of adequate parenting was the primary factor in the onset of autism. Infants with autism were seen as withdrawing into isolation to escape a hostile world, deeply lacking in warmth, love, and nurturance. Bruno Bettelheim, who established the Sonja Shankman Orthogenic School for severely emotionally disturbed children in 1944, adopted this line of thought. He interpreted autistic behaviour as a defence against a world perceived as hostile and rejecting. Bettelheim argued that children become autistic when their parents reject them or fail to respond to their attempts to influence their environment. Because children feel unable to exert any control over the external world, they withdraw into a private fantasy world and try to impose some order and consistency through an obsessive insistence on sameness.

Children who are autistic demonstrate severe self-isolation.

Bettelheim used the term "refrigerator mother" to characterize the mothers of autistic children (Csapo, 1981b). An even more devastating term, "the schizophregenic mother" laid direct responsibility for the child's condition on the mother's failure to provide love and nurturance. All the same, Bettelheim did not deny the possibility that genetic or organic causes might also contribute to infantile autism. In fact, although researchers tended to agree that parents created a climate that encouraged autism, few attributed the condition exclusively to parental behaviour.

During the 1970s, environmental theories were largely abandoned as emerging evidence indicated that children from emotionally deprived settings were not at higher risk for autism and that mothers of children with autism also had non-disabled offspring. With little to support environmental theories, autism emerged as an ideal candidate for biological study. Researchers turned their attention to investigating a range of biochemical, sensorimotor, neurological, and cognitive defects.

Today the evidence for biological causes is accumulating. Advances in neurobiology, brain imaging, and neuropsychology are allowing new insights into the possible brain basis of autism. A multifactorial neurobiological etiology is posited, yet it may be that such etiological diversity tends to cloud the issue simply because so many causes have been suggested.

Neurobiological investigations indicate that factors critical to the normal development of the central nervous system seem to have gone awry in autism. The condition almost certainly involves dysfunction of brain circuits that support the functioning of a variety of brain regions. Investigations have looked at brain lesions or pathological enlargement of the left temporal horn; have attempted to account for autism on the basis of dysfunction in the vestibular area of the brain, the area thought to modulate the interaction of sensory and motor functions; and have strongly implicated the medial temporal lobe. (See Dawson, Metzoff, Osterling, and Rinaldi, 1998, for a full discussion.)

As in the case of childhood schizophrenia, there is solid evidence to connect obstetrical problems and subsequent autism in children. On average, children with autism experience more pre- and perinatal complications than their siblings. In one early study (Kolvin, Ounsted, and Roth, 1971), 54 percent of children with infantile autism had demonstrable neonatal and perinatal abnormalities when given neurological examinations.

Maternal age may be a factor. In a small-sample study, Gillberg (1980) found the risk of having a child with autism to be nine times greater for mothers thirty-five or older than for mothers under thirty. Although Gillberg stresses that his small sample size makes generalizations difficult, the findings bolster earlier research on maternal age in the United States (Treffert, 1970), in Finland (Allanan, Arajar, and Vitamaki, 1964), and in Canada (Finnegan and Quarrington, 1979).

The importance of hereditary factors in the etiology of autism is well established. A number of researchers (e.g., Links, Stockwell, Abichandani, and Simeon, 1980) suggest a genetic factor; others point to the possibility of a genetic predisposition (see Gerdtz and Bergman, 1990). Some support is lent to genetic factors because autism is often accompanied by minor physical anomalies, such as fine hair, large head circumference, and malformed ears (Links et al., 1980).

Twin studies and the increasing number of reports on multiple incidence in siblings and second-degree relatives give further credence to the genetic hypothesis. The prevalence of infantile autism is far higher in siblings and second-degree relatives of children with the disorder than in the general population.

In family studies (e.g., Folstein and Rutter, 1988), only about 2 percent of the siblings of children who are autistic display the condition, but this is fifty times greater than the expectation for the general population. The incidence of autism in the identical twin of a child who is autistic is high. In one study (Steffenburg, Gillberg, Hellgren, Andersson, Gillberg, Jakonsson, and Bohman, 1989), nine of ten identical twin pairs were autistic, as were all three children in a set of identical triplets.

Infantile autism has also been associated with various X-linked chromosomal abnormalities, and in particular with the genetic subtype fragile X, which has the highest incidence of autism of any documented syndrome or chromosomal abnormality. Of the entire population diagnosed with infantile autism, it is estimated that 10 to 14 percent have fragile X syndrome. This makes fragile X syndrome the most commonly known organic cause of autism (Hagerman, 1988).

Other investigators are attempting to correlate the autistic syndrome with neurochemical measures. Measurement of blood serotonin levels has been a source of both optimism and frustration. Elevated platelet serotonin is the most consistently replicated biological abnormality found in subjects, occurring in roughly 30 percent of all cases (Piven, Tsai, Nehme, Coyle, Chase, and Folstein, 1991), but its origin and significance are unclear. In addition, autism is associated with PKU, an example of aberrant biochemistry (see Chapter 3 for more on PKU).

DEVELOPMENTAL CONSEQUENCES OF PERVASIVE DEVELOPMENTAL DISORDERS

Pervasive developmental disorders affect almost every domain of a child's development and seriously hinder all aspects of progress. Affected individuals exhibit a range of disordered behaviour and may appear to be severely retarded.

Much research has been directed toward autism; there is far less on childhood schizophrenia. However, many behaviours and developmental consequences are similar in the two conditions. This is especially true in behavioural manifestations. For example,

- *Social isolation.* Typically, these children live in their own isolated worlds, barely relating to others in the environment. Social development is minimal; even at their most developed, social interactions are limited in their quality and scope. Children with autism respond to other humans with aloofness and indifference, often becoming upset when interaction is demanded. Those with schizophrenia show a blunting of emotional responsiveness so that social relationships are invariably disturbed.
- *Maladaptive behaviour.* Children with autism or schizophrenia demonstrate maladaptive behaviours, which fall largely within two classes. The first is aggressive behaviour, either self-directed (self-injurious behaviour) or directed toward others. Some children who are severely disabled throw massive temper tantrums, during which they bite, kick, scratch, and strike out at others. Such aggressive behaviour can also sometimes cause serious physical harm to peers, parents, and teachers. It may result in a child being medicated and/or moved to a more restrictive environment (Lovaas and Favell, 1987). Many children inflict serious injury upon themselves: they bang their heads against sharp corners, bite themselves, and gouge their own eyes. Some children hurt themselves so often they must be kept in restraints for their own safety.

self-stimulation

The second class of maladaptive behaviour is **self-stimulation**, a persistent, stereotypic, repetitive mannerism. One of the defining characteristics of autism, it involves activities such as prolonged and repetitive body rocking, spinning, jumping, pacing, gazing at lights, twirling objects, excessive and repetitive vocalization, finger playing, flapping the hands, swishing saliva, patting the cheeks, and humming for hours on end. These behaviours do not possess the physical risks associated with aggressive behaviour, but they are socially stigmatizing and decrease a child's responsiveness to educational instruction.

Childhood Schizophrenia

Schizophrenia is a psychiatric illness characterized by serious loss of contact with reality and a marked deterioration in the ability to function. Children show delusions and hallucinations, emotional disturbance, apathy, and withdrawal.

Schizophrenia is extremely rare before the age of six, becomes a little more common in middle childhood, and is even more prevalent during adolescence. Because childhood schizophrenia typically does not take hold until early puberty, those affected escape early impairments of development in the realms of cognition, perception, and sensation. When the condition does take hold, however, affected children regress dramatically in their behaviour and demonstrate extreme withdrawal from the real world. Their close relationships are severely disrupted and they experience an overall deterioration in work, social relations, and self-care. They often lack or lose daily living skills, including such basic self-care as grooming, dressing, using the toilet, and feeding.

The behaviour of children with schizophrenia is extremely variable. According to Cantor (1989), the four characteristics most often found are:

- Sleep disturbance: a common symptom by the third year of life.
- Variable rather than short attention span. A child who is schizophrenic may attend for long periods of time to activities that are repetitive or perseverative.
- Variable behaviour: can vary from hyperactive to lethargic.
- Disturbances in thought processes.

Physical and Motor Development

Children who are schizophrenic tend to lag in physical and motor development. Individuals show serious deficits in gross motor areas but milder problems in the fine motor areas. As children with schizophrenia regress, acquired toilet and grooming skills may disappear.

Cognitive Development

This population of children shows great variability in cognitive functioning. On the Weschler scales, most youngsters who are schizophrenic achieve higher scores on the Performance than the Verbal subscales (Cantor, 1988).

Language Development

Language is intimately related to cognition and to social development, and therefore the properties of language usage vary considerably as a function of the general level of language and cognitive development. As children regress, their speech becomes limited and may reveal incoherent thinking.

Social and Emotional Development

Schizophrenia in childhood has its most devastating effects on a child's ability to monitor and test reality and on the ability to initiate and sustain interactions with others in the environment. Schizophrenia results in extreme withdrawal from the real world: affected children display a wide variety of disturbances in mood, thought, and behaviour.

Children who are schizophrenic show a marked reduction in interests and human attachments. They appear to live in a fantasy world and show emotional apathy, indifference, and withdrawal. Yet apathy can quickly give way to uncontrollable excitement or an enraged temper tantrum.

Infantile Autism

Autism is found in a heterogeneous group of individuals who show wide variability in the type, number, and severity of observed deficits in cognitive functioning, communication, social interaction, and overt behaviour (Soucy and Andrews, 1997). While children show a core group of symptoms, a further cluster of traits may not all be present in any given child. Children with autism demonstrate severe self-isolation, lack of appropriate use of language, stereotypical and inappropriate use of objects, a preoccupation with music, and abnormal motility patterns such as toe walking, body rocking, and bizarre choreoathetotic posturings. The most common behavioural problems are tantrums and non-compliance. These and other behaviours that appear as the child develops are presented in Table 13-2.

Affected children never begin to establish normal human attachments. They are extremely alone from earliest infancy, and are unresponsive to other people. As infants, children who are autistic show far less mutual gaze and facial responsiveness than other children. These children may be indifferent to physical contact, or may even show aversion to it.

Parents report that their children do not respond in normal ways to being held. Infants fail to make the usual anticipatory movements prior to being picked up and fail to make the usual body adjustment to adapt to the person carrying or holding. Between the fourteenth and eighteenth months, several disturbing symptoms begin to appear. These include prolonged rocking and head banging in the crib, apathy and disinterest in the surroundings, unusual fear of strangers, obsessive interest in certain toys or mechanical appliances, highly repetitive and ritualistic play, insistence on being left alone, demands that the physical environment remain unchanged, and very unusual language behaviour (Rimland, 1964).

In older children, autism reveals itself in fleeting eye contact, the failure to develop any relationships, and insistence on rituals and routines. Children fail to form attachments to other people. They seldom initiate contact and sometimes seem to look or walk through others. They appear distant, aloof, or in a shell, and are extremely alone. They have severely impaired communication skills and show an obsessive insistence on sameness. Objects are preferred to people; children's only strong attachments are toward inanimate things. Children who are autistic, for example, are fascinated by things that spin. They can sit for hours with a toy car upside down, endlessly spinning the wheels. Unlike other children, they are virtually impossible to distract from this behaviour.

Physical and Motor Development

Children with autism tend to be healthier than other children with pervasive disorders (Schreibman and Charlop, 1989). Motorically, they may show grace and normal motor skill development; however, it is not unusual to find ten-year-olds who are not yet toilet trained or capable of dressing themselves.

Table 13-2 Symptoms of infantile autism in the preschool child

Birth to eighteen months
• No mutual gazing
• Feeding problems, such as poor sucking
• Lack of smile response
• Apathy and unresponsiveness
• Rigidity and stiffness or limpness and hypotonia when held
• Constant crying or an unusual absence of crying
• Repetitive motor movements
• Obsessive interest in certain objects
• Great resistance to change
Eighteen months to two years
• Continued poor eye contact
• Withdrawal and isolation
• Difficulties in toilet-training
• Odd eating habits and food preferences
• Feeding problems, such as refusal to hold food in mouth, refusal to chew or swallow, or gagging
• Little or no development of speech
• Little or no receptive language skills
• Lack of interest in toys, but obsessive play with some items
After two years
• Continued withdrawal and isolation
• No development of co-operative play
• Continued problems with feeding, sleeping, and using the toilet
• Slow or precocious motor development
• Obsessive desire for sameness
• Development of repetitive habits, gestures, and mannerisms
• Tantrums at change or restriction of activities

Cognitive Development

Although there is no common theoretical base, conceptions of autism share the assumption that it stems from some deficient cognitive structure. Poor cognitive development affects children's ability to learn, while behaviour problems interfere with attention and motivation.

Some degree of mental disability is present in most individuals with infantile autism; 50 to 75 percent of individuals are mentally retarded (Goodman, 1987; Sigelman and Shaffer, 1991), and they often display an extremely low level of cognitive functioning.

Co-occuring conditions that further deflate cognitive functioning are very common. In a British Columbia survey of 152 children with autism, Marg Csapo (1979) found 85 percent to have additional conditions that included mental retardation (51.1 percent), speech dysfunction and retardation (14 percent), and epilepsy and retardation (9.6 percent). Of children showing autistic symptoms before age six, 21 percent have been found to develop seizure disorders by age eighteen (Deykin and MacMahon, 1979). For one in three children who are autistic, problems worsen with the onset of puberty.

Cognitive development appears to differ from that observed in typical retardation; in youngsters with autism, IQ scores become stable over time, predictive of later functioning, and fail to rise with age-related improvements in clinical symptoms (Rutter, 1983). Evidence suggests that females with autism tend to be more seriously affected, with lower intelligence scores and greater problems in cognition and language (Konstantareas, Hamatidis, and Busch, 1989).

Perceptual Development and Sensory Response

Children with pervasive developmental disorders, especially those diagnosed as autistic, may display abnormal responses to visual stimuli. They seem to suffer from constraints in attending to relevant cues and may exhibit a generalized over- or under-responsiveness to incoming stimuli. While fixating on an object or lights, they may flutter their hands, cross their eyes, glance to the side, or unfocus their eyes. They may try to smell new objects, or run their hands and tongues over rough and smooth surfaces. Sound may elicit indifference, distress, or intense fascination.

Faulty modulation of sensory input is an intrinsic feature of the pattern of autistic behaviour. To try to explain the disturbances of sensory input, a number of models have emerged. Some investigators believe that the child is overwhelmed by sensory input and unable to attend to pertinent environmental stimulation. Others see the child as showing overselectivity: he or she seems to select a part of a stimulus and maintain attention to that part. Once fixated on relatively few stimuli, the child becomes incapable of scanning the environment.

Language Development

Professionals have long been intrigued by children who are autistic and psychotic, especially their language patterns or, more often, lack of language. The central roles of deficits in language and cognitive factors in autism are well documented.

Research data indicate fairly conclusively that children with autism have incurred some damage to the brain, which may particularly affect the language centres. If this is the case, children with autism have a neurologically based language dysfunction that seriously interferes with their learning of expressive speech and abstract language.

It is the deviance in the quality and pattern of language usage, rather than language delay, that differentiates autism from other developmental disorders. Many children with autism seem to lack the awareness, intentionality, or competence to use language as a tool to convey messages to others. From infancy, children show little or no ability to analyze or make sense of sounds. As they mature, their language and communication skills remain impaired. Attempts to communicate are characterized by immaturity and abnormalities in grammatical constructions. Many children fail to speak at all.

Those who do speak show atypical language features: delayed echolalia, metaphorical language, pronoun reversals, and stereotypic utterances. Children with autism often use unusual words, with curious metaphors and odd expressions. They use **neologisms**, defined as non-words or words that are obviously peculiar.

neologisms

There are frequent pragmatic oddities, with language used in ways that are socially or contextually inappropriate. Children typically perseverate on topics and fail to recognize turn-taking rules. Pronoun usage is unusual. A child may say "You want ride," when he means "I want to ride."

Facial and gestural expression of emotions can also be abnormal. Children with autism are thought to have a visual motor imitation deficiency akin to dyspraxia, which interferes with the learning of normal body language and the understanding of non-verbal communication, so important during the pre-verbal stage of development (Cummings and Finger, 1980). Affected children fail to use gestures appropriately, and do not interpret such gestural clues as eye contact, body posture, tone of voice, and facial expression (Hobson, 1988).

If language is impaired, speech problems almost inevitably ensue. In their use of speech, children who are autistic are almost always delayed. Almost half of these children fail to develop functional oral language (Kauffman, 1997b), especially those who are also mentally retarded. In the other 50 percent, speech is severely delayed and, if present, frequently consists of meaningless repetitive and stereotypical utterances.

When learning speech, the process is abnormal and different from that seen in, say, children who are mentally retarded. Acquisition of first words is often delayed, and after that vocabulary often doesn't grow the way it does in other children. New words may appear but old ones are forgotten, resulting in a plateau. Some children with autism begin to speak and then lose all speech. Some then regain speech; others do not.

In children with speech, prosody is often peculiar; for instance, everything may be said staccato or in a monotonous drone. In spontaneous speech usage, children with autism display a lack of expressive intonational features, such as stress and pitch, although echolalic children can repeat sentences and phrases with uncanny accuracy of intonation.

Echolalia is the most frequently cited language characteristic of individuals with autism who are verbal. Of the estimated 50 to 60 percent of persons with autism who are verbal, 75 percent are echolalic (Rydell and Mirenda, 1991). Echolalic children may repeat whole sentences in parrot-like fashion as if the sentence were unanalyzable into smaller components: as if they had learned the behaviour and stored it in memory ever since. Children who use echolalia seem able to attend to a linguistic string. They may even use a response to a consistent stimulus, but fail to relate it enough to the content to associate it with anything but a vague and general meaning.

Language problems weaken the capacity of children with autism for symbolic thought and abstract reasoning. In discussions of their behavioural deviations, for example, play disorders are consistently cited. Children with autism demonstrate significant delays in the development of all forms of play, especially symbolic play. Evidence indicates that their play is quite different from that of mentally retarded and other exceptional children. For children with autism, it is not delayed play, but play that differs in topography, pleasure, and complexity. Even when intellectual level is allowed for, play is often obsessional, mechanical, and repetitive, with a marked absence of both co-operative play and innovative pretend play. For these youngsters, play as a vehicle for learning about objects and events and especially for engaging in make-believe does not appear to be intrinsically motivating (Lifter, Sulzer-Azaroff, Anderson, and Cowdery, 1993).

Perhaps because of the language deficits that invariably characterize infantile autism, the play is striking in its lack of fantasy and its sterile, repetitive, ritualistic, and solitary nature. These children do not seem to know how to use play forms. In a room full of toys, a child who is autistic is more likely to ignore the toys and engage in stereotypic self-stimulating body movements. If the child does play, toys are used in a deviant fashion. Unusual pre-occupations (such as memorizing timetables) are characteristically pursued single-mindedly to the detriment of other activities.

Social and Emotional Development

Impairments in social relatedness are increasingly considered to constitute some of the core symptoms of autism. Children with autism and other developmental disorders exhibit severe social interaction deficits. They demonstrate severely impaired relationships with parents, family members, and others in the environment. They do not attempt to gratify their needs through meaningful personal relationships; rather, they behave toward people as if they were inanimate objects.

Children who are autistic often resent parents and others who try to show affection. They demonstrate both aggressive and stereotypical behaviours, such as staring into space, body rocking, eye rubbing, and lip licking, that further interfere with social interactions.

ASSESSMENT OF CHILDREN WHO HAVE PERVASIVE DEVELOPMENTAL DISORDERS

Treatment programs for children with developmental disabilities relate to the accuracy and specificity with which the problems and deficits are initially identified. Without clear and precise information about the nature of disabilities and a child's current level of functioning, an effective treatment strategy cannot be developed. But even when the conditions can be readily diagnosed, their causes often remain a mystery, and the most efficient identification may not lead directly to the most effective programming.

In the diagnosis of childhood psychoses and infantile autism, we find interwoven currents of research and investigation. We also find that diagnosis has provoked unresolved controversy. Clinicians vary in their theoretical conceptions of the conditions and emphasize different aspects as essential for specific diagnostic labels. The presence of co-occurring conditions further muddies clear identification. Children with autism, for example, display a wide range of behaviours, many of them similar to those found in children with other disorders. Before they are correctly diagnosed, children who are autistic may be falsely labelled as blind or deaf. Mental retardation is often the initial diagnosis; however, this is not an either-or category, as a high percentage of children with autism are also retarded. Clinicians simultaneously try to determine whether a child is classically autistic, mildly autistic, or shows autistic features (Eaves, 1988).

Once assessment is begun, procedures are replete with difficulties. So much so that in the past children with developmental disabilities, especially those with infantile autism, were considered untestable through standardized tests. The complex and varied disabilities made such children exceptions to many of the rules by which psycho-educational tests are designed and administered and, as a result, standardized tests were seldom administered. When tests were given, incomplete results were often interpreted on the basis of the examiner's intuitive sense of a child's peak skills.

Testing of students who are psychotic and autistic is particularly difficult because

- Children often show a deficient ability to establish relationships;
- Regular systems of reinforcement may be inadequate for these children;
- Most of these children suffer impaired communication skills;
- Sensory abnormalities may result in unusual responses to sensory stimuli;
- Children have attention differences;
- Children may show abnormal motor behaviour;
- Clinicians must take into account the frequent co-existence of developmental disabilities, mental retardation, and neurological deficits;
- Children who are autistic especially have a need for sameness and often demonstrate an inability to switch tasks;
- Children with autism demonstrate marked variability on test performance. They may do poorly on tasks requiring abstract thought, symbolism, and sequential logic, but perform well on tasks that demand manual and visual spatial skills.

There is now a growing recognition that broad and thorough assessment of children who are psychotic and autistic is both possible and essential to provide the basis for educational and behavioural programming. Evaluation must be multidisciplinary and incorporate a variety of procedures, tools, and adaptations. Procedures require flexibility in administration, appropriate means of communication, alternation of free and structured time, motivation and reinforcers, predictable routines, and tools that limit the use of language to tasks that measure language skills. (See the appendix table, Tools for Assessment.)

Psycho-educational Assessment

Psychologists may administer both formal and informal assessment measures to students who are developmentally disabled. Specialized instruments are often needed to explore particular diagnostic and treatment questions. For example, the Autism Screening Instrument for Educational Planning (Krug, Arick, and Almond, 1980. 1993) has five components: sensory relating, body and object use, language, social skills, and self-help skills. (See also the appendix table, Tools for Assessment.)

Functional Assessment

Many assessors adopt a functional approach to testing, which we have discussed in Chapter 2 and in relation to students with behavioural disorders. In assessing students with pervasive developmental disorders, functional analysis serves similar purposes.

The aim is to find the purpose (function) of a behaviour and examine a child's performance within the context of naturalistic environments. Functional analysis looks at elements of the child's behavioural repertoire that interfere with instructional objectives; appropriate steps to reduce the skill-inhibiting elements of behaviour; and replacement behaviour—the conditions that motivate the child to attend or those that elicit a response; and ways to maintain consequences such as a token or food reward. The process is shown in Figure 13-1.

In assessing language, for example, the teacher would first identify the child's specific communication needs and interests. This includes the settings (when and where communication interactions occur); the people in them (with whom the most appropriate interactions occur); the purposes for communication (the reasons for the child to communicate); and why a child communicates (the objects and activities that the child prefers). Such an assessment allows a teacher to pinpoint specific communication needs as well as the vocabulary that the teacher and parents should include in instructional activities.

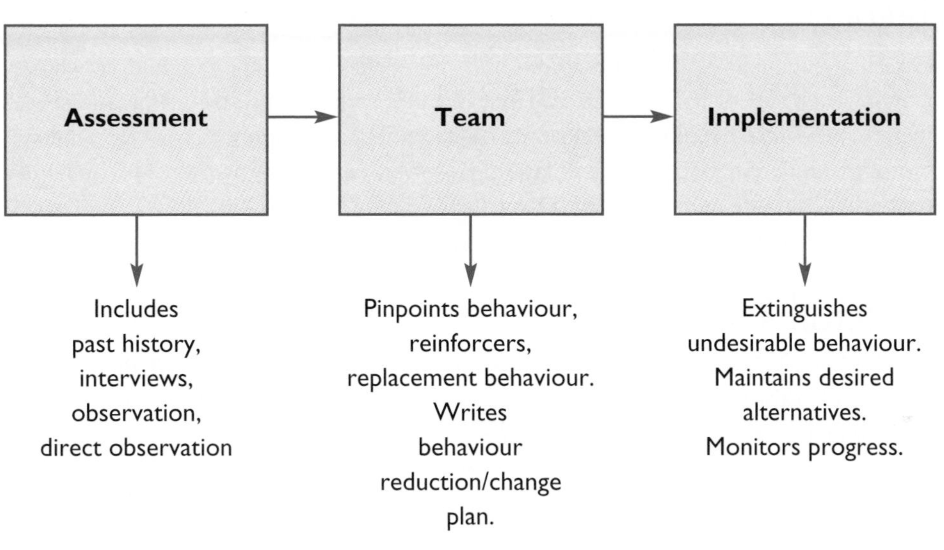

Figure 13-1 *Overview of the processes of functional assessment.*

INTERVENTION WITH CHILDREN WHO HAVE PERVASIVE DEVELOPMENTAL DISORDERS

Children with pervasive developmental disorders present many challenges to those who attempt to help them develop more meaningful lives. The field has attracted many passionate devotees—teachers, clinicians, and researchers—with widely varied views and very different treatment regimes. While there have been successes, they are not universally applicable and at present no specific treatment exists to help children who are psychotic or autistic reduce their anxiety and cope more effectively with reality. No one treatment method has proven notably effective with the entire group of children, and the outlook remains poor. For many children with infantile autism there is little likelihood of attaining normal functioning within the context of currently available treatment and educational techniques. Even after years of the most effective treatment, many children are likely to remain at the retarded level, requiring close supervision and care.

Medical Intervention

A wide variety of medications have proven useful in the treatment of youngsters with schizophrenia. Stimulants and tranquilizers are commonly administered. Antipsychotics used include haloperidol (Haldol), thioridazine (Mellaril), fluphenazine (Prolixin), and thiothixine (Navane).

In contrast, drug therapy has shown inconclusive but unpromising results in the treatment of autism. In general, there is little evidence that stimulants or tranquilizers significantly enhance the functioning of children who are autistic, although there has been some recent clinical success with new drugs such as Naloxone.

Therapy

Over the years, many different methods and approaches to therapy for children who are psychotic and autistic have been tried. These include psychotherapy, family therapy, speech therapy, residential treatment, psychiatric hospitalization, medication, megavitamin therapy, sensory stimulation, and sensory isolation. However, despite strong claims by individual researchers, no one method has been conclusively shown to substantially alleviate pervasive developmental disorders.

Technical Aids

For children who are not often interested in other people or comfortable with them, a computer may serve as a catalyst for social interaction. If children work in pairs, studies show that they spontaneously teach, help, and praise one another in computer environments, asking more questions of one another than of their teachers (Borgh and Dickson, 1986).

Educational Intervention

Historically, students presenting intensive educational challenges to our schools have been served outside the regular classroom and, in many cases, outside the community school. Residential schools or clinics were the mode. Today, the majority of children live at home with their families and a variety of educational settings are available. No evidence exists to favour one approach over another, especially for children who are autistic.

David's story is illustrative of the variety of placement options. He began school in a segregated setting but is moving more toward an inclusive classroom.

Service Delivery Models

Some children are placed in foster homes, group homes, or residential training centres. Children are enrolled in residential programs only when they are seriously delayed in feeding, toilet use, or other self-help skills; when their families badly need relief; or when they must be placed under extensive observation for assessment purposes.

Currently, a growing number of parents and educators are calling for the inclusion of all

Case Study

David (continued)

As soon as David was diagnosed, we contacted a local facility for autistic children. A therapist from the centre immediately began working with David in our home. When David was old enough, he attended a special preschool on a daily basis. All the children had some form of disability and the teachers were specially trained.

For David, they focused on trying to develop some social interactions, basic communication and language, and self-care skills, particularly toilet training. He did learn a few gestures to communicate his needs, but his progress was slow. He is still not fully toilet trained.

As success in the preschool setting was very limited, at school age David first went to a special school with a program and goals contiguous with the preschool. Through a very structured behavioural program the teachers worked on the same areas. To help David relate to others in the environment they continued to teach some basic communication. They worked on social skills training with the primary goal of helping David to get in touch and be more responsive to his environment and the people in it. They also stressed the self-help skills needed for independent functioning in relation to such basic needs as food, warmth, dressing, and toileting.

When he was nine years old, David moved from the special school into a special class in his local school. We did not feel that he was ready at that time for full inclusion but he is slowly joining his peers in the general classroom for more activities. When included in the regular classroom, the major aim is social interaction and opportunities to hear and respond to normal language. So far, his progress in speech and language development has been disappointing and we have seen few changes in David's responsiveness or use of language. There is more progress in the social domain. He seems to relate far more to his peers than in the past, is more co-operative with the teachers, and his temper tantrums have virtually disappeared when he is in the general classroom.

The school team developed a number of integration strategies for David to give him more opportunities to interact with his peers. They prepared an IEP focusing on goals for the regular classroom. An extract is shown below.

EXTRACT FROM DAVID'S IEP

Name David
School John Brown
Grade 4

Present Levels of Functioning

David has been diagnosed as autistic. No IQ levels have been estimated, but he is functioning at pre-academic levels. David has not developed any language or speech.

Placement

David is in a special class but there is to be increasing integration into the regular classroom for social purposes.

Annual Goal (Regular Classroom)

To increase interactions with others in the environment and awareness of environmental stimulation.

Long-Range Goals

- David will develop gaze-to-gaze behaviour.
- David will respond to others in the environment.
- David will use simple speech when it is modelled for him.
- David will participate in art classes with his peers on a daily basis.

Objectives

- When assisted to the correct hallway, David will locate and enter the art room independently.
- When given a visual cue by the teacher, he will sit in his assigned place.
- At the beginning of the class, he will respond to communication by waving or saying "Hi" to a peer.
- When presented with a choice of paints and a gestural cue for each option, David will select the colours he wishes to use.
- At the end of the class before clean-up, he will tap the arm of a peer at the table and will point to his own artwork to show it to the peer.
- When prompted by other students, he will look at their artwork.
- When cued, David will place the finished work in his own folder.
- David will return to his own classroom with a peer.

students within the mainstream of regular education, including those with severe disabilities. Nevertheless, there is acute disagreement within the field as to whether students with intensive educational needs belong in general education classrooms. In fact, one of the major placement issues of the day is whether such students should be based in regular or special education classrooms or in home schools.

Many argue for regular school placement. Others contend that children who show extreme symptoms are probably not suitable for integration. Children with severe and multiple disabilities, they say, may be at odds with a system that has few resources and little inclination to meet their needs. Link (1991), for example, argues that there is a population of students—those with severe and multiple disabilities—who, despite any currently popular instruction, will not be capable of functioning in the general classroom, will not be completely self-sufficient, and will not live independently within our society. Arguments and cautions surrounding the inclusion of students with severe disabilities are shown in the Debate box.

A Matter of Debate

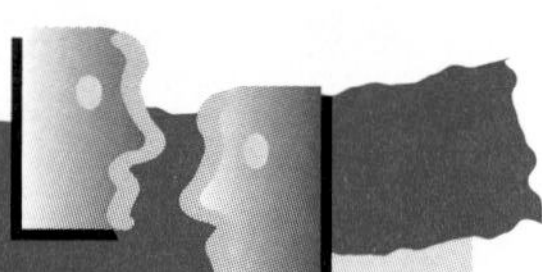

The Inclusion of Students with Severe Disabilities

Arguments for inclusion	Cautions about inclusion
General class placement will remove the stigma associated only with segregated placements.	Inclusive settings are potentially harmful. Not only may the physical environment of the public school present barriers, but also there is a lack of medical intervention.
Facilitates the modelling of appropriate social behaviour.	Deviant behaviours such as resistance to change, an inability to generalize from one situation to another, and stereotypical and aggressive

Arguments for inclusion	Cautions about inclusion
	behaviour seriously jeopardize a child's functioning in a normalized environment.
Social benefits accrue to students with severe disabilities in inclusive settings (Fryxell and Kennedy, 1995; Kennedy, Shukla, and Fryxell, 1997).	Children with disabilities do not interact with peers unless they are supported and encouraged to do so (Frea, Craig-Unkefer, Odom, and Johnson, 1999).
Inclusion in general classrooms increases the communicative interactions of students with severe disabilities.	Natural supports may mean that some important aspects of education are lost because of lack of specialization.
In segregated settings, children have few opportunities to associate with non-disabled peers and less opportunity to practise, refine, and expand their skill repertoires, thereby reducing the likelihood that they will develop friendships (Hendrickson, Shookoohi-Yekta, Hamre-Nietupski, and Gable, 1996).	The regular school may inhibit children's development by imposing educational models and social demands that do not meet their needs.
Anecdotal reports of successful inclusion of children with severe and profound disabilities are emerging consistently in the literature (e.g., Janney, Snell, Beers, and Raynes, 1995; Kozleski and Jackson, 1993).	The intense needs of children with severe disabilities challenge the boundaries of practitioner knowledge and organizational supports and, for some, their commitment to integration and inclusion.
Curriculum can be modified.	Training often emphasizes early developmental skills usually thought of as too routine or too basic to be part of a regular instructional program.
Students for whom traditional task requirements are not relevant can still learn social skills and see that they are full class members, not inferior to others.	The curricula proposed for students with significant disabilities are often vague, inconsistent, and show wide swings in emphasis (Fuchs and Fuchs, 1995b).
Studies (e.g., Janney et al., 1995; Kozleski and Jackson, 1993) find increases in positive teacher attitudes following the experience of including children with severe disabilities.	Teachers who are asked to include students with severe or profound disabilities may feel that they have limited resources and are not properly trained. A survey of special educators (Izen and Brown, 1991) found that many teachers did not feel adequately trained by university teacher training programs to work with children with severe disabilities.

Arguments for inclusion	Cautions about inclusion
With support, general education teachers can include all students.	There is limited availability of trained personnel as well as budgetary constraints. Schools and districts will likely have trouble finding enough personnel specifically trained to work with these students. These students may take an inordinate amount of time away from their peers without disabilities because of the traditionally required high learner/teacher ratios (Schaffner and Buswell, 1991).

Although the tide is flowing very strongly toward inclusion, the norm within most North American schools is still for students who are intensively challenged to be educated in schools or classrooms other than those of their neighbours' children. In both Canada and the United States, the full integration of students with severe disabilities has not been realized in many school districts. Two major barriers are a lack of trained classroom teachers and physical barriers in the schools.

Teachers may benefit from a general model such as the Autism Mainstream Collaboration Model (Simpson and Myles, 1993), which is designed to support general educators. It stresses collaboration and shared responsibility among special and regular educators and support personnel. It includes additional planning time for teachers and paraprofessionals.

Educational Approaches

Various conceptual models have been used in the education and training of children with developmental disorders. Three major approaches have traditionally been applied. The psychodynamic and behavioural approaches are the most popular, but a psycho-educational approach is also employed.

Psychodynamic Approaches

Before the 1960s, almost all intervention with children who were psychotic or autistic was founded on psychodynamic principles. This approach is still used, though it is not nearly as popular.

Children are given individual therapy within a therapeutic placement designed to promote and sustain emotional growth. Psychodynamic treatment is usually conducted in a residential setting away from the parents and typically lasts several years. Treatment may also be given through outpatient clinics or day treatment centres.

The psychodynamic approach tries to help children understand the inner forces that guide their behaviour. By responding to the child in ways that are consistent, positive, and accepting, the therapist builds the child's confidence and trust. At the same time, the therapist helps the child to understand the sources of conflicting ambivalent emotions. Art, play, pet, and music therapy may be part of the psychodynamic approach. (See Chapter 7.)

Behavioural Approaches

Autism and schizophrenia are extremely difficult to treat; affected children pose a variety of complex management problems. Although very resistant to psychotherapy, many children do respond to behaviour modification techniques, and the research literature is flooded with positive reports of the use of behaviour therapy and highly structured learning procedures with children categorized as psychotic or autistic. For children with autism, for example, behavioural approaches have been used to teach children to focus attention, to imitate actions, to develop basic speech skills such as vocalizing and word imitation, to label objects and pictures, and to extinguish temper tantrums.

Behaviour therapists do not claim to cure autism and give no promise of normalization or intellectual improvement. Rather, they attempt to modify deficits and excesses in behaviour patterns. However, "the long-term effectiveness of behavioural therapy for autism remains much in question, at times sparking intense debate even among investigators using it" (Bower, 1989, p. 312).

Behaviourists claim that behaviour modification trains children who are autistic to lead a more useful existence. Critics respond that behavioural techniques program children to perform like robots, unable to generalize their training to other situations. These critics claim that the child's trained responses are much too closely linked to the original training situation. Light (1983) found that a child trained to answer "Fine, thank you," to one trainer's "How are you?" does not necessarily respond the same way when the question is asked by another trainer.

Despite these criticisms, the general evaluation of behaviour therapy has been cautiously optimistic. But even with behaviour modification, many children with autism still need supervision.

Curriculum

The major goals of intervention with children with pervasive developmental disorders are to decrease the behavioural symptoms that interfere with the individual's functioning and to promote the development of skills in language, adaptive behaviour, social interaction, self-care, and independent living.

The 1980s saw many new curriculum developments that built on longitudinal, age-appropriate skills taught in domestic, recreational, vocational, and social contexts, and in integrated educational programs. But with their unresponsiveness and lack of communication skills, children with psychoses and infantile autism are very hard to train. Few receive academic training beyond basic levels.

At the outset, curriculum reflects all areas of development. Training may begin with the sensorimotor levels. (It clearly matches the curriculum we describe in Chapter 14 for children with multiple disabilities.) Many students need to be taught a wide range of basic daily living skills such as independent eating, dressing, and using the toilet. They must also learn how to relate effectively to others through training in social interaction and communication. Some students will need help to decrease inappropriate behaviours such as severe aggression or strong and persistent ritualistic and stereotyped behaviours.

Communication is a focus, particularly for children who are autistic. Speech and language development is related to general prognosis; the outcome appears to depend on the child's intellectual functioning at diagnosis and communicative speech development prior to the age of six (Gillberg and Steffenberg, 1987). Unless children achieve some use of spontaneous language by age five or six, the outlook is likely to be poor even for those with a relatively high level of non-verbal skills.

In some children, echolalic speech is decreased by non-attention, and normal speech is gradually shaped by food rewards for imitation of the therapist's vocalizations (Lovaas and Smith, 1988). Some behavioural methods to stimulate communication focus on reinforcing the utterances and demanding closer and closer approximations to real words to obtain a reinforcer (Kaplan, 1996). There is a new stress on teaching pragmatics, as performing expected social behaviours relates to increased social acceptance. But, as we pointed out earlier, doubts have been raised about the effectiveness of speech training with all children with autism.

An alternative approach, relying on the simultaneous use of speech and sign language, has been attempted with some success. One study (Konstantareas, 1984) found that sign and speech produced better results than speech alone, possibly because sign language relies primarily on visual and kinesthetic modalities and circumvents the auditory.

Another approach, facilitated communication, was introduced to North America in 1990. Since then, its use has become an area of intense controversy, with confirmations and rebuttals abounding. We outline the issues surrounding facilitated communication in the Research Notes.

Research Notes

Facilitated Communication

Perhaps because special education concerns itself with individuals who often cannot advocate for themselves, and with parents who are often desperate for guidance, if not cures, the field has long been the arena for fads, untried methods, and questionable treatments for which it is not uncommon for developers to overstate the efficacy. The penchant to promise more than can be delivered has a long history and we often embrace untried treatments, "only to find out subsequently that they were ineffectual, and in some cases, actually fraudulent" (MacMillan, Gresham, and Forness, 1996, p. 145).

This is not to suggest that facilitated communication is fraudulent. What it does suggest is that there is enormous discord in the professional literature on the subject. Some research results are negative; most are ambiguous; only a few are clear.

Facilitated communication was developed in the 1970s by Rosemary Crossley, an Australian educator, originally for persons with cerebral palsy. It soon came to be used with those with developmental disabilities and mental retardation. The technique was pioneered in the United States by Douglas Biklen in 1990.

Facilitated communication is a technique for some children and adults with autism who cannot talk and who do not point independently and reliably (Molnar, 1993). In this method of augmentative communication, someone physically assists an individual who is disabled to communicate through typing. A facilitator provides physical support under the forearm or hand of the individual and at the same time tries to minimize extraneous actions, redirect visual attention, and convey emotional support. With the assistant physically supporting his or her arm, wrist, or hand, the individual hunts and pecks for letters, words, or pictures on a keyboard (Molnar, 1993).

Although an unvalidated methodology, facilitated communication has been widely disseminated and reported in the popular media, including *Frontline* and *60 Minutes*. Promoted as a breakthrough for autistic and other communication-impaired individuals, it is little surprising that facilitated communication has "generated a level of interest and emotion rarely matched" (Simpson and Myles, 1995, p. 8).

The fulcrum of the controversy: Whose words are they? Those of the person with the disability or those of the facilitator? Advocates herald facilitated communication as a kind of key that has unlocked the imposed silence of autism. However, detractors say that it is far too easy for the assisted person to be led by the facilitator, that the method virtually puts words into his or her mouth whether it be intentional or not (Molnar, 1993).

Testimonies of parents and facilitators and some observational work show effectiveness. One study (Salomon-Weiss, Wagner, and Bauman, 1996) offered evidence of valid facilitated communication from a thirteen-year-old boy diagnosed with autism. Others (e.g., Simon, Toll, and Whitehair, 1994; Vasquez, 1994) demonstrate that individuals can produce their own messages.

Such evidence lacks robust and vigorous scientific investigation. In controlled studies it has often been difficult to confirm that successful independent communication was indeed happening. Careful empirical studies (e.g., Mulick, Jacabson, and Kobe, 1993) indicate that the facilitator, not the disabled individual, is the communicator in all but a very small number of cases. (For further details of the debate see Braman, Brady, Lineham, and Williams, 1995; Simpson and Myles, 1995.)

Historical Notes

It was not until the closing decades of the 19th century that the psychotic child became an object of study. Psychiatrists and others initiated careful efforts to observe, describe, and classify the disordered behaviours demonstrated by child patients, and collected and organized the existing material in monographs on psychic disorders, mental diseases, and insanity in children. By 1900, there was an assortment of data demonstrating that children displayed psychotic disorders (see Winzer, 1993).

In 1906, Sante de Sanctus named the psychotic problems observed in youngsters *dementia praecoxissima* (dementia of childhood). Then in 1911, Eugen Blueler, a Swiss psychiatrist, renamed dementia praecox as *schizophrenia*. The work of de Sanctus and others contributed to the identification of a distinct condition known as *childhood schizophrenia*. By 1935 schizophrenia in children was well documented and distinguished, although not clearly, from the adult condition.

Credit for first identifying autistic behaviours in children and adults also goes to Eugen Blueler, who isolated specific non-verbal and non-relating behaviours in 1906. Blueler used the word *autistic* as an adjective; it was not until Leo Kanner's major study in 1943 that an autistic syndrome, with autism as a noun, was identified in children.

Early authorities viewed childhood psychoses as one inclusive category, ignoring distinctions among specific syndromes. Research was simply generalized from one population to another. This became seriously evident in the disproportionate number of studies that focused on infantile autism and led to generalization of data that had little direct relevance to the schizophrenic group.

Even after recognition of psychoses in children

and the formulation of methods for identification, diagnosis, and intervention, the problems remained largely the bailiwick of psychiatrists and psychologists, and not the school system. The behaviour of children with psychoses and autism placed them in the category of the uneducable. Well into the 20th century, children with severe and multiple disabilities were excluded from public school segregated classes and often not accepted into residential settings. When treatment was given, institutionalization was the common mode, as many psychiatrists and other professionals believed that children who were autistic and psychotic could most effectively be treated away from their homes.

In the 1960s, interest in returning many previously institutionalized children to the community mounted and education began to assume responsibility for children with serious disturbances. For example, children with autism were integrated into classes in Toronto as early as 1956 (Lovatt, 1962).

By the 1970s, the education of children with developmental disorders was firmly entrenched in the school system, and professionals began to encourage parents to keep their children at home. Today, some children with severe developmental disabilities are taught in special day schools or residential settings, but increasing numbers of these youngsters are attending classes in their neighbourhood schools.

SUMMARY

1. *Pervasive developmental disorders* are exceedingly complex conditions. To many people, children who are psychotic and autistic are beyond comprehension. Their behaviour is bizarre, their emotions intense, and their isolation total. These children usually have difficulty developing language skills, learning to communicate, and learning to relate to others. They display unusual bodily movements, inordinate fears, and extreme resistance to change. Many children function at pre-academic levels and fail to develop, or lose, basic self-care skills or language.
2. Although infantile autism is generally considered the most devastating of developmental disorders, childhood schizophrenia is also extremely incapacitating. Schizophrenia is variously characterized by qualitative changes in functioning such as association disturbances, delusions, hallucinations, attention deficits, and inappropriate social interaction. Autism is a pervasive developmental disorder stemming from biophysical impairment. It reveals itself in fleeting eye contact, the failure to form attachments, disrupted relationships, and difficulty developing language skills.
3. Even after intense research efforts, the etiology of childhood psychoses and infantile autism remains vague, the symptoms severe and complex, the diagnosis difficult, the treatments unclear, and the prognosis uncertain at best. At the moment, the stress is on medical causality; serious biomedical research on autism is ongoing. While there is no irrefutable proof of causation, efforts have led to a much clearer understanding of the diagnosis of autism; today the condition is generally viewed not as a psychosis but as a developmental disability of neurological origin.
4. Of all assessment procedures, many researchers prefer functional assessment. This is a method for identifying the variables that reliably predict and maintain problem behaviour. The focus is on environmental events and intervention that brings changes in the environment.

5. For children with autism, poverty of language is a major factor that interferes with adjustment. Some children fail to develop speech; others have great difficulty following the conventions of conversation and interpreting linguistic and non-linguistic contextual rules. Poor language development spills over to affect many other areas, such as play and imaginative skills. Instead of language, children with autism turn to less problematic, more predictable, inanimate objects. They may sit for hours spinning or twirling an object, such as a shiny ashtray.
6. Children who are psychotic or autistic pose a variety of complex management problems. Of all the interventions that have been attempted, most children respond best to behaviour modification techniques. Nevertheless, these and other current educational treatments are unlikely to cure the disorders, although they alleviate the symptoms. Even with structured intervention procedures, the prognosis is poor. Many children continue to exhibit disordered behaviour as adults. Instead of becoming self-sufficient, they require continuous care.
7. Controversy still surrounds the placement of these children in regular schools. Some contend that children with severe and multiple disabilities may be at odds with a system that has few resources and little inclination to meet their needs. Today, however, children are placed in a range of settings, with inclusion in general classrooms becoming much more common.
8. Children with pervasive developmental disorders have a low repertoire of social interaction behaviours. The educational prognosis improves as they learn social skills. Children must first learn basic social behaviours, such as communication, and be trained to refrain from socially unacceptable actions.

WEBLINKS

Autism Society Manitoba **www.enable.mb.ca/enable/asm**

Center for the Study of Autism **www.autism.org/**

Ontario Association of Children's Mental Health Centres
www.oacmhc.org/

Schizophrenia: Youth's Greatest Disabler
www.mentalhealth.com/book/p40-sc02.html

Chapter 14

Children with Severe and Multiple Disabilities

Learning Outcomes

After reading this chapter, you should be able to:

Recognize the various ways in which multiple disabilities are described;

Relate the etiology of multiple disabilities to other etiologies described in the text;

Understand the developmental consequences of dual or multiple disabilities;

Discuss educational intervention for students with multiple disabilities;

Identify various types of augmentative communication.

Introduction

Children with severe and profound disabilities are those school-aged students who function intellectually within the lowest one percent of their particular age-groups or have delays of two or three standard deviations in two or more areas of development (TASH, 1986). Many, if not most, of these students are also multiply disabled. Children with multiple disabilities show evidence of independent and interdependent deficits in two or more areas of functioning.

With definitions so broad, and people with severe or multiple disabilities such an extremely heterogeneous population, we cannot paint any general portrait of students with severe and multiple disabilities. For one thing, the more severe the disabilities, the more unique the child. Children's development is integrated and organized across the various developmental domains—cognitive, language, physical, social, and emotional. With multiple disabilities, we cannot look at the impact of a single disability in isolation, but must instead realize that the interaction of disabilities results in the appearance of unique developmental and behavioural patterns. The conditions are not additive but cumulative and present a completely unique condition that may affect all the mind/body systems in different ways and to different degrees. For example, a deaf child with severe mental retardation may have independent deficits in cognitive functioning, in producing language, in understanding language, and in social interaction, as well as deficits resulting from a combination of these individual impairments.

Secondly, innumerable combinations of impairments are possible, although some appear more often than others, and some are more difficult to cope with. Individuals may suffer multisensory impairments such as deaf-blindness, or they may have conditions that combine sensory disorders with physical, neurological, or mental disabilities. Impairments of vision or hearing occur much more frequently among children with multiple disabilities than among other children. It has been estimated that one in five can be expected to have impaired hearing and two in five impaired vision (Orelove and Sobsey, 1987).

Students with severe and multiple disabilities present a range of special educational and psychosocial needs. Because of their complex conditions, these children require the services of many disciplines, most importantly education, psychology, physiotherapy, occupational therapy, speech pathology, audiology, and medicine. As a result, a transdisciplinary approach to their treatment and education is essential.

We encountered children with severe and profound intellectual disabilities in Chapter 6.

Case Study

Juanita

Juanita's mother had a difficult first pregnancy. The baby was born early after a contracted and arduous labour. Even though Juanita's mother was afraid that the child would suffer some adverse effects, she was stunned and frightened to soon find that the infant seemed to have a host of as-yet-unspecified developmental problems.

Consistent medical monitoring and assessment throughout the infant months confirmed the presence of severe difficulties and it was soon found that Juanita had serious visual and hearing difficulties, probably joined to mental retardation. Although early assessments indicated that she was not totally deaf or completely blind, physicians could not predict her future mental ability, the amount of residual hearing or vision, or Juanita's functional potential with sight and hearing.

By the time she was a year old, further assessment found that Juanita had quite a lot of usable vision although her hearing loss was in the severe to profound range. Both amplification and glasses were prescribed. Not that Juanita took kindly to either the hearing aid or the glasses. Despite the intensity of her disabilities, she had a mind of her own, and it took many months of perseverance on the part of her mother and many types of primary reinforcers before she would tolerate either appliance.

At about the same time, home-visiting teachers came to show her mother a range of activities to stimulate Juanita's mobility, communication, and interpersonal interactions. When she was three years of age, Juanita began attending a local preschool class on a part-time basis.

When she was ready for school, her mother enrolled her in the neighbourhood school, which had a special class for children with severe and multiple disabilities. For the first little while, Juanita remained in her special class, but soon the teacher worked to integrate her into a regular classroom for increasingly longer periods of the day. The teacher facilitated a "Circle of Friends" to assist Juanita's integration and worked co-operatively with the classroom teacher on planning specific activities that Juanita could accomplish in a small group setting.

As well, many of the other children that we have met in this text could be considered multiply disabled. The child with Down syndrome who has a speech disability, the youngster who is deaf and also emotionally disturbed, the child who is cerebral palsied with language disorders, and the child who is profoundly retarded and has autism, for example, have conditions that, taken together, severely disrupt their learning. And, while multiple disabilities are usually conceptualized as severe disabilities, it should be remembered that children can suffer from combinations of minor disabilities that can be devastating to their learning and behaviour. In this chapter, however, we focus on children with severe disabilities and debilitating multiple impairments.

DEFINITIONS OF SEVERE AND MULTIPLE DISABILITIES

Terminology and definitions are as confusing in this area as they are throughout special education. Apart from the terms *severely disabled* or *multiply disabled*, children may be described as physically disabled, dual sensory impaired; deaf-blind; autistic or psychotic; dependent multiply handicapped; and moderately, severely, or profoundly mentally retarded.

In the area of severe and multiple disabilities, the differences among students are greater than the similarities. This makes the formulation of precise definitions a complex and virtually impossible task. The heterogeneous nature of the population and the combinations of disabilities mean that we would not have one but dozens of definitions.

To overcome the problem, broad and encompassing generic definitions that attempt to include the entire range of possible combinations of conditions have evolved. The generic category of multiple disabilities under IDEA (1990) refers to

> A combination of impairments (such as mental retardation-blindness, or mental retardation-physical disabilities) that causes such severe educational problems that the child cannot be accommodated in a special education program solely for one of the impairments. The term does not include deaf-blindness.

This definition includes children who are severely and profoundly retarded; deaf-blind; mentally retarded and deaf-blind; physically disabled; and severely emotionally disturbed. It focuses on the combinations of problems possibly present as well as the range of interventions and allied disciplines necessary if children are to achieve their potential.

Criticisms of generic definitions abound, specifically because they tend to use very broad parameters that may obscure the effects of particular disabilities, making it harder to clinically interpret the needs of an individual child. Moreover, generic definitions do not lead to precise programming. For example, children with visual or hearing impairments who are enrolled in generic programs do not have access to specialist services, such as orientation and mobility training, low-vision services, or communication training.

Critics argue that more appropriate definitions could be generic but worded in terms of children's behaviours and needs. When individuals who are severely or multiply disabled are defined by their service needs, they are people "who require ongoing support in several major life areas in order to participate in the mainstream of community life and who are expected to require such support throughout life" (Bellamy, 1985, p. 6).

Some educators avoid generic definitions altogether, preferring more specificity for particular broad groupings of individuals who are severely or multiply disabled. They use *multisensory impaired* to describe children with sight and hearing handicaps. Included here are children who may also be developmentally delayed or have neurological impairments. *Multiple dependent handicapped* refers to children who are severely mentally handicapped and who also have sensory and/or other physical handicaps (see Orelove and Sobsey, 1987). Children described as multiple dependent handicapped display a wide variety of visual, auditory, and physical/neurological handicaps.

Dual sensory impairment refers to deaf-blind children, those whose disabilities are a complex of auditory, visual, communication, and language factors, often accompanied by other conditions that interfere with their learning. An individual who is deaf-blind is described under IDEA (1990) as having

> A combination of hearing and visual impairments causing such severe communication, developmental, and educational problems that the child cannot be accommodated in either a program specifically for the deaf or a program specifically for the blind.

Under this definition, children who are deaf-blind suffer impairments in both vision and hearing, and will not have their needs met if they are placed in special education programs for students who are only deaf or only visually impaired. Programs for students who are deaf rely heavily on the use of vision, while instruction for students with visual impairment depends on auditory instruction; but children who are deaf-blind suffer deficits in both these modalities. For many of these children, the sensory impairments co-exist with other challenging cognitive, physical, health, and behavioural characteristics.

PREVALENCE OF SEVERE AND MULTIPLE DISABILITIES

Estimating the true incidence and prevalence of almost any disability is an onerous, if not impossible, task. In the case of severe and multiple disabilities, a number of factors combine to hamper prevalence estimates. Difficulties arise because:

- Interpretations of the definition of certain populations have changed dramatically. For example, the number of persons with deaf-blindness has not increased substantially since 1974. Today, however, individuals categorized as deaf-blind can represent those with moderate to profound auditory and visual impairments with or without other educationally disabling conditions, who need services to increase independence; those with central processing problems that result in cortical blindness or central auditory dysfunctions; or those with progressive sensory impairments such as Usher's syndrome (Michael and Paul, 1991).
- As we mentioned earlier, children with combined disabilities may be registered for services with a variety of agencies so that the same child might be identified within the service delivery systems of any of these agencies.
- Probably the greatest difficulty in obtaining prevalence figures arises as children are counted in terms of their primary disability. In some school districts, children who are severely or multiply disabled may be entered into classes designed for mentally retarded, hearing impaired, or visually impaired children, and are then defined and counted by what is presumed to be the primary disability.

CLASSIFICATION OF SEVERE AND MULTIPLE DISABILITIES

As we just explained, the complexity and variety of severe and multiple disabilities has spawned a number of definitions and descriptions. The heterogeneous population also means that classification systems and service delivery are beset with confusion. Generally, services have been administered on the basis of labels and discrete categories, and this tendency has resulted in the creation of a number of overlapping classification systems.

primary disability
secondary disabilities

The most common way to classify multiple disabilities is in *primary* and *secondary* terms. The major condition that causes a child to differ in learning or behaviour is referred to as the **primary disability**; other conditions that arise or are present are known as **secondary disabilities.** A child who is both visually impaired and mentally retarded may be judged to suffer visual disabilities as the primary disabling condition, with mental retardation being the secondary disability.

Approaches that focus on presumed primary and secondary disabilities have their own built-in set of problems. For one thing, many children have more than one set of pertinent characteristics, and the primary disability is often impossible to identify. Children who are both blind and retarded, for example, may be visually inattentive because they do not see or because they are intellectually unaware of the visual environment.

Second, and perhaps more importantly, viewing multiple disabilities as primary and secondary overlooks the cumulative nature of the conditions. Children cannot be appropriately classified under the category of a single impairment because the combination of conditions creates an entirely new disability that requires access to special services for all the child's impairments, whether sensory, physical, mental, or behavioural. Children who suffer from visual impairments as well as mental disabilities, for example, cannot be appropriately accommodated in programs for mentally disabled children who don't have sight problems.

Sometimes children are classified and counted according to the agency that serves them. This also leads to problems, as the same child may be identified within the service delivery system of a number of agencies. Sometimes, too, children are simply classified by the type of educational program they attend.

ETIOLOGY OF SEVERE AND MULTIPLE DISABILITIES

The major causes of childhood disabilities that we have outlined throughout this text are also causes of multiple disabilities in children. In fact, with the exception of rubella, the etiology of multiple disabilities almost parallels that of physical impairments. This is especially true for central nervous system damage that results in severe motor impairment.

In the past, rubella was the culprit in many childhood conditions. At its most devastating, rubella caused deaf-blindness and severe multiple disabilities.

Chromosomal and genetic disorders account for only a tiny number of multiple disabilities. When they do appear, children often have complex disorders affecting several different body systems. In terms of numbers, injuries to the central nervous system account for significant numbers of multiple disabilities.

Neurological impairments result from damage or dysfunction of the brain and/or the spinal cord incurred before, during, or after birth. Other nervous system disorders resulting in multiple disabilities stem from trauma, accident, or child abuse. Hydrocephalus is frequently associated; if treatment is unsuccessful or only partly successful, the child may have damage to the optic nerve as well as motor impairments (see Chapter 12).

New medical technology, intensive care nurseries, and lifesaving techniques are saving many infants who would have perished just a few years ago. Children who are premature, especially those with birth-weights less than 1500 grams, are particularly vulnerable to insults of the central nervous system (Fenichel, 1980).

Meningitis contracted immediately after birth is a major cause of multiple disabilities. Fifty percent of infants who survive the disease suffer significant neurological impairments that include cerebral palsy, hydrocephalus, convulsive disorders, and hearing and visual handicaps (Fenichel, 1980).

Syndromes

Usher's syndrome

Usher's syndrome is a condition of familial nerve deafness associated with pigment degeneration of the retina. The incidence of Usher's syndrome in the general population is no greater than one in 15 000 to 30 000 births. Nevertheless, Usher's syndrome is the most common etiology of deaf-blindness, accounting for more than half of the deaf-blindness found in adults. It also accounts for 3 to 6 percent of all the profound prelingually deaf population, almost always born to hearing parents (Miller, 1985; Miner, 1995).

Usher's syndrome is transmitted through an autosomal recessive trait. The child is born deaf and gradually loses sight due to retinitis pigmentosa, which is most often diagnosed in the early teen years (Miner, 1995). As well as hearing loss and retinitis pigmentosa, a significant number of persons with Usher's syndrome show other symptoms, such as abnormal vestibular functioning, seizures, mental retardation, abnormal EEGs, schizophrenia, and autism (Davenport, O'Nuallian, Omenn, and Wilkus, 1978).

Not all individuals who are genetically deaf-blind suffer from Usher's syndrome. The single conditions may be caused by different genes or infections. There are other syndromes, such as Refsum's and Laurence-Moon, that involve both deafness and visual impairment; however, additional pathology such as obesity, retardation, diabetes, or scaly skin clearly distinguishes these from Usher's.

A number of other syndromes that involve mental retardation are mentioned in Chapter 3. Many of these have been identified and defined due to very recent genetic research.

DEVELOPMENTAL CONSEQUENCES OF SEVERE AND MULTIPLE DISABILITIES

Severe disabilities involving mental retardation imply, by definition, a low level of cognitive functioning. More often than not, persons who are severely retarded also show multiple disabilities—they have two or more exceptional conditions that hinder the attainment of their full potential. As we have stressed, the variety and combinations of disorders presented by children who are multiply disabled make generalizations about developmental consequences virtually impossible. These students may have orthopedic or health impairments, or hearing or speech disabilities. They may use unconventional behaviour to communicate a basic need or they may exhibit a combination of behaviours (Jones and Carlier, 1995).

Physical Development

Many domains of learning depend upon a child's ability to interact with the environment. As a result, many children with severe or multiple disabilities are very late in reaching developmental milestones. Walking, using first words, and toilet training may be quite delayed. In some children, they never emerge.

During the period when normal children are developing most rapidly, multiple deficits prevent children from interacting with the environment in ways that are critical for the subsequent development of social, motor, cognitive, and communication skills. They are then doubly limited by their delayed physical development and by their limited ability to engage with the environment in ways that can stimulate development.

Students who are deaf-blind are particularly disadvantaged. Deprivation in one distance sense tends to increase reliance on the other. Deprivations in the senses of both vision and hearing place reliance on the near senses of taste, touch, and smell. Children who are deaf and blind therefore have an infinitely more complex task in gaining information about their environments.

Cognitive Development

Poor cognitive development characterizes students with severe and profound disabilities. However, depressed cognitive development is not a necessary concomitant of other multiple disabilities. Nevertheless, the disabilities can be so severe that many children function in very low ranges. For example, although 94 percent of children who are deaf-blind have some usable vision and usable hearing (Chen and Haney, 1995), many of these children function in the severe to profound ranges of mental retardation as a result of their inability to perform basic skills (Orlansky, 1981).

Students with multiple disabilities usually have a range of special educational and psychosocial needs.

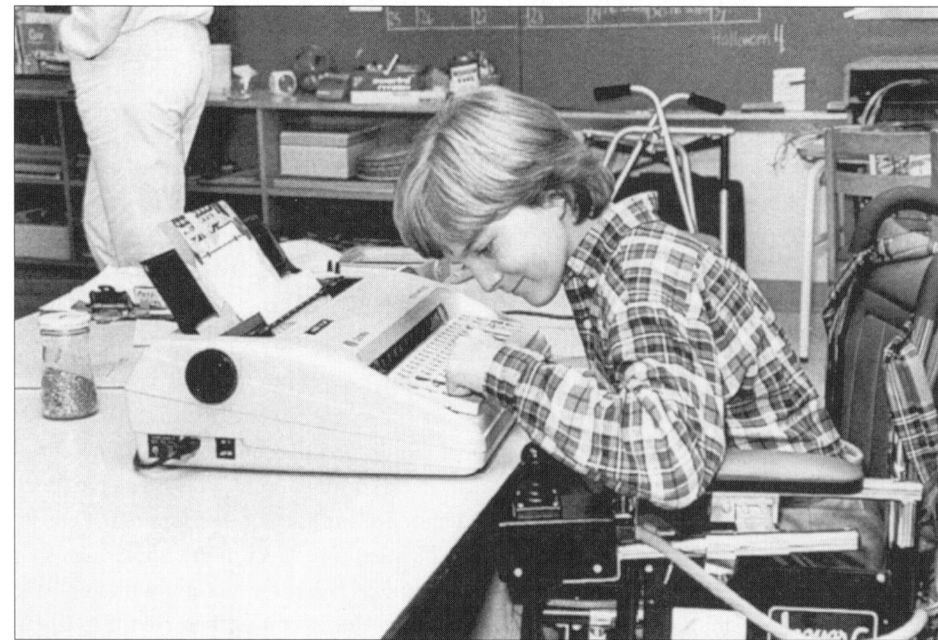

Communication

For most children, the ready acquisition of their culture's language and speech is a natural part of early maturation. But for those young children with disabilities, learning to communicate is not a simple or a naturally occurring task. Communication demands so much of the human organism that language learning is vulnerable to all the problems that can and do affect children. Almost invariably, those with severe or multiple disabilities display serious developmental lags in speech and language.

Children lacking efficient communication are often divided into two groups. The first group, *presymbolic children*, do not use signs, words, or pictures for communication. They may not possess a recognizable communication system or may use gestures such as pointing or touching or moving objects. The second group is made up of *minimally symbolic* children, who use some visual, verbal, or tactile symbols alone or in combinations (Owens, 1991).

Persons who are deaf-blind are diverse in their communication abilities. Some students with deaf-blindness retain some residual vision and hearing and can use speech. Some are nonverbal and rely on touch and gestures; others combine the use of signs, speech, and gestures in a total communication approach. Many children find it very difficult to acquire the complex symbol system of language without enough sensory data to make language meaningful. They appear to have no awareness of linguistic symbols and may communicate only through body movements (Engleman, Griffin, Griffin, and Maddox, 1999).

Academic Achievement

The learning and educational attainments of children who are severely or multiply disabled depend upon a matrix of factors. Not the least of these are the quality of education, the age at which education begins, the age of onset of the conditions, the nature of the combination of disabilities, and the severity of each condition. Also important are factors such as the family's response to the child, the educational setting, the amount of integration with non-disabled peers, the related services available for both the child and the family, and the amount of acceptance by the community.

Some children who are multiply disabled achieve well in school. But many function at pre-academic levels. Because their perception of events is impaired, they find it hard to develop awareness, attention, anticipation, and purpose—all skills needed for efficient learning. Hence, the academic competencies of general education are not within the purview of most children with severe and profound disabilities. The needs of these students extend beyond the normal developmental curriculum.

Social and Emotional Development

From the very beginning of life, the onset of attachment behaviours and social interactions may be very delayed as a child's physical and behavioural deficits disrupt the natural interchange between caregiver and child that is essential to early interactions. In addition, the baby's first months may be dominated by periods of hospitalization, feeding problems, and an inability to maintain a wakeful state.

Young children may appear not to recognize other family members, or they may be obsessively engaged in such self-stimulating behaviours as light gazing or hand flapping. In older children, emotional difficulties may be manifested in any or all of the following personality traits: frequent panic reactions, hyperkinesis, autism, withdrawal, and frequent tantrums (Van Dijk, 1982).

Problem behaviours are the rule rather than the exception in this population. The self-stimulation discussed in Chapters 6 and 13 is ubiquitous. In many cases the cause of problem behaviours is unknown. Some behaviours seem related to the type of brain damage a child has sustained; in other cases, behaviours may reflect the intense frustration caused by a child's inability to communicate.

ASSESSMENT OF CHILDREN WHO HAVE SEVERE AND MULTIPLE DISABILITIES

Whether diagnosis is medical or psycho-educational, the assessment of children with severe or multiple disabilities taxes the ingenuity of clinicians. Because data generation is so difficult, a diverse range of measures are used. All attempt to assess the child's disabilities, as well as the impact of the combination of disabilities, the possible etiology, the prognosis, and the strengths a child possesses.

Assessment of Hearing

It is often difficult to distinguish whether children fail to respond to an auditory stimulus because they do not hear it or because they are simply inattentive. This is particularly true of children with multiple disabilities, who require a wide range of sophisticated techniques for the assessment of auditory status. For these children, audiological assessment is divided into two major methods—electrophysiological and behavioural.

As we explained in Chapter 9, *electrophysiological measures* include impedance audiometry (the drum and the middle ear) and electroencephalography-evoked response audiometry, the measurement of various evoked electrical potentials that are responses to auditory stimuli. *Behavioural testing* includes observations and play audiometry.

Assessment of Vision

Determining whether a child with multiple disabilities has usable vision employs a number of procedures, particularly when children have neurological impairments and seem unable to establish normal visual contacts. A child who does not respond to conventional testing may be a candidate for several physiological tests that are administered by qualified clinical or medical personnel. Diagnosticians use electrophysiological procedures, behavioural measures, and functional tests.

Electrodiagnostic procedures assess the electrical activity of the optic pathway and occipital cortex of the brain. The presence of electrical activity indicates that an active pathway exists. Behavioural measures include field tests that use gross objects or lights. The Bailey-Hall Cereal Test for visual acuity (Bailey and Hall, 1983) is a behavioural technique that uses picture cards including one of cereal; if the child selects the correct picture, he or she is rewarded with praise and a piece of cereal (Bailey and Hall, 1983). Functional tests assess the visual behaviour of an individual rather than just the physiological condition of the eyes. Assessed are the ability to track objects, use visual fields, develop eye–hand coordination, and perform other functions that reflect visual development.

Psycho-educational Assessment

With their obvious disabilities, most students with severe and multiple problems are not screened; assessment begins with diagnostic testing. Assessment is never a one-time affair; administration is on a regular basis, usually once or twice a year.

The psycho-educational assessment of children who are severely or multiply disabled has a number of separate but equally important goals, which include measurement of the overall level of intellectual function and exploration of the individual child's impairments and abilities. Assessment data are used to decide on the most appropriate educational placement and to formulate an individual educational plan. Specifically, assessment attempts to answer some critical questions:

- Is the child attentive to auditory language and symbolic code systems?
- Does the child respond to communication? This includes receptive language comprehension to determine if the child responds appropriately to gestures, words, and short and complex sentences, as well as expressive language and vocabulary to check whether the child uses gestures, noises, jargon, baby talk, and concrete or abstract words.
- How are the child's hands used? Are they limp, like wet sponges, or are they actively employed for exploration and manipulation?
- How does the child respond to training?
- Does the child refuse to learn because of poor motivation or is the material too complex and confusing?
- Does the child use vision and hearing fully?
- Does the child indulge in stereotypical behaviours? These may serve as indicators of ability. For example, light gazing or hand flapping in front of a light indicates that the child has some vision (Hammer, 1984).

As mentioned, the assessment of children who are severely or multiply disabled is an arduous and challenging task requiring skilled practitioners, input from care providers, and many hours of observation and testing. Even so, results are always tenuous not only because of a child's complex disabilities but also due to untrained personnel and a lack of appropriate tools. For example, in a comprehensive study of assessment practices of special education staff serving students with severe disabilities in five school districts (Sigafoos, Cole, and McQuarter, 1987), researchers reported that special educators lacked training in the assessment of students with severe disabilities, were limited by the unavailability of appropriate assessment tools, and were dependent on norm-referenced instruments.

We point out in Chapter 13 some of the child behaviours that make assessment so difficult. Similar concerns surround students with severe or multiple disabilities. These children may show limited or absent expressive and/or receptive language and limited hand use. Many children have severe cognitive delays. Children are likely to withdraw from social interaction and to have short attention spans and limited co-operation in testing situations. They may perform certain behaviours in one milieu but not during testing, and may perform tasks for a known person but not an unknown tester.

Diagnosticians need to first arrange the setting in order to enhance the assessment situation for both the child and the tester. Some environmental adaptations (which are also relevant to the children discussed in Chapters 11 through 13) are listed below.

- A natural environment is an advantage to children. Psychological and educational assessments of children with severe or multiple disabilities are best made in familiar surroundings using familiar tasks and materials.
- The foundation of an accurate and appropriate assessment is the establishment of rapport with the child and the family. Having parents present may add to a child's feeling of security. Parents should also be involved during the assessment process as sources of information.
- Interdisciplinary assessments should be conducted. The size and nature of the team involved will vary according to the child's disabilities.
- No single assessment tool can meet all the needs of a population as diverse as that of children with severe or multiple disabilities. Specific instruments should vary according to the needs of the individual and to the areas being assessed. It is now common practice to use a functional approach that assists in determining the specific reinforcers of a particular behaviour and then in designing appropriate interventions. Included are a combination of direct observation; informant interviews; adaptive behaviour scales; measures of prelinguistic communication behaviour and alternate methods of communication; developmental scales; and observational checklists. Formal intelligence tests may also be administered.

arena testing

Within the assessment paradigm, the collection of observational data is a first step. Direct observation techniques permit assessment of children's behaviour and achievements in their normal daily routine. **Arena testing** can be used. This is an observational assessment approach in which people from several disciplines focus on their particular domains, such as motor skills or language, within the context of play.

A number of questionnaires and interview schedules have been constructed for use with parents, teachers, and other key informants who can provide important information about aspects of a child's progress. Parent interviews are strong indicators of a child's level of skills and awareness.

Language and communication assessment is critical. Many children are either prelinguistic or minimally linguistic. They meet problems in responding to interactions, in imitating, and in using basic communication.

Informal language assessment largely focuses on measures of prelinguistic communication behaviour. It attempts to determine a child's understanding of sounds and gestures, and includes observation of the child's response to environmental sounds, response to speech sounds, and response to gestures, names, and requests. Assessment also examines communication use—how a child gains the attention of others; how he or she initiates play with caregivers and peers; whether the child anticipates and takes turns; and how the child interacts in routine communication events. Important to note are the settings, people, and purposes for communication. These are assessed by looking at the reasons for the child to communicate, the objects and activities that the child prefers, and when and with whom the most appropriate interactions occur.

Educational assessment focuses on functional areas of competence in the domains of communication, social behaviour, self-help, and independence skills. For some children, educational assessment also measures areas of academic competence, such as reading, writing, and mathematics.

Psychometric tests are not suitable for a large proportion of children who are severely multiply disabled. If they are used, a number of adaptations to standard routines may need to be considered, as discussed in Chapter 12. Many of the tasks that are used in tests must be eliminated because of motor difficulties, sensory impairments, and special problems present in the children being assessed.

To assess mental ability, diagnosticians usually select scales of infant development because the sensorimotor behaviours tapped are often in the repertoires of these children. Although infant scales are known to be poor predictors of later development in non-disabled children, these measures with children who are severely disabled give IQs that have proven to be good predictors of later development (Fewell and Cone, 1983). Perhaps the most widely used test of cognition for children functioning in the sensorimotor period is the Ugiris and Hunt Scale of Infant Psychological Development or its adaptations (Dunst, 1980).

INTERVENTION WITH CHILDREN WHO HAVE SEVERE AND MULTIPLE DISABILITIES

In the past, persons with severe and multiple disabilities were excluded from educational services. Over the last forty years, education and treatment for this population has undergone considerable revision and expansion.

Treatment generally hinges on two major factors—etiology and the specific combination of disabilities. Although etiology is of less overall significance for educators, critical program modifications must be made for such secondary spin-offs as sensory problems and the psychological adjustments precipitated by Usher's syndrome.

Medical Intervention

A medical examination, a routine part of the diagnostic process, is undertaken with the child who is severely or multiply disabled as early as possible. Procedures are used to determine the exact nature and sometimes the underlying causes of the multiple disabilities. These include a careful medical history; laboratory tests to detect metabolic disorders; cytogenetic studies to identify possible causes; clinical neurophysiological investigation through electroencephalogram (EEG) tests of auditory and visual potential and electromyograms to test nerve conduction; and neuroradiology, which involves skull x-rays, echoencephalography, radio-isotope brain scans, and PET and CAT scans that can pinpoint the presence of brain lesions (Rogow, 1987).

Therapy

Physical and occupational therapists can help children to develop hand skills, body coordination, and other physical skills, and aid in gross motor development, muscle relaxation, and fine motor control (see Chapter 12). Speech and language therapy assists a child's development of speech and language. This form of therapy may also be used with children who have difficulty in controlling the fine motor muscles needed for eating. Therapists may also develop appropriate augmentative communication, discussed below, for children who cannot talk.

Technical Aids

Improved equipment and adaptive devices have been developed to enrich education and improve the quality of life for individuals of all ages. (See Chapter 13.)

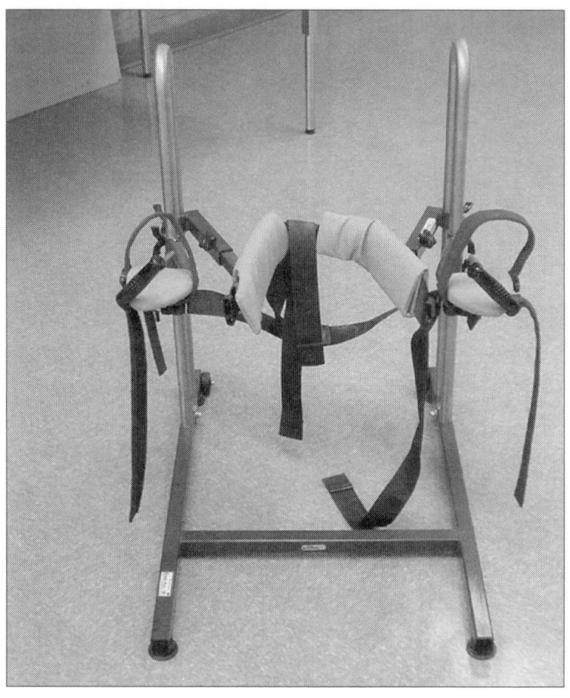

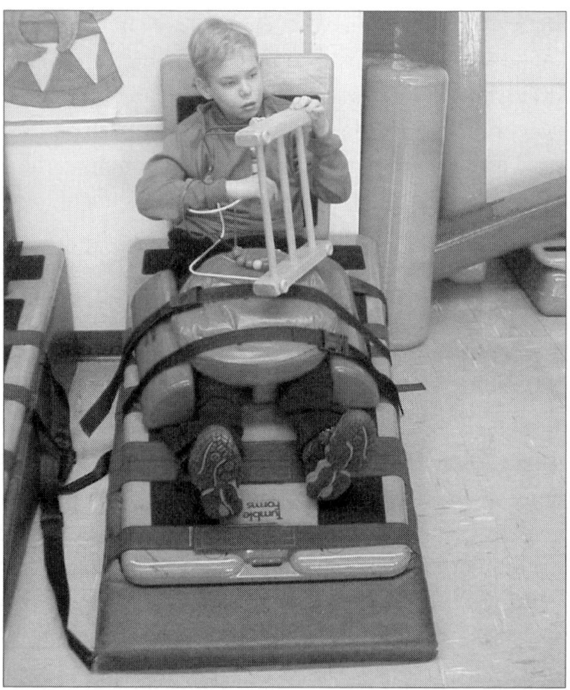

Standing frame (top left).
Longsit-supplemental (top right).
Wheelchair (right).

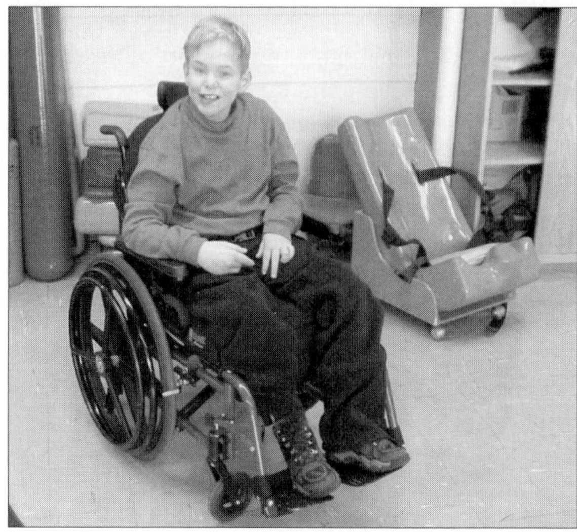

Educational Intervention

Children who are severely or multiply disabled take education beyond its traditional boundaries. These children may show different learning characteristics and developmental patterns. The instructional process may be hindered by maladaptive behaviour, the need to adapt technology and materials, and the difficulty in identifying appropriate reinforcers (Sisson, Van Hasselt, and Hersen, 1987).

Children's academic and social development is predicated on many factors. They need a responsive environment capable of providing appropriate stimulation and opportunities for interaction. Further needs include sensory stimulation; well-planned, consistent habilitative and educational programs; and multiple treatment modalities.

Many new successful education strategies have emerged in the field recently. Peters Goessling (2000) points to concepts of generalization, community-referenced instruction, social skills training, and supported employment.

Service Delivery Models

Children who are severely or multiply disabled need an extensive network of services to enable them to thrive and learn. The difficulties and potentialities resulting from each unique disability or combination of disabilities represent the decision point in placement and programming, so we find that students with multiple disabilities are educated in a variety of settings.

Some students may learn in clinics, special schools, residential placements, special classes, or general classrooms. With the current stress on inclusion, there has been a movement away from the traditional residential school model. Policy in the United States is instructive in this regard. American courts have decided that residential programming is necessary when more than six hours of instruction are required to meet the child's educational needs; when the severity of the child's language deficiency precludes meaningful benefit from peer group learning and interaction with non-disabled peers in a mainstream setting; or when social and emotional adjustment are poor in the normal setting.

Some children with mild physical or sensory impairments can learn well in the regular classroom, provided they receive additional support. These children are able to participate in academic programs, and benefit from interaction with non-disabled peers. In addition to regular instruction, they may need the services of speech therapists, physical therapists, audiologists, mobility and orientation specialists, and specialist teachers of the hearing or visually impaired.

On the other hand, including children with more severe disabilities in general classrooms continues to be controversial. It is difficult to find a school district where families and educators totally agree on the best way to educate these students (see Peters Goessling, 2000).

Those who actively promote less restrictive environments justify their position with arguments based on the potential social and emotional benefits. The defensible reasons for placing children with severe and multiple disabilities in regular classrooms are, they say, access to social relationships with peers and access to normalized learning environments. Students for whom traditional task requirements are not relevant can still learn social skills and feel that they are full class members, not inferior to others. The educational agenda is to promote students' freedom and responsibility to create an autonomous self, rather than to prepare students to perform in employment and other settings (see Reid, Robinson, and Bursen, 1995).

An opposing side warns that educators must guard against imprudent general education placement. Successful inclusive programs are those in which outcomes of both academic and social participation in a school are accomplished (Welch and Goetz, 1998).

Many students who are severely or multiply disabled require the expertise of specially trained staff, more intensive staffing allocations, community referenced curricula, and/or prosthetic techniques. These and other factors make it difficult to accommodate the needs of children who are deaf-blind, for example (Malloy, 1997). Children's educational rights must be at the forefront; it is unacceptable to place a child in a class solely for social skills and ignore the child's total functioning and future needs and the need for alternative and specialized curricula and experiences.

Further, inclusion means that students are full members of a class. However, a study of the instructional contexts of students with severe disabilities (Logan and Malone, 1998) found that although there were some similarities in instructional contexts different contexts existed for students with severe disabilities when compared with those without disabilities in the general education classroom. Children with severe disabilities had significantly more one to one, non-verbal instruction, instruction from special education staff and general education peers, and instructional in functional activities. There were fewer intervals of academic activity, whole class instruction, instruction by the general classroom teacher, and independent seat work. The instructional contexts were not a part of the general education classroom but provided by special education personnel.

Educators themselves are often in disagreement about whether inclusion is appropriate for students with significant disabilities. The attitudes of teachers toward particular students seems to be more important than the general attitude toward inclusion, which makes the nature and degree of a child's disability germane to issues of placement and curriculum. Teachers regard students with disabilities in the context of procedural classroom concerns and, overall, teacher willingness to teach students with disabilities, consistent with their support for inclusion, appears to co-vary with the severity of the disability and the amount of additional teacher responsibility required (Scruggs and Mastropieri, 1996). Generally, the more severe the disability, the more negative the attitudes teachers have toward inclusion (Wisniewski and Alper, 1994).

Readers are urged to revisit the Debate in Chapter 13 on the pros and cautions of inclusion for students with significant disabilities.

Educational Approaches

The learning characteristics and needs of children who are severely or multiply disabled vary widely. In general, these students require extensive ongoing support in more than one major area (mobility, communication, self-care, learning) in order to participate in school and community.

The following components are, however, generic to a comprehensive system of education:

- Early and continuous intervention. Early intervention can ameliorate at least some of the consequences of sensory deprivation and emotional withdrawal. (See Chapter 15.)

- Transdisciplinary models (team approaches) that rest on consultation and collaboration.
- Appropriate curricula. Children require both educational and psychosocial development founded on a carefully task-analyzed individual education plan. The more disabled the child, the more detailed and precise the task analysis and the goals and objectives need to be. Each child's educational plan (which will probably span five years) should include ongoing assessment of the child's progress and a detailed evaluation of the educational program. Curriculum materials should then be developed to meet the individualized educational goals of each child.
- Functional skills, those skills that are useful to a student in many current and future environments.
- Systematic instructional procedures. As students who are severely or multiply disabled miss so much incidental learning, they must be helped to develop a foundation for later and more complex learning.
- Stress on introducing or enhancing communication.
- Critical program modifications must be made because children suffer from combinations of conditions that interact in such a way as to depress or block the emergence of normal patterns of interaction with the environment.
- Support services. These include the provision of medical and therapeutic services to individual children. Associated professionals may also provide specific training and instruction to parents.

Team Approaches

The training and education of children with severe or multiple disabilities cannot rely on one person. Different disciplines bring unique skills and knowledge to intervention, and the nature of the child necessitates a partial blending of roles, skills, and knowledge across disciplines. When professionals in diverse roles function co-operatively to help students achieve their goals, this may be framed in the context of a *transdisciplinary model.*

transdisciplinary model

A **transdisciplinary model** is a team approach in which it is assured that the team members will perform the various services together. This means that the expertise of different types of agencies serving children with disabilities can be shared so that services are enriched, expanded, and made more comprehensive. A team approach enables everyone involved to see the child as a total being rather than concentrating on one aspect of that child's development. On a team, roles and expectations are shared by more than one member and experts on the team train other members (see Landerholm, 1990).

Teamwork demands *collaboration,* which is a generic term used to describe a style of interacting in which persons with diverse expertise voluntarily agree to work together to generate creative solutions to mutually defined problems (Idol, Paolucci-Whitcomb, and Nevin, 1986). In collaboration, the ownership of a problem is always shared and the consulting relationship is characterized by a sense of parity demonstrated through two-way communication and the sharing of knowledge and skills. The key hypothesis behind the process is that the group, functioning together, is greater than the sum of its individual parts.

Typically, a team is composed of the family and professionals from a variety of disciplines who collaborate in assessment and program planning. One individual, in consultation with other team members, works to carry out the individual program so that the case manager is both primary provider and service coordinator. Generally, in school settings, the teacher assumes the role of service provider (Orelove and Sobsey, 1987).

Certain attributes seem important to efficient team functioning:

- Each team must have a leader who may involve himself or herself in specific tasks related to team functioning.
- The size of the team will vary according to the child's disabilities.
- While the composition of a team will differ from case to case, certain core people are usually involved. These include teachers, therapists, aides, and other paraprofessionals such as an audiologist. Family members should be encouraged to join the team; not only do they have the right to be included, but they are the people most familiar with the child.
- Each team member has a role and each role has a set of skills and certain expectations associated with it.
- Effective teams develop over time and they need nurturance. When the membership of the team changes frequently, implementation and maintenance of child and family goals are jeopardized.
- The way people respond to others' communication directly determines the extent to which people on the team can continue the interchanges and initiate further dialogue. Personal characteristics that can assist in developing good communication and collaboration on the team include being empathetic and open, being able to establish good rapport, respecting different points of view, and being positive and enthusiastic (West and Cannon, 1987).

Curricula

Curricula designed for children who are multiply disabled must reflect all areas of development. Educational needs include language development, visual and auditory training, mobility training, and self-care skills. Psychosocial needs include adaptive behaviour, group activities, life skills, and a range of socialization experiences (Hammer, 1984). For children who are deaf-blind, additional stress must be placed on visual stimulation and visual perception skills as a basis for cognitive and academic tasks.

For many children with severe or multiple disabilities, training emphasizes early developmental skills usually thought of as too routine or too basic to be part of a regular instructional program. Most curricula for children with severe disorders have tended to adhere to a biological-developmental or cognitive-developmental approach. That is, developmental milestones are emphasized and skills must be developed in a specific hierarchical order regardless of the ages of the children. The developmental order of skills corresponds to what has been observed in younger children without disabilities.

While popular, there are problems associated with an approach based on the attainment of developmental milestones. For one thing, the sequences of behaviour typical for non-disabled students may not be relevant for a child with severe problems because such children may not develop or acquire skills in a normal sequence. When a pathology of the central nervous system exists, or when there are severe sensory losses, the organization of behaviour is disturbed and a child's early development is often uneven. Children with severe or multiple disabilities may learn in a different sequence and the relationship between skills may be different (Snell, 1987). For example, a child with multiple disabilities may walk at a relatively early age, but be severely delayed in the acquisition of language.

A number of commercial programs have been developed for youngsters who are deaf-blind; for example, the Assessment-Intervention Model for Deaf-Blind Students (AIM) (Schein, Kates, Wolf, and Theil, 1983) is a curriculum consisting of specific self-care and independence skills: drinking and pouring; dressing and undressing; using the toilet; personal care; kitchen preparation and cleanup; and housekeeping. It provides very low starting points and tiny steps in the sequence of reaching behavioural objectives.

Functional Skills

Apart from the uneven development seen in students with severe or multiple disabilities, a curriculum based on developmental sequences is likely to have little impact upon the ultimate attainment of self-sufficiency. The skills taught are not functional enough.

functional skills

Functional skills are those that help children to get along in their current and future environments, and are skills such that have a high probability of being required at home, in school, at work, or in the community, and that will increase self-sufficiency in those environments.

Self-help skills are functional. They include the ability to care for oneself, which is fundamental in achieving independence and self-sufficiency. The collected nouns for self-help skills are divided into those related to eating, dressing, bathing, grooming, and toileting.

Functional skills are displayed throughout a lifetime and tend to be performed in progressively more complex and varied forms as children grow. Together with the self-help skills of dressing, eating, and toileting, children need skills to participate in routine home and community activities such as playing with siblings, helping with simple chores, and eating at a fast-food restaurant. More advanced skills include functional math, such as telling the time, calendar use, and vending machine use; literacy skills that include reading maps, newspapers, and menus; mobility skills such as using public transportation or lockers; and other basic life skills such as personal hygiene and nutrition and cooking. Personal and social skills include consideration for others, common courtesy, obedience, and self-judgment.

Within a functional approach, targets for instruction are selected by analyzing the child's environment. Teachers identify specific skills to immediately improve the child's ability to interact with the environment and to increase the probability that the child will perform functionally critical behaviours for success and survival in future environments. Important skills are then broken down into small, building steps in a task analysis. Skills are taught for generalization as well as for functional usefulness.

Training is undertaken in such skills as independent eating, dressing, toileting, washing, combing hair, brushing teeth, and using a handkerchief. Students also learn simple homemaking skills, such as dusting, sweeping, setting and clearing a table, washing and drying dishes, washing and ironing clothes, sewing, using simple tools, and using the telephone. They are taught safety rules and how to use public transportation.

Mealtime is ideal for such instruction because it naturally occurs on a consistent, daily basis in school, at home, and in community environments. Instruction centres on providing the student with structured opportunities for selecting foods by offering a series of choices among familiar, meaningful, and disparate options (Gothelf, Crimmins, Mercer, and Finocchiaro, 1994).

The skills presented must be generalizable, developmentally appropriate, and age appropriate. Teaching a child to grasp a toy may, for example, generalize to grasping a hairbrush or a toothbrush, both necessary self-help skills. Sorting shapes to corresponding pictures of shapes is not a skill that a child is likely to use during daily activities, whereas the child is likely to use the skill of matching various shaped lids to corresponding containers. While both skills involve matching, recognizing, and sorting shapes, the use of functional objects such as containers and lids enables the child to learn a necessary skill that will foster independence in real-life situations (Notari-Syverson and Shuster, 1995). Similarly, placing pegs in a board may aid in fine motor development, but it is not really related to future needs. On the other hand, putting coins in a vending machine will develop the same motor areas and also provide a living skill. Or, if the objective is to teach students to operate a musical device during their leisure time, it is more functional and age appropriate for a fifteen-year-old to use a CD player than a gaily coloured Fisher-Price music box.

Can functional skills be taught in general classrooms or do they require special placements? Writers assert that in general classrooms, curricular items of practical utility such as daily life and functional skills need not be eliminated. Some skills can be taught incidentally, and students who require opportunities to learn practical living, working, and social skills can be provided guidance and opportunities to do so at natural times throughout the day. Susan Stainback and colleagues suggest that lunch and snack times and home economics can provide opportunities to learn about food preparation and eating and dining skills; dressing and grooming skills are learned when students do this before and after school or for gym class; and bus riding skills can be taught when students need to travel back and forth to school. Functional and vocational skills can be learned at natural times such as in after-school jobs and on weekend shopping trips with family and friends and in integrated, general education work-study programs, home economics, and other such classes (Stainback, Stainback, and Stefanich, 1996).

Communication Training

Of all the needs of children with severe or multiple disabilities, the acquisition of communication skills is one of the greatest. Training may take place in one-to-one, highly structured environments, but more generally in natural contexts such as the classroom.

Because language is the product of all aspects of development—physical, sensory, social, and neurological—the development of communication skills is a simultaneous activity. The major goal of language intervention is the initiation of effective communication. Two general strategies are used in communication training programs for presymbolic and minimally symbolic children, often in tandem. These are presymbolic training and communication-first approaches (Owens, 1991).

Presymbolic training is based on the belief that there are cognitive prerequisites for language acquisition. Teaching programs begin with assessment. Subsequent training is related to the cognitive, perceptual, social and/or communication targets identified as significant in the assessment process. Skills are usually those characteristic of the sensorimotor stage of development. Training begins with the development of basic sensorimotor skills such as object permanence, causality, means–end behaviour, spatial relationships, schemas for relating to objects, and imitation.

A *communication-first* approach is a functional approach to language that stresses nurturant and naturalistic language. Communication-first approaches place the initial emphasis on the establishment of a communication system that can later be expanded to symbol use. Elaborated forms of communication are built on simpler forms. The progression of communication moves from signals (cries, for example), to the use of sign (systematic, consistent gesturing to indicate wants), to the use of increasingly complex linguistic forms, to the metalinguistic uses of language. The major skills taught are initial communication; turn-taking skills; generalized imitation skills; lexical growth and establishment of a basic vocabulary; early symbol communication rules; and participation in interactions that occur outside the training context (see Owens, 1991).

Not all children will acquire speech, especially those beginning at prelinguistic levels. They may need an alternative communication system, referred to as a **communication mode**—"the form in which the content of a message is expressed" (Sailor, Guess, Goetz, Schuler, Utley, and Baldwin, 1980, p. 72).

communication mode

The selection of a communication mode and the strategies for teaching its use should be an interdisciplinary task. The choice of an adjunct to communication is ideally made in conjunction with family and therapists. Multiple factors must be considered: long-term linguistic needs; people with whom the child needs to communicate; and the most appropriate mode based on a child's mental ability, motivation, visual perception, motor control, and behavioural problems.

For students who are deaf-blind, repeated reports from parents, professionals, and people who are deaf-blind themselves indicate the fundamental need for boosting communication skills for participation in normal daily life activities (see Engleman et al., 1999). Students who are deaf-blind require very specialized techniques to compensate for the dual disabilities in the distance senses. Speech is the first option; all children who are capable of speech should undergo intensive speech training. Other children need training in the use of a specific communication system. Whatever the mode selected, it must be familiar to all those working with the child and to the parents.

Alternative Methods of Communication

Relatedness to others in the environment depends on some basic communication. When speech is delayed, or when there is reason to think that it may be delayed or not develop at all (for example, when the child has multiple disabilities including a significant hearing loss), alternative means of communication, referred to *augmentative communication*, are considered.

In general, anything that augments speech or accomplishes communication function is termed augmentative communication. More specifically, **augmentative communication** refers to a general group of procedures designed to support, enhance, or augment the communication of non-speaking individuals or utilize and supplement whatever vocal skills an individual possesses. The various procedures that make up augmentative communication are used chiefly by individuals whose speech communication is impaired by hearing impairments; individuals with severe language deficits; individuals with severe neuromuscular or physical disabilities; and those with severe and multiple disabilities.

augmentative communication

Augmentative communication is used to receive and transmit messages. There are two main types of augmentation: unaided and aided approaches. *Unaided approaches* rely on gestural communication; *aided approaches* depend on a device of some kind such as communication boards, mechanical or electrical devices, and computers. Table 14-1 outlines some alternative methods of communication.

Unaided Approaches

The major types of unaided approaches in augmentative communication are:

- Signal communication, which includes the use of a simple yes/no system and audio-signalling. Yes and no signals may be indicated by movements of head, hands, face, or

Table 14-1 Alternative methods of augmentative communication

Signal/code	Symbol	Manual
Yes/no	Rebus systems	Idiosyncratic gesturing
Audio-signalling	Blissymbolics	Amerind
Gesturing	Pictorial Ideographic Communication (PIC)	American Sign Language (ASL)
Morse code		School-based manual systems

eye. A portable audio-oscillator that emits a loud tone has been used to teach four simple signals (need, help, yes, no).

- Code communication, which uses Morse code as a method of communication.
- Natural gestures are simple movements of one or both hands used to convey meaning to the child. For example, the word *eat* is indicated by tapping the lips with the fingertips of one hand. Although natural gestures are often used with children who are deaf-blind, they may also be part of communication training for children with severe or multiple disabilities who are not hearing impaired. Natural gestures vary from child to child. If a child consistently points to the mouth to indicate hunger, then everyone working with that child should use the same gesture.
- Tactile sign language is used with students who are deaf-blind. In this, the learner's hands are placed on top of the communicator's hands so a gesture, sign, or finger spelling is felt.
- The Tadoma (vibration) method is also used with persons who are deaf-blind. The student places a thumb on the speaker's lips, an index finger on the speaker's jaw, and three fingers on the speaker's neck. This allows the learner to manually perceive the vibrations of the speaker's voice, the tension of the speaker's face, and the shape of the speaker's lips.
- Sign language is typically associated with deaf people; however, studies suggest that manual communication may be beneficial to a much larger population in improving communication skills. Its use may potentially offer unlimited opportunities for language development and may facilitate the onset and development of spoken language in prelinguistic children (Kouri, 1989).
- Amerind is a simpler system and more suitable for low-functioning individuals for whom sign language may prove too difficult. Amerind was adapted by Madge Skelly (1979), a speech and language pathologist and full-blooded Indian, from the system she learned from her grandfather. Amerind is built on the hand signals used by Native Americans and contains about 250 hand signals that may be arranged in any combination.

Aided Approaches

Augmentative devices are operated by an individual to communicate basic needs. They can be easily activated by movement of the head or hand, or even by an eye blink. The Vocaid is an example of an augmentative device suitable for functional needs, such as a call for assistance. Some augmentative devices make use of speech synthesis. Children with good intellectual ability might use a system where the child spells a message on a grid using row-column scanning with an electronic device. Other high-technology aids sometimes include the use of pre-recorded messages, such as greetings or farewells, that users can select by striking a predetermined key.

Blissymbolics has been successful with children with severe motor disabilities. Charles Bliss, a refugee from Hitler's concentration camps, went to Shanghai where he learned the Chinese writing system, in which each symbol stands for an idea rather than a sound. Based on this, Bliss developed an ideographic universal writing system. It was not popular until discovered by Shirley McNaughton at the Ontario Crippled Children's Centre in Toronto.

Today Blissymbolics is a complete language system. Even though it can be used for general conversation, the symbols are simple enough to be learned by children too young to read alphabetic writing. Bliss is used by 25 000 people in Canada, of whom one-quarter have cerebral palsy (Reich, 1986). Depending on a child's abilities, vocabularies of up to 400 terms may be learned. Figure 14-1 shows examples of Bliss symbols.

Pictorial systems were designed to enhance oral communication among intellectually impaired non-verbal and limited-verbal individuals. They use pictures rather than the styl-

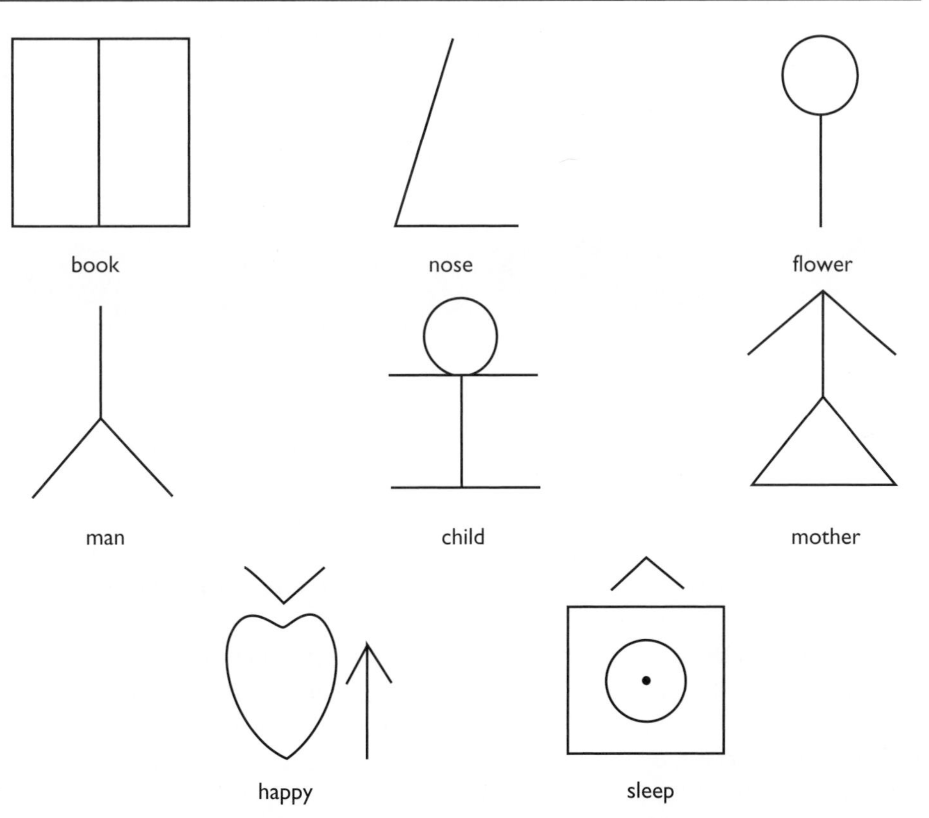

Figure 14-1
Bliss symbols

ized symbols of Blissymbolics. For example, Pictorial Ideographic Communication (PIC) is presented on a communication board and consists of pictures and symbols that represent objects and actions.

Studies have compared Blissymbolics and picture symbols (Mezriko, 1987). They report that non-disabled preschoolers find picture symbols to be more transparent and more learnable than Blissymbolics.

Both Blissymbolics and other picture systems are displayed on communication boards. Some current boards are sophisticated; they may have voice outputs that provide prerecorded or programmed speech in the form of words, phrases, or sentences.

Some children need an even simpler method. Picture communication boards have clear pictures or photographs depicting basic needs and activities such as an item of food, a cup, a toilet or pot, a bed, and a toy. The child communicates by pointing to the appropriate pictures.

Orientation and Mobility Training

Orientation and mobility training teaches individuals who have multiple disabilities that include blindness a basic knowledge of the environment and how to find their way to specific locations, such as the schoolroom or the workshop. The goals of orientation and mobility training are the same as for other children who are visually impaired, but some of the teaching techniques may differ. Children who are multiply disabled often need alternative methods that provide safety and information and yet are within their capabilities. Some specialists introduce cane travel before the child is technically ready in the hope of developing greater confidence. This has proved very successful with low-functioning blind children.

Case Study

Juanita (continued)

Juanita is now nine years old. She still spends part of her time learning specific skills in the special class, but she is also comfortable and welcome in the regular classroom and has a small group of friends who share with her both in and out of school.

Juanita's regular classroom teacher looked at both formal and informal ways to provide multiple interactions daily in the classroom. She helped to develop informal peer supports and friendships for Juanita by fostering respect for individual differences and by providing a positive model. She stressed proximity through peer tutoring, co-operative learning, buddy systems, and involvement in extra-curricular activities. Juanita's modified program kept her with the class but at her own developmental level. An extract from her IEP is shown below.

In one lesson, for example, the teacher read a book to the class. Juanita's objective was to sit on the floor in an assigned spot and direct her attention to the teacher. The second part of the lesson was to colour a picture from the story. The other children chose their colours, but a peer handed

Juanita a marker and instructed her where to colour. As the other children then wrote a story about their pictures, they read them aloud to Juanita and, using signs and natural gestures, prompted her to point to the pictures.

EXTRACT FROM JUANITA'S IEP

Present Levels of Functioning

Deaf, visually impaired, low cognitive functioning. Pre- to minimally linguistic. No intelligible speech and a few gestures for wants. Very interested in other children in the class.

Placement

Special class and general classroom part-time with paraprofessional assistance.

Current Progress

Growing awareness of classmates. Will wave with assistance. Interest in signing as used by other class members.

Strategies for Inclusion

Paraprofessional; simple signs used by all in environment; modified program stressing communication and life skills; out-of-class daily therapy.

Personnel

Classroom teacher, paraprofessional, therapist.

Goals and Objectives

- Co-operating with others
- Following classroom directions
- Adhering to the rules and routines of the classroom
- Waving on command
- Using basic sign communication
- Developing life skills (special class)

Program Modifications

Placing a child with a severe or multiple disability in an inclusive setting means a stress on natural supports; that is, supports in the environment the person would have access to if he or she did not have a disability (home, neighbourhood, local school, regular classroom, job site) and relying on persons in the environment (family members, classmates, general education teachers). For example, classmates can help students to feel welcome, accepted, and secure.

A school may elect one person, often a special education teacher, to act as a support facilitator. This person not only works with the severely disabled students but helps regular classroom teachers adapt instruction and aids in facilitating peer acceptance (see Stainback and Stainback, 1988). Programs and models such as the Circle of Friends (Snow and Forest, 1987) and the McGill Action Planning Systems (MAPS) (Forest and Lusthaus, 1989) foster positive relationships and support networks to include individuals with severe disabilities in school and community life.

SUMMARY

1. A number of useful definitions of severe or multiple disabilities have evolved. Some attempt to offer comprehensive generic descriptions; others describe the parameters of types of disabling conditions. More specific definitions have developed for particular combinations of disabling conditions.
2. In discussing children with severe or multiple impairments, it must be remembered that conditions are not additive. Each multiple disability is an entirely new category of ex-

Historical Notes

History tells us very little about persons with multiple disabilities. Deaf-blindness is the most known. In the middle of the 18th century, the Scots philosopher Dugald Stewart told of a deaf-blind lad named James Mitchell who responded to educational intervention. In Paris in the 1760s the Abbé de l'Épée experimented with a system of raised-print blocks to use with individuals who were deaf-blind. In 1789 in Paris Victorine Morriseau was the first deaf-blind woman to receive education (Collins, 1995).

In 1837 Laura Bridgman was admitted to the Perkins Institution for the Blind in Boston, where Samuel Gridley Howe undertook her education. Laura had lost her sight, hearing, taste, and smell to scarlet fever at the age of two. Howe taught her the manual alphabet and eventually Laura read embossed books, did simple arithmetic, and mastered needlework and other kinds of handicrafts. Howe's extensive reports of Laura Bridgman's education and development left an outstanding legacy to the entire field of special education, and to teachers of the deaf-blind in particular (Hallahan and Kauffman, 1991). His son-in-law, Michael Aganos, used Howe's directives when Helen Keller became a pupil at the Perkins Institution (Winzer, 1993).

Between 1900 and 1950, only a few programs opened. Most children with multiple disabilities were excluded from the residential schools because they had conditions that cut across several categories of impairment and they tended to fall between the cracks. Public schools did not take the responsibility for providing education on the assumption that these people were uneducable, that they could not learn.

The worldwide rubella epidemic between 1962 and 1964 left thousands upon thousands of children multiply disabled. While the needs of huge numbers meant that many programs were established, the historical legacy of special education means that students with intense needs were chiefly served in some form of special services. Today, most parents, teachers, and school administrators agree that the days of total segregation and institutionalization are long over. However, the manner in which the inclusion of students with severe or multiple disabilities can be most effectively attained has still not been worked out in practice.

ceptionality. Each child, therefore, must be considered individually to an even greater degree than for children with single disabilities. The special and diverse needs caused by the unique combinations of conditions challenge all those charged with training and educating severely or multiply disabled children.

3. The assessment of children who are severely or multiply disabled is difficult for even the most experienced clinicians. Because the value of IQ scores for diagnosis is relatively limited for this population, and no one measure or battery of measures is suitable for all, a range of assessment measures must be employed. Functional assessment and analysis is key. Assessment serves to generate data for program and placement decisions.
4. The needs of these children are varied and complex; interventions involve a wide range of techniques and personnel.
5. Education may take place in residential schools, special classes, clinics, or through school programs in hospitals. Many people promote the full inclusion of children with severe and

multiple disabilities. But the increasing availability and growing support for placement in general education classes has not stilled the disagreement within the field as to whether students with intensive educational needs belong in general-education classrooms. Inclusion is a choice for students with severe or multiple disabilities but it is not always the first choice of teachers and parents.

6. A variety of services are needed to support the students in general settings. Children with severe or multiple disabilities require the services of physical, occupational, and speech and language therapists. For the child who is deaf-blind, there may be an interpreter-tutor who acts as interpreter and facilitator. He or she needs skills in orientation and mobility, communication, and sign language if necessary.
7. When teaching students with severe or multiple disabilities, a good approach is to focus on functional skills. A functional approach ensures that the selection of objectives is based on their future usefulness.
8. There are cognitive prerequisites for language acquisition. Some researchers suggest organizing a teaching program around the initial assessment of and subsequent training in cognitive skills such as object permanence, classification, imitation, and representational play with objects. Others stress a communication-first approach.
9. In the education of children who are deaf-blind, no aspect of language development can be ignored. A primary goal is to teach students to communicate in the easiest possible way. Many children who are deaf-blind have learned to perceive speech through the Tadoma (vibration) method, where the hand of the listener is placed on the face and neck of the speaker to monitor the actions of speech.
10. Children who are unable to acquire oral language may learn other communication methods. Several systems of augmentative communication may be used in place of speech.

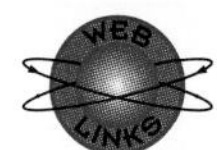

WEBLINKS

Home of Blissymbolics **www.symbols.net/bhome/1blisshome.htm**

Laurence-Moon-Bardet-Biedl Syndrome
www.avalon.nf.ca/~merbland/LMBB/home.html

Meningitis Research Foundation **www.meningitis.org**

Usher's Syndrome **deafed.educ.kent.edu/laurie.htm**

In the Classroom

As we have stressed, low-incidence conditions, especially those that involve multiple disabilities, are often unique. Therefore, generic teaching strategies are less applicable than in the case of students with high-incidence conditions.

Behavioural manifestations, needs	**Tips**
Needs adaptive equipment for learning, mobility, daily life.	• Use prosthetic aids to enhance active involvement. • Become familiar with any special equipment that a student uses in the classroom, such as wheelchairs and other mobility devices, visual and travel aids, amplification systems, catheterization equipment, ventilators, and so on. • Use magnetized rulers and instruments on the equipment chair table. • Use pencil holders; to assist children who have motor problems with grip, use a pencil grip made of a piece of clay or foam material wrapped around the pencil or pen. • Use large chunks of sponge for painting. • Use marking pens for free flow. • Anchor paper by taping it to the table or easel. • Make paintbrushes out of roll-on deodorant bottles by removing the tops, filling the bottle with tempera paint, and snapping the top back in place.
Needs special handling	• Learn about handling—how the child is picked up, carried, held, and assisted. • Do not pull the child by the arms; lift the child under the arms. • When helping a child dress, put clothes on the more affected side first. • To straighten a limb, push it out at shoulder and elbow or hip and knee first. • Don't try to pull a hand or foot through clothing—the limb will only bend tighter.
Needs regular positioning	• Be constantly aware of positioning and know how to position children in wheelchairs. This refers to providing support for the child's body, changing the child's sitting position in the chair, and arranging instructional or play materials in certain ways. • Constantly check on sitting position; reposition the child at least every half hour. • Tell the child what you are going to do at all times, whether in positioning or moving.

	• When moving the child in a wheelchair, always ensure that the child's feet are on the footrest. • Wear rubber-soled shoes. • Do not place the wheelchair too close to heaters.
Needs special seating	• Modify classroom routines and physical environment to keep the student situated near peers in similar seating. • At a desk, make sure that the child's heels touch the floor, knees are bent, and back is supported. • Use an abduction block; don't let feet dangle.
Special mobility needs	• Many children have difficulty moving from one place to another in the school. Within the entire school, attention must be paid to modifications such as widened doorways.
Requires a teacher knowledge base	• Learn as much as you can about the condition, including the etiology, developmental consequences, and the prognosis. Establish a building team, a kind of SWAT team of medical conditions to address the complex health needs. • Be aware of the treatment procedures being used, the potential side effects of certain medical treatments on appearance and behaviour, and the approximate schedule of upcoming treatments. • Keep an emergency protocol. • Check your school district's procedures for drug administration. • List and display special needs for substitute teachers.
Asthmatic	• Guard against common asthma triggers. These include cold air; chalk dust; dust in the classroom or gymnasium; photocopy toner fumes; science class chemicals; perfumes, cosmetics, and hairspray; cleaning fluids; paint fumes; and viral infections such as colds. • If a child has an asthma attack, remove the child from the trigger area if it is known. • Try to relax the child by sitting with him or her while you model deep breathing exercises. Then have the child use the inhaler. If the child is not responding to medication, seek medical advice immediately.
Diabetes	• Be aware of the child's food regimen and insulin schedule. • Always allow bathroom or water breaks.
Hygienically safe learning environment	• Especially if a child has AIDS, immediately clean up blood and bodily fluids. • Wear latex gloves. • Use paper towels to clean up and rinse spill area. Disinfect spill area with bleach solution (1/4 cup regular household bleach to one gallon of water).

	• Wash hands well and carefully.
Needs greater peer acceptance	• One way to increase positive attitudes and social acceptance is to answer accurately questions asked by other children about the differences in appearance and behaviour of the special child. This should be done at the time questions are asked, whether or not the special child is present. The questions children ask most often are: What is cancer? Can our friend die from it? What does it feel like to have cancer? (Peckham, 1993, p. 28). • Provide time for children to talk about the disease and its treatment.
May be isolated	• Develop a Circle of Friends. • Modify teacher roles so that the student belongs to the classroom teacher but receives support. • Treat the student the same as the group as much as possible • Make children feel a part of the class even if illness keeps them absent for long periods. • Be sympathetic to the child's feelings about hospital and separation.
Limited vitality	• Adjust classroom schedules for students with limited vitality to create maximum on-task learning time. • Develop short- and long-range goals that stress the child's self-help capabilities. • Provide frequent rest periods.
Difficulty in dealing with many different stimuli at once.	• Avoid overload. A serene classroom with a stress on routine is critical. • Stress social skills, communication, and stable, consistent discipline. Provide an environment with little visual and auditory stimulation. • Provide a personal workspace free from distractions. • Explain ahead of time what will happen, when it will happen, and what is expected. If there is to be a change in the schedule of the class or in an activity, the child should be warned in advance. • Speak using whispers.
Insistence on sameness and routine	• Children feel anxious and frustrated when confronted with unfamiliar experiences and variations in their routine. Be consistent. • Keep change to a minimum—establish stable routines in the classroom. • Have a clear schedule • Provide a structured day.

Needs more appropriate behaviours	• Model the behaviours you want the child to learn. • Have publicly posted rules. • Establish realistic goals and expectations. • Use direct instruction, modelling, role playing, and social interaction scripting to teach specific social skills. • Teach social skills in small groups.
Short attention span	• Give precise requests. • Give only one specific task at a time. Provide a lot of structure. • Break assignments into small pieces and provide extra time to complete tasks. • Provide many concrete examples and use concrete objects. • Overteach. • Use many diagrams, charts, and other graphic cues.
Difficulties with concepts, abstractions, generalizations	• Use many concrete materials. • Avoid long verbal instructions. • Provide appropriate wait time in questioning.
Limited, deficient, or absent language	• Most training efforts should be conducted in natural environments. For children with more severe deficits in speech and language, formal language training may involve lessons a few brief times daily. However, communication training with children who are severely impaired need not, and should not, be confined to one-to-one therapy sessions. • Activities should contain multiple components that can provide numerous opportunities within a single activity. Painting, for example, would provide at least three opportunities for communication: obtaining access to the paint, the water, and the brush. • Activities should lend themselves to repetitive action. If the child desires repeated actions, repeated opportunities exist for language use. Examples include playing catch and being pushed on a swing. • Accompany communication with rhythmic body actions, touch sensations, or actions that engage a number of senses simultaneously. • Reinforce vocalizations as consistently and frequently as possible. Provide vocal reinforcement for a short time after the child stops vocalizing. This offers a model dialogue, ensures that the child is not interrupted, and reinforces turn-taking patterns. Vocal reinforcement should include imitation of the child's sounds, whether verbal or pre-verbal. • Improve the quality of language stimulation by interspersing short bursts of speech with short periods of silence. Use playful social routines, rhyming verses, and other communication games that

are enjoyable for you and the child. For older students, try using rock and roll and other rhythmic patterns.

- Children who are multiply disabled are often able to comprehend far more than they indicate; keep sentences short and use an expressive voice.
- For most deaf–blind children with other impairments, natural gestures offer the best foundation for communication. Natural gestures can be easily individualized.
- To stimulate speech, place your mouth on the child's cheek or hand when speaking so that the child can feel your speech. Continue to hold your mouth against the child's cheek or hand between vocalizations so the child can feel the silence.
- Encourage art and computer activities.
- Use much music and rhythm.
- Encourage spontaneity by rewarding spontaneous behaviour.

SECTION 7

Intervention with Infants, Preschoolers, and Young Adults

Educators sometimes think of the critical years for learning as those between about ages five and eighteen, the time when children and adolescents are within the formal school system. But learning is a life-long experience, of which an enormous amount takes place before children even reach school. By the time children are six years old, almost two-thirds of their ultimate cognitive ability is formed. And, after the age of six, the child's potential for further intellectual growth is slowed (Bloom, 1964).

Educators should know "where children are coming from" as well as where they are going. They need to be aware of the experiences of the preschool years, as this period of development lays the groundwork for what we see in formal classrooms. They should also be knowledgeable about the special requirements of students at the other end of the age spectrum—young adults who are leaving the school system.

For very young children, the family is the central focus. All families face stresses and strains, which are only multiplied when a child has a disability. Families may differ greatly in structure, cultural values, and economic status, but most families with a child who is disabled have to cope with additional emotional adjustments and caregiving demands.

Early childhood special education (ECSE) is a new discipline designed to ameliorate the effects of a disability in a very young child and to assist the parents and family in dealing with the associated stress. Early identification and early intervention are essential elements of ECSE.

Just as ECSE is a new discipline, so interest in the needs of students nearing the end of their school careers is a relatively new development. Essentially, initiatives arose from data that showed that youths with disabling conditions are not faring well in the adult world, especially in the workforce.

Equally important for very young children with disabilities and for older adolescents is the concept and practice of *transition,* an umbrella term for all activities and opportunities that prepare students for significant changes in their lives. For young children and their parents, transition is the movement from preschool to school. In older students, transition means the movement from elementary to junior high school, or to secondary school. The most important meaning relates to secondary school students moving to new environments, most often from school to work. More often today, schools are becoming involved in assisting adolescents to negotiate the transition to independent adult living.

This section addresses students with disabilities at both ends of the age spectrum. Discussion focuses on the manner in which a child affects the family, the influence the family has on the child's development and progress, types of early intervention that are available to help parents cope with and enhance prospects for optimal development for their exceptional child, parent involvement and parent training, and transition. For students at the end of their school careers, the concepts and practices of transition form the major focus of Chapter 16.

Chapter 15

Early Intervention

Learning Outcomes

After reading this chapter, you should be able to:

- Differentiate among the models used to look at family functioning;
- Understand the concepts and processes of early identification and early intervention;
- Understand the link between early childhood education and education in the regular school system.

Introduction

All parents want their children to be born healthy, normal, and perfect, with sturdy bones, good vision, working organs and the promise of growing into a normal, intelligent, and happy person. For most parents, the wish is fulfilled; the chances are huge that a child will be born in superlative condition.

While most children are born healthy and well formed, some parents must reduce the expectations they hold for their new infant. For them, the not-so-perfect child has been born. Their children are not like other children; they have problems that potentially threaten their physical, intellectual, social, or emotional functioning. When this happens, parents face frustrations stemming from broken dreams; the goals and hopes for the child are no longer clear and the entire family functioning is affected.

No family, regardless of wealth, education, religious persuasion, race, or physical and mental health, is immune. About 3 percent of newborn infants have a condition that can be considered a developmental delay or developmental disability. Another 3 percent are born with significant conditions capable of causing medical or social disabilities (Berlin, 1983). For other children, problems appear later as a result of disease or accident.

The child with a disability has a major impact on the family, which usually requires modifications in family structure and roles. It has been only during the past few decades that professionals have begun to fully appreciate the parental pain and stress that accompany the diagnosis of a disabling condition in a child and the degree of courage and external support that parents need to retain their equilibrium. They now realize that family problems arising from the presence of a child with a disability require as much professional attention as the educational and medical treatment of the child. Parents require assistance in areas such as understanding the nature and prognosis of the condition; in handling the child; in stimulating mobility, locomotion and communication; and in responding appropriately to different or unexpected behaviours.

early identification
early intervention

In the broadest terms, work with very young children and their families is referred to as *early childhood special education.* It takes in two main processes. **Early identification** is designed to find the childhood disability as soon as possible. **Early intervention** includes a variety of educational, psychological, or therapeutic procedures aimed at infants and preschoolers.

Generally, the children who benefit from early intervention are the at-risk groups we discussed in Chapter 3. Early intervention is directed toward children between birth and age eight in three groups:

- Disabled or developmentally delayed children who have known congenital disorders, sensory impairments, neurological dysfunctions, or significant delays in major areas of functioning;
- Medically or biologically at-risk children who have a history of health factors, such as prematurity, known to be a potential threat to development;
- Environmentally at-risk children who are biologically sound but whose physical or social circumstances (such as poverty, neglect, abuse) may indicate a high probability of delayed development.

PARENTS AND FAMILIES

Parenting should be counted among the most esteemed professions. But while there are many apprenticeships available for professions and careers, none exist for that most difficult job: parenting. Few study the art—or craft—and there are no courses to teach really practical methods of child-rearing, or to teach parents how to weather the crises, frustrated ambitions, and periods of high stress that are common to most families. Nonetheless, most parents manage to raise their children remarkably well. They willingly endure many trials, problems, and moments of despair, secure in the hope that one day their children will become self-sufficient adults.

Expecting parents have great dreams for their unborn child. They hope for intelligence and physical beauty and plan ahead for later accomplishments and successes. By the time the baby is born, parents are ready to provide for the infant's physical needs and have probably consulted one of the hundreds of volumes on child care and child rearing. Typically, the birth of a child brings joy and excitement. When a parent holds a newborn close for the first time, feelings of belonging, togetherness, and attachment are cemented. The birth ends the period of expectations about the child and brings new challenges and responsibilities for parents as they adjust to the new family member.

The diagnosis of a disabling condition in a child shatters parental aspirations. The perfect child has died and in its place is a baby with apparent and frightening problems and unknown prospects for the future. When a disability is found, a void is created that is bridged only as the family reformulates its expectations to accommodate reality. The entire family undergoes a crisis, the resolution of which determines whether its members will live together in relative peace and contentment or in frustration, anger, and guilt.

The characteristics of the family—cultural background, socio-economic status, size, even religion—shape its ability to cope with a child who is exceptional. Each family's unique combination of strengths, stressors, vulnerabilities, and coping styles comes into play as the discovery of a disability in a child creates intense and conflicting feelings among the members of a family.

Looking at Families

There are a number of ways to look at families and to conceptualize the relationship of family members, the child with a disability, the care and treatment of the disabled member, the extended family, and the wider culture. Each of the theoretical frames used to view families is a little different, although they should be seen as a continuum with a different emphasis on certain factors and components of family functioning rather than different variables. Moreover, each of these ways of looking at families is important because these frameworks undergird the manner in which professionals present early intervention programs and interact with parents. Table 15-1 outlines ways of looking at families.

Table 15-1 Looking at families

Model	Principles	Major focus
Stage theory	Parents pass through discrete stages from grief to acceptance	Parent counselling Parent therapy Parent self-help groups Information about the condition
Life-cycle theory	Families pass through cycles in which there may be crises transition points	Transition support Liaison with other agencies Family support Intervention with the child
Systems theory	The family is a system within the larger social context	Priorities set by the family Stress on all family members Functional skills for the child Improved functioning within family needs
Social support theory	Families are systems of themselves	Families helping themselves Families setting priorities Advocating for child

Stage Theories

Stage theories represent the most traditional way of examining a family that includes a member with a disability. Stage theories hold that parents pass through discrete stages before they can fully accept the child's condition (see Table 15-2). Not all parents pass through all of these stages, and each person works through them at a different rate; however, most pass through similar stages before they accept the reality of their child's condition.

Acute initial (crisis) reactions accompany the diagnosis of a child's condition. These are mediated by the severity of the disability, the parents' socio-economic status, their religious orientation, and the quality of external and intrafamily support systems.

When first confronted with their child's condition, most parents react with shock, often accompanied by denial and disbelief. The period of shock is usually brief because of the necessity for making decisions regarding treatment. Parents must be concerned with the provision of daily care for their child. They may have to arrange transportation to treatment, alter methods of scheduling time, meet new financial costs, and assimilate technical information about the disability. Parents may also have to provide support for other family members.

In instances of clear-cut organic damage or with conditions such as Down syndrome, the child will probably be diagnosed at birth or shortly afterwards and the parents will learn about the problem immediately. Other parents may discover a problem more slowly. As a child matures and tends to lag behind others of the same age, parents may start to suspect some problem or disability.

Parents of children with severe disabilities may not deny the handicap, especially if they themselves were the first to recognize the child's disability, as in the case of deafness (Kroth, 1987). They may even respond positively when they find that they were not imagining problems. Some mothers have described feelings of relief on the confirmation of their suspicions, not defensive reactions (Faerstein, 1986). Once the problem is verbalized and labelled, some parents find that they can mobilize both the defensive and coping mechanisms available to them. For other parents, the confirmation of a diagnosis results in a compelling need for knowledge (Hobbs, Perrin, and Ireys, 1985).

Parents' initial grief may be more intense when the diagnosis is made well after the birth of the child. By this time, their hopes for the child have lasted longer and their bonds of affection have grown stronger (Fortier and Wanlass, 1984). The period of denial may be more protracted, especially if the condition is not readily obvious to the parents. Denial may operate as a protective device, giving parents additional time to adjust to the pain and disappointment of lost expectations. Denial becomes maladaptive when it results in the withholding of treatment necessary to ensure a child's optimal development. Unwittingly, family, friends, and even professionals may support parental denial. Anxious to relieve the parents' worries, they may suggest that the child will "grow out" of the condition, and parents may delay proper treatment as a result.

Parents may also feel anger when they learn of their child's condition. In fact, anger can be the most enduring emotion among parents of children with disabilities (Hall and Richmond, 1984). Some come to believe that the world is against them, as health practitioners, teachers, neighbours, and relatives confront them with a reality they do not want to accept.

Initially parents may direct their anger at the child as the obvious source of frustration. When parents turn the anger inward, they can react with fear, guilt, and shame. Fear arises when parents hold unfounded apprehensions and incorrect information about the disability, the implications, and the prognosis. Some parents feel that the condition might be of a genetic nature and worry about their future children; others view the disability as a defect in themselves. Many parents develop understandable apprehensions about their child's future life. Major concerns are sexual, social, and occupational exploitation of their offspring.

Parents who feel shame see their child who is disabled as a threat to the family's prestige. They worry about social stigma and anticipate social rejection. Some parents feel guilt because they think the condition could have been avoided if they had done something differently. Others believe the disability serves as retribution for some misdeed. Parents ask, "Why us?" and seek answers in factors such as marital discord, prenuptial pregnancy, unusual sex practices, use of drugs, and unusual events during pregnancy.

Sometimes parents project guilt on others. They direct resentment and hostility at their spouses, their other children, the doctor, the counsellor, society in general, even God. Some parents question their religious beliefs; others find solace in them.

Studies have found parents with a strong religious affiliation to be more accepting; their religious beliefs seem to sustain them through difficult situations in raising a child with an impairment. A study of African American families (Rogers-Dulan, 1998) found that religious experiences functioned, for the most part, in positive ways in affecting adjustment for most families. For other parents, having a child with a disability destabilizes their religious beliefs; they begin to question a previously held belief in God. Preconceived notions about God, fate, a just world and their implications for personal existence are often challenged (Erin, Rudin, and Njoroge, 1991).

Feelings of isolation are common. Gill (1994) notes that parents may be subjected to rude questions, crude comments, and withdrawal, even from formerly close friends. Once the initial sympathy fades, friends sometimes reveal a lack of understanding or interest.

Mourning or grief is a natural reaction to the disappointment of having a child with a disability. Like anger, denial, and guilt, grief follows the initial diagnosis and takes on different forms in different families. For some parents, grief results in withdrawal and depression. Others take recourse in bargaining—trying to make a deal with God, science, or society to cure their child. Grief may continue to some extent throughout the parent's life, never disappearing completely.

With a severe disability, the family's adjustment to the idea of future dependency can be made fairly easily. But with a milder disability, the family may find itself on a roller coaster of expectations, with hopes for the future alternately dashed and raised as the child progresses or falls back.

Some parents are never able to completely accept their child's condition. They may accept the diagnosis but reject the prognostic implications. Such parents are vulnerable to even the most unsubstantiated claims for cures or relief. They may embark on a trek from doctor to doctor and clinic to clinic in search of a more promising prognosis, miracle drugs, a new operation, a novel form of psychotherapy, or a radically new diet. Probably as many parents seek other opinions not because they reject or cannot handle their child but because they are simply seeking clarity about the problem. If a parent visits five professionals and obtains five different diagnoses, the ensuing confusion and need for clarification become obvious.

Some parents may reject the child as well as the condition. They may treat the child with open hostility, or use more subtle ploys, such as setting unrealistic goals or failing to praise positive behaviour. Other parents may develop positive and accepting attitudes, but nevertheless harbour resentment toward the child. Every parent must occasionally feel ambivalent about restricted activities, additional responsibilities, disappointments, and anxieties. If parents feel guilty about their ambivalent feelings, they may become overprotective and oversolicitous and try to compensate for their negative feelings with a life of martyrdom and self-sacrifice.

Such attitudes can foster an overdependency in the child, which will eventually become circuitous. In the course of investing themselves emotionally in the child, these parents exaggerate the child's needs and promote an overly dependent attitude. Then, to prove their worth as parents, they allow their whole lives to become centred on the child. Such parents may actually resist attempts by others to ease the burden.

Most parents reach a stage of mature adaptation, which is the end of the crisis period. However, acceptance does not come all at once; it begins fleetingly and goes on to fluctuate at different levels in different situations. Parental sadness may resurface at critical junctures in the life of the child and the family. A re-occurrence of sorrow and frustration may be triggered by milestones such as reaching school age, attaining puberty, and watching other children graduate from school or marry.

When parents have reached this stage, they can accept the child, the disability, and themselves. They become reconciled to the fact that their child's condition deeply affects, and will continue to affect, the entire family. As one mother explains,

> The whole process of having a handicapped child hurts. It's not the greatest thing on the face of the earth, but life throws these little curves at us and we can make our adjustments if we have good supports. Then, having a handicapped child becomes just like having any other child in the family. You deal with the problems that come along just as for any child. (Wilgosh, 1990, p. 302)

Parents do not differ significantly in their level of acceptance (McLinden, 1990). Some earlier studies indicated lack of involvement with and acceptance of the child by the father (e.g., Farber and Ryckman, 1965). Investigators found that fathers, more than

Table 15-2 Parental reactions to the diagnosis of a disability

Acute initial reaction	Chronic adaptive reaction	Mature adaptation
Shock	Withdrawal and isolation	Refashioning expectations
Denial and disbelief	Depression	Coping with everyday practical problems
Anger	Ambivalence	Maximizing the child's potential
Bitterness and shame	Rejection	Protecting the interests of the whole family
Loss of self-esteem	Overprotectiveness; self-sacrifice; defensiveness	Interaction with others
Inappropriate guilt, projection of blame	"Doctor shopping"	
Disappointment, sadness, grief, and bargaining		

mothers, were affected in the social domain. Fathers had more difficulty coping with the child, were more vulnerable to social stigma, and encountered more difficulty living with the uncertainty of the child's impairment and discussing the problem with friends. Later, Moran (1982) reported fathers to be positively involved with the child with a disability, playing and helping with their daily care. However, it still seems that fathers are more likely to show extreme patterns of great involvement or withdrawal than mothers; such extreme patterns are found more often when a son rather than a daughter has a disability (Lamb and Meyer, 1991).

Life-cycle Approach

Instead of adopting a stage approach, some researchers tend to view the family and the impact of a member with a disability through a *life-cycle* or *life-span approach.* A life-cycle perspective sees the family as a unit that is moving through time and experiencing a series of events, tasks, and transitions. By looking at the family life cycle, it can be seen that the impact of the child with a disability on the family changes over time.

All families experience life-cycle transitions, and there seem to be specific periods that result in increased stress (Wikler, Wasow, and Hatfield, 1981). For all families with children, these are the age at which the child should begin to walk; the age at which the child should begin to talk; entry into the public school system; onset of puberty; and the twenty-first birthday. When a child with a disability is a member of the family, transitions may also include events such as first encountering the disability; early childhood; school entry; when the development of a younger sibling surpasses that of the child who is disabled; when placement outside the home is considered; when a child-management crisis occurs; adolescence; beginning adult life; maintaining adult life; and when guardianship issues are discussed. These events can serve to magnify a child's special needs and create heightened stress in the family.

Systems Approach

Currently, a *systems approach* is seen as the most appropriate way to view families with a disabled member. A systems theory or perspective sees a family as more than individuals bound by a biological relationship. It recognizes that actions in any part of the system affect the other parts and that solutions to problems can be found only when the problem is properly defined in its larger environmental context.

Under a systems model, influences are seen as multidirectional. Each adult and child influences every member of the household and each family relationship affects all the other family members. Therefore, whether the family is nuclear, single-parent, or extended, it plays a powerful role in the child's social, emotional, behavioural, and academic development and progress. The outcomes of any child-rearing patterns on any child depend on many factors that interact with each other. These include the child's age, sex, and temperament; the parents' personality characteristics, personal history, economic circumstances, and so on; the needs of family members; and the values of the culture.

The relationship between the child who is exceptional and the family is reciprocal; the child deeply affects the family climate, while the family, in turn, affects the child. Interaction with family members deeply influences the child's opportunities and barriers, challenges and expectations, ambitions and frustrations, and general quality of life.

Social Support Approach

In many ways, the *social support approach* overlaps the systems approach; the difference is mainly one of emphasis. Whereas a systems approach focuses chiefly on the social context of the family, a social support approach focuses on a family's functioning in four family subsystems: marital, sibling, parental, and extra-familial (Carter and McGoldrick, 1980). It stresses families helping themselves and sees informal supports such as the extended family and church as more important than formal support.

Family support approaches include two major concepts—embeddedness and social networks influence. Embeddedness refers to the way that a developing child is enveloped within the family system and its members, and the way that the family unit is embedded in broader social units consisting of relatives, friends, neighbours, church members, and so on.

These people—the family's social network—directly and indirectly influence both the family and the child. Social support networks may be more important for mothers than fathers. A study investigated the differences between mothers and fathers in the areas of social support and family satisfaction, and in their reported frequency-of-occurrence and degree-of-problem of events and feelings related to the presence of a child with special needs. It found that mothers had a higher frequency of demands placed on their lives than did fathers and also experienced more negative physical and emotional states (McLinden, 1990).

Status of Disability

Another way to look at families is on the basis of the *type of condition*. This is not a theoretical model or approach, but it does recognize that the nature of a child's disability can have a substantial impact on parental stress and levels of acceptance. Researchers (Frey, Greenberg, and Fewell, 1989) have found that a child's characteristics predict the amount of stress that parents report and the amount of psychological stress reported by fathers.

Most observers conclude that raising a child with a disability is often burdensome, tiresome, and frustrating. High levels of family stress may be created by a particular child's slower progress, more difficult temperament, lack of social responsiveness, stereotypical behaviour patterns, or additional or unusual caregiving needs. Research in families with infants indicates that role confusion, social isolation, fatigue, financial worries, and lack of information on child development are cited by new mothers as primary causes of stress (Salisbury, 1987).

Behaviours that parents of disabled infants have identified as most difficult, stressful, or uncomfortable are crying, resisting being held, being hard to soothe, passive non-responsiveness, tuning out, and emitting atypical motor responses. Symptoms of stress are more evident among parents of children with delayed rather than prompt diagnoses and with unknown rather than specified etiologies (Goldberg, Marcovitch, MacGregor, and Lojkasek, 1986). Stress is also more evident among families when the child has a severe or profound rather than a mild or moderate condition. Studies have found greater stress reported by parents of boys and of children with limited communication skills (Frey, Greenberg, and Fewell, 1989). Parents of children with dual disabilities seem to be doubly stressed (Hintermaier, 2000).

Stress may occur from the outset if the attachment process between infants with disabilities and their parents is disrupted. Premature and disabled infants may be kept in neonatal intensive care for up to twelve weeks, depending on birth weight, gestational age, physical anomalies, respiration, and weight gain. Later, children who show disturbed interactions include preterm, Down syndrome, blind, autistic, and failure-to-thrive infants (Field, 1983). Such infants are less responsive than others, and parents need to work harder to focus their attention and generate smiles and contented vocalizations.

Children with problems such as Fetal Alcohol Syndrome, Down syndrome, and cleft palate may have feeding problems and limited abilities to suck, bite, chew, or swallow. Feeding problems are common among infants who are autistic, beginning with poor nursing habits and continuing through infancy and childhood.

Some disruption may arise from the medical needs of a child. Children with chronic conditions such as cystic fibrosis require intense medical and therapeutic intervention. The age of the child may also be related to the condition. As children grow older, they become harder to manage. At the same time, the gap between the progress of children who are exceptional and their peers becomes more noticeable.

Parents with children who are exceptional must also take on new roles: educator, lobbyist, advocate, therapist, and, of course, chauffeur. In addition, financial burdens can cause parents constant concern and frustration. The need for special equipment, special medical care, and special programs often brings financial hardship. Economic pressures can distort the family's emotional response to their child, particularly in families with limited financial resources.

Specific Conditions

The discovery that a child is severely intellectually disabled causes great stress for the parents and other family members. Across all socio-economic levels, mothers of children who are mentally retarded report depression (Breslau and Davis, 1986). Parents must eventually confront three critical issues. They must decide how to train and educate the child, accept that the child may never be self-sufficient, and plan for the child's future.

Family functioning is a factor in outcomes. Research has discovered that highly functional families have children with Down syndrome who, over time, demonstrate significant benefits in communicating and socializing with others and in their ability to engage in independent self-care tasks (Hauser-Cram, Warfield, Shonkoff, Krauss, Lipshur, and Sayer, 1999).

The experiences of families with a member with a learning disability are not well understood because of equivocal and sparse information (Dyson, 1996). But it may seem at first glance that parents of children with learning disabilities are much more fortunate than parents of children with more severe disabilities. In fact, when a child is identified as learning disabled, parents may feel relieved, hoping this identification will lead to solutions that will eliminate the child's learning or behaviour problem (Bos and Vaughn, 1998).

It appears, rather, that learning disabilities create much confusion within a family. Dyson (1996) found increased parental stress and some altered family routines, although there was not family dysfunction or altered sibling self-concept.

Lack of a clear diagnosis causes great concern and anxiety, resulting in high levels of stress for parents. Few learning disabilities are severely disabling to children younger than five years, and therefore their detection before a child enters school is quite difficult (Vaughn, Bos, and Schumm, 1997). Parents, however, may detect subtle signs that lead them to suspect a difficulty. Even so, Faerstein (1986) found that a gap of 3.5 years elapsed between the time a learning disability was suspected and its diagnosis. This gap was not due to the mother's lack of responsibility, but more often to others who denied the child's problem and averred that he or she would outgrow it.

The receptive and expressive language problems of children who are learning disabled may cause them to appear slow, confused, impulsive, inattentive, or even obstinate. Parents may react to these problems with guilt, overprotection, rejection, or concern. Thinking they are assisting the child, some parents may disrupt a child's activities by using more responses and initiations. Or parents may react by placing too much responsibility on the child, by denying the gravity of the problem, or by placing responsibility on themselves and accepting failure.

Deafness is often suspected when children are about twelve months of age and expected to say their first words. Ross (1990) found that many mothers, especially of children with profound deafness, suspected a loss before the child was one year old. Deaf children with hearing parents comprise more than 90 percent of the deaf population. Hearing parents are much more likely than deaf parents to view their child's diagnosis as a tragic crisis. Hearing parents often express feelings of incompetence, self-doubt, and sorrow. In some cases, the birth of a child with a hearing impairment threatens family integration and destroys the balance of family relationships (Meadow, 1980).

Parents of children with clefts often worry about the physical manifestations and social stigma, while emotional and social development are harmed by parents' feelings of guilt that the deformity is their fault. Of particular concern to parents are the child's appearance; the need for immediate surgery and regular and protracted contact with physicians; speech development; fears that the child may choke during feeding; reaction of the spouse, siblings, family and friends; intellectual development; financial considerations; and a recurrence of the defect in future children. Very often, parents are anxious about possible mental retardation in the child as well as the physical defect (Vanpoelvoorde and Shaughnessy, 1991).

Many parents of infants with severe visual impairments feel anxious and apprehensive, even grief-stricken, when they learn of their child's disability. Parents may be worried and frustrated by the infant's responses, or seeming lack of responses.

From infancy, parent–child relationships may be harmed if the child has a visual impairment (Dote-Kwan, 1995). Hence, maternal interaction behaviour has been an important focus of research with children with visual impairments. Attachment behaviours between infants and parents are facilitated by the infant's ability to elicit parental responses, but very young visually impaired children do not always react to their parents in the same way that sighted children do. For example, babies who are blind do not reach out in the "Pick me up" gesture seen in sighted babies at about five months. The facial expressions of babies who are blind are less varied and less frequently seen; they smile significantly less frequently than sighted ones, and the mother's voice does not automatically and consistently evoke smiling. Babies who are blind vocalize much less frequently than do sighted babies, and their vocalizations to initiate contact with parents appear much later, even when families encourage such interaction and reward it.

Parents of older children with severe visual impairments tend to expect less of their children. This may lead to a child's lesser accomplishments and slower development (see McConnell, 1999).

Of all caretaking demands, none seems to have more impact than the demands of coping with a child who has a behavioural problem. When parents cannot handle or control the child fully, the integrity of the family is threatened. Parents can become physically and emotionally exhausted as their preschooler is fussy and irritable; exhibits irregular patterns of eating and sleeping; and displays abusive, destructive, and cantankerous behaviour that causes disruption and disharmony in the home.

Parents of children with special health care needs suffer many traumas and stresses. Family reactions include depression, denial, anxiety, resentment, and anger. Moreover, illnesses such as cystic fibrosis are an affront to an assumed developmental order for the family life cycle; parents must confront the abbreviated life expectancy of the child; some must handle the additional stress of a dying child.

When conventional medical treatment fails, parents of children with serious health disabilities sometimes hunt for miracle cures and faith healers. They may focus normal feelings of anger upon medical personnel, other family members, or any other available target. They may experience feelings of guilt, believing they should have noticed symptoms sooner or been more lenient in their discipline. Parents often transmit their anxiety to the child. They may also create conflict and jealousy among siblings by spending a disproportionate amount of time with the special child.

Raising and training a psychotic or autistic child can cause enormous stress for parents and family. Caregivers must contend with the bizarre withdrawn attitudes of autism or the clinging behaviours of schizophrenia. Children who are autistic are likely to ignore the presence of their mother or other family members, and the parents are continually faced with their children's failure to respond to interaction. The deviant gaze pattern, known as **gaze aversion** (the failure to look directly at another individual), is a conspicuous characteristic of children who are autistic and severely hinders parent–child interaction. As well, children

gaze aversion

Gifted children are advantaged in many ways, but they may cause disruption within the family.

tend to show little response to their mother's voice, do not anticipate being picked up, and do not adapt their body postures to the people holding them. These behaviours inevitably have a deep effect on parental interaction and are compounded in later years by the children's lack of verbal responsiveness and bizarre and inappropriate behaviours.

For the parents, the child who is gifted may be both a blessing and a burden. Although giftedness is socially acceptable, giftedness is not without stigma and other potentially troublesome psychosocial correlates (Kauffman, 1997b). Many parents of children who are gifted are bewildered and frustrated about issues related to both home and school.

The advent of a child who is gifted can alter normal parental roles. Ross (1979) hypothesized that the degree of a gifted child's impact on traditional family roles is directly related to the degree of discrepancy between the child's intellectual capacity and that of

Case Study

Gerry

Dear Gerry,
Sorry that I haven't written for a while but you know how it is; have been busy with the boys, especially Gerry the Younger. In fact, it's because of Gerry that I'm writing to you tonight. The boys got your package today. John really liked the whip. Made of elephant hair, eh? The African headgear that you sent Gerry, though! Now that was really something else. The interesting thing was that he knows all about the thing, how it was made, history, symbolism, the works. I gather he saw a picture of one of them in one of those books you left at the house and read up on it. It's downright disturbing what that kid knows. After all, he's only eight years old and in grade three but he reads better than John, who's two years older.

Now, I'm not saying that the kid can read a university book on Africa and extract all the information, but he did read some of it and understood a whole lot more. He remembers all of it, too. And he never shuts up about it. Question, question, question, talk, talk, talk!

The kid is really something special. I know that all parents say that but in this case it's true. He's a ball of energy, always poking into things, always doing or saying something weird. Always asking "Why?" Makes me feel like a jerk sometimes. Most of the stuff he asks I don't know "why."

You know what the young Mr. Spock's latest interest is? My computer. He and John started playing games on it but now the kid is building Web sites and can access anything on the Web. I've had the thing for three years and I don't have any of the skill he seems to come by quite naturally. Gerry said he learned how to do it in school. He's in grade three. I was in grade eleven before I learned to use a slide rule. I take that back—I never learned how to use a slide rule.

Mixed feeling time, old buddy. I feel kind of not up to the job of raising the kid. I know he'll be more on the ball than his old man ever was. But on the other hand, I'm proud of him.

Another thing is that I sometimes think I'm spending too much time and money on Gerry at the expense of Number One Son. I know John sometimes resents his kid brother, but then again he won't let anyone kick sand in the kid's face.
So long, buddy,
John

other family members. Parents sometimes have difficulty clarifying the differences between parent and child roles. They wonder whether they should treat their offspring as a child or as an adult. We can see this in the letter from a parent—the father's pride in his son, but also his confusion about how to handle such a precocious youngster.

Parents may treat the child differently. The family of a gifted child may wish to make special adaptations that can include costly and time-consuming measures, such as special schools and extra equipment. When special adaptations are made for the child, sibling competition and jealousy may result. Siblings may resent the extra money and attention spent by their parents. Moreover, if parents give the preschooler who is gifted too much attention, that child may later meet difficulties in coping with sibling and peer competition. Finally, parents of children who are gifted often have to choose between regular class placement and special programming: and even experts cannot agree on which is the best option.

Siblings

Brothers and sisters play important parts in the entire family drama; indeed, "The fabric of the family is hard to imagine without the complex, frustrating, joy-inducing realities of siblings" (Cramer, Erzkus, Mayweather, Pope, Roeder, and Tone, 1997, p. 47). Siblings have a profound influence on each other's social and emotional development. Of the huge host of variables that affect sibling relationships, some of the most important are family size, birth order, gender, responsibilities and roles of all family members, temperaments, feelings and perceptions of self, personalities and their match, personal values and attitudes, and style (Atkins, 1987).

Parent roles change with the advent of a child with a disability, and it is obvious that sibling relationships will also change and take on special significance when one sibling is disabled. Yet while the points of view of parents have been investigated in depth, research has largely overlooked the possible consequences to children who have a sibling with a disability. The general picture of sibling interaction is bland; it simply tells us that the outcomes can range from very little effect to very positive or very negative ones.

Some research has looked at more specific interactions and finds differences in the following groupings:

- Role confusion. The relationship between siblings is special and intimate, particularly during childhood when siblings serve each other as playmates, models for identification, caretakers, and socializing agents. When a child has a disability, the roles a sibling normally assumes are somehow altered. A child with a disability may not function as a playmate, a caretaker, or a socializing agent for his or her siblings. Equality in relationships decreases as disability increases.
- The kind and amount of attention the child who is disabled requires of parents and siblings. The parents' attempts to protect the child with a disability may result in various degrees of neglect for the other children in the family and may interfere with their normal child–parent relationship, with family activity, and with social life outside the home. Researchers (Cantwell, Baker, and Rutter, 1979) found that mothers spent twice as much time in concentrated interaction with the child with a disability as they did with normally developing siblings.
- Disappointment at not having a normal sibling. Children share their parents' anticipa-

tion and excitement about a new addition to the family; they also share the grief, stress, and pain that accompanies the birth of a brother or sister who is disabled (Seligman, 1991).

- The embarrassment of relating to the disabled sibling in the company of peers or in public. The presence of a sibling with a physical disability, for example, may lead to "de-identification" (see Neal and MacLean, 1995). Children may feel that they are viewed as flawed or weird by others because there is a disability in their family (Gill, 1994). One five-year-old asked, "Why does my baby sister have to go to school when the baby sister across the street gets to stay home and play?" A thirteen-year-old wanted to know, "Will my sister frighten my boyfriend away?" (Cramer et al., 1997).
- The heavy demands on normal siblings to care for the child. In some families, the child who is disabled may generate extra caretaking responsibilities. Siblings of children with disabilities often assume dominant leadership roles, even when younger than the child with a disability. They tend to display more nurturant and affectionate behaviour toward the disabled sibling (see Hiller, Gallagher, and Frederick, 1999). At the same time, siblings may become overworked caretakers. Females, especially older sisters, are more likely to be adversely affected. Older sisters with siblings who are intellectually disabled, for example, assume multiple caretaking responsibilities and frequently assume a teacher role (Brody, Stoneman, Davis, and Crapps, 1991).

  When normally developing siblings are required to supervise, care for, defend, and protect the child with a disability, resentment can develop. Excessive responsibility for caretaking by siblings is related to anger, guilt, increased sibling conflict, decreased opportunities for peer contacts and out-of-home activities and, quite possibly, subsequent psychological damage (Seligman, 1991).
- The pressure on the normal child to "make up for" the deficits in the child who is disabled. Siblings may find themselves recipients of uneven expectation standards as compensation for parental disappointment. Sometimes, children are made to bear unrealistically high parental expectations. Or they may be expected to repress their abilities so that they do not perform better than the child who is special.
- Some parents have different ways of treating the normally developing children and the child with a disability. Because parents feel uncertainty regarding the care and management of a child who is disabled, they may subject that child to patterns of socialization that are significantly different from those that operate in the case of the other children. They may allow two quite different disciplinary systems to run side by side: one for the siblings and a more lenient, permissive one for the child who is disabled.

  Some parents treat their children with disabilities as though they were ill; they give them fewer responsibilities, place fewer restrictions on behaviour, and are more tolerant of undesirable behaviour, often at the expense of other siblings. Two different sets of rules intensify sibling rivalry. A twelve-year-old sister of a child with a hearing impairment complained, "I have to clean up my room and Mom cleans up Sherry's. That's just not fair. Her ears don't work, but her hands do" (Atkins, 1987, p. 38).
- Resentment is aggravated when additional care expenses deprive the others of educational and recreational opportunities. Siblings share family resources and the sibling relationship may be negatively affected by the additional resources required by the special child.

- There are only a few empirical studies on the self-concept of the siblings of children with disabilities, and their results are conflicting. Some research has found that children who have siblings with disabilities scored more poorly than children with non-disabled siblings on almost every measure of internalized adjustment problems. Others have found lower than average self-concept in siblings of children with physical disabilities (Harvey and Greenway, 1984) and with diabetes (Ferrari, 1987).

  In contrast, a study of seventy-four American and Canadian children with disabilities and normal siblings (Dyson and Fewell, 1989) showed no differences in level of self-concept. Other research finds no difference in the self-concept of siblings of chronically ill (Ferrari, 1984) and developmentally disabled (Lobato, Barbour, Hall, and Miller, 1987) children. One study (Gayton, Friedman, Tavormina, and Tucker, 1977) found higher than average self-concept in the siblings of children with cystic fibrosis.

The Extended Family

Children with disabilities have a considerable influence on the extended family. At the same time, the extended family may influence the development of children who are disabled through direct interactions and through the nature of the support provided to their parents. But there exists relatively little research on the grandparents of normal children, much less the grandparents of children with disabilities.

In many ways, grandchildren provide a new lease on life for their grandparents. The sense of surviving through the grandchild may help soothe the increasing infirmities of advancing age and the approaching reality of death. Grandchildren also allow grandparents to relive the joys of their own early parenthood. Playing with and caring for young grandchildren supplies grandparents with a revitalized feeling of importance and purpose in life.

Like parents, grandparents hope for a healthy, normal baby. When a child is diagnosed as exceptional, they too may experience a death of expectations that can leave them with a diminished capacity to provide support for the child's parents (see Sandler, 1998). Generally, more support is provided by the maternal than the paternal grandmother (Harris, Handleman, and Palmer, 1985). Such support is consistent with the maternal grandmother's understanding of her daughter's distress.

On the other hand, some paternal grandmothers express their resentment toward their daughters-in-law. Pieper (1976) described how her mother-in-law lashed out in anger when presented with a grandchild with a disability. The grandmother blamed the daughter-in-law for having bad blood and burdening her husband with such a child.

EARLY CHILDHOOD SPECIAL EDUCATION

We use the phrase *early childhood special education* (ECSE) to encompass two major processes: early identification and early intervention. These processes are not exclusive but natural corollaries. Early identification serves no purpose if it is not followed by early intervention, and appropriate early intervention rests on accurate identification.

ECSE is a relatively new field. Although efforts to intervene early actually date from preschool programs in the 1880s for children who were deaf, the term and concept were only formalized in 1986. This is explained in the Research Notes.

Given the field's newness and rapid expansion, the education and training of infants

Research Notes

The Formalization of Early Intervention

In the late 1960s, the disciplines of regular early childhood education, special education, and ameliorative programs such as Head Start began to draw together. The result was an entirely new field, *early childhood special education*, formalized by federal legislation in the United States in 1986.

Public Law 99-457, the Handicapped Children's Protection Act, an amendment of PL94-142, together with IDEA of 1990, underlie the rights afforded parents of preschoolers with disabilities. IDEA contains three critical sections: Part H; Part B, section 619; and the Early Education Program for Children with Disabilities (EEPCD). These deal specifically with children with disabilities under the age of five and their families.

Of the many provisions in PL 99-457 and IDEA, one of the most important is the mandate for the full inclusion of families in any decisions relating to the preschool child or infant with a disability. To accomplish this, all intervenors must complete and comply with an Individual Family Services Plan (IFSP), which is akin to the IEP used for school-aged children.

PL 99-457 has been described as "the most important legislation ever enacted for developmentally vulnerable young children" (Shonkoff and Meisels, 1990, p. 19) and has intensified concerns and interest about early intervention in the United States, in Canada, and elsewhere. Canada does not have comprehensive legislation on service provision for children under the age of five with special needs. In Canada, programs for preschoolers generally fall under provincial departments of social services or health and are covered by provincial legislation in these areas. Nevertheless, the influence of PL 99-457 has seen ECSE become an important component of special education in this country.

and preschoolers with disabilities is an area characterized by innovation and creativity. It also encompasses a variety of program models, many trends and movements, and not a little controversy.

Studies of early intervention programs cannot conclusively document positive effects for a range of problems and disability groups. Although the integration of children with exceptionalities with their normally developing peers is clearly the most appropriate option for many children, dissension and discussion still cloud the issue. However, the major issues today do not revolve around the question of whether or not to provide early intervention programs but rather focus on the most effective and efficient types of intervention. We present some of the arguments in the Debate feature below.

Early Identification

early identification

Early identification is the practice of screening infants and young children in an attempt to identify those likely to experience problems in learning or behaviour. When compared to the practices used with school-aged children that we have discussed throughout the text, early identification is even broader. Involved personnel must be acquainted with procedures for

A Matter of Debate

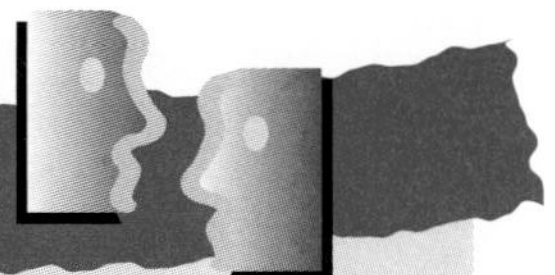

Early Intervention

Debates about early intervention do not concern whether or not to provide services. Rather, the question is efficacy. Critics of early intervention complain that too much has been claimed and too little proven concerning the efficacy of early intervention.

Arguments in favour of early intervention	Cautions about early intervention
In fifty-two reviews of early intervention efficacy studies, 92 percent of the reviews concluded that early intervention provided significant immediate effects for children who are disabled, at risk, or disadvantaged (White, Bush, and Casto, 1986).	Edmister and Ekstrand (1987) point out that "generally, the only documented benefit from integration of disabled and non-disabled preschool-aged children seems to be in the social domain" (p. 133).
Outcomes for children are better in integrated rather than segregated programs because of the potential social and cognitive benefits of integration.	Sustained social outcomes in integrated settings have been found only when interaction is frequent, planned, and carefully orchestrated by teachers.
Preschool personnel can learn and use the techniques needed for inclusion.	Preschool and day-care teachers are not trained to serve children with disabilities and most typical preschools do not have the rich training and staffing resources that might facilitate inclusion of children with special needs.
Language abilities improve in integrated programs. Studies document substantial changes in language abilities of preschool children with autism exposed to an intensive language stimulation program (Harris, Handleman, Kristoff, Bass, and Gordon, 1990).	Children in specialized settings obtain assistance for their specific disabilities. They require more intentional instruction to optimize their growth and development.
Contact with agemates with disabilities is associated with long-lasting positive gains in young children's attitudes toward people with disabilities (Esposito and Reed, 1986).	Very young delayed children find it extremely difficult to form friendships. They are highly interested in peers, discriminate among them, and develop preferences for specific playmates, but the friendships are usually unilateral, and rarely reciprocated. Few playmates whom they choose as friends choose them in return (Guralnick, 1990).
Segregated early intervention programs may make young children with disabilities overly	Successful teaching of children with disabilities demands that trained professionals be equipped

Arguments in favour of early intervention	Cautions about early intervention
dependent on adults and make their transition to school or kindergarten more difficult (Hamachek and Kauffman, 1994).	with skills for dealing with their unique characteristics and needs.
Increased hours of programming are associated with greater gains and earlier is better. Children do best if intervention is begun before thirty-six months of age. Mildly disabled children have better outcomes if enrolled in programs before six months of age (Shonkoff and Hauser-Cram, 1987).	Studies have failed to find adequate relationships between the intensity of intervention and the age of start and effect size. Casto and Mastropieri (1987) provided no support to the principle that "earlier is better" and found that children's progress did not differ based on the time that intervention was initiated.

assessing infants, toddlers, and preschoolers across a variety of domains, ways to assess family functioning, and ways to examine a child's environment.

The overarching aim of early assessment is to collect data so as to target skills that will increase options for the child's participation in present and future environments. The processes are based on the assumption that early identification will lead to an individual program plan that will either prevent or diminish the effects of an inappropriate education. Lacking early assessment, a child may experience years of failure before a diagnosis is reached. Children may also develop secondary conditions, such as behavioural disorders.

Infant Identification

The chief purpose of infant assessment is to provide information regarding an infant's strengths and weaknesses in order to plan intervention. *Observation* is a primary assessment strategy. A trained observer may be able to distinguish signs of sensory or neurological problems, for example. Observation also provides an assessment of the child's strengths and needs related to a particular home and/or community activity that is identified as a concern to families, such as feeding behaviours or behaviour while shopping.

There are no tests available that adequately assess intelligence in the newborn or reliably predict later intellectual development. Measures designed to assess an infant's developmental state make use of sensorimotor tasks: gross motor behaviour, vocalization, and language behaviour. Generally, a six-month-old would be assessed on recognition of people and objects, motor coordination, alertness, awareness of the environment, and vocalization.

Preschool Assessment

In infants and preschoolers, screening is used to look for maturational lags and problems that can be improved through early intervention. Before examiners can assess a child, they must know what behaviours they expect to observe. To test a three-year-old, they must focus on behaviour usually exhibited by two- to four-year-olds. These behaviours might include speaking in sentences of four to six words, building three-block pyramids, matching similar pictures, or buttoning. Problem behaviours might include poor attention span or failure to respond to oral language and visual symbols. A child who is out of touch with the environment may manifest poor motor control, low body image, and poor visual and auditory discrimination.

Observations of how a child functions in a setting such as a nursery school provides essential information about the child's progress and the effectiveness of the program. As well, it gives information to others involved with the child. An audiologist, for example, needs data on how a child is responding with specific amplification. Together with observations, early childhood personnel may use a variety of standardized measures. Diagnosticians involved in early identification frequently use developmental checklists, rating scales, readiness measures, basic concept inventories, and standardized measures.

Kindergarten Assessment

In kindergarten, as at the preschool level, the observation of behaviour serves as a valuable indicator of potential learning problems. Screening is used to identify children who do not possess the readiness skills needed to perform well in a structured school environment. Readiness tests attempt to assess a child's readiness for academic learning in specific areas of school achievement as well as potential academic difficulties. For example, reading readiness tests typically include subtests of letter recognition, shape perception, sound–symbol correspondences, and oral vocabulary.

Do remember our warning from Chapter 5 about children with maturational lags. Kindergarten screening procedures may identify maturational lags but they should not be used to inappropriately label children early in their school careers.

Family Needs Assessment

Family needs refers to a family's expressed desire for services to be obtained or outcomes to be achieved (Bailey and Blanco, 1990, p. 196). Family needs are determined by a *needs assessment*, a process that helps to identify and examine both values and information. A needs assessment evaluates current conditions and needs in a family and provides information on what the parents' goals are for their child and for potential parent involvement in the early intervention program.

A parent interview is one mechanism used to determine family needs. In interviews, intervenors can explore child-rearing methods, discipline, the opportunities for learning in the home, and parental attitudes and perceptions about the child's behaviour and skills. Professionals and family members can then discuss questions such as: Are there specific home and/or community activities that are concerns for family members? What skills would family members like the child to learn or to do more often? What behaviours would family members like the child to do less often? Which of these concerns are priorities for family members? (Cordesco and Laus, 1993).

Early Intervention

Early intervention occurs at much the same time as early identification. There are many types of intervention provided by different people in different settings.

The first issue in early intervention is encompassing. The question is, "Why intervene early?" The answer is complex and includes the following:

- Research in child development clearly demonstrates that the early years are a time of rapid learning. After Benjamin Bloom (1964) summarized a plethora of studies on intellectual growth, he suggested that a stimulating environment is critical to optimal cognitive growth. Bloom proposed that intellectual development can be seen as following a negative growth curve; as the child grows older, a rich and diverse environment has a decreasingly positive effect. Thus, children at the age of three will benefit more from enrichment activities than children aged eight to ten.
- Early intervention can "help ensure that all young children reach their full developmental potential; that they can become valued and full participants in their families, schools and communities; and that their families benefit from consistent and supportive collaboration with service providers" (see CEC Position, 1993).
- Early services can maximize skill development and reduce or alleviate the need for special services when a child enters school. Both developmental and educational intervention are likely to be more effective if they occur before the child's deficiencies become massive and are compounded by the numbing effects of extended school failure. In fact, the earlier intervention is started, the higher the rate of later educational attainment (Bloom, 1991).
- Intervention sustains growth. For example, among preschoolers Down syndrome is the most frequent specific diagnosis in the population of delayed children (Lojkasek, Goldberg, Marcovitch, and MacGregor, 1990). For children with Down syndrome, early and sustained intervention halts the decline in cognitive development that typically occurs during the first twelve to eighteen months of life and appears to prevent further decreases throughout the remaining early childhood years. Similar outcomes have been observed for the motor development of children with cerebral palsy (Palmer, Shapiro, Wachtel, Allen, Hiller, Harryman, Master, Meinert, and Capute, 1988).
- For the family, early intervention serves as a support that enhances family functioning, provides crucial information for parents, and makes parents the primary players in their child's developmental progress. Activities are designed to support families to the greatest extent possible. These family-centred activities optimally include the siblings and the extended family as well as the parents.
- For the school-age child, achievement levels in third grade seem to have particular predictive value. The prime time for intervention is before the end of grade three. Young children learn inappropriate strategies that soon become habitual and that can present an almost insurmountable obstacle to remediation. Teachers are well aware, for example, of how difficult it is to change the way children form letters once they have internalized incorrect formations.

Infants and preschoolers with disabilities may be served in the home, in clinic settings, in separate specialized programs, or within the regular complex of child care facilities. Those in the five to eight years of age range will be in regular schools and classrooms.

Infant Programs

Infants and toddlers are often served in centre-based (or clinic-based) programs, which are typically specialized, serving only children with disabilities and their families. In centre-

Very young exceptional children usually receive their education in regular classes.

based programs, families bring their infant or toddler to a program or an agency setting where appropriate services are provided by professionals and paraprofessionals.

Regular intervention sessions are scheduled either on an individual basis for infants or in small groups for toddlers. Most programs tend to follow developmental and therapeutic models in their curricula. A professional related to a discipline in the child's area of most significant need is the primary intervenor.

Equally popular today is early intervention that takes place in the home and/or uses the home as a basis for curricular objectives. Home-based programs are often referred to as **home visiting**: a process whereby a professional or paraprofessional provides help over an extended period of time to a family in its own home (Wasik, Bryant, and Lyons, 1990).

home visiting

In general, home-based early intervention involves a consistent contact in the client's home between the child and the family and a representative of a formal agency. The appeal of home visiting is based on the opportunity to work with individuals within the family context. This enables professionals to learn first-hand about the conditions of life for children and parents and means that instructional recommendations are practical and realistic because the teacher has the opportunity to observe the family's lifestyle and available resources.

Preschool Programs

Although segregated preschool programs are still to be found right across Canada, the current philosophy is that early childhood special education should generally not take place in settings separate from early childhood education. Early childhood special education should be thought of not as parallel care and education but as care and education that is embedded in and integral to early childhood education. The most appropriate settings for young children are comprehensive programs that promote regular contact.

The integration of children with disabilities into natural settings is predicated on the development of social interaction and friendship among children, the improvement in self-concept in children with disabilities; and opportunities for observation and imitation of the language, behaviour, and skills of normally developing youngsters. Children with special needs should be placed in a centre where they can achieve at their own level, where they are challenged to develop their potential but not swamped by a program beyond their grasp, where they can receive instruction in areas of need, and where they have opportunities to interact with normally developing children.

Children with disabilities need the same skills as their peers and they usually acquire the same skills in the same sequence. Therefore, it makes sense that the normal developmental processes of children provide the most critical reference for teachers of preschool children with mild disabilities. The regular early childhood curriculum includes communication, social and emotional development, self-care and physical development, the demands of the current environment, and the skills needed in the next environment. These curriculum objectives will be the same for young children with disabilities. Exceptions will probably be a somewhat expanded program to include early assessment, the development of an individualized program, the intervention of professionals and paraprofessionals, a range of teaching approaches and techniques, and adaptations to the environment.

Parent Involvement

Parents' discovery of their child's disability brings them into the orbit of a number of professional disciplines. Learning about the exceptionality is only the first of a lifelong series of interactions; many families are plunged into the world of infant stimulation, early intervention, preschools, respite services, medical intervention, and so on.

A wide range of services by professionals and paraprofessionals are available to support the parents and to help the child through various stages of development. Families will interact in some way with professionals from the disciplines of education, psychology, medicine, therapy, counselling, and allied public health and social work. Few children who are exceptional will require all, or even most, of these professional services. However, the child certainly will need some of these services at some time. A child diagnosed in infancy, for example, would encounter many of the medical personnel in hospital. Once the child is in the home, visiting personnel might provide infant stimulation, information for the parents, and the first steps for educational intervention.

Parents as Intervenors

Apart from teachers and other professionals, the primary intervenors in the early years are a child's own parents. *Parent involvement* does not mean that parents should do the job of professionals. Nor is parent involvement a specific set of activities such as parents' groups or teaching activities. Rather, parent involvement implies shared responsibility for a child's progress. As one worker said, "Effective parent involvement programs acknowledge the fact that parents are a child's earliest and most influential teachers. Trying to educate the young child without help and support from the home is akin to trying to rake leaves in a high wind" (Gough, 1991, p. 339).

Parents are trained to assist in program planning and/or teaching activities either at home or in a centre. They learn strategies for imparting specific skills and competencies to their own child in the belief that with instruction, modelling, and reinforcement they can become more effective teachers of their own children. Some specific areas of parent training include understanding the nature and prognosis of the condition; physical management; managing self-care and daily living activities; guidance and behaviour management; handling the child; stimulating mobility, locomotion, and communication; and responding appropriately to different or unexpected behaviours.

Treatment regimes depend on the special needs of a child. For example, parents of children with autism can learn how to manage their child and how to stimulate social, motor, and communicative development. Howlin (1981) trained parents of children with autism to use behavioural techniques to stimulate language at home and to deal with obsessions, rituals, phobias, temper tantrums, and hyperactivity. The parents also learned to teach constructive play and social skills. After a six-month period, the children spoke more than previously and used appropriate communicative language.

For a child with a hearing impairment, parents may be instructed as to the nature of hearing impairment, the stages of normal language development, the use of a hearing aid, and the various available modes of communication. Parents can be taught to reinforce their child's early vocalizations by responding with pleasure and attention through smiling, talking, and touching so that the child is encouraged to continue vocalization as a means of receiving positive reinforcement.

The developmental progress of children with Down syndrome appears to be best when parents and other regular companions are persistent in their attempts to stimulate the child while providing ample emotional support. With early support, children with Down syndrome can make remarkable progress. In the University of Washington Early Intervention Program for Down syndrome children, studies of experimental and control groups demonstrated that children lacking early intervention showed progressive declines in their performance compared to normally developing peers. In contrast, those children with early intervention showed positive developmental patterns. Initially they were able to perform only 62 percent of the tasks expected of their normal peers; those who participated in the program and were between three and four years of age typically performed approximately 95 percent of the tasks (Peterson, 1987).

For children with physical and health disorders, parents must be educated to promote their children's independence. This involves an acceptance of the disability as well as a recognition of the child's individual strengths and abilities.

Even though parent participation is highly valued, many difficulties remain. In fact, studies (e.g., Bricker, 1986) have found that only 20 to 40 percent of parents were actively involved in their child's early intervention program. Some parents cannot or will not play an active role, but the factors that influence parent involvement are diverse and often difficult to document.

The greater the number of unmet needs the parents have in their own lives, the less time, energy, and commitment they have to carry out educational and therapeutic interventions with their child. In other cases, parent intervention is hindered by limited knowledge bases, skill deficits, lack of self-confidence, impaired objectivity, economic considerations, and the needs of other family members.

The cultural background of the family is a major factor that can alter the intervention process, the role of professionals, and the amount of active parent participation. Culturally based beliefs affect the manner in which families adapt to the child, the family's willingness and ability to seek help, their communication styles with professionals, the level of trust given to caregivers and caregiving agencies, the amount and type of participation, the goals and outcomes they select for the child, and the family members who will participate in intervention activities (Hansen, Lynch, and Wayman, 1990; Schorr Ribera, 1987).

Other parents may be resentful if intervenors fail to take into consideration different family types and changing roles within families. Even though the traditional family is not as represented in today's society, infant and preschool programs are often directed toward the two-parent, one-mother, middle-class family. They assume that mothers are the primary caregivers, that children are raised by two biological parents, and that fathers show their concern for their children through participation in organized efforts such as fundraising, meeting with legislators, and so forth. These assumptions are not based on data (Atkins, 1987). Intervention should not become the sole concern of the mother.

Even for those parents eager for involvement, the process may be neither cheap nor convenient. Parents enter programs with the expectation of getting help for their child. When the assistance carries with it high explicit or implicit expectations of parent participation and time-consuming commitments by the parents, to not participate fully may make parents feel guilty. They feel that they are open to criticism for appearing not to have their child's interests at heart (Akerley, 1975).

TRANSITION

One common experience for each child and each family is the transition from a setting serving very young children to the formal school system. In early childhood special education, **transition** is the process of moving from one program to another, or from one service delivery mode to another (Chandler, 1992).

transition

The child's transition from a preschool to a public school program is a time of change for both the child and the family. Preschool and public school programs differ on a number of dimensions, including location, personnel, transportation options, schedules, family support services, and methods of communication between home and teacher.

Changing programs, systems, and personnel can be stressful for both child and parents. For the parents, the public school brings changing roles and expectations. For example, in public school the child is often labelled officially for the first time as being different. For the child, the separation from a child care or preschool program may be the most abrupt and permanent break with the past that he or she experiences before leaving home as a young adult. Transition means severing bonds with preschool staff, making new friends, generalizing old skills to new situations, acquiring new routines, and exploring new environments. Children face a group of strange people and inevitably experience separation fears along with the daunting tasks of learning the rules and consequences of an unfamiliar environment and learning their place in a new hierarchy.

The factors contributing to the success or failure of transitions are multiple and complex. They involve not only the child but also the quality of the sending and receiving programs, and the behaviour of the teachers, families, and communities. Especially important are the preparation, implementation, and follow-up that underlie the entire transition process. Preparing for transition involves a number of components:

- Preparing children and family members for the move to a new program;
- Minimizing the disruption caused by necessary changes in services;
- Supporting children and family members as they adjust to the new program;
- Making subsequent adjustments to new experiences for the child and the child's family;
- Providing the child with the skills to succeed in the new placement.

Preparation of the child focuses on the demands of the public school environment. These differ from those of the preschool, as do the skills that are needed for the child to function in a kindergarten program. For example, in kindergarten classrooms there is a predictable and consistent schedule of activities. Kindergarten teachers require children to respond to directions given once to a large group; preschool teachers often give children repeated individual directions in small groups or on a one-to-one basis. There are provisions for free play in kindergarten, but these differ from programs for younger children, as does the stress on academic subjects or academic readiness. Literacy behaviour is stressed.

The success of transition is influenced by the skills and behaviours a child has and the match between the child's skills and the expectations and requirements of the receiving program. Children who make the transition to kindergarten armed with the necessary survival skills and who use those skills in appropriate contexts are more likely to succeed in the regular classrooms than peers without these skills. But there can never be a universal list of transition skills because classroom and teacher expectations differ too much.

The research does indicate that in kindergarten the skills most crucial for success are not naming colours or recognizing the letters of the alphabet, but social skills. These are generally self-help skills, social interaction, play, the ability to function independently, and responding to group instruction.

Service Delivery Models

One of the most difficult choices for many parents is the location of the child's schooling. In concert with educators, many parents opt for inclusive classrooms; others are more cautious.

In the broadest terms, parents of children with significant disabilities are concerned with social integration, while parents of students with mild problems are more concerned with curricula and remediation. But even parents of children with significant disabilities hold widely divergent views about the efficacy of inclusion. Many parents seem confident about the social goals of inclusion, yet they are apprehensive about the impact on the quality of services their children receive (Palmer, Borthwick-Duffy, and Widaman, 1998).

When asked about inclusion, the concern of parents is whether the special child will receive adequate attention and instruction. With special services in place, some parents are reluctant to move a child from a special class to the regular classroom (Green and Shinn, 1995). They voice doubts about whether their children will receive the necessary help and may feel that their children's needs can be better met in a segregated setting with a structured curriculum and a low child–teacher ratio.

The views of parents of normally developing children must also be considered. In a longitudinal study (Leyser and Gottlieb, 1996) of parents of normally developing children, parents in both 1981 and 1991 expressed strong negative feelings toward the idea of including children with severe disabilities in classes with non-disabled peers. Parents of normally developing children may believe that their children are being denied teacher time and intervention. They fear that inclusion will negatively skew equitable distribution of instructional time in the classroom.

Teachers in early childhood settings are not one hundred percent committed. One study of parents and teachers of young children (Bennett, Deluca, and Burns, 1997) found that teachers' attitudes affect the success of the inclusionary process. Attitudes were influenced by general feelings about inclusion, confidence in skills, and the ability to access resources. Teachers who were themselves educated many years ago tended to have less positive attitudes toward inclusion.

PARENT SUPPORT

Before parents can effectively assist in the care and progress of their child with an exceptionality, they need to overcome their own emotional reactions. Many parents seek counselling or join self-help groups, especially in the period immediately following the initial diagnosis.

Counselling

Parent counselling differs from the usual conception of adult counselling, which is structured to facilitate changes in the client's behaviour. Parent counselling is not intended to change the personalities of family members; it is really closer to social work than to psychotherapy.

The major aims are to help the family face continuing periods of grief and provide assistance in handling the special problems and environmental adjustments that having a child with a disability entails. Counselling helps parents to understand the meaning of a child's diagnosis by focusing on information about the child, the nature and degree of the handicap, educational planning, and future prognosis. Sessions also provide a forum in which parents can openly express and work through their feelings of anger, fear, and anxiety. They offer coping self-help skills, group relaxation, self-praise and self-instruction, and opportunities to favourably contrast participants with each other.

As siblings are an important aspect of family-centred practice, in many cases the counselling sessions will actively involve siblings. Problems are explained simply and honestly, with a fair assessment of how the problems will affect family life.

Parent Self-Help Groups

Social supports complement personal coping skills for parents. Groups promote understanding and offer parents therapeutic involvement with people with similar problems; they provide a forum in which parents can discuss their concerns and exchange ideas with each other. It helps parents to talk about role changes, exhaustion, money problems, isolation, and so on with people who are going through the same experiences (Gill, 1994). Parents can channel their frustrations and anxieties into positive action for their children while gaining more realistic hopes for the future.

McMaster University researchers conducted a study of nine parent-run support groups in Ontario to explore the groups' perceived effect in providing parents with support, reducing parent stress, and improving parents' ability to deal with disability issues. Results indicated substantial benefits for those belonging to the groups. Parents were seen to gain increased skills, an increased sense of power, and a sense of belonging. Participants were able to connect with each other and provide support and skills to deal with the day-to-day issues of raising a child with special needs ("Many roads...," 1999).

Historical Notes

For most of the 19th century, educators saw early adolescence, not early childhood, as the formative years for both normal and exceptional populations. Most agreed that a commitment to mental discipline was incompatible with children under the ages of six or seven years and that school was physically, psychologically, and intellectually harmful to children younger than five or six years of age. The public schools catered to children from seven or eight years of age and up. Youngsters who were disabled went to institutional settings where they were admitted much later, at ten or twelve years of age.

In the final three decades of the 19th century, the view of the incapacity of young children was revised as part of the emerging child study movement. Infancy was distinguished from childhood as a discrete period of development. Children from birth to about six years of age were now seen to be active beings who required play rather than formal lessons, but this could be presented within the confines of educational settings. Kindergarten care, together with day care and nursery education, became a feature of American education in the 1880s.

Programs for young children with special needs were boosted early in the 1900s when Maria Montessori (1870–1962) began to work with retarded children in Italy. Montessori drew heavily on the sense training methods developed by Itard in his work with Victor. (See Chapter 4.)

Nineteenth-century parents had little say in their children's education; they deferred to educational experts. Throughout the 20th century, there was a rather slow but growing trend for parents to become more involved in the educational progress of their children. Parent–teacher groups sprang up in the opening decades. The first was the National Society for Crippled Children, formed in the United States in 1921. In 1933, an Ohio group of parents of children with mental disabilities established a parents' group to advocate the legal and educational rights of disabled children. The United Cerebral Palsy Association began in 1948.

Largely because of inadequate public and professional response to their children's educational and other needs, parents began to organize more formally on a local level in the 1940s and 1950s and on a national level in the 1960s. Often in uneasy alliance with professionals, they lobbied for more effective education and more humane treatment of persons with disabilities. Since then, parent organizations have had a tremendous impact on special education. Across Canada today, parent organizations exist at the local, provincial, and national level. Some of these groups are small, local, and casual; others are affiliated with professional organizations. Parent organizations have lobbied successfully for improved educational, social, recreational, and vocational services for their children. Parent advocacy has altered the standards of treatment in institutions, the development of community-based living facilities, personnel training, and research in prevention and amelioration of disabling conditions. Parent and professional activism has also brought to the courts the plight of children who are exceptional.

However, in the actual delivery of services, parents tended to be ignored. Until the early 1970s, they were not invited to participate to any degree but rather remained passive recipients of professional advice. Professionals made the major decisions about a child's needs and educational placement and then worked with the family and other agencies to attain the prescribed goals.

During the 1970s, professionals began to agree that parents could have a constructive impact, but involvement was typically limited to carrying out specific activities directed by the school. By the early 1980s, the traditional notion of professional expertise, which denied that parents are competent to take the initiative in regard to their child, began to change. Today, family-centred approaches emphasize that parents are the chief intervenors and advocates for their own children.

SUMMARY

1. Having a child with a disability has been acknowledged for many years to be a difficult situation for all family members. However, the emphasis on the family as the critical factor in the development of a child with a disability is a fairly new thrust. Today there is a greater commitment to provide comprehensive, coordinated, and family-focused services to children with disabilities and their families.
2. The effects of stress on the families of very young disabled or at-risk children are pervasive, multiple, and sometimes unsuspected. Families are as individual and unique as their children. With a child who is disabled, some families cope effectively and adaptively; others tend to feel helpless and experience less personal gratification and more child-related problems.
3. Over the years, families, family functioning, the impact of a member with a disability, and the provision of treatment and services have been looked at in different ways. Researchers examine family functioning in terms of a *stage-theory approach,* a *life-cycle approach,* a *systems approach,* or its first cousin, a *social-support approach.* Each of these ways of viewing families translates into practical models for actually intervening and working with families.
4. Although several authorities have questioned the validity of the stage theory in understanding parents' reactions to a child with a disability and prefer other approaches, it is still the most common and traditional way of looking at families with a disabled member. Stage theory suggests that the parents of children with disabilities pass through orderly stages before they accept the reality of their child's condition. Shock, denial, blame, guilt, depression, anger, and bargaining are all responses to the family member who is disabled.
5. The life-cycle approach sees families moving through time experiencing a series of events and tasks that include transitions. The currently favoured way of viewing families is through a systems approach or perspective that sees the family as a system; any event involving a change in the life of a family that has a disabled child can cause stress to the whole system. A family support system approach stresses how the family fits into the broader social context.
6. Each parent, each sibling, and each member of the extended family may reveal different reactions to the presence of a child with a disability in the family. However, studies on sib-

ling relationships are contradictory and inconsistent and those on the extended family sparse.

7. Both early intervention and its natural corollary, early identification, rest on the belief that children with disabilities can make positive gains if their problems are identified and diagnosed as early as possible and if they receive educational and therapeutic services attuned to their special needs. Early intervention activities are directed toward ameliorating problems in children with established disabilities and toward intervention with children who are at risk to prevent or hinder the development of conditions that impair learning or behaviour.
8. Early intervention is based on research evidence in child development, models of successful performance, the general observations of lay persons and experts, and the impetus from the American legislation, PL 99-452.
9. Early intervention allows treatment to begin; draws parents into the intervention process; may prevent the development of secondary conditions; and increases the chances that the child will achieve the greatest possible degree of independence. Parent involvement is critical. Research shows that early childhood special education is not as effective if parents are not involved and supported. As well, programs should be family-centred. They should establish the family as the focus of services; support and respect family decision making; and provide intervention services designed to strengthen family functioning.
10. Infant and toddler programs offer parents intensive participation and usually continue until the child is about three years of age. Programs in which workers visit the home are a promising mechanism used to provide for a growing population of children under the age of three receiving special services.
11. Programs try to enhance a child's development by helping the parents to become effective intervenors. The goal of training is to enable family members to achieve desired outcomes and to deal effectively with future concerns. For the child, the goal is optimal development in the motor, cognitive, language and communication, social, and self-help skill domains.
12. Today, many young children with disabilities are placed in normalized preschool settings (day-care or nursery school) under naturalistic curricula.
13. *Transition* is more than simply transferring records or relocating a child. It is a complex process as it relates to both the family and the child. For the child, moving from preschool involves a movement to a larger program with more children and new expectations. Children must practise co-operation, interdependence, sharing, teamwork, and group membership.

WEBLINKS

Beach Center on Families and Disability
www.lsi.ukans.edu/beach/research/pcp.html

The Canadian Association of Family Resource Programs
www.cafcc.on.ca/cafrp.htm

Canadian Early Childhood Care and Education Research and Policy **www.childcarecanada.org**

Canadian Parents Online **www.canadianparents.com/**

Family Centre on Technology and Disabilities **www.pacer.org**

Family Education Network **familyeducation.com/signup/cec**

Family Village **www.familyvillage.wisc.edu/**

National Parent Network on Disabilities **www.npnd.org/**

Parent Pals Gifted and Special Education Guide **parentpals.com/index2.html**

Parents Helping Parents **www.php.com/**

Chapter 16

Adolescents and Young Adults

Learning Outcomes

After reading this chapter, you should be able to:

- Understand the special needs of adolescents with disabilities;
- Relate the material in this chapter to earlier categorical chapters;
- Discuss models of inclusive schooling and their validity for adolescents with special needs;
- Appreciate the need for transition services and understand the transition process and its major components.

Introduction

It is only very recently that special education has begun to focus on early childhood and late adolescence. Currently, intense research is being directed toward very young children with special needs, and interest has grown dramatically in secondary-level students who are disabled and the schools' responsibilities to this population. Nevertheless, there remains a relative vacuum; research in the area of adolescents with learning or behavioural disorders is strikingly deficient compared to childhood groups.

Most program delivery models are found at elementary levels. Most inclusive projects occur at the preschool or elementary rather than high school or middle school levels: efficacy studies to support inclusion have been conducted in elementary schools, the professional literature focuses on the elementary level, and model programs described are elementary (see Cole and McLeskey, 1997). The number of students with disabilities served in general classes decreases with the age of the students, and the number served in separate classes, separate schools, and residential facilities increases (Hobbs and Westling, 1998). Only one-third the number of students with severe disabilities who are included in the elementary years remain included in secondary school (see Peters Goessling, 2000).

Why have secondary-level students in special education tended to be overlooked? There are a number of reasons. For one thing, most middle and high schools are organized on a departmental or subject-matter basis, and secondary schools are generally large places in which students are expected to function independently. As student bodies become larger, schedules become more complex and the system's ability to differentiate and individualize is compromised.

Student motivation and interest is different from that seen in elementary pupils. On average, the grades and attendance for all students, including those with special needs, decline after moving from elementary to junior high and high schools (see Roderick and Camburn, 1999). Teachers may feel that students show poor motivation and are at the end of their school careers, anyway.

Secondary teachers have different responsibilities and orientations than their peers at the elementary levels. They are trained as content specialists and may not offer students the same warm indulgence and social protection provided earlier. As well, elementary and secondary teachers differ on their views of integration and the kinds and numbers of accommodations they make (Olson, Chalmer, and Hoover, 1997). Findings show a tendency of secondary level teachers to be less accepting than others of students with special needs in regular classrooms (Savage and Wienke, 1989).

With the comparative lack of interest in the secondary experience, there is much that we still do not know about educational and counselling needs and transition planning at secondary levels and the needs of young adults with disabilities. While there is a far greater focus on the post-school experiences of young adults than there was even ten years ago, not enough is known about effective secondary-level programming, the experiences of young adults, and how schools can assist them as they enter the workforce or tertiary education.

What we do know about are the difficulties met by many young adults with disabilities. For them, the school experience, though tainted with frustration and failure, still offers some predictability. But the adult world does not have this predictability, and many tend to flounder in both occupations and independent living.

Of course, many people who are disabled develop into productive and self-sufficient adults. They marry, have children, assume mortgages, hold down jobs, and participate in social activities. But as adults, "the vast majority of students with disabilities never attain a satisfactory level of career development consistent with their capabilities" (Brolin and Gysbers, 1989, p. 155). Moreover, these students are not as adept in general independent living skills and may show deficits in areas such as knowledge about sexual conventions and behaviour.

transition

Contemporary educators are attempting to close the gap with a new thrust on **transition**, defined as "a systematic passage from school to adult life for students with disabilities" (Morningstar, Kleinhammer-Tramill, and Laltin, 1999, p. 1). Transition stresses academic achievement, social and personal adjustment, and post-school adjustment. In the school, counselling and sex education stand out as important elements contributing to adult life skills. There is also a greater focus on remedial education and a stress on programming designed to help students to obtain training, gain employment, and live productive, self-sufficient lives.

Transition services for young adults with disabilities are in their infancy; problems abound and there remain many barriers to the implementation of programs. There is a lack of a systematic approach to providing transition services, and not all school systems place priority on transition. For example, when the Canadian Council for Exceptional Children surveyed eight provinces and two territories on whether transition programs that support school-to-work programs exist in provincial policy, they found policies in five provinces or territories, no policy in three, and "under review" in two (Kasko, 2000).

ADOLESCENTS

In this final chapter we discuss the needs of adolescents and young adults with disabilities. We focus particularly on the need for transition planning and specific transition programming. This chapter also considers various types of post-secondary and employment options available to persons with disabilities.

In humans, the twenty-year developmental trajectory from birth on includes an extended and protracted childhood and the period known as *adolescence.* The adolescent years are characterized by major psychological, social, and physiological changes, and the biological capacity for adult relationships. With this rapid change emerges confusion, uncertainty, social anxiety, and acute self-awareness. Adolescence brings a period of identity crisis, intense peer-group relationships, and sometimes rebellion against established order. As adolescent students develop their own identities and their own expectations of the future, they begin to think of themselves as independent individuals, not their parents' children. They become less compliant with teachers and parents and more prone to question and criticize than younger children.

Every contemporary adolescent faces a daunting task in learning to become a competent adult, and the task is made more difficult if overlaid by an exceptional condition. Adolescence is a bad time to feel incompetent and unconfident. Small children can still feel comfortable being helped by adults and adults learn the limits of their abilities. But daily tests of personal competence against one's peers are the stuff of adolescence, and those who compete poorly meet a variety of problems in self-concept and interpersonal relationships.

Fulfilling the multiple tasks of adolescence is more difficult when a student has a disability: the characteristics specific to adolescents with disabilities simply exacerbate the normal difficulties of adolescence. Students with intellectual disabilities, for instance, may not have the cognitive ability to cope with the new developments within themselves and the new demands of the environment.

Environmental demands relate to the structure of secondary schools, including schedules and routines. Students with disabilities often have problems adjusting to the school and its expectations, classroom routines, the pressures of daily life, peer groups, and a range of different teachers. Students who have been successful in elementary school where there is some continuity between instructional areas and teachers often have difficulty in high school dealing with several different teachers and with compartmentalized instruction. Students may lack the plethora of survival skills that include going to class every day; arriving at school on time; bringing pencils and other supplies to class; turning in work on time; talking to teachers politely; and reading and following directions. For example, school attendance is a problem for adolescents who are learning disabled: more secondary students with learning disabilities fail regular courses because of attendance than for any other reason (Kaplan, 1996).

There is more to high school success than competency in academics. Social competence and peer acceptance are increasingly important. Between the ages of six and twelve, children spend an average of 40 percent of their waking hours in the company of peers, children of their own age and status (Cole and Cole, 1989). By adolescence, students spend far more time with friends and place special emphasis on the qualities of intimacy, mutual understanding, and loyalty.

Peers, being popular with peers, and belonging to the right crowd are a critical part of growing up. Adolescents are particularly vulnerable to the negative impact of having few or no friends, a situation that may be common for students with disabilities. One report (Polloway, Epstein, Patton, Cullinan, and Lueble, 1986) found that teacher ratings indicated that more than 20 percent of older students with mild intellectual disabilities were rejected by their peers.

For normally developing students, self-esteem increases steadily during adolescence and early adulthood; on the average, eighteen-year-olds have higher self-esteem than thirteen-year-olds. Social, physical, and cognitive deficits hinder this process in adolescents with disabilities. Physical disabilities, for example, reduce the rate of self-concept formation (Lawrence, 1991).

The gap between students with disabilities and their peers continues to widen the further they progress in school. Low-achieving students are frequently judged in relation to high achievers, and feelings of inferiority, lack of motivation, and interpersonal hostility often result. Teenagers who are disabled often become frustrated with their lack of progress; they may become caught in a spiral of failure and dissatisfaction, resign themselves to a poor view of their intelligence and their ability as a whole, and lose their self-esteem and motivation.

For teachers at the secondary level, the world of the adolescent raises issues that are far broader than those raised for the elementary-school child. These include the adolescent's emerging sexuality, vocational interests and talents, future expectations, range of leisure activities, and independent living skills. Teachers are also faced with negative attitudes toward school and academic learning that many adolescents have developed, the manifestations of disabilities, and the need for remedial programming.

CONCEPTS OF TRANSITION

Definitions of the term *transition* have in common the concept that a transition is a passage or an evolution, not simply a "here today gone tomorrow" phenomenon. In other words, transitions are not a fleeting proposition but rather represent recurrent, life-long processes that all individuals experience.

As used in relation to the needs of adolescents with disabilities, *transition* has a number of meanings and foci.

- Transition as an ongoing experience. For all students, the high-school experience represents a period of transition between the security of school and the complexity associated with the opportunities and risks of adult life. The quality of the secondary school experience and the decisions made during this time have significant implications for the quality of life experienced after students leave school.
- Transition as a movement. The general concept of transition has recently become a thrust in special education in the sense that transition is the movement from one service delivery system to another. For the adolescent with disabilities, this means moving from the school, with its services in education and counselling, to an adult world with com-

munity services and advocacy and self-help groups such as the Canadian Association for Community Living.

- Transition as a school program focus. Transition programs focus on the acquisition of life and vocational skills with the focus on the local community, and on both job preparation and job finding and maintenance. Programs seek the maximum development of intellectual, personal, social, and vocational skills necessary for independent functioning.

An emphasis on transition in the adolescent years is rather new in special education. It essentially developed from a number of interlinked thrusts. Historically, the secondary transition movement is grounded in the co-operative work/study programs of the 1960s and the career education initiative of the 1970s.

The obvious need for transition activities developed as follow-up studies of graduates of public school programs indicated that something had to be done about the poor post-school performance of many young adults with disabilities. Many students with special needs, despite special education programs, still experience major difficulties in bridging the gap from school to community work and living. They meet difficulties in independent living, occupational stability, and status within their communities. They do not utilize community services and resources effectively, and tend to be isolated from peers, both disabled and non-disabled.

Transition is similarly an appropriate response for families that sometimes feel abandoned. As students near the end of their school careers, parents realize that special education services are ending but hold little certainty that community services will begin and provide needed support.

In the early 1980s, the American government made commitments to transition services in terms of both policy and federal discretionary grants. First, amendments to PL 94-142 (PL 98-199) included a Secondary Education and Transition Services section in which Section 626 authorized funds to be spent on research, training, and demonstration in the transition area. A later amendment, the Individuals with Disabilities Education Act (IDEA, 1990, PL 101-476) provided a clear definition along with transition mandates and programming. According to IDEA, transition is

> a co-ordinated set of activities for a student, designed with an outcome-oriented process, which promotes movement from school to post-school activities, including post-secondary education, vocational training, integrated employment (including supported employment), continuing and adult education, adult services, independent living, or community participation. The co-ordinated set of activities shall be based upon the individual student's preferences and interests, and shall include instruction, community experiences, and development of employment and other post-school adult living objectives, and, when appropriate, acquisition of daily living skills and functional vocational evaluation. (PL101-476, Sec. 602 (a)(19))

The American definition makes a number of points that are salient to the Canadian situation:

- The transition process is a vehicle for alleviating the problems of youth with various disabilities and need levels through integrating planning, instruction, placement, and provision of ongoing support as and after they leave school.
- Effective transition planning is much more than the mere physical transfer of administrative responsibility for an individual's service program from the school to

adult service agencies. Successfully negotiating the transition through and out of high school is a process that requires varying degrees of assistance from family and school personnel.

- A basic objective during the transition period is to arrange for individuals with disabilities those services needed to support successful adult living. There may be many different agencies, depending on the nature and severity of the disability.
- Transition involves collaboration and coordination. The likelihood of meaningful post-secondary outcomes is possible only when stakeholders work together—including schools, community agencies, human service organizations, employers, and students and their families.
- The involvement of parents in secondary programs has been traditionally underemphasized. For transition to be successful, parents must be involved.
- Transition is founded on the premise that all persons with disabilities can perform meaningful tasks and assume valued roles within normal community settings.
- Transition initiatives enhance the prospects for economic stability for persons who are exceptional.
- Although community employment is the goal of transition planning and secondary-level vocational instruction, the placement of a graduating student into a job should not be considered an outcome in and of itself. It is also important to identify the quality of life outcomes that the student wishes to obtain through employment. Quality of life outcomes are the tangible and intangible results of employment that contribute to the enhancement of students' lifestyles.
- In transition, the school has two primary roles. First, it is the school's responsibility to develop and implement an effective program that will prepare students for life in their local communities. Second, the school must take the lead in coordinating the transition planning process (see Figure 16-1). This involves secondary programs for transition, linkages to post-secondary environments, and post-secondary services.
- A transition team should include all those providing services in both school and community—special educators, family members, general and vocational educators, adult service providers, employers, community leaders, and consumers. The team should target skills that the student may need to be successful after he or she leaves school. It should also address the student's strengths, the family's critical concerns, and other needs related to broad skill domains (such as non-verbal communication, language, social relationships, self-management, academics, personal care, community living, home living, vocational skills, and recreational interests and skills).
- Transition planning must be incorporated into the IEP planning process. The transition component, to be developed not later than the student's sixteenth birthday, is designed to provide instruction and community experiences that lead to post-school outcomes in a variety of areas, including post-secondary education, training, employment, independent living, and community participation (Furney, Hasazi, and De Stefano, 1997).
- Student participation, which includes self-evaluation, self-determination, student-identified post-school goals, and self-selected educational experiences, is important.

The goals to ensure a successful transition from high school to adult life require major commitments from schools, adult services, and communities. In the following section, we ex-

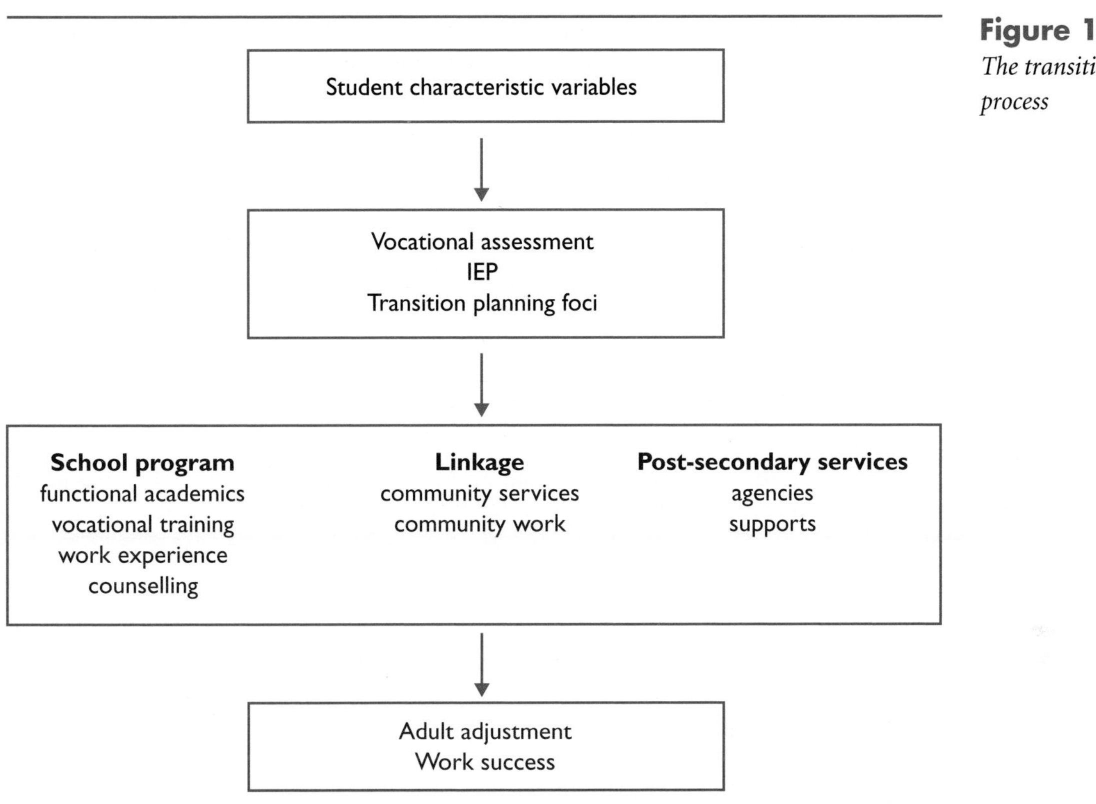

Figure 16-1
The transition process

amine various facets of the transition process. The focus is on the school's responsibilities; also mentioned are student participation, parent involvement, and post-school options.

The School's Responsibilities in Transition

At the school level, transition involves the provision of school experiences that will assist in locating and maintaining employment together with training in skills for successful adulthood. The school should also identify community resources to assist students and involve students and parents.

Preparation for Transition

Schools must prepare for transitions. Transition planning should start much sooner than high school; it should begin in the elementary grades. Career awareness can begin as early as the primary grades with discussions about what it means to work in a particular job (Bounds, 1997). Students also begin to learn the rudiments of community and vocational living skills in upper elementary school.

Formal Transition Plan

For secondary students with mild disabilities, there are three essential components in senior programming: work preparation skills, functional academics, and life-skills training, which includes counselling and sex education. For students with severe disabilities the curriculum should expose them to job options in the community in which they live; teach specific work skills such as using tools and equipment; and teach work-related skills, such as transportation and personal hygiene (McDonnell, Ferguson, and Mathot-Buckner, 1992).

Adolescents with disabilities need a comprehensive curriculum that leads to successful, satisfying employment. A variety of generic curriculum domains have been proposed during recent years as important components of secondary special education. The major areas of instruction are academic skills, specifically functional academics, to remediate deficient basic skills; vocational skills, which include career exploration and occupational knowledge and skills, such as job finding skills, work experience, and job maintenance; personal management skills, which include independent living knowledge and skills such as budgeting, home management, and social skills; and leisure skills.

Within these domains, instruction should occur throughout the school years, with the relative emphasis on the vocational domain increasing at secondary levels. Training in this area helps students to develop stronger self-concepts and to engage in self-supporting productive work.

Preparation should include an individual transition plan as part of a student's IEP. The plan will include goals and objectives, timelines, and designations of responsible persons and agencies. Educationally, the IEP will focus on a comprehensive curriculum that is functional in nature and that includes community-based vocational instruction. It will identify and teach activities that will maximize the individual's participation in community settings, such as vocational training, personal management, and recreation/leisure activities. The plan will also identify the types of community services that will be necessary to support the individual's participation, and complete the steps required to access community services.

Planned and systematic opportunities to interact with non-disabled peers help prepare young people with disabilities to function independently in the general community.

Service Delivery

Integration at the secondary levels is harder to implement than it is for young children. Various factors account for this:

- Younger children acclimatize more rapidly to integrated settings than do older students.
- The mental gap between non-disabled students and those with disabilities continuously widens with age.
- The grade level of the class is a proxy for a number of variables. For example, primary-grade students are more tolerant than are those of junior-high-school age, who are more likely to ostracize a child.
- The instructional emphasis at the secondary levels is different from that of the elementary school. Curriculum in secondary schools is no longer focused on the acquisition of basic skills but on the use of skills to acquire content knowledge.
- Teachers at the elementary level are more student oriented than subject-matter-oriented; the opposite goes for most high school teachers (MacMillan, Gresham, and Forness, 1996).
- The current needs and ultimate goals of students at the end of their school careers are different from those of younger children. As Figure 16-2 shows, the needs that must be addressed by secondary programming meld into after-school needs.

In many ways, inclusive practices are in direct conflict with what we know works for adolescent students with disabilities in terms of functional skill instruction and vocational training in the community. So it is not surprising that there is skepticism about whether inclusion is feasible or desirable for secondary students. Some researchers go so far as to contend that, at the secondary level, the full integration of all students is simply not appropriate; it is an invitation to failure (e.g., Edgar, 1987; Schumaker and Deshler, 1988). Wayne Nesbit (1990) points out that for senior students with special needs, a case can be made for special programming because it is the special aspects of the senior program that will do much to facilitate long-term normalization.

The argument circles around three interrelated themes: the characteristics of adolescent students with disabilities, the content of the regular curriculum, and the future needs of students. We discuss each of these themes below.

Student Characteristics

If we examine the characteristics of students, we find that adolescents do not outgrow their learning difficulties, nor is simple maturation matched with an increase in motivation and achievement. On the contrary. Factors correlated with students with mild disabilities include physiological and neurological problems, deficits in cognitive processes such as memory and metacognitive awareness, disorders of attention, social behaviour problems, communication problems, and perceptual problems. For example, of all disabilities, learning disabilities are the most open to the assumption that they can be cured and are not lifelong. This is, unfortunately, not true. Certainly, learning disabilities change form as students get older. But even with appropriate intervention, learning disabilities do not just go away; they tend to endure into adulthood.

Secondary students classified as learning disabled often retain subtle manifestations of

Figure 16-2
Needs of secondary students

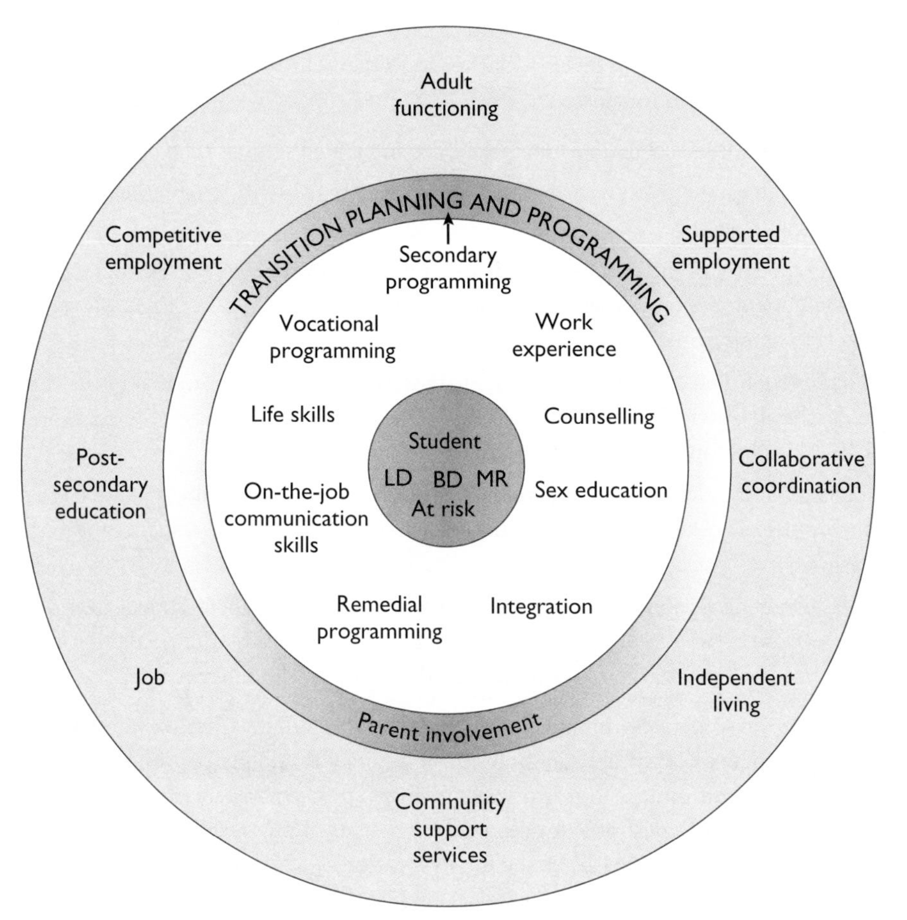

childhood traits, such as lack of coordination and hyperactivity. Academically, they tend to plateau at fourth or fifth grade. The result: almost all of these students lack functional proficiency in language, reading, handwriting, spelling, and arithmetic. They often cannot understand the abstract language of academic disciplines or comprehend the texts.

Adolescents with learning disabilities are at risk for emotional difficulties and are more likely to experience depression (Kaplan, 1996). They tend to demonstrate a high degree of anxiety, low expectations of future success, poor adaptive strategies for coping with normal stress and solving everyday personal problems, reduced motivation, and poor self-concept. Social deficits often create frustration and students become emotionally vulnerable and easily stressed.

With so many barriers to performance, adolescents with learning disabilities are often characterized as passive learners, lacking in motivation, underachieving in academic skills, lacking social skills, without the ability to comprehend the varied demands of secondary school, and lacking organizational skills. Homework, for example, accounts for about 20 percent of student time spent on academic tasks, but it is estimated that 56 percent of students with learning disabilities have difficulty completing homework (Bryan and Sullivan-Burstein, 1997).

Similarly, students with learning disabilities (and those with behavioural disorders) exhibit higher levels of test anxiety than do their non-disabled peers (Rizzo and Zabel, 1988). Test anxiety has been associated with depressed academic performance and self-defeating interpersonal and intrapersonal behaviour. It contributes to the development of detrimental motivational, coping, and task strategies such as dependence, self-deprecation, and conformity (Swanson and Howell, 1996), negative self-evaluation, difficulties in concentrating, and off-task thoughts.

Learning disabilities can embed individuals in a cycle of frustration and failure. The letter below was written many years after the person had left school, yet it offers a particularly

Case Study

Brian

Dear Teacher,

You will not, I am sure, remember me. I am the child you failed in the second grade many years ago. That failure had profound effects on my life. It was my first, but not my last, bitter taste of defeat. I never found out from my mother why I failed that year. I was told only that "it was thought best."

The full implication of repeating a grade did not dawn on me until the day school started that next autumn. I had once felt like my younger sister's smart older brother, but now I felt like her slow, retarded brother. From that day onward, she and I were both in the same grade until we parted company in high school.

I hated school after that first day of my second go-round in grade two. Teacher, I hated you. I hated being the same mental age as my younger sister. I hated authority. I had done my best to please you the year before and my best was not good enough. I quit trying to please anyone in school.

You never asked me why I was hyperactive and could not sit still. You never wondered how it felt to be in the "Blue Birds" slow reading group. You never asked how I felt about math, which I just could not do. I wanted to be good at numbers, but I could just not cope with the anger that math provoked in me.

To some people, numbers are friendly little creatures that love you. To me, numbers were mean ugly biters that bullied me every chance they got. Hell, I thought, must be having to do numbers forever by working them out in your head. Spelling was also a painful subject. I used to avoid your eyes, and prayed that you would not call on me.

As a young teenager, I thought I had found the answer to all my problems in the power of alcohol. I relied on alcohol to change my fear into temporary courage, and to turn my feelings of low self-worth into Superman-like confidence. At first my answer worked. But in time it became a one-way ticket to training school, jail, and personal defeat. Only by luck did I meet a counsellor who understood my learning problems and helped to set me on the right path.

In closing, I'd just like to say that today you have other children like me in your classroom. They may be the shy wallflower types or the loud performers that get on your nerves and disturb the rest of the class. They may be the ones with hidden secrets who daydream all day long. One thing is certain—they are already awake and the nightmare will not go away.

Thank you for listening, Teacher,
Brian

poignant example of a child whose learning disability was not identified during the school years and who met with great difficulties in adolescence and early adulthood.

While an estimated 50 percent of individuals classified as Attention Deficit Hyperactivity Disorder experience a brain maturational spurt of unknown etiology and do outgrow the condition, the other 50 percent have difficulties that persist into adulthood and cause concentration and attention problems. In a longitudinal study, Lambert (1988) identified more than 100 hyperactive children in elementary school, tracked them until they were seventeen or eighteen years old, and then compared them with non-hyperactive peers. He found that the students in the hyperactive group were less likely to have graduated from high school and more likely to have run away from home or become delinquent. They were more aggressive than their peers and more likely to be receiving treatment for psychological problems.

Long-term prospects for students who are both hyperactive and aggressive are even more bleak. Students with ADHD or learning disabilities combined with aggression, inattention, and impulsivity are at elevated risk for violent and antisocial behaviour (Lynam, 1996).

We point out in Chapter 7 that while the onset of aggressive behaviour can be gradual, extending over many years, the long-term effects are more serious when antisocial behaviour begins early. Patterns of early poor behaviour are often highlighted at school entry, magnified in the classroom setting, and then show escalating conflict and an increasing cycle of severity and intensity. About one half of the children with disruptive behavioural problems in preschool years continue to have problems in the school years; the other half improve (Campbell, 1995).

Continued antisocial behaviour in childhood places a student at substantial risk for a wide variety of negative outcomes. The continuation of antisocial behaviour in school is likely to lead to rejection and low levels of peer acceptance, increased risk of school failure, membership in deviant peer groups, dropping out of school, eventual delinquency, and poor adjustment and mental health in later years, especially for boys. Socially unacceptable behaviour in adulthood is most likely to be seen in individuals classified as conduct disordered.

Along with deviant behaviours, students identified as behaviourally disordered demonstrate academic deficits; they have lower grades, fail more courses, are often retained in one grade or more, and pass minimum competency tests at lower rates than do students with other disabilities. In the United States, less than 50 percent of these students graduate from high school (see Maag and Katsiyannis, 1998; Rylance, 1997).

Curriculum

The second argument against universal inclusion focuses on the content of the secondary school curriculum. Adolescents with disabilities who spend the majority of their school day in general education classes are expected to meet the same demands as their non-disabled peers. Students must be able to listen to lectures and take notes; complete many written assignments; read content-area information, often from poorly organized textbooks; and take tests that frequently do not facilitate students' responding.

In the general education classroom, students can experience success only when the teacher is able to meet their individual learning needs through appropriate curriculum adaptations and modifications. But curriculum adaptations are not a part of secondary classroom life. In general, general educators teach to single large groups and incorporate little or no differentiation based on student need. Few teachers make adaptations and, when they do, it is more often than not lowering their expectations of students rather than attempting to improve their programs (Fuchs, Fuchs, Hamlett, Phillips, and Karns, 1995). For example, a study of sixty social studies and science teachers who were seen as effective with students with learning disabilities by peers, principals, and self found that the teachers made few adaptations to meet special learning needs (McIntosh, Vaughn, Schumm, Haager, and Lee, 1994).

Even the special education curriculum, as it now stands, may be inappropriate. Researchers (Kaiser and Abell, 1997) observe that: "The traditional special education curriculum at the secondary level, driven by both graduation requirements and deficits in the students' present levels of performance, often does not meet the transitional needs of youth with mild disabilities" (p. 70). For example, students with learning disabilities enter secondary school severely deficient in basic reading and written expression skills; three or four years later they leave with little or no improvement in these areas (Espin and Foegen, 1996).

Future Needs

Finally, there are the future needs of students. In the educational mainstream, some of the necessary curricular elements are simply not present. The overall secondary curriculum is not congruent with the present needs of many senior students with disabilities; they do not have either the interest or the reading ability required for academic credit courses (Nesbit, 1990).

Traditional secondary-school subjects are generally not related to the future needs of students; preparation for independent living requires much more than academic goals for adolescents who are disabled. Their hope is to work, not to continue schooling, and there is less likelihood that their career development needs will be met in regular classrooms (Izzo, 1987). By this stage, the major goal of education should not be to compensate for intellectual and physical deficiencies per se. Rather, instruction must be directed toward the development of critical skills necessary for adulthood, for success in daily life, for citizenship, and for a future career.

Counselling

The needs of adolescents are quite different from those of younger children and, when the adolescent has a disability, the needs become even more intense. Both guidance and vocational/career counselling play important roles.

Guidance Counselling

guidance counselling

Guidance counselling assists students in selecting courses, in adapting to their disability, and in personal concerns. It may also slip over into the area of career plans, occupational choice, and job placement.

Adaptation to the disability is a major thrust. Students with physical disabilities, for example, reach an awareness of their disability and its implications at different ages. Generally, they move from a broad understanding of the disability at age six to a more acute realization of the implications by age eight (Dunn, McCartan, and Fugura, 1988). By the time they reach the adolescent years, students with physical disabilities hold deep concerns regarding social acceptance, sexuality, and career choices. Students may need instruction in social skills as they mature and may also have to deal with sexual needs.

Learning how to dress and use makeup to improve personal appearance can prove tricky for students who are blind. The problem is intensified if the appearance of the eyes is abnormal, while the unattractive appearance of optical aids may cause adolescents to reject them. Many adolescents with visual impairments try to mask their disabilities because they perceive visual impairments as a negative attribute (Sacks and Corn, 1996). Students often need assistance in dealing with the implications of visual impairment; personal counselling and sex education to develop greater social awareness; and help with more pragmatic concerns such as dress codes and the use of cosmetics.

For adolescents with hearing impairments, the problems of deciding on communication modes and on a cultural identity complicate life (Garbe and Rodda, 1988). Deafness is an invisible handicap, and students with hearing impairments do not receive much sympathy (Corywell, Holcomb, and Scherer, 1992). Counselling can assist in improving relations between students who are hearing impaired and their hearing peers.

In the case study below, two students, Gretchen and Christopher, are each dealing with a disability and its implications.

Case Study

Gretchen

Gretchen is now in grade ten at Point West School. She is severely visually impaired and has low vision, even with the use of strong correction. She has always been included in regular classrooms and has learned orientation and mobility from a special teacher. Gretchen reads large print but has only very recently started to learn braille and does not use it for classroom work.

In elementary school, and even into junior high, Gretchen was an average student. She needed, and received, much extra assistance with reading and math, and adaptations of assignments and tests. But now high school is proving arduous for Gretchen. She is falling far behind her peers, chiefly because she can't keep up with the reading in the content-area textbooks and with the homework. All her subjects are suffering, but in English she is failing badly. Her reading is slow, written language is poor, and her spelling shows gross deficits.

Gretchen is well aware that she is not doing well, but is reacting with defiance. She tells the teacher that there is too much homework and at home storms to her parents about the load. Adding to her academic deficits are developing social problems. Gretchen appears to be finding it difficult to accept her impairment, the needed optical aids, and the restraints on lifestyle. Her moodiness has seen her more and more ignored by her peers.

The school counsellor has spent much time with Gretchen. The major aim of counselling is to help Gretchen to accept her disability and its limitations while also stressing her strengths. Grooming and other self-care skills are also a part of the process. For classroom work, the amount of homework has decreased, Gretchen now has a computer with large print for all classroom work, and a note-taking buddy has been assigned.

Christopher

Christopher attends the same school. He comes from a home where both parents are deaf, and a younger sibling has a profound hearing impairment. Chris himself has been diagnosed as severely hard of hearing. He has a flat loss in both ears of 85 dB. He wears aids and has an interpreter in some classes (English, math, science, and social studies) to translate the teacher's message into sign language and to translate back the comments that Chris makes and questions he answers.

For most of his career, Christopher had been in special placements. For all of elementary school, he was in a residential school for deaf students. His parents agreed, with some trepidation, when the residential school suggested that Chris could be integrated. This is only the second year that Chris has been integrated into a classroom with normally hearing peers.

Chris uses sign as his main mode of communication but has developed quite acceptable speech. Both his language and reading are well below grade level, however, and he has great difficulty in keeping up with the work of the classroom. But it is his behaviour that is the chief concern. Recently, it has become worse and worse. In his homeroom and in the other classes, Chris shows overt acting-out behaviour. If reprimanded, he sulks and will not participate in the lesson at all. When the teacher speaks to him, he reaches up and turns off his aid and closes his eyes. The interpreter is at a loss; she never knows how many of Chris's "off the cuff" and rude remarks to interpret for the teacher and finds herself playing the role of mediator.

Because of the behaviour, both the school counsellor and the psychologist met with Chris at different times. They later reported that the residential setting was where Chris wanted to be. He found the competition with his peers too difficult, did not feel that he was accepted in the class, often could not understand what was going on, even with an interpreter, and missed his deaf friends. Most especially, Chris stressed that he was a "deaf boy" and wanted to use sign, not speech, and to identify more closely with the deaf community. If his parents wanted him to go to university, then he would choose Gallaudet.

The needs of students who are gifted cannot be overlooked in the counselling process. Some, but certainly not all, students who are gifted in high school consider their giftedness a social liability, and may need assistance in course selection and understanding the implications of potential.

The increases in antisocial and law-breaking behaviour, in truancy, the emotional conflicts, personal disturbances, and learning problems characteristic of students with behavioural disorders suggest the need for intervention in the areas of vocation and career, sexuality, and drug abuse. Counselling must be a long-term process: it needs an extended time frame to deal with students' affect, to increase their understanding of why they behave as they do, and to explore the possibility of change.

Vocational/Career Counselling

For all of us, career choices are limited by such factors as individual preferences, aptitude, and temperament. Career and vocational education are particularly important for students with disabilities who need to critically assess the competencies required in specific occupations and identify realistic vocational goals that match their maximum vocational potential.

Few adolescents, disabled or not, know about available occupations in their geographic area, the content of people's work, or their earnings. Students with disabilities often have even fewer and less diverse career-related experiences and learning opportunities than do their peers without disabilities. Individuals who are deaf, for example, know less than their hearing peers about different types of occupations (Schroedel, 1992).

Data suggest that students are aware of their lack of preparedness. A study of 106 students with severe physical disabilities (Liebert, Lutsky, and Gottlieb, 1990) found that graduates expressed a desire for more intensive guidance counselling (especially in the area of job placement), additional training in upgrading job skills, more help with transportation, and more access to social and recreational programs. In another study of students with and without learning disabilities, the learning-disabled group had a far greater desire for more information about how to find a job, keep a job, and live independently than did their non-disabled peers (Dowdy, Carter, and Smith, 1990).

Having some work experience before graduation helps adolescents with the transition to adult life.

For adolescents who are visually impaired, realistic career choices can be difficult. Those who are deaf need help in vocational training and counselling to assess their strengths, weaknesses, and interests. Counsellors can encourage students to consider a broad array of options and to take a major role in decision making.

Multipotential can be a mixed blessing; many youngsters who are gifted share a feeling of ambivalence about the future and their place in it. By ages thirteen or fourteen, some students are already conditioned to avoid failure at all costs. They are willing to pursue career choices far below their potential (Willings, 1983). Others cannot focus on career plans.

For average learners, career plans can change between seventeen and nineteen years of age. For those who are gifted, changes in career plans can occur between thirteen and fourteen, sixteen and eighteen, and twenty-one and twenty-three. A radical change in careers for the gifted develops between ages twenty-eight and thirty-two. (Talented children, on the other hand, often have fixed career goals prior to adolescence.) Gifted students need personal and career counselling, a networking system that links students to school and community resources, and appropriate role models.

For all students who are exceptional, a major aim of career counselling is a careful assessment and analysis of students' strengths and weaknesses, motivations and preferences, and performance in training programs. Counsellors need to establish students' present levels with regard to readiness for adult settings. For this, a vocational evaluation is required.

vocational evaluation

A **vocational evaluation** is a comprehensive and systematic process that utilizes work (real or simulated) to assess the vocational potential of people with disabilities. The process incorporates data such as test scores, medical data, information on education and work experience, and the needs and interests of the individual in setting vocational goals and service requirements (Pruitt, 1986).

Vocational evaluation helps students identify their functional capacities and limitations, formulate realistic vocational goals, and determine their needs for rehabilitation programming (Power, 1984). Sometimes the results of a vocational evaluation will suggest that the goals of the students (and sometimes their parents) are unrealistic. At other times, job choices may be below a student's capacity.

Counsellors may use instruments such as Becker's (1981) Vocational Interest Inventory, which requires no reading. Individuals select the jobs they would prefer from fifty-five black and white outline drawings depicting eleven categories of unskilled, semi-skilled, and skilled jobs. Students who are deaf can use the Transition Competence Battery (Bullis and Reiman, 1992, 1997) or the Self-Help InterPersonal Skills Assessment (Loeding and Crittenden, 1993).

Sex Education

Adolescents with disabilities are less likely to have accurate information about sex, are more subject to fears and myths, and are more likely to be sexually exploited than are their normally developing peers. Studies indicate that children with disabilities are 150 times more at risk than others for being sexually abused ("Increased ... ," 1993).

The problems are particularly acute for individuals with intellectual disabilities in the community who are exposed to all the contingencies of sexuality, including situations that involve sexual coercion (Podell, Kastner, and Kastner, 1996). It is reported that as many as 89 percent of persons with intellectual disabilities say they have been sexually abused ("Increased...," 1993). A study using structured interviews (Stromsness, 1993) found that just under 80 percent of the subjects had been sexually abused.

It is imperative that students be provided with sex education that includes instruction in social behaviour and self-protection. Participation in society has increased the risk of unwanted pregnancies, venereal diseases, and abuse. And, since most persons with mild and moderate retardation now live in the community and do not learn easily from non-directed observations, books, or friends, instruction in appropriate sexual behaviour is particularly important for them.

Equally compelling are the principles of normalization. The major goal of normalization is a normal family and community life for all individuals, and sexual activity is a normal part of human life. It is a myth that individuals who are physically disabled do not have sexual needs or that persons with intellectual disabilities are asexual or oversexed. People with mental and physical disabilities have the same range of sexual needs and drives as everyone else.

Persons who are intellectually disabled are likely to develop a strong and normal interest in the opposite sex. But, as with non-disabled people, some seem to have little need for physical contact, some express more need than the average, and the majority fall in the middle range (McClennen, 1988). If physical development is normal, sexual development follows chronological rather than cognitive development, although psychosocial development may be reached at a later chronological age (Martin and Forchuk, 1987). Because of this, some individuals who are disabled are more likely to express experimentation overtly. They may also have trouble figuring out where the boundaries are and when they should say no.

To understand sexuality, an individual must be educated about sexuality. Adolescent students may need to be made aware that their own sexuality is acceptable and that they have the same rights to sexual expression as do their peers. Sex education programs for adolescents who are physically and mentally disabled should include explanations of bodily functions, the mechanics of reproduction, social behaviour, dating skills, and preparation for marriage and family.

AIDS is also an issue for adolescents because adolescence is often a time of sexual confusion and experimentation (Sloane and Sloane, 1990). Effective AIDS education means talking about topics such as homosexuality, drugs, and condoms (although this makes many parents uneasy).

Functional Academics

Despite special education programming often offered throughout their school careers, many adolescent students with disabilities continue to function far below grade level. They often require a functional skill approach to improve functioning in present environments and facilitate transition to and participation in age-appropriate future environments.

Rather than focusing solely on the traditional three Rs, teachers of secondary students with disabilities must be concerned with targeting useful learning objectives. Students require functional skills and **functional academics**; that is, academics that have meaning and are relevant to the learner soon to enter community work and life.

functional academics

Functional academics include intense remedial instruction for skill deficits, such as basic knowledge and skills in reading, computation, study skills, and strategy training to enable older students to gain the knowledge of how to use skills to meet demands of the academic, occupational, and social environment. Functional skills are essentially all the components a student requires to successfully negotiate life as an adult. The myriad of skills are those in self-care, mobility training, communication, social interaction, health and safety, leisure time, vocational pursuits and skills such as filling out applications, and improving job related behaviour such as time on task, following directions, and dealing with authority (Maag and Katsiyannis, 1998).

Vocational Education and Work Experiences

Transition should focus on work personality (self-concept and motivation); work competencies (habits, physical and mental skills, and interpersonal skills); and work goals (career objectives) (see Szymanski, 1994). It should facilitate students' access to and participation in the receiving environment through job preparation that includes skills such as locating job openings in newspapers and displaying correct behaviour during a job interview.

Students are given opportunities to learn a trade through high-school-sponsored vocational training and on-the-job training in the context of full or part-time work-study programs. Course content includes a multitude of job search, job maintenance, and work-related interpersonal skills lesson formats including the following: obtaining documentation necessary to become employed; preparing a résumé; completing a job application; identifying jobs of interest; finding job leads; organizing a job search; contacting employers by telephone, in person, and in writing; interviewing for a job; and handling work-related paperwork such as timecards, paycheque stubs, work schedule, and tax returns.

Students are taught about being a good employee and getting along with others on the job. This includes skills such as understanding instruction; asking a question; asking for help; accepting criticism; ordering job responsibilities; accepting assistance; giving instruction; offering assistance; apologizing; convincing others; being punctual; and practising good attendance. They also need practice in getting to and from work, which includes telephoning for bus route information, reading bus maps and schedules, and practising appropriate and safe behaviour on public transit. There is also information on making positive job changes; setting realistic goals for the future; and being an effective self-advocate (Montague, 1988; Patton, Cronin, Polloway, Hutchinson, and Robinson, 1989).

Work-study experiences, founded on the premise that there should be some cross-coordination between schoolwork and vocational experiences, play a major role in the secondary curriculum and link the preparatory employment to the receiving environment through community-based instruction. Instruction is referenced directly to activities and performance demands in the local community. Students are placed in work situations in the community, and their academic programs are oriented to supplement the work experience.

For youth who are disabled, part-time jobs during school and enrollment in vocational classes correlate with increases in employability (Siegel, Robert, and Gaylord Ross, 1992). Students who have paid work as part of secondary school experiences are significantly more likely to have a competitive job than those without such experiences (62 percent versus 45 percent) (Bounds, 1997). Persons who are intellectually disabled, for example, who have been in school work experience programs tend to respond better to occupational demands and are more employable than those not in programs (Patton et al., 1989).

The reasons are fairly obvious. Work experiences allow individuals to try new things in an atmosphere that allows for a second chance (Nesbit, 1990). Students learn how to adapt to changes in the work environment and how to maintain acceptable levels of work performance. As well, training often gives students the boost they need to succeed in the work world. Not only do they learn specific job skills, but also they learn how to conduct themselves on the job, know the responsibilities that accompany employment, and gain a better idea of what it takes to succeed in a particular field (Bounds, 1997). Holding a paid job allows youth to hone their work skills and demonstrate their reliability to potential employers. Paid work experiences provide students an opportunity to apply classroom learning in the real world, gives meaning to their learning, and can be a great motivator (Bounds, 1997).

For students with severe disabilities, the school's vocational curriculum cannot be divorced from the community in which the child lives. Schools need to identify potential employment in early training conducted in the home community (Moon and Inge, 1993).

Social Skills Instruction

The existence of social skill deficits among populations of students who are disabled has been well documented in the professional literature. Adaptive behaviour is predictive of certain aspects of future vocational performance, and the absence of effective social skills is considered to be a major cause of the less than successful adjustment of students who are disabled to the regular competitive workforce.

Wayne Nesbit notes that when senior students finish school, their personalities must be marketable. "The reality," observes Nesbit, "is that they will not receive an academic high school certificate nor will they earn a university degree. It is their personality and ability to work co-operatively which determines their acceptance and success in the work world" (1990, p. 5).

Programs provide training in the social skills needed for job success. For students with intellectual disabilities, for example, targeted social skills range from isolated non-verbal responses such as eye contact and gestures to complex skills involved in asking questions, expressing appreciation and praise, and carrying on a conversation. Students may also need training in aspects of speech such as loudness, intonation, and intelligibility.

Self-management

Self-management refers to a multiplicity of skills needed for independence in the adult world. For example, students learn about apartment living, marriage, family responsibilities, budgeting, and community resources. Students with severe disabilities need instruction in life skills, which include basic hygiene, grooming and dressing, as well as mobility, money handling, shopping, housekeeping, and leisure skills. Even for those who can never achieve full independence, life skills training contributes to feelings of confidence, self-reliance, and personal satisfaction.

Futures Planning

Upon completion of their public schooling, many young people with disabilities still need additional assistance and support to negotiate the transition process successfully. Transition should ensure access to community support and continuity of services. The adult agency support component is designed to educate students and their family members about the procedures of becoming active clients of vocational rehabilitation, or other agencies, before graduation.

Students need to be trained in self-determination, defined as "an attitude expressed in determining one's goals and taking the initiative to meet those goals" (Holub, Lamb, and Bang, 1998, p. 185). Self-determination influences a person's ability to make choices and preferences about the future built on a realistic understanding of individual strengths and weaknesses.

Parent Involvement

In a survey of special educators in secondary schools, the activities they considered most important were teaching social skills and job skills, involving parents, and matching skills to the job (Morgan, Morre, McSweyn, and Salzberg, 1992). Nevertheless, parent involvement continues to be a major gap in successful transition services. The available evidence and collective experience of families suggest that current transition efforts are far from optimal. Rather, with a few exceptions, they are fragmented, disorganized, and largely ineffective.

The experiences of parents of students with blindness are illustrative. Researchers (Houser, Moses, and Kay, 1987) found that families are not actively involved in the transition process; are frequently isolated from information about available resources and possibilities for employment; are frequently isolated from emotional support that other families with similar needs can supply; in many cases are unaware of their own resources; rely on professionals to plan and implement services for them; and may not understand the differences between education and rehabilitation services.

POST-SCHOOL EXPERIENCES

Despite difficulties, many young people with disabilities move into post-secondary education or competitive employment with their non-disabled peers. Sadly, though, there remains a high proportion who are either underemployed or unemployed.

In its 1998 *Annual Report*, the Canadian Human Rights Commission chided that "Canadians with disabilities continue to be denied equal opportunities to jobs and services and full participation in our society" ("Access denied...," 1999, p. 12). According to the *Report*, the situation of people with disabilities in the workforce is abysmal. In fact, it has deteriorated. Representation lessened from 2.7 percent in 1996 to 2.3 percent in 1997 in the federally regulated private sector. "At this rate, it will take them 60 years to be equitably employed," concluded the report ("Access denied...," 1999, p.12).

Dropouts

From a sociological perspective, high school graduation may be seen as a rite of passage marking the successful movement of an individual from adolescence into adulthood. Dropouts voluntarily leave the system before completing their education. A general definition used by researchers identifies a **dropout** as any person who has left secondary school for any reason prior to graduation (Sullivan, 1988). There is a widespread belief that many students who drop out of school are capable of graduating.

dropout

Local, provincial, and national studies show a multiplicity of definitions and methodologies for calculating dropout rates. Generally, Canadian estimates give the proportion of grade-nine students who do not fulfill graduation requirements at 33 percent (Watt and Roessingh, 1993).

Factors correlated with dropping out include community type, single-parent family, attendance rate, low self-concept, low need for self-development, pregnancy, marriage, having a job, institutionalization or incarceration, delinquency, and drug use. Poverty, membership in a dysfunctional family, and poor mental and physical health serve to further disadvantage some youth and their expectations of high school graduation (Squires, 1992).

Students themselves give varied explanations for dropping out, although three major reasons surface in the dropout literature. First is a sense of alienation. Students' satisfaction with school, their sense that their classes are interesting and that teachers care, and teacher feedback and evaluation influence students' self-esteem (Hoge, Smit, and Hanson, 1990). School dropouts often feel that no one cares for them. Second is the belief that courses are irrelevant, which results in students being bored and unmotivated. Third is frustration born of poor academic concept, resulting in failure, grade retention, and poor self-concept (Canadian Council for Exceptional Children, 1992).

Predicting who will drop out is not easy, although poor reading performance and retention in a grade seem to be primary. According to Robert Slavin and his colleagues (1990):

> Reaching the third grade on time with adequate basic skills may not provide a guarantee that a student will complete his education, but it appears that children who do not reach third grade on time with adequate skills have little chance of educational success, regardless of the remedial or special education resources invested in them later in their school careers.

Only a small amount of literature deals specifically with dropping out by students identified as candidates for special education. In the United States, approximately 30 percent of students who are disabled drop out (Knight and Rieck, 1997). In Canada, there is evidence that the majority of students in only two categories of special education (gifted and physically disabled) graduate from high school.

The dropout percentage for students with disabilities has decreased steadily over the past five years, and the graduation percentage has shown a general upward trend (see

Blackorby and Wagner, 1996). More students go to college and more have access to some form of vocational education that contributes significantly to the probability of competitive employment.

Nevertheless, special education must still address the fact that an unacceptable percentage of students with disabilities drop out of school, and a significant number of those students who do graduate do not secure employment later or do not retain secured jobs. Generally, high unemployment, low income, and low educational levels characterize school leavers with disabilities. When Lichenstein (1989) followed a population of students with mild disabilities beyond high school, he found that dropping out was a greater factor in unemployment than the disability itself.

Other research findings consistently suggest that young adults at greatest risk for lifelong economic and social harm are those with disabilities who also dropped out of high school. These young people are seriously at risk because of their history of inadequate educational attainment, their chronic dependence on society, and their uncertain future in the job market (Edgar, Levine, and Maddox, 1985). Social costs are high. In the United States, for example, the price of prison, parole, and welfare for each high-school dropout is more than twice that of a high-school graduate and almost five times that of a college graduate (Lewis, 1996).

Competitive Employment

Competitive employment of persons with disabilities enhances feelings of self-worth and efficacy and increases the normalization of these persons, both in self-perception and the perception of society. The mere observation of individuals who are disabled engaging in functional, integrated, and age-appropriate activities appears to have effects on the development of a more respectful and optimistic attitude toward them from the public, one factor that contributes further to employment success.

When young adults with disabilities enter the workforce, they find many difficulties in obtaining and retaining employment. People with mild disabilities tend to be far less successful than their peers and to be employed less often. Follow-up studies have reported low levels of employment for those exiting special education; young people in virtually all disability groups are employed at a lower rate than the general population.

Jobs found are often at entry level but with few employee benefits, and they are often obtained through a self-family-friend network (Lombard and Newbert, 1992). In Vermont, a study of 459 youths exiting special education (Hasazi, Gordon, and Roe, 1985) showed an employment rate of only 54 percent. In Colorado, researchers (Mithaug, Horiuchi, and Fanning, 1985) found employment rates of 69 percent, but almost half of those employed were earning less than $3 an hour.

It is difficult to pinpoint the factors that contribute to failure for students with disabilities. Some problems certainly stem from conditions in the labour market, inadequate or inappropriate vocational and educational preparation, lack of transition support services, or other related factors, such as employer attitudes. Others relate to individual traits, work habits, and attitudes. Exactly how a disability affects an adult depends on the adult's past academic, social, and emotional experiences and the expectations of the settings in which he or she works.

For example, the research on learning disabilities in adulthood is fragmented and the lives of adults with learning disabilities are not well understood. Although there are not gender differences, studies show that these adults do less well than peers (Levine and Mouse, 1998). A 1992 project found that only 54 percent of young adults with learning disabilities had achieved independent living and stable roles (see Sitlington, Frank, and Carson, 1992).

As we pointed out earlier, learning disabilities do not disappear; many adults retain subtle or overt manifestations. Some adults with learning disabilities learn to compensate for their attention problems and find occupations that allow them to utilize their strengths while minimizing their shortcomings. Yet while people who had severe reading problems in childhood may be successful in many areas as adults, their substantial reading problems continue (Bruck, 1998).

For others, the disabling aspects of learning disabilities may become more firmly established in adulthood. The behaviours that characterize learning disabilities then contribute to the problems adults experience and may actually increase as the individual experiences new social and vocational expectations.

Adults with learning disabilities continue to have reading problems, to have difficulties with written expression, and to need help with math skills. Individuals may exhibit low motivation, distractibility, self-concept problems, and lack of organization. They feel frustrated, have little self-confidence, and have difficulty controlling emotions and/or temper; depression often follows (Hoffman, Shelson, Minskoff, Sautter, Steidle, Baker, Bailey, and Echols, 1987; Rogan and Hardman, 1990).

Adults who are learning disabled secure employment at nearly the same rate as their non-disabled peers. The jobs, however, have less social status, lower wages, and fewer regular hours than those of non-disabled groups (Okolo and Sitlington, 1986). When they find jobs, people with learning disabilities often cannot keep them. It seems to be the subtle invisible aspects of learning disabilities that impede success in the work world.

Little information is available on adults with Attention Deficit Hyperactivity Disorder, and treatment programs are virtually nonexistent. It is estimated that up to 70 percent of children diagnosed with ADHD continue to have symptoms in adolescence and adulthood, although the prevalence in adults is unknown (Burt, Parks-Charney, and Schwean, 1996; Heiligenstrin and Keeling, 1995; Richard, 1995). The disorders manifest in different ways in adults and may vary considerably depending on task and content (Brown, 1995). For example, the hyperactivity component often dissipates in adults, but it is replaced by inner feelings of restlessness.

Over one-third of students with ADHD fail to finish high school (Weiss and Hechtman, 1986). Young adults are then open to the problems we discussed for dropouts.

Transition from school to work is particularly difficult for adolescents who are behaviourally disordered; they have more difficulty in adjusting to young adulthood than those who are learning disabled or mentally retarded (Maag and Katsiyannis, 1998). Given the manner in which their problems manifest, it is not surprising that students with behavioural disorders are among those most likely to drop out of school and among the most difficult individuals to train in transition programs. Many lack the basic skills needed for employment. Students with behavioural disorders often use inappropriate strategies to solve conflicts and cope with frustration; they often behave in ways that prevent them from being accepted, liked, and helped by employers and co-workers. Only about 50 percent are likely to retain their jobs for more than six months (Sitlington, Frank, and Carson, 1992).

Many adults who are mildly retarded are able to merge into the community and work at a variety of semi-skilled and service positions. They have varying degrees of success in attaining and retaining employment, but most can partially or totally support themselves. However, persons with intellectual disabilities do less well at getting employment than learning-disabled or emotionally disturbed subgroups (Edgar, 1988). If not underemployed or unemployed, they are often the last hired and tend to hold unskilled and semi-skilled jobs.

Adults who are intellectually disabled seem to be particularly susceptible to changes in the economy. Job success is a function of attitudes and personality, not IQ. On the job, persons with intellectual disabilities often have problems with job responsibility, task production competence, and/or social competence (Salzberg, Lignugaris-Kraft, and McCuller, 1988).

Persons with severe visual impairments are underrepresented in the competitive labour market. Barriers include transportation, public awareness of visual impairments, attitudes, difficulties with reading print, obtaining adaptive equipment, and accommodations (see Crudden and McBroom, 1999).

Supported Employment

Supported employment, once referred to as *sheltered workshops*, is built on the belief that people with severe disabilities have the potential to work productively in a community of workers. Supported employment offers more structure and ensures that people receive continuous help managing the routines of living and working (see Kregel, 1997).

The term *supported employment* describes a wide variety of work situations and vocational rehabilitation programs that range from adult day programs to highly automated production factories. Three essential features characterize all types of supported employment. These are opportunities for paid productive work with ongoing support; training to ensure continued employment; and employment in a socially integrated environment (Sinnot-Oswald, Gliner, and Spencer, 1991).

Programs provide long-term support in a controlled and protected work environment where they offer work experience for those who cannot be in competitive employment. They serve to assess, improve, and stabilize vocational functioning, thus assisting a person who is disabled to progress to employment in the competitive labour market. Expectations are adjusted to each individual's ability. The workers have constant input and supervision and their personal differences are tolerated.

Post-secondary Education

As we mentioned earlier, the dropout rate among students with disabilities has decreased. At the same time, there has been a tremendous growth in the number of students with disabilities completing their high school and continuing their education at college or university.

When the Canadian National Education Association of Disabled Students conducted a survey of seventy service providers, they found that the largest group in post-secondary educational institutions was those with learning disabilities, a ratio of 36:1 to other groups with disabilities. Indeed, in any Canadian college or university of 10 000 students, as many as 1000 may have some type of learning disability (Cox and Klas, 1996). Keep in mind that these numbers are tenuous. Because students in post-secondary institutions are typically asked to self-identify, many disabilities remain hidden (Cox and Klas, 1996).

Students with learning disabilities represent the largest numbers. However, those who have suffered traumatic brain injuries represent the fastest-growing segment of the disabled population entering post-secondary institutions (Cook, 1991).

Students with learning disabilities and other disabilities can succeed in college and university if they are given reasonable accommodations. Cox and Klas (1996) mention that Ontario has been the most responsive to the needs of students with learning disabilities but also note that specially designed programs are found at St. Mary's University, Memorial University of Newfoundland, the University of British Columbia, the University of Alberta, the University of Western Ontario, and York University.

To assist students with disabilities, typical approaches include modified tests, more time to complete tests, many short examinations rather than one long one, alternate assignments, and assistive devices such as computer access. Generally, faculty members seem willing to make accommodations.

In the United States, it is reported that 60 percent of deaf and hard of hearing students choose to pursue a post-secondary education (Blackorby and Wagner, 1996). In contrast, Jermome Schein reported in 1994 that only 3 percent of Canadians who are deaf attend university (Schein, 1994). Students with deafness can both succeed and compete in public post-secondary institutions if provided with adequate support services such as note taking and sign language interpreting.

Historical Notes

For most of the 19th century, special education catered to discrete age groups. Schooling was not designed for young children, although a high proportion of older students were instructed within the institutional complex. The Ontario Institution for the Deaf, for example, was established in 1870; by 1879 about 7 percent of the student population was between the ages of twenty-one and forty. In the schools for the blind, students were allowed to remain up to their thirtieth birthdays (Winzer, 1993).

Adult attendance at school was voluntary and indicated the imperative need of disabled lads—getting a job and keeping it. Some adults were early school leavers who wanted more skills for the workforce; others had never before been offered the opportunity for education and training. When students were admitted for upgrading in trades they received no wages for their work but were given free room and board (Winzer, 1993).

The adult experiences of persons with disabilities have not been of great interest to historians. The formation of deaf communities is probably the most widely studied. It seems that wherever there were schools for the deaf a community flourished, with deaf adults tending to marry other deaf people, send their children to residential schools for the deaf, and confine their social relations to their community. There are some scattered indications of blind communities in the late 19th century, but they seem to have been short-lived.

When persons with intellectual disabilities were institutionalized, it was usually for life. However, in the early 1920s, Walter Fernald conducted a study of the later lives of persons who had left his institution at Waverley. His findings on their occupational status and independent living were generally pessimistic (see Winzer, 1993).

While 57 percent of students with visual impairments chose post-secondary education (Blackorby and Wagner, 1996), there is also a high number of dropouts—32 percent in one study (cited by McBroom, 1997). To retain students with severe visual impairments, a program must be matched to student needs and accommodations provided.

SUMMARY

1. Consistent and structured programming for adolescents with disabilities has not traditionally been a prominent feature of special education. Although the field has had access to well-articulated models of high school programs for students with disabilities for more than two decades, adolescents and young adults have received less than their share of special education services.
2. The needs of adolescents are quite different from those of younger children and, when the adolescent has a disability, the needs become even more intense. Adolescents and young adults with disabilities have complex support needs such as finding and keeping employment, living independently, planning post-secondary education, recreation, and friendships. As educators have begun to appreciate that the needs of students with disabilities do not stop at the school door, various means of assisting young adults are being implemented.
3. As both a concept and a process, *transition* is relatively new in special education. The need for transition services arose from data demonstrating less than complimentary outcomes from special education. Once out of school, youth with disabilities experience high rates of unemployment, and if they do find jobs they often cannot keep them. In addition to problems with job finding and retention, young adults with disabilities may not possess adequate functional skills.
4. Transition serves the needs of parents and students and conforms to the principles of normalization. Transition services are intended to provide young people with disabilities with access to relevant post-secondary education opportunities, employment in competitive settings, residential independence, and future self-sufficiency with a focus on the school-to-community scenario.
5. School practices attempt to establish relationships between educational variables and better employment and independent living outcomes. Programs should match the skills needed by individuals in the community so as to better prepare students for post-school life. Included are counselling, sex education, and functional academic skills— the tool skills needed for reading, writing, and math.
6. Some necessary skills can be taught in regular settings; some cannot. Many adolescents with disabilities reach secondary school with severe deficits in the core areas of reading and math. There is often a mismatch between their abilities and the requirements of the system. As curriculum expectations and outcomes may not match the needs of older learners who are disabled, full academic inclusion may not be what is needed at the senior level. A number of educators argue that despite the current emphasis on inclusion, the regular classroom may not be the most suitable setting for late-secondary students. They contend that we need to pay more attention to bettering the lives of students than to their school address. The acquisition of requisite employment skills cannot be left to chance or viewed as a peripheral adjunct to mainstream curricula.

7. In concert with their non-disabled counterparts, students with disabilities experience a wide variety of post-secondary outcomes. Young people with disabilities may enroll in university or community college; they may enter competitive employment or military service; or they may be supported in more restrictive employment and sheltered workshops. Post-secondary institutions in Canada have responded to the needs of students with disabilities.

WEBLINKS

The Canadian Vocational Association **www.cva-acfp.org**

Global Applied Disability Research and Information Network on Employment and Training **www.gladnet.org/**

Institute on Disability Culture Newsgroup Archive **www.dimenet.com/cgi-bin/getindex?disculture,1R**

Literacy skills **www.ups.edu/community/tofu**

The Opportunity of Adolescence **www.winternet.com/~webpage/adolescence.html**

Sexuality and persons with disabilities **idt.net/~mauro/alindasx.html**

APPENDIX

Tools for Assessment

Process	Developmental domain	Typical population(s)	Procedure	Sample tool(s)
Screening, medical	All	All	Amniocentesis, sonar scan, etc.	
	Hearing	Hearing impaired	Sweep test	
	Vision	Visually impaired	Eye examination	
Diagnosis, medical	Hearing	Hearing impaired	Auditory brainstem evoked response Reflex audiometry Impedence audiometry Play audiometry Pure-tone audiometry Speech audiometry	
	Visual acuity	Visually impaired	Visual Evoked Potential (VEP) Visually Evoked Response (VER), also known as Electroretinogram (ERG) Electro-oculogram	
	Visual acuity	Visually impaired		UC-Berkeley Preferential Looking Test (Bailey and Hall, 1984)
Screening, educational	All	All	Case histories	
		Behaviour problems	Direct observation	
		All	Interviews: family, student, teachers	
		Gifted	Nominations: teacher, parent, peer, self	
		All	Observations	
		All	Portfolios	

Process	Developmental domain	Typical population(s)	Procedure	Sample tool(s)
		All	School grades	
		All	School records	
		Behaviour problems	Sociometric measures	
		All	Teacher-made measures	
	All	Mental retardation, severe disabilities, young children	Developmental	Battelle Developmental Inventory (Newborg, Stock, and Wnek, 1984) Developmental Activities Screening Inventory 2 (Fewell and Langley, 1984)
Screening/ diagnosis	Adaptive behaviour	Mental retardation, severe disabilities	Observation, interviews	Vineland Adaptive Behaviour Scale (Sparrow, Balla, and Cicchetti, 1984)
	Adaptive behaviour	Mental retardation, severe disabilities	Rating scales	AAMD Adaptive Behavior Scales (Lambert and Windmiller, 1981) Balthazar Scales of Adaptive Behavior (Balthazar, 1973, 1976)
	Adaptive behaviour	Mental retardation, severe disabilities	Checklists	Adaptive Behavior Checklist (Allen, Cortazzo, and Adams, 1970)
	Behaviour problems	Behaviour disorders	Rating scales	Behavior Rating Profile 2 (Brown and Hammill, 1990) Draw a Person: Screening Procedures for Emotional Disorders (Naglieri, 1991) Conners Teacher Rating Scale (Conners, 1973)

Process	Developmental domain	Typical population(s)	Procedure	Sample tool(s)
				Devereux Behavior Rating Scales—School Form (Naglieri, LeBuffe, and Pfiefer, 1993) Devereaux Scales of Mental Disorders (Naglieri, LeBuffe, and Pfiefer, 1994)
	Behaviour problems	Behaviour disorders	Checklists	Behavioral Assessment System for Children (Reynolds and Kamphaus, 1992) Behavior Problem Checklist—Revised (Quay and Peterson, 1987) Battelle Developmental Inventory (Newborg, Stock, and Wnek, 1984) Systematic Screening for Behavior Disorders (Walker and Severson, 1990)
	Creativity	Gifted	Various	Creativity Assessment Package (Williams, 1980) Group Inventory for Finding Creative Talent (GIFT) (Rimm and Davis, 1976) Torrance Tests of Creative Thinking (Torrance, 1966)
Screening	Language	Speech/language difficulties, learning disabled, mentally retarded, limited English proficient, hearing impaired	Language sampling, spontaneous and elicited	

Process	Developmental domain	Typical population(s)	Procedure	Sample tool(s)
			Criterion-referenced	Clinical Evaluation of Language Functions (CELF) (Semel and Wiig, 1980)
			Standardized language tests	Test of Adolescent Language—3 (Hammill, Brown, Larsen, and Wiederholt, 1994) Test of Language Development 2 (Hammill and Newcomer, 1988) Peabody Picture Vocabulary Test III (Dunn and Dunn, 1997) Woodcock Language Proficiency Battery-R (Woodcock, 1991) Woodcock-Munoz Language Survey (Woodcock and Munoz-Sandoval, 1993)
Screening	Language	Pre- and minimally linguistic	Standardized language tests	Preschool Language Scale (Zimmerman, Sheener, and Pond, 1979) Sequenced Inventory of Communication Development (Hedrick, Pratter, and Tobin, 1975)
Screening	Motor	Significant disabilities	Developmental	Peabody Developmental Motor Scales and Activity Cards (Folio and Fewell, 1983)
	Social skills	Behavioural problems	Rating scales	School Social Behavior Scales (Merrell, 1993)

Process	Developmental domain	Typical population(s)	Procedure	Sample tool(s)
				Social Skills Rating System—Elementary and Secondary (Gresham and Elliott, 1990) Walker-McConnell Scale of Social Competence and School Adjustment (Walker and McConnell, 1988)
	Social skills	Visually impaired	Rating scales	Maxfield-Buchholz Social Maturity Scale (an adaptation of the original Vineland Social Maturity Scale) (Doll, 1941)
Screening	Academics	Milder disabilities	Readiness	Brigance Kindergarten and 1 Screen 3rd ed. (Brigance, 1992)
Screening	Academics	Milder disabilities	Achievement tests	Canadian Test of Basic Skills Differential Ability Scales (Elliott, 1990) Peabody Individual Achievement Test (Markwardt, 1989) Stanford Achievement Tests
Screening	Academics	Visually impaired	Achievement tests	Stanford Achievement Tests (adaptations in large print or braille)
Screening	Reading	Mild disabilities	Inventory	Informal Reading Inventory 5 (Burns and Roe, 1999)
Screening	Reading	Mild disabilities	Standardized tests	Gates-MacGinitie Reading Tests-2 (MacGinitie and MacGinitie, 1992)

Process	Developmental domain	Typical population(s)	Procedure	Sample tool(s)
				Test of Reading Comprehension 3rd ed. (Brown, Hammill, and Wiederholt, 1995) Woodcock Diagnostic Reading Battery (Woodcock, 1997)
Screening	Phonological awareness	Mild disabilities	Standardized tests	Test of Awareness of Language Segments (Sawyer, 1987)
Screening	Giftedness	Gifted	Standardized tests	Test of Phonological Awareness (Torgesen and Bryant, 1994) Screening Assessment for Gifted Elementary Students (Johnsen and Corn, 1987)
Diagnosis	Giftedness	Gifted	Rating scale	Scale for Rating Behavioral Characteristics of Superior Students (Renzulli, Hartman, and Callahan, 1975)
Screening	All	Autism	Checklist	Autism Behavior Checklist (Krug, Arick, and Almond, 1993)
Screening	All	Pervasive developmental disorders	Rating scales	Pervasive Developmental Disorder Rating Scale (Eaves, 1993) Childhood Autism Scale (Schopler, Reichler, De Vellis, and Daly, 1980)
Screening	All	Deaf-blind	Rating scales	Callier-Azusa Scale (Stillman, 1978)
Diagnosis	Vocational	Hearing impaired	Standardized tests	Transition Competence Battery (Bullis, Reiman,

Process	Developmental domain	Typical population(s)	Procedure	Sample tool(s)
				Davis, and Reid, 1997)
Formal	Intelligence	All	Standardized tests	Canadian Cognitive Abilities Test (1998) Universal Nonverbal Intelligence Test (Bracken and McCallum, 1998) Wechsler Intelligence Scale for Children 3 (Wechsler, 1991) Woodcock-Johnson Psycho- Educational Battery (Woodcock and Johnson, 1989/1990)
Formal	Intelligence	Gifted	Standardized tests	Stanford-Binet Individual Intelligence Test—4 (Thorndike, Hagen, and Sattler, 1986)
Formal	Intelligence	Hearing impaired, difficult to test	Standardized tests	Goodenough-Harris Draw-a-Person Test (Harris, 1963) Leiter International Performance Scale (Leiter, 1948) Raven's Progressive Matrices (Raven, 1948)
Formal	Intelligence	Young children, difficult to test	Standardized tests	Bayley Scales of Infant Development (Bayley, 1993) McCarthy Scales of Children's Abilities (McCarthy, 1972)

GLOSSARY

Academic ability: intellectual ability measured by performance on IQ and standardized tests of academic achievement.

Academic underachievers: those about whom we can make a reasonable prediction of academic potential that is not fulfilled.

Academically talented students: those scoring at the 95th percentile or higher on IQ and standardized tests of academic achievement.

Acoupedic (unisensory) approach: an oral method that aims to develop intelligible speech through the maximum development of listening skills.

Adaptations (instructional): how teachers change instruction; changes to the regular curriculum that retain the same outcomes as those for normally developing children.

Adaptive (assistive) equipment: any device designed or modified to lead individuals with disabilities to independence.

Adaptive behaviour: how well a person is able to adapt to environmental demands according to the individual's age group and particular situation.

Adventitious hearing losses: acquired some time after birth, through accident or disease.

Adventitious low vision: conditions caused by accident or disease some time after birth.

Albinism: a condition carried as an inherited autosomal recessive trait.

Allergy (hypersensitivity): an abnormal and varied reaction that occurs following a contact with substances or agents that normally do not cause symptoms in other individuals.

Anoxia: deprivation of oxygen.

Anxiety: a fear with a future reference.

Aphasia: conditions (trauma) that occur after language has been developed.

Aphonia: the condition where there is no voice.

Apnea: lack of oxygen.

Apraxia: the inability to program, position, and sequence the muscle movements involved in speech.

Arena testing: an observational assessment approach in which people from several disciplines focus on their particular domains such as motor skills or language within the context of play.

Articulation disorder: the condition when a child cannot actually make or produce a sound.

Assessment: the process of gathering valid evidence to guide decisions about curriculum and in struction, and to evaluate the outcomes of instruction.

Asthma: a variable, reversible obstruction of the airway characterized by the narrowing of bronchial tubes, swelling of tissues, and clogging of mucus.

Astigmatism: the result of an irregularity in the curvature of the cornea or lens of the eye.

At risk: more vulnerable to biological or environmental insult.

Atopic allergies: allergies associated with hereditary and/or familial factors.

Attention: the process of tuning in to sensory information, and with engagement or active participation.

Attributions: the reasons that people give for what happens to them.

Atypical youngsters: those who do not reach the norm in some functional area or areas.

Audiology: the science of detecting and correcting hearing impairment.

Auditory atresia: missing or undeveloped auditory canals.

Augmentative communication: a general group of procedures designed to support, enhance, or augment the communication of nonspeaking individuals or utilize and supplement whatever vocal skills an individual possesses.

Babbling: an almost universal response during infancy; random sound play of almost infinite variety.

Behaviour management: all the ways in which teachers control inappropriate and disruptive behaviour as well as ways in which children are taught discipline and to control their own behaviour.

Bibliotherapy: a procedure based on the concept that books serve a therapeutic purpose, especially for children with disabilities.

Biological risk: relates to infants and toddlers with a history of prenatal, perinatal, neonatal, or early developmental events resulting in biological insults to the developing nervous system.

Blindness: vision of 20/200 or less with correction.

Body image: a person's awareness of the body, its capabilities, the interrelationship of body parts, and the relationship of bodies to the environment.

Carrying: the way that a child with a physical or motor disability is moved.

Cataract: an opacity of the lens or its capsule that restricts the eye's ability to receive light and interferes with central and peripheral visual acuity.

Child advocacy: any social, political, or legal action that is intended to achieve a better life for children from infancy to late adolescence.

Child advocate: anyone who pleads a child's cause or defends a particular child-related cause.

Child with a visual impairment: those with serious visual problems ranging from an inability to read newsprint with the use of ordinary glasses to total blindness.

Childhood psychoses: a heterogeneous group of clinical syndromes characterized by any number of maladaptive behaviours or clusters of behaviours that affect various aspects of adaptive behaviour and the success of interpersonal relations.

Childhood schizophrenia: one of the *childhood psychoses.*

Children with exceptionalities: those who have difficulty in realizing their full human potential. Their intellectual, emotional, physical, or social performance falls below or rises above that of other children. The differences may be related to physical, psychological, cognitive, emotional, or social factors, or a combination of these.

Classroom management: the way in which teachers manipulate the classroom environment to minimize disruptions and give all children the optimum opportunity to engage in appropriate behaviour and reach learning and social goals.

Cochlea: a tiny, snail-shaped structure filled with a fluid similar to cerebral spinal fluid.

Cognition: the process of recognizing, identifying, associating, and inferring meaning beyond the figural information provided by the environment that allows an understanding of a concept and application to new conditions.

Cognitive development: orderly changes that occur in the way children understand and cope with their world.

Collaboration: any mutual effort to plan, implement, or evaluate educational programs for a student or students.

Colour blindness: a rare, sex-linked, hereditary disorder found almost always in males. Defects of colour vision arise from the absence or malfunctioning of the cone cells of the retina.

Communication: the process of exchanging information and ideas between participants.

Communication mode: the form in which the content of a message is expressed.

Communicative competence: when individuals know how to interact, how to communicate appropriately in various situations, and how to make sense of what others say and do in communicative interactions.

Comorbidity: the simultaneous occurrence of two or more unrelated conditions.

Conductive hearing losses: caused by problems in the mechanical transmission of sound waves through the outer and middle ear.

Congenital abnormalities: abnormalities present at birth.

Congenital amputation: A child born with a limb deficiency that includes the loss or absence of entire limbs or parts of limbs.

Congenital hearing impairment: one that is present at birth.

Congenital low vision: conditions that are diagnosable at birth or shortly thereafter.

Continuum of reproductive casualty: problems may range from relatively minor through to major difficulties.

Contracture: a permanent shortening of the muscles, tendons, and ligaments that results in postural distortion and decreased joint mobility.

Cooing: infants' production of clear vowels, often in isolation.

Curriculum-based assessment: (CBA): a standardized measurement system used to monitor a student's academic growth and to improve instructional programs.

Cytogenetics: the study of the location and organization of genetic material from chromosomes.

Deaf community: describes social and other associations of persons who are deaf and bound together by a common language and culture.

Deaf person: one whose hearing disability precludes successful processing of linguistic information through audition, with or without a hearing aid.

Decibel: the smallest difference in loudness intensity that can be perceived.

Delinquency: a legal term applied by the criminal justice system to indicate that a youth has been adjudicated by the courts and found guilty of criminal behaviour.

Developmental disability: a significant lag in development.

Diabetic retinopathy: a disease of the retina's blood vessels.

Differential diagnosis: the precise specification that a given set of symptoms is indicative of one disorder rather than another.

Direct testing (psycho-educational assessment): testing children across a variety of domains relevant to social and educational performance.

Directionality: an awareness of left and right in the environment outside the body.

Disabilities: reflect the consequences of impairments in terms of functional performance and activity by the individual.

Discipline: helping children to learn to guide their own behaviour in a way that shows respect and caring for themselves, other people, and the physical environment.

Dropout: any person who has left secondary school for any reason prior to graduation.

Dysarthria: a group of speech disorders resulting from disturbed muscular control over the speech mechanisms.

Dysfluency: conditions in which the flow of speech is interrupted with blocking, repetitions, or prolongations of sounds, words, phrases, or syllables.

Dysnomia: forgetting words or word meanings.

Dyssynchrony: uneven development.

Ear drum: a tough, tightly stretched tissue that separates the outer from the middle ear.

Early identification: the practice of

screening infants and young children in an attempt to identify those likely to experience problems in learning or behaviour.

Early intervention: a variety of educational, psychological, or therapeutic interventions provided for handicapped, at-risk, or disadvantaged infants and preschoolers to prevent or ameliorate developmental delays of disabilities or to provide support to children and families in cases where disabilities exist.

Echolalic speech: speech that is an immediate imitation of some other speaker.

Educational setting: a child's placement for instruction.

Emotional overlay: an adverse reaction to learning problems and academic failure.

Enrichment: providing special activities in the regular classroom setting.

Environmental risk: applies to families and their infants and toddlers who are considered biologically sound but whose early life experiences (including maternal and family care, health care, nutrition, opportunities for expression of language, adaptive behaviour, and patterns of physical and social stimulation) are sufficiently limited that there is a high probability of delayed development.

Epidemiology: the study of the distribution and determinants of diseases and handicapping conditions in a population.

Established risk: a diagnosed medical disorder with a known *etiology* (cause) that bears relatively well known expectancies for developmental outcomes within varying ranges of developmental disabilities.

Etiology: the process of finding causes to explain how a particular problem came into existence.

Event sampling: used to determine the frequency or length of a specific behaviour.

Expressive disorders: those that affect the formulation of grammatic utterances.

First trimester: the opening third of pregnancy.

Flaccid paralysis: an inability to move the muscles because the neural impulses needed for muscle contractions are lacking.

Functional academics: academics that have meaning and are relevant to the learner soon to enter community work and life.

Functional skills: those skills that help children to get along in their current and future environments.

Gaze aversion: the failure to look directly at another individual.

Glaucoma: a condition caused by interocular pressure on the eyeball.

Goal: a stated outcome desired as the result of some action.

Group therapy: the simultaneous treatment of several clients, usually in the same age range.

Guidance counselling: assists students in selecting courses, in adapting to their disability, and in personal concerns. May include career plans, occupational choice, and job placement.

Habilitation: to restore to normal functioning.

Handicaps: environmental or functional demands placed on a disabled person in a particular situation that are not met.

Hard-of-hearing person: one who, generally with the use of a hearing aid, has residual hearing sufficient to enable successful processing of linguistic information through audition.

Hearing impairment: a generic term indicating a hearing disability that may range in severity from mild to profound. It includes the subsets of deaf and hard-of-hearing.

Hereditary anomalies: genetic disorders present at birth.

Hertz: measurement of cycles of sound per second.

Holophrasic: a single word is used to express a more complex idea.

Home visiting (home-based programs): a process whereby a professional or paraprofessional provides help over an extended period of time to a family in its own home.

Hydrocephalus: a condition characterized by an excessive accumulation of cerebrospinal fluid in the brain due to an obstruction of its flow.

Hyperactive children: children who display rates of motor behaviour that are too high for their age groups.

Hyperglycemia: high blood sugar (diabetes).

Hyperopia: farsightedness caused by too short an eye or too flat a corneal surface.

Hypoglycemia: low blood sugar (diabetes).

Impairments: abnormalities of body structure and with system function resulting from any cause.

Impulsivity: a child's difficulty in withholding active responses, such as blurting out statements or grabbing materials.

Incidence: the number of new cases of a particular condition ascertained over a given period of time, usually a year.

Incidental teaching: instruction that occurs within naturally occurring situations.

Incus: small bone in the middle ear.

Independent studies: individualized learning experiences that allow students to select a topic, define problems or questions, gather and analyze information, apply skills, and create a product to show what has been learned.

Individualization: individual planning for students with special needs.

Intelligence quotient: (IQ): the relationship between a child's mental age (MA) and chronological age (CA).

Intervention: a general term for the application of professional skills to maintain or improve a child's potential and functioning; care and education aimed at influencing the direction and scope of children's developmental processes.

Labelling: the categorizing of children on the basis of their primary disability.

Labyrinth: the inner ear, which contains the cochlea and the vestibular mechanism.

Language: a system of symbols organized into conventional patterns to communicate meaning.

Language delays: seen in children who demonstrate significant lags but whose language is still progressing according to the stages of normal language development.

Language disorders: impairment or deviant development of comprehension or the use of a spoken, written, or other symbol system.

Language problems: a range of difficulties with the linguistic code, or with the rules and concentrations for linking the symbols and the symbol sequences.

Laterality: an internal knowledge of the differences between left and right.

Law: a system of rules and regulations relating to the behaviour of individuals and society as a whole.

Learning strategies: an individual's approach to tasks that are either generic or domain specific.

Least restrictive environment: the most appropriate placement in which a student can receive instruction and services.

Legislation: laws that underlie special education.

Litigation: involves an individual or a small group of people filing a lawsuit against another group.

Low vision: vision of 70/200 with correction.

Low-vision aids: those that augment residual vision by increasing the size of the retinal image.

Macrocephaly: an enlargement of the head.

Malleus: small bone in the middle ear.

Maturational lag: a child is slow to reach some developmental milestones.

Medically fragile children: those with special health management needs; includes children who demonstrate a wide range of chronic and progressive illnesses and severe disabilities.

Ménière's disease: caused by a buildup of endolymphatic (inner ear) fluid that creates increased pressure on the inner ear.

Metacognition: the awareness of basic learning strategies and one's own awareness of how one learns.

Metalinguistics: the ability to think about and talk about language.

Microcephaly: a rare phenomenon in which brain development is impaired by an abnormally small cranium.

Mobility: negotiating space.

Morphology: the system of word building in a language.

Motherese: child–adult communicative interaction characterized by unique alterations in speech, meaning, form, and even language usage.

Motor development: the process through which a child acquires movement patterns and skills.

Motor: a term used to denote muscular movement.

Muscular dystrophy: a group of inherited conditions characterized by degeneration of muscle fibres without neurological deficit.

Mutism: absence of speech due to severe emotional problems.

Myopia: nearsightedness; the greatest single cause of defective vision in children and young adults.

Neologisms: non-words or words that are obviously peculiar.

Neurological impairments: those that result from damage or dysfunction of the brain and/or the spinal cord.

Non-atopic allergies: do not have a hereditary component but result from antibodies produced in response to allergens in the environment.

Normalization: the philosophical belief that all exceptional individuals, no matter what their level and type of disability, should be provided with an education and living environment that is as close to normal as possible.

Nystagmus: a rhythmic involuntary movement of the eyes.

Oppositional defiant disorder: a condition in which children argue repeatedly with authority figures, show resentment, and often throw temper tantrums, although physical aggression is limited.

Orientation: an individual's knowledge of his or her position in space.

Orthotic devices: those that assist a limb's action.

Otitis media: a condition in which the mucosal lining of the middle ear becomes inflamed and the cavity filled with fluid.

Otosclerosis: a hereditary condition characterized by the destruction of the capsular bone in the middle ear and the growth of a weblike bone that attaches to and restricts the stapes.

Pediatric AIDS: AIDS contracted by children under thirteen years of age.

Perception: the use of the senses to recognize, discriminate, and interpret stimuli; it forms a link between sensation and perception.

Perseverate: to purposelessly and sometimes disadvantageously repeat an activity.

Phenylketonuria: (PKU): an enzymatic problem that, uncorrected, leads to mental retardation.

Phobia: an anxiety reaction that is specific to one stimulus, an intense fear with no rational basis.

Phonetics: the description of the speech sounds of a language.

Phonological awareness: the ability

to blend, segment, rhyme, or in other ways manipulate the sounds of spoken words.

Phonological problem: when a child has a sound and pronounces it correctly in some contexts but not in others.

Phonology: the sound system of language; the rules for using the sounds of language.

Photophobia: a condition in which very bright light blinds the individual and thus decreases acuity.

Pinna: the cartilage structure on the side of the head.

Positioning: how the child is seated or otherwise positioned.

Post-lingual deafness: those who became deaf after the development of speech and language.

Pragmatics: the ways in which we use language, the role of context in communicative interactions.

Precocity: remarkable early development.

Prelingual deafness: those who were deaf prior to the development of speech and language.

Premature babies (pre-term): those born before the completion of thirty-seven weeks.

Pre-referral intervention: adaptations undertaken before referral for special education.

Presbycusis: deafness of age, the most common cause of auditory defect.

Presbyopia: a condition in which the lens of the eye loses its ability to accommodate to near objects.

Prevalence: the total number of existing cases, old and new.

Preventative discipline: strategies and procedures that militate against any discipline problems arising.

Primary disability: the first or chief disability.

Primary prevention: procedures concerned with removing the causative factors that account for the initial occurrence of the disorder or strengthening the well being of individuals in the population as a form of inoculation against the causes of subsequent problems.

Probes: brief samples of academic behaviour.

Prosocial behaviour: voluntary behaviour intended to aid or benefit others.

Prosthetic devices: functional devices that substitute for missing body parts.

Psychological processing: how an individual processes sensory information and puts it to meaningful intellectual use.

Receptive disorders: those that interfere with the comprehension of spoken language.

Reflexes: automatic, involuntary motor patterns that are triggered by specific stimuli.

Rehabilitation: procedures that endeavour to restore an individual to normal or optimal functioning.

Remediation: helping a child to overcome, or compensate for, specific deficits in learning and development.

Retinitis pigmentosa: a hereditary condition that causes degeneration of retinal tissues and loss of peripheral vision.

Retinoblastoma: results from a malignant tumour on the retina that may spread to the optic nerve and other areas.

Retinopathy of prematurity (retrolental fibroplasia): a condition affecting the retina and the vitreous humour.

Risk factors: the causes of potential disabilities.

Risk status: a mechanism for describing the likelihood that a particular individual will experience a specific outcome, given certain conditions.

Role playing: participants assume a specific role in a demonstration or simulation.

Rubric: a generic scoring tool used to evaluate the quality of products and performance in a given area.

School law: the legislation, regulations, by-laws, and judicial decisions that apply primarily to all or part of the public school system.

Screening: developmental and health activities that are intended to identify those children who have a high probability of exhibiting delayed or abnormal development.

Secondary disabilities: problems that occur because of the primary disability.

Secondary prevention: ascertaining, as early as possible, the evidence of disorders that may cause disabilities as well as allied attempts to reduce, remove, or reverse substantially complex aspects of disabilities.

Self-concept: a person's description of him- or herself in relation to roles, attributes, or characteristics.

Self-discipline: being able to consider an outcome and select the behaviour that will achieve it.

Self-injurious behaviour: any self-inflicted, repetitive action that leads to laceration, bruising, or abrasions of the client's own body,

Self-stimulation: a persistent, stereotypic, repetitive mannerism.

Semantics: word meaning.

Sensorineural hearing impairments: impairments that interfere with the conversion of sound waves to neural impulses for the brain.

Service delivery model: plans for bringing students, teachers, instruction, and learning together.

Sociability: a child's willingness to engage others in social interaction and to seek their attention or approval.

Social cognition: the knowledge and cognitive activities employed by people in dealing with the social world.

Social competence: the ability of children to successfully and appropriately select and carry out their interpersonal goals.

Social skills: those responses that prove effective within a given situation.

Socialization: the means by which individuals become reasonably acceptable and competent members of their society.

Socially competent individuals: those who perform behaviours that they believe will effect rewarding outcomes and avoid acting in ways that might cause negative outcomes.

Special education: instruction that is specially designed to meet the unique needs of children and youth who are exceptional.

Special health care needs: relates to diseases and conditions that affect the lives and functioning of children and adults.

Special needs: an educational term used to designate pupils who require special education.

Speech disorders: problems encountered in the oral production of language; an impairment of verbal communication such that the intelligibility of spoken language is reduced.

Speech reading (lip reading): the skill of understanding speech through watching the lips and face.

Speech reception threshold (**SRT**): the level at which an individual actually understands speech.

Speech: the mechanical production of language.

Speech range: the range of pitch of most human speech.

Spina bifida: a congenital midline defect of the spinal column.

Stapes: small bone in the middle ear.

Strabismus: one of the most common oculomotor problems, resulting from inefficient ocular motor mobility.

Story grammar: the description of the typical elements frequently found in stories such as theme, characters, and setting.

Stuttering: speech flow disorder; a major category of dysfluency.

Support services: services designed to assist a child with a disability and his or her teacher.

Syndrome: a constellation of findings similar from patient to patient.

Syntax: the network of organizational principles underlying linguistic expression.

Talent: above-average performance.

Task analysis: analyzing the behavioural components and prerequisite skills of a task; breaking skills down into their component parts.

Tay-Sachs disease: a fatal deterioration of brain function.

Telegraphic speech: reduced speech that resembles a telegram in that only the essential aspects of the message, those possessing meaning, are included.

Teratogens: environmental agents that may harm the developing infant.

Teratology: the study of the agents involved in major congenital malformations.

Tertiary prevention: intervention strategies used after a negative outcome has been attained.

Therapy: the treatment of an illness or disabling condition.

Threshold of hearing: the level at which a person can first detect a sound.

Trait plasticity: when IQ can be changed.

Transdisciplinary models: models that rest on consultation and collaboration.

Transition: the process of moving from one program to another, or from one service delivery mode to another.

Traumatic Brain Injury (TBI): an insult to the brain caused by an external physical force that results in impairment of cognitive abilities or physical functioning and that may result in disturbances of behaviour or emotional functioning.

Tympanic membrane (**ear drum**)**:** a tough, tightly stretched tissue that separates the outer from the middle ear.

Usher's syndrome: a condition of familial nerve deafness associated with pigment degeneration of the retina.

Vestibular mechanism: lies behind the cochlea; composed of three fluid-filled, semi-circular canals.

Visual functioning (**visual efficiency**)**:** what the impaired person is doing with his or her residual vision.

Vocational evaluation: a comprehensive and systematic process that utilizes work (real or simulated) to assess the vocational potential of people with disabilities.

BIBLIOGRAPHY

Abang, T.B. (1980). *Teaching visually handicapped children in Nigeria.* Ibadan, Nigeria: Cleverianum Press.

Abroms, K.I. and Bennett, J.W. (1983). Current findings in Down's syndrome. *Exceptional Children, 49,* 449–450

Access denied. (1999, May). Premiers' Council on the Status of People with Disabilities. Canadians with disabilities still lack equal opportunities, according to watchdog report. *Status Report: Quarterly Newsletter on Disability Issues in Alberta,* p. 12.

Achenbach, T.M. (1991). *Child Behavior Checklist and Revised Child Behavior Profile.* Burlington, VT: University of Vermont.

Adams, K. and Markham, R. (1991). Recognition of affective facial expressions by children and adolescents with and without mental retardation. *American Journal on Mental Deficiency, 96,* 21–28.

Adams, J.W. and Tidwell, R. (1989). An instructional guide for reducing the stress of parents of hearing impaired children. *American Annals of the Deaf, 134,* 323–328.

Adams, M.J. (1990). *Beginning to read: Thinking and learning about print.* Cambridge, MA: MIT Press.

Address of Trustees of the New England Institute for the Education of the Blind to the Public. (1836). In C. Dunscombe, Report upon the subject of education made to the Parliament of Upper Canada 25 February 1836, through the Commissioners, Doctors Morrison and Bruce, appointed by a resolution of the House of Assembly in 1835 to obtain information upon the subject of education, etc. (pp. 95–109) Upper Canada: M.C. Reynolds.

Agnew, J. (1986). Tinnitus: An overview. *Volta Review, 88,* 215–221.

Akamatsu, C.T. and Cole, E. (2000). Meeting the psychosocial needs of deaf immigrant and refugee children. *Canadian Journal of School Psychology,* 15, 1–18.

Akerley, M.S. (1975). Parents speak. *Journal of Autism and Childhood Schizophrenia, 5,* 373–380.

Alberta Education Response Centre. (1989). *A teacher's guide to allergies in the classroom.* Edmonton: Alberta Education.

Alberta Teachers Association. (1993). *Trying to teach.* Edmonton: Author.

Alderson, D. (1993, February). Attention Deficit Disorder. *Keeping in Touch,* p. 2.

Aleman, S.R. (1991). CRS report for Congress: Special education for children with attention deficit disorders: Current issues. Washington, DC: Congressional Research Services.

Algozzine, B., Morsink, C.V., and Algozzine, K.K. (1988). What's happening in self-contained special education classrooms? *Exceptional Children, 55,* 259–265.

Allanan, Y.O., Arajar, T., and Vitamaki, R.O. (1964). Psychoses in childhood. *Acta Psychiatrica Scandinavica,* Supp. 174.

Allen, R.E. and Wasserman G.A. (1985). Origins of language delay in abused infants. *Child Abuse and Neglect, 9,* 335–340.

Allen, R.M., Cortazzo, A.D., and Adams, C. (1970). Factors in an adaptive behavior checklist for use with retardates. *Training School Bulletin, 67,* 144–157.

Allum, N. (1975). *Spina bifida: The treatment and care of spina bifida children.* London: George Allen and Unwin.

Alper, S.K., Schloss, P.J., and Schloss, C.N. (1994). *Families of students with disabilities.* Boston, MA: Allyn and Bacon.

Ambrose, N.G., Cox, N.J., and Yairi, E. (1997). The genetic basis of persistence and recovery in stuttering. *Journal of Speech, Language and Hearing Research, 40,* 567–580.

American Association on Mental Deficiency. (1959). *Manual of terminology and classification in mental retardation.* Washington, DC: Author.

American Association on Mental Retardation. (1993). *Mental retardation: Definition, classification, and systems of support* (9th ed.) Washington, DC: Author.

American Psychiatric Association (1968, 1982, 1987) *Diagnostic and statistical manual of mental disorders* (2nd ed., 3rded., 3rd ed., revised) Washington, DC: Author.

American Psychiatric Association. (1994). *Diagnostic and statistical manual of mental disorders.* (4th ed.) Washington, DC: Author.

American Speech-Language-Hearing Association. (1982). Definitions: Communicative disorders and variations. *ASHA, 24,* 949–959.

Anderson, J. (1990). *Cognitive psychology and its implications* (3rd ed.) New York: Freeman.

Andrews, G.A., Craig, A., Feyer, A., Hoddinott, S., Howie, P., and Neilson, M. (1983). Stuttering: A review of research findings and theories. *Journal of Speech and Hearing Disorders, 48,* 226–246.

Andrews, J. and Violato, C. (1996). A structural equation model of learning approaches and strategies. Canadian Journal of School Psychology, 12, 60–73.

Andrews, J.W. and Mason, J.M. (1991). Strategy usage among deaf and hearing readers. *Exceptional Children, 57,* 536–545.

Aplin, D.Y. (1987). Social and emotional adjustment of hearing-impaired children in ordinary and special schools. *Educational Research, 29,* 56–64.

Archambault, F. and Hallmark B.W. (1992). Regular classroom practices: Results of a national survey. In J.S. Renzulli, Chair, Regular classroom practices with gifted students: Findings from the National Research Center on the Gifted and Talented Symposium conducted at the American Educational Research Association, San Francisco.

Archambault, F., Westberg, K., Brown, S., Hallmark, B., Zhang, W., and Emmons, C. (1993). Classroom practices used with gifted third and fourth grade students. *Journal for the Education of the Gifte*d, 16, 103–119.

Arnold, K.M. and Hornett, D. (1990). Teaching idioms to children who are deaf. *Teaching Exceptional Children, 22,* 14–17.

At a glance: Qualifications of paraprofessionals (1999, spring/ summer). *Keeping in Touch*, p. 6.

Atkins, D.V. (1987). Siblings of the hearing impaired: Perspectives for parents. *Volta Review, 89,* 32–45.

Atkinson, M.A. and MacLaren, N.K. (1990). What causes diabetes? *Scientific American,* pp. 63–71.

Augoustinos, M. (1987). Developmental effects of child abuse: Recent findings. *Child Abuse and Neglect, 11,* 15–26.

Augusto, C.R. and McGraw, J.M. (1990). Humanizing blindness through public education. *Journal of Visual Impairment and Blindness, 84,* 397–400.

Badian, N.A. (1988). The prediction of good and poor reading before kindergarten entry: A nine-year follow up. *Journal of Learning Disabilities, 21,* 98–103.

Bailey, D.B. Jr. and Blanco, P.M. (1990). Parents' perspectives of a written survey of family needs. *Journal of Early Intervention, 14,* 196–203.

Bailey, D.B. Jr. and Brochin, H.A. (1989). Tests and test development. In D.B. Bailey and M. Wolery (Eds.) *Assessing infants and preschoolers with handicaps* (pp. 22–46) Columbus, OH: Merrill.

Bailey, I.L. and Hall, A. (1983). *Bailey-Hall Cereal Test for the Measurement of Visual Acuity in Children.* Berkeley, CA: Multimedia Center, School of Optometry, University of California.

Bailey, I.L. and Hall, A. (1984). *U.C. Berkeley Preferential Looking Test.* Berkeley, CA: Multimedia Center, School of Optometry, University of California.

Bailey W.J. (1996, June 13). Factline on nonmedical use of Ritalin. <www.drugs.indiana. edu/pubs/factline/ritalin.html>

Bain, D.A. (1980). Gifted and enriched education in Canada. In M. Csapo and L. Goguen (Eds.) *Special education across Canada: Issues and concerns for the '80s.* Vancouver: Centre for Human Development and Research.

Baird, S.M., Mayfield, P., and Baker, P. (1997). Mothers' interpretations of the behavior of their infants with visual and other impairments during interactions. *Journal of Visual Impairment and Blindness, 91,* 467–483.

Bak, J.J., Cooper, E.M., Dobroth, K.M., and Siperstein, G.N. (1987). Special class placements as labels: Effects on children's attitudes toward learning handicapped peers. *Exceptional Children, 54,* 151–155.

Baker, D. (1983). Justin Clark: Legal implications of the Mental Incompetency Act for Citizens of the World. *Canadian Journal on Mental Retardation, 33,* 14–20.

Baker, J.M. and Zigmond, N. (1990). Are regular education classes equipped to accommodate students with learning disabilities? *Exceptional Children, 56,* 515–526.

Baker, J.M. and Zigmond, N. (1995). The meaning and practice of inclusion for students with learning disabilities: Theories and implications from five cases. *Journal of Special Education,* 29, 163–180.

Baker, L. and Cantwell, D.P. (1982). Psychiatric disorders in children with different types of communication disorders. *Journal of Communication Disorders, 15,* 113–126.

Baker, L. and Cantwell, D.P. (1987). A prospective psychiatric follow-up of children with speech/language disorders. *Journal of the American Academy of Child and Adolescent Psychiatry, 26,* 546–553.

Balakrishnan, T.R. and Wolf, L.C. (1976). Life expectancy of mentally retarded persons in Canadian institutions. *Journal of Abnormal Psychology, 80,* 211–224.

Balthazar, E.E. (1973). *The Balthazar Scales of Adaptive Behavior: Scale 2, Scales of Social Adaptation.* Palo Alto, CA: Consulting Psychologists Press.

Balthazar, E.E. (1976). *The Balthazar Scales of Adaptive Behavior: Scale 1, Scale of Functional Independence.* Palo Alto, CA: Consulting Psychologists Press.

Banarji, M. and Dailey, R. (1995). A study of the effects of an inclusion model on students with specific learning disabilities. *Journal of Learning Disabilities,* 28, 511–522.

Banbury, M.M. and Wellington, B. (1989). Designing and using peer nomination forms. *Gifted/Creative/Talented* , 33, 161–164.

Bank-Mikkelson, N.E. (1969). A metropolitan area in Denmark: Copenhagen. In R. Kugel and W. Wolfsenberger (Eds.) *Changing patterns in residential services for the mentally retarded.*Washington, DC: President's Committee on Mental Retardation.

Barden, R.C., Ford, M.E., Jensen, A.G., Rogers-Salyer, M., and Salyer, K.E. (1989). Effects of craniofacial deformity in infancy on the quality of mother–infant interactions. *Child Development, 60,* 819–824.

Barkley, R.A. Fisher, M., Newby, R., and Breen, M. (1988). Development of multi-method clinical protocol for assessing stimulant drug responses in ADHD children. *Journal of Clinical Child Psychology, 17,* 14–24.

Barkley, R.A., Du Paul, G., and McMurray, M. (1990). Comprehensive evaluation of attention deficit disorder with and without hyperactivity as defined by research criteria. *Journal of Consulting and Clinical Psychology, 58,* 775–789.

Barnett, W.S. (1986). Definition and classification of mental retardation: A reply to Zigler, Balla and Hodapp. *American Journal on Mental Deficiency, 91,* 111–116.

Barringer, D.C., Strong, C.J., Blair, J.C., Clark, T.C., and Watkins, S. (1993). Screening procedures used to identify children with hearing loss. *American Annals of the Deaf, 138,* 420–426.

Barrington, K., Papageorgiou, A., and Usher, R. (2001, January 24). Better early than never. *Globe and Mail,* p. A13.

Bassett, D.S., Jackson L., Ferrel, K., Luckner, J., Hagerty, P., Bussen T., and MacIsan, D. (1996). Multiple perspectives on inclusive education: Reflections of a university faculty. *Teacher Education and Special Education, 19,* 355–386.

Bateman, B. (1993). Learning disabilities: The changing landscape. *Journal of Learning Disabilities,* 25, 29–63.

Bates, J.E. (1987). Temperament in infancy. In J.D. Osofsky (Ed.) *Handbook of infant development* (pp. 1101–1149). New York: Wiley.

Batshaw, M.L. and Perrett, Y.M. (1986). *Children with handicaps: A medical primer.* Baltimore, MD: Brookes.

Bauer, A.M. and Shea, T.M. (1989). *Teaching exceptional students in your classroom.* Toronto: Allyn and Bacon.

Baum, C. (1989). Conduct disorders. In T.H. Ollendick and M. Hersen (Eds.) *Handbook of child psychopathology* (2nd ed.) New York: Plenum.

Baum, S. (1995). Gifted but learning disabled: A puzzling paradox. ERIC Digest, No 479. Reston, VA: Council for Exceptional Children.

Baum, S. and Owen, S. (1988). Learning disabled students: How are they different? *Gifted Child Quarterly, 32,* 321–326.

Baumeister, A.A., Kupstas, F., and Klindworth, L.M. (1990). New morbidity: Implications for prevention of children's disabilities. *Exceptionality, 1,* 1–16.

Bay, E. (1975). Ontogeny of stable speech areas in the human brain. In E.H. Lenneberg and E. Lenneberg (Eds.) *Foundations of language development: A multidisciplinary approach* (vol. 2). New York: Academic Press.

Bayley Scales of Infant Development. (2nd ed.) (1994). New York: Psychological Corporation.

Beakley, B.A. and Yoder, S.L. (1998). Middle schoolers learn community skills. *Teaching Exceptional Children, 30,* 16–21

Beare, P.L. (1991). Philosophy, instructional methodology, training and goals of teachers of the behaviorally disordered. *Behavioral Disorders, 16,* 211–218.

Bearison, D.J. and Muhern, R.L. (Eds.) (1994). *Pediatric psychooncology: Psychological perspectives on children with cancer.* New York: Oxford University Press.

Beattie, L. (1993, summer). Conductive education: Renewing the integration vs segregation debate. *Disability Today,* pp. 51–53.

Becker, W.C. (1981). *Becker Reading Tree Vocational Interest Inventory.* Washington, D.C.: American Association on Mental Deficiency.

Beckman, P. J. and Lieber, J. (1994). The Social Strategy Rating Scale: An approach to evaluating social competence. *Journal of Early Intervention, 18,* 1–11.

Befring, E. (1997). The enrichment perspective: A special educational approach to an inclusive school. *Remedial and Special Education, 18,* 182–187.

Begley, S. (1996, February 19). Your child's brain. *Newsweek,* pp. 55–62.

Behar, L. and George P. (1994). Teachers as change agents: Implications for how teachers use curriculum knowledge. *Educational Researcher Quarterly,* 16, 8–11.

Belcostas, F.P. (1987). Elementary pull-out programs for the intellectually gifted: Boon or bane? *Roeper Review, 9,* 41–55.

Bell, L.M. (1986). Evaluation and implementation of innovation in gifted/enrichment programs. *Gifted Education International, 4,* 120–127.

Bell, R., Fisher, M., and Rodriguez, J. (1994, October 30). Ritalin use sparks concern. *Calgary Sun,* pp. 3, 16–17.

Bellamy, T. (1985). Severe disability in adulthood. *Newsletter for the Association for Persons with Severe Handicaps, 11,* 1–6.

Benbow, C.P. (1991). Meeting the needs of gifted students through use of acceleration. In M.C. Wang, M.C. Reynolds, and H.J. Walberg (Eds.) *Handbook of special education* (vol. 4, pp. 23–36). Elmsford, NY: Pergamon.

Bender, W.N. and Smith, J.K. (1990). Classroom behavior of children and adolescents with learning disabilities: A meta-analysis. *Journal of Learning Disabilities, 23,* 298–305.

Benedict, H. (1979). Early lexical development: Comprehension and production. *Journal of Child Language, 6,* 183–200.

Bennett, T., Deluca, D., and Burns, D. (1997). Putting inclusion into practice: Perspectives of teachers and parents. *Exceptional Children, 64,* 115–131.

Bentley, K.M. and Li, A.K.F. (1995). Bully and victim problems in elementary schools and students' beliefs about aggression. *Canadian Journal of School Psychology, 11,* 153–165.

Berglund, M. and Hoffbauer, D. (1996). New opportunities for students with traumatic brain injuries. *Teaching Exceptional Children, 28,* 54–56.

Berkow, R. (Ed.) (1982). *The Merck manual of diagnosis and therapy.* Rahway, NJ: Merck, Sharp and Dohme.

Berkson, G. and Tupa, M. (2000). Early development of stereotypes and self-injurious behavior. *Journal of Early Intervention,* 23, 1–19.

Berlin, C.M. Jr. (1983). Biological causes of exceptionality. In R.M. Smith, J.T. Neisworth, and F.M. Hunt (Eds.) *The exceptional child: A functional approach.* New York: McGraw-Hill.

Bernard, H. (1973). *Child development and learning.* Boston, MA: Allyn and Bacon.

Bernthal, J. and Bankston, N. (1981). *Articulation disorders.* Englewood Cliffs, NJ: Prentice-Hall.

Betts, G.T. (1985). *Autonomous learner model for the gifted and talented.* Greeley, CO: Autonomous Learning Publications and Specialists.

Bickett, L. and Milich, R. (1990). First impressions formed of boys with attention deficit disorders. *Journal of Learning Disabilities, 23,* 253–259.

Bidwell, N. (1997). *The nature and prevalance of bullying in elementary schools.* Regina: Saskatchewan, Research Report 97-06, Saskatchewan School Trustees Assocation.

Bigelow, A. (1987). Early words of blind children. *Journal of Child Language, 14,* 47–56.

Bigelow, A. (1991). Spatial mapping of familar locations in blind children. *Journal of Visual Impairment and Blindness, 85,* 113–117.

Bingol, N., Schuster, C., Fuchs, M., and Iosub, S. (1987). The influence of socioeconomic factors in the occurrence of fetal alcohol syndrome. Advances in Alcohol and Substance Abuse, 6, 105–118.

Bishop, V. (1986). Identifying the components of success in mainstreaming. *Journal of Visual Impairment and Blindness, 80,* 939–946.

Bishop, W. (1968). Successful teachers of the gifted. *Exceptional Children, 34,* 317–325.

Blackorby, J. and Wagner, M. (1996). Longitudinal postschool outcomes of youth with disabilities: Findings from the national longitudinal transition study. *Exceptional Children, 62,* 399–413.

Bleck, E.L. and Nagel, D.A. (1982). *Physically handicapped children: A medical atlas for teachers.* New York: Grune and Stratton.

Blomquist, H., Gustavson, K.H. Holmgren, S. Nordenson, I., and Paslsson-Strade, U. (1983). Fragile X syndrome in mildly mentally retarded children in a northern Swedish county: A prevalence study. *Clinical Genetics, 24,* 393–398.

Bloodstein, O. (1975). *A handbook on stuttering* (rev. ed.) National Easter Seal Society for Crippled Children and Adults.

Bloom, B.S. (Ed.) (1956). *Taxonomy of educational objectives: Handbook 1: cognitive domain.* New York: David McKay.

Bloom, B.S. (1964). *Stability and change in human characteristics.* New York: Wiley.

Bloom, B.S. (1985). *Developing talent in young people.* New York: Ballantine Books.

Bloom, B.S. and Sosniak, L.A. (1981). Talent development vs schooling. *Educational Leadership, 39,* 86–94.

Bloom, D.T. (1991, winter). Mainstreaming remains the goal. *Day Care and Early Education, 18,* 44–45.

Bluestone, D.C. (1982). Otitis media in children: To treat or not to treat. *New England Journal of Medicine, 306,* 1399–1404.

Blumstein, A., Cohen J., and Farrington, D.P. (1988). Criminal career research: Its value for criminology. *Criminology, 26,* 1–35.

Bogie H. (1997, fall). Eaton versus Brant County Board of Education: The Supreme court of Canada decision, released Feb. 6, 1997. *Keeping in Touch,* p. 6.

Bonvillian, J.D., Orlansky, M.D., and Novack, L.L. (1983). Developmental milestones: Sign language acquisition and motor development. *Child Development, 54,* 1435–1445.

Booth, T. and Ainscow, M. (Eds.) (1998). *From them to us: An international study of inclusion in education.* London: Routledge.

Borgh, K. and Dickson, W.P. (1986). Two preschools sharing one microcomputer: Creating prosocial behavior with hardware and software. In P.F. Campbell and G.G. Fein (Eds.) *Young children and microcomputers* (pp. 37–44). Reston, VA: Reston.

Borland, J.H. (1989). *Planning and implementing programs for the gifted.* New York: Teachers College Press.

Bos, C.C. and Vaughn, S. (1998). *Strategies for teaching students with learning and behavior problems.* Boston, MA: Allyn and Bacon.

Bouchard, T.J. Jr. and McGue, M. (1981). Familial studies of intelligence: A review. *Science, 212,* 1055–1059.

Bounds, B. (1997, April/May). Should special education students be paid for vocational training? *CEC Today,* p. 14.

Bourque, J. and Li, A.K. (1987). Perceived competence, social adjustment and peer relations of intellectually gifted children in segregated versus regular-classroom settings. *Canadian Journal of Special Education, 3,* 191–200.

Bowe, F. (1992). Radicalism vs reason: Directions in the educational issues of ASL. In M. Walworth, D. Moores, and T. J. O'Rourke (Eds.) *A free hand* (pp.182–197). Silver Spring, MD: TJ Publishers.

Bower, B, (1989). Remodeling the autistic child. *Science News, 136,* 312–313.

Bowley, A. and Gardner, L. (1980). *The handicapped child.* London: Churchill Livingstone.

Boyle, R. and Yeager, N. (1997). Blueprints for learning: Using cognitive frameworks for understanding. *Teaching Exceptional Children. 29,* 26–31.

Bracken, B.A. and McCallum, R.S. (1998). *Universal nonverbal intelligence test.* Toronto: Nelson.

Bracken, B.A. and Newman, V.L. (1994). Child and adolescent interpersonal relations with parents, peers, and teachers: A factor analytic investigation. *Canadian Journal of School Psychology,* 10, 108–122.

Braden, J.P. (1987). An explanation of the superior performance IQs of deaf children of deaf parents. *American Annals of the Deaf, 132,* 263–266.

Bradley, C. (1937). The behavior of children receiving Benzedrine. *American Journal of Psychiatry, 94,* 577–585.

Bradley, D.F. and West, J.F. (1994). Staff training for the inclusion of students with disabilities: Visions from school-based educators. *Teacher Education and Special Education,* 17, 117–128.

Braman, B.J., Brady, M.P., Lineham, S.L., and Williams, R.E. (1995). Facilitated communication for children with autism: An examination of face validity. *Behavioral Disorders, 21,* 110–119.

Bransky, T. (1987). Specific program information: A key to attitudes about the gifted education program. *Gifted Child Quarterly, 31,* 20–24.

Breslau, N. and Davis, G.C. (1986). Chronic stress and major depression. *Archives of General Psychiatry, 43,* 309–314.

Bricker, D. (1986). *Early education of at-risk and handicapped infants, toddlers and preschool children.* Glenville, IL: Scott, Foresman.

Bricker, D. and Squires, J. (1989). Low cost system using parents to monitor the development of at-risk infants. *Journal of Early Intervention,* 13, 50–60.

Brigance A (1992). B*rigance K and 1 screen* (3rd ed.) North Bellerica, MA: Curriculum Associates.

Brigham, E.J. and Kauffman, J.M. (1998). Creating supportive environments for students with emotional and behavioral disorders. *Effective School Practice, 17,* 25–35.

Brinthaupt, G.P. (1991). Cystic fibrosis and parental adjustment. In M. Seligman (Ed.) *The family with a handicapped child* (2nd ed.) (pp. 295–336) Boston, MA: Allyn and Bacon.

British Columbia Ministry of Health. (1978). *Epilepsy: The causes, the treatment, the hope.* Victoria: B.C. Ministry of Health.

Brod, N. and Hamilton, D. (1973). Binocularity and reading. *Journal of Learning Disabilities, 6,* 574–576.

Brody, G.H., Stoneman, Z., Davis, C.H., and Crapps, J.M. (1991). Observations of the role relations and behavior between older children with mental retardation and their younger siblings. *American Journal on Mental Retardation, 95,* 527–536.

Brody, L.E. and Mills, C.J. (1997). Gifted children with learning disabilities: A review of the issues. *Journal of Learning Disabilities,* 30, 282–296.

Brokx, J.P. (1987). The integration of hearing aid rehabilitation in the management of young hearing-impaired children. *Audiology in Practice, 4,* 7–8.

Brolin, D. and Gysbers, N. (1989). Career education for students with disabilities. *Journal of Counseling and Development, 68,* 155–159.

Brown, L.L. and Hammill, D.D. (1990). *The Behavior Rating Profile-2.* Austin, TX: Pro-Ed.

Brown, T.E. (1995). Differential diagnosis of ADD versus ADHD in adults. In K.G. Nadeau (Ed.) *A comprehensive guide to attention deficit disorder in adults: Research, diagnosis, treatment* (pp. 93–108). New York: Brunner/Mazel.

Brown, V.L., Hammill, D.D. and Wiederholt, J.L. (1995). *The Test of Reading Comprehension—3rd ed.* Austin, TX: Pro-Ed.

Brubacher, R.G. (1994). Acculturative stress: A useful framework for understanding the experiences of deaf Americans. *Journal of Rehabilitation of the Deaf, 28,* 1–15.

Bruck, M. (1998). Outcomes of adults with childhood histories of dyslexia. In C. Hulme and R.M. Joshi (Eds.) *Reading and selling: Development and disorder* (pp. 179–200). Mahwah, NJ: Erlbaum.

Bruininks, R.H. (1977). Manual for the Bruininks-Osteresky Test of Motor Proficiency. Circle Pines, MI: American Guidance Service.

Bruininks,R.H., Woodcock, R.W., Weathernan R.F., and Hill, B.K. (1996). *Scales of independent behavior-revised.* Toronto: Nelson.

Bryan, T.H. and Sullivan-Burstein, K. (1997). Homework how-to's. *Teaching Exceptional Children, 29,* 32–37.

Bryan, W.H. and Jeffrey, D.L. (1982). Education of visually handicapped students in the regular classroom. *Texas Teachers Journal of Education, 9,* 125–131.

Bryson, S. (1996). Brief report: Epidemiology of autism. *Journal of Autism and Developmental Disabilities, 26,* 165–167.

Buescher, T.M. (1991). Gifted adolescents. In N. Colangelo and G.A. Davis (Eds.) *Handbook of gifted education* (pp. 382–401). Boston, MA: Allyn and Bacon.

Bullis, M. and Reiman, J. (1992). Development and preliminary psychometric properties of the Transition Competence Battery for deaf adolescents and young adults. *Exceptional Children, 59,* 12–26.

Bullis, M., Reiman, J.W., Davis, C., and Reid, C. (1997). National field testing of the 'mini' version of the Transition Competence Battery for adolescents and young adults who are deaf. *Journal of Special Education, 31,* 347–361.

Bunch, G.O. (1994). Inclusion. *American Annals of the Deaf, 139,* 150–152.

Burns, P.C. and Roe, B.D. (1999). *Informal reading inventory.* 5th ed. Toronto: Nelson.

Burt, K.L., Parks-Charney, R., and Schwean, V.L. (1996). The AD/HD skills and strategies program: A program for AD/HD adults in postsecondary education. *Canadian Journal of School Psychology, 12,* 122–134.

Caffey, J. (1946). Multiple fractures in the long bones of infants suffering from chronic subdural hematoma. *American Journal of Roentgenology, 56,* 163–173.

Calfee, R.C. (1977). Assessment of independent reading skills: Basic research and practical applications. In A.S. Reber and D.L. Scarborough (Eds.) *Toward a psychology of reading.* Hillsdale, NJ: Erlbaum.

Calfee, R.C. (1987). The school as a context for assessment of literacy. *The Reading Teacher, 40,* 738–743.

Camp, B. (1973). Psychiatric tests and learning tests in severely disabled readers. *Journal of Learning Disabilities,* 6, 512–517.

Campbell, M. (1997, August 9). A pill before lunch at Camp Ritalin. *The Globe and Mail,* p. 30C.

Campbell, M., Grange, M., Cernetig, M., Ha, T.T., and Galt, V. (1997, October 4). Shakedowns in the schoolyard. *The Globe and Mail,* pp. 1, 6.

Campbell, S.B. (1995). Behavior problems in preschool children: A review of recent research. *Journal of Psychology and Psychiatry and Applied Disciplines, 36,* 113–149.

Canadian Association for the Mentally Retarded. [1980]. *Questions and answers about mental retardation.* Pamphlet, n.p., CAMR.

Canadian Cognitive Abilities Test (CCAT) New edition. (1998).Toronto: Nelson.

Canadian Council for Exceptional Children. (1992, March). *Monograph one: Staying in school initiatives.* Toronto:

Canadian Council for Exceptional Children. (1998). Standards testing. *Keeping in Touch,* p. 7.

Canadian Lung Association. (1997). Asthma. Toronto: Author.

Canadian National Education Association of Disabled Students. (2000). National approach to services project: Executive summary. http://www.indie.ca/needs.

Canadian National Institute for the Blind. (1980). Brochure. Toronto: CNIB.

Canadian Office for Disability Issues. (1997). In Global Applied Disability Research and Information Network on Employment and Training. www.gladnet.org/.

Canadian Pediatric Society. (1988). Hyperactivity in children. *Canadian Medical Association Journal, 139,* 211–212.

Cantor, S. (1988). Childhood schizophrenia. *American Journal on Mental Retardation, 94,* 688–690.

Cantor, S. (1989). *Childhood schizophrenia.* New York: Guilford Press.

Cantwell, D.P., Baker, B.L., and Rutter, M. (1979). Families of autistic and dysphonic children: Family life and interaction patterns. *Archives of General Psychiatry, 36,* 682–687.

Carey, S. T. (1978). The child as word learner. In M. Halle, J. Bresnan, and G. Miller (Eds.) *Linguistic theory and psychological reality.* Cambridge, MA: MIT Press.

Carney, A. (1986). Understanding speech intelligibility in the hearing impaired. *Topics in Language Disorders, 6,* 47–59.

Carpenter, D. (1985). Grading handicapped pupils: Review and position statement. *Remedial and Special Education, 6,* 54–59

Carpenter, S.L. and McKee-Higgins, E. (1996). Behavior management in inclusive classrooms. *Remedial and Special Education, 17,* 195–203.

Carrow-Woolfolk, E. (1985). *Test of Auditory Comprehension.* Toronto: Nelson.

Carter, D.E. and Rogers, W.T. (1989). Diagnostic and placement practice for mildly educable mentally handicapped students. *Canadian Journal of Special Education, 5,* 15–23.

Carter, E.A. and McGoldrick, M. (Eds.) (1980). *The family life cycle: A framework for family therapy.* New York: Gardner Press.

Carter, S., Janzen, H., and Paterson, J.G. (1999). The psychopathology of school violence. In G. Malicky, B. Shapiro, and K. Mazurek (Eds.) *Building foundations for safe and caring schools: Research on disruptive behaviour and violence.* Edmonton: Duval House.

Casby, H.W. (1997). Symbolic play of children with language impairment: A critical review. *Journal of Speech, Language, and Hearing Research, 40,* 468–479.

Caspi, A., Elder, G.H., and Bern, D.J. (1987). Moving against the world: Life-course patterns of explosive children. *Developmental Psychology, 23,* 308–313.

Casto, G., and Mastropieri, M.A. (1987). The efficacy of early intervention programs: A meta-analysis. *Exceptional Children, 52,* 417–424.

Cataracts: Some facts you should know. (1990). Alberta: CNIB.

Cazden, C.B. (1988). *Classroom discourse: The language of teaching and learning.* Portsmouth, NH: Heinemannn.

Center for Assessment and Demographic Studies. (1991). *Stanford Achievement Test, eighth edition: Hearing-impaired norms booklet.* Washington, DC: Gallaudet University.

Chall, J.S., Jacobs, V., and Baldwin, L. (1990). *The reading crisis: Why poor children fall behind.* Cambridge MA: Harvard University Press.

Chandler, L.K. (1992). Promoting young children's social competence as a strategy for transition to mainstreamed kindergarten programs. In S.L. Odon, S.R. McConnell, and M.A. McEvoy (Eds.) *Social competence of young children with disabilities* (pp. 245–276). Baltimore, MD: Brookes.

Chasnoff. I.J. (1987, May). Prenatal effects of cocaine. *Contemporary OB/GYN,* pp. 163–179.

Chasnoff, I. J., Burns, K.A., Burns, W.J., and Schnoll, S. (1988). Prenatal drug exposure: Effects on neonatal and infant growth and development. *Neurobehavioral Toxicology and Teratology, 8,* 357–362.

Chasnoff, I.J., Chisum, G., and Kaplan, W. (1988). Maternal cocaine use and genitourinary malformation. *Teratology,* 201–204.

Chen, D. and Haney, M. (1995). An early intervention model for infants who are deaf-blind. *Journal of Visual Impairment and Blindness, 89,* 213–221.

Cheney, D. and Muscott, H.S. (1996). Preventing school failure for students with emotional and behavioral disoders through responsible inclusion. *Preventing School Failure,* 40, 109–116.

Children should see more and more each day. (1980). Toronto: National Retinitis Pigmentosa Foundation of Canada.

Children with communication disorders. (1995). ERIC Digest, H 470. Reston, VA: Council for Exceptional Children.

Chomsky, N. (1965). *Aspects of the theory of syntax.* Cambridge, MA: MIT Press.

Chorost, S. (1988). The hearing-impaired child in the mainstream: A survey of the attitudes of regular classroom teachers. *Volta Review, 90,* 7–12.

Clark, B. (1988). *Growing up gifted* (3rd ed.) Columbus OH: Merrill.

Clark, G.M., Tong, Y.C., and Patrick. J.F. (Eds.) (1990). *Cochlea prothesis.* New York: Churchill Livingtone.

Coggins, T.E. and Morrison, J.A. (1981). Spontaneous imitations in Down's syndrome children: A lexical analysis. *Journal of Speech and Hearing Research, 24,* 303–308.

Coie, J. (1985). Fitting social skills intervention to the target group. In R.H. Schnider, K.H. Rubin, and J.E. Ledingham (Eds.) *Peer relationships and social skills in childhood: Issues in assessment and training.* New York: Springer-Verlag.

Colangelo, N. (1989). Moral dilemmas as formulated by gifted students. *Understanding Our Gifted, 1,* 10–12.

Colangelo, N. and Fleuridas, C. (1986). The abduction of childhood. *Journal of Counseling and Development, 64,* 561–563.

Cole, C. and McLeskey, J. (1997, February). Secondary inclusion programs for students with mild disabilities. *Focus on Exceptional Children,* 1–16.

Cole, C.K., Jones, M.K., and Sadofsky, G.S. (1990). Working with children at risk due to prenatal susbstance exposure. *PRISE Reporter—Issues in the Education of Students with Handicaps, 21,* 1–6.

Cole, E. (1992). Depression and the risk for suicide in children and adolescents. In S. Miezitis (Ed.) *Creating alternatives to depression in our schools.* Toronto: Hogrefe and Huber.

Cole, E. and Brown, R. (1996). Multidisciplinary school teams: A five-year follow-up study. *Canadian Journal of School Psychology, 12,* 155–168.

Cole, H. and Sarnoff, D. (1980, June). Interactive creativity: Explorations of basic meanings and their implications for teaching and counselling. Paper at the Twenty-sixth Annual Creative Problem Solving Institute, Buffalo.

Cole, M. and Cole, S.R. (1989). *The development of children.* San Diego, CA: Scientific American Books.

Coleman, J.M. and Minnett, A.M. (1992). Learning disabilities and social competence: A social ecological perspective. *Exceptional Children, 59,* 234–246.

Coleman, M.C. (1992). *Behavior disorders: Theory and practice* (2nd ed.) Boston, MA: Allyn and Bacon.

Coles, C. and Zsargo, L. (1998). Conductive education: Towards an "educational model." *British Journal of Special Education,* 25, 70–73.

Coles, G. (1978). The learning disabilities test battery: Empirical and social issues. *Harvard Educational Review, 48,* 313–340.

Collins, M.T. (1995). History of deaf-blind education. *Journal of Visual Impairment and Blindess, 89,* 210–212.

Colvin, G., Ainge, D., and Nelson, R. (1997). How to defuse confrontations. *Teaching Exceptional Children* 29, 47–51.

Conn-Blowers, E.A. and McLeod, H.J. (1989). Special education in Alberta. In M. Csapo and L. Goguen (Eds.) *Special education across Canada* (pp. 19–27) Vancouver: Centre For Human Development and Research.

Conners, C.K. (1973). Rating scales for use in drug studies with children. *Psychopharmocology Bulletin, 9,* 24–81.

Conroy, M.A., Clark, D., Gable, R.A., and Fox, J. (1999, summer). Building competence in the use of functional behavioral assessment. *Preventing School Failure,* pp. 140–143.

Conte, R., Andrews, J., Loomer, M., and Hutton, G. (1995). A classroom-based social skills inventory for children with learning disabilities. *Alberta Journal of Educational Research, 41,* 84–102.

Cook, J. (1991). Higher education: An attainable goal for students who have sustained head injuries. *Journal of Head Trauma Rehabilitation, 6,* 64–72.

Cooper, D.H. and Speece, D.L. (1990). Maintaining at-risk children in regular education settings: Initial effects of individual differences and classroom environment. *Exceptional Children,* 57, 117–126.

Copeland, E.D. (1994). *Medications for attention disorders (ADHD/ADD) and related medical problems (Tourette's syndrome, sleep apnea, seizure disorders): A comprehensive handbook.* Atlanta, GA: Resurgens.

Copeland, M.E. and Kimmel, J.R. (1989). *Evaluation and management of infants and young children with developmental disabilities.* Baltimore, MD: Brookes.

Cordesco, L.K. and Laus, M.K. (1993). Individualized training in behavioral strategies for parents of preschool children with disabilities. *Teaching Exceptional Children, 25,* 43–47.

Corn, A.L. (1980). Optical aids in the classroom. *Education of the Visually Handicapped, 12,* 114–121.

Cornell, D. (1983). Gifted children: The impact of positive labelling on the family system. *American Journal of Orthopsychiatry, 53,* 322–355.

Cornell, D.G., Callahan, C.M., and Loyd, B.H. (1991). Socioemotional adjustments of adolescent girls enrolled in a residential acceleration program. *Gifted Child Quarterly, 35,* 58–66.

Cornwell, A. and Bawden, H.N. (1992). Reading disabilities and aggression: A critical review. *Journal of Learning Disabilities, 25,* 281–289.

Corywell, J., Holcomb, T.K., and Scherer, M. (1992). Attitudes towards deafness: A collegiate perspective. *American Annals of the Deaf, 137,* 299–302.

Cotler, S. (1986). Epidemiology and outcome. In J.M. Reisman (Ed.) *Behavior disorders in infants, children, and adolescents.* New York: Random House.

Council for Exceptional Children. (1993). Position paper. Division for Early Childhood: Council for Exceptional Children.

Council of Administrators of Special Education (CASE) Inc. Position paper on delivery of services to students with disabilities (1997, fall) *Keeping in Touch,* p. 3.

Council of Administrators of Special Education (CASE) Inc. (2000). Position paper on delivery of services to students with disabilities, revised. *Keeping in Touch,* p. 3.

Cowan, W.M. (1979). *The brain.* San Francisco, CA: Freeman.

Cox, D.H. and Klas, L.D. (1996). Students with learning disabilities in Canadian colleges and universities: A primer for service provision. *Journal of Learning Disabilities, 29,* 93–97.

Craig, W.M. and Peplar, D.J. (1997). Observations of bullying and victimization in the school yard. *Canadian Journal of School Psychology,* 13, 41–60.

Cramer, S., Erzkus, A., Mayweather, K., Pope, K., Roeder, J. and Tone, T. (1997). Connecting with siblings. *Teaching Exceptional Children, 30,* 46–51.

Cramond, B. and Martin, C.E. (1987). Inservice and preservice teachers' attitudes toward the academically brilliant. *Gifted Child Quarterly, 31,* 15–19.

Cratty, B. (1986). *Perceptual and motor development in infants and children* (3rd ed.) Englewood Cliffs, NJ: Prentice-Hall.

Crawford, L.V. (Ed.) (1982). *Pediatric allergic diseases.* Garden City, NY: Medical Examination Publishing Company.

Crealock, C. (1983). Teacher and student behaviours in regular and special education settings. *B.C. Journal of Special Education, 7,* 321–330.

Crealock, C. (1984). The JD/LD link: Causation or condition? Report prepared for the Solicitor General of Canada. Ottawa: Solicitor General.

Crealock, C. (1986) *The learning disabilities/juvenile delinquency link: Causation or correction.* Ottawa: Ministry of the Solicitor-General.

Crockenberg, S.R. and Litman, C. (1990). Autonomy as competence in two year olds: Maternal correlates of child defiance, compliance, and self-assertion. *Developmental Psychology, 26,* 961–971.

Crystal, D., Fletcher, P., and Garman, M.G. (1976). *The grammatical analysis of language disability: A process for assessment and remediation.* London: Edward Arnold.

Crudden, A. and McBroom, L. (1999). Barriers to employment: A survey of employed persons who are visually impaired. *Journal of Visual Impairment and Blindness, 93,* 341–350.

Csapo, M. (1979). Prevalence and needs assessment study of autistic children in British Columbia. *B.C. Journal of Special Education, 3,* 159–191.

Csapo, M. (1981a). The emotionally disturbed child in Canada's schools. *Behavior Disorders, 6,* 139–149.

Csapo, M. (1981b). Educational provisions for emotionally disturbed children in British Columbia: A status report. *B.C. Journal of Special Education, 5,* 357–367.

Csapo, M. (1988). Sexual abuse of children. *B.C. Journal of Special Education, 12,* 121–159.

Cullinan, D., Epstein, M.H., and Lloyd, J.W. (1991). Evaluation of conceptual models of behavior disorders. *Behavioral Disorders, 16,* 148–157.

Culross, R.D. (1997). Concepts of inclusion in gifted education. *Teaching Exceptional Children, 29,* 24–26.

Cummings, S.T. and Finger, D.C. (1980). Emotional disorders. In H.E. Rie and E.D. Rie (Eds.) *Handbook of minimal brain dysfunction.* New York: Wiley.

Curci, R.A. and Gottlieb, J. (1990). Teachers' instruction of noncategorically grouped handicapped children. *Exceptionality, 1,* 239–248.

Curlee, R.F. and Yairi, E. (1997). Early intervention with early childhood stuttering: A critical examination of the data. *American Journal of Speech-Language Pathology, 6,* 8–18.

D'Alonzo, B.J., Giordano, G., and Vanleuven D.M. (1997). Perceptions by the teacher about the benefits and liabilities of inclusion. *Preventing School Failure,* 42, 4–11.

Dao, M. (1991). Designing assessment procedures for educationally at-risk southeast Asian-American students. *Journal of Learning Disabilities, 24,* 594–601, 629.

Darwin, C. (1859). *On the origin of the species.* London: Murray.

Dauber, S.L. and Benbow, C.P. (1990). Aspects of personality and peer relations of extremely talented adolescents. *Gifted Child Quarterly,* 34, 10–14.

Davenport, S.L., O'Nuallian, S., Omenn, G.S., and Wilkus, R.J. (1978). Usher's syndrome in four hard-of-hearing siblings. *British Journal of Opthomology,* 7, 484–488.

David, J. (Ed.) (1990). *Our forgotten children: Hard of hearing pupils in the schools* (2nd ed.) Washington: Self Help for the Hard of Hearing.

Davis, G.A. and Rimm, S.B. (1985). *Education of the gifted and talented.* Englewood Cliffs. NJ: Prentice Hall.

Davis, G.A. and Rimm, S.B. (1994). *Education of the gifted and talented* (3rd ed.) Boston, MA: Allyn and Bacon.

Dawson, G., Metzoff, A.N., Osterling, J., and Rinaldi, J. (1998). Neurophysiological correlates of early symptoms of autism. *Child Development, 69,* 1276–1285.

de Bettencourt, L.U. (1987). Strategy training: A need for clarification. *Exceptional Children, 54,* 24–30.

Decker, S.N. and DeFries, J.C. (1980). Cognitive abilities in families with reading disabled children. *Journal of Learning Disabilities, 13,* 517–522.

Decker, S.N. and DeFries, J.C. (1981). Cognitive ability profiles in families of reading disabled children. *Developmental Medicine and Child Neurology, 23,* 217–227.

Dei, G.J., James, I.M., James-Wilson, S., Karumanchery, L.L., and Zine, J. (2000). *Removing the margin: The challenges and possibilities of inclusive schooling.* Toronto: Canadian Scholars' Press Inc.

De La Paz, S. and Graham, S. (1997). Strategy instruction in planning efforts on the writing performance and behavior of students with learning disabilities. *Exceptional Children, 63,* 167–181.

de Mause, L. (1975). Our forefathers made childhood a nightmare. *Psychology Today, 8,* 85–88.

De Pompei, R. and Blosser, J. (1987). Strategies for helping head-injured children successfully return to school. *Language, Speech and Hearing Services in the Schools, 18,* 292–300.

Derevensky, J. and Coleman, E. (1989). Gifted children's fears. *Gifted Child Quarterly, 33,* 65–68.

DeRuiter, J.A. and Wansart, W. (1982). *Psychology of learning disabilities.* Rockville, MD: Aspen Systems.

Destad, L. (1987). A personal legacy. *Phi Delta Kappan, 68,* 744–745.

Detterman, D.K. and Thompson, L.A. (1997). What is so special about special education? *American Psychologist, 52,* 1082–1090.

Developmental delay: Questions and answers. (1991). *DEC Communicator, The Council for Exceptional Children, 17,* 1–4.

de Villiers, J.G. and de Villiers, P.A. (1978). *Language acquisition.* Cambridge, MA: Harvard University Press.

De Witt, K. (1991, May 12). How best to teach the blind: A growing battle over braille. *New York Times,* pp. 1, 18.

Deykin, E.Y. and MacMahon, B. (1979). The incidence of seizures among children with autistic symptoms. *American Journal of Psychiatry, 116,* 1310–1312.

Diabetic retinopathy. (1990). Alberta: Canadian National Institute for the Blind.

Diamond, G.W. and Cohen, H.J. (1987, December). *AIDS and developmental disabilities: Prevention update of the National Coalition in Prevention on Mental Retardation.* Silver Spring, MD: American Association of University Affiliated Programs for Persons with Developmental Disabilities.

Dikmen, S., Matthews, C.G., and Harley, J.P. (1975). The effect of early versus late onset of major motor epilepsy upon cognition-intellectual performance. *Epilepsia, 76,* 73–81.

Diller, L.H. (1996). The run on Ritalin: Attention deficit disorders and stimulant treatment in the 1990s. *The Hastings Center Report, 26,* 12–18.

Dimitrovsky, L., Spector, H., Levy-Shiff, R., and Vakil, E. (1998). Interpretation of facial expressions of affect in children with learning disabilities with verbal or nonverbal deficits. *Journal of Learning Disabilities, 31,* 286–292, 312.

The discipline problem—and ways to deal with it. (1996). *CEC Today, 3,* 1, 9, 14.

Dishion, T.J., Andrews, D.W., and Crosby, L. (1995). Antisocial boys and their friends in early adolescence: Relationship characteristics, quality, and interactional process. *Child Development, 66,* 139–151.

Dodge, K.A., Bates, J.E., and Pettit, G.S. (1990). Mechanisms in the cycle of violence. *Science, 250,* 1678–1683.

Dodge, K.A., Pettit, G.S., and Bates, J.E. (1994). Socialization mediators of the relation between socioeconomic status and child conduct problems. *Child Development, 65,* 649–665.

Dodge, K.A., Pettit, G.S., McCloskey, C.L., and Boron, M.M. (1986). Social competence in children. *Monographs of the Society for Research in Child Development, 51,* 2. Serial 213.

Dohrn, E. and Bryan, T. (1994). Attibution instruction. *Teaching Exceptional Children, 26,* 61–63.

Dokecki, F., Baumeister, A.A., and Kupstas, F.D. (1989). Biomedical and social aspects of pediatric AIDS. *Journal of Early Intervention, 13,* 99–113

Doll, E. (1941). The essentials of an inclusive concept of mental deficiency. *American Journal of Mental Deficiency, 46,* 214–219.

Dolmage, W.R. (1999). Lies, damned lies and statistics: The media's treatment of youth violence. *Education and Law Journal, 10,* 4–46.

Dolnick, E. (1993). Deafness as culture. *Atlantic Monthly, 272,* 37–53.

Donaldson, E.L. (1999). A comparative study of educational policies and effective school-based strategies to reduce violence in schools: Canada, Finland and Scotland. In G. Malicky, B. Shapiro, and K. Mazurek (Eds.) *Building foundations for safe and caring schools: Research on disruptive behaviour and violence* (pp. 199–220) Edmonton: Duval House

Dote-Kwan, J. (1995). Impact of mothers' interactions on the development of their young visually impaired children. *Journal of Visual Impairment and Blindness, 89,* 46–58.

Dowdy, C.A., Carter, J., and Smith, T.E.C. (1990). Differences in transitional needs of high school students with and without learning disabilities. *Journal of Learning Disabilities, 23,* 343–348.

Downey, G. and Walker, E. (1989). Spatial cognition and adjustment in children at risk for psychopathology. *Developmental Psychology, 25,* 835–845.

Downey, J., Elkin, E.J., Ehrhardt, A.A., Meyer-Bahlberg, H., Bell, J.J., and Morishima, A. (1991). Cognitive ability and every day functioning in women with Turner syndrome. *Journal of Learning Disabilities,* 24, 32–39.

Drew, C.J., Logan, D.R., and Hardman M.L. (1992). *Mental retardation: A life cycle approach* (5th ed.) New York: Macmillan.

Dunn, L.M. and Dunn, L. (1997). *Peabody Picture Vocabulary Test— III.* Circle Pines, MN: American Guidance Service.

Dunn, N.L. McCartan, K.W., and Fugura, R.W. (1988). Young children with orthopedic handicaps: Self-knowledge about their disability. *Exceptional Children, 55,* 249–252.

Dunn, W. (1989). Integrated related services for preschoolers with neurological impairments. *Remedial and Special Education, 10,* 31–39.

Dunner, G.M. Connor-Kuntz, F.J., and Goodway, J.D. (1995). A physical education curriculum for all preschool students. *Teaching Exceptional Children, 27,* 28–34.

Dunst, C.J. (1980). *A clinical and educational manual for use with the Ugiris and Hunt Scales of Infant Psychological Development.* Baltimore, MD: University Park Press.

DuPaul, G.J. and Stoner, G. (1994). *ADHD in the schools: Assessment and intervention strategies.* New York: Guilford Press.

Dworet, D. and Rathberger, A.J. (1990). Provincial and territorial government responses to behaviourally disordered students in Canada. *Behavioral Disorders, 15,* 201–209.

Dykens, E. (1996). DNA meets DSM: The growing importance of genetic syndromes in dual diagnoses. *Mental Retardation, 34,* 125–127.

Dykens E. and Kasari, C. (1997). Maladaptive behavior in children with Prader-Willi syndrome, Down syndrome, and nonspecific mental retardation. *American Journal on Mental Retardation, 102,* 228–237.

Dykens, E., Leckman, J., Paul, R., and Watson, M. (1988). Cognitive, behavioral and adaptive functioning in fragile X and non–fragile X retarded men. *Journal of Autism and Developmental Disorders,18,* 41–52.

Dyson L.L. (1996). The experiences of families of children with learning disabilities: Parental stress, family functioning, and sibling self-concept. *Journal of Learning Disabilities, 29,* 280–286.

Dyson, L.L. and Fewell, R.R. (1989). The self-concept of siblings of handicapped children: A comparison. *Journal of Early Intervention, 13,* 230–238.

Easterbrooks, S. (1999). Improving practices for students with hearing impairments. *Exceptional Children, 65,* 537–554.

Easterbrooks, S. and Baker-Hawkins, S. (Eds.) (1995). *Deaf and hard of hearing students: Educational services guidelines.* Alexandria, VA: National Association of State Directors of Special Education. ERIC Doc. No. 377-614.

Eaves, L.C. (1988). Prevalence and needs survey of autistic preschool children in the lower mainland of British Columbia. *B.C. Journal of Special Education, 12,* 29–39.

Eaves, R.C. (1993). *The Pervasive Developmental Disorders Rating Scale.* Opelika, AL: Small World.

Eber, L., Nelson, C.M., and Miles, P. (1997). School-based wraparound for students with emotional and behavioral challenges. *Exceptional Children, 63,* 539–555.

Ecklund, J. (2000, February 26). Number of "difficult kids" on the rise. *Lethbridge Herald,* p. A3.

Edelbrock, C. (1979). Empirical classifications of children's behavior disorders: Progress based on parent and teacher ratings. *School Psychology Digest, 8,* 355–369.

Edgar, E. (1987). Secondary programs in special education: Are many of them justifiable? *Exceptional Children, 53,* 555–561.

Edgar, E. (1988). Employment as an outcome for mildly handicapped students: Current status and future directions. *Focus on Exceptional Children, 21,* 1–8.

Edgar, E., Levine, P., and Maddox, M. (1985). *Washingon State follow-up data of postsecondary special education students.* Seattle: Networking and Evaluation Team, University of Washington.

Edlind, E.P. and Heansly, P.A. (1985). Gifts of mentorship. *Gifted Child Quarterly, 29,* 55–60.

Edmister, P. and Ekstrand, R. (1987). Preschool programming: Legal and educational issues. *Exceptional Children, 54,* 130–136.

Einfield, S.L. and Tonge, B.J. (1995). The Develomental Behavioral Checklist: The development and validation of an instrument to assess behavioral and emotional disturbance in children and adolescents with mental retardation. *Journal of Autism and Developmental Disabilities, 25,* 81–104.

Elbaum, B., Vaughn, S., Hughes, M., and Moody, S.W. (1999). Grouping practices and reading outcomes for students with disabilities. *Exceptional Children, 65,* 399–415.

Elksnin, L.K. (1997). Collaborative special education language services for students with learning disabilities. *Journal of Learning Disabilities, 30,* 414–426.

Elksnin, L.K. and Elksnin, N. (1989). Facilitating successful vocational/special education programs for mildly handicapped adolescents through collaborative consultation with parents. In *Conference proceedings of the fifth international conference of the division of career de-*

velopment, Atlanta. ERIC Doc. Ed. No. ED 320 363.

Elksnin, L.K. and Elksnin, N. (1997). Issues in the assessment of children's social skills. *Diagnostique, 22,* 75–86.

Elliott, C.D. (1990). *Differential Ability Scales: Administration and scoring manual.* San Antonio, TX: Psychological Corporation.

Elliott, L. (1993, 18 May). Mainstreaming opposed by deaf community. *ATA News,* p. 11.

Elliott, R. and Worthington, L.A. (1995). *ADHD project facilitate: An inservice education program for educators and parents.* Tuscaloosa, AL: University of Alabama.

Engleman, M.D., Griffin, H.C., Griffin, L.W., and Maddox, J.I. (1999). A teacher's guide to communicating with students with deaf-blindness. *Teaching Exceptional Children, 31,* 64–70.

Englemann, S.E. (1977). Sequencing cognitive and academic tasks. In R.D. Kneedler and S.G. Tarner (Eds.) *Changing perspectives in special education.* Columbus, OH: Merrill.

Englert, C.S. and Mariage, T. (1991). Making students partners in the comprehension process: Organizing the reading POSSE. *Learning Disabilities Quarterly, 14,* 123–138.

Epanchin, B.C. and Paul, J.L. (1986). *Emotional problems of children and adolescents. A multidisciplinary perspective.* Columbus, OH: Merrill.

Epilepsy Canada Scientific Council. [1994]. *Statistics.* Ottawa: Author.

Erickson, M.T. (1992). *Behavior disorders in children and adolescents* (2nd ed.) Englewood Cliffs, NJ: Prentice Hall.

Erin, J., Rudin, D., and Njoroge, M. (1991). Religious beliefs of parents of children with visual impairments. *Journal of Visual Impairment and Blindness, 85,* 157–162.

Erin, J. and Koenig, A. (1997). The student with a visual impairment and a learning disability. *Journal of Learning Disabilities, 30,* 309–320.

Erting, C.J., Prezioso, C., and Hynes, M. (1990). The interactional content of deaf mother–infant communication. In V. Volterra and C.J. Erting (Eds.) *From gesture to language in hearing and deaf children* (pp. 97–106). New York: Springer-Verlag.

Espin, C.A. and Foegen, A. (1996). Validity of general outcome measures for predicting secondary students' performance on content-area texts. *Exceptional Children, 62,* 497–514.

Esposito, B.G. and Reed, T.M. (1986). The effects of contact with handicapped persons on young children's attitudes. *Exceptional Children, 53,* 221–229.

Evans, S., Tickle, B., Toppel, C., and Nichols, A. (1997). Here's help for young children exposed to drugs. *Teaching Exceptional Children, 29,* 60–62.

Evenson, B. (1999, August 7). Schoolyard bullies are victims, too: Researchers. *National Post,* pp. 1, A2.

Ewing-Cobbs, L.E., Fletcher, J.M., and Levin, H.S. (1985). Neuropsychological sequelae following pediatric head injury. In M. Ylvisaber (Ed.) *Head injury rehabilitation: Children and adolescents* (pp. 118–137). San Diego, CA: College Hill Press.

Faerstein, L.M. (1986). Coping and defence mechanisms of mothers of learning disabled children. *Journal of Learning Disabilities, 19,* 8–11.

Famularo, R., Stone, K., Barnum, R., and Wharton, R. (1986). Alcoholism and severe child maltreatment. *American Journal of Orthopsychiatry, 56,* 481–485.

Farber, B. and Ryckman, D.B. (1965). Effects of severely mentally retarded children on family relationships. *Mental Retardation Abstracts, 2,* 1–17.

Farber, S. (1981). *Identical twins reared apart: A re-analysis.* New York: Basic Books.

Farmer, T.W. and Farmer E.M. (1996). Social relationships of students with exceptionalities in mainstream classrooms: Social networks and homophily. *Exceptional Children, 62,* 431–450.

Farmer, T.W. and Hollowell, J.H. (1994). Social networks in mainstream classrooms: Social affiliations and behavioral characteristics of students with EBD. *Journal of Emotional and Behavioral Disorders, 7,* 143–155, 163.

Farrington, D.P. (1983). Offending from 10 to 25 years of age. In K.T. Van Dusen and S.A. Mednick (Eds.) *Prospective studies of crime and delinquency* (pp. 17–37). Boston, MA: Kluwer-Nijhoff.

Farrington, D.P. (1987). Early precursors of frequent offending. In J.Q. Wilson and G.C. Loury (Eds.) *From children to citizens (vol. 3) Families, schools, and delinquency prevention* (pp. 27–51) New York: Springer Verlag.

Farrington, D.P., Gallagher, B., Morley, L., St. Ledger, R., and West, D.J. (1986). *Cambridge study in delinquent development: Long term follow-up.* Cambridge, England: Cambridge Institute of Criminology.

Fausti, S.A. [1987]. Pure tone audiology and high frequencies. *Audiology in Practice, 4,* 4–6.

Feingold, B.F. (1975). Hyperkinesis and learning disabilities linked to artificial food flavors and dyes. *American Journal of Nursing, 75,* 797–803.

Feingold, B.F. (1976). Hyperkenesis and learning disabilities linked to the ingestion of artificial food colors and flavors. *Journal of Learning Disabilities, 9,* 551–559.

Feitler, F. and Tokar, E. (1982). Getting a handle on teacher stress: How bad is the problem? *Educational Leadership, 39,* 456–458.

Feldhusen, J.F. (1989). Why the public schools will continue to neglect the gifted. *Gifted Child Today, 12,* 55–59.

Feldhusen, J.F. and Clinkenbeard, P.A. (1987). Creativity instructional materials: Review of research. *Journal of Creative Behavior, 20,* 1153–1182.

Feldhusen, J.F. and Hoover, S.M. (1986). A conception of giftedness: Intelligence, self-concept and motivation. *Roeper Review, 8,* 140–143.

Feldhusen, J.F. and Moon, S. (1992). Grouping gifted students: Issues and concerns. *Gifted Child Quarterly, 36,* 63–67.

Feldman, D. (1993). Child prodigies: A distinctive form of giftedness. *Gifted Child Quarterly, 37,* 188–193.

Fencham, F.D., Hokada, A., and Sanders, R. Jr. (1989). Learned helplessness, test anxiety, and academic achievement: A longitudinal analysis. *Child Development, 60,* 138–145.

Feniak, C.A. (1988). Labelling in special education: A problematic issue in England and Wales. *International Journal of Special Education, 3,* 117–124.

Fenichel, G.H. (1980). *Neonatal neurology.* New York: Churchill Livingstone.

Fenson, L., Dale, P., Reznick, S., Bates, E., Thal, D., and Pethick, S. (1994). Variability in early communicative development. *Monographs of the Society for Research in Child Development, 59* (5, Serial No. 242).

Ferguson, D.L. (1998). Changing tactics: Embedding inclusion reforms within general education restructuring efforts. In S. Vitello and D. Mithaug (Eds.) *Inclusive schooling: National and international perspectives* (pp. 35–53) New York: Erlblum.

Ferrari, M. (1984). Chronic illness: Psychological effects on siblings: 1, Chronically ill boys. *Journal of Child Psychology and Psychiatry, 25,* 459–476.

Ferrari, M. (1987). The diabetic child and well siblings: Risk to the well child's self-concept. *Children's Health Care, 15,* 141–147.

Fetal Alcohol Syndrome: The misdiagnosed disability (1997, October) CEC Today, pp. 12–13, 15.

Fewell, R.R. and Cone, J.D. (1983). Identification and placement of severely handicapped children. In M. Snell (Ed.) *A systematic approach for instruction of moderately, severely and profoundly handicapped children* (pp. 46–73). Columbus, OH: Merrill.

Fewell, R.R. and Langley, B. (1984). *Developmental Activities Screening Inventory, 11.* Austin, TX: Pro-Ed.

Fichten, C.S., Judd, D., Tagalikis, V., Amsel, R., and Robillard, K. (1991). Communication cues used by people with and without visual impairments in daily conversations and dating. *Journal of Visual Impairment and Blindness, 85,* 371–377.

Fiedler, C.R. and Simpson, R.I. (1987). Modifying the attitudes of nonhandicapped high school students toward handicapped peers. *Exceptional Children, 53,* 342–349.

Field, T. (1983). High risk infants 'have less fun' during early interactions. *Topics in Early Childhood Special Education, 3,* 77–87.

Fink, A.H. and Janssen, K.N. (1992). The management of maltreated adolescents in school settings. *Preventing School Failure, 36,* 32–36.

Finn, J.D., Pannozzo, G.M., and Voelkl, K.E. (1995). Disruptive and inattentive: Withdrawn behavior and achievement among fourth graders. *Elementary School Journal, 95,* 421–433.

Finnegan, J.A. and Quarrington, B. (1979). Pre-, peri- and neonatal factors and infantile autism. *Journal of Child Psychology and Psychiatry, 20,* 119–128.

Fisher, D. (1999). According to their peers: Inclusion as high school students see it. *Mental Retardation, 37,* 458–467.

Fitzgerald, R. (1996). *Assaults against children and youth in the family, 1996.* Ottawa: Statistics Canada, Canadian Centre for Justice Statistics.

Fitzgerald, R. (1999). *Family violence in Canada: A statistical profile.* Ottawa: Statistics Canada, Canadian Centre for Justice Statistics.

Flaxbeard, R. and Toomey, W. (1987). No longer deaf to their needs. *British Journal of Special Education, 14,* 103–105.

Fokes, J. (1976). *Fokes Sentence Builder.* Boston, MA: Teaching Resources Corporation.

Folio, M.R. and Fewell, R.R. (1983). *Peabody Developmental Motor Scale and Activity Cards.* Hingham, MA: Teaching Resources Corporation.

Folstein, S.E. and Rutter, M.L. (1988). Autism: Familial progression and genetic implications. *Journal of Autism and Developmental Disorders, 18,* 3–29.

Forest, M. and Lusthaus, E. (1989). Promoting educational equality for all students: Circles and maps. In S. Stainback, W. Stainback, and M. Forest (Eds.) *Educating all students in the mainstream of regular education* (pp.43–57). Baltimore, MD: Brookes.

Forness, S.R. and Kavale, K.A. (1994). The balkanization of special education: Proliferation of categories for 'new' behavioral disorders. *Education and Treatment of Children, 17,* 215–277.

Forness, S.R., Kavale K.A., Sweeney, D.P., and Gresham T.M. (1999). The future of research and practice in behavioral disorders: Psychopharmocology and its school implications. *Behavioral Disorders, 24,* 305–318.

Fortier, L.M. and Wanlass, R.L. (1984). Family crisis following the diagnosis of a handicapped child. *Family Relations, 33,* 13–24.

Foster, S. (1988). Life in the mainstream: Deaf college freshmen and their experiences in mainstreamed high school. *Journal of the American Deafness and Rehabilitation Association, 22,* 27–35.

Foster, S.L. and Ritchey, W.L. (1979). Issues in the assessment of social competence in children. *Journal of Applied Behavior Analysis, 12,* 625–638.

Frea, W., Craig-Unkefer, L., Odom, S .,and Johnson, D.

(1999). Differential effects of structured social integration and group friendships activities for promoting social interaction with peers. *Journal of Early Intervention, 22,* 23–242.

Freeland, A. (1989). *Deafness: The facts.* Oxford: Oxford University Press.

French, D.B. and MacDonnell, B.M. (1985). A survey of questions posed by regular classroom teachers integrating hearing impaired students in Nova Scotia and New Brunswick. *ACEHI Journal, 11,* 12–33.

French, K.F. and Pickett, A.L. (1997). Paraprofessionals in special education: Issues for teacher education. *Teacher Education and Special Education, 20,* 61–73.

Freund, J., Casey, P.H., and Bradley, R.H. (1982). A special education course with pediatric components. *Exceptional Children, 48,* 348–351.

Frey, K.S., Greenberg, M.T., and Fewell, R.R. (1989). Stress and coping among parents of handicapped children: A multidimensional approach. *American Journal of Mental Retardation, 94,* 240–249.

Friesen, J.W. (1997). The concept of giftedness in First Nations context. *Multicultural Education Journal, 15,* 26–35.

Frodi, A. M. (1981). Contributions of infant characteristics to child abuse. *American Journal on Mental Deficiency, 85,* 341–349.

Frymier, J. and Gansneder, B. (1989, October). The Phi Delta Kappa study of students at risk. *Phi Delta Kappan, 71,* 142–151.

Fryxell, D. and Kennedy, C.H. (1995). Placement along the continuum of services and its impact on students' social relationships. *Journal for the Association for Persons with Severe Handicaps, 20,* 259–269.

Fuchs, D. and Fuchs, L.S. (1994). Inclusive schools movement and radicalization of special education reform. *Exceptional Children, 60,* 294–309.

Fuchs, D. and Fuchs, L.S. (1995a). Special education can work. In J.M. Kauffman, J.W. Lloyd, D.P. Hallahan, and T.A. Astuto (Eds.) *Issues in educational placement* (pp. 363–377). Hillsdale, NJ: Erlbaum.

Fuchs, D. and Fuchs, L.S. (1995b, January). Sometimes separate is better. *Educational Leadership,* pp. 22–24.

Fuchs, L.S., Fuchs, D., Hamlett, C.L., Phillips, N.B., and Karns, K. (1995). General educators' specialized adaptations for students with learning disabilities. *Exceptional Children, 61,* 440–459.

Furney, K.S., Hasazi, S.B., and De Stefano L. (1997). Transition policies, practices, and promises: Lessons from three states. *Exceptional Children, 63,* 343–355.

Gadd, J. (1997, March 28). 10,000 child abuse cases tallied: Toronto police investigated an average of 10 incidents a day in past 3 years. *The Globe and Mail,* p. A1.

Gadow, K. (1986). *Children on medication (vol 1.): Hyperactivity, learning disabilities, and mental retardation.* Boston, MA: College Hill.

Gagné, F. (1985). Giftedness and talent: Reexamining an examination of the definitions. *Gifted Child Quarterly, 29,* 103–112.

Gagné, F. (1989). Peer nominations as a psychometric instrument: Many questions asked but few answered. *Gifted Child Quarterly, 33,* 53–58.

Gagné, F. (1991). Toward a differential model of giftedness and talent. In N. Colangelo and G.A. Davis (Eds.) *Handbook of gifted education* (pp. 65–80). Needham Heights, MA: Allyn and Bacon.

Gallagher, J.J. (1975). *The gifted child in the elementary school.* Washington, DC: American Educational Research Foundation.

Gallagher, J.J. (2000). Unthinkable thoughts: Education of gifted students. *Gifted Child Quarterly,* 44, 5–12.

Galligan, B. (1990). Serving people who are dually diagnosed: A problem evaluation. *Mental Retardation, 28,* 353–358.

Galt, V. (1997, 28 August). Teachers support disabled in classes: Fiscal, social realities prevent student integration. *The Globe and Mail,* pp. A1, A10.

Galton, F. (1869). *Hereditary genius: An enquiry into its laws and consequences.* London, New York: Appleton, 1870.

Garbe, B. and Rodda, M. (1988). Growing in silence: The deaf adolescent. *ACEHI Journal, 14,* 59–69.

Garcia, E.E. (1988). Attributes of effective schools for language minority students. *Education and Urban Society, 20,* 387–398.

Gardner, H. (1983). *Frames of mind: The theory of multiple intelligences.* New York: Basic Books.

Gayton, W.F., Friedman, S.B., Tavormina, J.F., and Tucker, F. (1977). Children with cystic fibrosis: 1. Psychological test findings of patients, siblings, and parents. *Pediatrics, 59,* 888–894.

Gdowski, B.S., Sanger, D.D., and Decker, T.N. (1986). Otitis media: Effect on a child's learning. *Academic Therapy, 21,* 283–291.

Gearheart, B., Mullen, R. C., and Gearheart, C.J. (1993). *Exceptional individuals: An introduction.* Pacific Grove, CA: Brooks/Cole.

Gedye, A. (1989). Extreme self-injury attributed to frontal lobe seizure. *American Journal on Mental Retardation,* 94, 20–26.

George, N.L., George, M.P., Gersten, R., and Grasenick, J.K. (1995). To leave or to stay? An exploratory study of teachers of students with emotional and behavioral disorders. *Remedial and Special Education, 16,* 227–236

Gerard, J.A. and Junkula, J. (1980). Task analysis, handwriting, and process based instruction. *Journal of Learning Disabilities, 13,* 49–58.

Gerber, M.M. (1988). Tolerance and technology of instruction: Implications for special education reform. *Exceptional Children, 54,* 309–314.

Gerdtz, J. and Bergman, J. (1990). *Autism: A practical guide for those who help others.* New York: Continuum.

Gersh, E.S. (1991a). What is cerebral palsy? In E. Geralis (Ed.) *Children with cerebral palsy.* New York: Woodbine.

Gersh, E.S. (1991b). Medical concerns and treatment. In E. Geralis (Ed.) *Children with cerebral palsy.* New York: Woodbine.

Gersten, R. (1990). Enemies real and imagined: Implications of teachers' thinking about instruction for collaboration between special and general educators. *Remedial and Special Education, 11,* 50–53.

Geschwund, N. and Galaburda, A.M. (1978). *Cerebral lateralization.* Cambridge, MA: MIT Press.

Getch, V.Q. and Newharth-Pritchett, S. (1999). Children with asthma: Strategies for educators. *Teaching Exceptional Children,* 31, 30–36.

Giangreco, M.F., Edelman, S.W., MacFarland, S., and Luiselli, T.C. (1997). Attitudes about educational and related service provisions for students with deaf-blindness and multiple disabilities. *Exceptional Children, 63,* 329–342.

Giddan J.J., Melling, L., and Campbell, N.B. (1996). Unrecognized language and speech deficits in predolescent psychiatric patients. *American Journal of Orthopsychiatry, 66,* 85–92.

Gill, C. (1994, February). Disability and the family. *Mainstream,* pp. 30–35.

Gillberg, C. (1980). Maternal age and infantile autism. *Journal of Autism and Developmental Disorders, 10,* 293–297.

Gillberg, C. and Steffenburg, S. (1987). Outcomes and prognostic factors in infantile autism and similar conditions: A population based study of 45 cases followed through puberty. *Journal of Autism and Developmental Disorders, 17,* 273–287.

Glassberg, L.A. (1994). Students with behavioral disorders: Determinants of placement outcomes. *Behavioural Disorders, 19,* 181–191.

Gleason, J.B. (1985). *The development of language.* Columbus, OH: Merrill.

Glenn, H.S. and Nelson, J. (1987). *Raising children for success.* Fair Oaks, CA: Sunrise Press.

Goertz, M. and Friedman, D. (1996). *State education reform and students with disabilities: A preliminary analysis.* New Brunswick, NJ: Rutgers University Consortium on Policy Research in Education and Center for Policy Research on the Impact of General and Special Education Reform.

Gogel, E.M., McCumsey, J., and Hewitt, G. (1985, November/December). What parents are saying. *Gifted Talented Creative,* pp. 7–9.

Goguen, L. (1993). Right to education for the gifted in Canada. In K.A. Keller, F.J. Monks, and A.H. Passow (Eds.) *International handbook of research and development of giftedness and talents* (pp. 771–777) New York: Pergamon.

Goldberg, S., Marcovitch, S., MacGregor, D., and Lojkasek, M. (1986). Family responses to developmentally delayed preschoolers: Etiology and the father's role. *American Journal on Mental Deficiency, 90,* 610–617.

Goldring, E.B. (1990). Assessing the status of information on classroom organizational frameworks for gifted students. *Journal of Educational Research, 83,* 313–326.

Goldwin-Meadow, S. and Morford, M. (1985). Gestures in early child language: Studies of deaf and hearing children. *Merrill-Palmer Quarterly, 31,* 145–176.

Golledge, R.G. (1991). Tactual strip maps as navigational aids. *Journal of Visual Impairment and Blindness, 85,* 296–301.

Good, W.V. (1992, summer). Cortical visual insufficiency: *Awareness.* Newsletter of the National Association for Parents of the Visually Impaired.

Goodlad, J.I. and Field S. (1993). Teaching for renewing schools. In J.I. Goodlad and T.C. Lovitt (Eds.) *Integrating general and special education* (pp. 229–252). New York: Merrill Macmillan.

Goodman, R. (1987). Infantile autism: A syndrome of multiple primary deficits. *Journal of Autism and Developmental Disorders, 19,* 409–424.

Goodman, R. and Sevenson, J. (1989). A twin study of hyperactivity 2: The etiological role of genes, family relationships, and perinatal adversity. *Journal of Child Psychology and Psychiatry, 30,* 691–709.

Goreau, M., Kennedy, C., and Sawalzty, D. (1996). "Conquering heroes:" A study of childhood cancer survivors. *Early Childhood Education, 29,* 67–73.

Gothelf, G.R., Crimmins, D.B., Mercer, C.A., and Finocchiaro, P.L. (1994). Teaching choice-making skills to students who are deaf-blind. *Teaching Exceptional Children, 26,* 13–15.

Gottesman, I.I. and Shields, J. (1976). A critical review of recent adoption, twin, and family studies of schizophrenics: Behavioral genetic perspectives. *Schizophrenia Bulletin, 2,* 360–401.

Gough, P.B. (1991). Tapping parent power. *Phi Delta Kappan, 75,* p. 339.

Granowelter, L. (1994). Pediatric oncology: A medical overview. In D.J. Bearison and R.K. Mulhern (Eds.) *Pediatric psychooncology: Psychological perspectives on children with cancer.* New York: Oxford University Press.

Gray, C.D. (1989). Opening comments on the conference on developmental disabilities and HIV infection. *Mental Retardation,* 27, 199–200.

Green, S.K. and Shinn, M.R. (1995). Parent attitudes about

special education and reintegration: What is the role of student outcomes? *Exceptional Children, 61,* 269–280.

Gregory, S., Bishop, J., and Sheldon, L. (1995). *Deaf young people and their families.* Cambridge: Cambridge University Press.

Grenwood, C.R., Carta, J.J., and Hall, R.V. (1988). The use of peer tutoring strategies in classroom management and educational instruction. *School Psychology Review, 17,* 258–275.

Gresham, F. (1997, November/December). We need a better way to identify students with learning disabilities. *CEC Today,* p. 14.

Gresham, F. and Elliott, S. (1990). *Social skills rating system.* Circle Pines, MI: American Guidance Services.

Griffiths, P., Smith, C., and Harvie, A. (1997). Transitory hyperphenylalaninaemia in children with continuously treated phenylketonuria. *American Journal on Mental Retardation, 102,* 27–36.

Grossman, H. (Ed.) (1977). *Manual on terminology and classification in mental retardation.* Washington, DC: American Association on Mental Deficiency.

Grossman, H. (1995). *Special eduction in a diverse society.* Boston, MA: Allyn and Bacon.

Grover, R., Shahidi, S., Fisher, B., Goldberg, D., and Wethers, D. (1983). Current sickle cell screening program for newborns in New York City, 1979–1980. *American Journal of Public Health, 73,* 249–252.

Groves, P.M. and Rebec, G.V. (1988). *Introduction to biological psychology* (3rd ed.) Dubuque, IA: Brown.

Growing challenge for teachers — Providing medical procedures for students. (1998). *CEC Today, 5,* 1, 5,15.

Gualtieri, G.J., Koriath, U., Van Bourgondien, M., and Saleeby, N. (1983). Language disorders in children referred for psychiatric services. *Journal of the American Academy of Child Psychiatry, 22,* 165–171.

Gubbins, E.J. (1991, April). Research needs of gifted and talented through the year 2000. In J. Renzulli (Chair) The National Research Center on the Gifted and Talented: Present activities, future plans, and an invitation for input and involvement. At American Educational Research Association, Chicago.

Guerra, N.G. and Slaby, R. (1990). Cognitive mediators of aggression in adolescent offenders. 2. Intervention, *Developmental Psychology,* 26, 269–277.

Guetzloe, E. (1999a). Inclusion: The broken promise. *Preventing School Failure,* 43, 92–98.

Guetzloe, E. (1999b, April/May). What can we do to stop students killing students? *CEC Today,* pp. 5, 14.

Guilford, J.P. (1988). Some changes in the Structure of Intellect model. *Educational and Psychological Measurement, 48,* 1–4.

Guitar, B. (1998). *Stuttering: An integrated approach to its nature and treatment.* Baltimore, MD: Williams and Wilkins.

Guralnick, M. (1981). Programmatic factors affecting child–child social interactions in mainstreamed preschool programs. *Exceptional Education Quarterly, 1,* 71–91.

Guralnick, M. (1986). The peer relations of young handicapped and nonhandicapped children. In P.S. Stein, M.J. Guralnick, and H.M. Walter (Eds.) *Children's social behavior: Development, assessment, and modification* (pp. 93–140). New York: Academic Press.

Guralnick, M. (1988). Efficacy research in early childhood intervention programs. In S.L. Odom and M.B. Karnes (Eds.) *Early intervention for infants and children with handicaps: An empirical base* (pp. 75–88) Baltimore, MD: Brookes.

Guralnick, M. (1990). Social competence and early intervention. *Journal of Early Intervention, 14,* 3–14.

Guralnick, M. and Bricker, D. (1987). The effectiveness of early intervention for children wih cognitive and general developmental delays, In M. J. Guralnick and C. Bennett (Eds.) *The effectiveness of early intervention for at-risk and handicapped children* (pp. 115–173). New York: Academic Press.

Hagerman, R.J. (1988). Fragile x syndrome: An overview. *Early Childhood Update, 4,* 1, 6.

Hagerman, R.J. and Sobesky, W.E. (1989). Psychopathology in fragile X syndrome. *American Journal of Orthopsychiatry, 59,* 142–152.

Hall, C.W. and Richmond, B.O. (1984). Consultation with parents of handicapped children. *Exceptional Children, 31,* 185–191.

Hallahan, D.P. and Kauffman, J.M. (1991). *Exceptional children: Introduction to special education* (5th ed.) Englewood Cliffs, NJ: Prentice-Hall.

Hallahan, D. P., Kauffman, J. M., and Lloyd, J. W. (1999). *Introduction to learning disabilities.* Boston, MA: Allyn and Bacon.

Hamachek, B. and Kauffman, J. (1994). Special education in the United States. In K. Mazurek and M. Winzer (Eds.) *Comparative studies in special education.* Washington, D.C.: Gallaudet University Press.

Hammer, E. (October, 1984). Quality of life for the multiply handicapped child. Paper prepared for the Helen Keller Seminar on the Multiply Handicapped, New York City.

Hammill, D.D. and Newcomer, P.L. (1988). *Test of Language Development—2, Intermediate.* Austin, TX: Pro-Ed.

Hammill D.D. and Wiederholt, J.L. (1995). *Test of Reading Comprehension.* Austin, TX: Pro-Ed.

Hammill, D.D., Brown, V.L., Larsen, S.C. and Wiederholt, J.L. (1994). *Test of Adolescent Language—3.* Austin. TX: Pro-Ed.

Hancock, L. (1996, March 18). Mother's little helper. *Newsweek,* pp. 51–56.

Handel, R.D. (1983). Teachers of gifted girls: Are there differences in classroom management? *Journal for the Education of the Gifted, 6,* 86–97.

Hansen, H. (1978). Decline of Down's syndrome after abortion reform in New York State. *American Journal on Mental Deficiency, 83,* 185–188.

Hansen, M.J., Lynch E.W., and Wayman, L.I. (1990). Honoring the cultural diversity of families when gathering data. *Topics in Early Childhood Special Education, 10,* 112–131.

Hanson, L. (1996, October). Are special educators still struggling to gain respect? *CEC Today,* p. 14.

Hanson, M.J. and Carta, J.J. (1995). Addresing the challenges of families with multiple risks. *Exceptional Children,* 62, 201–212.

Harber, J.R. (1980). Issues in the assessment of language and reading disorders in learning disabled children. *Learning Disability Quarterly, 3,* 20–28.

Hardman, M.L., Drew, C.J., Egan, M.W., and Wolf, B. (1993). *Human exceptionalty: Society, school, and family* (4th ed.) Boston, MA: Allyn and Bacon.

Harris, D.B. (1963). *Goodenough-Harris Drawing Test Manual.* New York: Harcourt, Brace and World.

Harris, S.L., Handleman, J.S., and Palmer, C. (1985). Parents and grandparents view the autistic child. *Journal of Autism and Developmental Disorders, 15,* 127–137.

Harris, S.L., Handleman, J.S., Kristoff, B., Bass, L., and Gordon, R. (1990). Changes in language development among autistic and peer children in segregated and integrated preschool settings. *Journal of Autism and Developmental Disorders, 20,* 23–31.

Harris, M. and Curran, C.M. (1998). Knowledge, skills, and concerns about portfolio assessment: An exploratory study. *Teacher Education and Special Education, 21,* 83–94.

Harrison R. and Philips, B. (1971). Observations on hearing levels of preschool cleft palate children. *Journal of Speech and Hearing Disorders, 36,* 252–256.

Harrison, T. R. (1980). *Harrison's principles of internal medicine* (9th ed.). New York: McGraw-Hill.

Harry, B. (1992). Making sense of disability: Low-income, Puerto Rican parents' theories of the problem. *Exceptional Children, 59,* 27–40.

Hart, S.N. and Brassard, M.R. (1987). A major threat to children's mental health: Psychological maltreatment. *American Psychologist, 42,* 160–165.

Hartup, W.W. (1974). Aggression in childhood: Developmental perspectives. *American Psychologist, 29,* 336–341.

Harvey, D.H.P. and Greenway, A.P. (1984). The self-concept of physically handicapped children and their nonhandicapped siblings: An empirical investigation. *Journal of Child Psychology and Psychiatry, 25,* 273–284.

Hasazi, S.B., Gordon, L.R., and Roe, C.A. (1985). Factors associated with the employment status of handicapped youth exiting from high school from 1979–1983. *Exceptional Children, 51,* 455–469.

Hatcher, P.J., Hanline, C., and Ellis A.W. (1994). Ameliorating early reading failure by integrating the teaching of reading and phonological skills: The phonological linkage hypothesis. *Child Development, 65,* 41–58.

Hatton, D.D., Bailey, D.B., Burchinal, M.R., and Ferrell, K.A. (1997). Developmental growth curves of preschool children with vision impairments. *Child Development, 68,* 788–806.

Hauser-Cram, P., Warfield, M., Shonkoff, J., Krauss, M., Lipshur, C.C., and Sayer, A. (1999). Family influences on adaptive development in young children with Down syndrome. *Child Development,* 70, 979–989.

Hay, H. (1990). Allergies and the teacher. Unpublished paper, University of Lethbridge.

Haywood Gear, G. (1976). Accuracy of teacher judgment in identifying intellectually gifted children: A review of the literature. *Gifted Child Quarterly, 20,* 478–487.

Hazel, J.S., Schumaker, J.B., Sherman, J.A., and Sheldon-Wildgren, J. (1981). *ASSET: A social skills program for adolescents.* Champaign, IL: Research Press.

Healey, W. (1999). Focus on disability — Williams syndrome. *CEC Today, 6,* p. 11.

Hearing loss and surgery. (1982). *Lifeline Magazine, 4,* 8–10.

Hedrick, D.L., Pratter, E.M., and Tobin, A.R. (1975). *Sequenced Inventory of Communication Development.* Seattle, WA: University of Washington Press.

Heflin, L.J. and Bullock, L.M. (1999). Inclusion of students with emotional/behavioral disorders: A survey of teachers in general and special education. *Preventing School Failure,* 43, 103–111.

Heiligenstrin, E. and Keeling, R.P. (1995). Prevention of unrecognized attention deficit hyperactivity disorder in college students. *Journal of American College Health, 43,* 226–228.

Helfer, R.E. (1987). The developmental basis of child abuse and neglect: An epidemiological approach. In R.E. Helfer and R.S. Kempe (Eds.) *The battered child* (4th ed.) Chicago, IL: University of Chicago Press.

Heller, K.W., Frederick, L.D., Dykes, M., Best, S., and Cohen, E.T. (1999). A national perspective on competencies for teachers of individuals with physical and health disabilities. *Exceptional Children 65,* 219–234.

Henderson, R.A. (1989). PKU and maternal PKU: The cure and the problem. *BC Journal of Special Education, 13,* 253–257.

Hendrickson, J.M., Shookoohi-Yekta, M., Hamre-Nietupski, S., and Gable R.A. (1996). Middle and high school students' perceptions of being friends with peers with severe disabilities. *Exceptional Children, 63,* 19–28.

Henig, R.M. (1982, February 28). Saving babies before birth. *New York Times Magazine,* pp.19–22.

Henker, B. and Whalen, B. (1980). The changing faces of hyperactivity: Retrospect and prospect. In C. K. Whalen and B. Henker (Eds.) *Hyperactive children: The social ecology of identification and treatment.* New York: Academic Press.

Herbst, D.S. and Baird, P.A. (1983). Non-specific mental retardation in British Columbia as ascertained through a registry. *American Journal on Mental Deficiency, 87,* 506–513.

Herronkohl, R.C., Egolf, B.P., Ellen, C., and Herrenkohl, E.C. (1997). Preschool antecedents of adolescent assaultive behavior: A longitudinal study. *American Journal of Orthopsychiatry, 67,* 422–432.

Hessler, G. and Kitchen, D. (1980). Language characteristics of a purposive sample of early elementary learning disabled students. *Learning Disability Quarterly, 3,* 36–41.

Hetherington, E.M. and Parke, R.D. (1986). *Child psychology: A contemporary viewpoint* (3rd ed.) New York: McGraw-Hill.

Hicks, L. (1987). Unpublished paper, St. John's: Memorial University of Newfoundland.

Hiebert, E. and Raphael, T. (1996). Psychological perspectives on literacy and extensions to educational practice. In D. Berliner and R. Calfe (Eds.) *Handbook of educational psychology* (pp. 55–602). New York: Macmillan.

Higginbotham, D.J., and Baker, B.M. (1981). Social participation and cognitive play differences in hearing-impaired and normally hearing preschoolers. *Volta Review, 83,* 135–149.

Higginbotham, D.J., Baker, B.M., and Neill, R.D. (1980). Assessing the social participation and cognitive play abilities of hearing-impaired preschoolers. *Volta Review, 82,* 261–270.

Hiller, K.W., Gallagher, P., and Frederick, P. (1999). Parents' perceptions of siblings: Interactions with their brothers and sisters who are deaf-blind. *Journal of the Association for Persons with Severe Handicaps, 24,* 33–43.

Hinshelwood, J. (1917). *Congenital word blindness.* London: H.K. Lewis.

Hintermaier, M. (2000). Children who are hearing impaired with additional disabilities and related aspects of parental stress. *Exceptional Children, 66,* 327–332.

Hobbs, N., Perrin, J.M., and Ireys, H.T. (1985). *Chronically ill children and their families.* San Francisco, CA: Jossey Bass.

Hobbs, T. and Westling, D.L. (1998). Inclusion, inclusion, inclusion: Promoting successful inclusion. *Teaching Exceptional Children, 31,* 12–19.

Hobson, R.P. (1988). Beyond cognition: A theory of autism. In G. Dawson (Ed.) *Autism: New perspectives on diagnoses, nature and treatment.* New York: Guilford.

Hodapp, R.M. and Fidler, D.J. (1999). Special education and genetics: Connections for the 21st century. *Journal of Special Education, 33,* 130–137.

Hoffman, F.J., Shelson, K.L., Minskoff, E.M., Sautter, S.W., Steidle, E.F., Baker, D.P., Bailey, M.B., and Echols, L.D. (1987). Needs of learning disabled students. *Journal of Learning Disabilities, 20,* 43–53.

Hoge, R.D, Smit, E.K., and Hanson, S.L. (1990). School experiences predicting changes in self-esteem of sixth and seventh grade students. *Journal of Educational Psychology, 82,* 117–127.

Hoge, R.D. and Andrews, D.A. (1992). Assessing conduct problems in the classroom. *Canadian Psychology Review,* 1–20.

Hoge, R.D. and McSheffrey, R. (1991). An investigation of self-concept in gifted children. *Exceptional Children, 57,* 238–245.

Holahan, C. K. (1991). Lifetime achievement patterns, retirement and life satisfaction of gifted aged women. *Journal of Gerontology,* 36, 741–749.

Holder, H.B. and Kirkpatrick, S.W. (1991). Interpretation of emotion from facial expressions in children with and without learning disabilities. *Journal of Learning Disabilities, 24,* 170.

Holland, A.L., Swindell, C.S., and Ruinmuth, O.M. (1990). Aphasia and related adult disorders. In G.H. Shames and E.H. Wiig (Eds.) *Human communication disorders* (3rd ed.) (pp. 424–462). Columbus, OH: Merrill.

Holmgren, R.A., Eisenberg, N., and Fokes, R.A. (1998). The relation of children's situational empathy-related emotions to dispositional prosocial behavior. *International Journal of Behavioral Development, 22,* 169–194.

Holt, J. (1994). Classroom attributes and achievement test scores of deaf and hard of hearing students. *American Annals of the Deaf, 139,* 430–437.

Holub, T.M., Lamb, P., and Bang, M.Y. (1998). Empowering all students through self-determination. In C.M. Jorgensen (Ed.) *Restructuring high schools for all students* (pp. 183-208) Baltimore, MD: Brookes.

Horner, R.H. and Carr, E.G. (1997). Behavioral support for students with severe disabilities: Functional assessment and comprehensive intervention. *Journal of Special Education, 31,* 84–104.

Horowitz, E. (1981). Popularity, decentering ability, and role-taking skills in learning disabled and normal children. *Learning Disability Quarterly, 4,* 23–30.

Houser, L., Moses, E., and Kay, J.L. (1987). A family orientation to transition. *Education of the Visually Handicapped, 19,* 109–119.

Howard, I. and Templeton, W. (1966). *Human spatial orientation.* New York: Wiley.

Howe, M.L. and O'Sullivan, J.T. (1990). The development of strategic memory: Coordinating knowledge, metamemory, and resources. In D. F. Bjorklund (Ed)

Children's strategies: Contemporary views of cognitive development. Hillsdale, NJ: Erlbaum.

Howlin, P. (1981). The results of a homebound language training program with autistic children. *British Journal of Disorders of Communication, 16,* 73–87.

Howse, H. (1988). Asthma in children. Unpublished paper, St. John's: Memorial University of Newfoundland.

Huebner, K.M. (1985). The challenges in providing appropriate educational services to rural visually impaired children and their families. *Rural and Special Education Quarterly, 6,* 2–4.

Huessman, L.R., Eron, L.D., and Yarmel, P.W. (1987). Intellectual functioning and aggression. *Journal of Personality and Social Psychology, 52,* 232–240.

Hughes, M., Dote-Kwan, J., and Dolendo, J. (1998). A close look at the cognitive play of preschoolers with visual impairments in the home. *Exceptional Children,* 64, 451–462.

Hugh-Jones, S. and Smith P.K. (1999). Self-reports of short-and long-term effects of bullying on children who stammer. *British Journal of Educational Psychology, 69,* 141–158.

Hutchinson, J. (1997, September). Is your child safe at school? *Readers Digest, 151,* pp. 46–53.

Hynd, G.W. and Semrud-Clikeman, M. (1989). Dyslexia and brain morphology. *Psychological Bulletin, 106,* 447–482.

Hysert, L. (1993a, fall). Read it on television. *Disability Today,* pp. 49, 59.

Hysert, L. (1993b, fall). Voiceprint presents the information age to the blind. *Disability Today,* pp. 41–42.

Iber, F.L. (1980). Fetal alcohol syndrome. *Nutrition Today,* pp. 4–11.

Idol, L., Paolucci-Whitcomb, P., and Nevin, A. (1986). *Collaborative consultation.* Austin, TX: Pro-Ed.

Immen, W. (1995, April 19). The truth about selective vision. *The Globe and Mail,* p. A8.

Inclusion: Where are we today? (1996). *CEC Today 1,* pp. 1, 5, 15.

Increased threat of sexual abuse facing kids with disabilities. (1993, summer). *Disability Today,* p. 8.

Injuries at a glance. (1994, fall). *Disability Today,* pp. 73–74.

Innes, J.J. (1994). Full inclusion and the deaf student: A deaf consumer's review of the issue. *American Annals of the Deaf, 139,* 152–156.

Isabell, R.A. and Barber, W.H. (1993). Respiratory disorders: An update and status report for educators. *B.C. Journal of Special Education, 17,* 244–255.

Izen, C.L. and Brown, E. (1991). Education and treatment needs of students with profound multiple handicaps and medically fragile conditions: A survey of teachers' perceptions. *Journal of the Association for Persons with Severe Handicaps, 16,* 94–103.

Izzo, M.V. (1987). Career development of disabled youth: The parents' role. *Journal of Career Development, 13,* 47–55.

Jack, S.L., Shores, R.E., Denny, R.K., Gunter, P.L., DeBriere, T., and DePaepem, P. (1996). An analysis of the relationship of teachers' reported use of classroom management strategies and types of classroom interactions. *Journal of Behavioral Education, 6,* 67–87.

Jacobs, L. (1991). Assessment concerns: A study of cultural differences, teacher concepts, and inappropriate labelling. *Teacher Education and Special Education, 14,* 43–48.

Jacobs, P.A., Mayer, M., and Abruzzo, M.A. (1986). Studies of the fragile (x) syndrome in populations of mentally retarded individuals in Hawaii. *American Journal of Medical Genetics, 23,* 567–572.

Janney, R.E., Snell, M.E., Beers, M.K., and Raynes, M. (1995). Integrating students with moderate and severe disabilities into regular education classrooms. *Exceptional Children, 61,* 425–439.

Jaussi, K.R. (1991). Drawing the insiders in: Deaf students in the mainstream. *Perspectives in Education and Deafness, 9,* 12–15.

Jenkins, J.R. and Heinen, A. (1989). Students' preferences for service delivery: Pull-out, in-class, or integrated models. *Exceptional Children,* 55, 516–526.

Jensema, C.J., Karchmer, M.A., and Trybus, R.J. (1978). The rated speech intelligibility of hearing impaired children: Basic relationships and a detailed analysis. Series R, No. 6. Washington, DC: Gallaudet College, Office of Demographic Studies.

Johns, B.H. and Car, V.G. (1995). *Techniques for managing verbally and physically aggressive students.* Denver, CO: Love.

Johnsen, S.K. and Corn, A. (1987). *Screening Assessment for Gifted Elementary Students.* Austin, TX: Pro-Ed.

Johnsen, S.K., Ryser, G., and Dougherty, E. (1993). The validity of product portfiolios in the identification of gifted students. *Gifted International: A Talent Development Journal,* 8, 40–43.

Johnson, D.G. (1989). An unassisted method of psychological testing for visually impaired individuals. *Journal of Visual Impairment and Blindness, 83,* 114–118.

Johnson, G.M. (1998). Principles of instruction for at-risk learners. *Preventing School Failure,* 42, 107–113.

Jonassen, D., Hannum, W., and Tessmer, M. (1989). *Handbook of task analysis procedures.* New York: Praeger.

Jones, B.E., Clark, G.M., and Soltz, D.F. (1997). Characteristics and practices of sign language interpreters in inclusive education programs. *Exceptional Children, 63,* 257–268.

Jones, C.S. (1987). Cerebral palsy. In C.E. Reynolds (Ed.) *Encyclopedia of special education* (pp. 293–296). New York: Wiley.

Jones, K.L. and Smith, D.W. (1973). Recognition of the fetal alcohol syndrome in early infancy. Lancet, pp. 999–1001.

Jones, K.N. and Bender, W.N. (1993). Utilization of paraprofessionals in special education: A review of the literature. *Remedial and Special Education, 14,* 7–14.

Jones, M.H. (1983). Cerebral palsy. In J. Umbriel (Ed.) *Physical disabilities and health impairment: Assessment, treatment, education.* Baltimore, MD: University Park Press.

Jones, M.M. and Carlier, L.L.(1995). Creating inclusionary opportunities for learners with multiple disabilities: A team-teaching approach. *Teaching Exceptional Children, 27,* 23–27.

Jones, V.J. (1996). "In the face of predictable crisis:" Developing a comprehensive treatment plan for students with emotional or behavioral disorders. *Teaching Exceptional Children, 29,* 54–59.

Juel, C. (1988). Learning to read and write: A longitudinal study of fifty-four children from first through fourth grade. *Journal of Educational Psychology, 80,* 437–447.

Kaiser, D. and Abell, M. (1997). Learning life management in the classroom. *Teaching Exceptional Children, 30,* 70–75.

Kapell, D., Nightingale, B., Rodriguez, A., Lee, J.H., Zigman, W.B., and Schupf, N. (1998) Prevelance of chronic medical conditions in adults with mental retardation: Comparison with the general population. *Mental Retardation, 36,* 269-279.

Kaplan, P.S. (1996). *Pathways for exceptional children: School, home, and culture.* Minneapolis/St. Paul, MI: West Publishing.

Kaplan, R.M. and Saccuzzo, D.P. (1993). *Psychological testing: Principles, applications, and issues* (3rd ed.) Pacific Grove, CA: Brooks/Cole.

Karnes, M.B. and Strong, P.S. (1978). *Nurturing leadership talent in early childhood.* Urbana, IL: Institute for Child Behavior and Development, University of Illinois.

Kasko, J. (2000). *Keeping in Touch.*

Kauffman, J.M. (1991a). *Characteristics of children's behavior disorders* (3rd ed.) Columbus, OH: Merrill.

Kauffman, J.M. (1991b). Restructuring in sociopolitical context: Reservations about the effects of current reform proposals on students with disabilities. In J.W. Lloyd, A. C.Repp, and N.N. Singh (Eds.) *The regular education initiative: Alernative perspectives on concepts, issues, and models* (pp. 57–66) Sycamore, IL: Sycamore Publishing Co.

Kauffman, J.M. (1993). How we might achieve the radical reform of special education. *Exceptional Children, 60,* 6–16.

Kauffman, J.M. (1997a). Caricature, science, and exceptionality. *Remedial and Special Education, 18,* 130–132.

Kauffman, J.M. (1997b). *Characteristics of emotional and behavior disorders in children and youth* (6th ed.) Columbus, OH: Merrill.

Kauffman, J.M. (1999). How we prevent the prevention of emotional and behavioral disorders. *Exceptional Children,* 65, 338–468.

Kauffman, J.M. (2001). *Characteristics of emotional and behavior disorders in children and youth* (7th ed.) Upper Saddle River, NJ: Merrill Prentice-Hall.

Kauffman, J.M. and Wong, K.L.H. (1991). Forum: Effective teachers of students with behavioral disorders: Are generic teaching skills enough? *Behavioral Disorders, 16,* 225–237.

Kauffman J.M., Lloyd, J.W., Baker, J., and Riedel, T.M. (1995). Inclusion of all students with emotional or behavioral disorders? Let's think again. *Phi Delta Kappan, 76,* 542–546.

Kaufman, F.A and Sexton, D. (1983, September). Some implications for home–school linkages. *Roeper Review,* pp. 49–51.

Kaufman, J. and Zigler, E. (1989). The intergenerational transmission of child abuse. In D. Cicchetti and V. Carlson (Eds.) *Child maltreatment: Theory and research on the causes and consequences of child abuse and neglect* (pp. 129–151). New York: Cambridge University Press.

Kavale, K.A. and Forness, S.R. (1995). Social skills deficits and training: A meta-analysis of the research in learning disabilities. In T.E. Scruggs and M.A. Mastropieri (Eds.) *Advances in learning and behavioral disorders* (pp. 119–160). Greenwich, CT: JAI Press.

Kavale, K.A. and Forness, S.R. (1997). Defining learning disabilities: Consonance and dissonance. In J.W. Lloyd, E. Kameenui, and D. Chard (Eds.) *Issues in educating students with disabilities* (pp. 3–25) Mahawk, NJ: Erlbaum.

Kaye, K., Elkind, L., Goldberg, D., and Tytum, A. (1989). Birth outcomes for infants of drug abusing mothers. *New York State Journal of Medicine, 89,* 256–261.

Kazdin, A.E. (1987). Treatment of antisocial behavior in children: Current status and future directions. *Psychological Bulletin, 102,* 187–203.

Kazdin, A.E. (1989). *Behavior modification in applied settings* (4th ed.) Pacific Grove, CA: Brooks/Cole.

Keating, D.P. (1980). Four faces of creativity: The continuing plight of the intellectually underserved. *Gifted Child Quarterly, 24,* 56–61.

Keele, M.C., Dangel, H.L., and Owens, S.H. (1999, April). Selecting instructional interventions for students with mild disabilities in inclusive classrooms. *Focus on Exceptional Children,* 1–16.

Keilitz, L. and Dunivant, N. (1986). The relationship beween learning disabilities and juvenile delinquency: Current state of knowledge. *Remedial and Special Education, 3,* 18–26.

Keller, H. (1933). *Helen Keller in Scotland.* London: Methuen.

Kemp, M. (1998). Why is learning American Sign Language a challenge? *American Annals of the Deaf, 143,* 255–259.

Kempe, C., Silverman, F., Steele, B., Droegemueller, W., and Silver, H. (1962). The battered child syndrome. *Journal of the American Medical Association, 181,* 17–24.

Kennedy, C.H., Shukla, S., and Fryxell, D. (1997). Comparing the effects of educational placement on the social relationships of intermediate school students with severe disabilities. *Exceptional Children,* 64, 31–47.

Kennedy, G.H. and Meyer, K.A. (1998). The use of psychotropic medication for people with severe disabilities and challenging behavior: Current status and future directions. *Journal of the Association for Persons with Severe Handicaps, 23,* 83–97.

Kerms, K.A., Don, A., Mateer, C.A., and Streissguth, A.P. (1997). Cognitive defects in nonretarded adults with fetal alcohol syndrome. *Journal of Learning Disabilities, 30,* 685693.

Kerr, B.A. (1988). Raising career expectations of gifted girls. *Vocational Guidance Quarterly, 32,* 37–43.

Kerr, M.M. and Nelson, C.M. (1998). *Strategies for managing behavior problems in the classroom* (3rd ed.). Upper Saddle River, NJ: Prentice-Hall.

Kessler, J. (1977). Parenting the handicapped child. *Pediatric Annals, 6,* 654–661.

Khatena, J. (1982). *Educational psychology of the gifted.* New York: Wiley.

Khoury, J.T. and Appel, M.A. (1979). Gifted children: Current trends and issues. In A. Lane (Ed.) *Readings in human growth and development of the exceptional individual.* Connecticut: Special Learning Corporation.

King-Sears, M.E. (1997, March) Best academic practices for inclusive classrooms. *Focus on Eceptional Children,* 1–24.

Kirk, S. (1963, April 16). Behavioral diagnosis and remediation of learning disabilities. In Proceedings of the Conference on Exploration into the Problems of the Perceptually Handicapped Child: First annual meeting (vol. 1). Chicago.

Klien, R.G. and Last, C.G. (1989). *Anxiety disorders in children.* Newbury Park, CA: Sage.

Klesner, H. (1994). *ESL achievement project: Development of English as a second language achievement criteria as a function of age and residence in Canada.* North York, Ont.: North York Board of Education.

Klinger, J.K., Vaughn, S., Schumm, J.S., Cohen, P., and Forgan J.W. (1998). Inclusion or pull-out? Which do students prefer? *Journal of Learning Disabilities, 31,* 148–158.

Knight, D. and Rieck, W. (1997). Contracts for careers. *Teaching Exceptional Children, 29,* 42–46.

Knitzer, J., Steinberg, Z., and Fleisch, B. (1990). *At the schoolhouse door.* New York: Bank Street College of Education.

Kolata, G. (1988, January 5). New treatments may aid women who have miscarriages. *New York Times,* p. C5.

Kolvin, I., Ounsted, C., and Roth, M. (1971). Cerebral dysfunction and childhood psychoses. *British Journal of Psychiatry, 118,* 407–414.

Konstantareas, M.M. (1984). Sign language as a communication prosthesis with language-impaired children. *Journal of Autism and Developmental Disorders, 14,* 9–25.

Konstantareas, M.M., Hamatidis, S., and Busch, J. (1989). Cognitiion, communication, and social diferences betwen autistic boys and girls. *Journal of Applied Developmental Psychology,* 10, 411–424.

Kopp, C.B. (1983). Risk factors in development. In P.H. Mussen (Series ed.), M.M. Haith, and J. Campos (vol. eds.) *Handbook of child psychology. Vol. 2. Infancy and developmental psychobiology.* (pp. 1081–1088). New York: Wiley.

Korbin, J.E. (1987). Child abuse and neglect: The cultural context. In R.E. Helfer and R.S. Kempe (Eds.) *The battered child* (4th ed.) (pp. 23–41). Chicago, IL: University of Chicago Press.

Kouri, T. (1989). How manual sign acquisition relates to the development of spoken language: A case study. *Language, Speech and Hearing Services in the Schools, 20,* 50–62.

Kovacs, M. (1989). Affective disorders in children and adolescents. *American Psychologist, 44,* 209–215.

Kozleski, E.B. and Jackson, L. (1993). Taylor's story: Full inclusion in the neighborhood elementary school. *Exceptionality, 4,* 153–175.

Kraus, J.F., Fife, D., and Conroy, D. (1987). Pediatric brain injury: The nature, clinical course, and early outcomes in a defined United States population. *Pediatrics, 79,* 501–507.

Kregel, J. (1997). Supported employment. *Remedial and Special Education, 19,* 194–196.

Kroth, R.L. (1987). Mixed or missed messages between parents and professionals. *Volta Review, 89,* 1–10.

Krug, D.A., Arick, J.R., and Almond, P.J. (1980). Behavior checklist for identifying severely handicapped individuals with high levels of autistic behavior. *Journal of Child Psychology and Psychiatry,* 21, 221–229.

Krug, D.A., Arick, J.R., and Almond, P.J. (1993). *Autism Screening Instrument for Educational planning.* Austin, TX: Pro-Ed.

Krupp, M.A. and Chatton, M.J. (1983). *Current medical diagnosis and treatment.* Los Altos, CA: Lange Medical Publications.

Kulik, J.A. (1992). *An analysis of the research on ability grouping: Historical and contemporary perspectives.* Storrs, CT: National Research Center on the Gifted and Talented, University of Connecticut.

Kulik, J.A. and Kulik, C.L. (1984). *Effects of accelerated in-*

struction on students. Review of Educational Research, 54, 409–425.

Kulik, J.A. and Kulik, C. (1991). Research on acceleration. In N. Colangelo and G.A. Davis (Eds.) *Handbook of gifted education* (pp. 190–191) Boston, MA: Allyn and Bacon.

Kulik, J.A. Kulik, C.C. (1992). Meta-analytic findings on grouping. *Gifted Child Quarterly, 36,* 73–78.

Kurant, J.E. and Sever, J.L. (1977). Infectious diseases. In J.G. Wilson and F.C. Fraser (Eds.) *Handbook of teratology (vol. 1) General principles of etiology.* New York: Plenum Press.

Kuzemko, J.A. (1978). *Allergy in children.* Kent, England: Pittman Medical.

Lagercrantz, H. and Slotkin, T.A. (1986, April). The "stress" of being born. *Scientific American,* pp. 100–107.

Lahey, B. and Carlson, C. (1991). Validity of the diagnostic category of attention deficit disorder without hyperactivity: A review of the literature. *Journal of Learning Disabilities, 24,* 11–120.

Lahey, B.B. and Ciminero, A.R. (1980), *Maladaptive behavior: An introduction to abnormal psychology.* Glenview, IL: Scott Foresman.

Lahey, B.B., Hammer, D., Crumrine, P.L., and Forehand, R.L. (1980). Birth order x sex interactions in child development problems. *Developmental Psychology, 16,* 608–615.

Lamb, M.E. and Meyer, D.J. (1991). Fathers of children with special needs. In M. Seligman (Ed.) *The family with a handicapped child* (2nd ed.) (pp. 151–180). Boston, MA: Allyn and Bacon.

Lambert, N. (1988). Adolescent outcomes for hyperactive children: Perspectives on general and specific patterns of childhood risk for adolescents' educational, social, and mental health problems. *American Psychologist, 43,* 786–799.

Lambert, N. and Windmiller, M. (1981). *AAMD Adaptive Behavior Scale—School edition.* Washington, D.C.: American Association on Mental Deficiency.

Lamond, M.B. (1995). Should inclusion of children with emotional and physical disabilities in regular classrooms be a good idea even when teachers are given limited support? *Education Update, 37.*

Lamont, I.L. and Hill, J.L. (1991). Roles and responsibilities of paraprofessionals in the regular elementary classroom. *BC Journal of Special Education, 15,* 1–24.

Landau, B. (1983). Blind children's language is not 'meaningless.' In A.E. Mills (Ed.) *Language acquisition in the blind child.* (pp. 62–76) San Diego, CA: College Hill Press.

Landerholm, E. (1990). The transdisciplinary team approach in infant intervention programs. *Teaching Exceptional Children, 22,* 66–70.

Landesman-Dwyer, S., Martin, J.C., Smith D.W., and Streissguth, A.P. (1980). Teratogenic effects of alcohol in human and laboratory animals. *Science,* 209, 353.

LaSasso, C. and Davey, B. (1987). The relationship between lexical knowledge and reading comprehension for prelingually, profoundly hearing-impaired students. *Volta Review, 89,* 211–220.

Lawrence, B. (1991). Self-concept formation and physical handicap: Some educational implications for integration. *Disability, Handicap, and Society, 6,* 139–146.

Leavitt, A. and Ioannides, A. (1993). Using character development to improve story writing. *Teaching Exceptional Children, 25,* 41–45.

Lefebrue, A. (1983). The child with physical handicaps. In P.D. Strenhauser and Z. Rae-Grant (Eds.) *Psychological problems of the child in the family* (2nd ed.). New York: Basic Books.

Leffert, J.S. and Siperstein, G.N. (1996). Assessment of social-cognitive processes in children with mental retardation. *American Journal on Mental Retardation, 100,* 441–455.

Leffert, J.S., Siperstein, G.N., and Millikan, E. (2000). Understanding social adaptation in children with mental retardation: A social-cognitive perspective. *Exceptional Children, 66,* 530–545.

Leiter, R. (1948). *The Leiter International Performance Scale.* New York: Wiley.

Lemon, L.A. and Barber, W.H. (1991). Gilles de Tourette syndrome: A review and implications for educators. *B.C. Journal of Special Education, 15,* 146–158.

Lepper, M.R. and Gurtner, J. (1989). Children and computers: Approaching the twenty-first century. *American Psychologist, 44,* 170–178.

Lerner, J., Mardell-Czudnowski, C., and Goldenberg, D. (1981). *Special education for the early childhood years.* Englewood Cliffs, NJ: Prentice-Hall.

Le Roy, C.H., Powell, T.H., and Kelber, P.H. (1994). Meeting our responsibilities in special education. *Teaching Exceptional Children, 26,* 37–44.

Leuenberger, J. and Morris, M. (1990). Analysis of spelling errors by learning disabled and normal college students. *Learning Disability Focus, 5,* 103–118.

Levine, E. (1981). *The ecology of early deafness: Guides to fashioning environments and psychological assessments.* New York: Columbia University Press.

Levine, P. and Mouse, S.W. (1998). What follow-up studies say about postschool life for young men and women with learning disabilities: A critical look at the literature. *Journal of Learning Disabilities, 31,* 212–233.

Lewis, A.C. (1996). Words about the future. *Phi Delta Kappan, 77,* 460.

Lewis, R.B. and Doorlag, D.H. (1991). *Teaching special students in the mainstream.* New York: Macmillan.

Lewis, T.J., Chard, D., and Scott T.M. (1994). Full inclusion and the education of children and youth with emotional/behavioral disorders. *Behavioral Disorders, 19,* 277–293.

Lewis, T.J., Heflin, J. and DiGangi, S. (1991). *Teaching students with behavioural disorders. Basic questions and answers.* Reston, VA: Council for Exceptional Children.

Leyser, L. and Gottlieb, J. (1996). Reactions of parents of nondisabled children to mainstreaming over time: Implications for education practitioners. *International Journal of Special Education, 11,* 73–87.

Li, A.K. (1985). Changing preservice teachers' attitudes toward emotionally disturbed children. *Canadian Journal of Special Education, 1,* 73–82.

Li, A.K. and Adamson, G. (1992). Gifted secondary students' preferred learning style: Cooperative, competitive, or individualistic. *Journal for the Education of the Gifted, 16,* 46–54.

Lichenstein, S. (1989). Post-school employment patterns of handicapped and nonhandicapped graduates and dropouts. *International Journal of Educational Research, 15,* 501–513.

Liebert, D., Lutsky, L., and Gottlieb, A. (1990). Postsecondary experiences of young adults with severe physical disabilities. *Exceptional Children, 57,* 56–63.

Lifter, K., Sulzer-Azaroff, B., Anderson, S.R., and Cowdery, G.E. (1993). Teaching play activities to preschool children with disabilities: The importance of developmental considerations. *Journal of Early Intervention, 17,* 139–159.

Light, J.C. (1983). Language intervention programs for autistic children. *Special Education in Canada, 57,* 11–14.

Lindfors, J. (1987). *Children's language and learning* (2nd ed.) Englewood Cliffs, NJ: Prentice-Hall.

Link, M.P. (1991). Is integration really the least restrictive environment? *Teaching Exceptional Children, 23,* 63–64.

Links, P.S., Stockwell, M., Abichandani, F., and Simeon, E. (1980). Minor physical anomalies in childhood autism. Part II: Their relationship to maternal age. *Journal of Autism and Development Disorders, 10,* 287–292.

Linn, R.J., Algozzine, B. Mann, L., and Schwartz, S.E. (1987). Communication skills of learning disabled adolescents. *BC Journal of Special Education, 11,* 301–312.

Lipp, M. (1988, May). Educating gifted students. Paper presented at Canadian Education Association Meeting, Fredericton.

Lipsky, D. and Gartner, A. (1991). Restructuring for quality. In J.W. Lloyd, N.N. Singh, and A.C. Repp (Eds.) *The regular education initiative: Alternative perspectives on concepts, issues, and models* (pp. 43–46). Sycamore, IL: Sycamore.

Little, D. M. (1980). Learning disabilities and the severely learning disabled—Status quo in B.C. *B.C. Journal of Special Education, 4,* 155–163.

Lloyd, J.W. (1975). The pedagogical orientation: An argument for improving instruction. *Journal of Learning Disabilities, 8,* 74–78.

Lloyd, J.W. (1988). Direct instruction. In M.C. Wang, M.C. Reynolds, and H.J. Walberg (Eds.) *Handbook of special education (vol. 2): Mildly handicapping conditions.* New York: Pergamon.

Lloyd, J.W., Keller, C.E.I., Kauffman, J.M., and Hallahan, D.P. (1988, January). What will the regular education initiative require of general education teachers? Washington, DC: Office of Special Education Programs, Department of Education.

Lloyd, J.W., Kauffman, J.M., Lundrum, T., and Roe, D.L. (1991). Why do teachers refer pupils for special education? An analysis of referral reports. *Exceptonality, 2,* 115–126.

Lobato, D., Barbour, L., Hall, L.J., and Miller, C.T. (1987). Psychosocial characteristics of preschool siblings of handicapped and nonhandicapped children. *Journal of Abnormal Child Psychology, 15,* 329–338.

Loeber, R. (1982). The stability of antisocial and delinquent child behavior: A review. *Child Development, 53,* 1431–1446.

Loeber, R. (1985). Patterns and development of antisocial child behavior. *Annals of Child Development, 2,* 77–116.

Loeber, R. (1990). Developmental and risk factors of juvenile antisocial behavior and delinquency. *Clinical Psychlogy Review, 10,* 1–41.

Loeber, R. and Stouthamer-Loeber, M. (1996). Family factors as correlates of juvenile conduct problems and deliquency. In M. Tonry and N. Morris (Eds.) *Crime and justice* (vol. 7). Chicago, IL: University of Chicago Press.

Loeber, R. and Stouthamer-Loeber, M. (1998). Development of juvenile aggression and violence: Some common misconceptions and controversies. *American Psychologist, 53,* 242–259.

Loeding, B.L. and Crittenden, J.B. (1993). *The Self-Help InterPersonal Skills Assessment (SHIPS).* Tampa, FL: University of South Florida.

Logan, K.R. and Malone D.M. (1998). Comparing instructional contexts of students with and without severe disabilities in general education classrooms. *Exceptional Children, 64,* 343–358.

Logan, K.R., Bakeman, R., and Keefe, E.B. (1997). Effects of instructional variables on engaged behavior of students with disabilities in general classrooms. *Exceptional Children, 63,* 481–497.

Lojkasek, M., Goldberg, S., Marcovitch, S., and MacGregor, D. (1990). Influences on maternal responsiveness to developmentally delayed preschoolers. *Journal of Early Intervention, 14,* 236–273.

Lombard, R.C. and Newbert, D. (1992). Collaborative transition planning: Federal mandates and local solutions. *International Journal of Special Education,* 7, 123–132.

Louis, B. and Lewis, M. (1992). Parental beliefs about giftedness in young children and their relationship to actual ability level. *Gifted Child Quarterly, 36,* 27–31.

Lourie, N.V. (1975). The many faces of advocacy. In I.N. Berlin (Ed.) *Advocacy for child mental health.* New York: Brunner/Mazel.

Lovaas, O.I. and Favell, J.E. (1987). Protection for clients undergoing aversive/restrictive intervention. *Education and Treatment of Children, 10,* 311–325.

Lovaas, O.I. and Smith, T. (1988). Intensive behavioral treatment for young autistic children. In B.B. Lahey and A.E. Kazdin (Eds.) *Advances in clinical child psychology* (vol. 2) New York: Plenum.

Lovatt, M. (1962). Autistic children in a day nursery. *Exceptional Children, 29,* 103–108.

Lowenbraun, S. and Thompson, M.D. (1982). Hearing impairments. In N.G. Haring (Ed.) *Exceptional children and youth* (3rd ed.). Columbus, OH: Merrill.

Lowey, M. (1993, summer). 3-D image and laser camera improving prostheses for amputees. *Disability Today,* pp. 7–9.

Lowman, D.K. (1998). Preschoolers with complex health care needs in preschool classrooms. *Young Excepional Children, 1,* 2–6.

Luetke-Stahlman, B. and Luckner, J. (1991). *Effectively educating students with hearing impairments.* New York: Longman.

Luftig, R.L. (1988). Assessment of the perceived school loneliness and social isolation of mentally retarded and nonretarded students. *American Journal of Mental Retardation, 92,* 472–475.

Lupart, J. (1998). Setting right the delusion of inclusion: Implications for Canadian schools. *Canadian Journal of Education,* 23, 251–264.

Lynam, D. (1996). Early identification of chronic offenders: Who is the fledgling psychopath? *Psychological Bulletin, 120,* 209–234.

Lynch, M.A. and Roberts, J. (1982). *Consequences of child abuse.* London: Academic Press.

Lyon, G.R. (1994) *Frames of reference for assessment of learning diabilities: New views on measurement issues.* Baltimore, MD: Brookes.

Lyon, G.R. (1995). Research initiatives in learning disabilities: Contributions from scintists supported by the National Institute of Child Health and Development. *Journal of Child Neurology, 10,* 5120–5126 (supplement 1).

Lyon, M.E. (1997). Symbolic play and language development in young deaf children. *Deafness and Education, 21,* 10–20.

Maag, J.W. and Katsiyannis, A. (1998). Challenges facing successful transition for youths with E/BD. *Behavioral Disorders, 23,* 209–221.

MacAnally, P., Rose, S., and Quigley, S. (1987). *Language learning practices with deaf children.* Boston, MA: College Hill Press.

Maccoby, E.E. (1980). *Social development: Psychological growth and the parent-child relationship.* New York: Harcourt Brace Jovanovich.

MacCuspie, P.A. (1993). Short-term placements: A crucial role for residential schools. *Journal of Visual Impairment and Blindness,* 87, 193-198.

MacDonald, I.M. (1995). Junior high school student perceptions on the nature and extent of school violence. Masters thesis, Edmonton, University of Alberta.

MacDonald, I.M. (1997). Violence in schools: Multiple realities. *Alberta Journal of Educational Research,* 43, 142-156.

MacGinitie, W.H. and MacGinitie R.K. (1992). *Gates-MacGinitie Reading Tests* (Canadian ed.) Toronto: Nelson.

MacKay, A.W. (1987). The Elwood case: Vindicating the educational rights of the disabled. *Canadian Journal of Special Education, 3,* 113-116.

MacMillan, D.L., Gresham F.M., and Forness S.R. (1996). Full inclusion: An empirical perspective. *Behavioral Disorders,* 21, 145-159.

Maddux, C. (2000). Technology and special education. In M. Winzer and K. Mazurek (Eds.) *Special education in the 21st century: Issues of inclusion and reform* (pp. 83-105) Washington, DC: Gallaudet University Press.

Main, M. and George, C. (1985). Responses of abused and disadvantaged toddlers to distress in agemates: A study in the day care setting. *Developmental Psychology, 21,* 407-412.

Maker, J.C. (1993). Creativity, intelligence, and problem soving: A definition and design for cross-cultural research and measurement related to giftedness. *Gifted Education International, 9,* 68-77.

Maker, J.C., Nielson, A.B., and Rogers, J.A. (1994). Giftedness, diversity, and problem-solving. *Teaching Exceptional Children, 27,* 4-19.

Makin, K. (1997, February). Classroom exclusion acceptable, court days. *The Globe and Mail,* p. A 7.

Malloy, P. (1997). Communication and culture: How they relate to service development and advocacy for people who are deaf-blind: A report on a presentation by Dr. Harlan Lane at the Perkins National Conference on Deaf-Blindness. *Deaf-Blind Perspectives, 5,* 7-9.

Maloney, J. (1995). A call for placement options. *Educational Leadership, 53,* 25.

Manfredini, D. (1988). Down syndrome. ERIC Digest, No. 457. Reston, VA: Council for Exceptional Children.

Manset, G. and Semmel, M.I. (1997). Are inclusive programs for students with mild disabilities effective? A comparative review of program models. *Journal of Special Education,* 31, 155-180.

Many roads to one place: Clear benefits of parent support

groups: Status report (1999, May) *The Quarterly Newsletter on Disability Issues in Alberta*, p. 10

Mar, H.H. and Sall, N. (1995). Enhancing social opportunities and relationships of children who are deaf-blind. *Journal of Visual Impairment and Blindness, 89*, 280-286.

Marano, H.E. (1995, September/October). Big bad bully. *Psychology Today*, pp. 50-57, 62-70, 74-82.

March of Dimes. (1987). Down syndrome: Public Health Education Information Sheet, Genetic Series.

March of Dimes. [1986]. *Crisis for the unborn.* Videotape.

Mark, R., Beal, A.L., and Dumont, R. (1998). Validation of a WISC-III short-form for the identification of Canadian gifted students. *Canadian Journal of School Psychology, 14*, 1-10.

Markwardt, F.C. (1989). *Peabody Individual Achievement Test-Revised.* Circle Pines, MN: American Guidance Services.

Marland, S.P. Jr. (1972). Education of the gifted and talented: Report to the Congress of the United States by the Commission of Education. Washington, DC: U.S. Government Printing Office.

Marschark, M. (1993). *Raising and educating a deaf child: A comprehensive guide to the choices, controversies, and decisions faced by parents and educators.* New York: Oxford University Press.

Marston, D. (1996). A comparison of inclusive only, pull-out only, and combined service models for students with mild disabilities. *Journal of Special Education, 30*, 121-132.

Martin, A.J., Linfoot, K., and Stephenson, J. (1999). How teachers respond to concerns about misbehavior in their classroom. *Psychology in the Schools, 36*, 347-358.

Martin, M.L. and Forchuk, C. (1987). Sexuality and the developmentally handicapped: Health education strategies. *Canadian Journal of Special Education, 3*, 181-189.

Martinson, R.A. (1975). *The identification of the gifted and talented.* Reston, VA: Council for Exceptional Children.

Maurer, H. and Newbrough, J. (1987). Facial expressions of mentally retarded and nonretarded children: 1: Recognition by mentally retarded and nonretarded adults. *American Journal on Mental Deficiency, 91*, 505-510.

Mayberry, R., Woodlinger, Cohen, R., and Goldwin-Meadow, S. (1987). Symbolic development in deaf children. In D. Cicchetti and M. Beeghly (Eds.) *Symbolic development in atypical children* (pp. 109-126). San Francisco, CA: Jossey Bass.

Mayer, C. (1999). Shaping at the point of utterance: An investigation of the composing processes of deaf student writers. *Journal of Deaf Studies and Deaf Education, 4*, 37-49.

Mayne, A., Yoshinaga-Itano, C., Seday, A.L., and Carey, A. (2000). Expressive vobabulary development of infants and toddlers who are deaf or hard of hearing. *Volta Review, 100*, 1-28.

Mazurek, K. and Winzer, M. (1994). *Comparative studies in special education.* Washington, DC: Gallaudet University Press.

McBride, H. and Seigel, L.S. (1997). Learning disabilities and adolescent suicide. *Journal of Learning Disabilities, 30*, 652-659.

McBroom, L.W. (1997). Making the grade: College students with visual impairments. *Journal of Visual Impairment and Blindness, 91*, 261-270.

McCarthy, D. (1972). *Manual for the McCarthy Scales of Children's Abilities.* New York: Psychological Corporation.

McCarthy, M.M. (1994). Inclusion and the law: Recent judicial developments. *PDK Research Bulletin*, 13.

McClennen, S. (1988). Sexuality and students with mental retardation. *Teaching Exceptional Children, 20*, 58-61

McCombs, B.G. and Manzano, R.J. (1990). Putting the self in self-regulated learning: The self as agent in integrating skill and will. *Educational Psychologist, 25*, 51-70.

McConnell, J. (1999). Parents, adolescents, and career plans of visually impaired students. *Journal of Visual Impairment and Blindness, 93*, 498-515.

McCormick, L. (1987). Comparison of the effects of a microcomputer activity and toy play on social and communication behaviors of young children. *Journal of the Division of Early Childhood, 11*, 195-205.

McCrindle, K. (1995, summer). War on words: Label vs euphemism. *Disability Today*, pp. 16-22.

McDonnell, J., Ferguson, B., and Mathot-Buckner, C. (1992). Transition from school to work for students with severe disabilities: The Utah comunity employment placement project. In F. Rusch, L. De Stefano, J. Chadsey-Rusch, L.A. Phelps, and E. Szymanski (Eds.) *Transition from school to adult life: Models, linkages, and policy* (pp. 33-50). Sycamore,IL: Sycamore Publishing.

McFadden, M. and Ellis, J. (2000). What happens to gifted education within inclusive schooling? In M. Winzer and K Mazurek (Eds.) *Special education in the 21st century: Issues of inclusion and reform* (pp. 142-162). Washington, DC: Gallaudet University Press.

McGee, L.M. and Richgels, D.J. (1990). *Literacy's beginings: Supporting young readers and writers.* Boston, MA: Allyn and Bacon.

McIntosh, K. (1984). Viral infections of the fetus and newborn. In M. Avery and H.W. Taeusch Jr. (Eds.) *Schaffer's diseases of the newborn* (5th ed.) Philadelphia, PA: Saunders.

McIntosh, R., Vaughn, S., Schumm, J.S., Haager, D., and Lee, O. (1994). Observations of students with learning disabilities in general education classrooms. *Exceptional Children, 60*, 249-261.

McKinney, J.D., McLure, S., and Feagans, L. (1982).

Classroom behavior of learning disabled children. *Learning Disability Quarterly, 5,* 45-51.

McKinney, J.D., Montague, M., and Hocutt, A.M. (1993). Educational assessment of students with attention deficit disorders. *Exceptional Children, 60,* 125-131.

McLaren, J. and Bryson, S.E. (1987). Review of recent epidemiological studies of mental retardation: Prevalence, associated disorders, and etiology. *American Journal on Mental Retardation, 92,* 243-254.

McLaughlin, M. and Henderson, K. (2000). Defining US special education into the twenty-first century. In M. Winzer and K. Mazurek (Eds.) *Special education in the 21st century: Issues of inclusion and reform* (pp. 41-61) Washington, DC: Gallaudet University Press.

McLean, L.K., Brady, N.C., and McLean, J.E. (1996). Reported communication abilities of individuals with severe mental retardation. *American Journal on Mental Retardation, 100,* 580-591.

McLeskey, J., Henry, D., and Hodges, D. (1999). Inclusion: What progress is being made across disability categories? *Teaching Exceptional Children, 31,* 60-64.

McLinden, S. (1990). Mothers' and fathers' reports of the effects of a young child with special needs on the family. *Journal of Early Intervention, 14,* 249-259.

McNeill J., and Fowler, S. (1996). Using story reading to encourage children's conversations. *Teaching Exceptional Children, 28,* 44-46.

McWilliams, B., Morris, H., and Shelton, R. (1990). *Cleft palate speech* (2nd ed.). Philadelphia, PA: B.C. Decker, Inc.

Meadow, K.P. (1980). *Deafness and child development.* Berkely, CA: University of California Press.

Meadows, N.B., Neel, R.S., Scott, C.M., and Parker, G. (1994). Academic performance, social competence, and mainstreaming: A look at mainstreamed and nonmainstreamed students with serious behavior disorders. *Behavioral Disorders, 19,* 170–180.

Meeker, M.N. (1979). *Teachers' guide to the Structure of Intellect Learning Abilities Test.* El Segundo, CA: SOI Systems.

Meents, C.K. (1989). Attention deficit disorder: A review of the literature. *Psychology in the Schools, 26,* 168–178.

Mehas, K., Boling, K., Sobieniak, S., Sprague, J., Burke, M.D., and Hagan, S. (1998). Finding a safe haven in middle school. *Teaching Exceptional Childen,* 30, 20–23.

Mercer, C.D. (1987). *Students with learning disabilities* (3rd ed.) Columbus OH: Merrill.

Mercer, J.R. (1973). *Labelling the mentally retarded: Clinical and social system perspectives on mental retardation.* Berkeley, CA: University of California Press.

Merrell, K.W. (1993). *School social behavior scales.* Brandon, VT: Clinical Psychological Publishing.

Metcoff, J., Cristiloe, P., Crosby, W.M., Sandstread, H.H., and Milne, D. (1989). Smoking in pregnancy: Relation of birth weight to maternal plasma carotene and chlosterol levels. *Obsterics and Gynecology, 102,* 302–308.

Meyers, E. (1984). A study of concerns of classroom teachers regarding a resource room program for the gifted. *Roeper Review, 7,* 32–36.

Mezriko, M. (1987). Transparency and ease of learning of symbols represented by Blissymbols, PCS and Picsyms. *Augmentative and Alternative Communication, 3,* 129–136.

Michael, M.G. and Paul, P.V. (1991). Early intervention for infants with deaf-blindness. *Exceptional Children, 57,* 200–210.

Miller, C.A. (1985). Infant mortality in the United States. *Scientific American, 235,* 31–37.

Miller, M.S. and Moores, D.F. (2000). Bilingual/bicultural education for deaf students. In M. Winzer and K. Mazurek (Eds.) *Special education in the 21st century: Issues of inclusion and reform* (pp. 221–237). Washington, DC: Gallaudet University Press.

Miller, S.P., Butler, F.M., and Lee, K. (1998, September). Validated practices for teaching mathematics to students with learning disabilities: A review of the literature. *Focus on Exceptional Children,* pp. 1–24.

Mills, J.R. and Jackson, N.E. (1990). Predictive significance of early giftedness: The case of precocious reading. *Journal of Educational Psychology, 82,* 410–419.

Miner, I.D. (1995). Psychosocial implications of Ushers Syndrome Type 1 throughout the life cycle. *Journal of Visual Impairment and Blindness, 89,* 287–296.

Minke, K.M., Bear, G.G., Deiner, S.A., and Griffin S.M. (1996). Teachers' experiences with inclusive classrooms: Implications for special education reform. *Journal of Special Education, 30,* 152–186.

Minner, S. (1989). The use of a paraprofessional to work with parents in a rural school. *Rural and Special Education Quarterly, 10,* 38–43.

Mira, M. P. and Tyler, J. S. (1991). Students with Traumatic Brain Injury: Making the transition from hospital to school. *Focus on Exceptional Children, 23,* 1–6.

Mithaug, D.Z., Horiuchi, C.N., and Fanning P.N. (1985). A report on the Colorado statewide follow-up survey of special education students. *Exceptional Children, 51,* 397–404.

Moffitt, T. (1993). "Life course persistent" and "adolescent limited" antisocial behavior: A developmental taxonomy. *Psychological Review, 100,* 674-701.

Molnar, M. (1993, November). Whose words are they anyway? *Mainstream,* pp. 18–22.

Monkman, H. and Baskind, S. (1998). Are assistants effectively supporting hearing-impaired children in mainstream schools? *Deafness and Education, 22,* 15–22.

Monroe, E. (1991). Who's the teacher? *ATA Magazine,* 71, 25–26.

Montagu, A. (1977). *Life before birth.* New York: Signet Books.

Montague, M. (1988). Job-related social skills training for adolescents with handicaps. *Career Development for Exceptional Individuals, 11,* 26–41.

Montague, M. and Graves, A. (1993). Improving students' story writing. *Teaching Exceptional Children, 25,* 36–37.

Moon, M.S. and Inge, K. (1993). Vocational preparation and transition. In M.E. Snell (Ed.) *Instruction of students with severe disabilities* (4th ed.) (pp. 556–588) New York: Merrill.

Moore, K.L. and Persaud, T.V.N. (1993). *Before we are born.* Philadephia, PA: Saunders.

Moore, P. (1986). Voice disorders. In G. Shames and E. Wiig (Eds.) *Human communication disorders* (2nd ed.) (pp. 183–229). Columbus, OH: Merrill.

Moore, S.E. and Perkins, W.R. (1990). Validity and reliability of judgments of authentic and simulated stuttering. *Journal of Speech and Hearing Disorders,* 55, 383–391.

Moores, D.F. (1982). *Educating the deaf: Psychology, principles and practices* (2nd ed.). Boston, MA: Houghton Mifflin.

Moran, M. (1982, April). Living with a handicapped child: Findings on families and early intervention. Paper presented at CEC, Houston, Texas.

Moran, M.J. and Pentz, A.L. (1995). Helping the child with a cleft palate in your classroom. *Teaching Exceptional Children, 27,* 46–48.

Morgan, R.L., Morre, S.C., McSweyn, C.A., and Salzberg, C.L. (1992). Transition from school to work: Views of secondary special educators. *Education and Training in Mental Retardation, 27,* 315–323.

Morningstar, M.E., Kleinhammer-Tramill, P., and Laltin, D.L. (1999, May). Using successful models of student-centered transition planning and services for adolescents with disabilities. *Focus on Exceptional Children,* 1–20.

Mossish, R. (1997). Gambling with discipline. *Keeping in Touch,* pp. 1,4.

Mulick, J.A., Jacabson, J.W., and Kobe, F.H. (1993). Anguished silence and helping hands: Autism and facilitated communication. *Skeptical Enquiries, 17,* 270–287.

Murphy, D. (1986). The prevalence of handicapping conditions among juvenile delinquents. *Remedial and Special Education, 7,* 7–17.

Murphy, J. and Slorach, N. (1983). The language development of pre-school hearing children of deaf parents. *British Journal of Disorders of Communication, 18,* 118–126.

Murphy, K.R. and Barkley R.A. (1996). Parents of children with attention deficit-hyperactivity disorder: Psychological and attentional impairment. *American Journal of Orthopsychiatry, 66,* 93–102.

Myers, G., Cerone, S., and Olson, A. (1981). *A guide for helping the child with spina bifida.* Springfield, IL: Charles C. Thomas.

Myers, P., and Hammill, D.D. (1990). *Learning disabilities: Basic concepts, assessment practices and instructional strategies.* (4th ed.) Austin, TX: Pro-Ed.

Naeyaert, K.M. and Grace, G. (1990). Prevalence and causes of blindness and visual impairment in Canada. *Journal of Visual Impairment and Blindness, 84,* 361–363.

Naglieri, J.A. (1991). *Draw a person screening procedures for e.d. Examiner's manual.* Austin,TX: Pro-Ed.

Naglieri, J.A., Lebuffe, P.A., and Pfiefer, S.I. (1993). *Devereaux Behavior Rating Scale— School Edition.* San Antonio, TX: Psychological Corporation.

Naglieri, J.A., Lebuffe, P.A., and Pfiefer, S.I. (1994). *Devereaux Scales of Mental Disorders.* New York: Psychological Corporation.

National Advisory Committee on Dyslexia and Related Reading Disorders. (1969). *Reading disorders in the United States.* Washington, DC: Department of Health, Education and Welfare.

National Association. (1991). *Liaison Bulletin, 17,* 2.

National Joint Committee on Learning Disabilities. (1988). Letter to NJCLD member organizations.

Neal, S. and MacLean, W. (1995). Disrupted lives: Siblings of disturbed adolescents. *American Journal of Orthpsychiatry, 65,* 274–281.

Nealis, J.T. (1983). Epilepsy: In J. Umbriel (Ed.) *Physical disabilities and health impairments: An introduction* (pp. 74–85). Columbus, OH: Merrill.

Neihart, M. (1999). The impact of giftedness on psychological well-being: What does the empirical literature say? *Roeper Review, 22,* 10–17.

Nelkin, D. and Tancredi, L. (1989). *Dangerous diagnostics: The social power of biological information.* New York: Basic Books.

Nelson, C.M., Rutherford, R.B. Jr., Center, D.B., and Walker, H.M. (1991). Do public schools have an obligation to serve disabled children and youth? *Exceptional Children, 57,* 406–413.

Nelson, K.B. and Ellenberg, J.H. (1986). Antecedents of cerebral palsy: Multivariate analysis of risk. *New England Journal of Medicine, 315,* 81–86.

Nelson, J.R., Ferrante, C., and Mantella, R.C. (1999). Children's evaluations of the effectiveness of in-class and pull-out service delivery models. *International Journal of Special Education, 14,* 77–91.

Nesbit, W. (1990, March). The efficacy of integrated senior programs. *Keeping in Touch,* pp. 3–4.

Nessner, K. (1990, winter). Children with disabilities. *Canadian Social Trends.* pp. 18–20.

Newacheck, P.W. and Taylor, W.R. (1992). Childhood chronic illnesses: Prevalence, severity, and impact. *American Journal of Public Health, 82,* 364–371.

Newborg, J., Stock, J.R., and Wnek, L. (1984). *Battelle Developmental Inventory.* Allen, TX: DLM Teaching Resources.

New Brunswick Department of Education. (1994). *Teacher assistant guidlines for standards and evaluation.* New Brunswick: Author.

New development: New strategies for ADHD. (1995). *CEC Today, 2,* p. 12.

New developments in ADD/ADHD (1997, September). *CEC Today,* pp. 12–13.

New developments. (1995). *CEC Today.*

New developments. (1996). *CEC Today.*

New developments: We can't — and we shouldn't —treat all our students the same. (1996). *CEC Today, 3,* p. 3.

Neuwirth, S. (1994). *Attention deficit hyperactivity disorder.* National Institute of Mental Health Publication No. 94-3572.

Nicholls, A. C. and Martin, Y. M. (1983). Judicial decisions and the public schools. *Canadian Journal of Education/Revue canadienne de l'education, 8,* 97–116.

Nirje, B. (1979). Changing patterns in residential services for the mentally retarded. In E. L. Meyen (Ed.) *Basic readings in the study of exceptional children and youth.* Denver, CO: Love Publishing.

Notari-Syverson, A.R. and Shuster, S.L. (1995). Putting real-life skills into IEPs? IPSPs for infants and young children. *Teaching Exceptional Children, 27,* 29–32.

Oderkirk, J. (1993, winter). Disabilities among children. *Canadian Social Trends,* pp. 22–25.

Odom, S.L. Kohler, F.W. and Strain, P.S. (1987). *Teaching strategies for promoting social interaction skills.* Pittsburgh, PA: The Early Childhood Research Institute, University of Pittsburgh.

Ohlsen, M.M. (1977). *Group counseling* (2nd ed.). New York: Holt, Rinehart and Winston.

Okolo, C.M. and Sitlington, P. (1986). The role of special education in LD adolescents' transition from school to work. *Learning Disability Quarterly, 9,* 141–155.

Ollendick, T. H. and King N.J. (1999). Child behavior assessment and cognitive-behavior intervention in schools. *Psychology in the Schools, 36,* 427–436.

Olson, M.R., Chalmer, L., and Hoover, J.H. (1997). Attitudes and attributes of general education teachers identified as effective inclusionists. *Remedial and Special Education, 18,* 28–35.

Olweus, D. (1987, fall). Schoolyard bullying: Grounds for intervention. *School Safety,* pp. 4–11.

O'Melia, M.C. and Rosenberg, M.S. (1994). Effects of cooperative homework teams on the acquisition of mathematics skills by secondary students with mild disabilities. *Exceptional Children, 60,* 538–548.

Ontario Council for Exceptional Children. (1997, September). Ontario CEC develops a position paper on professional standards and competencies for educational assistants. *CEC Today,* p. 7.

Ontario Ministry of Health (1978). *You and your hearing.* Toronto: Ontario Ministry of Health.

Oppenheimer, T. (1997, July). The computer delusion. *The Atlantic Monthly,* pp. 45–48, 50–56, 61–66.

Orelove, F.P. and Sobsey, D. (1987). *Educating children with multiple disabilities: A transdisciplinary approach.* Baltimore, MD: Brookes.

Orlansky, M.C. (1981). The deaf-blind and the severe/profoundly handicapped: An emerging relationship. In S.R. Walsh and R. Holzberg (Eds.) *Understanding and educating the deaf-blind/severely and profoundly handicapped* (pp. 5–23). Springfield, IL: Thomas.

Osher, D., Osher, T., and Smith, C. (1994). Toward a national perspective on emotional and behavioral disorders: A developmental agenda. *Beyond Behavior, 61,* 6–17.

Orton, S. (1927). Studies in stuttering. *Archives of Neurology and Psychology, 18,* 671–672.

OTA, Office of Technology Assessment, U.S. Congress. (1987). Technology dependent children: Hospital vs. home care—a technical memorandum. OTA-TM-H-38. Washington, D.C.: Author.

Otto, T.L. and Barber, W.H. (1992). Prader-Willi syndrome: Causes, characteristics, intervention, long-term consequences. *BC Journal of Special Education, 16,* 38–50.

Overton, T. (1992). *Assessment in special education: An applied approach.* Columbus, OH: Merrill.

Owens, R.J. Jr. (1991). *Language disorders: A functional approach to assessment and intervention.* New York: Merrill.

Owens, R.J. Jr. (1996) Language development: An introduction. (4th ed.) Boston, MA: Allyn and Bacon.

Ozanne, A.E., Kaimmer, H., and Murdoch, B.E. (1990). Speech and language skills in children with early treated phenylketonuria. *American Journal on Mental Retardation, 94,* 625–632.

Pagliaro, L.A. (1995). Adolescent depression and suicide: A review and analysis of the literature. *Canadian Journal of School Psychology, 11,* 191–201.

Painter, K. (1997, August 10). Tumor gene identified by scientists. *Calgary Sun,* p. 13.

Palinscar, A.S. and Brown, A.L (1984). Reciprocal teaching of comprehension: Fostering and comprehension monitoring activities. *Cognition and Instruction, 2,* 117–175.

Palmer D.S., Borthwick-Duffy, S.A., and Widaman, K. (1998). Parent perceptions of inclusive practices for their children with significant cognitive disabilities. *Exceptional Children, 64,* 271–282.

Palmer, F.B., Shapiro, B.F., Wachtel, R.C., Allen, M.C., Hiller, J.E., Harryman, S.E., Master, B.S., Meinert, C.L., and Capute, A.J. (1988). The effects of physical therapy on cerebral palsy. *New England Journal of Medicine, 318,* 803–808.

Palmer, B. and Sellars, M. (1993). The integration of hearing-impaired people in ordinary schools. *Education Today,* 43, 28–31.

Pardeck, J.T. (1990). Children's literature and child abuse. *Child Welfare, 69,* 83–88.

Parker, W.D. (1997). An empirical typology of perfectionism in academically talented children. *American Educational Research Journal, 34,* 545–562.

Patten, B.M. (1973). Visually mediated thinking: A report of the case of Albert Einstein. *Journal of Learning Disabilities, 6,* 415–420.

Patterson, D. (1987, August). The causes of Down syndrome. *Scientific American,* pp. 52–57, 60.

Patterson, G.R. (1982). *Coercive family process.* Eugene, OR: Castalia Press.

Patterson, G.R., De Baryshe, B.D., and Ramsey, E. (1989). A developmental perspective on antisocial behavior. *American Psychologist, 44,* 322–335.

Patton, J.R., Cronin, M.E. Polloway, E.A., Hutchinson, D., and Robinson, G.A. (1989). Curricula considerations: A life skills orientation. In G.A. Robinson, J.R. Patton, E.A. Polloway, and L.R. Sargent. *Best practices in mild mental disabilities.* Reston, VA: Council for Exceptional Children.

Paul, J.L. (1987). Defining behavior disorders in children. In B.C. Epanchin and J.L. Paul (Eds.) *Emotional problems of childhood and adolescence* (pp. 15–29). Columbus, OH: Merrill.

Pearl, R. (1987). Social cognitive factors in learning disabled children's social problems. In S.J. Ceci (Ed.) *Handbook of cognitive, social, and neurological aspects of learning disabilties* (vol. 2) Hillsdale, NJ: Erlbaum.

Peckham, V.C. (1993). Children with cancer in the classroom. *Teaching Exceptional Children, 26,* 26–32.

Pennington, B.F. (1990). *Diagnosing learning disorders: A neuropsychological framework.* New York: Guilford.

Perkins Institution for the Blind. (1839). Annual reports of the Trustees of the New England Institution for the Education of the Blind to the Corporation. Boston, MA: J.T. Buckingham.

Perkins, W.H. (1990). What is stuttering? *Journal of Speech and Hearing Disorders, 55,* 370–382.

Perks, B. (1984). Identification of gifted children. Ed.D. thesis, University of British Columbia.

Perl, J. (1995). Improving relationship skills for parent conferences. *Teaching Exceptional Children, 28,* 29–31.

Perlmutter, B. (1986). Personality variables and peer relations of children and adolescents with learning disabilities. In S.J. Ceci (Ed.) *Handbook of cognitive, social and neoropsychological aspects of learning disabilities* (vol. 1) (pp. 339–359) Hillsdale, NJ: Erlbaum.

Peterson, N.L. (1987). *Early intervention for handicapped and at-risk children.* Denver, CO: Love.

Peters Goessling, D. (2000). From tolerance to acceptance and celebration: Including students with severe disabilities. In M. Winzer and K. Mazurek (Eds.) *Special education in the 21st century: Issues of inclusion and reform* (pp. 175–197). Washington, DC: Gallaudet University Press.

Pettito, L.A. and Marenette, P.F. (1991). Babbling in the manual mode: Evidence for the ontogeny of language. *Science, 251,* 1493–1495.

Pfeffer, C.R. (1986). *The suicidal child.* New York: Guilford.

Pfeuti, M. (1997). Asthma: A chronic illness in the classroom. Unpublished paper, University of Lethbridge.

Pfeiffer, S.I. (1980). The influence of diagnostic labelling on special eduation placement decisions. *Psychology in the Schools, 17,* 346–350.

Phelp, M. (2000, November 11). The promise of hope. *The Globe and Mail,* pp. A14–15.

Phillips, K. (1990). Why can't a man be more like a woman—and vice versa. *Omni,* 42–48, 68.

Phipps. (1982). The learning disabled learner is often a boy—Why? *Academic Therapy, 17,* 425–430.

Pickett, A.L. (1989). Restructuring the schools: The role of paraprofessionals. *Results in education.* Washington, DC: National Governor's Association.

Pieper, E. (1976). Grandparents can help. *Exceptional Parent, 6,* 7–10.

Pierce, B.A. (1990). *Family genetic sourcebook.* New York: Wiley.

Piirto, J. (1994). *Talented children and adults: Their development and education.* New York: Merrill.

Pilecka, A. (1995, July). Childhood allergies. Lecture presented at University of Lethbridge.

Pirro, J.F. (1993, September). Gallaudet football: "The difference is in the hear" for the up-and-down Bisons. *Mainstream,* p. 16.

Pituch, M. and Bruggeman, J. (1982). Lungs unlimited. *Children Today, 11,* 6–10.

Piven, J. Tsai, G., Nehme, E. Coyle, J.T. Chase, G.A., and Folstein, S.E. (1991). Platelet serotonin, a possible marker for familial autism. *Journal of Autism and Developmental Disorders, 21,* 51–54.

Planta, R.C. (1990). Widening the debate on educational reform: Prevention as a viable alternative. *Exceptional Children, 56,* 306–313.

Plomin, R. (1989). Environment and genes: Determinants of behavior. *American Psychologist, 44,* 105–111.

Plomin, R., De Fries, J.C., and McClearn, G.E. (1990). *Behavioral genetics: A primer* (2nd ed.) New York: Freeman.

Plowman, P.D. (1981). Training extraordinary leaders. *Roeper Review, 3,* 13–16.

Podell, D.M., Kastner, J., and Kastner, S. (1996). Adolescents with mental retardation: Perceptions of sexual abuse. *American Journal of Orthopsychiatry, 66,* 103–110.

Poikkurs, A. Ahoren, T., Nahri, V., Lytimen, P., and Rusku-Puttonen, H. (1999). Language problems in children with learning disabilities: Do they interfere with maternal communication? *Journal of Learning Disabilities*, 32, 22–35.

Pollack, D. (1980). Acoupedics: An approach to early management. In G.T. Mencher and S.E. Gerber (Eds.) *Early management of hearing loss.* New York: Grune and Stratton.

Polloway, E.A., Epstein, M.H., Patton, J.R., Cullinan, D., and Lueble, J. (1986). Demographic, social, and behavioral characteristics of students with educable mental retardation: A survey of the field. *Education and Training of the Mentally Retarded,* 21, 27–34.

Pope, A.M. and Tarlov, A.R. (Eds.) (1991). *Disability in America: Toward a national agenda for prevention.* Washington, DC: National Academy Press.

Powell, S. and Dalley, M. (1995). When to intervene in selective mutism: The multimodel treatment of a case of persistent selective mutism. *Psychology in the Schools, 32,* 114–123.

Power, P.W. (1984). *A guide to vocational assessment.* Austin, TX: Pro-Ed.

Prasher, V.P., Chowdhury, T.A., Rowe, B., and Bain, S.C. (1997). ApoE genotype and Alzheimer's disease in adults with Down syndrome: Meta-analysis. *American Journal on Mental Retardation, 102,* 103–110.

Pre-natal care [1987]. Pamphlet, n.p. Available at Lethbridge Health Unit.

Prendergast, D.E. (1995). Preparing for children who are medically fragile in educational programs. *Teaching Exceptional Children, 27,* 37–41.

Prevalence of disability in Canada rises. (1995, winter). *Disability Today,* p. 7.

Pruitt, W. (1986). *Vocational evaluation* (2nd ed.) Menomonie, WI: Walt Pruitt Associates.

Quay, H.C. (1972). Patterns of aggression, withdrawal, and immaturity. In H.C. Quay and J.S. Werry (Eds.). *Psychopathological disorders of childhood.* New York: Wiley.

Quay, H.C. (1986). Classification. In H.C. Quay and J.S. Werry (Eds.) *Psychopathological disorders in childhood* (3rd ed.) New York: Wiley.

Quay, H.C. and Peterson, D.R. (1987). *Manual for the Revised Behavior Problem Checklist.* Coral Gables, FL: University of Miami.

Quinsland, L.K. and Vanginkel, A. (1990). Cognitive processing and the development of concepts by deaf students. *American Annals of the Deaf, 135,* 280–284.

Rathegerber, A.J. (1981). Manitoba vision screening study. *Journal of Visual Impairment and Blindness, 75,* 239–243.

Rathus, S. (1988). *Understanding child development.* New York: Holt, Rinehart and Winston.

Raven, J. (1948). *Progressive matrices.* New York: Psychological Corporation.

Reading difficulties versus learning disability. (1997, November/December). *CEC Today,* pp. 1, 9, 13.

Reading summit sheds new insights on teaching reading to students with disabilities. (1999). *CEC Today,* 5, 1, 9, 15.

Reagan, T. (1988). Multiculturalism and the deaf: An educational manifesto. *Journal of Research and Development in Education, 22,* 1–6.

Reagan, T. (1997) When is a language not a language? Challenges to "linguistic legitimacy" in educational discourse. *Educational Foundations, 11,* 5–28.

Reich, P.A. (1986). *Language development.* Englewood Cliffs, NJ: Prentice-Hall.

Reid, D.K., Robinson, S.J., and Bursen, T.D. (1995). Empiricism and beyond: Expanding the boundaries of special education. *Remedial and Special Education,* 16, 131–141.

Reid, R., Maag, J.W, and Vasa, S.F. (1993). Attention deficit hyperactivity disorder as a disability category: A critique. *Exceptional Children, 60,* 198–214.

Reinert, H. (1980). *Children in conflict* (2nd ed.) St. Louis, MO: Mosley.

Reinert, H. and Huang, A. (1987). *Children in conflict.* Columbus, OH: Merrill.

Reis, S.M. (1989). Reflections on policy affecting the education of gifted and talented students: Past and future perspectives. *American Psychologist, 44,* 399–408.

Reis, S.M. (1995). *Curriculum compacting communicator.* 28(2), 1, 27–32. Mansfield Center, CT: Creative Learning Press, Inc.

Reis, S.M. and O'Shea, A.A. (1984). An innovative enrichment program: The Enrichment Triad/Revolving Door Model. *Special Education in Canada, 58,* 135–138.

Reis, S.M. and Purcell, J. (1992). *An analysis of content elimination and strategies used by elementary classroom teachers in the curriculum compacting process.* Storrs, University of Connecticut, National Research Center on the Gifted and Talented.

Reis, S.M. and Westberg, K.L. (1994). The impact of staff development on teachers' ability to modify curriculum for gifted and talented students. *Gifted Child Quarterly, 38,* 127–135.

Reiss, A.L. and Freund, L. (1990). Fragile X syndrome. *Biological Psychiatry, 27,* 223–240.

Reist, M. (1991, March). The Young Offenders Act and how it impacts upon educators. *Keeping in Touch,* pp. 2–3.

Rempel, R.G. (1992, winter). Let the buyer beware: Integration is more than just a word. *Disability Today,* pp. 46–48.

Renzulli, J.S. (1978). What makes giftedness? Reexamining a definition. *Phi Delta Kappan, 60,* 180–184, 261.

Renzulli, J.S. (1979). What makes giftedness? Los Angeles: National/State Leadership Training Institute on the Gifted and Talented, Brief no. 6. Report (1981).

Renzulli, J.S. and Reis, S. (1991). The reform movement

and the quiet crisis in education. *Gifted Child Quarterly, 35,* 26–35.

Renzulli, J.S. and Reis, S.M. (1991). The schoolwide enrichment model: A comprehensive plan for the development of creative productivity. In N. Colangelo and G. Davis (Eds.) *Handbook of gifted education* (pp. 111–141) Boston, MA: Allyn and Bacon.

Renzulli, J.S. and Smith, L.H. (1984). Revolving door: A truer turn for the gifted. *Learning, 9,* 91–93.

Renzulli, J.S., Hartman, R.K.,and Callahan, C.M. (1975). Scale for Rating the Behavioral Characteristics of Superior Students. In W.B. Barbe and J.S. Renzulli (Eds.) *Psychology and education of gifted children* (2nd ed.) New York: Irvington.

Reschley, D.J. (1989). Incorporating adaptive behavior deficits into instructional programs. In G.A. Robinson, J.R. Palton, E.A. Polloway, and L.R. Sargent (Eds.) *Best practices in mental retardation* (pp. 39–63). Reston, VA: Council for Exceptional Children.

Reschly, D.J. and Ysseldyke, J.E (1995). School psychology paradigm shift. In A. Thomas and J. Grimes (Eds.) *Best practices in school psychology* (pp. 17–31) Washington, DC: National Association of School Psychologists.

Resistance and acceptance: Educator attitudes to inclusion of students with disabilities. (1997, fall). *Keeping in Touch,* pp. 1,4.

Rest, M.C. (1990, July). The shadow children: Preparing for the arrival of crack babies in school. *Phi Delta Kappan Research Bulletin,* pp. 1–6.

Reynolds, C.R. and Kamphaus, R.W. (1992). *Behavior Assessment System for Children.* Circle Pines, MN: American Guidance Service.

Reynolds, M.C., Wang, M., and Walberg, H.J. (1987). The necessary restructuring of special and regular education. *Exceptional Children, 53,* 391–398.

Rich, Y. (1986). Curriculum development for co-operative learning in mixed ability classes. *Journal of Curriculum Studies, 18,* 339–341.

Richard, M.M. (1995). Students with attention deficit disorders in postsecondary education: Issues in identification and accommodation. In K.G. Nadeau (Ed.) *A comprehensive guide to attention deficit disorder in adults: Research, diagnosis, treatment* (pp. 284–307). New York: Brunner/Mazel.

Richards, C.M., Symons, D.K., Greene, C.A., and Szuskiewicz, T. (1995). The bidirectional relationship between achievement and externalizing behavior problems and students with learning disabilities. *Journal of Learning Disabilities, 28,* 8–17.

Richert, E.S., Alvino, J.J., and McDonnell, R.C. (1982). National report on identification: Assessment and recommendations for comprehensive identification of gifted and talented youth. Sewell, NJ: Information Resource Center.

Rimland, B. (1964). *Infantile autism.* New York: Appleton-Century-Crofts.

Rimland, B. (1983). The Fiengold diet: An assessment of the reviews by Mattes, by Kavale and Forness and others. *Journal of Learning Disabilities, 16,* 331–333.

Rimm, S. and Davis, G.A. (1976). GIFT: An instrument for the identification of creativity. *The Journal of Creative Behavior, 10,* 178–182.

Rimm, S. and Lowe, B. (1988). Family environments of underachieving gifted students. *Gifted Child Quarterly, 32,* 353–359.

Ritchey, D. (1993, June). Frustration of a parent of gifted children. *Keeping in Touch,* pp. 3–4.

Rittenhouse, R.K. (1987). The attitudes of teachers toward mainstreaming of hearing impaired high schoolers. *Journal of Rehabilitation of the Deaf, 20,* 11–13

Rizzo, J.V. and Zabel, R.H. (1988). *Educating children and adolescents with behavioral disorders: An integrative approach.* Boston, MA: Allyn and Bacon.

Roach, V. (1995). Supporting inclusion: Beyond the rhetoric. *Phi Delta Kappan,* 77, 295–299,

Robert, L.J. (1995). An epidemiological study of behaviour disorders in the Saskatoon Tribal council student population. M.Ed. thesis, University of Saskatchewan.

Roberts, C., Pratt, C., and Leach, D. (1991). Classroom and playground interactions of students with and without disabilities. *Exceptional Children, 57,* 212–224.

Roberts, J. (2000). Pediatric HIV/AIDS: A review of neurological and psychosocial implications of infection. *Canadian Journal of School Psychology,* 15, 19–34.

Roberts, J.E., Burchind, M.R., Koch, M.A., Fodto, M.M., and Henderson, F.W. (1988, November). Otitis media in early childhood and its relationship to later phonological development. *Journal of Speech and Hearing Disorders,* pp. 424–432.

Roberts, K. (1997). A preliminary account of the effects of otitis media on 15-month-olds' categorization and some implications for early language learning. *Journal of Speech, Language and Hearing Research, 40,* 508–518.

Roberts, R. and Mather, N. (1995). The return of students with learning disabilities to regular classrooms: A sellout? *Learning Disabilities Research and Practice,* 10, 46–58.

Robins, L.N. and Earls, F. (1985). A program for preventing antisocial behavior for high-risk infants and presechoolers: A research prospectus. In R.L. Hugh, P.A. Gongla, V.B. Brown, and S.E. Goldston (Eds.) *Psychiatric epidemiology and prevention: The possibilities* (pp. 73–84) Los Angeles, CA: Neuropsychiatric Institute.

Robinson, D.O., Allen, D.V., and Root, L.P. (1988). Infant tympanometry: Differential results by race. *Journal of Speech and Hearing Disorders, 53,* 341–346.

Robinson, G.A., Palton, J.R., Polloway, E.A, and Sargent, L.R. (Eds.). (1989). *Best practices in mental retardation.* Reston, VA: Council for Exceptional Children.

Rock, E.E., Fessler, M.A., and Church, R.P. (1997). The concomitance of learning disabilities and emotional/behavioral disorders: A conceptual model. *Journal of Learning Disabilities, 30,* 245–263.

Rockefeller, N.A. (1976, October 16). Don't accept anyone's verdict that you are lazy, stupid or retarded. *TV Guide,* pp. 12–14.

Rodda, M., Grove, C., and Finch, B.M. (1986). Mainstreaming and the education of deaf students. *Alberta Journal of Educational Research, 32,* 140–153.

Roderick, M. and Camburn, E .(1999). Risk and recovery from course failure in the early years of high school. *American Educational Research Journal,* 36, 303–343.

Rodger, N.W. and Hunt, J.A. (1980). *Research horizons.* Toronto: Canadian Diabetic Association.

Rodin, D. (1989). Prognisis of cognitive function in children with epilepsy. In B.P. Hermann and M. Seidenberg (Eds.) *Childhood epilepsies: Neurophysiological, psychosocial and intervention aspects* (pp. 33–50). New York: Wiley.

Rogan, L.L. and Hardman, L.D. (1990). Adult outcome of learning disabled students 10 years after initial follow-up. *Learning Disability Focus, 5,* 91–102.

Rogers, K.B. (1990, November). Using effect size to make good decisions about acceleration. Paper presented at the National Association for Gifted Children, Little Rock, Arkansas.

Rogers, S.J. (1988). Cognitive characteristics of handicapped children's play: A review. *Journal of the Division for Early Childhood, 12,* 161–168.

Rogers-Dulan, J. (1998). Religious beliefs among urban African-American families who have a child with a disability. *Mental Retardation, 36,* 91–103.

Rogow, S. (1987). Children with multiple handicaps. In M. Winzer, S. Rogow, and C. David. *Exceptional children in Canada.* Toronto: Prentice-Hall.

Rosenblith, J.F. and Sims-Knight, J.E. (1985). *In the beginning: Development in the first two years.* Monterey, CA: Brooks/Cole.

Ross, M. (1990). Implications of delay in detection and management of deafness. *Volta Review, 92,* 69–79.

Ross, R. (1979). A program model for altering children's consciousness. *Gifted Child Quarterly, 23,* 109–117.

Roth, M., McCaul, E. and Barnes, K. (1993). Who becomes an "At-risk" student? The predictive value of a kindergarten screening battery. *Exceptional Children, 59,* 348–358.

Rovet, J.F., Erlich, R.M., and Hoppe, M. (1988). Specific intellectual deficits in childhood with early onset diabetes mellitus. *Child Development, 59,* 226–234.

Ruppert, E.S. and Buhrer, K. (1992). Ohio's infant hearing screening and assessment program. *Clinical Pediatrics, 31,* 19–22.

Russell, A.T., Bott, L., and Sammons, C. (1989). The phenomonology of schizophrenia occurring in childhood. *Journal of the American Academy of Child and Adolescent Psychiatry, 28,* 399–407.

Rutherford, R.B. (1997, July). Why doesn't social skills training work? *CEC Today,* p. 14.

Rutter, M. (1983). Cognitive defects in the pathogenesis of autism. *Journal of Child Psychology and Psychiatry, 24,* 513–531.

Rydell, P.J. and Mirenda, P. (1991). The effects of two levels of linguistic constraint on echolalia and generative language production in children with autism. *Journal of Autism and Developmental Disorders, 21,* 131–157.

Rylance, B. J. (1997). Predictors of high school graduation or dropping out for youths with severe emotional disturbance. *Behavioral Disorders,* 23, 5–17.

Sacks S.Z. and Corn A.L. (1996). Students with visual impairments: Do they understand their disability? *Journal of Visual Impairment and Blindness, 90,* 412–422.

Sadker, D. (1999). Gender equity: Still knocking on the classroom door. *Educational Leadership, 56,* 22–26.

Safer, D.J. and Krager, J.M. (1988). A survey of medication treatment for hyperactive/inattentive students. *Journal of the American Medical Association, 260,* 2256–2258.

Safran, S.P. and Safran, J.S. (1987). Teachers' judgment of problem behaviors. *Exceptional Children, 54,* 240–244.

Sagal, R., Rosenbaum, P., Stotskopf, B., and Milner, R. (1982). Follow-up of infants 501 to 1500 gm birth weight delivered to residents of a geographically defined region with perinatal intensive care facilities. *Journal of Pediatrics, 100,* 606–613.

Sailor, W., Guess, D., Goetz, L., Schuler, A., Utley, B., and Baldwin, M. (1980). Language and severely handicapped persons: Deciding what to teach to whom. In W. Sailor, B. Wilcox, and L. Brown (Eds). *Methods of instruction for severely handicapped students.* Baltimore, MD: Brookes.

Salend, S.J., and Andress, M. (1984). Decreasing stuttering in an elementary level student. *Journal of Language, Speech and Hearing Services in the Schools,* 15, 133–140.

Salend, S.J. and Longo, M. (1994). The roles of the educational interpreter in mainstreaming. *Teaching Exceptional Children, 26,* 22–28.

Salisbury, C.L. (1987). Stressors of parents with young handicapped and nonhandicapped children. *Journal of the Division for Early Childhood, 11,* 154–160.

Salisbury, C.L. (1991). Mainstreaming during the early childhood years. *Exceptional Children, 58,* 146–155.

Salisbury C.L., Evans, I.M., and Palombaro, M.M. (1997). Collaborative problem-solving to promote the inclusion of young children with significant disabilities in primary grades. *Exceptional Children, 63,* 195–209.

Salkind, N. (1990). *Child Development* (6th ed.) Fort Worth, TX: Holt, Reinhart and Winston.

Salomon-Weiss, M.J., Wagner, S.H., and Bauman M.L.

(1996). A validated case of facilitated communication. *Mental Retardation, 34,* 220–230.

Salt, P., Galler, J.R., and Ramsey, F.C. (1988). The influence of early malnutrition on subsequent behavioral development. *Developmental and Behavioral Pediatrics,* 9, 1–5.

Salzberg, C.L. and Morgan, J. (1995). Preparing teachers to work with paraeducators. *Teacher Education and Special Education, 18,* 49–55.

Salzberg, C.L., Lignugaris-Kraft, B., and McCuller, G.L. (1988). Reasons for job loss: A review of employment termination studies of mentally retarded workers. *Research in Developmental Disabilities, 9,* 153–170.

Samson, G.E. (1985). Effects of training in test-taking skills on achievement test performance: A quantitative synthesis. *Journal of Educational Research, 78,* 261–266.

Sancilio, M.F.M, Plumment, J.M., and Hartup, W.W. (1989). Friendships and aggressiveness as determiners of conflict outcomes in middle children. *Developmental Psychology, 25,* 812–819.

Sanders, D. (1971). *Aural rehabilitation.* Englewood Cliffs, NJ: Prentice-Hall.

Sandler, A.M.G. (1998). Grandparents of children with disabilities: A closer look. *Education and Training in Mental Retardation and Developmental Disabilities, 33,* 350–356.

Sandor, G. (1981). Fetal alcohol syndrome: Cardiac malformations. *BC Medical Journal, 23,* 326–327.

Sandoval, J. (1998). Neuromuscular diseases. In L. Phelps (Ed.) *Health-related disorders in children and adolescents: A guidebook for understanding and educating* (pp. 463–473). Washington, D.C.: American Psychological Association.

Santos, K.E. (1992). Fragile X Syndrome: An educator's role in identification, prevention, and intervention. *Remedial and Special Education, 13,* 32–37.

Sapon-Shevin, H. (1984). The tug-of-war nobody wins: Allocations of educational resources for handicapped, gifted, and 'typical' students. *Curriculum Inquiry, 14,* 57–81.

Savage, H. (1983). The Canadian Charter and the rights of handicapped persons: The moral imperative of blood, sweat and tears. *Canadian Journal on Mental Retardation, 33,* 28–31.

Savage, L.B. and Wienke, W.D. (1989). Attitude of secondary teachers toward mainstreaming. *High School Journal,* 73, 70–73.

Savage, R.C. (1988). Introduction to educational issues for students who have suffered traumatic brain injury. In R.C. Savage and G.F. Wolcott (Eds.) *An educators' manual: What educators need to know about students with traumatic brain injury.* Scarborough, MA: National Head Injury Foundation.

Savage, R.C. and Wolcott, G.F. (1994). Overview of acquired brain injury. In R.C. Savage and G.F. Wolcott (Eds.) *Educational dimensions of acquired brain injury* (pp. 3–12). Austin TX: Pro-Ed.

Sawyer, D.J. (1987). *Test of awareness of language segments.* Frederick, MD: Aspen.

Scaldwell, W.A. and Frame, J.E. (1985). Prevalence of otitis media in Cree and Ojibway school children in six Ontario communities. *Journal of American Indian Education, 25,* 1–5.

Scarborough, H. (1989). Prediction of reading disability from familial and individual differences. *Journal of Educational Psychology, 81,* 101–108.

Scarborough, H. (1990). Very early language deficits in dyslexic children. *Child Development, 61,* 1728–1743.

Scaringi, M. (1994, fall). A study in pediatric brain injury. *Disability Today,* pp. 75–77.

Scarr-Salapatek, S. (1975). Genetics and the development of intelligence. In F.D. Horowitz (Ed.) *Review of child development research* (Vol. 4) Chicago, IL: University of Chicago Press.

Schaffner, B. and Buswell, B. (1991). *Opening doors: Strategies for including all students in regular education.* Colorado Springs, CO: Peak Parent Center, Inc.

Schein, J.D. (1989). *At home among strangers: Exploring the deaf community in the United States.* Washington, DC: Gallaudet University Press.

Schein, J.D. (1994). *Deafness in Canada and the United States.* Deaf American Monographs, pp. 93–99.

Schein, J.D., Kates, L., Wolf, E.G., and Theil, L. (1983). Assessing and developing communication abilities of deaf-blind children. *Journal of Visual Impairment and Blindness, 77,* 152–157.

Schick, B. and Moeller, M. (1989). The expressive English language of deaf students exposed to SEE 1. Paper presented at American Speech and Language Association annual meeting, St. Lois, Missouri.

Schiff, N.B. and Ventry, I.M. (1976). Communication problems in hearing children of deaf parents. *Journal of Speech and Hearing Disorders, 41,* 348–358.

Schildroth, A.N. and Hotto, S. (1996). Annual survey of hearing impaired children and youth: 1991-92 school year. *American Annals of the Deaf, 138,* 163–171.

Schlesinger, H.S. and Meadow, K.P. (1972). *Sound and sign: Childhood deafness and mental health.* Berkely, CA: University of California Press.

Schneider, B.H., Clegg, M.R., Byrne, B.M., Ledingham, J.E., and Crombie, G. (1992). Social relations of gifted children as a function of age and school program. In S. Towson (Ed.) *Educational psychology: Readings for the Canadian context.* Peterborough, ON: Broadview.

School-wide behavior management systems: A promising practice for safer schools (1997). *Research Connections in Special Education,* 1, whole issue.

Schopler, E., Reichler, R.J., De Vellis, R.F., and Daly, K.

(1980). Toward objective classification of childhood autism: Childhood Autism Rating Scale (CARS). *Journal of Autism and Developmental Disorders, 19,* 91–103.

Schorr, L.B. (1988). *Within our reach.* New York: Doubleday.

Schorr Ribera, H.K. (1987). Ethnicity and culture as relevant rehabilitation factors in families with children with disabilities. In M. Seligman (Ed.) *The family with a handicapped child* (2nd ed.) Boston, MA: Allyn and Bacon.

Schreibman, L. and Charlop, M.H. (1989). Infantile autism. In T.H. Ollendick and M. Hersen (Eds.) *Handbook of child psychopathology* (2nd ed.) New York: Plenum.

Schroedel, J. (1992). Helping adolescents and young adults who are deaf make career decisions. *Volta Review, 93,* 37–46.

Schroeder, F.K. (1996). Perceptions of braille usage by legally blind adults. *Journal of Visual Impairment and Blindness, 90,* 210–218.

Schumaker, J.B. and Deshler, D.D. (1988). Implementing the Regular Education Initiative in secondary schools: A different ball game. *Journal of Learning Disabilities, 21,* 36–42.

Schunk, D.H. (1987). Peer models and children's behavioral change. *Review of Educational Research, 57,* 149–174.

Schwartz, L.L. (1980). Advocacy for the neglected gifted: Females. *Gifted Child Quarterly, 24,* 113–117.

Schwartz M.F. (1988). *Stuttering solved.* New York: National Center for Stuttering.

Schwartz, M.H., Wolfe, J.N., and Cassar, R. (1997). Predicting teacher referrals of emotionally disturbed children. *Psychology in the Schools, 34,* 51–61.

Scruggs, T.E. and Mastropieri, M.A. (1989). Reconstructive elaborations: A model for content area learning. *American Educational Research Journal, 26,* 311–327.

Scruggs, T.E. and Mastropieri, M.A. (1990). The case for mnemonic instruction: From laboratory investigations to classroom applications. *Journal of Special Education, 24,* 7–32.

Scruggs, T.E. and Mastropieri, M.A. (1996). Teacher perceptions of mainstreaming/inclusion: A research synthesis. *Exceptional Children, 63,* 59–74.

Schvaneveldt, J.D., Lindauer, S.L.K., and Young, M.H. (1990). Childrens' understanding of AIDS: A developmental viewpoint. *Family Relations,* 39, 33–335.

Sciutto, M.J., Terjesen, M.D., and Bender Frank, A.S. (2000). Teachers' knowledge and misconceptions of attention deficit/hyperactivity disorder. *Psychology in the Schools, 37,* 115–122.

Seidel, V.P., Chadwick, O.F.D., and Rutter, M. (1975). Psychological disorders in crippled children: A comparative study with and without bone damage. *Genetic Psychology Monograph, 75,* 255–335.

Seidenberg, P.L. (1997). Understanding learning disabilities. In D.K. Bernsteinad and E. Tiegerman-Farker (Eds.) *Language and communication disorders in children* (4th ed.) Boston, MA: Allyn and Bacon.

Seligman, M. (1991). Siblings of disabled brothers and sisters. In M. Seligman (Ed.) *The family with a handicapped child* (2nd ed.) Boston, MA: Allyn and Bacon.

Semel, E. and Wiig, E. (1980). *Clinical Evaluation of Language Functions.* Columbus, OH: Merrill.

Semmel, M.I., Abernathy, T.V., Butera, G., and Lesar, S. (1991). Teacher perception of the regular education initiative. *Exceptional Children, 58,* 9–23.

Sexton, M., Harris, K.R., and Graham, S. (1998). Self-regulated strategy development and the writing process: Effects on essay writing and arttributions. *Exceptional Children, 64,* 295–311.

Shames, G.H. and Wiig, E. (1990). *Human communication disorders* (3rd ed.) Columbus, OH: Merrill.

Shaver, K., Boughman, J., and Nance, W. (1985). Congenital rubella syndrome and diabetes: A review of epidemiologic, genetic, and immunologic factors. *American Annals of the Deaf, 85,* 526–532.

Shaywitz, S.E. and Shaywitz, B.A. (1987). Attention deficit disorder: Current perspectives. Paper presented at the National Conference on Learning Disabilities. Bethesda, MD: National Institute for Child Health and Human Development.

Shonkoff, J. and Hauser-Cram, P. (1987). Early intervention for disabled infants and their families: A quantative analysis. *Pediatrics, 80,* 650–658.

Shonkoff, J. and Meisels, S. (1990). Early childhood intervention. In S. Meisels and J. Shonkoff (Eds.) *Handbook of early intervention* (pp. 3–32) New York: Cambridge University Press.

Shore, B. and Tsiamis, A. (1986). Identification by provision: Limited field test of a radical alternative for identifying gifted children. In K. Heller and J. Feldhusen (Eds.) *Identifying and nurturing the gifted* (pp. 93–102). Toronto: Hans Huber.

Siegel, S., Robert, M., and Gaylord Ross, R. (1992). A follow-along study of participants in a longitudinal transition program for youths with mild disabilities. *Exceptional Children, 58,* 346–356.

Siegler, R.S. and Kotovsky, K. (1985). Two levels of giftedness: Shall ever the twain meet? In R.J. Sternberg and J.E. Davidson (Eds.) *Conceptions of giftedness* (pp. 417–435) New York: Cambridge University Press.

Sigafoos, J., Cole, D.A., and McQuarter. (1987). Current practices in the assessment of students with severe handicaps. *Journal of the Association for Persons with Severe Handicaps, 12,* 264–273.

Sigelman C.K. and Shaffer, D.R. (1991). *Life-span human development.* Pacific Grove, CA: Brooks/Cole.

Silberman, R. (1981). A comparison of visual functioning in

hearing-impaired children and normally hearing children. *Volta Review, 83,* 95–104.

Silva, P.A. (1980). The prevalence, stability and significance of developmental language delays in preschool children. *Developmental Medicine and Child Neurology, 22,* 768–777.

Silverman, L.K. (1989). Invisible gifts, invisible handicap. *Roeper Review, 12,* 37–42.

Simen, R.J. and Rogers, R.C. (1989). School psychology and medical diagnosis: The fragile x syndrome. *Psychology in the Schools, 26,* 380–388.

Simner, M. L. (1997). *Predicting and preventing early school failure: Classroom activities for the preschool child.* Ottawa: Canadian Psychological Association.

Simner, M.L. and Eidlitz, M.R. (2000). Towards an empirical definition of developmental dysgraphia: Preliminary findings. *Canadian Journal of School Psychology, 16,* 103–110.

Simon, E.W., Toll, D.M., and Whitehair P.M. (1994). A naturistic appproach to the validation of facilitated communication. *Journal of Autism and Developmental Disorders, 24,* 647–657.

Simpson, R.L. and Myles, B. S. (1993). Successful integration of children with autism in mainstreamed settings. *Focus on Autistic Behavior, 7,* 1–13.

Simpson, R.L. and Myles, B. (1995, May). Facilitated communication and children with disabilities: An enigma in search of a perspective? *Focus on Exceptional Children,* 1–16.

Simpson, R.L. and Myles, B. (1998). Aggression among children and youth who have Asperger's syndrome.: A different population requiring different strategies. *Preventing School Failure,* 42, 149–153.

Simonds, R.J. and Rogers, M.F. (1992). Epidemiology of HIV in children and other populations. In A. Crocker, H. Cohen, and T. Kastner (Eds.) *HIV infection and developmental disabilities: A resource for service providers* (pp. 3–13). Baltmore, MD: Brookes.

Sinclair, E. (1998). Head Start children at risk: Relationships of prenatal drug exposure to education of special needs and subsequent special education kindergarten placement. *Behavioral Disorders, 23,* 125–133.

Singer, J.D. (1988). Should special education merge with regular education? *Educational Policy, 2,* 409–424.

Singleton, J., Supalla, S., Lotchfield, S., and Schley, S. (1998). From sign to word: Considering modality constraints in ASL/English bilingual education. *Topics in Language Disorders,* 18, 16–29.

Sinnot-Oswald, M., Gliner, J.A., Spencer, K.C. (1991). Supported and sheltered employment: Quality of life issues among workers with disabilities. *Education and Training in Mental Retardation, 9,* 388–397.

Siperstein, G.N. and Leffert, J.S. (1997). Comparisons of socially accepted and rejected children with mental retardation. *American Journal on Mental Retardation, 101,* 339–351.

Sisson, L.A., Van Hasselt, V.B., and Hersen, M. (1987). Psychological approaches with deaf-blind persons: Strategies and issues in research and treatment. *Clinical Psychology Review, 7,* 303–328.

Sitlington, P.L., Frank, A.R., and Carson, R. (1992). Adult adjustment among high school graduates with mild disabilities. *Exceptional Children, 59,* 221–233.

Sivin-Kachala, J. and Bialo, E.R. (1995). *Report on the effectiveness of technology in schools, 1990-1994.* Washngton, DC: Software Publishers Association.

Siwolop, S. and Mohs, M. (1985, February). The war on Down syndrome. *Discover,* pp. 67–73.

Skelly, M. (1979). *Amer-Ind gestural code based on universal American Indian hand talk.* New York: Elsivien.

Slate, J.R. and Jones, C.H. (2000). Assessment issues in special education. In M. Winzer and K. Mazurek (Eds.) *Special education in the 21st century: Issues of inclusion and reform* (pp.69-81). Washington, DC: Gallaudet University Press.

Slavin, R.R., Madden, N.E., Kariviet, N.L., Liverman, B.J., and Dolan, L. (1990). Success for all: First year outcomes of a comprehensive plan for reforming urban education. *American Education Research Journal, 27,* 255–278.

Slee, R. (1997). Inclusion or assimilation? Sociological explorations of the foundations of theories of special education. *Educational Foundations, 11,* 55–71.

Sleeter, C.E. (1986). Learning disabilities: The social construction of a special education category. *Exceptional Children, 53,* 46–54.

Sleeter, C.E and Grant, C.A. (1994). *Making choices for multicultural education: Five approaches to race, class, and gender.* New York: Merrill.

Sloane, D.C. and Sloane, B.C. (1990). AIDS in schools: A comprehensive initiative. *McGill Journal of Education, 25,* 205–228.

Smith, A.J., Del'aunne, W., and Geruschat, D.R. (1992). Low vision mobility problems: Perceptions of O and M specialists and persons with low vision. *Journal of Visual Impairment and Blindness, 86,* 58–62.

Smith, B. (1995, June). Implications of the Eaton case. *Alberta CEC,* 5, p. 7.

Smith, D.D. and Luckasson, R. (1995). *Introduction to special education: Teaching in an age of challenge* (2nd ed.) Needham Heights, MA: Allyn and Bacon.

Smith, D.D. and Robinson, S. (1986). Educating the learning disabled. In R.J. Morris and B. Blatt (Eds.) *Special education: Research and trends* (pp. 222–248). New York: Pergamon.

Smith, P.K. and Thompson D. (1991). *Practical approaches to bullying.* Great Britain: David Fulton.

Smith, S.D. and Pennington, B.F. (1987). Genetic influences. In K.A. Kavale and S.R. Forness (Eds.) *Handbook of learning disabilities (vol. 1) Dimensions and diagnosis* (pp. 49–75). San Diego, CA: College-Hill.

Smith, S.P. (1978). Some (not all) facts about asthma. *Journal of School Health, 48,* 311.

Smith W.J. (1994). *Equal educational opportunity for students with disabilities: Legislative action in Canada.* McGill University, Office of Research on Educational Policy.

Snell, M.E. (1987). *Systematic instruction of persons with severe handicaps* (3rd ed.) Columbus, OH: Merrill.

Snow, C. (1987). Relevance of the notion of a critical period of language acquisition. In M.H. Bornstein (Ed.) *Sensitive periods in development: Interdisciplinary perspectives* (pp. 183–210). Hillsdale, NJ: Erlbaum.

Snow, J. and Forest, M. (1987). Circles. In M. Forest (Ed.) *More educational intervention* (pp. 169–176) Downsview, Ontario: G. Allan Roeher Institute.

Soare, P.L. and Raimondi, A. (1977). Intellectual and perceptual-motor characteristics of treated myelomeningocele children. *American Journal of Diseases in Children, 131,* 199–204.

Soucy, M. and Andrews, J. (1997). The underlying structures of autism: An exploratory factor analytic study. *Canadian Journal of School Psychology, 13,* 85–98.

Southern, W.T., Jones, E.D., and Fiscus, E.D. (1989). Practitioner objections to the academic acceleration of gifted children. *Gifted Child Quarterly, 33,* 29–35.

Spafford, C. and Grosser, G. (1996). *Dyslexia: Research and resource guide.* Boston, MA: Allyn and Bacon.

Spain, B. (1972). Verbal and performance ability in preschool spina bifida children. *Developmental Medicine and Child Neurology, 27,* 155.

Sparrow, S.S., Balla, D.A., and Cicchetti, D.V. (1984). *Vineland Adaptive Behavior Scale.* Circle Pines, MN: American Guidance Services.

Speaking out on the model for delivery of support to students with exceptionalities (1999, spring/summer) *Keeping in Touch,* p. 7.

Speltz, M.L., Endriga, M.C., Fisher, P.A., and Mason, C.A. (1997). Early predictors of attachment in infants with cleft lip and/or palate. *Child Development, 68,* 12–25.

Spitz, R.V., Tallal, P., Flax, J., and Benasich A.A. (1997). Look who's talking: A prospective study on familial transmission of language impairments. *Journal of Speech, Language and Hearing Research, 40,* 990–1001.

Spradlin, J.E. and Siegel, G.M. (1982). Language training in natural and clinical environments. *Journal of Speech and Hearing Disorders, 47,* 2–6.

Sprague, J. and Walker, H. (2000). Early identification and intervention for youth with antisocial and violent behavior. *Exceptional Children, 66,* 367–379.

Spring, C. and Sandoval, J. (1976). Food additives and hyperkenesis: A critical evaluation of the evidence. *Journal of Learning Disabilities,* 9, 560–569.

Sprinthall, N.A. and Sprinthall, R.C. (1990). *Educational psychology: A developmental approach* (5th ed) New York: Random House.

Squires, D. (1992, June). Forum 11: An overview, *Keeping in Touch,* pp. 2–3.

Sridhar, D. and Vaughn, S. (2000). Bibliotherapy for all: Enhancing reading comprehension, self-concept, and behavior. *Teaching Exceptional Children, 33,* 74–82.

Stainback, S. and Stainback, W. (1988). Educating students with severe disabilities. *Teaching Exceptional Children, 21,* 16–19.

Stainback, W., Stainback, S., and Stefanich, G. (1996). Learning together in inclusive classrooms: What about the curriculum? *Teaching Exceptional Children,* 28, 14–19.

Stanley, J.C. and Benbow, C.P. (1986). Extremely young college gaduates: Evidence of their success. *College and University, 58,* 361–371.

Statement of policy approved for bilingual/bicultural program Ontario. (1993). *Deaf Education, 2,* 1–2.

Staub, D. and Hunt, P. (1993). The effects of social interaction training on high school peer tutors of schoolmates with severe disabilities. *Exceptional Children, 60,* 41–57.

Steele, B.F. (1986). Notes on the lasting effects of early child abuse throughout the life cycle. *Child Abuse and Neglect, 10,* 283–291.

Steffenburg, S., Gillberg, C., Hellgren, L., Andersson, L., Gillberg, I.C., Jakonsson, G., and Bohman M. (1989). A twin study of autism in Denmark, Finland, Iceland, Norway, and Sweden. *Journal of Child Psychology and Psychiatry, 30,* 405–416.

Stephens, O. (1989). Braille—Implications for living. *Journal of Visual Impairment and Blindness, 83,* 288–289.

Sternberg, R.J. (1987). A unified theory of intellectual exceptionality. In J.D. Day and J.G. Borkowski (Eds.) *Intelligence and exceptionality: New directions for theory, assessment and instructional practices* (pp. 135–172). Norwood, NJ: Ablex.

Sternberg, R.J. and Davidson, J.E. (1986). (Eds.) *Conceptions of giftedness.* New York: Cambridge University Press.

Sternberg, R.J and Lubart, R. (1995). *Defying the crowd.* New York: Free Press.

Stevens, D.D. and Englert, C.S. (1993). Making writing systems work. *Teaching Exceptional Children, 26,* 34–39.

Stewart, D.A. (1984). Mainstreaming deaf children: A different perspective. *The ACHEI Journal, 10,* 91–104.

Stewart, D.A. and Akamatsu, C.T. (1988). The coming of age of American Sign Language. *Anthropology and Education Quarterly, 19,* 235–252.

Stillman, R. (Ed.) (1978). *The Callier-Azusa Scale.* Dallas, TX: Callier Center for Communication Disorders, University of Texas at Dallas.

Stokoe, W.C., Jr. and Battiston, R. (1975). *Sign language, mental health and satisfactory interaction.* Linguistic Research Laboratory, Gallaudet College, Washington, DC.

Stoll, C. (1995). *Silicon snake oil: Second thoughts on the information highway.* New York: Doubleday.

Stone, P. and Adam, A. (1986). Is your child wearing the right hearing aid? Principles for selecting and maintaining amplification. *Volta Review, 88,* 45–54.

Story, C.M. (1985). Facilitation of learning: A micro-ethnographic study of the teacher of the gifted. *Gifted Child Quarterly, 29,* 155–159.

Stough L.M. and Baker L. (1999). Identifying depression in students with mental retardation. *Teaching Exceptional Children, 31,* 62–66.

Stratz, E. (1994). Cross-Canada survey of programs for behaviourally disordered children and youth. M. Ed. thesis, University of Saskatchewan.

Stromsness, M.M. (1993). Sexualy abused women with mental retardation: Hidden victims, absent resources. *Women and Therapy, 14,* 139–152.

Strong, K. and Sandoval, J. (1999). Mainstreaming children with neuromuscular disease: A map of concerns. *Exceptional Children, 65,* 353–366.

Subsotnik, R. (1997). Teaching students in a multicultural society. In J. Banks and C. Banks (Eds.) *Multicultural education: issues and perspectives* (3rd ed.) (pp. 361–382) Boston, MA: Allyn and Bacon.

Sugai, G. and Horner, R. (1994). Including students with severe behavioural problems in general edcuation settings: Assumptions, challenges, and solutions. In J. Marr, G. Sugai, and G. Tindel (Eds.) *The Oregon Conference Monograph* (vol. 6) (pp. 109–120). Eugene, OR: University of Oregon.

Sullivan. M. (1988). *A comparative anaylsis of dropouts and non-dropouts in Ontario secondary schools.* Toronto: Ontario Ministry of Education.

Supalla, S. (1992). Equal educational opportunity: The Deaf version. In M. Walworth, D. Moores, and T.J. O'Rourke (eds.) *A free hand* (pp. 17–181). Silver Spring, MD: T,J. Publishers.

Swanson, J.M. and Kinsbourne, M. (1980). Artificial food colourings impair the learning of hyperactive children. Report to the Nutrition Foundation, Hospital for Sick Children, Toronto.

Swanson, S. and Howell, C. (1996). Test anxiety in adolescents with learning disabilities and behavior disorders. *Exceptional Children, 62,* 389–397.

Swanwick, R.A. (1998). Learning English as a second language: Opportunities and challenges for sign bilingual deaf children. *Deafness and Education, 22,* 3–9.

Swiatek, M.A. and Benbow, C.P. (1991). Ten-year longitudinal follow-up of ability-matched accelerated and unaccelerated gifted students. *Journal of Educational Psychology, 83,* 528–538.

Sylvester, R. (1997, February). The neurobiology of self-esteem and aggression. *Educational Leadership, 54,* 75–79.

Szymanski, E.M. (1994). Transition: Life-span and life-space considerations for empowerement. *Exceptional Children, 60,* 402–410.

Tannenbaum, A.J. (1962). *Adolescent attitudes toward academic brilliance.* New York: Bureau of Publications, Teachers College, Columbia University.

Tannenbaum, A.J. (1986). The enrichment matric model. In J. S. Renzulli (Ed.) *Systems and models for developing programs for gifted and talented* (pp. 391–428) Mansfield Center, Conn: Creative Learning Press.

TASH, The Association for Persons with Severe Handicaps. (1986). Definition of the people TASH serves. In L. Myer, C.Peck, and L. Brown (Eds.) *Critical issues in the lives of people with severe disabilities.* Baltimore, MD: Brookes.

Taylor, R.L., Richards, S.B., Goldstein, P.A., and Schilit, J. (1997). Teacher perceptions of inclusive settings. *Teaching Exceptional Children, 29,* 50–54.

Telford, C. W. and Sawrey, J. M. (1981). *The exceptional individual* (4th ed.) Englewood Cliffs, NJ: Prentice-Hall.

Teplin, S.W. (1995). Visual impairment in infants and young children. *Infants and Young Children, 8,* 18–51.

Terman, L.M. (1926). *Genetic studies of genius: Mental and physical traits of a thousand gifted children* (2nd ed.) Stanford, CA: Stanford University Press.

Terman, L.M. and Oden, M.H. (1951). The Stanford studies of the gifted. In P. Witty (Ed.) *The gifted child.* Lexington, MA: D.C. Heath.

Terman, L.M. and Oden, M.H. (1959). *Genetic studies of genius: The gifted population at mid-life* (vol. 5). Stanford, CA: Stanford University Press.

Tew, B. and Lawrence, K. (1975). The effects of hydrocephalus on intelligence, visual perception, and school attainment. *Developmental Medicine and Neurology, 17* (supp. 35), 129–134.

Thompson, L.J. (1971). Language disabilities in men of eminence. *Journal of Learning Disabilities, 4,* 34–44.

Thorndike, R., Hagan, E. and Sattler, J. (1986). *The Stanford-Binet Intelligence Scale* (4th ed.) Chicago, IL: Riverside.

Tiessen, J. (1996, winter). Orthotics and prosthetics: Fit and fashion join a tradition of function. *Disability Today,* pp. 23–25.

Tomlinson C.A., Callahan, C.M., Tomchin, E.M., Eiss, N. Imbeau, M., and Lundrum, M. (1997). Becoming architects of communities of learning: Addressing academic diversity in contemporary classrooms. *Exceptional Children, 63,* 269–282.

Topping, K. (1989, March). Peer tutoring and paired reading: Combining two powerful techniques. *The Reading Teacher*, pp. 488–494.

Torgenson, J.K. (1988). Studies of children with learning disabilities who perform poorly on memory span task. *Journal of Learning Disabilities, 21,* 605–612.

Torgenson, J.K. (1998 spring summer) Catch them before they fall. *American Educator*, pp 32-41.

Torgesen, J.K. and Bryant, B. (1994). *Test of phonological awareness.* Austin, TX: Pro-Ed.

Torrance, E.P. (1966). *The Torrance Tests of Creative Thinking: Norms and technical manual.* Princeton, NJ: Personnel Press.

Torrance, E.P. (1969). Creative positives of disadvantaged children and youth. *Gifted Child Quarterly, 13,* 71–81.

Treffert, D.A. (1970). Epidemiology of infantile autism. *Archives of General Psychiatry, 23,* 431–438.

Treffinger, D. (1986). Research on creativity. *Gifted Child Quarterly, 30,* 15–19.

Trief, E., Duckman, R., Morse, A.R., and Silberman, R.K. (1989). Retinopathy of prematurity. *Journal of Visual Impairment and Blindness, 83,* 500–504.

Turnbull, A.P. and Ruef, M. (1997). Family perspectives on inclusive lifestyle issues for people with problem behavior. *Exceptional Children, 63,* 211–227.

Tyler, J.S. and Colson, S. (1994, December). Common pediatric disabilities: Medical aspects and educational implications. *Focus on Excepional Children*, 1–16.

Tyler, J.S and Mira, M.P. (1993). Educational modifications for students with head injuries. *Teaching Exceptional Children, 25,* 24–27.

United States Department of Health, Education and Welfare. (1977). Education of Handicapped Children: Implementation of Part B of the Education of the Handicapped Act. Federal Register, 42(163).

United States, Individuals with Disabilities Education Act amendments of 1997, 20 USC, #14000 (1997). ERIC Doc. No. Ed. 419-322.

United States, PL 101-476, Sec. 602 (a)(19)), IDEA, 1990.

Vallecorsa, A.L. and Garriss, E. (1990). Story composition skills of middle grade students with learning disabilities. *Exceptional Children, 57,* 48–54.

Van Dijk, J. (1982). *Rubella handicapped children: The effects of bilateral cataract and/or hearing impairment on behavior and learning.* The Netherlands: Swets and Zeitlinger.

Van Dyke, D.C. and Fox, A.A. (1990). Fetal drug exposure and its possible implications for learning in the preschool and school age population. *Journal of Learning Disabilities, 23,* 160–163.

Van Osdol, W.R. and Shane, D.B. (1982). *An introduction to exceptional children.* Dubuque, IA: William C. Brown.

Vanpoelvoorde, L. and Shaughnessy, M.F. (1991). Parental reactions to cleft palate children. *B.C. Journal of Special Education, 15,* 276–283.

Van Rijn, N. (2000, July 14). Guidelines suggest limited use of behaviour-altering drug in kids. *Lethbridge Herald*, p. A15.

Van Riper, C. and Emerick, L. (1990). *Speech correction: An introduction to speech pathology and audiology* (8th ed.) Englewood Cliffs, NJ: Prentice Hall.

Van Tassel Baska, J. (1987). The ineffectiveness of the pull-out model in gifted education: A minority perspective. *Journal for the Education of the Gifted, 10,* 255–264.

Van Tassel Baska, J. (1989). Appropriate curriculum for gifted learners. *Educational Leadership, 4,* 13–15.

Van Tassel Baska, J. (1994). *Comprehensive curriculum for gifted learners* (2nd ed.) Denver, CO: Love.

Van Tassel Baska, J. (1995). The development of talent through curriculum. *Roeper Review, 18,* 98–102.

Van Tassel-Baska J., Landau, M., and Olszewski, P. (1985). Toward developing an appropriate math/science curriculum for gifted learners. *Journal for Education of the Gifted, 7,* 257–272.

Vasquez, C.A. (1994). Brief report: A multitask controlled evaluation of facilitated communication. *Journal of Autism and Developmental Disorders, 24,* 369–379.

Vaughn, S., Bos, C., and Schumm, J.S. (1997). *Teaching mainstreamed, diverse, and at-risk students in the general education classroom.* Boston, MA: Allyn and Bacon.

Vaughn, S.E., Erlbaum, B.E., Schumm, J.S., and Hughes, M.T. (1998). Social outcomes for students with and without learning disabilities in inclusive classrooms. *Journal of Learning Disabilities, 31,* 428–436.

Vaughn, V.L., Feldhusen, J.F., and Asher, J.W. (1991). Meta-analyses and review of research on pull-out programs in gifted education. *Gifted Child Quarterly, 35,* 92–98.

Vaughn, S., Schumm, J.S., and Kouzekanani, K. (1993). What do students with learning disabilities think when general education teachers make adaptations? *Journal of Learning Disabilities,* 26, 545–555.

Vaughn, S., Schumm, J.S., Jallad, B., Slushar, J., and Saunell, L. (1996). Teachers' views of inclusion: *Learning Disabilities Research and Practice, 11,* 96–106.

Vergason, G.A. and Anderegg, M.L. (1993). Rich and Ross: A mixed message. *Exceptional Children, 59,* 475–476.

Vergason, G.A. and Anderegg, M.L. (1997). The ins and outs of special education terminology. *Teaching Exceptional Children, 29,* 34–39.

Verhaaran, P. and Connor, F.P. (1981). Physical disabilities. In J.M. Kauffman and D.P. Hallahan (Eds.) *Handbook of special education* (pp. 248–289). Englewood Cliffs, NJ: Prentice Hall.

Villaruel, B.A., Martin, C.A., and Dickson, W.P. (1985). Using a microcomputer to create social interactions among handicapped and nonhandicapped children in a mainstream preschool. Paper presented at AAMD conference, Denver.

Vitello, S.J. and Soskin, R.M. (1985). *Mental retardation: Its social and legal context.* Englewood Cliffs, NJ: Prentice-Hall.

Voignier, R.R. and Bridgewater, S.C. (1980). Allergies in young children. *Young Children, 35,* 67–70.

Vorhees, C.V. and Mollnow, E. (1987). Behavioral terategenesis: Long-term influences from early exposure to environmental agents. In J.D. Osfosky (Ed.) *Handbook of infant development* (pp. 913–972). New York: Wiley.

Wade, S.L., Taylor, H.G., Drotar, D., Stancin, T., and Yeates, K.O. (1996). Childhood traumatic brain injury: Initial impact on the family. *Journal of Learning Disabilities, 29,* 652–661.

Wagner, M., Newman, L., D'Amico, R., Jay, E.D., Butler-Nalin, P., Marder, C., and Cox, R. (1991, September). Youth with disabilities: How are they doing? The first comprehensive report from the National Longitudinal Transition Study of Special Education Students. Menlo Park, CA: SRI International.

Wagner, S. (1999). Focus on disablity — Asperger's syndrome. *CEC Today, 6,* p. 11,

Walberg, H.J. (1991). Improving school science in advanced and developed countries. *Review of Educational Research, 61,* 25–69.

Walker, H.M., and McConnell, S.R. (1988). *Walker-McConnell Scale of Social Competence and School Adjustment.* Austin, TX: Pro-Ed.

Walker, H.M. and Severson, H.H. (1990). *Systematic screening for behavior disorders (SSBD): A multiple gating procedure.* Longmont, CO: Sopris West.

Walker, H.M., Colvin, G., and Ramsey, E. (1995). *Antisocial behavior in schools: Strategies and best practices.* Pacific Grove, CA: Brooks/Cole.

Walmsley, S.A. and Allington, R.L. (1995). Redefining and reforming instructional support programs for at-risk students. In R.L. Allington and S.A. Walmsley (Eds.) *No quick fix* (pp. 19–44). New York: Teachers College Press.

Warren, D. (1984). *Blindness and early child development.* New York: American Foundation for the Blind.

Warren, P. (1988). *Teachers and the law.* St. John's: Memorial University of Newfoundland.

Warren, W. and Hasenstab, S. (1986). Self concept of severely to profoundly hearing-impaired children. *Volta Review, 88,* 289–295.

Wasik, B.H., Bryant, D.M., and Lyons, C.M. (1990). *Home visiting: Procedures for helping families.* Newbury Park, CA: Sage.

Watt, D.L.E. and Roessingh, H. (1993, October). Dropout—Fall out—Push out: Results from a longitudinal study of the educational progress of high school ESL students. Paper presented at the Alberta Teachers Association ESL Council, Calgary.

Webb, J.T., Meckstroth, E.A., and Tolan, S.S. (1982). *Guiding the gifted child: A practical source for parents and teachers.* Columbus, OH: Ohio Psychology Publishing.

Webb, T.P., Bundey, S.E., Thake, A.I., and Todd, J. (1986). Population incidence and segregation ratios in Martin-Bell syndrome. *American Journal of Medical Genetics, 23,* 573–580.

Weber, K. (1994). *Special education in Canadian schools.* Canada: Highland Press.

Wechsler, D. (1991). *Wechsler Intelligence Scale for Children,* 3rd ed. New York: Psychological Corporation.

Weiner, J. Harris, P.J., and Shirer, C. (1990). Achievement and social behavioral correlates of peer status in LD children. *Learning Disability Quarterly, 13,* 114–127.

Weiner, L. and Septimus, A. (1991). Psyhosocial consideration and support for the child and family. In P.A. Pizzo and C.M. Wilfert (Eds.) *Pediatric AIDS: The challenge of HIV infants, children and adolescents* (pp. 577–594). Baltimore, MD: Williams and Wilkins.

Weishaar, M.K. and Boyle, J.R. (1997, fall). Notetaking for students with disabilities. *CEC Today,* pp. 12.

Weiss, G. and Hechtman, L. (1979). The hyperactive child syndrome. *Science, 205,* 1348–1353.

Weiss, G. and Hechtman, L.T. (1986). *Hyperactive children grown up.* New York: Guilford.

Weiss, J.B. and Weiss, J. (1981). Use of the talking calculator to improve mathematical skills. *Journal of Visual Impairment and Blindness, 75,* 61–63.

Welch, T. and Goetz, L. (1998). Issues and concerns related to inclusive education of students who are deaf blind: Findings of the task force of a model demonstration project. *Deaf Blind Perspectives, 4,* 1–6.

Wenar, C. (1994). *Developmental psychopathology* (3rd ed.). New York: McGraw Hill.

Wenz-Gross, M. and Siperstein, G.N. (1997). Importance of social support in the adjustment of children with learning problems. *Exceptional Children, 63,* 183–193.

Wesanko, E. (1990, June). Long term consequences of communication disorders. *Keeping in Touch,* p. 2.

West, J.F. and Cannon, G. (1987). Essential collaborative consultation competencies for regular and special educators. *Journal of Learning Disabilities, 21,* 56–63.

Westat Inc. (1994). *Issues and options in outcome-based accountability for students with disabilities.* College Park, MD: Center for Policy Options in Special Education.

Whinnery, K.H., King, M., Evans, W.H., and Gable, R.A. (1995). Perceptions of students with learning disabilities: Inclusion versus pull-out services. *Preventing School Failure, 40,* 5–9.

White, K.R. Bush, D., and Casto, G. (1986). Let the past be

prologue: Learning from previous reviews of early intervention efficacy research. *Journal of Special Education, 19,* 417–428.

Whitlock, M.S. and Du Cette, J.P. (1989). Outstanding and average teachers of the gifted: A comparative study. *Gifted Child Quarterly, 33,* 15–21.

Whitman, B.C., Simpson, G.B., and Compton, W.C. (1986). Relationship of otitis media and language impairment in adolescents with Down syndrome. *Mental Retardation, 24,* 353–356.

Whitman, T.L. and Scibak, J.W. (1979). Behavior modification research with the severely and profoundly retarded. In N.R. Ellis (Ed.) *Handbook of mental deficiency: Psychological theory and research* (2nd ed.) Hillsdale, NJ: Erlbaum.

Whitmore, J.R. (1979). The etiology of underachievement in highly gifted young children. *Journal for the Education of the Gifted, 3,* 38–51.

Whitmore, J.R. (1980). *Giftedness, conflict and underachievement.* Boston, MA: Allyn and Bacon.

Whitmore, J.R. (1985, November). Creating appropriate conditions for gifted students in the regular school program. Paper presented at the British Columbia Council for Exceptional Children conference.

Whitmore, J.R. (1988). Gifted children at risk for learning difficulties. *Teaching Exceptional Children, 20,* 10–14.

Whitmore, J.R. and Maker, J. (1985). *Intellectual giftedness in disabled persons.* Rockville, MD: Pen.

Wicks-Nelson, R. and Israel, A.C. (1991). *Behavior disorders of childhood* (2nd ed.) Englewood Cliffs, NJ: Prentice-Hall.

Widom, C.S. (1989). Does violence beget violence? A critical examination of the literature. *Psychological Bulletin, 106,* 3–28.

Wiggins, S.B. and Behrmann, M.M. (1988). Increasing independence through community learning. *Teaching Exceptional Children, 21,* 20–24.

Wiig, E.H. and Semel, E. (1976). *Language disabilities in children and adolescents.* Columbus, OH: Merrill.

Wikler, L., Wasow, M., and Hatfield, E. (1981). Chronic sorrow revisited: Parent vs professional depiction of the adjustment of parents of mentally retarded children. *American Journal of Orthopsychiatry, 51,* 63–70.

Wilczenski, F.L. (1992). Measuring attitudes toward inclusion. *Psychology in the Schools,* 29, 306–312.

Wilgosh, L. (1990, December). Issues in education and daily living for families of children with disabilities. *Alberta Journal of Educational Research, 36,* 299–309.

Will, M. (1986). Educating students with learning problems: A shared responsibility. *Exceptional Children, 52,* 405–411.

Will, G. (1999, December 5). Don't just reach for Ritalin: New research finds old truth— sometimes, boys will be boys. *Calgary Sunday Sun,* p. C6.

Willard-Holt, C. (1998). Academic and personality characteristics of gifted students with cerebral palsy: A multiple case study. *Exceptional Children, 65,* 37–50.

Williams, D.F. (1999). The child who stutters: Guidelines for the educator. *Our Young Exceptional Children, 2,* 9–14.

Williams, B.F., Howard, V.F., and McLaughlin T.F. (1994). Fetal alcohol syndrome: Developmental characteristics and directions for further research. *Education and Treatment of Children, 17,* 86–97.

Williams, F. (1980). *Creativity Assessment Package.* Buffalo, NY: D.O.K. Publishers.

Williams, J., Sharp, G., Bates, S., Griebel, M., Lange, B., Spence, G.T., and Thomas, P. (1996). Academic achievement and behavioral ratings in children with absence and complex partial epilepsy. *Education and Treatment of Children, 19,* 143–152.

Willig, A.C. and Greenberg, H.F. (1986). *Bilingualism and learning disabilities: Policy and practice for teachers and administrators.* New York: American Library.

Willings, D. (1983). Issues in career choice for gifted students. *Teaching Exceptional Children, 15,* 266–233.

Wilson, R.J. and Humphries, T. (1986). The impact of recent legislation on the role of Canadian school psychologists. *Canadian Journal of School Psychology, 2,* 1–6.

Wingert, P. and Kantrowitz, B. (1997, October 27). Why Andy couldn't read. *Newsweek,* pp. 56–64.

Winzer, M.A. (1993). *The history of special education: From isolation to integration.* Washington, DC: Gallaudet University Press.

Winzer, M.A. (1995). *Educational psychology in Canadian classrooms* (2nd ed.) Toronto: Allyn and Bacon.

Winzer, M.A. (1997). *Special education in early childhood: An inclusive approach.* Toronto: Allyn and Bacon.

Winzer, M.A. and Mazurek, K. (1998). *Special education in multicultural contexts.* Columbus, OH: Merrill.

Winzer, M.A. and Mazurek, K. (2000). Multicultural special education for increasingly diverse societies. In M. Winzer and K. Mazurek (Eds.) *Special education in the 21st century: Issues of inclusion and reform* (pp. 238–256). Washington, DC: Gallaudet Univeristy Press.

Wisniewski, L. and Alper, S. (1994). Including students with severe disabilities in general education settings. *Remedial and Special Education,* 15, 4–13.

Wolman, B.B. (1978). *Children's fears.* New York: Grosset and Dunlap.

Woodcock, R.W. (1991). *Woodcock language proficency battery, revised.* Toronto: Nelson.

Woodcock, R.W (1997). *Woodcock diagnostic reading battery.* Circle Pines, MN: American Guidance Service.

Woodcock, R.W. and Johnson, M.B. (1989/90). *The Woodcock Johnson Psychoeducational Battery—Revised.* Allen TX: DLM Teacher Resources.

Woodcock, R. and Munoz-Sandoval, A. (1993). *Woodcock-Munoz Language Survey.* Chicago,IL: Riverside Publishing Company.

World Health Organization. (1980). *International classification of impairments, disabilities and handicaps.* Geneva: World Health Organization.

Yairi, E. and Ambrose, N. (1992). A longitudinal study of stuttering in children. *Journal of Speech and Hearing Research, 35,* 755–760.

Yell, M.l. and Shriner, J.G. (1997). The IDEA amendments of 1997: Implications for special and general education teachers. *Focus on Exceptional Children, 30,* 1–19.

Yewchuk, C. (1984). Gifted education in Alberta: Current developments. *Special Education in Canada, 58,* 142–143.

Ylvisaker, M. (1986). Language and communication disorders following pediatric injury. *Journal of Head Trauma Rehabilitation, 1,* 48–56.

Yoshingata-Itano, C. (1994). Language assessment of infants and toddlers with significant hearing losses. *Seminars in Hearing, 15,* 128–147.

Ysseldyke, J.E. (1987). Classification of handicapped students. In M.C. Wang, M.C Reynolds, and H.J. Walberg (Eds.) *Handbook of special education: Research and practice. vol. 1: Learner characteristics and adaptive education* (pp. 253–272). New York: Pergamon.

Ysseldyke, J.E. and Algozzine, B. (1990). *Introduction to special education* (2nd ed.) Boston, MA: Allyn and Bacon.

Ysseldyke, J.E., Algozzine, B., and Thurlow, M.L. (2000). *Critical issues in special education* (3rd ed.). Boston, MA: Houghton and Mifflin.

Zammitt, N.O., Hare, A., Mason, J., and Elliott, G. (1999). Use of low vision aids by children attending a centalized multidiscilpinary visual impairment service. *Journal of Visual Impairment and Blindness, 93,* 351–359.

Zemlin, W.R. (1990). Anatomy and physiology of speech. In G.H. Shames and E.H. Wiig (Eds.) *Human communication disorders* (3rd ed.) Columbus, OH: Merrill.

Zentall, S.S. (1993). Research on the educational implications of attention deficit hyperactivity disorder. *Exceptional Children, 60,* 143–153.

Zetlin, A. and Murtaugh, M. (1988). Friendship patterns of mentally handicapped and nonhandicapped high school students. *American Journal on Mental Retardation, 92,* 447–454.

Zetlin, A. and Murtaugh, M. (1990). Whatever happened to those with borderline IQs? *American Journal on Mental Retardation, 94,* 463–469.

Zigmond, N., Jenkins, J., Fuchs, L.S., Deno, S., Fuchs, D., Baker, J.N., Jenkins, L., and Couthino, M. (1995). Special education in restructured schools: Findings from three multi-year studies. *Phi Delta Kappan, 76,* 531–540.

Zigmond, N., Levine, E., and Laurie, T.E. (1985). Managing the mainstream: An analysis of teachers' attitudes and student performance in mainstream high school programs. *Journal of Learning Disabilities, 18,* 535–541.

Zigler, E., Balla, D., and Hodapp, R. (1984). On the definition and classification of mental retardation. *American Journal of Mental Deficiency, 89,* 215–230.

Zimmerman, I., Sheener, V., and Pond, R. (1979). *The Preschool Language Scale* (Revised ed.). Columbus, OH: Merrill.

Zirpoli, T.J. (1990). Physical abuse: Are children with disabilities at greater risk? *Intervention in School and Clinic, 26,* 6–11.

Zirpoli, T.J. and Melloy, K.J. (1997). *Behavior management: Applications for teachers and parents.* (2nd ed.) Columbus, OH: Merrill.

Zoccolillio, M., Tremblay, R., and Vilano, F. (1996). DSM-III-R and DSM-III criteria for conduct disorders in preadolescent girls: Specific but insensitive. *Journal of American Academy of Child and Adolescent Psychiatry, 35,* 461–470.

SUBJECT INDEX*

*Entries in **bold** are defined in the glossary.

AUTHOR INDEX